VITAMIN D3

The publishers are indebted to the following contributors for their expertise and collaboration, and for their texts.

Rahel Aima: 18, 70, 124, 178, 232, 262.
Skye Arundhati Thomas: 164, 192, 234, 248, 292, 296
Paige K. Bradley: 86, 132, 258,
Paul Carey-Kent: 194, 250, 264, 278, 284
Elbé Coetsee: 48, 152, 180, 188, 274
Ellen Mara De Wachter: 34, 66, 160, 210, 290
Louisa Elderton: 118, 212, 270, 282
Charles Green: 20, 110, 136, 236
Catalina Imizcoz: 40, 54, 96, 166, 184
Natalie King: 26, 38, 92, 230, 268
Carol Yinghua Lu: 204, 242, 246, 276
Kathleen Madden: 80, 168, 216
Rosanna Mclaughlin: 106, 108, 116, 134, 142, 238, 254, 298
Sean O'Toole: 50, 94, 104, 112, 126, 128, 174, 224
Hili Perlson: 44, 140, 148, 172, 190, 198, 200, 206
Matt Price: 156, 158, 252, 286, 294
Michele Robecchi: 74, 146, 196
James Smith: 100, 120, 130, 154
David Trigg: 22, 32, 36, 64, 68, 72, 228, 266
George Vasey: 52, 60, 90, 162, 202
Christian Viveros-Fauné: 170, 220, 222, 240, 244
Kristian Vistrup Madsen: 28, 30, 56, 58, 78, 84

We are most grateful to Michela Parkin, Joanne Murray and Hilary Bird for editorial services.

And finally, we extend our thanks to all the nominators, artists and galleries, for their participation and support.

Phaidon Press Limited
2 Cooperage Yard, London E15 2QR

Phaidon Press Inc.
111 Broadway, New York, NY 10006

Phaidon SARL
55, rue Traversière, 75012 Paris

phaidon.com

First published 2021
Reprinted in paperback 2022, 2025

ISBN 978 1 83866 571 5

A CIP catalogue record for this book is available from the British Library and the Library of Congress.

Commissioning Editor: Rebecca Morrill
Project Editor: Louisa Elderton
Production Controller: Adela Cory
Design and cover illustration: Julia Hasting
Typesetting: Studio Chehade

Printed in China

VITAMIN D3

TODAY'S BEST IN CONTEMPORARY DRAWING

Φ

NOMINATORS.......

RAHEL AIMA.......
Art critic and writer, New York

SHEIKHA HOOR AL-QASIMI.......
President, Sharjah Art Foundation and International Biennial Association, UAE

MAISA AL-QASSIMI
Programmes Manager, Solomon R. Guggenheim Foundation, Abu Dhabi Project, UAE

MESKEREM ASSEGUED
Curator, Zoma Museum, Addis Ababa, Ethiopia

DAVID AYALA-ALFONSO.......
Independent curator and artist, Bogotá and London

ÇELENK BAFRA.......
Independent curator and Director of SAHA–Supporting Contemporary Art from Turkey

LAURA BARLOW.......
Curator, Qatar Museums, Doha

UTE META BAUER.......
Founding Director, NTU Centre for Contemporary Art Singapore

OMAR BERRADA.......
Director, Dar al-Ma'mûn, Marrakech, Morocco

IWONA BLAZWICK.......
Director, Whitechapel Gallery, London

KIMBERLY BRADLEY.......
Critic and writer, Berlin and Vienna

LOUISA BUCK.......
Contemporary Art Correspondent, *The Art Newspaper*, London

ZOE BUTT.......
Artistic Director, The Factory Contemporary Arts Centre, Ho Chi Minh City, Vietnam

AARON CEZAR.......
Founding Director, Delfina Foundation, London

ELBÉ COETSEE.......
Director, Mogalakwena Craft Art Development Foundation, Limpopo Province, South Africa

MARK COETZEE.......
Director, Gay Contemporary Art Institute

SUSAN CROSS.......
Senior Curator, MASS MoCA (Massachusetts Museum of Contemporary Art), North Adams

MAX DELANY.......
Artistic Director and Chief Executive Officer, ACCA – Australian Centre for Contemporary Art, Melbourne

MAURIN DIETRICH.......
Director, Kunstverein München, Munich

MARK DOYLE.......
Co-Head of Culture, Touchstones Art Gallery, Rochdale, UK

TOM ECCLES.......
Executive Director, Center for Curatorial Studies, Bard College, New York

REEM FADDA.......
Director, Cultural Foundation, Department of Culture and Tourism Abu Dhabi, UAE

MARINA FOKIDIS.......
Director, Kunsthalle Athena, Athens

MAGNOLIA DE LA GARZA.......
Director, Coppel Collection, Mexico City

CLAIRE GILMAN.......
Chief Curator, The Drawing Center, New York

THELMA GOLDEN.......
Director and Chief Curator, The Studio Museum in Harlem, New York

CATHERINE GOODMAN.......
Artistic Director, Royal Drawing School, London

KETTY GOTTARDO.......
Martin Halusa Curator of Drawings, The Courtauld Gallery, London

MARY GRIFFITHS.......
Curator, The Whitworth, Manchester

MARTIN HERBERT
Writer and critic, Berlin

LAURA HOPTMAN.......
Executive Director, The Drawing Center, New York

KATYA INOZEMTSEVA.......
Senior Curator, Garage Museum of Contemporary Art, Moscow

GEETA KAPUR.......
Independent writer and critic, New Delhi

MAMI KATAOKA.......
Director, Mori Art Museum, Tokyo

RACHEL KENT.......
Chief Curator, Museum of Contemporary Art Australia, Sydney

KATI KIVINEN.......
Chief Curator, Kiasma Museum of Contemporary Art, Helsinki

EDOUARD KOPP.......
John R. Eckel, Jr. Foundation Chief Curator, Menil Drawing Institute, Houston, TX

VIVIANA KURI.......
Director, MAZ – Museo de Arte de Zapopan, Guadalajara, Mexico

PABLO LEÓN DE LA BARRA.......
Curator at Large, Latin America Solomon R. Guggenheim Museum, New York, and Chief Curator, Museu de Arte Contemporânea (MAC) Niterói, Rio de Janeiro

BRETT LITTMAN.......
Director, The Isamu Noguchi Foundation and Garden Museum, New York

JENNI LOMAX.......
Independent curator and former Director of Camden Art Centre, London

MIGUEL LÓPEZ.......
Co-director and chief curator, TEOR/éTica, San José, Costa Rica

ANNA LOVATT.......
Assistant Professor of Art History (Modern and Contemporary), Southern Methodist University, Dallas

CARLA LUCINI.......
Art historian, New York

CHRISTINE MACEL.......
Chief Curator, Centre Pompidou, Paris

KATE MACFARLANE.......
Co-Director, Drawing Room, London

KATHLEEN MADDEN.......
Independent writer, and Adjunct Faculty, MA Contemporary Art and Summer Study, Sotheby's Institute of Art, New York

EVA MCGOVERN-BASA.......
Independent curator and writer, Manila

ELINOR MORGAN.......
Senior Curator, MIMA (Middlesbrough Institute of Modern Art), UK

GERARDO MOSQUERA.......
Independent curator and critic, Havana

HELEN NISBET.......
Independent curator, and Artistic Director, Art Night, London

YATES NORTON.......
Curator, Rupert – Centre for Art, Residencies and Education, Vilnius, Lithuania

MICHAL NOVOTNÝ.......
Director, Modern and Contemporary Art Collection, National Gallery Prague

HANS ULRICH OBRIST.......
Artistic Director, Serpentine Galleries, London

ZANE ONCKULE.......
Programme Director and Curator, Kim? Contemporary Art Center, Riga, Latvia

SEAN O'TOOLE.......
Writer and editor, Cape Town

ANDREW RENTON.......
Professor of Curating, Goldsmiths, University of London

GABRIEL RITTER.......
Curator and Head of Contemporary Art, Minneapolis Institute of Art, MN

FRIDA SANDSTRÖM.......
Independent writer and critic, and PhD fellow at the University of Copenhagen

ISABEL SELIGMAN.......
Bridget Riley Art Foundation Curator, British Museum, London

JILL SILVERMAN VAN COENEGRACHTS.......
Founder, Draw Art Fair, London

DIRK SNAUWAERT.......
Artistic Director, Wiels, Contemporary Art Centre, Brussels

OLGA SPEAKES.......
Curator, South African National Gallery, Cape Town

ROCHELLE STEINER.......
Chief Curator and Director of Curatorial Affairs and Programs, Palm Springs Art Museum, CA,

RUSSELL STORER.......
Senior Curator, National Gallery Singapore

KATHARINE STOUT.......
Director, Focal Point Gallery, Southend-on-Sea, UK, and Associate Director, Drawing Room, London

KATE STRAIN.......
Director, Grazer Kunstverein, Graz, Austria

DR STEPHANIE STRAINE.......
Senior Curator, Modern and Contemporary Art, National Galleries of Scotland, Edinburgh

SUHEYLA TAKESH.......
Curator, Barjeel Art Foundation, Sharjah, UAE

CLAIRE TANCONS.......
Curator and writer, Berlin

CHRISTINE TOHMÉ.......
Founding Director, Ashkal Alwan – The Lebanese Association for Plastic Arts, Beirut

MARIANNA VECELLIO.......
Curator, Castello di Rivoli Museum of Contemporary Art, Turin, Italy

SABINE B. VOGEL.......
Independent writer and critic, Vienna

ZOÉ WHITLEY.......
Director, Chisenhale Gallery, London

SAMANTHA WOODS.......
Exhibitions Curator, Fruitmarket Gallery, Edinburgh

HEIDI ZUCKERMAN JACOBSON.......
Director and Chief Curator, Aspen Art Museum, CO

....

WRITERS.......

RAHEL AIMA.......
Art critic and writer, New York

SKYE ARUNDHATI THOMAS.......
Writer and editor, Mumbai, India

PAIGE K. BRADLEY.......
Artist, writer and editor, New York

PAUL CAREY-KENT.......
Writer and curator, Southampton, UK

ELBÉ COETSEE.......
Director, Mogalakwena Craft Art Development Foundation, Limpopo Province, South Africa

ELLEN MARA DE WACHTER.......
Writer, London

LOUISA ELDERTON.......
Writer and editor, and Curatorial Editor, Gropius Bau, Berlin

CHARLES GREEN.......
Professor, Art History, School of Culture and Communication, University of Melbourne, Australia

CATALINA IMIZCOZ.......
Researcher and editor, London and Buenos Aires

NATALIE KING.......
Curator, writer and Enterprise Professorial Fellow at the Victorian College of the Arts, University of Melbourne, Australia

CAROL YINGHUA LU.......
Writer and curator, Beijing and Melbourne, Australia

KATHLEEN MADDEN.......
Independent writer, and Adjunct Faculty, MA Contemporary Art and Summer Study, Sotheby's Institute of Art, New York

ROSANNA MCLAUGHLIN.......
Writer and editor, London

SEAN O'TOOLE.......
Writer and editor, Cape Town, South Africa

HILI PERLSON.......
Writer, editor and lecturer, Berlin

MATT PRICE.......
Curator and writer, London

MICHELE ROBECCHI.......
Curator, writer and editor, London

JAMES SMITH.......
Writer, Ramsgate, UK

DAVID TRIGG.......
Critic and writer, Bristol, UK

GEORGE VASEY.......
Writer, and Curator, Wellcome Collection, London

CHRISTIAN VIVEROS-FAUNÉ.......
Writer and curator, Brooklyn, New York

KRISTIAN VISTRUP MADSEN.......
Writer and critic, Berlin

.... This is the third in the series of 'Vitamin' books devoted to contemporary artists who have made significant contributions to the medium of drawing, following *Vitamin D* (2005) and *Vitamin D2* (2013). Drawing is arguably the most direct and immediate of all art processes – humankind's instinctive way of representing the world and externalising thoughts and emotions into visual expression. Our distant ancestors made sketches on cave walls, and while subsequent advances in knowledge, science and technology have endlessly changed how we live, the appeal of this simple mode of expression endures.
....

.... 'Drawing' is a deceptively complex word. As a verb it is easily understood. Most people drew in childhood, and many of us still do, though often so subconsciously that it needs its own special term: doodling. But what of the noun? What defines a drawing? Sometimes it is indisputable, for example, when a dry medium – graphite pencil, charcoal or pastel – is applied by hand to a surface, such as paper or a wall. But what if it is a wet medium – ink or watercolour – applied in equally careful lines using a brush? Must mark-making be planned and controlled, or can a drawing be made with arbitrary marks achieved randomly through chance, using a machine or the forces of gravity? Or if there's no applied medium at all and the work is created using paper alone, by piercing holes, folding, tearing or burning? Can this still be called a drawing?
....

.... In this book's introductory essay, Anna Lovatt builds upon essays by Emma Dexter and Christian Rattemeyer, in *Vitamin D* and *Vitamin D2* respectively, to discuss the complex interplay of cognitive, somatic and material conventions that define drawing today. She considers the tensions that exist in drawing between blankness and trace, its multifaceted identity and fundamentally relational character, and reflects on how drawing responds to the complex temporalities structuring our everyday lives.
....

.... The longlist of living artists put forward by our esteemed international panel of nominators, many of whom are specialists in the field of drawing, featured practitioners working in a vast range of processes and materials. The simplest way to shortlist would have been to keep definitions narrow and disregard all but those whose work epitomised drawing in the most conventional sense. Yet this seemed a betrayal of the way in which this medium – historically employed by artists as a preparatory stage in the service of the more highly-prized painting and sculpture – has matured into an art form in its own right, and as such, has continually pushed boundaries and diversified. So we ultimately deferred to how artists defined themselves or how they were described by their representatives. This enabled us to include drawing-related installations, animations and performances alongside work made using more conventional mark-making processes. Today's best in contemporary drawing is revealed to be a remarkable diversity of approaches and results made by artists across the globe.
....

.... Louisa Elderton and Rebecca Morrill, Editors

INTRODUCTION.......BY ANNA LOVATT

DRAWING AS WORLD MAKING....... In spring 2020, Rashid Johnson began a series of 'Untitled Anxious Red Drawings' (fig.1). Confined to the house by a stay-at-home order designed to slow the spread of COVID-19, Johnson returned to the 'Anxious Men' that had inhabited his drawings since 2015.[1] Departing from his earlier use of black soap, wax or oil stick (p.124), he used red oil stick to cover sheets of cotton rag with densely packed boxes. Two ovoid forms at the top of each box and a horizontal scrawl underneath anthropomorphized these repetitive units until they resembled a crowd of faces, held tight by the drawing's gridded structure. Johnson's red drawings appeared more rapidly executed than their predecessors, with the frenetic movement of his hand unravelling the grid and its fraught countenances. These were drawings for an anxious time, Johnson said, a time that felt radical and urgent.[2]

.... During the pandemic, artists, nurses, journalists, teachers and schoolchildren began to draw. As social distancing and stay-at-home orders were put in place throughout the world, drawings appeared on pavements, in windows, on walls and on the Internet. Artists and teachers led online drawing sessions, while museums released colouring sheets based on works in their shuttered collections.[3] Initiatives like the Artist Support Pledge enabled practitioners who had lost exhibitions, teaching jobs and technical support to sell their work and purchase the work of others.[4] Johnson's drawings were exhibited and sold online, with a percentage of the profits donated to the World Health Organization's COVID-19 Solidarity Response Fund.......

.... Why drawing now? The answers are complex and manifold. With limited access to studios, materials, fabricators and studio assistants, artists known for their work in other media have turned to drawing. People draw to pass the time or to calm the mind, harnessing the therapeutic properties of drawing, long recognized in the field of psychology. In public spaces and liminal zones such as windows, doorways, porches and balconies, drawings express frustration, hope or solidarity to passers-by. Drawings can function as journals or documents – poignantly, as in the sketches (fig.2) made by South Korean critical care nurse Oh Young-jun.[5] For some, drawing is simply a means of psychological or economic survival. Referring to his experiences as a West African asylum seeker in the United States, Sanou Oumar (p.188) has said of his scintillating drawings: 'The reason I am alive is because of them.'[6] ....

.... What is drawing now? Museums continue to define drawing in terms of a set of materials, with the Museum of Modern Art (MoMA), New York describing it as: 'a unique work of art, often on paper, made with dry or wet mediums including pencil, charcoal, chalk, pastel, crayon, pen, ink, watercolour, or oils'.[7] For others, like curators Catherine de Zegher and Cornelia H. Butler, the practice of drawing is rooted in formal and relational qualities including linearity and surface tension.[8] Their exhibition 'On Line: Drawing Through the Twentieth Century', presented at MoMA in 2010–11, included works that might be otherwise categorized as painting, sculpture, dance, performance, film and installation, but which were united by their nonrepresentational use of line.......

.... Drawing has long been understood as a conceptual process that elides definition in material terms, 'the parent of our three arts, Architecture, Sculpture and Painting'.[9] In this sense, a building by Kazuyo Sejima, a sculpture by Nina Canell or a painting by Julie Mehretu could all be understood in terms of drawing – as could a performance by Francis Alÿs or an

1.

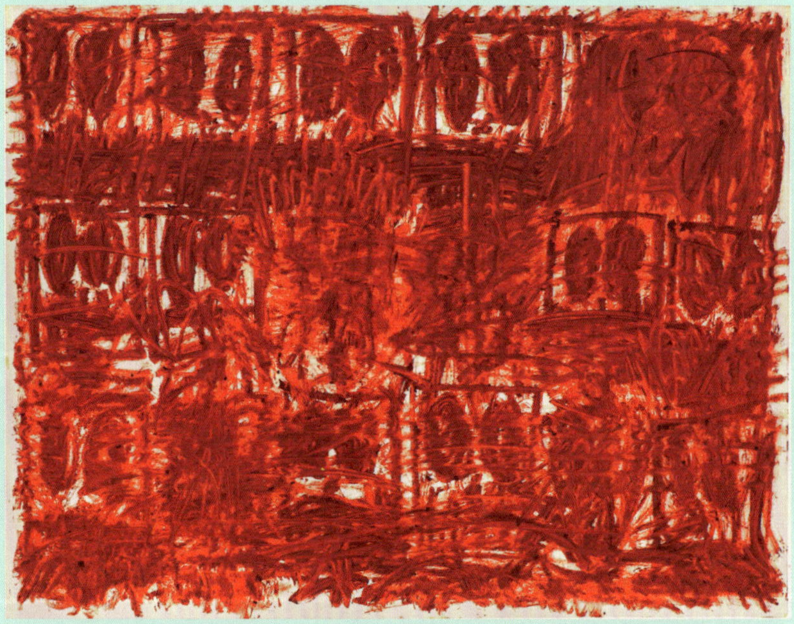

1. Rashid Johnson, *Untitled Anxious Red Drawing*, 2020, oil on cotton rag, 97.2 × 127 cm (38 ¼ × 50 in)
2. Oh Young-jun, from the series 'Nursing Story', 2020, digital drawing
3. Jacques-Louis David, *Marie Antoinette Led to Her Execution*, 1793, pen and ink, 15 × 10 cm (6 ⅞ × 4 in)

Internet project by Rafaël Rozendaal. These diverse works share an interest in linearity, mobility, projection and erasure, rather than a fixed set of materials. Yet other artists, including some featured in this book, such as Susan Collis (p.64) and Mauro Giaconi (p.96), use materials traditionally associated with drawing to create a sense of planarity or volume rather than line. Instead of defining drawing in purely material or solely conceptual terms, we can think of it as a complex interplay of cognitive, somatic and material conventions. These conventions include processes of conceptualization and delineation, mark-making and erasure; particular supports, substances and tools of inscription; and the tension between blankness and the trace. Drawing cannot be reduced to any one of these qualities – it is fundamentally relational and deceptively complex. ....

.... Does drawing have a purchase on the 'now', on the condition of contemporaneity? When Jacques-Louis David attempted to record one of the pivotal events of the French Revolution in his painting *The Tennis Court Oath* (1790–4), events overtook him and the painting was left unfinished.[10] Yet his caustic 1793 sketch (fig.3) of Marie Antoinette on her way to the guillotine – drawn from a window as the convoy passed by – captured the unfolding scene in a few deft strokes of ink. With the invention of photography a few decades later and the more recent proliferation of camera phones, drawing is no longer the fastest or most common way of documenting historical events. But the viciousness and urgency of David's sketch shows how the graphic trace can register emotional and psychological impulses in real time, existing 'always in the present tense, in the time of its unfolding, the ongoing time of a present that constantly presses forward'.[11] This introduction to *Vitamin D3: Today's Best in Contemporary Drawing* will survey developments in drawing since 2013, when *Vitamin D2: New Perspectives in Contemporary Drawing* was published. I will frame this discussion within a broader analysis of drawing's relationship with contemporaneity, exploring its ability to respond to the complex temporalities that structure our lives today. ....

DRAWING NOW, AGAIN .... In the catalogue for the exhibition 'Drawing Now: 1955–1975' at the Museum of Modern Art, New York in 1976, curator Bernice Rose argued that drawing – often perceived as a conservative, retrograde or subsidiary practice – had become a field of radical experimentation.[12] Beginning with Robert Rauschenberg's *Erased de Kooning Drawing* (1953), Rose demonstrated how drawing had become central to North American and European art of the post-war period, including Neo-Dada and Pop art, Minimal, Post-Minimal and Conceptual art. As I have argued elsewhere, the artists in Rose's exhibition engaged in a rigorous critique of drawing's presumed relationship with subjective expression.[13] Using strategies of delegation, reproduction and the ready-made, they questioned the autographic potential of the drawn mark so cherished by the earlier generation exemplified by de Kooning. ....

.... Rose's description of the 'emotive cooling' of the line has become canonical in accounts of modern and contemporary drawing.[14] Less discussed is the conclusion of her essay, in which she argues that such drawings carved out a space in response to the 'crisis and noise' of the late 1960s and early 1970s.[15] The abstract works in 'Drawing Now' can be seen as strategic acts of withdrawal, restraint and reorientation in response to the tumultuous period in which they were produced. That moment can now be understood as a transitional one, embodying a shift from modern to contemporary art. In some ways, the post-Minimal and Conceptual drawings

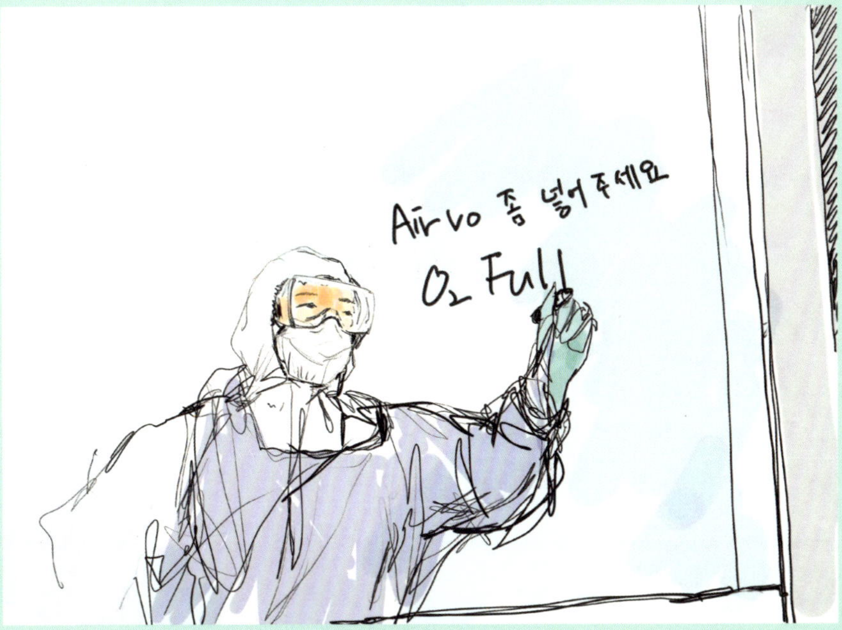

2.

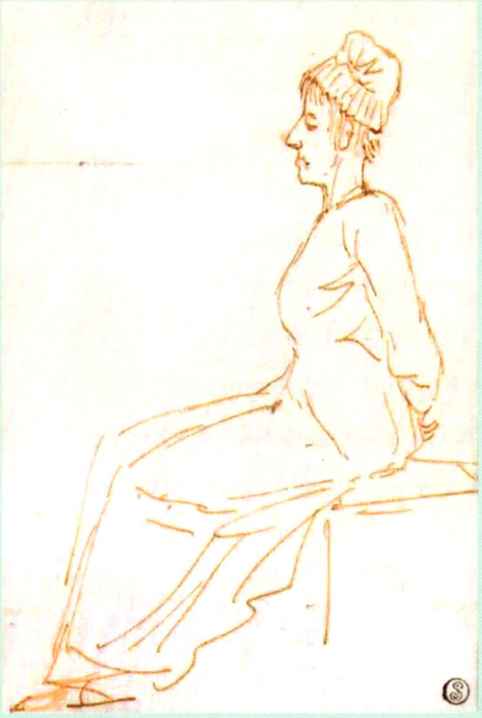

3.

in Rose's exhibition, such as Dorothea Rockburne's *Drawing Which Makes Itself* (1972, fig.4), can be seen as the culmination of the reflexivity and experimentality that had driven modernist art for over a century. Yet the site-specificity of many of these works, and their prioritization of conceptual processes over manual virtuosity, broke with the modernist emphasis on the autonomous art object. Moreover, the fact that they were drawings – a practice marginalized in narratives of modernism and within art history more broadly – worked against previous notions of the modernist masterpiece as monumental and enduring.

The time involved in planning large-scale museum surveys meant that the state of contemporary drawing had shifted by the time 'Drawing Now' opened in January 1976. In a public dialogue with Rose, the critic Lucy Lippard contended:

> Bernice organized a good historical show, but should not have called it 'Drawing Now' because I don't think it expresses drawing now. If it had been drawing now, for one thing, there would have been a great many more women in it. There would have been people like Michelle Stuart, Nancy Spero, Brenda Miller, Pat Steir [who] are doing beautiful interesting personal drawings.[16]

Shortly after Rose's show left MoMA to begin an international tour, Corinne Robins curated 'Drawing Now: 10 Artists', at the SoHo Center for Visual Artists, New York. Presenting the work of nine women artists and one man, Robins prioritized the 'individual, idiosyncratic statement', in direct contrast to the conceptual works in Rose's exhibition.[17] Robins argued for a more expansive understanding of drawing in the mid-1970s, one that could accommodate Nancy Grossman's virtuoso studies of masked and bound figures (fig.5), alongside Howardena Pindell's numbered circles cut by a hole punch, or Michelle Stuart's graphite rubbings made at outdoor sites.

Despite the eclectic appearance of 'Drawing Now: 10 Artists', all the practitioners included in the exhibition lived in New York City. The Brooklyn Museum looked elsewhere with 'Korean Drawing Now', curated by Gene Baro in 1981.[18] Adapting Rose's title, this exhibition introduced a North American audience to the artists associated with the Dansaekhwa movement, such as Chung Sang-Hwa and Park Seo-Bo, and a younger generation including Il Lee. (Minjung Kim (p.134) has extended this trajectory into the twenty-first century). The gridded structures and repetitive gestures on display bore some formal resemblance to works by North American Minimal and Post-Minimal artists, but they were rooted in an entirely different set of material and spiritual concerns. To suggest that Dansaekhwa was simply 'influenced' by Western movements fails, in the words of Simon Morley, artist and Professor at Dankook University, 'to take into account the differentials within the temporality of modernity as it impacted on, and unfolded within, East Asia itself'.[19] Drawing 'now' was beginning to be understood not as a single entity, but in terms of multiple, global currents shaped by industrialization, urbanization, secularization and coloniality.

A more phenomenological understanding of drawing and temporality was explored in 'Afterimage: Drawing Through Process' organized by Butler at the Museum of Contemporary Art, Los Angeles, in 1999. Responding to a resurgence of interest in Process art, the exhibition included several of the artists featured in Rose's 'Drawing Now' and Robins's feminist riposte. Butler and essayist Pamela Lee argued that Process art articulated 'a desire to move outside traditional means/ends dichotomies, rejecting the idea of formal composition and con-

4.

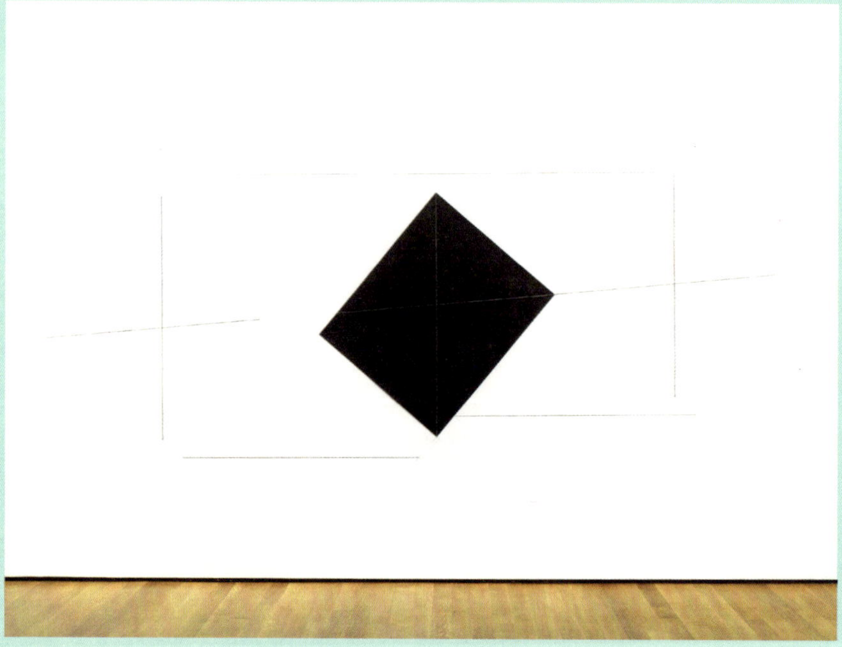

4. Dorothea Rockburne, *Drawing Which Makes Itself: Nesting*, 1972, carbon paper and pencil on wall, 294.6 × 426.7 cm (116 × 168 in)

5. Nancy Grossman, *Santa*, 1971, mixed-media collage with oil and graphite on paper, 55.2 × 73.7 cm (21 ¾ × 29 in)

ventions through which to circumscribe matter'.[20] 'Afterimage: Drawing Through Process' was a historical exhibition, focusing exclusively on drawings produced in the late 1960s and early 1970s. Yet by the late 1990s, this prioritization of dynamism over fixity had acquired new meaning in the work of a younger generation of artists who linked processes of dispersal and decline to the precarity of human life during the AIDS pandemic.[21] ....

.... Rose's title was recycled once more for 'Drawing Now: Eight Propositions', curated by Laura Hoptman at MoMA in 2002. At the turn of the twenty-first century, Hoptman argued that the drawings in her exhibition shared a 'rejection of the orientation toward process, exhibiting more affinities with nineteenth-century drawings than with the graphic effusions of North American artists in the 1970s'.[22] Emphasizing figuration, appropriation, narrative, fantasy, decoration and satire, these drawings had much in common with the alternative strategies foregrounded by Robins in 1976 – suggesting a more complex set of trajectories than the generational divide Hoptman proposed. The miniature heads that make up Chris Ofili's drawings might be productively compared to the paper chads produced by Pindell's hole punch, while the sadistic imagery of Kara Walker resonates with Grossman's figurative drawings. An important development was the broader geographical reach of 'Drawing Now: Eight Propositions', which featured the work of Toba Khedoori, Los Carpinteros, Yoshitomo Nara and Shahzia Sikander, alongside a preponderance of European and North American artists. Hoptman's selection was formative and many of these artists featured in the first *Vitamin D* book, which was published three years later. ....

.... The beginning of the twenty-first century saw unprecedented growth in the global art market, with the establishment of Art Basel Miami in 2002 and the Frieze Art Fair the following year. The 'Drawing Now' art fair was initiated in Paris in 2007 and the 'Draw Art Fair' was launched in London in 2019, both focusing on modern and contemporary drawing. During the 1960s, collectors Dorothy and Herbert Vogel built a major collection of Minimal, Post-Minimal and Conceptual drawings at a point when museums and galleries considered these works inconsequential. The emergence of the global super-rich and speculation in the art market make it hard to imagine middle-class civil servants like the Vogels amassing a comparable collection today.[23] Yet drawing is still held up to fledgling collectors as an accessible, affordable and compact alternative to artwork in other media.[24] Art fairs dedicated to drawing are both responding to and fostering an interest in this practice among a new generation of collectors. ....

.... In his introduction to *Vitamin D2*, Christian Rattemeyer, then Associate Curator in the Department of Drawings and Prints at MoMA, New York, contrasted the limited internationalism of the early 2000s – which centred on artists born in diverse locations but working in first-world cities – with the more thoroughgoing globalization of the art world that followed. Looking back on the first *Vitamin D* book, he wrote:

> What in 2005 could still be read as a dichotomy of Western normalcy and non-Western exception (with Latin America as the most obvious example of another modernism), has unfolded into a more global dialogue, where methods and materials, subjects and traditions are exchanged and employed regardless of national boundaries, and where the world that inspires artists is increasingly understood as a shared, complex whole.[25]

.... In the first decade of the new millennium, these dynamic flows were embodied in the drawings and paintings of Julie

5.

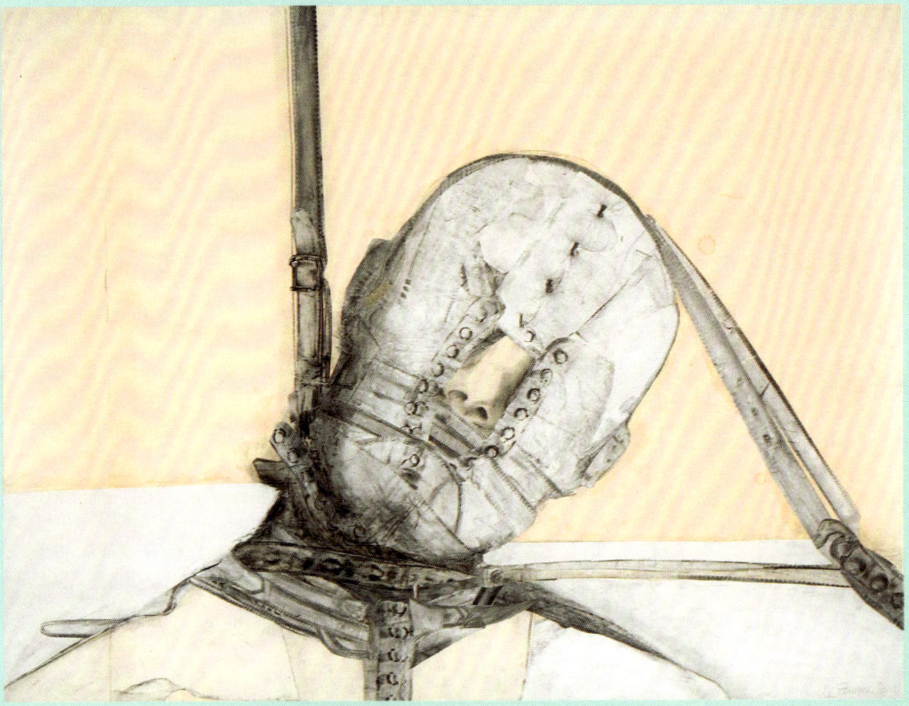

Mehretu, which featured in the first *Vitamin D,* in Rattemeyer's essay for the second book and on the cover of the *On Line* exhibition catalogue. But the unfettered progress of globalization has since been challenged, and the obliviousness to national boundaries described by Rattemeyer now elicits pangs of nostalgia. In the short time since *Vitamin D2* was published, globalization has come under siege: by the resurgence of nationalism, populism and xenophobia; ruptures within the European Union and the Paris Agreement; the abandonment of multilateral trade agreements and the instigation of trade wars; and, most recently, the disruption of international travel and trade in an effort to slow the spread of COVID-19.…….

WORLDS WITHIN WORLDS……. How have artists visualized this crisis of globalization? Describing the globe on stilts that totters through William Kentridge's drawings and animated films (fig.6), contemporary art theorist Terry Smith admires Kentridge's ability to picture 'the world as a whole, with many worlds nested within it, and many connections among them; yet, each world is a place in itself, with, in turn, many places within it. Connections among these worlds are dynamic and can take varied forms, all the way from mutual sustenance to apocalypse.'[26] In Kentridge's work, these nested worlds unfurl around a cast of idiosyncratic characters who process through the postcolonial, post-industrial landscape on the outskirts of Johannesburg. Instead of delineating sweeping vectors, Kentridge registers global forces as they act on flawed individuals, exposing networks of complicity and mutual vulnerability.…….

……. Although Kentridge has been working since the 1970s (his work featured in the first *Vitamin D*), his engagement with global concerns via the minutiae of individual experiences resonates with many of the drawings in *Vitamin D3*. Smith's conception of placemaking, world-picturing and connecting as ways of understanding what it means to be contemporary proves useful in this respect.[27] Drawing has a unique ability to carve out worlds in the margin of a page or to distil unimaginable suffering into the curve of a graph. This nimble capacity to shift from the microcosmic to the macrocosmic makes the ancient practice of drawing well suited to articulating contemporaneity as a multiplicity of worlds within worlds.…….

……. Several of the artists in *Vitamin D3* stake out visionary microcosms in response to experiences of suffering and persecution. In 1975 Ibrahim El-Salahi was wrongfully accused of being involved in an anti-government coup in his native Sudan. He was arrested and held for six months without trial in Khartoum's Kober Prison, where he made small drawings in secret and buried them in the sand. Following his release, El-Salahi was held under house arrest, during which he filled a small notebook (fig.7) with drawings, poetry and prose documenting his time in prison.[28] In one drawing, a figure has a barred window for a body, with the caption 'each window has two faces'. El-Salahi describes the window as a membrane between the hopes and aspirations of the individual and external forces beyond their control. He envisages these nested worlds interacting with one another through the windows, doors, rooms and boxes that recur throughout his *Prison Notebook* (1976).…….

……. El-Salahi's recent 'Pain Relief Drawings' (p.74) offer a different kind of escape, from the chronic back pain he now experiences. These diminutive drawings on the reverse of medicine packets follow the improvisational ethos of the doodle, which opens up a space of distraction and release from a particular situation. This ethos can also be found in Teresa Burga's 'Insomnia Drawings', which she produced during bouts

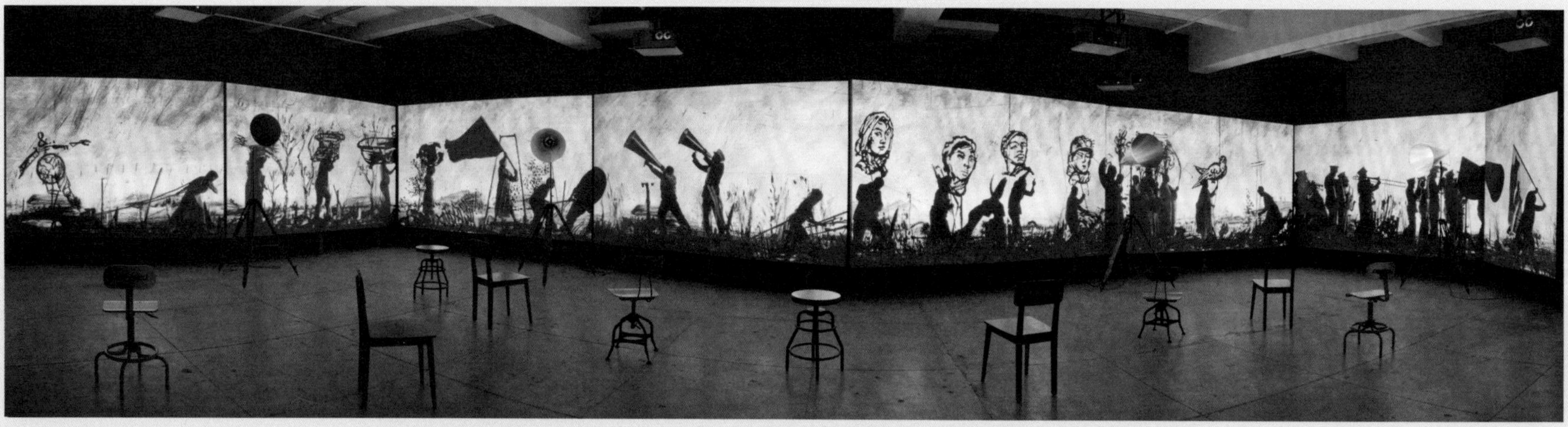

6.

6. William Kentridge, *More Sweetly Play the Dance*, 2015, 8-channel HD video installation with 4 megaphones, sound, 15 mins
7. Ibrahim El-Salahi, *Prison Notebook*, 1976, notebook with 38 ink on paper drawings, each page *c.*28.7 × 17 cm (11 ¼ × 6 ¾ in)

of sleeplessness from the late 1970s to the early 1990s. During this period Burga worked in the General Customs Office in Peru, while mobilizing Conceptual art's 'aesthetic of administration' to highlight broader processes of systematization and control.[29] The dizzying, automatist patterns that characterize Burga's 'Insomnia Drawings' recur in her more recent depictions of young indigenous women from Peru's Andean region, on which she logs the dates and times of her artistic labour.......

.......Other artists in this book use drawing's ability to open a portal on to another world to address questions of displacement, exile and longing. The home is a recurrent theme in the work of Zarina, who experienced the partition of India when she was ten years old and led a nomadic existence following her marriage to an Indian diplomat in the late 1950s. Works like *Spinning House* (2013) use a minimal vocabulary to meditate on the idea of home, referencing a plethora of buildings Zarina had known. Her understanding of home as a concept we carry with us rather than a fixed abode relates to her use of paper – a fragile, portable material she likened to a second skin.[30] This nomadic understanding of drawing resonates with the work of younger artists like Sanou Oumar, whose mandala-like structures are rendered with humble materials such as coloured pencil, pen and marker, using his ID card, disposable spoons and washers as stencils. These geometric drawings reference the architectural structures, tilework and textiles of his birthplace, Burkina Faso in West Africa. Their intricate patterns relate to the drawings of Johanna Unzueta, which are traced with the embroidery hoops used by Chilean textile workers......

.......Worldbuilding, Smith suggests, usually takes place 'around oneself and one's family, friends, neighbors and colleagues – that is, from the connections close to hand'.[31] This focus on kinship and community is evident in the work of several artists in *Vitamin D3*. Some, including Vernon Ah Kee, Claudette Johnson and Barbara Walker, have been picturing marginalized communities for decades, revitalizing the elitist genre of portraiture by prioritizing subjects excluded from its history. In recent years, this reinvigoration of portraiture has continued in the work of Phoebe Boswell, Kenturah Davis and Pierre Mukeba. Other figurative drawings envisage alternative models of kinship, from the scenes of queer sociality envisaged by Hannah Quinlan and Rosie Hastings, to the human/non-human interactions diagrammed in the work of Otobong Nkanga.......

.......Resisting the homogenizing tendencies of globalization, some artists in the book prioritize specific landscapes, traditions and vernaculars, while acknowledging their susceptibility to external forces. Nilima Sheikh draws on medieval poetry, Kashmiri folktales and miniature painting, arguing for the continued relevance of these traditions in the twenty-first century. Like Sheikh, Wael Shawky has made historical research a central component of his artistic practice, interweaving fact and fantasy in his stories of the Arab peninsula. Abel Rodríguez and Miriam de Búrca invest meticulous botanical drawings of native plants in Colombia and Ireland respectively with references to guerrilla violence and institutional abuse. In all these drawings, an abundance of detail functions to summon a specific locality. But rather than supporting a kind of parochialism, this painstaking evocation of place is conditioned by feelings of loss, longing and remembrance.......

.......Smith proposes that in contemporary circumstances, 'location is possible only with the surround of potential dislocation'.[32] This dislocation is foregrounded in drawings of diasporic subjects, including in this volume Mounira Al Solh's drawings of Middle Eastern and North African migrants, inscribed on yellow legal paper to indicate the bureaucratic

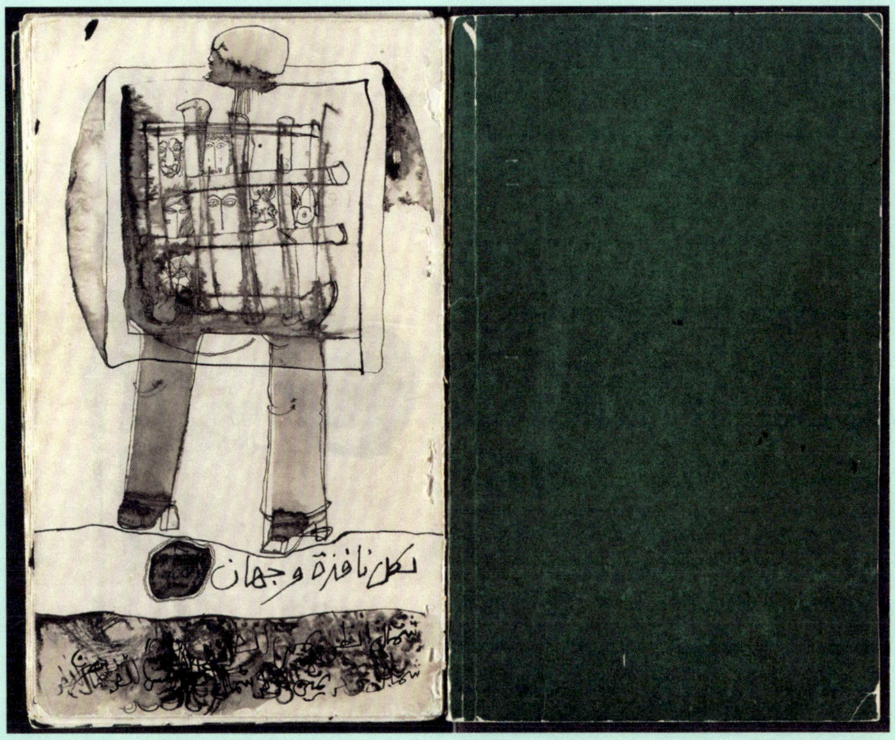

7.

procedures they are subjected to in their quest for citizenship. Miriam Cahn's *MARE NOSTRUM (Henry Moore)* (2015) revisits Henry Moore's celebrated drawings of figures sheltering from the Blitz, but instead of crowding into a London Underground tunnel her displaced figures lie prone on a Mediterranean shore. Like his installations, Barthélémy Toguo's lyrical watercolours address racist violence, conflict and exile on an epic scale in his monumental frieze *Dynastie* of 2012. ....

.... The 1990s and 2000s saw artists including Guillermo Kuitca (fig.8), Mark Lombardi and Julie Mehretu deploy cartographic and diagrammatic drawings to visualize a networked world. In contrast to these overarching worldviews, the artists in *Vitamin D3* offer more idiosyncratic and partial perspectives. Adriana Bustos's expansive mural *Venus Planisphere* (2018) takes the form of a celestial planisphere that could be used to read the sky from any point on earth. Yet Bustos anchors her sky to a specific time and place – Jerusalem, in the first hour of the first day of the Common Era. Around the planisphere, she charts an alternative history shaped entirely by women and people of colour. Qiu Zhijie's maps connect ideas, individuals and historical events, drawing on traditions of cartography and landscape painting. Despite their grand scale, the multiple panels of each map and the expansion of the series over time suggest that our attempts to understand the world are necessarily subjective and piecemeal. ....

.... Finally, contemporary artists are using drawing to visualize our embattled planet, charting geological, meteorological and astronomical phenomena. These artists extend the work of pioneers like Michelle Stuart and Agnes Denes (fig.9), which emerged at the intersection of feminism and environmentalism in the 1970s. Emma McNally has described her drawings as a 'weather system of graphite' and these atmospheric fields conjure processes of vaporization, condensation, turbulence and drift.[33] In Tania Kovats's 'Evaporation' series, a kind of self-generating drawing is achieved by soaking blotting paper in a solution of salt, ink and water and allowing it to dry, referencing geological processes and the looming threat of climate change. The globes, exploratory vessels and images of outer space drawn by Hondartza Fraga hold the human quest for knowledge in delicate tension with our scientific and epistemic limitations. ....

.... Shortly after Johnson completed his 'Untitled Anxious Red Drawings', cities across the United States and Europe erupted in protest following another police killing of an unarmed Black man. This event continued an unending cycle of suspicion, hostility and brutality, now painfully replayed in the midst of a pandemic that disproportionately affected African Americans. Although Johnson's 'Untitled Anxious Red Drawings' preceded these events, the 'Anxious Men' series of which they are part grew out of his ongoing engagement with Black cultural identity and the potent blend of fear and rage voiced by the protestors.[34] The ability of Johnson's drawings to speak to the specificity of this anguish, while evoking more diffuse forms of societal unease, is what makes them so compelling. Similarly, drawing's capacity to pivot between particularity and abstraction – from the most introspective gesture to the diagramming of immeasurable forces – makes it responsive to the volatile temporalities of contemporary life. .....

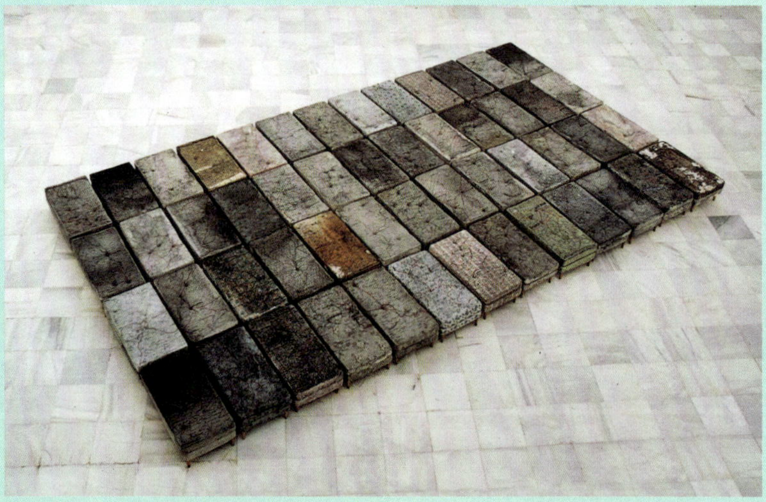

8.

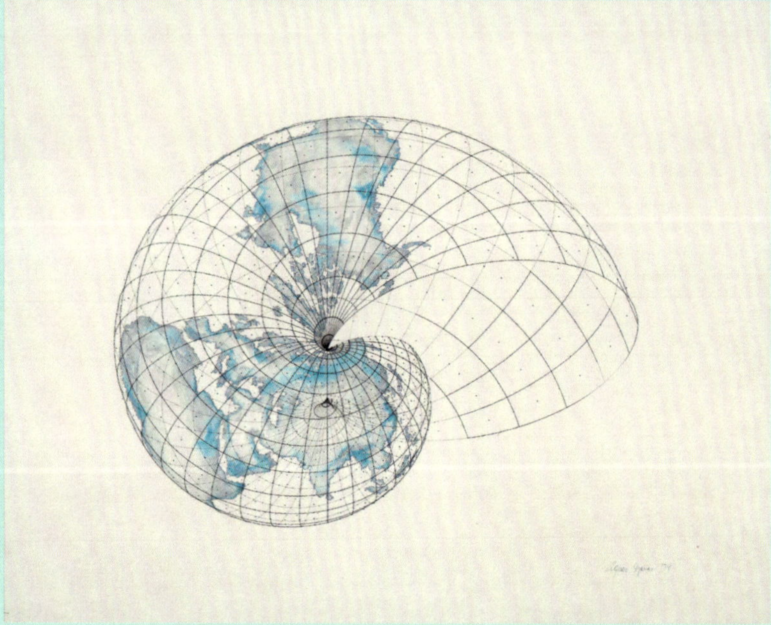

9.

8. Guillermo Kuitca, *Le Sacre*, 1992, acrylic on mattress with wood and brass legs: 54 beds, each c.40 × 60 × 120 cm (15 ¾ × 23 ⅝ × 47 ¼ in)
9. Agnes Denes, *Isometric Systems in Isotropic Space – Map Projections: The Snail*, 1979, watercolour, metallic pigments and pen and ink on paper with screenprint on plastic overlay, 61 × 76.2 cm (24 × 30 in)

NOTES

1. The 'Anxious Men' series was first shown at The Drawing Center, New York in 2015. Claire Gilman (ed.), *Rashid Johnson: Anxious Men* (New York: The Drawing Center, 2015).
2. 'Rashid Johnson: Untitled Anxious Red Drawings', video accompanying the online exhibition organized by Hauser & Wirth, https://www.vip-hauserwirth.com/rashid-johnson-untitled-anxious-red-drawings/. Accessed 15 May 2020.
3. 'Color in Quarantine with Artists like Daniel Heidkamp, KAWS and Rashid Johnson', *The Art Newspaper* blog, 7 April 2020, https://www.theartnewspaper.com/blog/colouring-in-quarantine. Accessed 8 April 2020.
4. 'Emerging Artists are Pledging to Support One Another During the Health Crisis By Buying Each Other's Art Through Instagram', *artnet news*, 19 March 2020, https://news.artnet.com/art-world/artist-support-pledge-instagram-1807881. Accessed 25 March 2020.
5. Victoria Kim, 'An ICU Nurse Sketches the Heroes and Fighters inside a Coronavirus Isolation Ward', *Los Angeles Times*, 9 April 2020, https://www.latimes.com/world-nation/story/2020-04-09/sketches-from-the-coronavirus-fight. Accessed 9 April 2020.
6. Frieze Art Fair 2019, 'Frame: Sanou Oumar, Gordon Robichaux, New York (F16)', https://frieze.com/fair-programme/sanou-oumar. Accessed 20 May 2020.
7. The phrase 'often on paper' is qualified by the following sentences in MoMA's definition: 'In addition to paper, drawings may be made on other organic or synthetic supports, including parchment, vellum, or acetate. Drawings that are site-specific can be executed directly on a wall, floor, or other surface.' Museum of Modern Art Collection Terms, https://www.moma.org/collection/terms/117. Accessed 15 April 2020.
8. Cornelia H. Butler and Catherine de Zegher (eds.), *On Line: Drawing Through the Twentieth Century* (New York: Museum of Modern Art, 2010).
9. Giorgio Vasari, original introduction to *The Lives of the Most Excellent Painters, Sculptors, and Architects*, 1550, published as *Vasari on Technique* (New York: Dover Publications, 1960), p.205.
10. Thomas Crow, 'Patriotism and Virtue: David to the Young Ingres', in Stephen F. Eisenman, *Nineteenth Century Art: A Critical History* (London: Thames and Hudson, 2007), pp.34–5.
11. Norman Bryson, 'A Walk for a Walk's Sake', in Catherine de Zegher (ed.), *The Stage of Drawing: Gesture and Act* (London and New York: Tate Publishing and The Drawing Center), p.149.
12. Bernice Rose, *Drawing Now: 1955–1975* (New York: Museum of Modern Art, 1976), p.9.
13. Anna Lovatt, *Drawing Degree Zero: The Line from Minimal to Conceptual Art*, (Pennsylvania: Penn State University Press, 2019).
14. Rose, *Drawing Now*, p.14.
15. ibid., p.91.
16. Bernice Rose, 'A Dialogue with Lucy Lippard', audio recording of a public dialogue on 28 February 1976, Museum of Modern Art, New York. MoMA curatorial exhibition files, exh. #1117, 7" reel, 3 ¾ ips, sound recordings, Museum of Modern Art Archives, 76.6.
17. Corinne Robins, *Drawing Now: 10 Artists* (New York: SoHo Center for Visual Artists, 1976), unpaginated.
18. Gene Baro (ed.), *Korean Drawing Now* (New York: Brooklyn Museum, 1981).
19. Simon Morley, 'Dansaekhwa: Korean Monochrome Painting', *Third Text*, vol. 27, 2013, pp.194–5.
20. Pamela Lee, 'Some Kinds of Duration: The Temporality of Drawing as Process Art', in Cornelia Butler (ed.), *Afterimage: Drawing Through Process*, (Los Angeles: Museum of Contemporary Art, 1999), p.48.
21. Here I am thinking of artists including Felix Gonzalez-Torres, Zoe Leonard and Kiki Smith.
22. Laura Hoptman (ed.), *Drawing Now: Eight Propositions* (New York: Museum of Modern Art, 2002), p.12.
23. Scott Reyburn, 'Feeling the Pinch: Why the Middle Class Art Collector is a Dying Breed', *The Art Newspaper*, 16 September 2019, https://www.theartnewspaper.com/feature/middle-class-collectors. Accessed 5 April 2020.
24. Reyburn, 'Want to Buy Art Without Breaking The Bank? Consider a Drawing', *New York Times*, 29 March 2018, https://www.nytimes.com/2018/03/29/arts/paris-drawing-art-collectors.html. Accessed 30 March 2020.
25. Christian Rattemeyer, 'Drawing Today', in *Vitamin D2: New Perspectives in Drawing* (London: Phaidon, 2013), p.13.
26. Terry Smith, *Art to Come: Histories of Contemporary Art* (Durham and London: Duke University Press, 2019), p.205.
27. ibid., pp.198–227.
28. Salah Hassan (ed.), *Ibrahim El-Salahi: Prison Notebook* (New York: Museum of Modern Art, 2018).
29. The phrase 'aesthetic of administration' was first used by Benjamin Buchloh in 'Conceptual Art 1962–1969: From the Aesthetic of Administration to the Critique of Institutions', *October*, vol. 55, Winter 1990, pp.105–43. In the context of Burga's work, see: Dorota Biczel, 'Cracking Open the Systems: Media, Materiality and Agency in Teresa Burga's *Self-Portrait. Structure. Report. 9. 6. 72*, *alter/nativas: Latin American Cultural Studies Journal*, no. 3, 2015, https://alternativas.osu.edu/en/issues/autumn-2014/visual-culture1/biczel.html.
30. Allegra Pesenti (ed.), *Zarina: Paper Like Skin* (Los Angeles: Hammer Museum, University of California; New York: DelMonico Books, 2012).
31. Smith, *Art to Come*, p.199.
32. ibid., p.207.
33. Emma McNally, 'Interviews: Emma McNally', *Artforum*, 28 December 2014, https://www.artforum.com/interviews/emma-mcnally-talks-about-her-drawings-in-mirrorcity-at-the-hayward-gallery-49602. Accessed 30 May 2020.
34. When Johnson's 'Anxious Men' were shown at The Drawing Center in New York in 2015, the exhibition included an auditory component. Melvin Van Peebles's 1970 song 'Love, That's America' played in the exhibition space: 'This ain't America, is it? / In America, folks don't run through the streets / Blood streamin' from where they've been beaten / In the park for the people / And the cop in the good ol' U.S.A. / Don't think they some kinda gods either.'

DR. ANNA LOVATT
is Assistant Professor of Art History at Southern Methodist University, Dallas. She has published extensively on modern and contemporary drawing and is the author of *Drawing Degree Zero: The Line from Minimal to Conceptual Art* (Pennysylvania: Penn State University Press, 2019) and *Michelle Stuart: Drawn from Nature*, (Berlin: Hatje Cantz, 2013), which accompanied an exhibition of the same name.

JUMANA EMIL ABBOUD .... In Jumana Emil Abboud's practice, drawing becomes a way to access memory and guard against erasure and loss; she also works with installation, video and performance. At its heart is an emphasis on homeland and displacement – Palestine in her case – the long shadow of history and the many ways that the latter is both interpreted and replicated. Another common theme is the tension and sometimes conflict between individual and collective memory, inspired by her own difficult return to Palestine as an adult after over a decade abroad. In her work, line functions as a thread of resilience that mirrors the struggles of her compatriots: the fight for Palestinian culture to survive even as its people are being killed, their land encroached upon and their institutions systematically decimated. .... Abboud adopts storytelling strategies of telling, retelling and mythmaking to consider the transmissions of history and culture. Her practice draws heavily from Palestinian folklore, incorporating tales of demons, spirits and other magical entities that haunt displaced and exiled populations as much as they do the trees, caves, wells and springs. Much of this comes from a 1920 publication that documented this rich oral tradition entitled *Haunted Springs and Water Demons in Palestine*. However, Abboud supplements this with oral history interviews, recording the different variations and personal memories of these tales to build a multifaceted compound-eye narrative that offers new interpretations of old stories. .... This research unspools in numerous ways: films in which Abboud visits these watery haunts, performances and a suite of mixed-media drawings. These drawings are loose and colourful. Many, like *The Dig* (2015), hold a certain opacity that leaves them open to interpretation, albeit one that relies on the implicit associations that a viewer might have between colour and various forms of natural life. That green must be grass, the gushing blue eruptions of underground springs, and the branch-like brown shapes trees, but is the white a stream, and are the yellow blobs ghosts? Or tree canopies? Even more figurative works, like *Ein Ayoub Bride* (2015), resist immediate interpretation. Here, a nude woman reclines, in a pose not dissimilar to an Orientalist *odalisque*, in a natural landscape that fades to baby pink. The title, partly repeated in Arabic on one corner loosely translates to 'eye of Job' – a Biblical reference perhaps? Other drawings, like *Things that make you laugh and cry at the same time* (2018), rehash history in a different way – by literally rewriting upon archival images. Its parent series 'God's Army and other floods' draws comparisons between calamitous events like the 1915 invasion of locusts in Palestine and the later destruction of the *Nakba* – the catastrophic 1948 exodus from Palestine – even as they pay tribute to the lives lost.
.... Rahel Aima

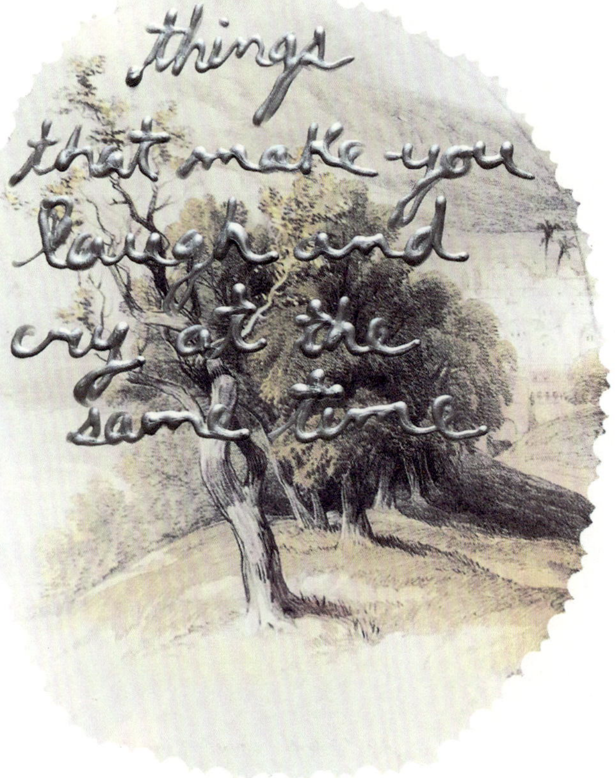

1.

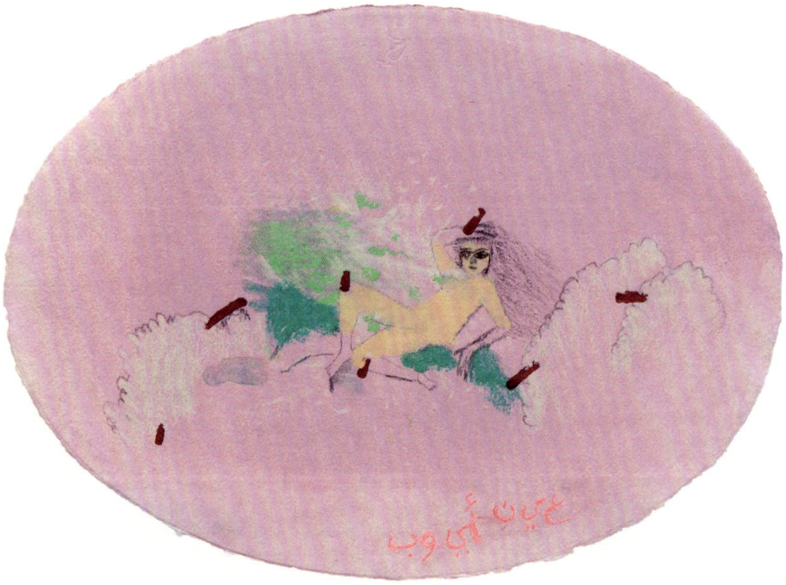

2.

Born 1971, Nazareth. Lives and works in London and Al-Quds, Jerusalem.

1. *Things that make you laugh and cry at the same time* from 'God's Army and other floods', 2018, gel ink paste on archival print, 16.5 × 14.5 cm (6 ¾ × 5 ¾ in)
2. *Ein Ayoub Bride*, 2015, pencil and gouache on paper, 28 × 39 cm (11 × 15 in)
3. *Two cubs* (drawing for performance series), 2016, ink on archival image print, 29.5 × 21 cm (11 ⅝ × 8 ¼ in)
4. *The Dig*, 2015, pencil, pastel, ink, acrylic and gouache on paper, 73 × 95 cm (28 × 37 in)
5. *Faithful* (drawing for performance series), 2016, ink on archival image print, 21 × 29.5 cm (8 ¼ × 11 ⅝ in)

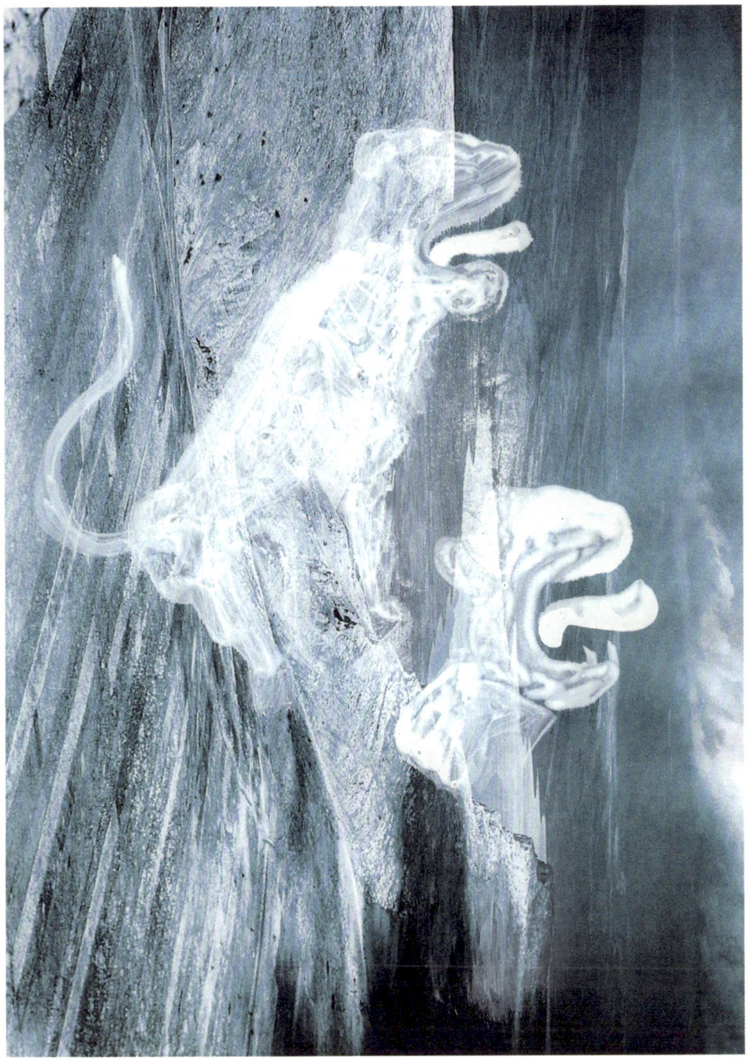

3.

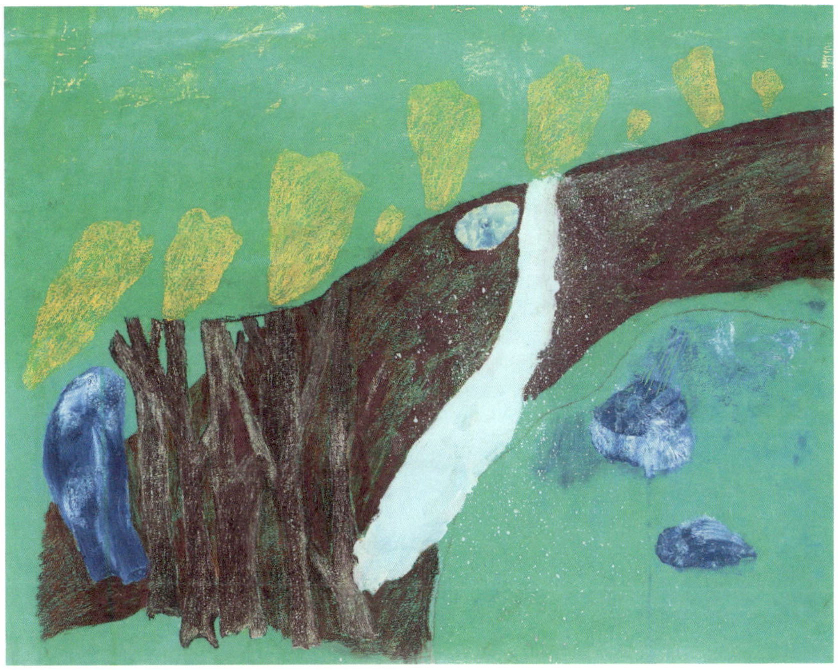

4.

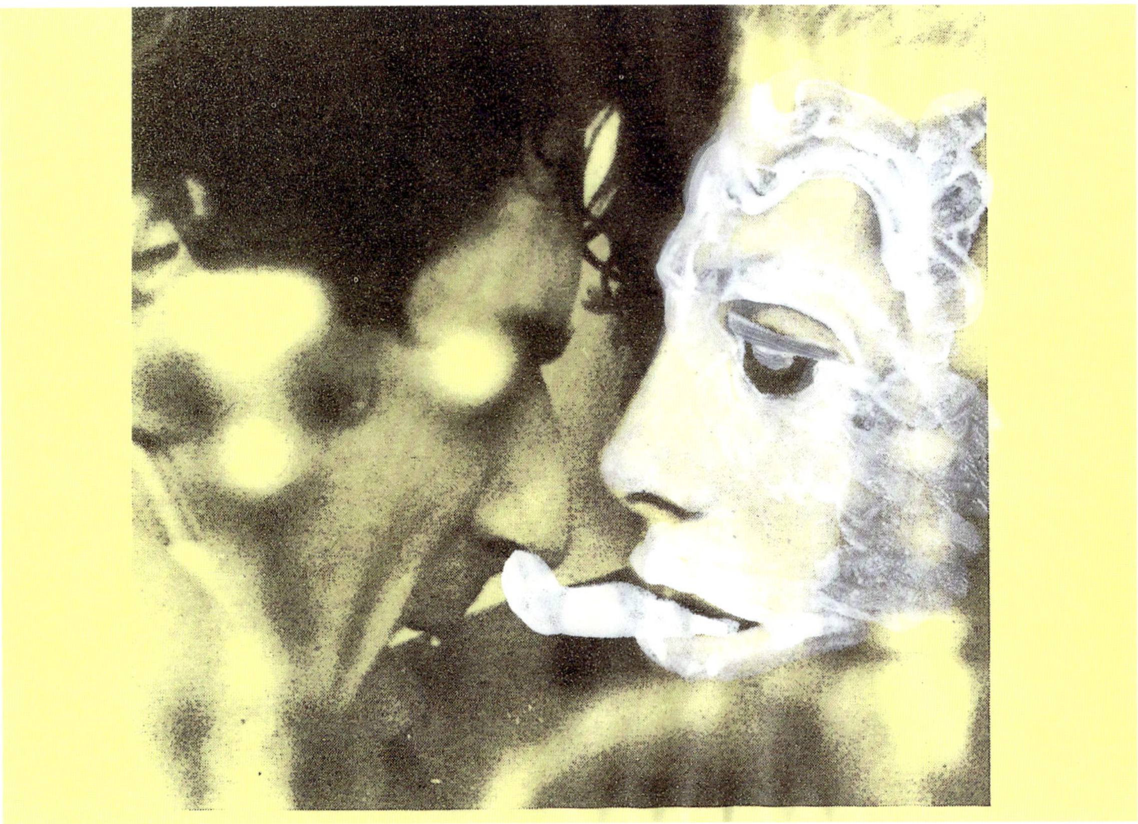

5.

VERNON AH KEE .... Art is conditioned by history, and Vernon Ah Kee's charismatic drawings call in historical debts that art can't merely acknowledge and then move past. These grand works on paper open up a vertiginous concatenation of history, photography, racial stereotyping and mnemonics. Always underlying their reception are words like 'identity', given his prominence as a fiercely intelligent and outspoken First Nations artist. So, for example, the sheer presence of *Michael* (2017), a large close-toned drawing of a man's impassive face, starts out as a portrait, a genre whose anachronism is neither offset by Ah Kee's ability to create extraordinary iconicity from low-tech, old-fashioned drawing materials nor by his implicit indictment, as an Aboriginal artist, of racialized stereotyping in his subject's performance of an identikit photograph, emphasized by the artist's tight cropping. Even so, this extraordinary drawing cannot merely be read as the illustration of his decolonizing drive, and manages to do even more. .... Ah Kee's ten-year-long series of drawings, 'Unwritten', makes this clearer still, just as photographs of his drawings always fail to do justice to their complicated materiality. *Unwritten #4* (2017) at first seems straightforward like an indeterminately repellent alien from Ridley Scott's 1979 sci-fi film. In common with *Alien*'s extraterrestrial intruder, *Unwritten #4*'s face is memorable for the suspense it conjures because, like other works in the series, it is far from clear what race is depicted or even if the face's physiognomy is complete. *Unwritten #4* is informed by an undisclosed image history and many collisions between semi-moving artistic parts: white guilt, black implacability and paper's obduracy. In exactly the same way, attention oscillates on three fronts when we look at *Michael*. We move from theory to experience, from implacable icon to Ah Kee's elegantly restrained, almost anonymous pencil marks; from the post-human to an enigmatic, asexual formalism remarkable for its just-enough personal resemblance. .... So too *Lynching 1* and *Lynching 2* (both 2015) are only just mimetic, worryingly abundant with the same complications. Two blurry, glowing figures depicted from waist up, they hover in a cloud of marks. The faces are nothing more than auras and the effect is neither uncanny nor ghostly but is completely unexpected. Ah Kee's marriage of horrific title to idealized bodies is neither repugnant nor didactic. The impact is an odd double vision. In the same way, the separate parts of *Unwritten #4*'s face only just look like they fit together. Such fractured, fissured representation can be traced further than the histories of art to a wider field of violent culture and anthropology. Ah Kee's environmental drawings demonstrate on the one hand the emulation of literature – of the visual arts' longing for narrative – and on the other the explosive, messy fragmentation of racism.
.... Charles Green

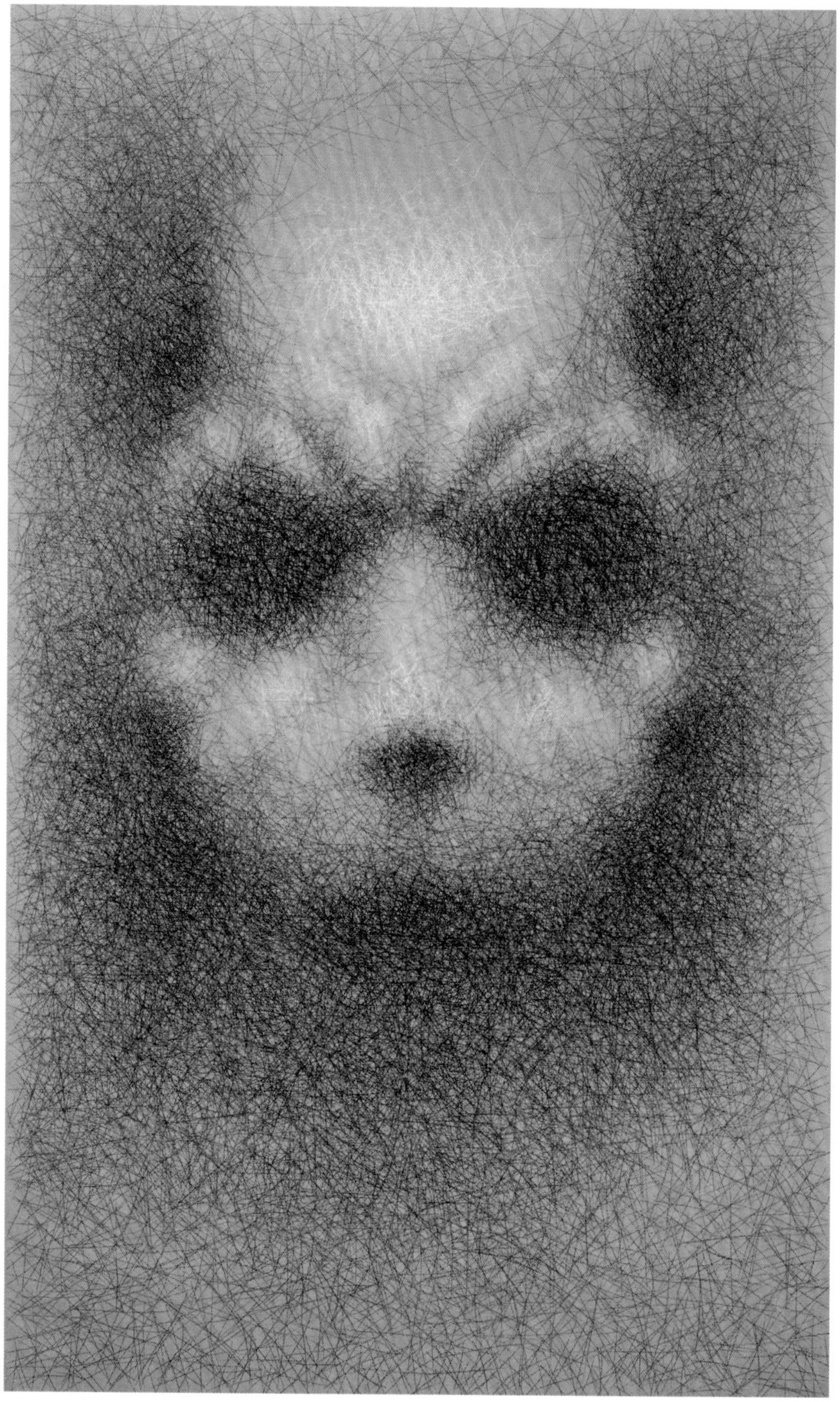

1.

Born 1967, Innisfail, Australia. Lives and works in Brisbane, Australia.

1. *Unwritten #4*, 2017, charcoal, pastel and acrylic on linen, 150 × 90 cm (59 × 35 ⅜ in)
2. *Michael*, 2017, acrylic, charcoal and crayon on linen, 180 × 240 cm (70 ⅞ × 94 ½ in)
3. *Lynching 1* and *Lynching 2*, 2015, charcoal and crayon on linen, each 300 × 200 cm (118 ⅛ × 78 ¾ in), installation view at Griffith University Art Museum, Brisbane, Australia ....

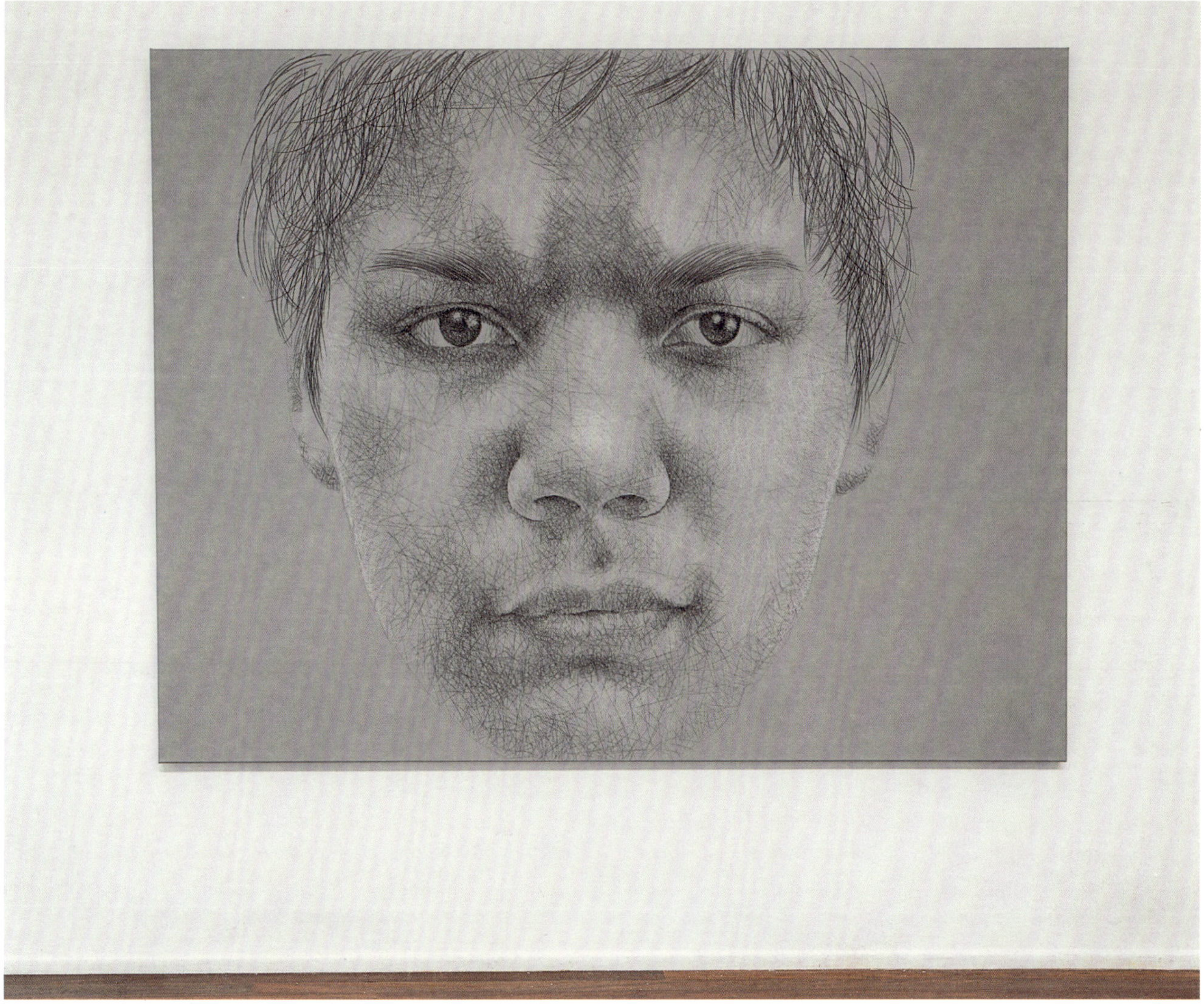

2.

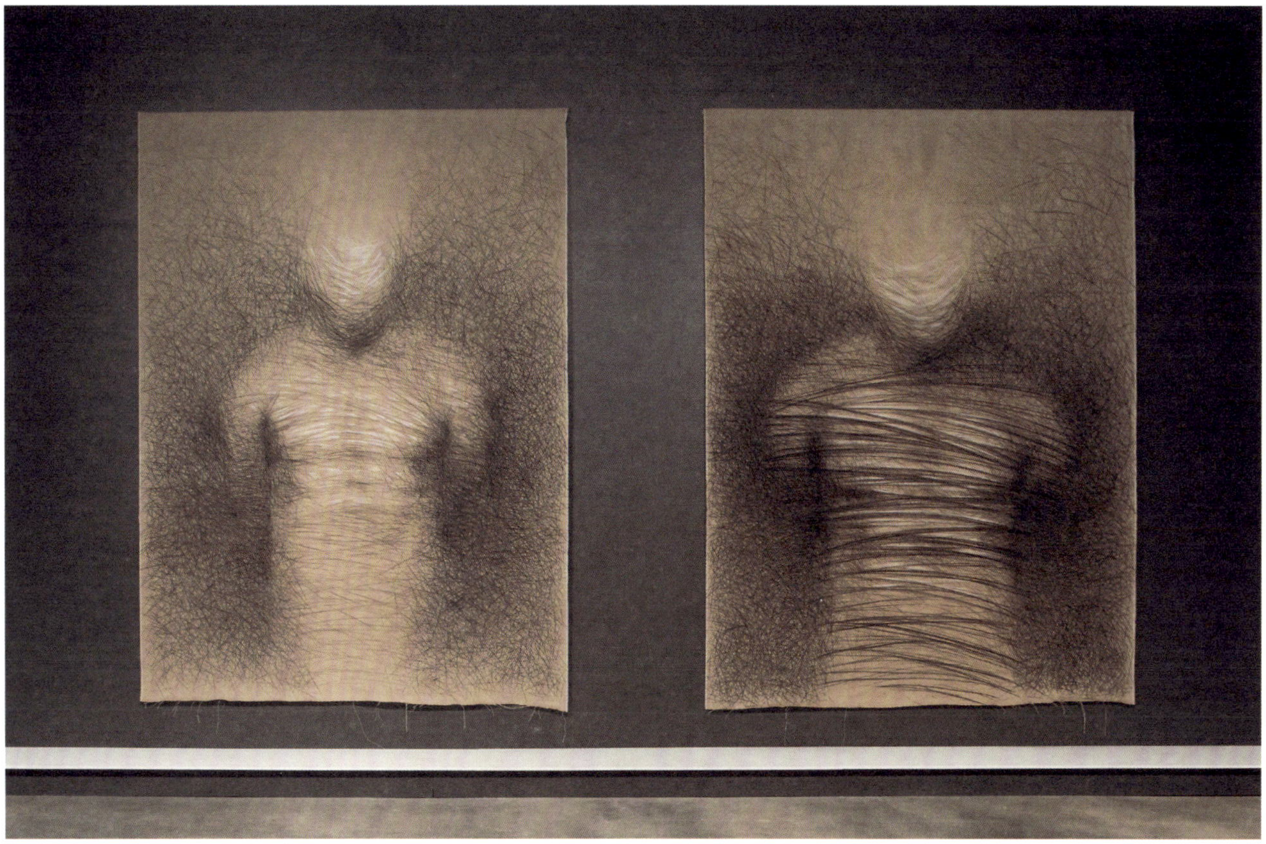

3.

DENIZ AKTAŞ .... Deniz Aktaş is no stranger to conflict. The Turkish artist has known political instability and war for as long as he can remember. As a child in the early 1990s, he and his family were forced to migrate when their village was evacuated, while in 2016 his home city of Diyarbakır in south-eastern Turkey became the focal point of the long-running armed conflict between the Turkish state and Kurdish militants. Such experiences feed his rich drawing practice, informing works such as the 'No Man's Land' series (2016–18) in which he depicts in photographic detail the bleak remnants of ruined buildings in lonely landscapes. These war-torn sites in predominantly Kurdish areas continue his long-standing interest in the impact – both positive and negative – that humans have on their surroundings, from cultural and environmental destruction to urbanization and regeneration. Aktaş composes his ink drawings, in subtle hues of grey and beige, with small linear strokes, giving them a uniform, grainy appearance. In *No Man's Land II* (2018) a crumbling wall with windows and fireplace stands exposed to the elements amid mounds of rubble. Tinged with sadness, it reflects the strange feeling that Aktaş had of being both inside and outside of Diyarbakır as he witnessed its buildings being levelled. Earlier images from the series show formerly inhabited sites returning to nature; a heap of stones or the foundations of a dwelling overgrown by grass and weeds are all that remains of some homes. Though born from conflict, these drawings belong to a broader engagement with notions of construction and destruction. Aktaş's ruins bear traces of violence, yet also suggest the potential for transformation. As his earlier drawings and paintings showing scaffolded structures and soaring cranes acknowledged, the loss of one building may engender the birth of another. .... Aktaş is a prominent figure in Diyarbakır's art scene and, with fellow artists Şener Özmen (b. 1971), Erkan Özgen (b. 1971) and Cengiz Tekin (b. 1977), is a founding member of Loading, an independent art space that, since 2017, has offered professional support to young Kurdish artists. As an act of resistance in the face of government hostility, the project attempts to make a constructive contribution to Kurdish culture in the midst of suppression and censorship. .... More recently, Aktaş has radically increased his scale with *Ruins of Hope 1* (2019). Unframed and tacked to the wall, the enormous drawing depicts a sea of discarded rubber tyres. Alluding to Caspar David Friedrich's (1774–1840) painting *The Wreck of Hope* (1823–4), showing a sinking ship smashed on polar ice, Aktaş similarly points to humanity's precarious relationship with nature. His ocean of rubber speaks urgently to ecological imbalance and, as with all of his works, highlights the inextricable link between progress and destruction.
.... David Trigg

1.
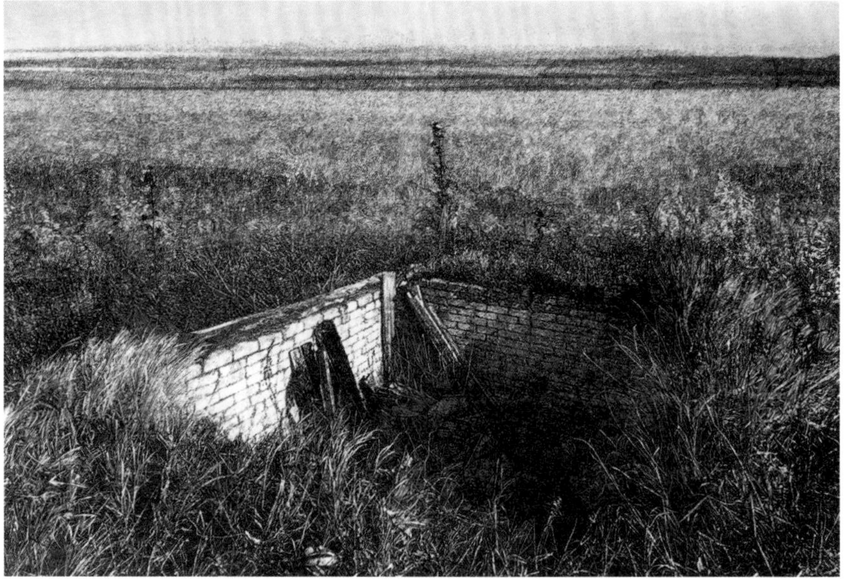

2.
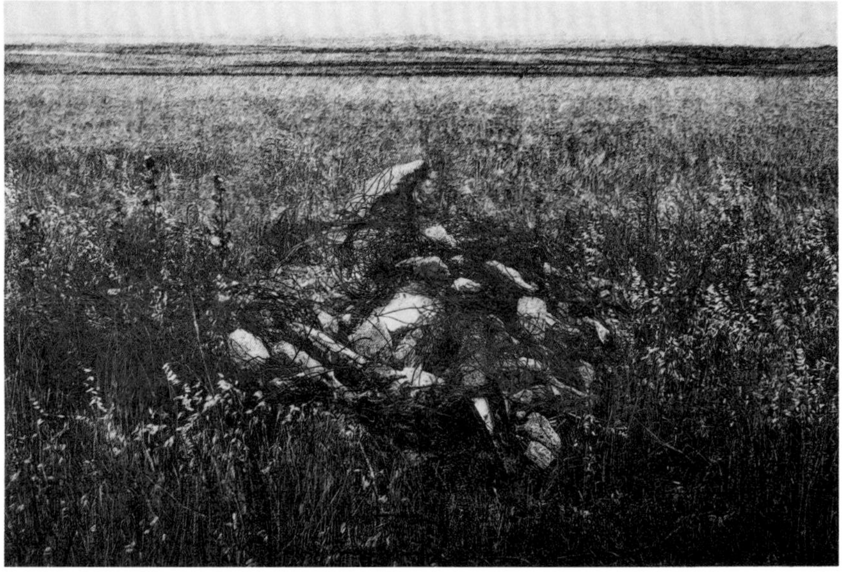

Born 1987, Diyarbakır, Turkey. Lives and works in Istanbul and Diyarbakır.

1. *No Man's Land*, 2017, ink on paper, 100 × 130 cm (39 ½ × 51 in)
2. *No Man's Land*, 2016, ink on paper, 70 × 100 cm (28 × 40 in)
3. *No Man's Land II*, 2018, ink on paper, 100 × 150 cm (39 ⅜ × 59 in)
4. *No Man's Land III*, 2018, ink on paper, 130 × 200 cm (51 × 78 ¾ in)

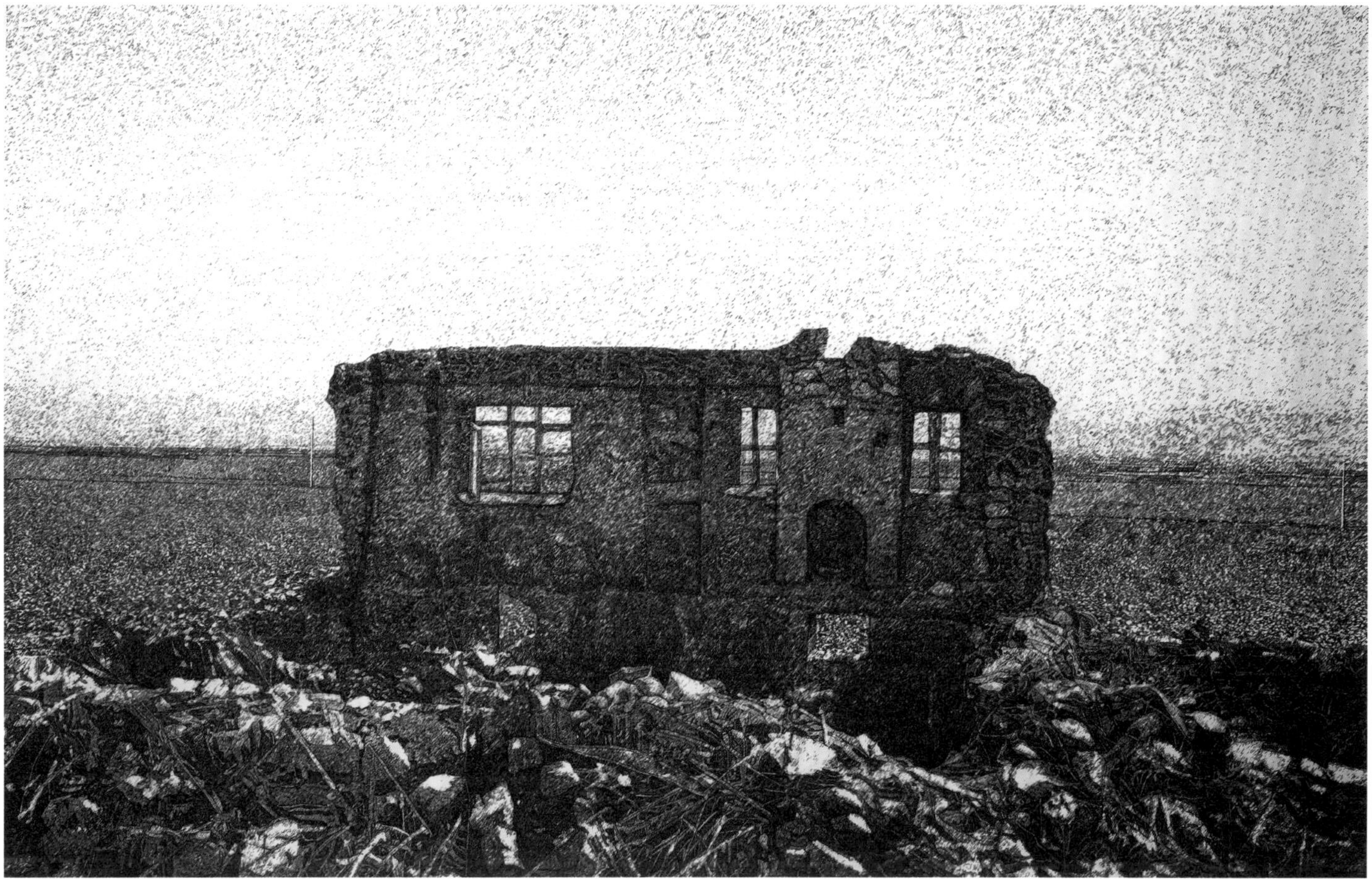
3.

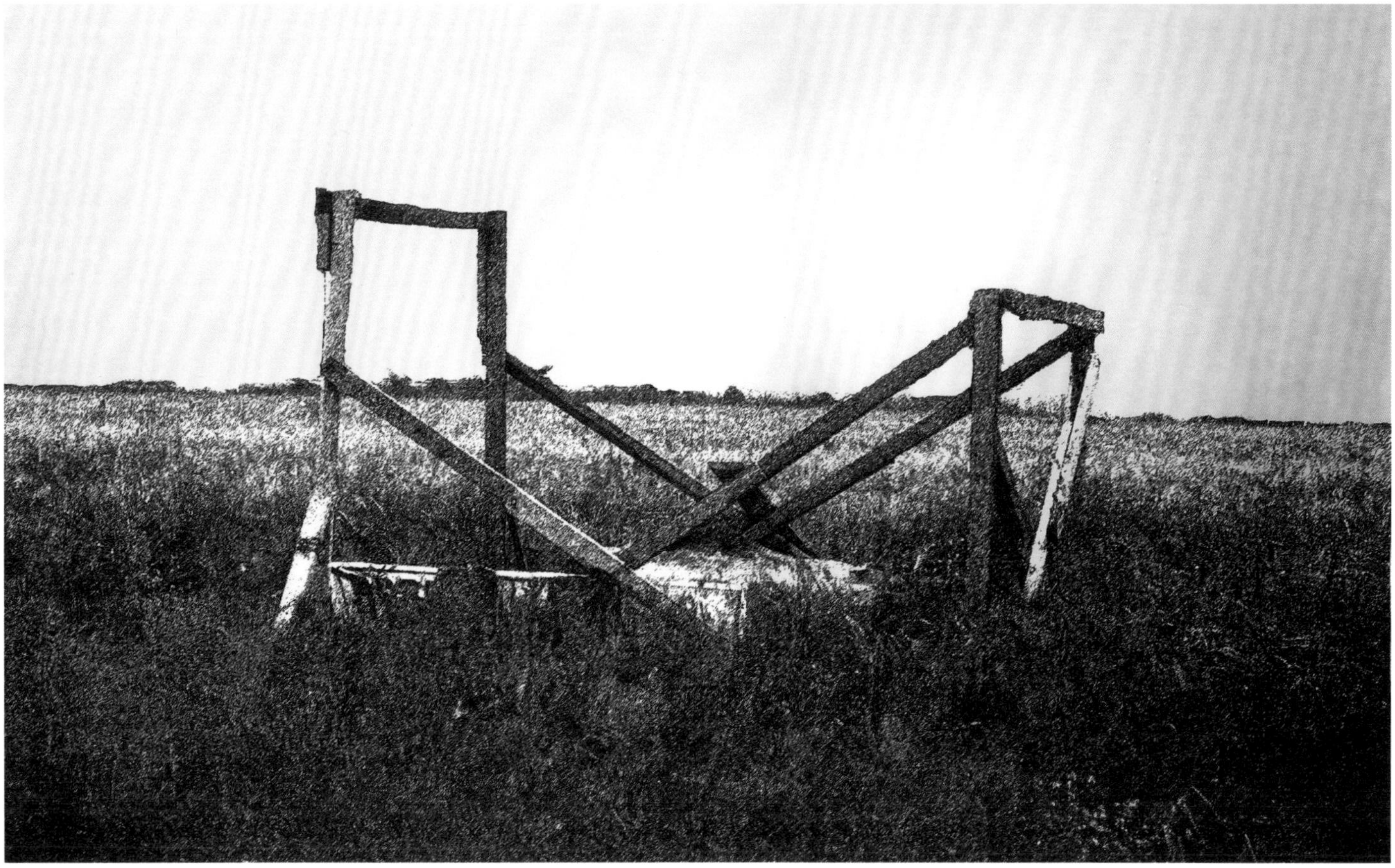
4.

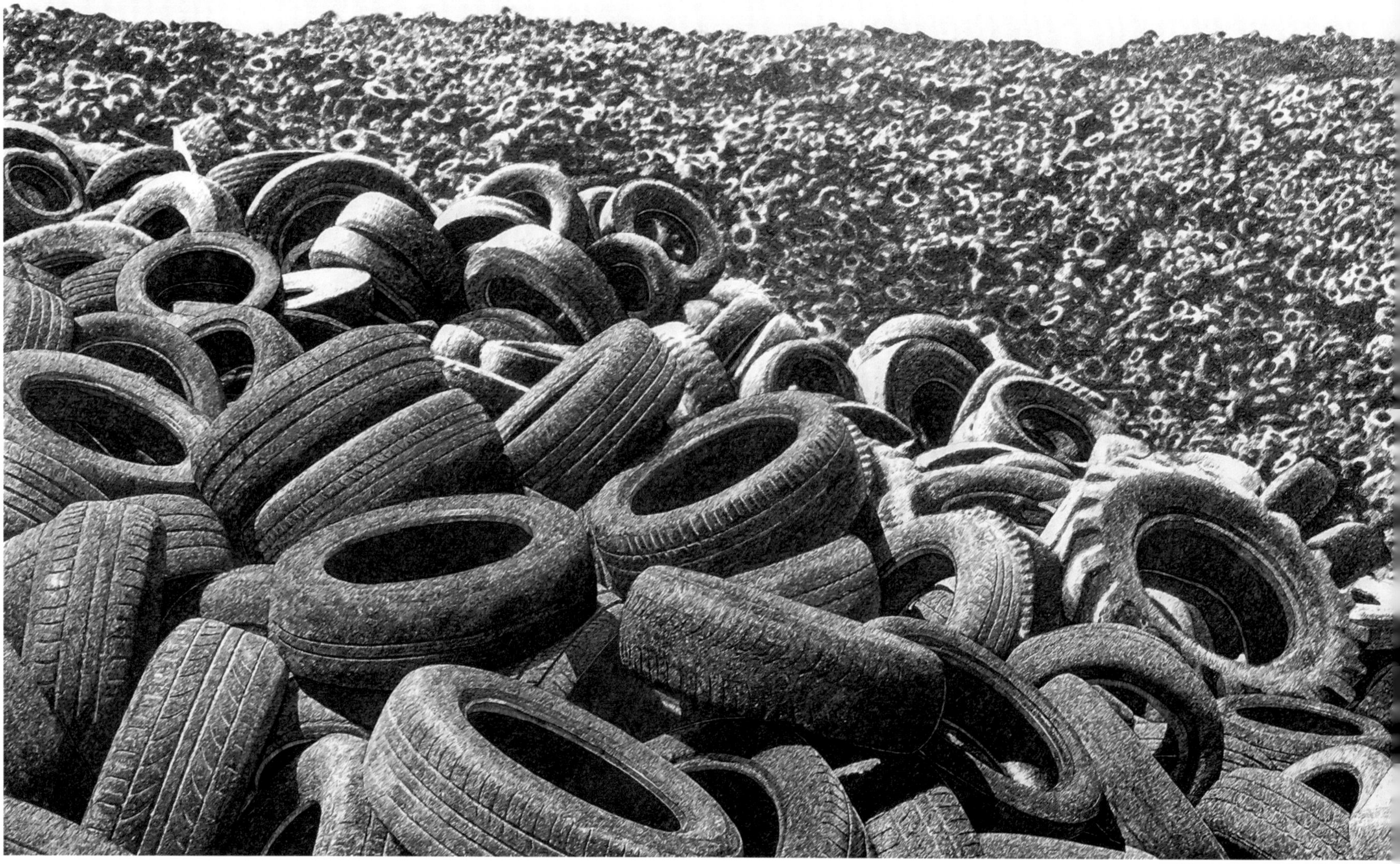

5.

5. *Ruins of Hope 1*, 2019, ink on paper, 120 × 310 cm (47 ¼ × 122 in)

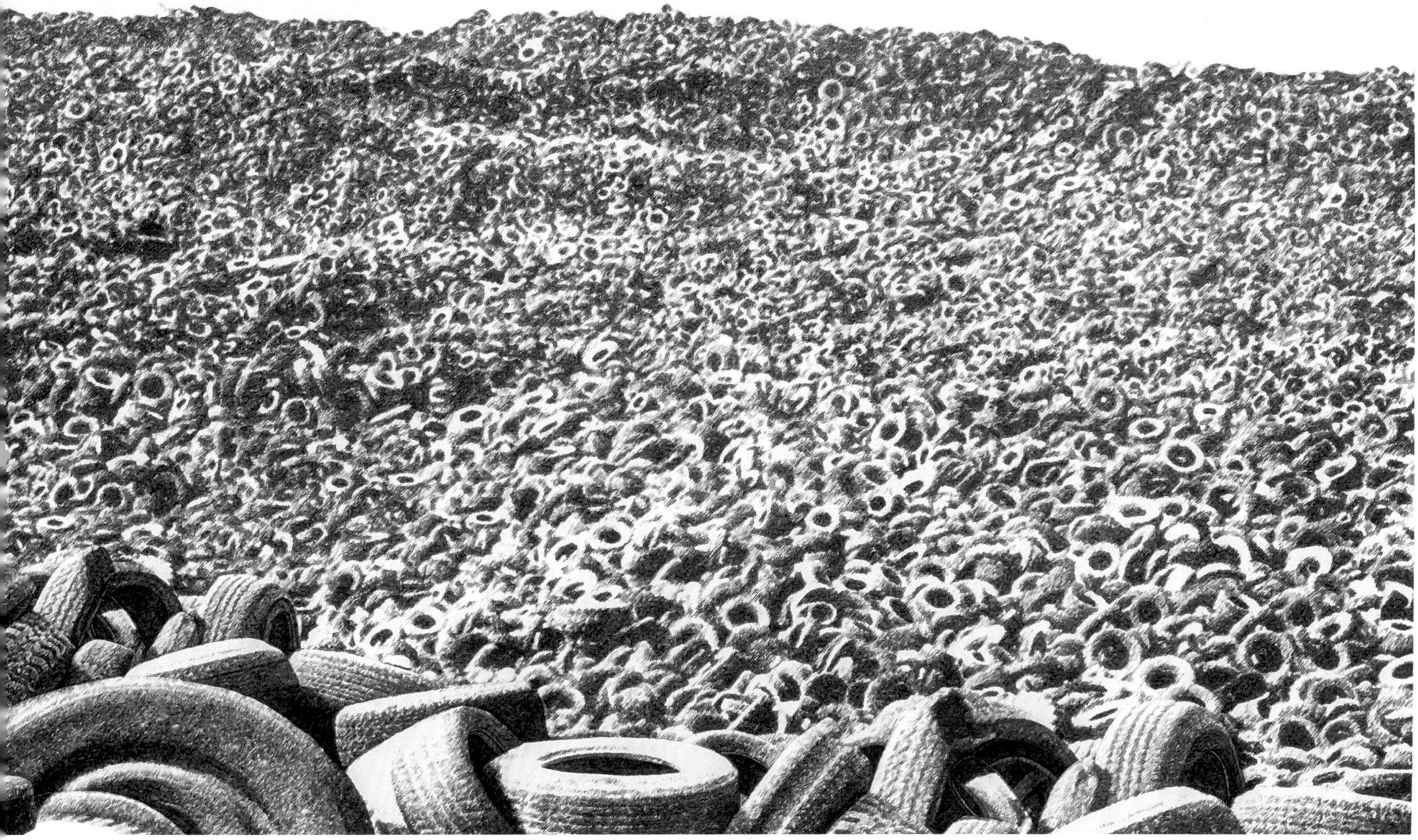

MOUNIRA AL SOLH .... 'Is right not always victorious? Perhaps not.' This concise and conversational jotting is inscribed as a handwritten note in Arabic on Mounira Al Solh's portrait of a young woman, sketched on yellow, lined legal paper, which forms part of *I strongly believe in our right to be frivolous*, an ongoing suite of biographical mini portraits of refugees begun in 2012. Blotches of paint, a red-stained mouth and searing eyes, set within a few deft lines suggesting her headscarf, engage the viewer. Another portrait depicts an older woman also wearing a headscarf, the mother of five daughters, her face covered in wrinkles rendered in dense, black gouache. .... Raised in Beirut, Lebanese-Dutch artist Al Solh works across video, installation and socially engaged community projects, but deploys drawing as a mode to tell stories of forced migration, conflict, assassination and struggle alongside everyday occurrences such as watching TV and eating walnut cake at Starbucks. Her intimate portraits and accompanying written notations capture the plight of displaced migrants by intertwining personal accounts with political scenarios: 'you left on 07/12/2011. We understood you are with the revolution and there are people dying.' .... The title of *I strongly believe in our right to be frivolous* is derived from a statement by Mahmoud Darwish, a Palestinian poet known for writing about the turmoil of exile. In an interview with Eva Heisler in *Asymptote*, Al Solh commented: 'I personally wanted to recollect my Syria through the stories of the people, but also to live its diversity, its love stories, and its little unwritten matters that happen on the side of the war. When people came over, we spoke about everything! Also, we spoke about frivolous matters.' The series numbers more than 450 portraits or conversational sketches and up-close depictions in pen, pencil, ink and watercolour. Al Solh invited displaced peoples to her studio to share their experiences, hearing their stories and drawing their portraits. Mainly Syrians but also Afghans, Bengalis, Somalis and Ethiopians, her sitters recounted personal, political and social narratives, alluded to in the artist's handwritten annotations. The series of drawings has been exhibited in Documenta 14 (2017) in Kassel, Germany and as part of the artist's first solo exhibition in the United States, at the Art Institute of Chicago in 2018. .... Whether using bureaucratic, yellow lined paper or a graph pad, Al Solh's image and text portraits are intimate and immediate, part of an exchange and sharing of histories that reflects the artist's personal plight. Her maternal family was from Syria and her paternal family from Lebanon, but in 1958 her grandfather was assassinated. In her work displacement, war, torture, danger, detention and massacre are interwoven with everyday reflections and ordinary accounts.
.... Natalie King

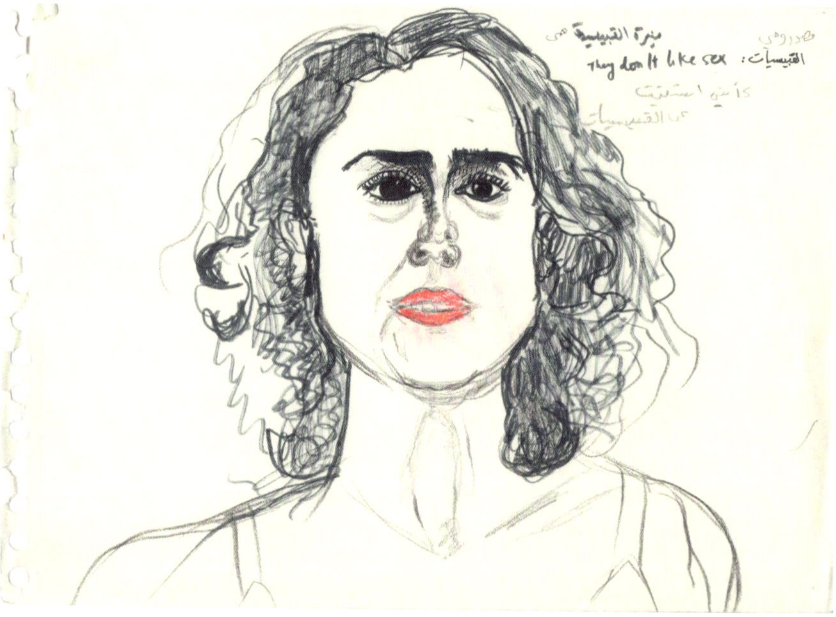

1.

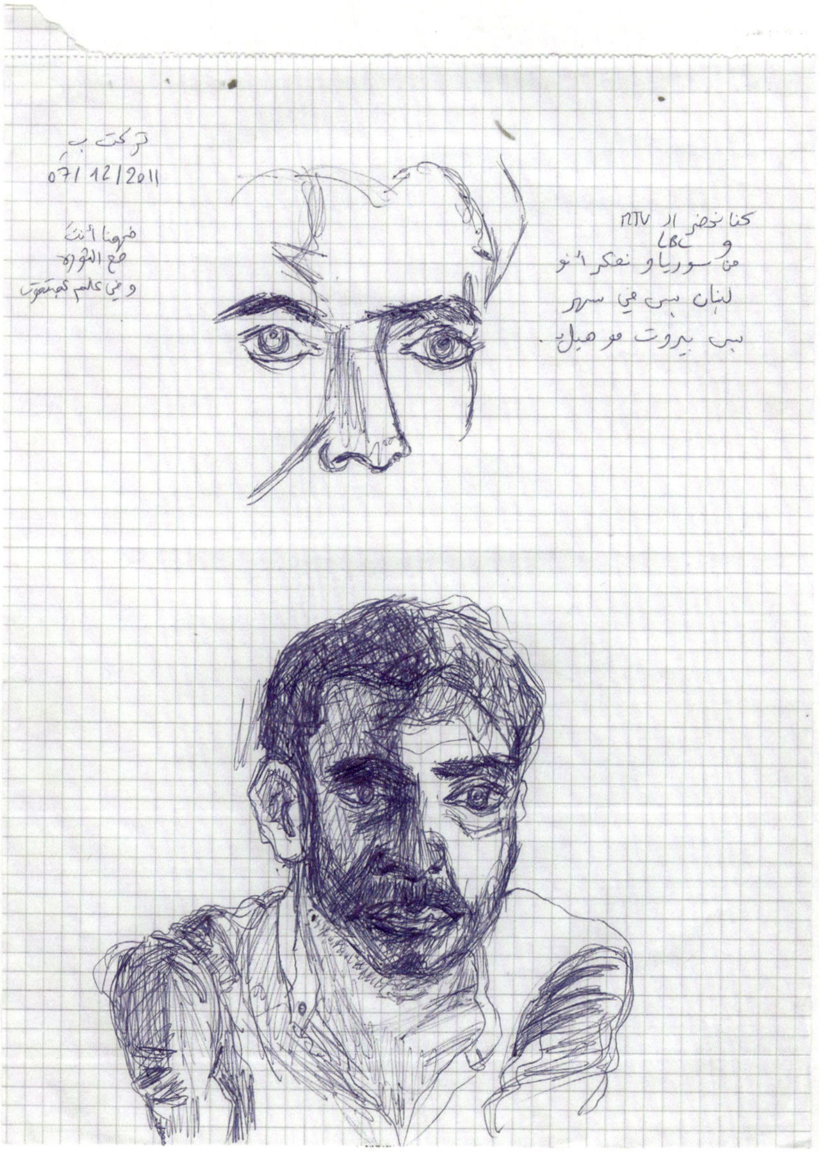

2.

Born 1978, Beirut. Lives and works in the Mediterranean Sea, Lebanon, and the IJssel River, the Netherlands.

1–6. *I strongly believe in our right to be frivolous*, 2012–ongoing, mixed media on legal paper, 1: 22 × 32 cm (8 ⅝ × 12 ⅝ in); 2: 35 × 22 cm (13 ¾ × 8 ⅝ in); 3 & 4: 28.6 × 21 cm (11 ¼ × 8 ¼ in); 5: 28 × 21.4 cm (11 × 8 ⅜ in); 6: 28.6 × 21 cm (11 ¼ × 8 ¼ in)

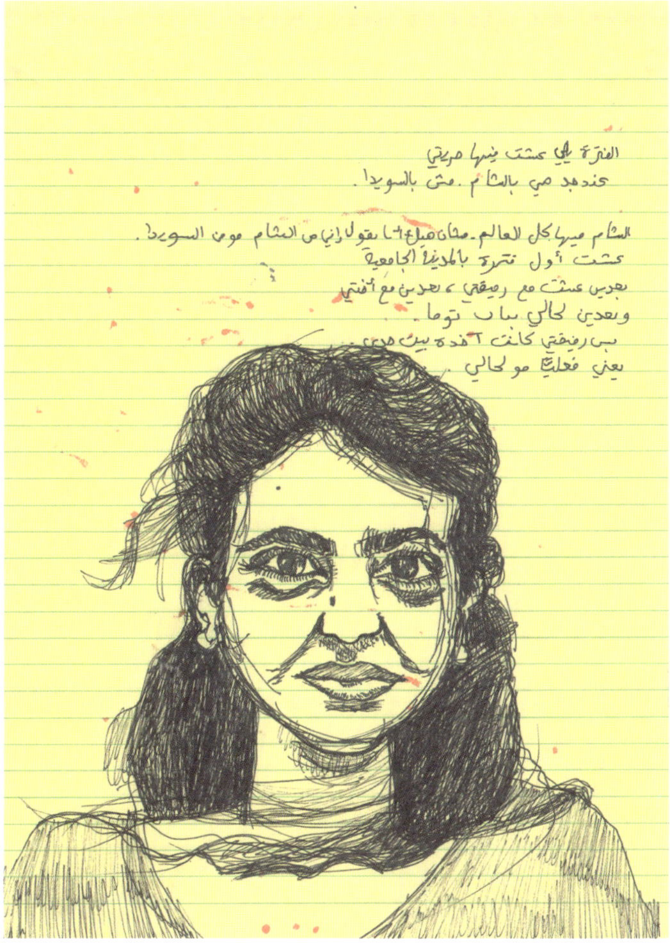
الفترة يلي عشت فيها حريتي
عندجد هي بالشام. مش بالسويد.
الشام فيها كل العالم. مشان هيك بقول إني من الشام مو من السويد.
عشت أول فترة بالمدينة الجامعية
بعدين عشت مع رفيقتي، بعدين مع أختي
وبعدين لحالي بباب توما.
بس رفيقتي كانت آخدة بيت حدي
يعني فعلياً مو لحالي.

3.

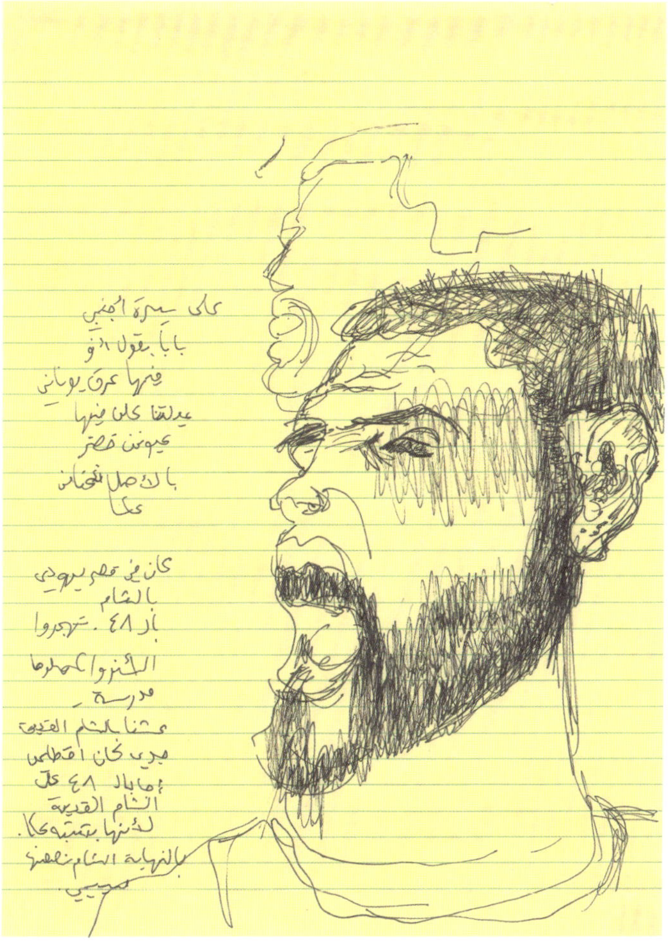

4.

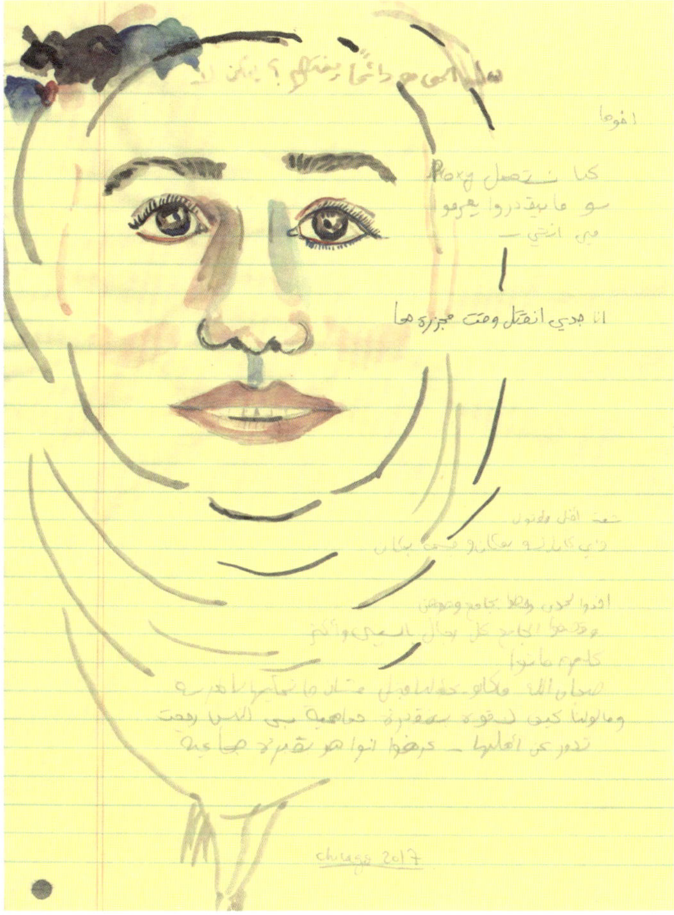

5.

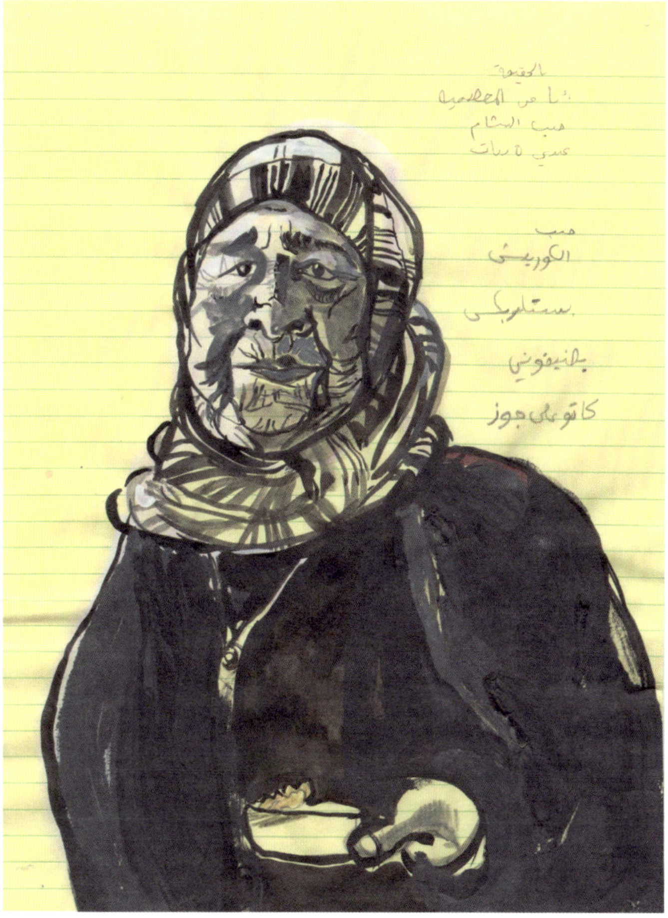

6.

r u b y o n y i n y e c h i a m a n z e .... ruby onyinyechi amanze, who prefers to have her name in all lowercase, creates large drawings on paper that exist in a cosmology entirely their own. Ordinary conventions of proportion, gravity and space have been released from duty to form new and liquid illogics. Scooters, potted plants, birds and flowers swerve through the white without reference to ground or horizon. Even the boundaries of the characters that inhabit her world are porous and elastic. The series titled 'aliens, hybrids and ghosts' (2013–ongoing) features two protagonists: ada, an alien who looks not unlike the artist herself, rendered with great detail in pencil, and audre, a leopard with a human body, mostly conjured by collage. In *audre and ada [pas de deux]* (2019) the two are sharing a dance, while in *the garden palace and the folly of innocence* (2014) audre is doing ada's hair, though, curiously, with ada's signature yellow hands. The two are of the same piece, as if different aspects of a single life. amanze was born in Nigeria, grew up in Britain and now resides in the United States. Her works are often read as a comment on home and belonging as hybrid and interchangeable concepts – a constant tango between body and place. That she chooses to write her name, as well as the names of her characters and the titles of her works, using only lowercase letters, speaks to this understanding of identity as indeterminate. 'Home can be many different places,' she explained on the occasion of being named the Deutsche Bank featured artist at Frieze New York in 2019, 'not just geographical places with borders and points on a map, but mental, emotional and spiritual places that you can go between very easily.' .... Drawing on paper has historically been for sketches and studies, and therefore lends itself well to amanze's provisional and amorphous compositions. But works on paper are also often small and modest in ambition, whereas amanze's tend towards the monumental. *with the galaxy beneath her, she remembered the magic of soaring amidst coconut clouds* (2014) is roughly two by three metres (six and a half by ten feet) large. It depicts yellow ada on a blanket of geometric shapes, gazing into the distance through a thin frame as her cloud of hair morphs into a row of palm trees. Here, a personal and introspective moment, wavering and doubtful, without narrative clarity, is given immense room to breathe. And room, or the ample space left empty in the artist's drawings, is just as important as the motifs themselves. While the juxtaposition of the serious and intricate drawings and the lighter collage elements brings a tongue-in-cheek atmosphere to the pieces, it is the white in-between space that delivers their poetry. In amanze's work, blank paper is a promise of continuous transformation.
.... Kristian Vistrup Madsen

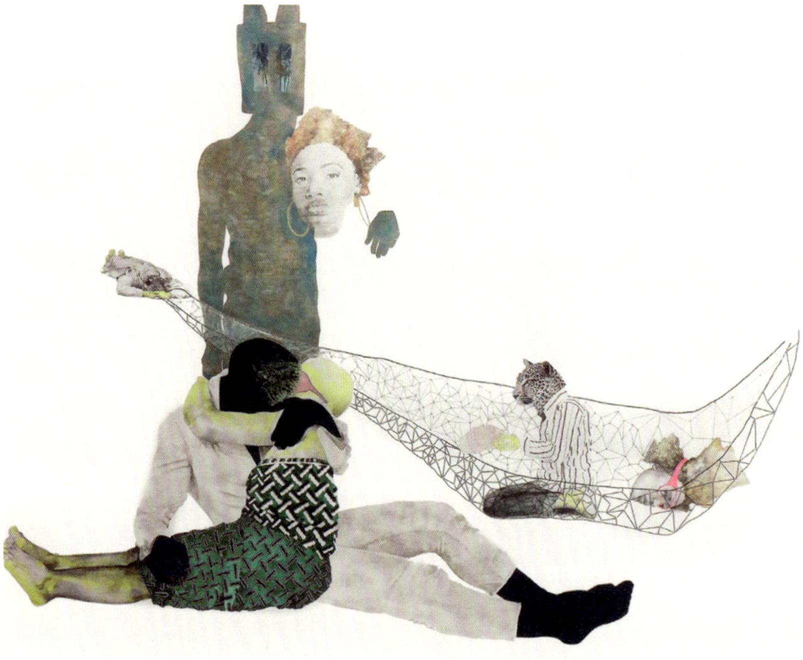
1.

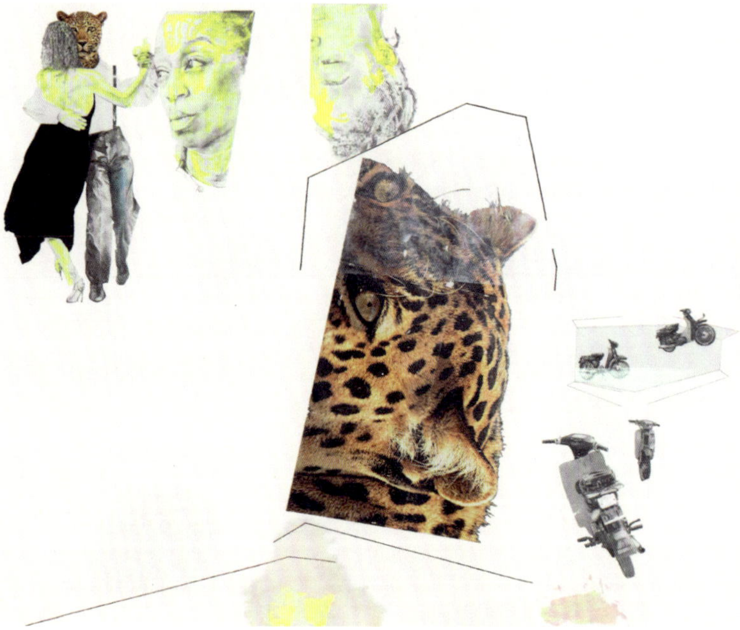
2.

Born 1982, Port Harcourt, Nigeria. Lives and works in Philadelphia and Brooklyn.

1. *kisses at a beach with a hammock for audre [to learn to pray]*, 2015, graphite, ink, coloured pencils, fluorescent acrylic and photo transfers on paper, 183 × 244 cm (72 × 96 in)
2. *audre and ada [pas de deux]*, 2019, graphite, photo transfers, ink and gouache on paper, 101 × 140 cm (39 ¾ × 55 ⅛ in)
3. *either way, you'll be in a pool of something*, 2015, graphite, ink and photo transfers on paper, 102 × 152 cm (40 ⅛ × 59 ⅞ in)

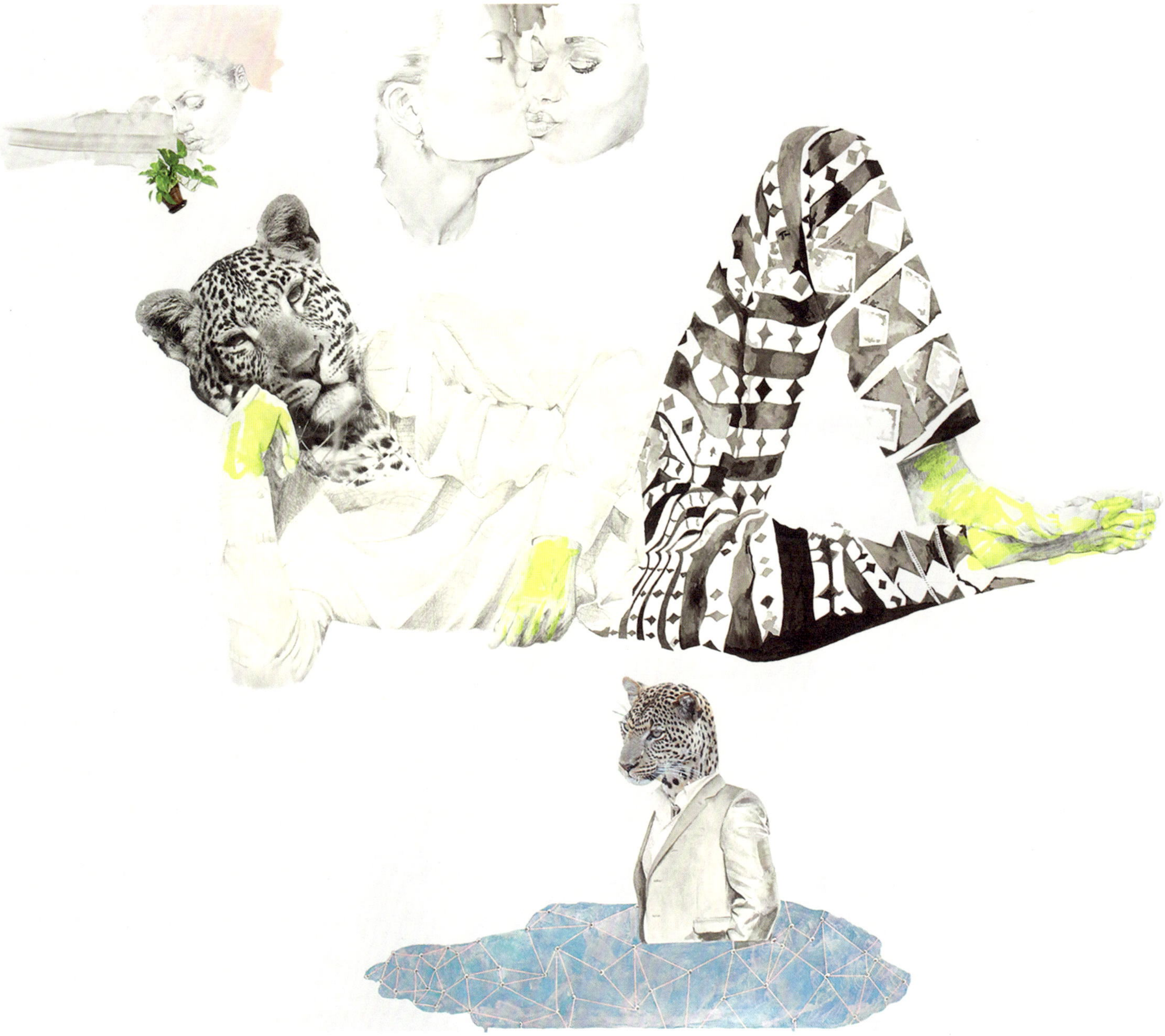

3.

CATHERINE ANYANGO GRÜNEWALD ....
In 2010 Catherine Anyango Grünewald published a graphic novel adaptation of Joseph Conrad's classic, *Heart of Darkness* (1899). Her menacingly dense black and white drawings depict limbs like flashes of light and boats like bullets shooting from the river and into the forest. One picture looks at a table from the perspective of a seemingly enormous lamp, covered in flies. Such 'surreal mismatches of scale,' Michael Faber wrote in *The Guardian*, 'allude to colonialism's distortions of moral perspective'. With her illustrations Anyango renders the rot of Conrad's narrative self-reflexive, without having to change it at all. This is her pictorial recipe for engaging with histories of colonialism as well as ongoing racism: do not shy away from a painful scene, or tarnished tale, but look at it harder, draw it thicker. .... The many murders of unarmed Black men by police in the United States, which garnered media attention after the lethal shooting of Florida high school student Trayvon Martin in 2012, are among the subjects of Anyango's series 'Last Seen' (2012–). Her large drawings are based on the last known recorded image of the victim, often glitchy or pixelated, taken by a phone or CCTV camera. In these pictures, there is no composition or framing, only this questionable relationship to a brutal, widely circulated and forensic image. Countless layers of pencil make a flickering effect, at once shiny and matte, that gives the work a real material texture. 'The ethics here are blurred, the rights of who owns these images debatable,' Anyango has written about the series, 'and I hope by drawing them to elevate the photographs into something beautiful, at least, an homage to the victims.' .... While 'Last Seen' deals with the complicated politics of representing those who have lost control of their own image to death or systemic oppression, the series 'Black Beds' depicts the absence of those same bodies. In a set of dark and haunting drawings, such as *Burnt Bed* (2013), Anyango shows empty bed frames that recall the black mouth of a grave. What are the traces we leave behind where we toss and turn, rest and sleep? Here, the pencil is laid on so thick as to transfer the lead on to the paper, making a metallic surface that cracks to resemble burnt wood. This goes beyond the remits of drawing to a kind of fusion of pencil and paper into something entirely other. A compensation, perhaps, for the bed's missing occupant.
.... Kristian Vistrup Madsen

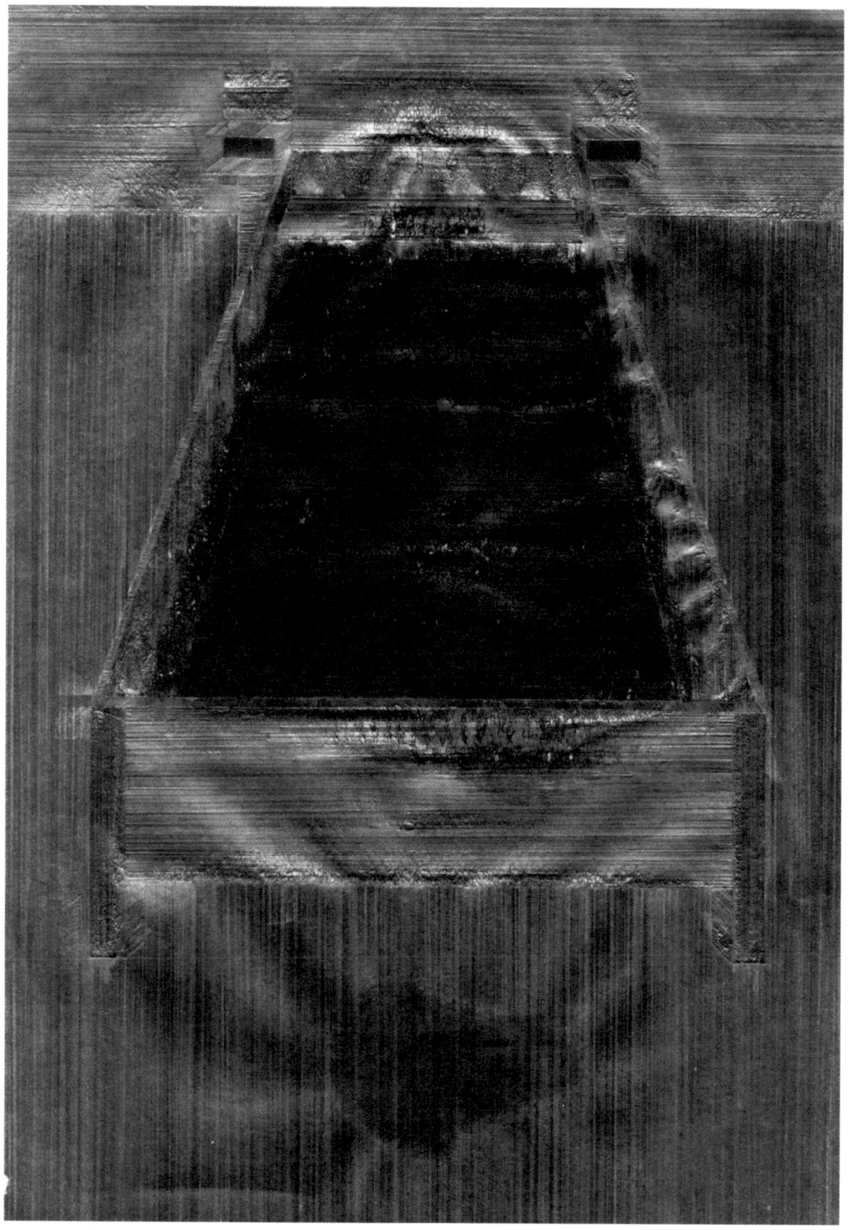

1.

Born 1982, Nairobi, Kenya. Lives and works in Stockholm.

1. *Burnt Bed*, 2013, pencil on paper, 42 × 29.7 cm (16 ½ × 11 ⅝ in)
2. *Bad Dream: The Death of Walter Scott, 4.4.15*, 2017, pencil and charcoal on watercolour paper, 76 × 111 cm (30 × 43 ¾ in)
3. *The Death of Trayvon Martin, Florida, 26.2.12*, 2012, pencil on paper, 66 × 101.6 cm (26 × 40 in)

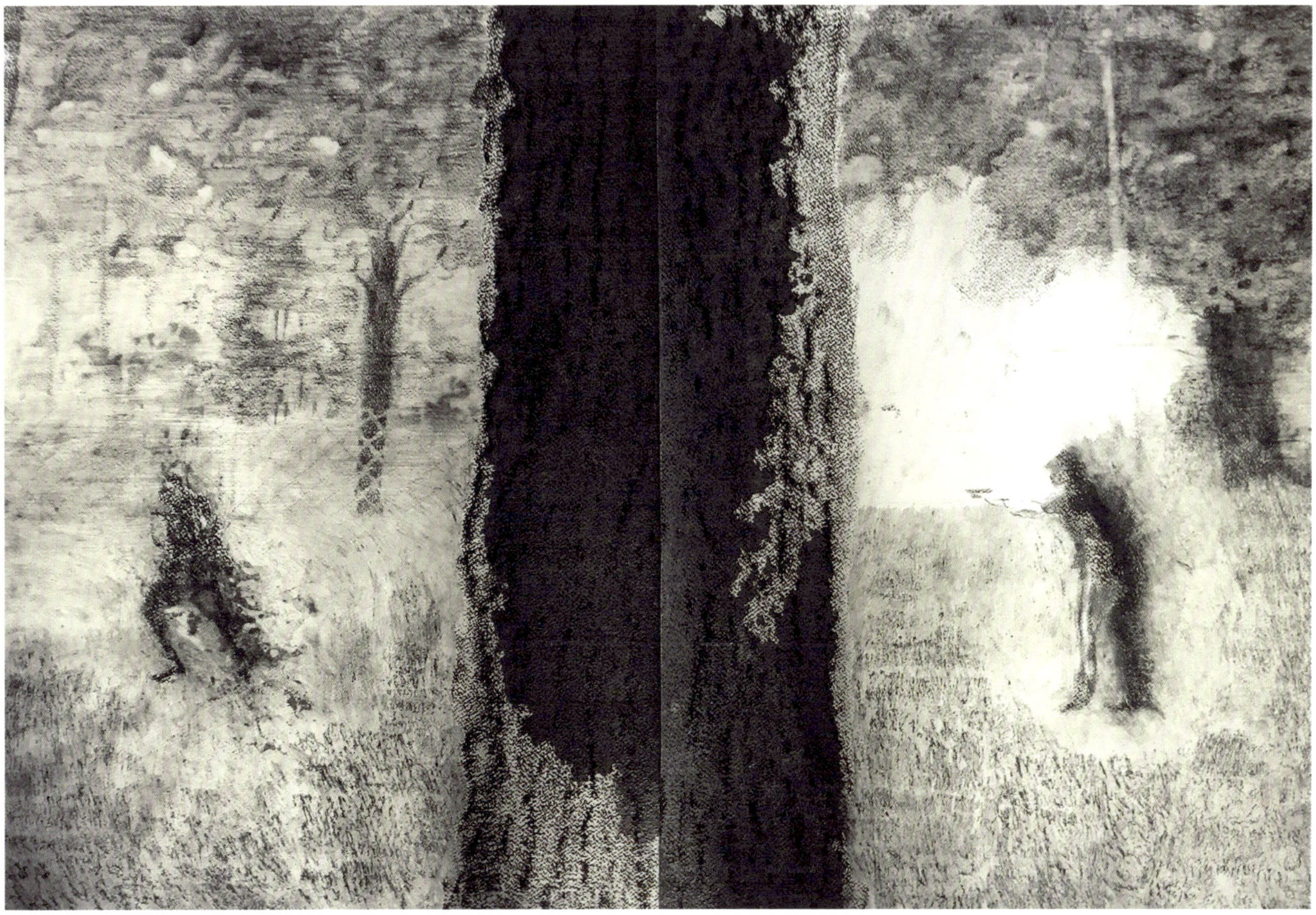
2.

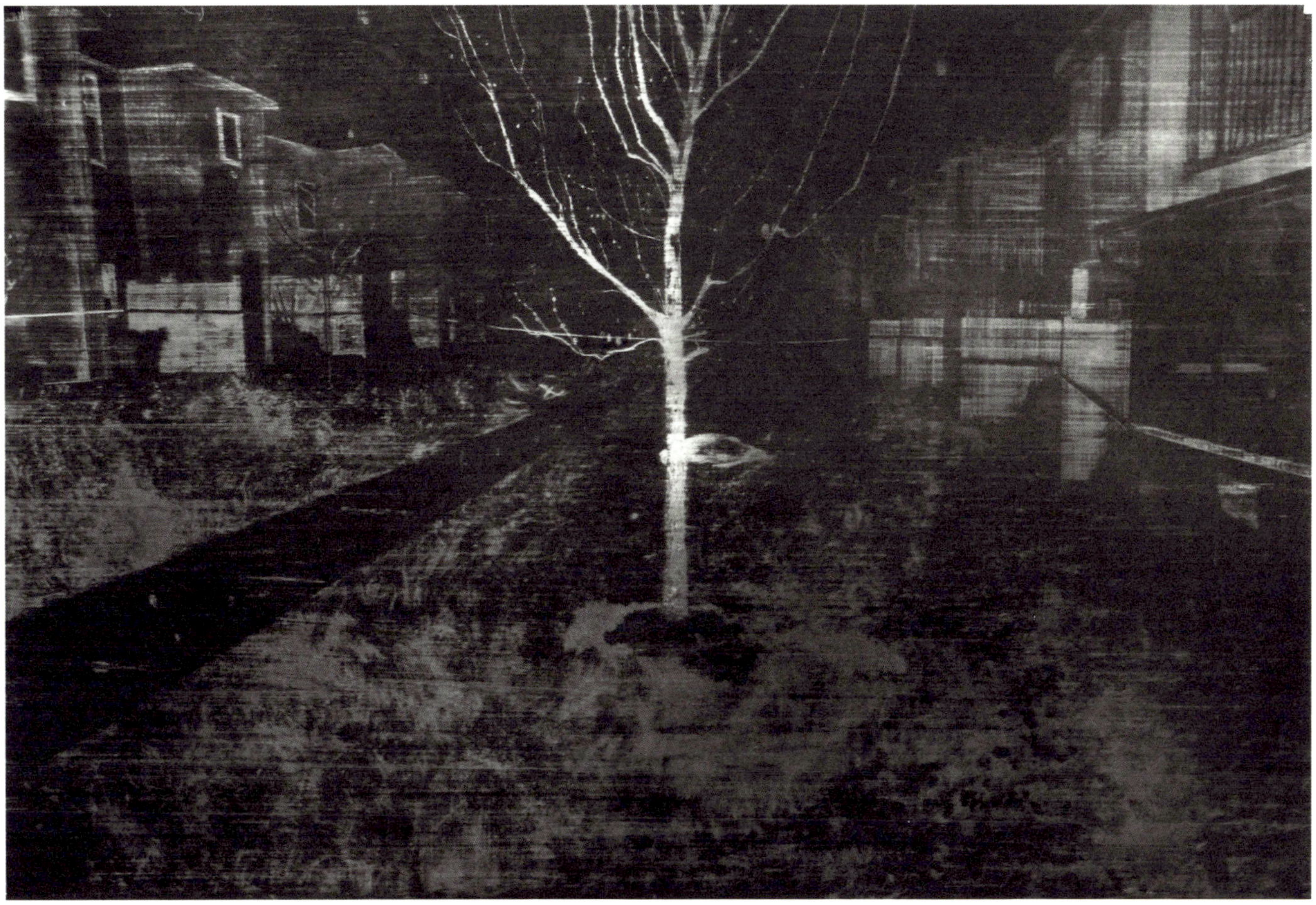
3.

KATE ATKIN .... Once primarily a photographer, Kate Atkin found the camera's capacity for verisimilitude unable to satisfy her penchant for exoticism and the fantastic. Turning her hand instead to drawing, the immediacy of the medium, coupled with the imaginative freedom it occasions, proved irresistible. Now working predominantly with graphite, Atkin spends days and sometimes weeks on her densely worked chiaroscuro drawings and related sculptures. Natural forms such as trees, roots, shells and rocks dominate her works, but these are made strange and unfamiliar, often appearing as if deformed or mutated. In many of Atkin's more recent drawings, trees seem to be disintegrating, their leaves turning to dust. In others, isolated trunks bulging with unsightly growths evoke the human body; gnarled, twisted roots become intestines, while thick, rugged bark morphs into skeletal structures. Sometimes phantasmic faces emerge, such as the skull-like head in *Study: Tree Head* (2016). Its mass of swirling marks is redolent of thick foliage or perhaps billowing plumes of smoke emanating from a deadly explosion. Straying into horror film territory is *Study: Seed Head* (2016), a more sinister visage formed from ghastly fissures in a grisly seed head. While Atkin's fascination with the natural world can be attributed to her upbringing in the New Forest in southern England, her preoccupation with damaged and diseased plants relates to a larger concern with mortality prompted by her father's premature death from cancer. Reminding us of nature's capacity for both beauty and ugliness, these images also hint at environmental concerns, suggesting a fragile world on the brink of ecological breakdown. .... Given Atkin's evident interest in structures and sculptural forms, it was inevitable that her two-dimensional drawings should start occupying three-dimensional space. *A Face Like Julius Caesar and Pale Green Hair* (2012) is a towering, wing-like structure constructed from plywood and designed to rest against the wall. Covered with twisted root forms and wispy, sinuous lines familiar from Atkin's works on paper, it is, in fact, based on a mussel shell in reference to the work of Marcel Broodthaers (1924–76), an artist whom Atkin has always admired for his incongruous juxtapositions and visual paradoxes. Occasionally, man-made objects, such as wagon wheels or hubcaps, inform her sculptures, but these too reflect an interest in change, transformation and transition. .... Like the organic forms that inspire them, Atkin's drawings could go on growing endlessly. For that reason, she often stops working on them before they are fully complete, thereby lending them an intriguing, unresolved quality. While photography continues to play a role in her practice (each drawing begins with a snapshot), it is through the humble pencil that her fanciful images grow and develop in ways that could never be achieved with a camera.

.... David Trigg

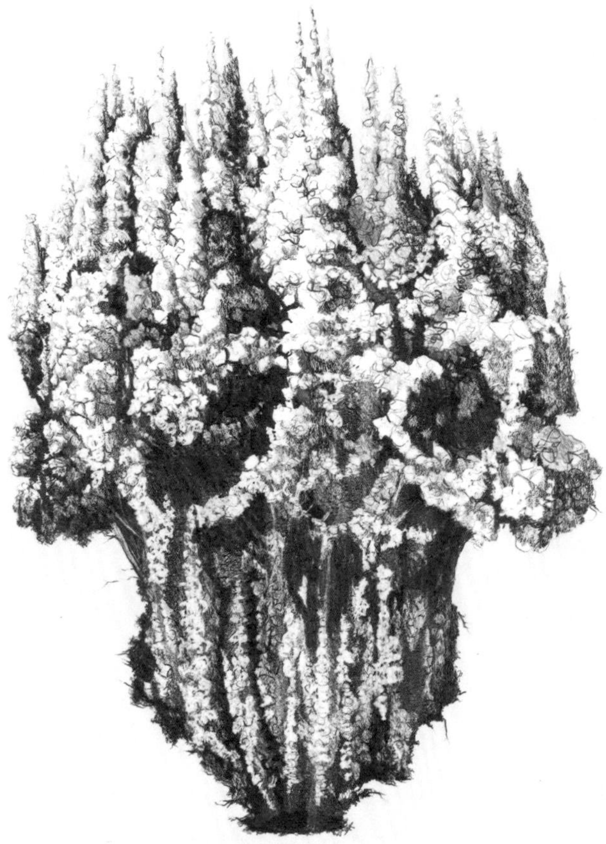

1.

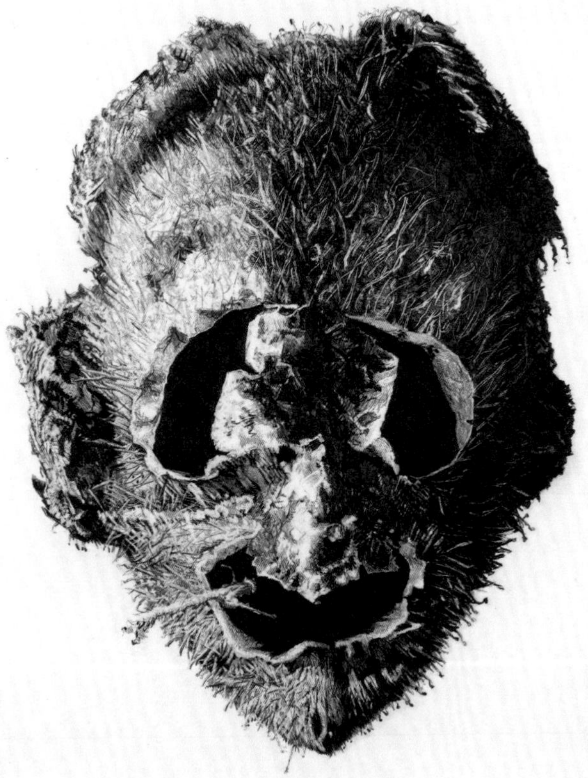

2.

Born 1981, Wiltshire, UK. Lives and works in London.

1. *Study: Tree Head*, 2016, pencil on paper, 46 × 38 cm (18 ⅛ × 15 in)
2. *Study: Seed Head*, 2016, pencil on paper, 43.8 × 39.2 cm (17 ¼ × 15 ½ in)
3. *A Face Like Julius Caesar and Pale Green Hair*, 2012, charcoal, gesso, Structura, birch plywood, screws, glue and varnish, 260 × 156 × 50 cm (102 ⅜ × 61 ⅜ × 19 ¾ in)

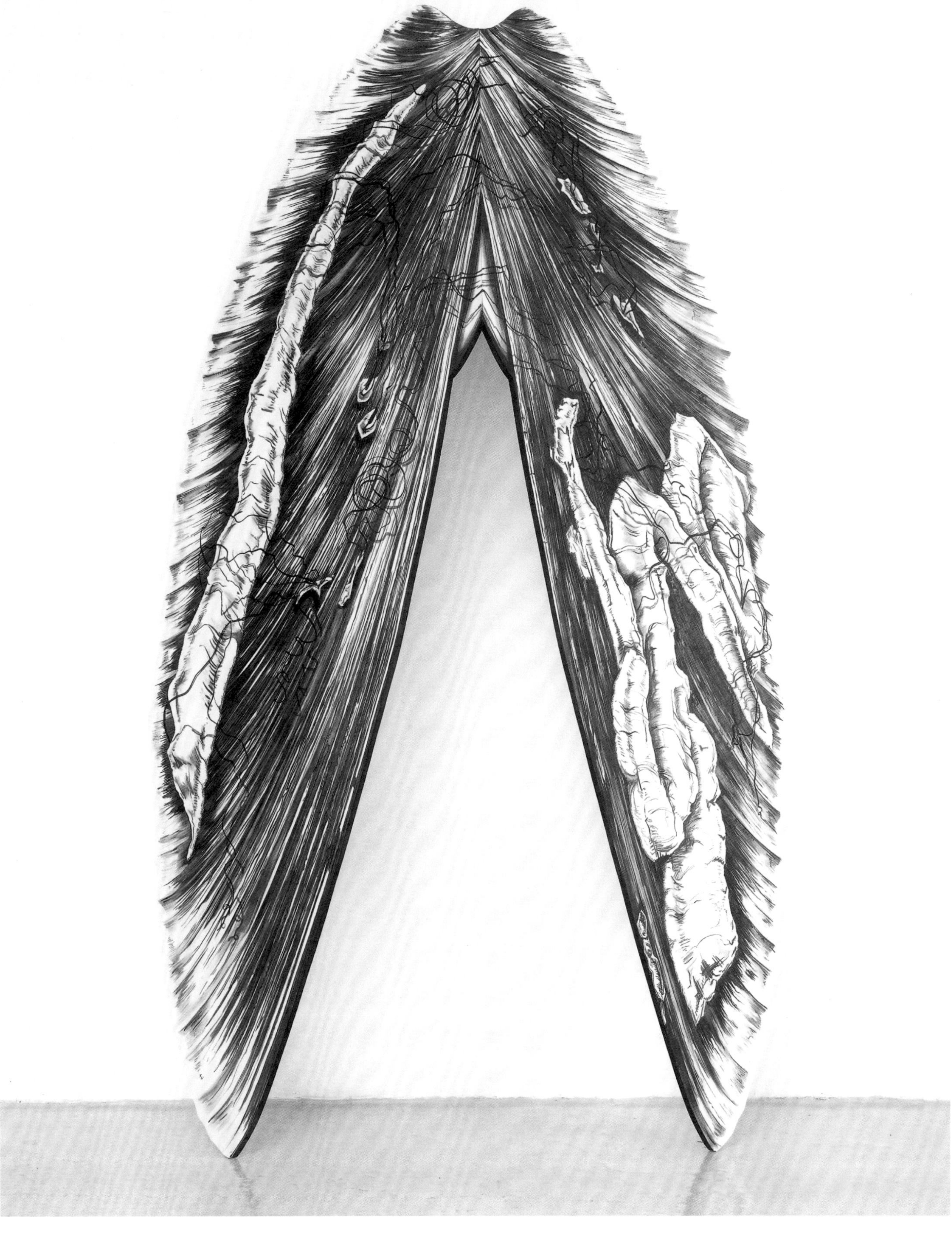
3.

TAUBA AUERBACH .... Early on in her career, Tauba Auerbach worked as a sign painter in California, and her knowledge of calligraphy and typography has infiltrated much of her art. Although she is prolific across a wide range of materials and techniques, including painting, photography, sculpture, weaving, books, jewellery and glass, drawing remains an important tool with which Auerbach pursues investigations into the nature of the physical world. Her insatiable curiosity motivates her ongoing endeavour to research the complex relationships between ideas and material structures. This includes academic disciplines such as physics, philosophy and anatomy, as well as magnetism and molecular biology, but also more freethinking and esoteric fields related to ancient knowledge, such as traditional medicine, puzzles and games. As she told *The Brooklyn Rail* in 2018: 'I want to hang out with ideas that aren't just a stretch for me, but a stretch for us collectively – just at the edge of our understanding in general.' Indeed, Auerbach's work, which often sparks an optical thrill in the viewer, invites us to try to make sense of what we are seeing, and perhaps even to reverse-engineer the processes by which she has produced it. .... Auerbach is interested in how different areas of study connect in such a way as to create a topology of knowledge that also includes the arts, and she regularly collaborates with mathematicians, scientists, musicians and designers. Her interest in the interconnections between materials and ideas extends to the edges of fields of knowledge, where things might begin to fray and come apart. Pattern provides a gateway to these enquiries, especially when the systematic arrangement of elements within a pattern gives way to the unexpected – to variation or accident. The state of imperfection that manifests in patterns displaying errors or changes of direction, as in *Ligature Drawing, 1 February 2019* (2019), is the product of an attitude that values process over outcome, interested in flaws and what they might reveal about a wider context. .... Auerbach's series of 'Ligature Drawings' and 'Marble' works are part of an ongoing investigation into fluid dynamics. Through a process of improvised calligraphy, these works on paper combine controlled mark-making and gestural abstraction. They evoke patterns of flow and ornament, orderliness and irregularity, and suggest that an established system has been recruited for the production of new forms and meanings. In making them, Auerbach hones in on forms that have the most rhythmic qualities. She has compared the flowing process of making the 'Ligature Drawings' to automatic writing, explaining, on the occasion of a 2019 exhibition at the Artist's Institute in New York, 'I don't want to just *draw* the rhythm, I want to be the rhythm, to sense the rhythms I already am.'
.... Ellen Mara De Wachter

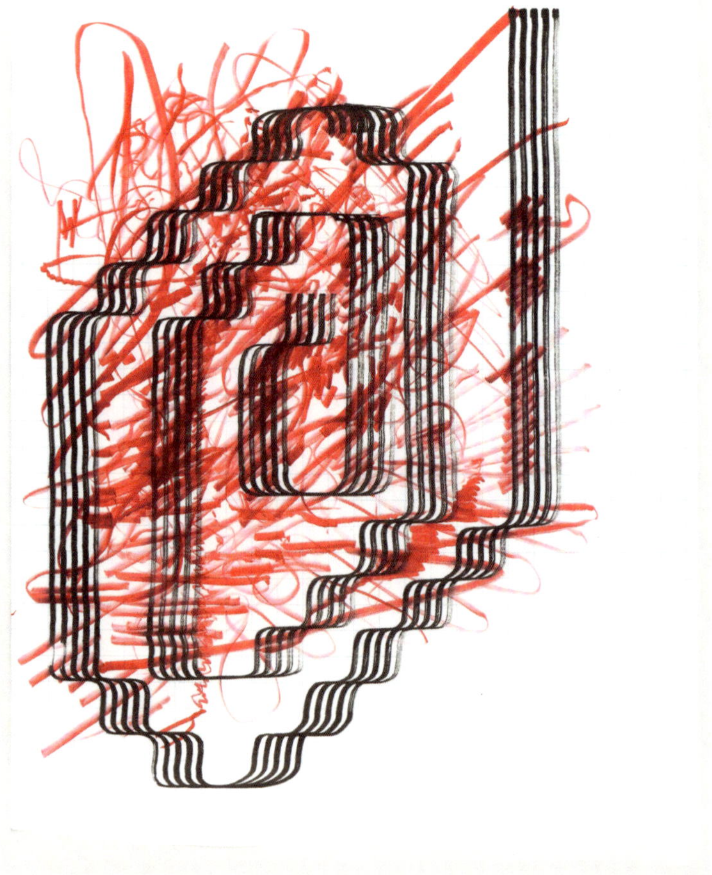
1.

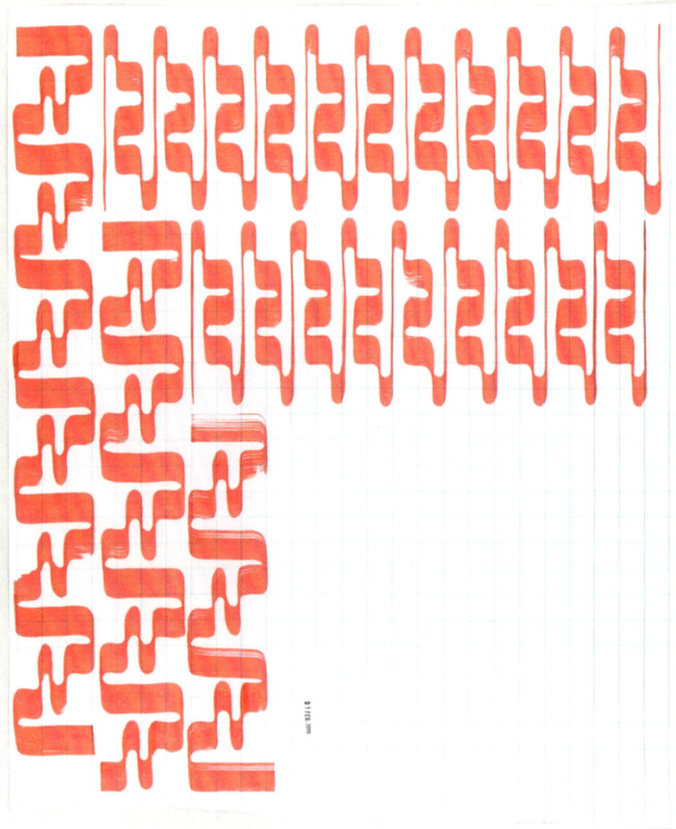
2.

Born 1981, San Francisco. Lives and works in New York.

1. *Ligature Drawing, 8 June 2018*, 2018, ink on paper with date stamp, 82.6 × 68.6 cm (32 ½ × 27 in)
2. *Ligature Drawing, 1 February 2019*, 2019, ink on paper with date stamp, 81.3 × 68.6 cm (32 × 27 in)
3. *Untitled*, 2019, ink on paper, 65.4 × 48.9 cm (25 ¾ × 19 ¼ in)

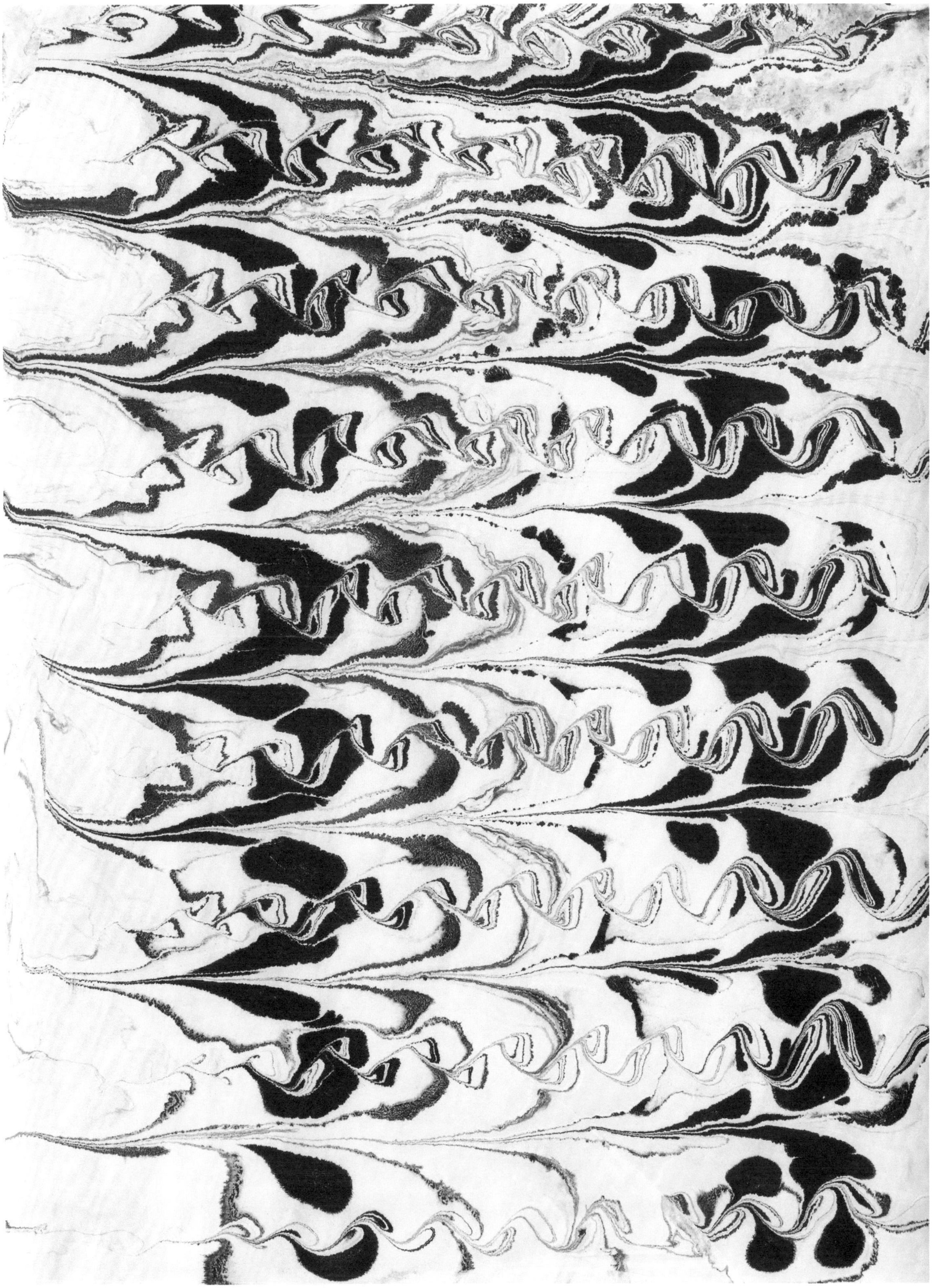

3.

VANESSA BAIRD .... The bloated and haggard faces in Vanessa Baird's 'Red Herring. Prednisolon, ciclosporin' series (2014–18) seem to show different victims of a disfiguring disease, yet each one is a self-portrait. The small watercolour drawings show the effects on the artist's body of prednisolone and cyclosporine, the drugs she takes for a chronic kidney condition that has seen her hospitalized many times. In each image her face is distorted but, whether swollen with red and blotchy skin or appearing gaunt, grey and pasty, she remains recognizable. These uncompromising portraits confront pain and suffering head-on, exemplifying the warts and all approach to art-making that has earned Baird significant acclaim and notoriety in her native Norway. .... In contrast to her small, sketch-like watercolours, Baird's large-scale pastel drawings teem with elaborate detail, melding intimate, personal narrative with larger existential concerns. *You are something else* (2017) comprises thirty-eight nightmarish scenes drawn onto long strips of paper that hang like wallpaper from ceiling to floor. The immersive installation confronts viewers with a procession of grotesque characters, abused women, drowning migrants, exhausted mothers and the artist's own father lying on his deathbed. Polluted waters and diseased trees allude to environmental breakdown, while mental torment is ostensibly embodied by a gang of psychotic Smurfs. Elsewhere, domestic disarray is represented by crockery and chairs strewn on a red carpet and a flurry of white pages that drift across the composition. Filled with perversion, excrement, chaos and despair, the drawing conveys a dark vision of a world gone awry. But it is not entirely hopeless – the final panel, which depicts sleeping babies and children, suggests new life and the potential for change. .... Autobiographical detail is often included in Baird's surreal fantasies. The drudgery of caring for children and elderly parents are recurring themes, as is the experience of losing her father to cancer, referenced by an emaciated figure sinking wearily into an armchair. With no studio, she works at home, often spending months producing her pastel drawings on the bedroom floor. Her turbulent domestic arrangements seep into her drawings and many reflect the mess of sharing her family home with her husband, children, mother, sister and nieces. It is hardly surprising, then, to learn that Baird rarely plans her drawings, allowing imagery to pour forth almost subconsciously. Describing them as 'rants', she acknowledges her works as cathartic vehicles by which she expresses her anger and frustration at the state of the world. As she commented in a 2017 interview with *Studio International*: 'It's like sticking everything together in your own life, mending things, putting all your frustrations and whatever down on the papers.' What emerges are ugly and intensely personal visions that captivate and repel in equal measure. .... David Trigg

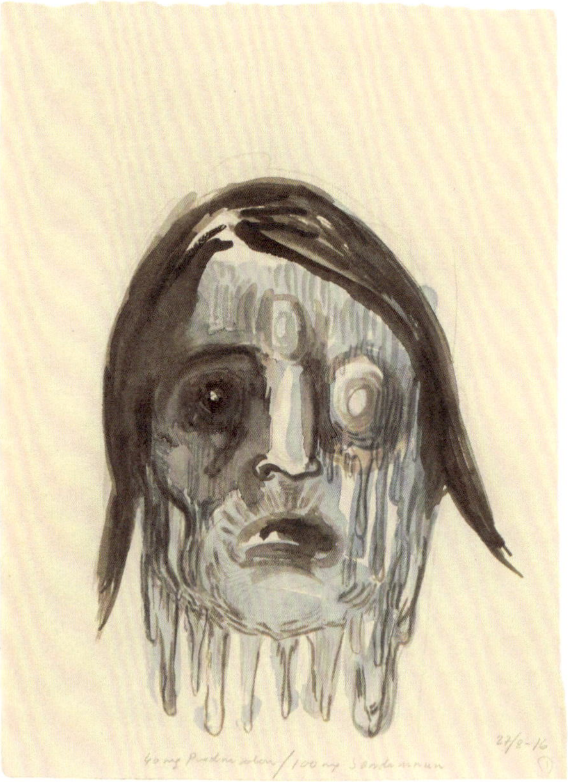

1.

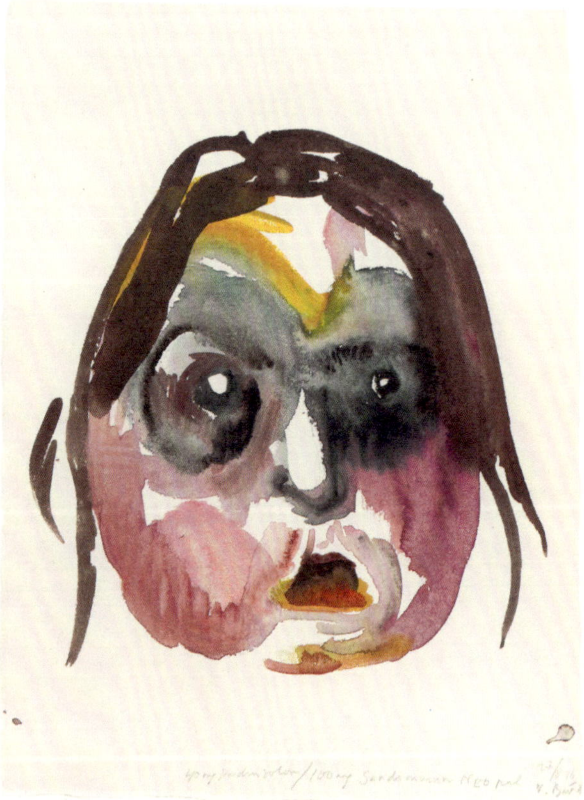

2.

Born 1963, Oslo. Lives and works in Oslo.

1. From the series 'Red Herring. Prednisolon, ciclosporin', 2014–18, watercolour on paper, 38 × 28.5 cm (15 × 11 ¼ in)
2. From the series 'Red Herring. Prednisolon, ciclosporin', 2014–18, watercolour on paper, 38 × 28.5 cm (15 × 11 ¼ in)

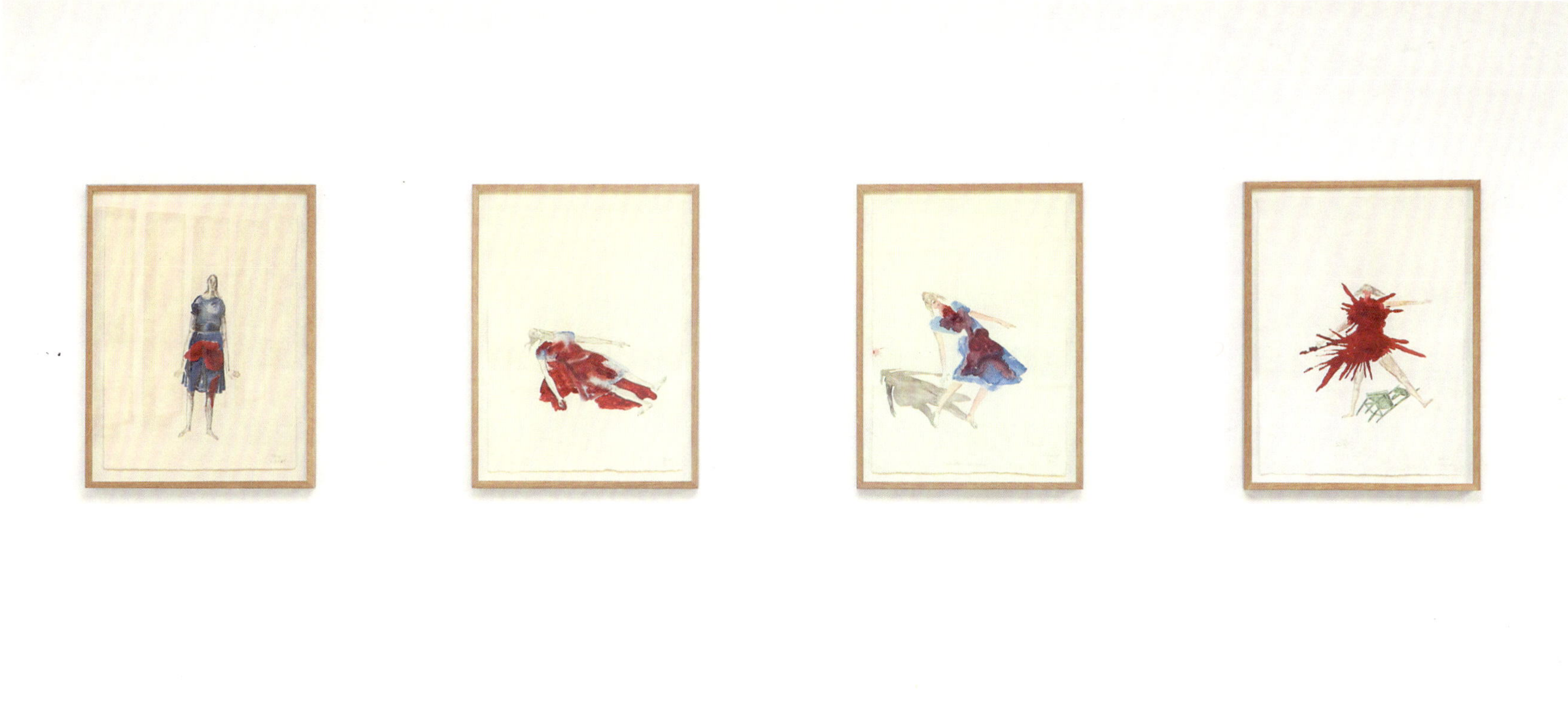

3.

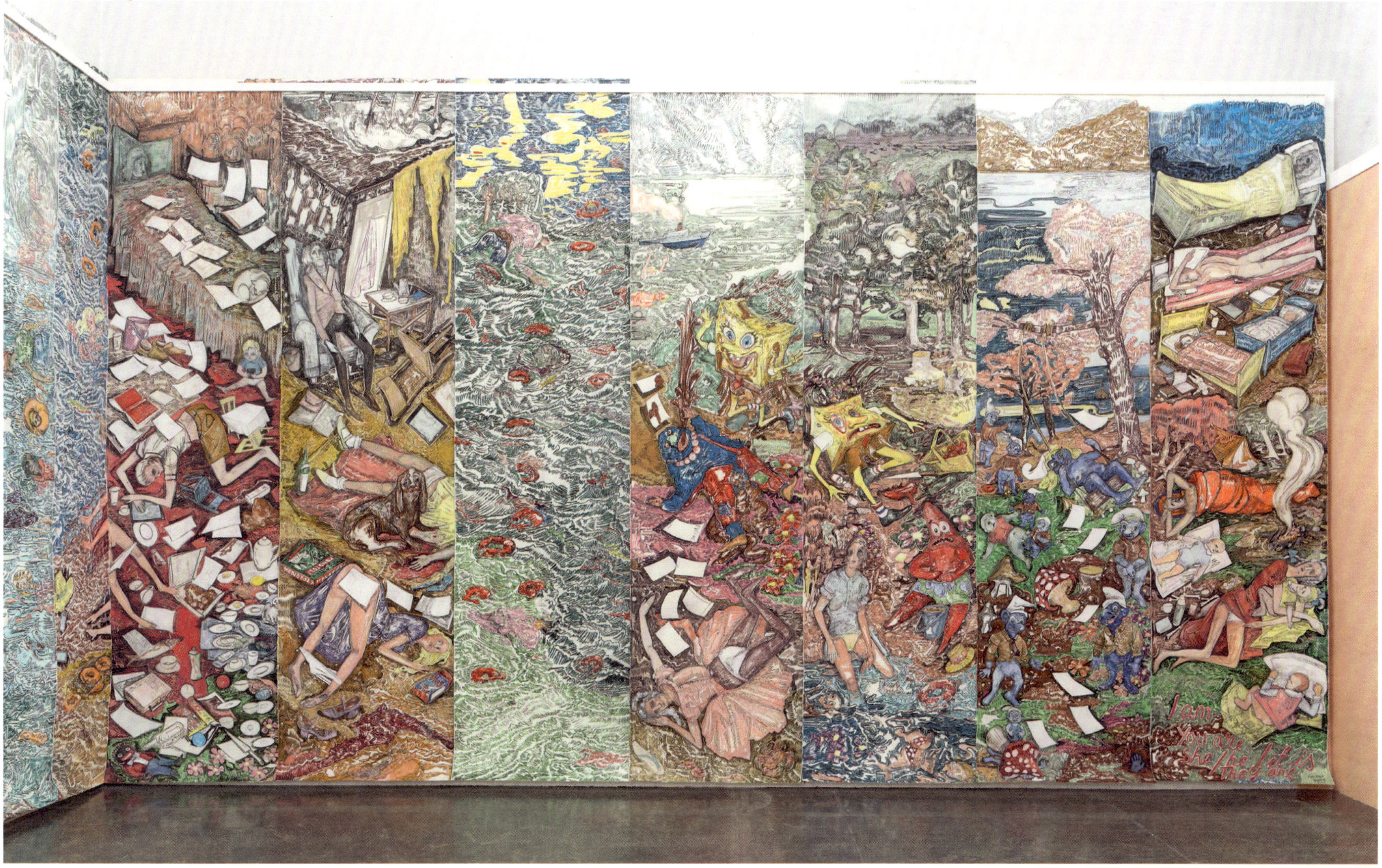

4.

3. *Here we go again…*, 2013, watercolour on paper, each 53 × 38.5 cm (20 ⅞ × 15 ⅛ in)
4. *You are something else*, 2017 (detail), soft pastel on 38 sheets printing paper, each 400 × 124 cm (157 ½ × 48 ⅞ in), installation view at Kunstnernes Hus, Oslo

NADIAH BAMADHAJ....... When Nadiah Bamadhaj delivered her lecture-performance *A King in a Republic* as part of 'FIELD MEETING Take 5: Thinking Projects' at Asia Contemporary Art Week in New York in 2017, she stridently critiqued the archipelago of Indonesia and the district of Yogyakarta where she lives with her husband and son. Bamadhaj's practice explores the socio-political issues confronting South East Asia, such as propaganda, independence, ruling versus the unruly, land, governance, status and Javanese cosmology. As such, her cultural context seeps into her densely rendered charcoal and collage drawings. She implicitly interrogates the region's restrictive societal mores in her large-scale drawings and detailed observations of the social intricacies of Yogyakarta's society, melding myth, monarchy, patterns and female forms....... Born to a Malaysian father and New Zealander mother, Bamadhaj studied weekly life-drawing classes as part of her degree at Canterbury University's School of Fine Arts in Christchurch, New Zealand. Even though she has a foundation in drawing, her practice spans digital media, performance lectures, installations and collage. Her drawings are distinctly sculptural, with heavy shading, weighty contours, dense figures and drapery set against stark white backgrounds. In *No Really, I'm Fine I* (2014) she interrogates the role of women and patriarchy with a Medusa-like head shaded with topographical contours and an anguished look of defiance. Surrounded by menacing and monstrous snakes in place of hair, Bamadhaj's Medusa incarnates female rage and authority....... In an interview with Naima Morelli in *Qantara* in 2019, Bamadhaj elaborated on her ongoing exploration of gender, sexuality and taboos in marginalized communities while working in a transgender-run shelter for people living with HIV: 'My exposure to issues of sex and sexuality of people with different genders and sexual orientation, and the stigma and shaming they face, has encouraged me to do more reading and research on the subject, the ideas of which have made their way into my work. I have met some amazing, resourceful and resilient people at the shelter, and I'm better off for it, not only as an artist, but in my life in general.'....... Another image that explores power and dominance is *The Misogynist's Throne I* (2015), a depiction of an ornately carved throne whose seat and legs become a human form draped in heavy cloth. Bamadhaj metaphorically references the position of the sultan and governance within a South East Asian cultural context. In doing so, she alludes to dominant moralities, discipline and religion in Indonesia. Based in the cultural city of Yogyakarta, a monarchy within a republic, Bamadhaj was awarded the Nippon Foundation's Asian Public Intellectual Fellowship in 2002 to spend a year in this communal and creative place where she now resides. Here, she can undertake fieldwork and scrutinize gender structures, power imbalances and overlooked histories.
.... Natalie King

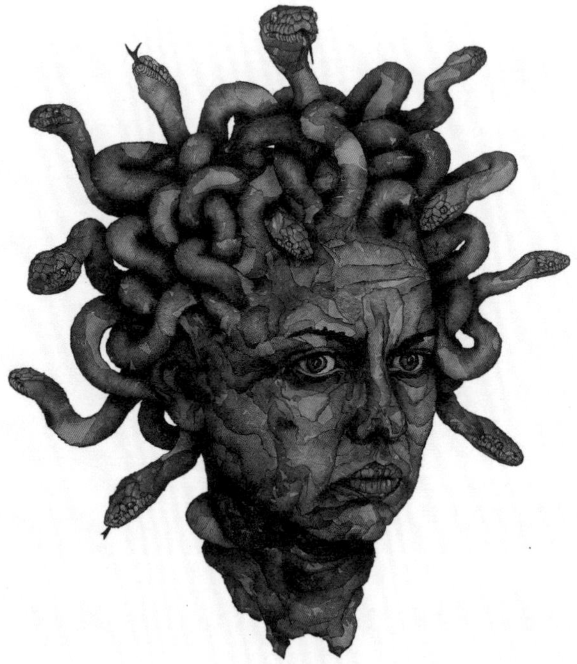

1.

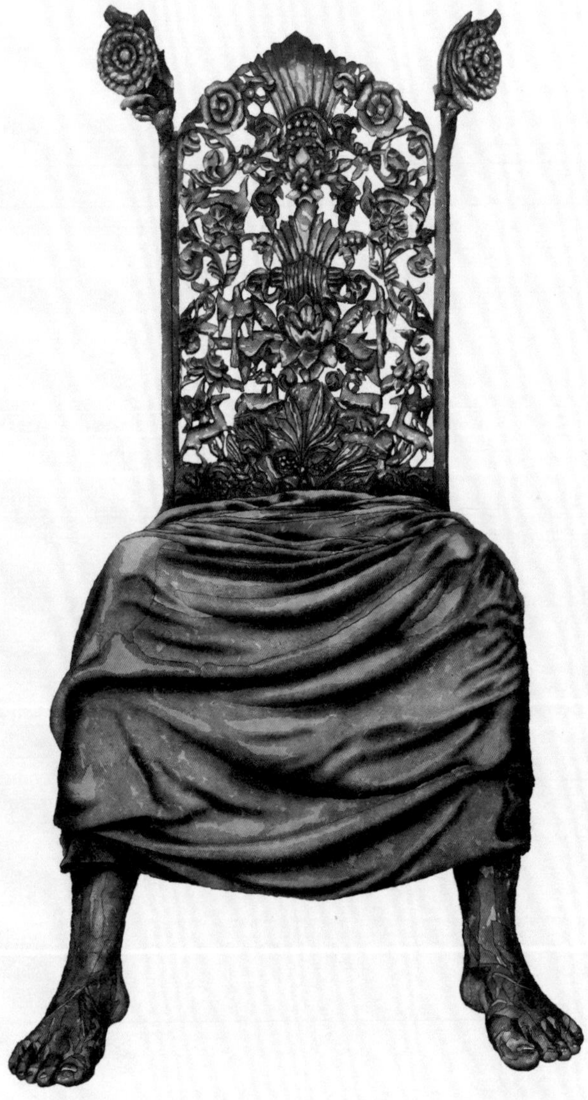

2.

Born 1968, Petaling Jaya, Malaysia. Lives and works in Yogyakarta, Indonesia.

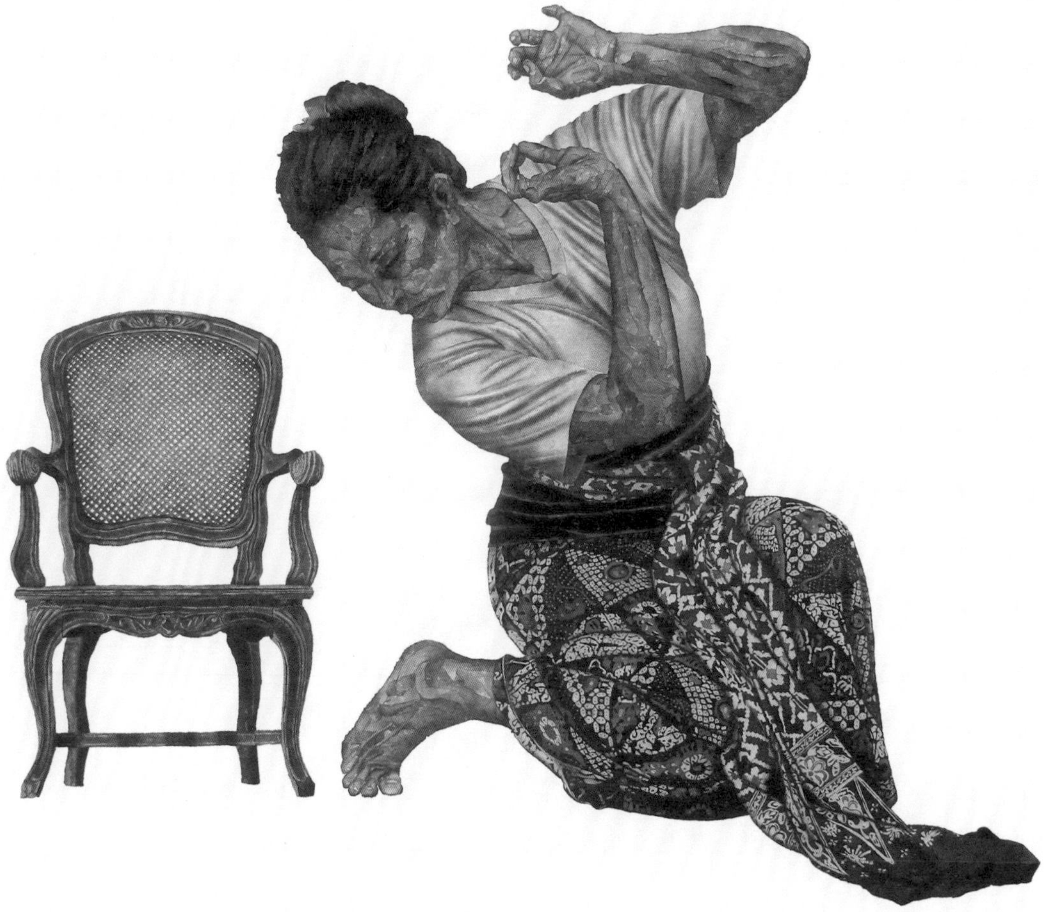

3.

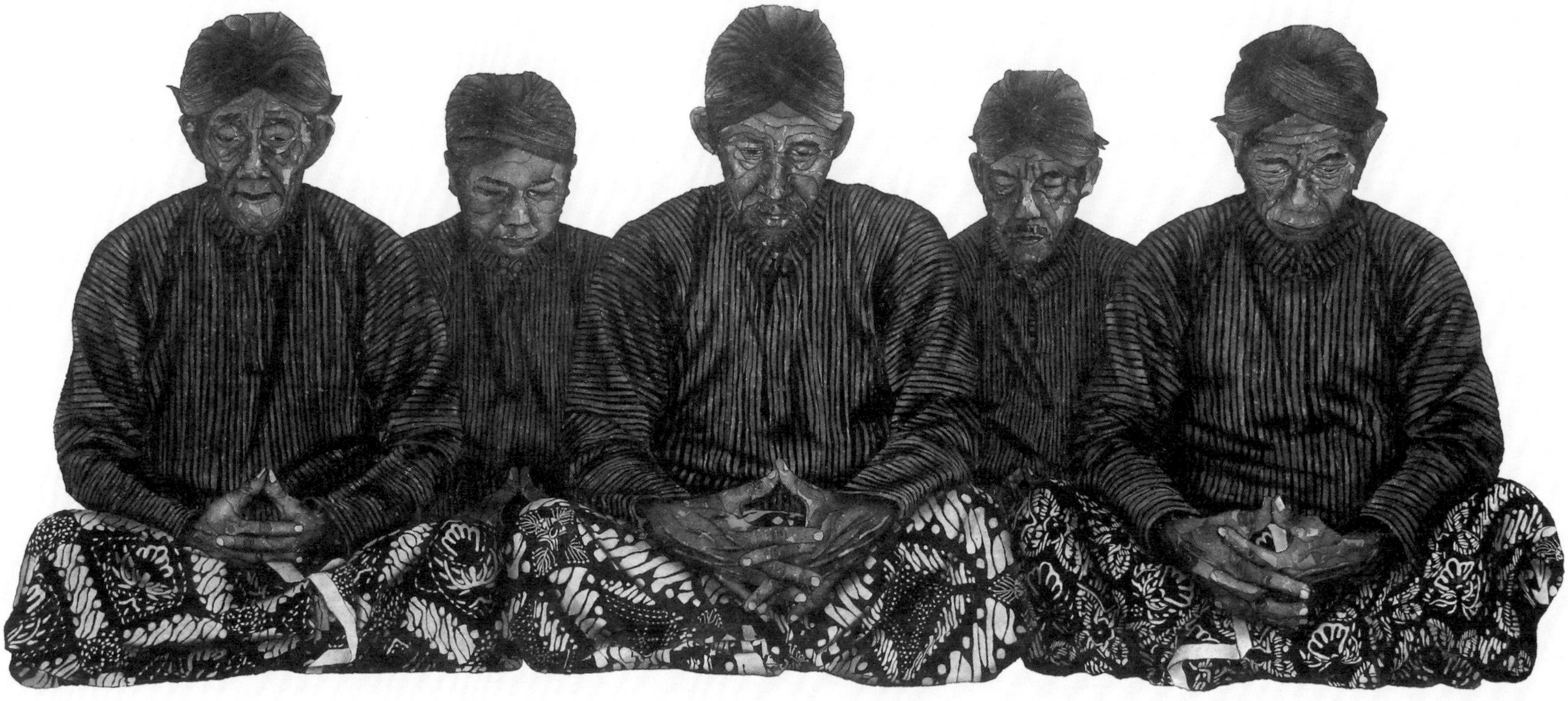

4.

1. *No Really, I'm Fine I*, 2014, charcoal and collage on paper, 114 × 114 cm (44 ⅞ × 44 ⅞ in)
2. *The Misogynist's Throne I*, 2015, charcoal and collage on paper, 198 × 111 cm (78 × 43 ¾ in)
3. *The Height of Ambivalence*, 2016, charcoal and collage on paper, 228 × 271 cm (89 ¾ × 106 ¾ in)
4. *Protestations of the Subservient*, 2016, charcoal and collage on paper, 117 × 272 cm (46 × 107 in)

THIAGO BARBALHO .... It was in 2015–16 that Thiago Barbalho turned to the medium of drawing. Crossovers between disciplines are fundamental to Barbalho's practice – he confesses that he first resorted to drawing in order to express that which became lost within the limits of language. The artist initially worked with the written word, having authored three books that range from poetry to a novel and short stories, and edited many more as part of Ediciones Vira-Lata – the independent press he founded after completing his philosophy studies in São Paulo. The publishing project produced visual arts fanzines and participated in artists' book fairs like the city's well-known Feira Tijuana. He also created and edited a magazine called *Revista Rosa*, in which queer art and literature intermingled. .... In *Monkey's Words* (2017) the artist gives the floor to a shouting baboon. Barbalho's explosive compositions appear to reference the Post-Impressionist painter Henri Rousseau's (1844–1910) naive art, while incorporating a street art psychedelia and at the same time paying tribute to the Brazilian modernist Tarsila do Amaral's (1886–1973) organic, rounded figures. Yet none of these comparisons does his work justice. Fiercely colourful and fully improvised, his drawings have a life of their own. Symbols, images, characters and fields of colour come together in what the artist has referred to as 'unplanned compositions'. His repertoire includes regional and aboriginal symbolisms, mixing human and non-human beings against fuchsia landscapes. Given his philosophical background, it is tempting to think that Barbalho is presenting us with his own personal depiction of the multitude – this political agent that is everyone and everything, self-organized and inherently revolutionary. .... From February to April 2019, the experimental-slash-institutional space Kunsthalle Lissabon in Lisbon hosted a three-person exhibition featuring the works of Flora Rebollo and Yuli Yamagata alongside Barbalho's. The trio had met during a residency at the São Paulo-based non-profit space Pivô. The resulting exhibition, 'Rocambole', united three practices in which irreverent combinations and anamorphic distortions seemed to be a common element. Barbalho often looks to his community and immediate context to further his practice: working as Alexandre da Cunha's (b. 1969) assistant was a pivotal moment that shaped his interest in the visual arts, not to mention the way he discovered his competence in drawing, affirmed by friends who found works on his desk. Using the pen and paper that was readily available on his writing table – as seen in *Instant VII* (2019) or *Instant II* (2017) – Barbalho's art has evolved out of an instinctive reaction, or perhaps a need, to give visible form to thoughts. The nebulous designs emerge from infinite pencil strokes lined tightly against each other. Their mantric quality might be the reason why they are so mesmerizing.
.... Catalina Imizcoz

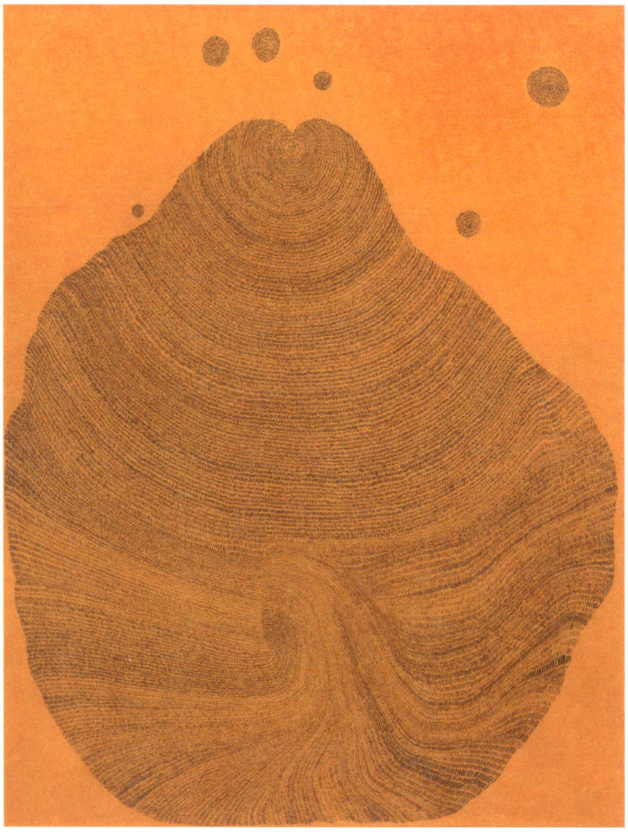
1.

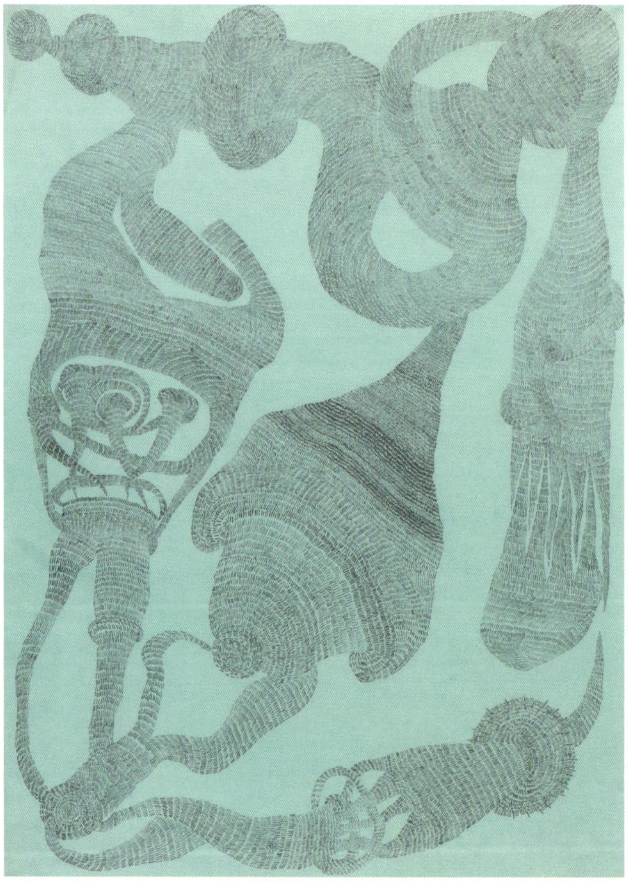
2.

Born 1984, Natal, Brazil. Lives and works in São Paulo.

1. *Instant VII*, 2019, pencil on coloured paper, 65 × 47.5 cm (25 ⅝ × 18 ¾ in)
2. *Instant II*, 2017, pencil on coloured paper, 65 × 47.5 cm (25 ⅝ × 18 ¾ in)
3. *Monkey's Words*, 2017, crayon, acrylic, coloured pencil, pencil, ballpoint pen, permanent marker, oil pastel and spray paint on paper, 120 × 80 cm (47 ¼ × 31 ½ in)

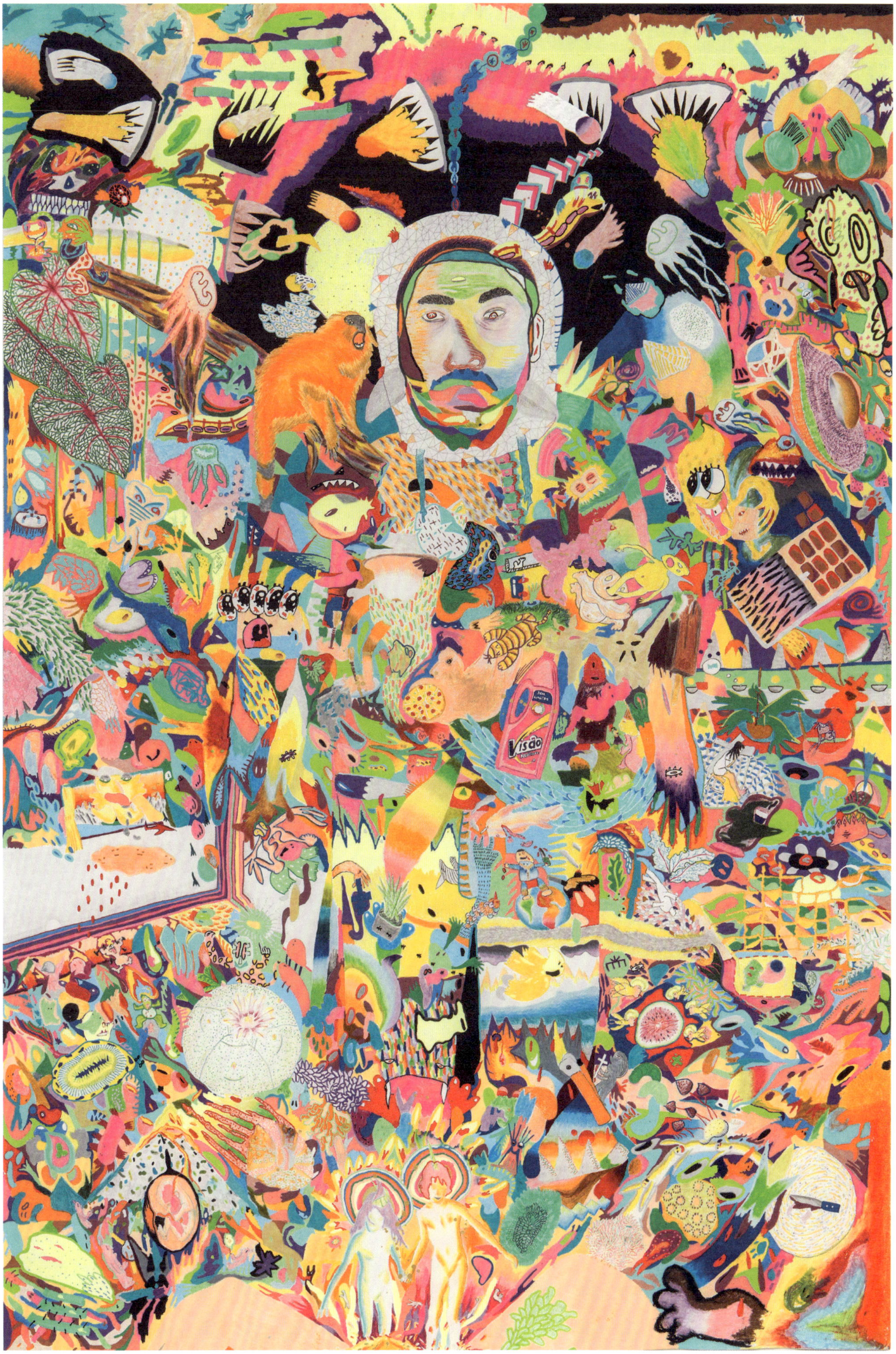

3.

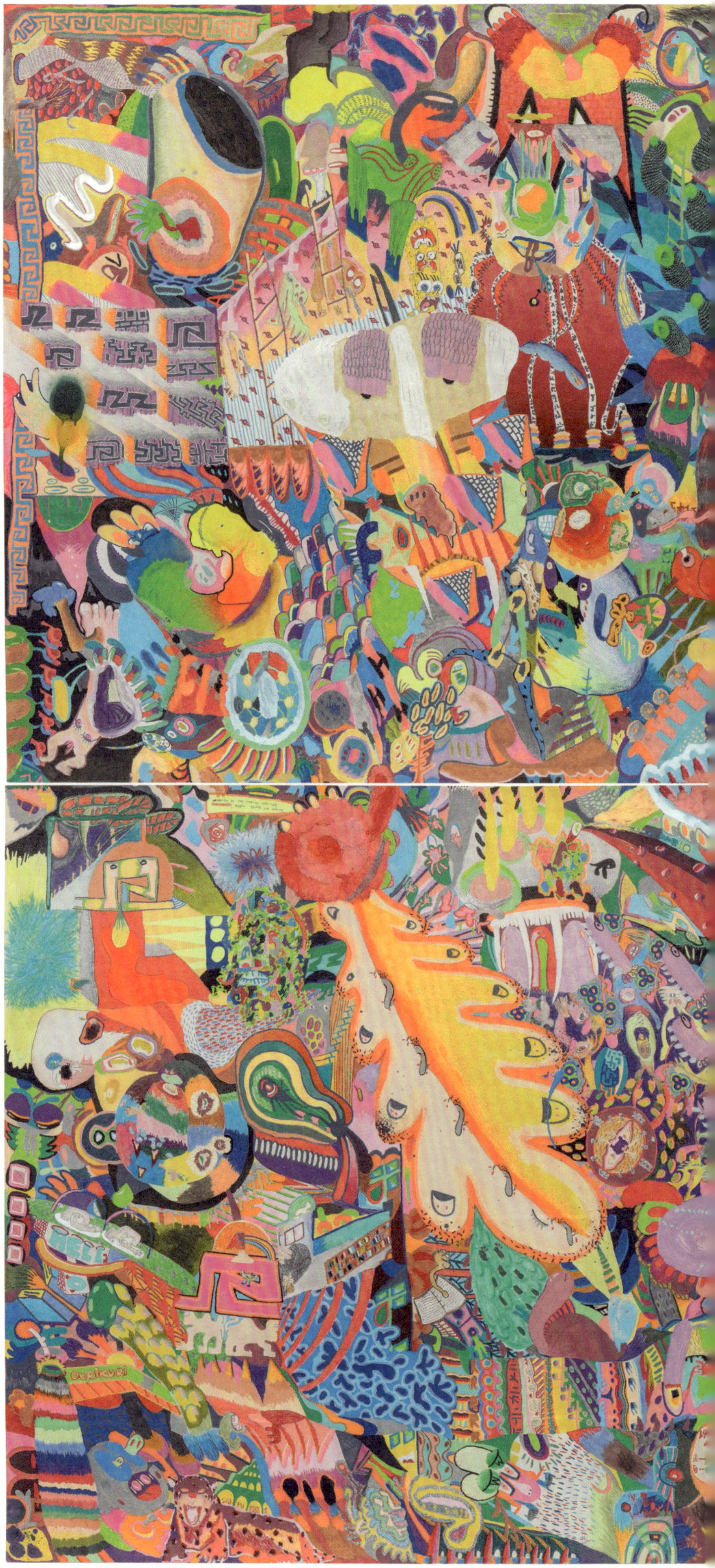

4.

4. *The Idiotic Redemption*, 2019, crayon, coloured pencil, pencil, ballpoint pen, permanent marker, oil pastel, acrylic, oil and spray paint on paper, 160 × 234 cm (63 × 92 in)

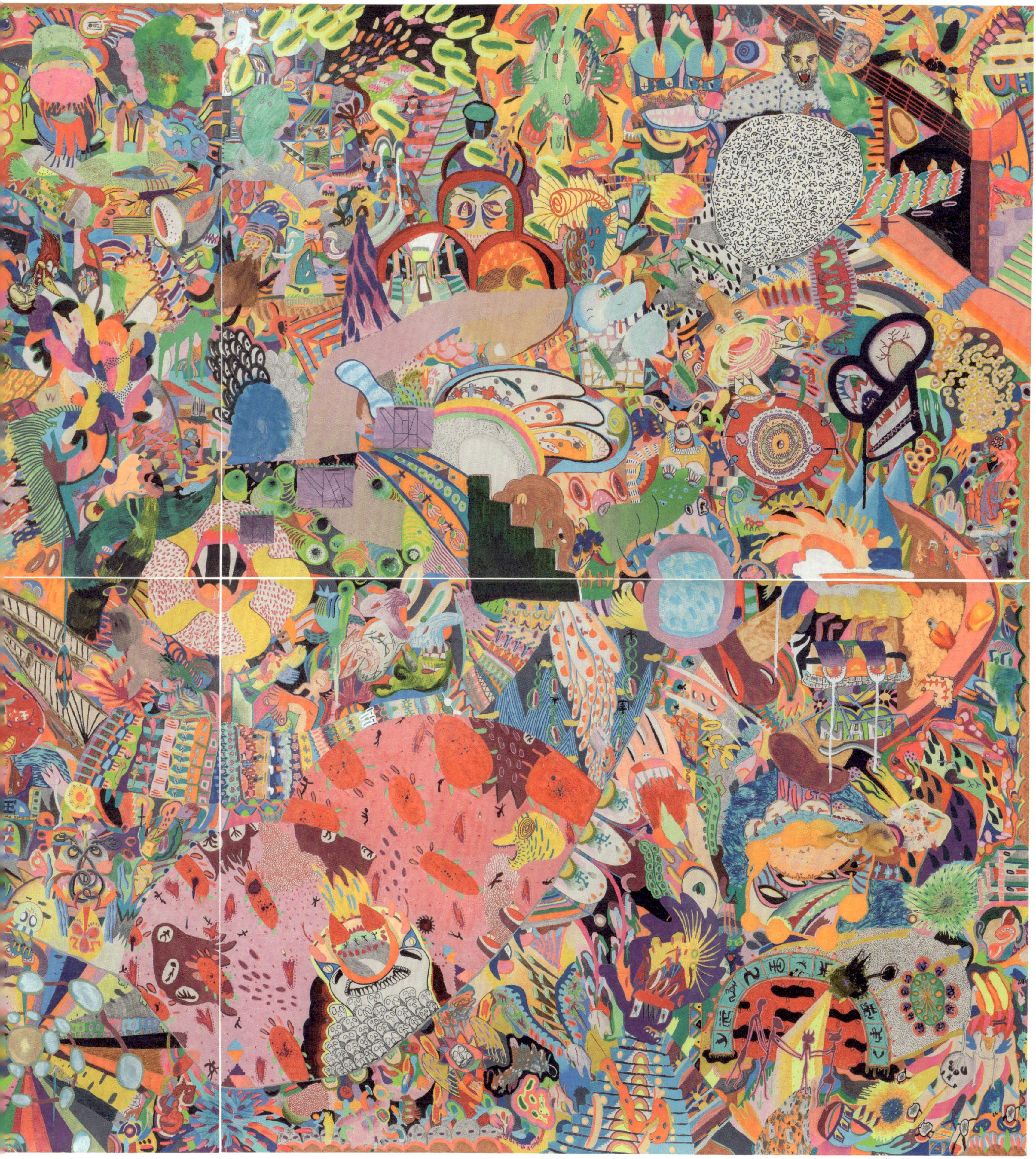

EDOUARD BARIBEAUD .... Edouard Baribeaud creates fantastical intricate universes using the classical techniques of ink and watercolour on paper. With a background in book illustration and printmaking, Baribeaud's drawing style is meticulously detailed and vibrant. It also reveals a host of art-historical techniques and influences, ranging from pointillism to *grisaille*, Orientalism and even botanical illustrations. Often, several of these styles coexist in wonderous anachronism within a single work. Baribeaud's drawings are frequently narrative-driven, though the stories they tell remain enigmatic, as unreliable as matted memories or dreams, existing only as fragments within multi-part series. 'I like to juxtapose the mundane with the mythical,' he said in an interview in 2015. 'And in doing so, I blend real personal experiences with invented memories.' .... *Homer*, which features the artist's self-portrait, is part of the 2018 series 'An Old Story for Our Modern Times' in which each drawing takes its title from a figure in Greek mythology – the series also includes the works *Danaë* and *Minotaur*. The man in the portrait is gazing downwards, supporting his head with his left hand. A source of light illuminates the man's forehead. The lower part of his face is shadowy and the contours of his upper body are almost indistinguishable in a dark sweater. Behind him, a wallpaper design of lush shrubbery in deep greens and greys evokes a particularly photogenic interior style now popular on social media. (Other works in the series also feature distinctive interior decor.) The portrait is framed by another layer in the drawing, rendered to appear like candy-coloured terrazzo. Eight motifs captured in circular frames surround the figure, each featuring an object such as a cloud, a watchtower or a disembodied arm throwing a lightning bolt. All these elements have appeared in Baribeaud's previous series, referencing a personal creative odyssey, as the work's titular Homer might suggest. .... There is ample use of recurrent motifs throughout Baribeaud's body of work, one of them being a trompe-l'oeil effect of a set design. Some drawings are made to resemble a life-size diorama, appearing as if there were several movable layers of scenery that can be wheeled on and off a stage. *The Nocturnal Vault* (2016), from the sixteen-part series of the same name, depicts three long-haired rock musicians on a wooden platform. A backdrop featuring fiery orange skies and a jungle in black and white is hung behind them, while a different element on the right of the stage shows a colour version of the same lush vegetation. The foreground, yet another prop, is made to look like a craggy opening of a cave, as if the viewer were watching the musical act from inside a cold and dark hollow.
.... Hili Perlson

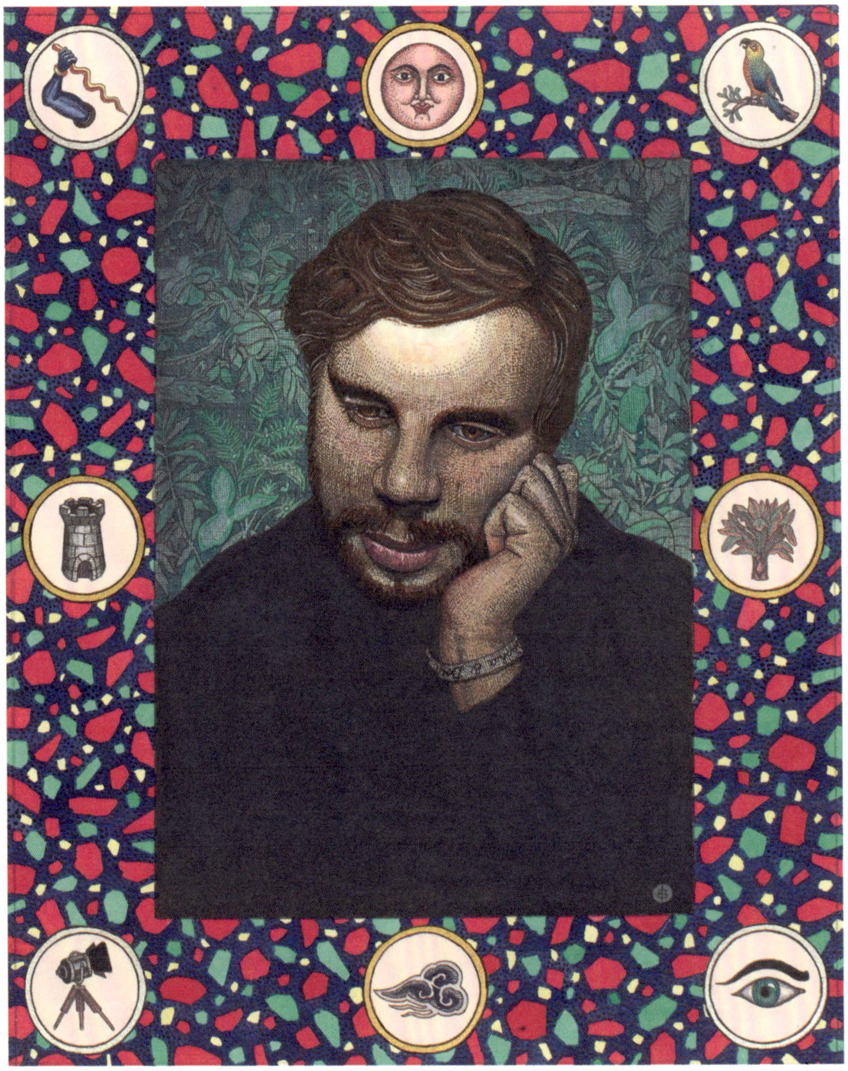
1.

Born 1984, Versailles, France. Lives and works in Berlin.

1. *Homer*, 2018, India ink, watercolour, gold leaf on paper, 49.5 × 39.5 cm (19 ½ in × 15 ½ in)
2. *The Decline*, 2015, India ink and watercolour on paper, 36 × 51 cm (14 ⅛ × 20 in)
3. *The Nocturnal Vault*, 2016, India ink and watercolour on paper, 29.5 × 46 cm (11 ⅝ × 18 ⅛ in)

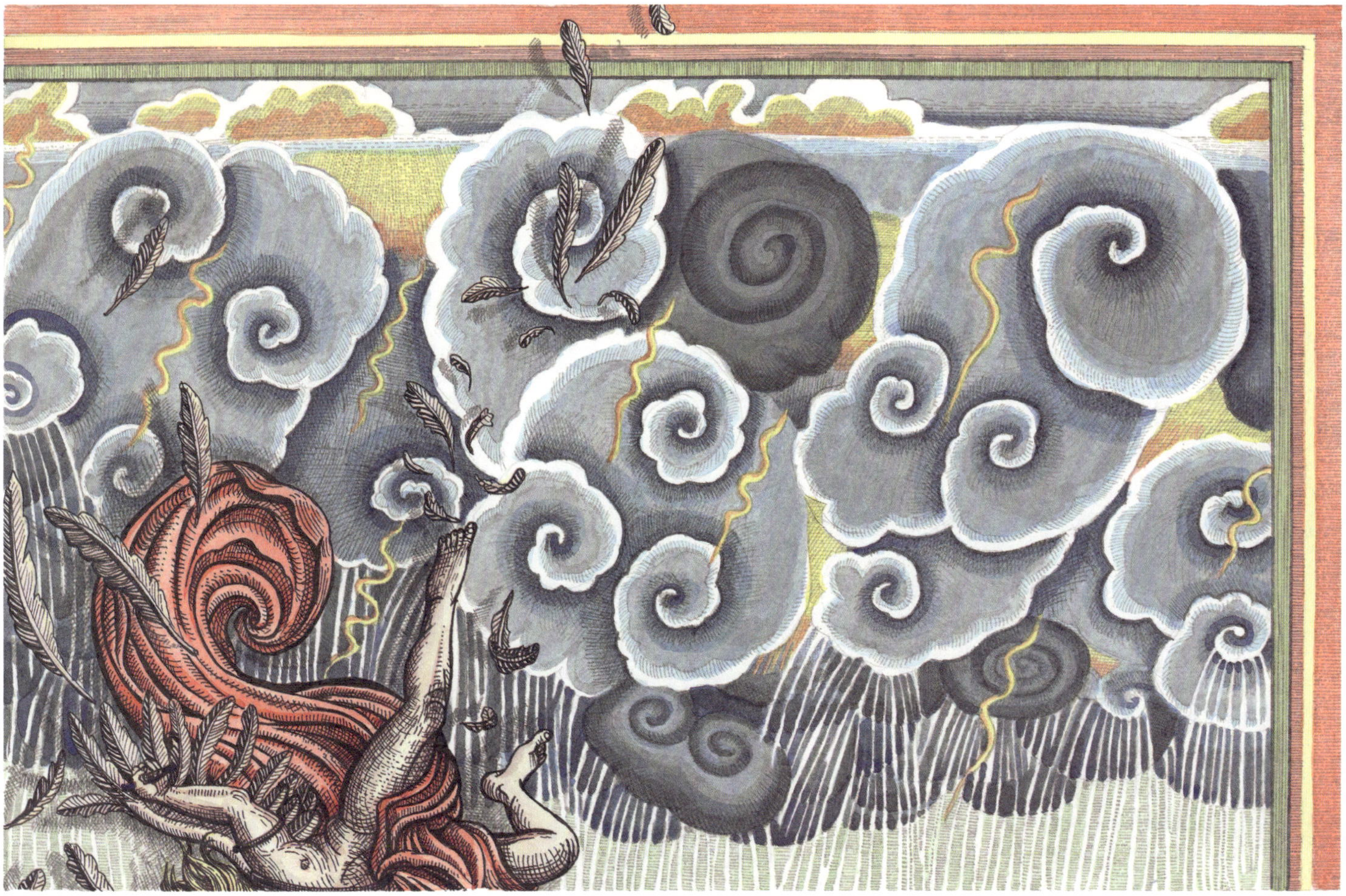

2.

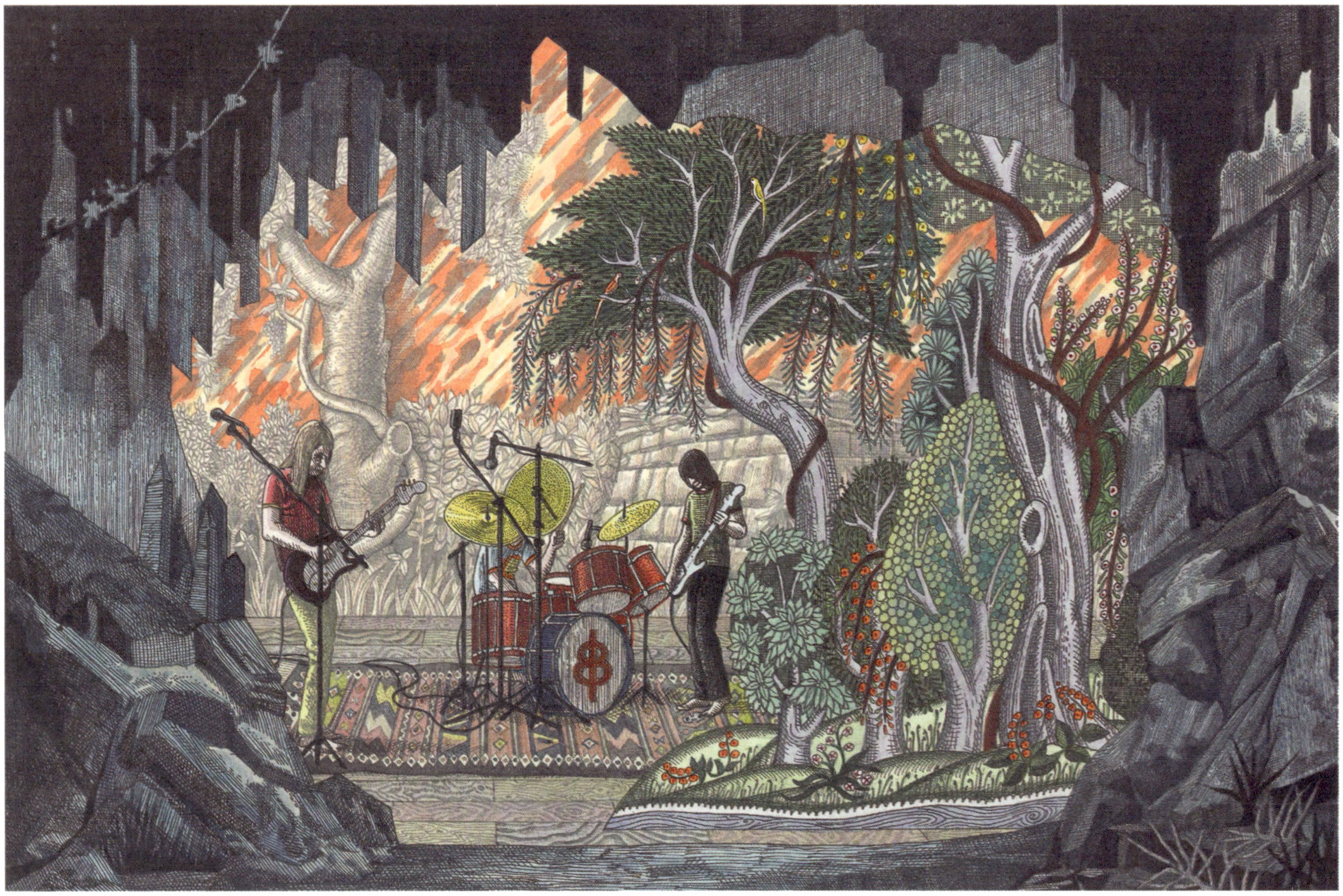

3.

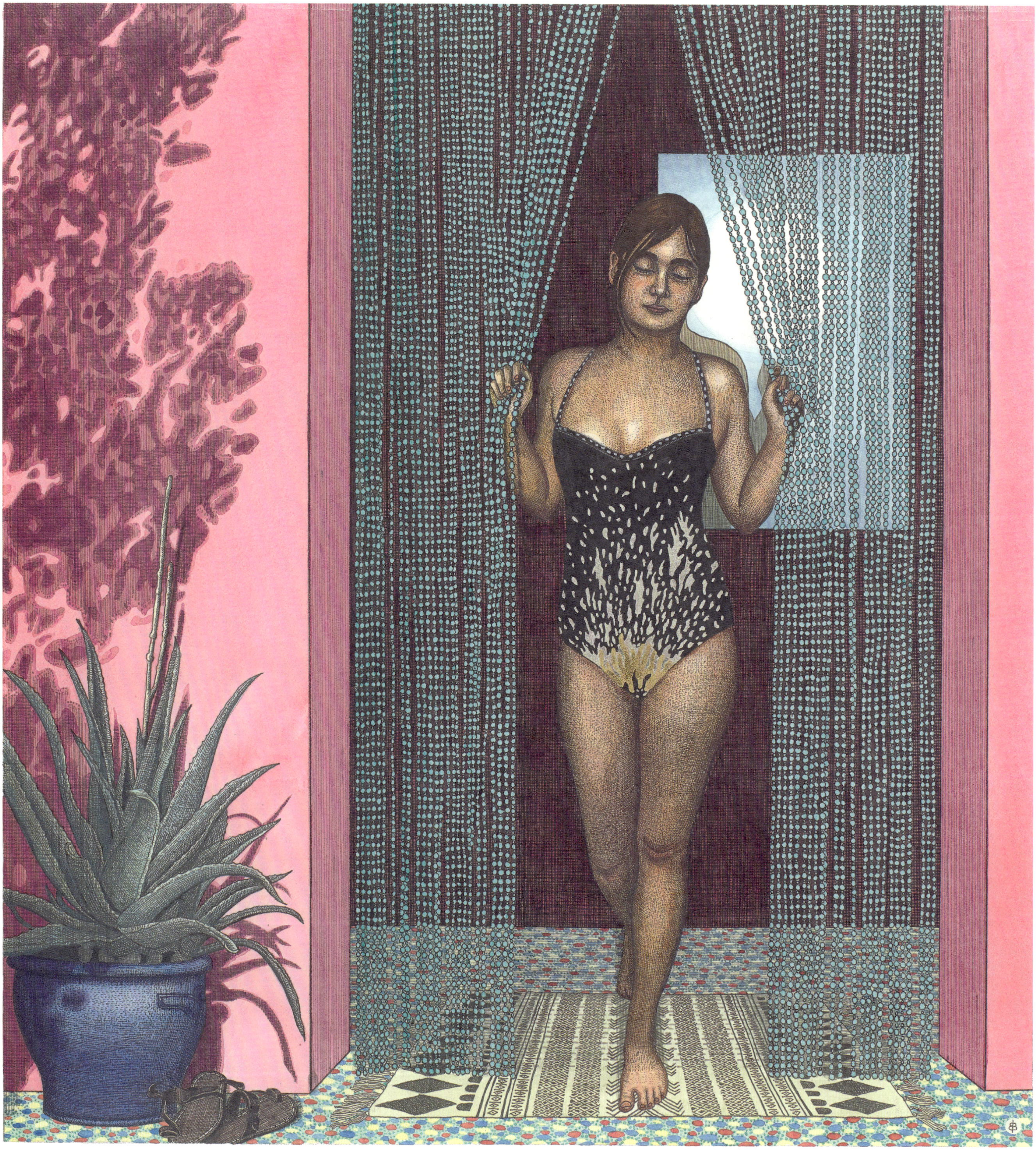

4.

4. *Danaë*, 2018, India ink, watercolour, gold and silver leaf on paper, 80 × 72 cm (31 ½ × 28 ⅜ in)

5. *Minotaur*, 2018, India ink and watercolour on paper, 77.5 × 71 cm (30 ½ × 28 in)

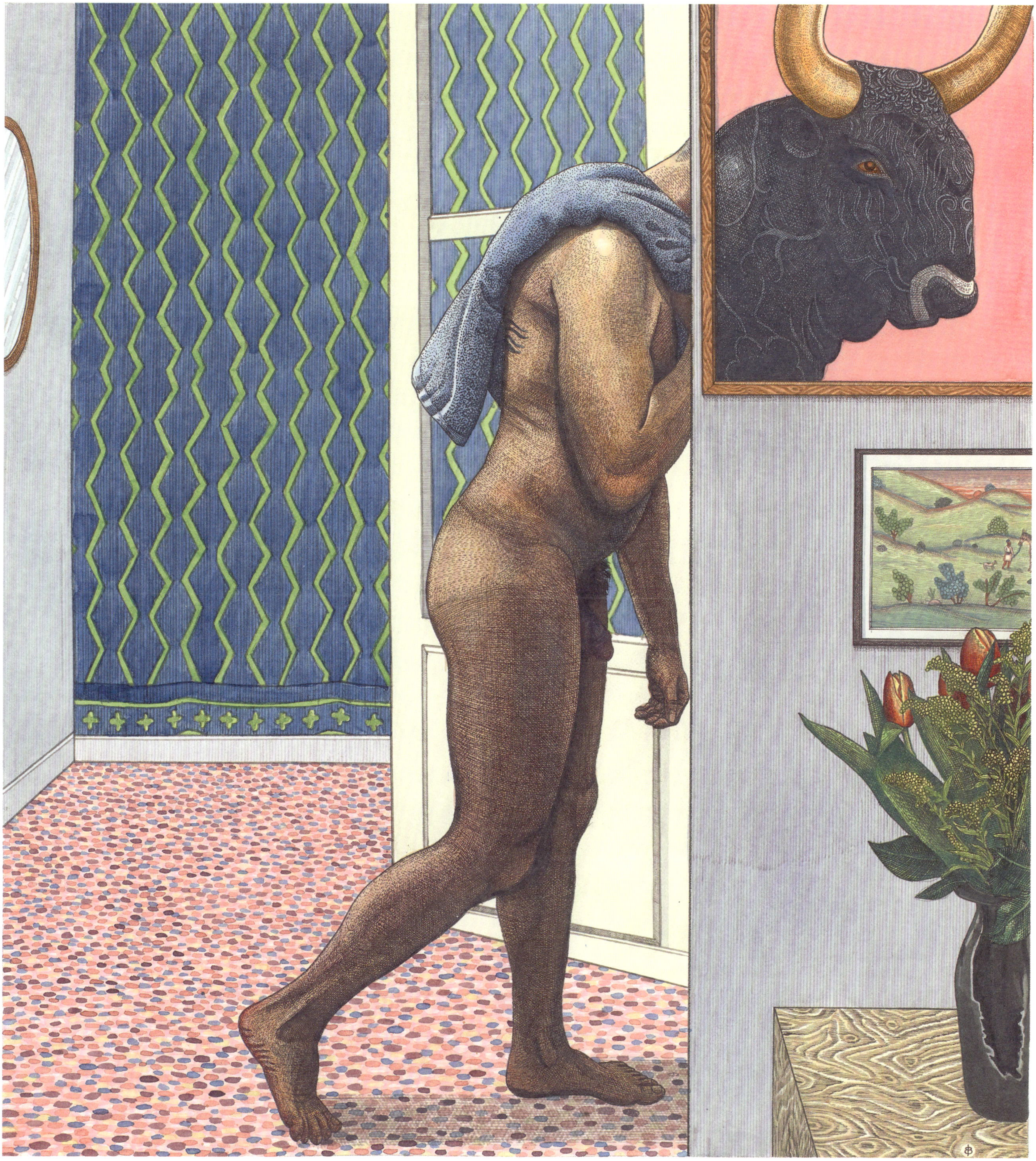

5.

.......Phoebe Boswell's finely drawn portraits shrug off stereotypical perceptions and interpretations, revealing their subjects with realistic honesty.. She draws with willow charcoal as well as pencil, and sometimes expands her technique by involving digital technology to create animations and installations. Her work reflects a multi-layered approach to creativity and communication, the result in part of a diasporic consciousness informed by her life across three disparate cultures – born in Nairobi, she grew up in the Arabian Gulf before moving to London to study and practise art. The search for roots, home, identity and a sense of belonging remains for her a constant endeavour, as it does for so many others. The series 'For Every Real Word Spoken' (2017) includes various pencil portraits of Boswell's friends, acquaintances, fellow artists and colleagues. The figures, almost life-size, are naked and hold mobile phones in front of them with the screens facing out towards the viewer. Each phone presents an interactive QR code, hand-drawn by the artist, which, when scanned with a mobile device, activates a URL, song, article or thought chosen by the person in the drawing. Exhibited at Tiwani Contemporary in London in 2017, this powerful installation of digitally active pencil portraits revealed that each of the subjects inhabiting these meticulously drawn bodies has their own voice, and message, separate from the viewer's subjective perception or preconceived frame of reference. The substance of the series lies in its spirit of collaboration. Another series, 'Eye' (2018), relates to a traumatic incident the artist experienced, resulting in a serious eye injury and consequential cardiac emergency. Presented in her exhibition 'Take Me To The Lighthouse' at Sapar Contemporary, New York in 2018, this group of dramatic drawings depicting her injured right eye illustrates her suffering and anguish in a painfully honest manner. Extending from this, *On the Line* (2018), commissioned for her institutional solo exhibition 'The Space Between Things' at Autograph, London, in 2018–19, is a willow charcoal drawing made directly upon the wall of the gallery. At twenty-five metres (eighty-two feet) in length, it portrays the artist's nude body in several positions – curled, elongated, twisted, lying on her side, or on her back, breasts bare, arms stretched upwards. Using her personal experience of this life-altering physical and emotional trauma as subject matter, in these self-portraits Boswell bravely confronts her condition and brilliantly portrays her distress. Although blinded in her right eye, the creative process of making these painstaking drawings assisted her recovery and healing. Expanding beyond the medium, she also created a series of accompanying video recordings of her eye and heart surgeries. And yet this is not just a personal tragedy but one that connects to the wider human condition, allowing her to relate to others in similarly painful circumstances. Boswell offers up her art as a form of individual and collective therapy.
.... Elbé Coetsee

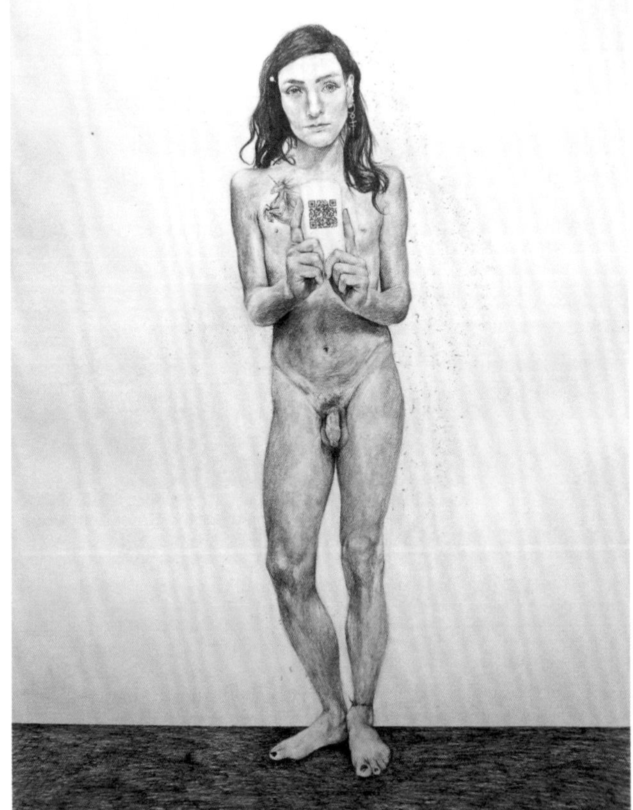

1.

2.

Born 1982, Nairobi, Kenya. Lives and works in London

1. *Pieces of a (Wo)man* from the series 'For Every Real Word Spoken', 2017, pencil on paper with hand-drawn interactive QR code, 150 × 120 cm (59 × 47 ¼ in)

2. *Is that a...? (creature of Myth)* from the series 'For Every Real Word Spoken', 2017, pencil on paper with hand-drawn interactive QR code, 150 × 120 cm (59 × 47 ¼ in)

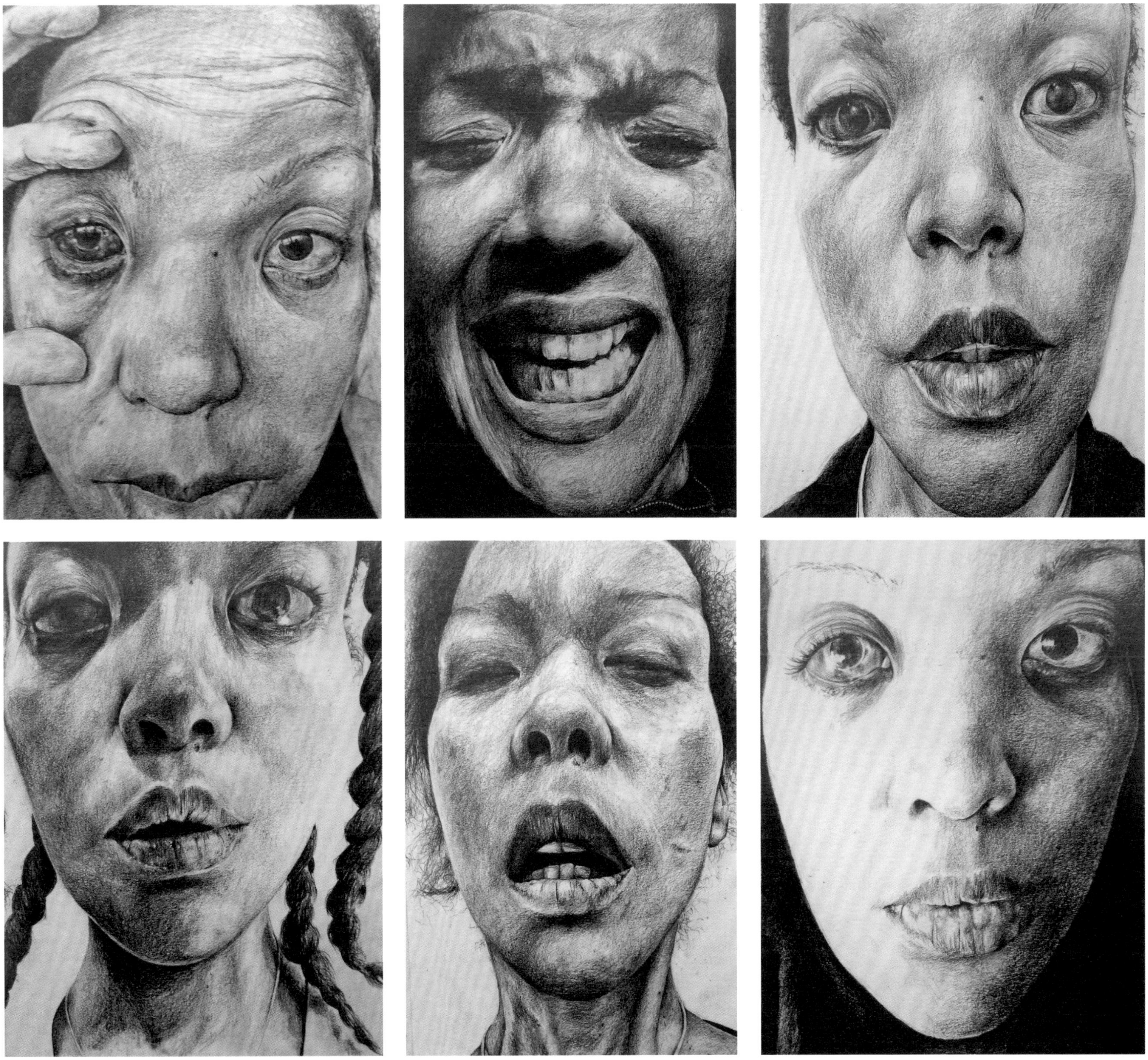

3.

3. *Eye (series)*, 2018, pencil on paper, each 38 × 28 cm (15 × 11 in)

CONRAD BOTES .... In 1989, during the twilight of white-minority rule in South Africa, Conrad Botes made a poster poking fun at the moral puritanism of his birth country's state-sanctioned Calvinist ideology. The subject of the poster was libidinal: 'Nice boys don't do it, Say NO to masturbation!' Over the course of the next decade, while pursuing his post-graduate studies in illustration in Stellenbosch and The Hague, Botes continued to probe the bounds of propriety in his erotic drawings. The earliest published examples appeared in *Gif (Poison*, 1994), a thirty-two-page comic Botes produced in collaboration with Anton Kannemeyer (p.128); it was the first publication to be banned in post-apartheid South Africa. .... A 2020 exhibition in Cape Town tracked the fixity of erotica in the artist's practice, as well as revealing the prominence of self-portraiture. Botes often evidences a cyclic and iterative approach to image-making. Figures, motifs and themes recur, endlessly. The artist's sketchbooks are an important source of his ribald ideas. The sketches *CB 01 (our people)* (2017) and *CB 02 (Bosch)* (2014) are consistent – in style, line and colour – with more scurrilous drawings like *The Passion of the White Zombie* (2010), which depicts the titular subject, a mute surrogate for the white male in Africa, surrounded by five demonic figures either defecating or ejaculating. Botes's pungent work exceeds mere psychosexual melodrama; his transgressive practice draws from a deep well of unsettlement and flagrancy in the history of art. The huddled, zombie-like figures in *CB 02 (Bosch)* reappear in his nearly seven metre (twenty-three foot) canvas painting *Sabbath* (2019), which also quotes Francisco Goya's (1746–1828) *Saturn Devouring His Son* (1819–23). An admirer of Goya's bleaker work, Botes has also cited underground comics artists Robert Crumb (p.66) and Jean 'Mœbius' Giraud (1938–2012) as influences. His succinct illustrations using hatchings bear out his comics background, although the artist's output includes expressionist drawings and mural installations portraying simplified figures with thick black lines reminiscent of A. R. Penck (1939–2017). .... Narrative is important to an appreciation of Botes's output. 'With his robust, incendiary style and unerring eye for character, [Botes] has emerged as a visionary storyteller capable of capturing agonized moments of Afrikaner history in powerful iconic images,' noted art historian Andy Mason in 2002, highlighting his noirish retellings of South African history as standout examples. Works such as *Master's Voice* (2018) and *Untitled: Pavement* (2017) chart yet another aspect of his practice. They form part of an evolving body of work started in the early 2000s in which portrayals of sex, religion and authority are overlaid on to contemporary and historical landscape photographs, including *Valley of the Shadow of Death* (1855) by Roger Fenton (1819–69) The figure-ground polemic in these allegorical works explores a long-standing concern: human action exhibits worldly biases and flaws, but causality is often informed by place.
.... Sean O'Toole

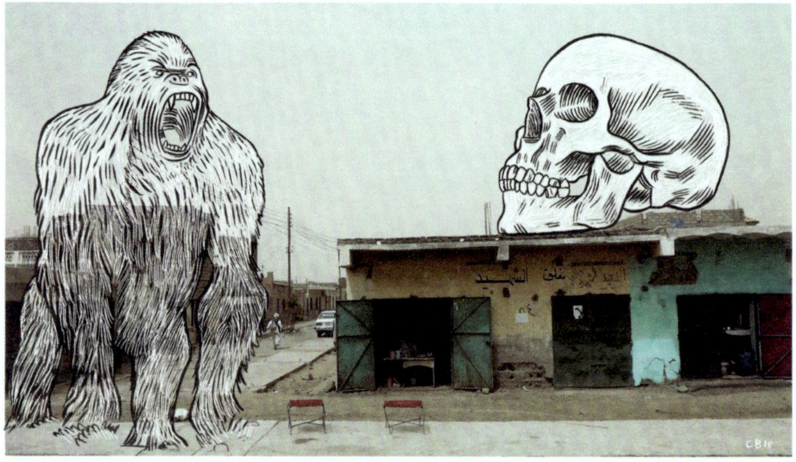

1.

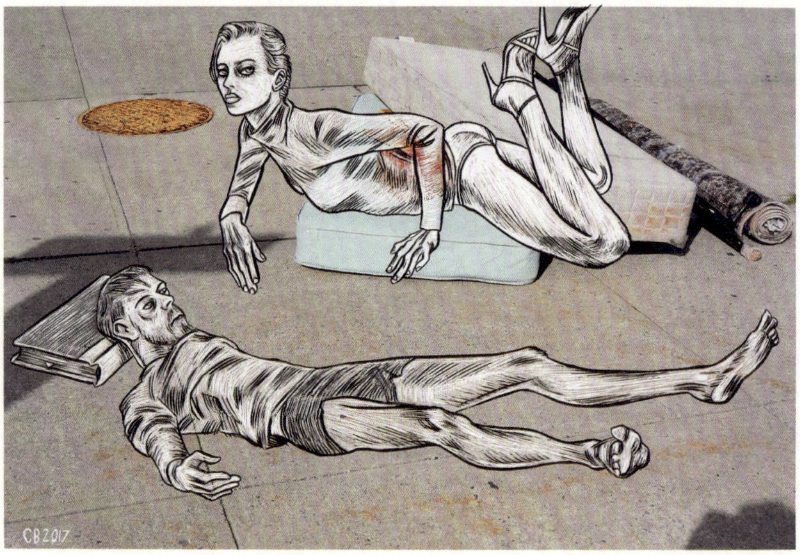

2.

Born 1969, Ladismith, South Africa. Lives and works in Cape Town.

1. *Master's Voice*, 2018, ink drawing on C-print, 39 × 60 cm (15 ⅜ × 23 ⅝ in)
2. *Untitled: Pavement*, 2017, ink drawing on C-print, 39 × 60 cm (15 ⅜ × 23 ⅝ in)
3. *CB 05 (self-portraits) Extract from Zerkall-Ingres drawing book*, 2019, pencil and ink on paper, 21 × 58 cm (8 ¼ × 22 ⅞ in)
4. *CB 01 (our people) Extract from Moleskine drawing book*, 2017, pencil and ink on paper, 13.5 × 41 cm (5 ⅜ × 16 ⅛ in)
5. *CB 02 (Bosch) Extract from Zerkall-Bütten drawing book*, 2014, pencil and ink on paper, 21 × 53 cm (8 ¼ × 20 ⅞ in)

3.
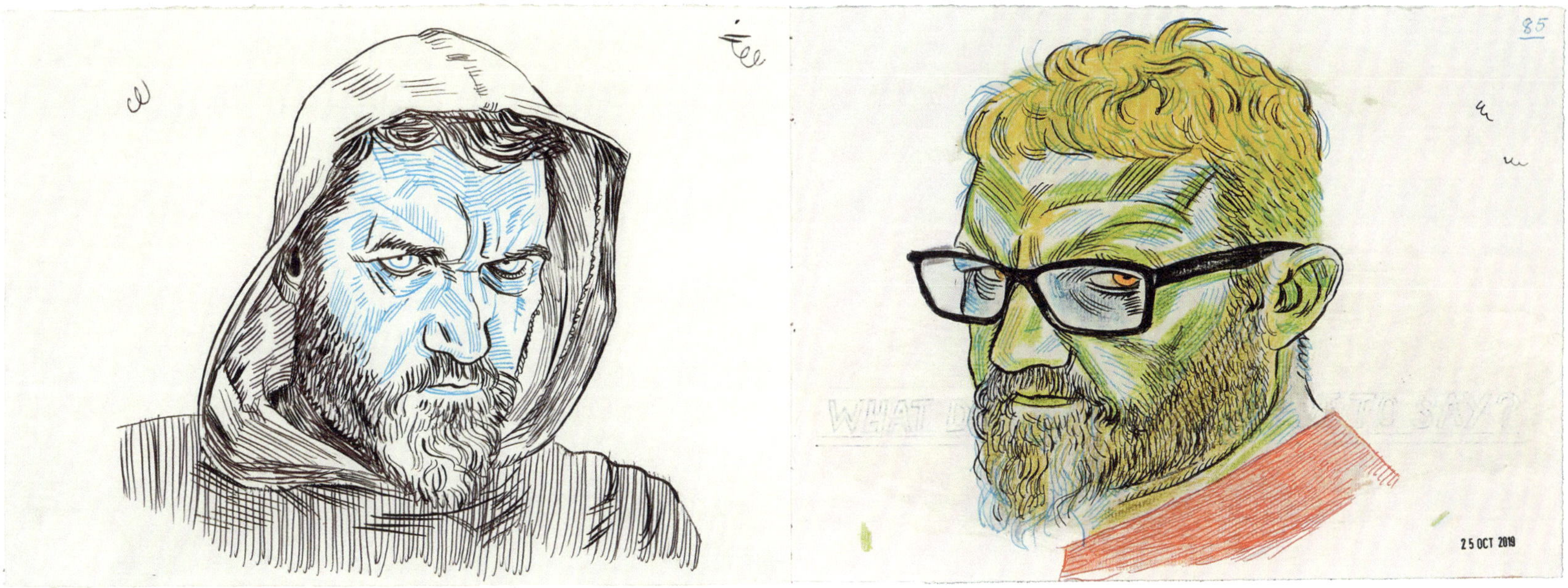
85
25 OCT 2019

4.
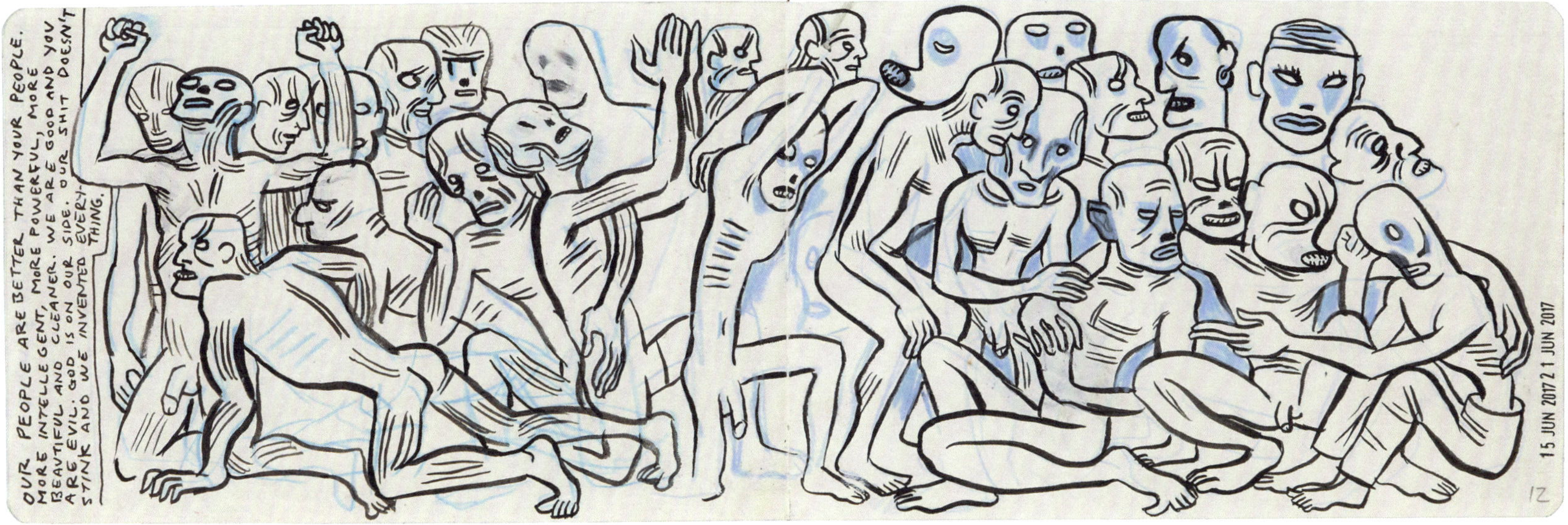
OUR PEOPLE ARE BETTER THAN YOUR PEOPLE. MORE INTELLEGENT, MORE POWERFUL, MORE BEAUTIFUL AND CLEANER. WE ARE GOOD AND YOU ARE EVIL. GOD IS ON OUR SIDE. OUR SHIT DOESN'T STINK AND WE INVENTED EVERYTHING.
15 JUN 2017 21 JUN 2017
12

5.
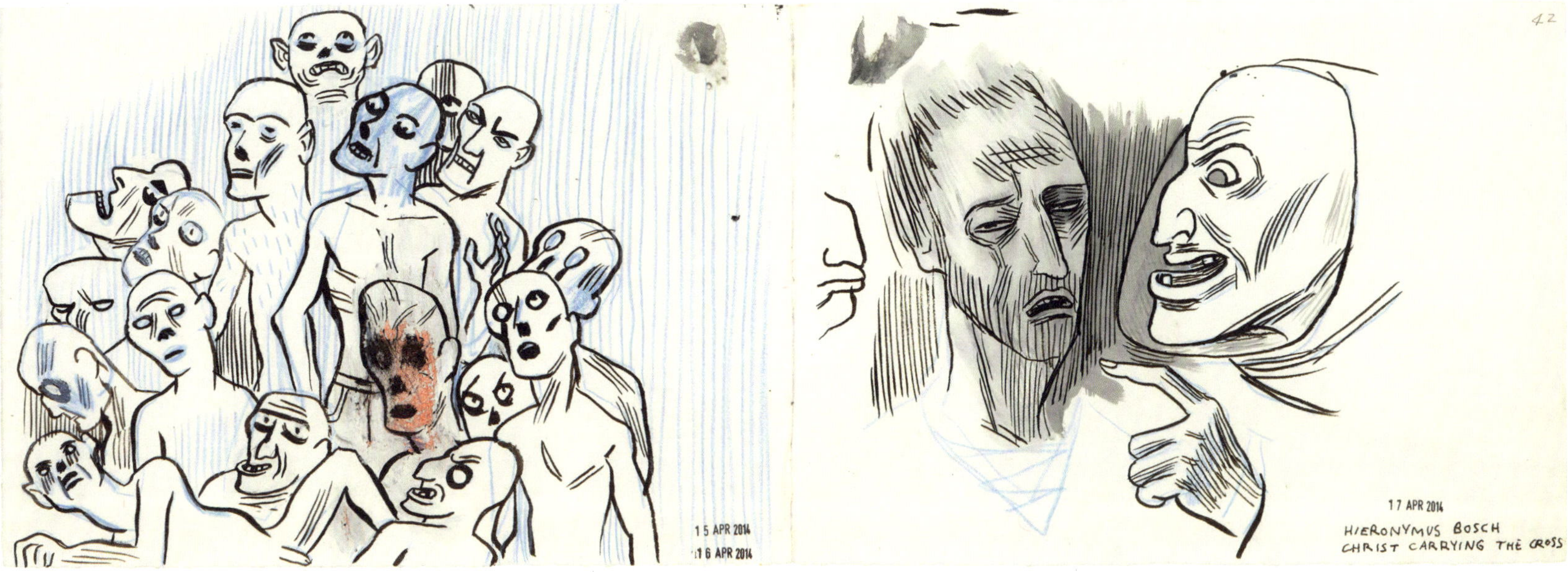
42
15 APR 2014
16 APR 2014
17 APR 2014
HIERONYMUS BOSCH
CHRIST CARRYING THE CROSS

T E R E S A   B U R G A .... Teresa Burga is a central figure in Latin American art history. In the late 1960s she was associated with Arte Nuevo, a group of artists who advanced avant-garde artistic ideas in Peru. During an increasingly hostile environment led by the nationalistic military regime, Burga pursued a radical practice that incorporated Pop and Conceptual art. She retreated from the art world in the mid-1980s and found international acclaim late in her career, with audiences finally catching up with her pioneering practice. .... In her early works Burga fused images of femininity and domesticity with bold colours. Her ambitious project *Perfil de la mujer Peruana* (*Profile of the Peruvian Woman*), (1980–1) epitomizes the range of her practice. Collaborating with the psychotherapist Marie-France Cathelat, Burga surveyed 290 women in Lima about their personal and political identities. The resulting statistics were translated into a series of sculptures, installations and books that satirized the mainstream construction of female subjectivity. .... Burga's more recent works on paper – combining drawing and collage – depict women in traditional clothing. The series 'Acqua Alta' (High Water) (2019) portrays figures in Venetian costumes. There is a folksy and childlike quality to the images with their wonky lines, bright hues and vibrant patterning that merges the characters with their indistinct surroundings. As documents of indigenous dress, they feel sociological and recall the imagery found in ethnographic museums. The works pose numerous questions: are these actors or women dressed for a party? Are they observed from everyday life or imagined? They stare straight back at us but we are unsure who they are performing for. Burga's fine pen conveys the detail of their costumes, taking obvious delight in the tailoring. .... Under the images Burga has noted the amount of labour that has gone into each work, writing out the days of the week and time taken to complete them. The tally provides a bureaucratic addition to the cheerful and seemingly carefree images. For an artist who has long interrogated themes of labour and domesticity, the merging of the administrative and the decorative is significant. Unlike artistic activity, which tends to bleed into every aspect of an artist's life, the recording of her labour suggests a clear boundary between work and rest. There is a tension between productive work that is measured and compensated and artistic work that resists quantitative remuneration. Burga's joyous depictions of women and fashion embrace pleasure, colour and decoration and, as such, feel slyly political. These themes have historically been associated with home craft traditions and, by extension, denigrated as feminine and beyond critical appraisal. Burga reclaims and proudly attests to their renewed potential. Burga has made a career of challenging conventions and expectations and, with these works, she continues to make her points with a wry smile.
.... George Vasey

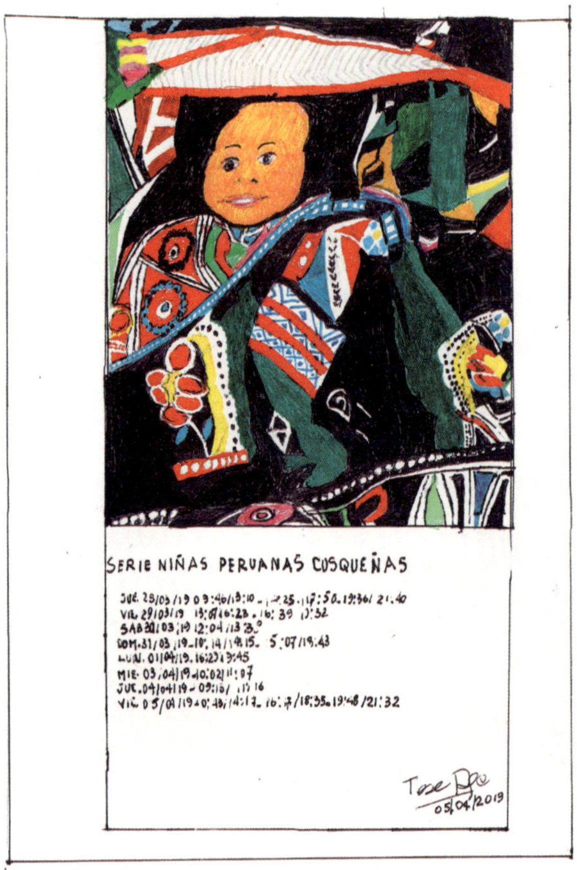

1.

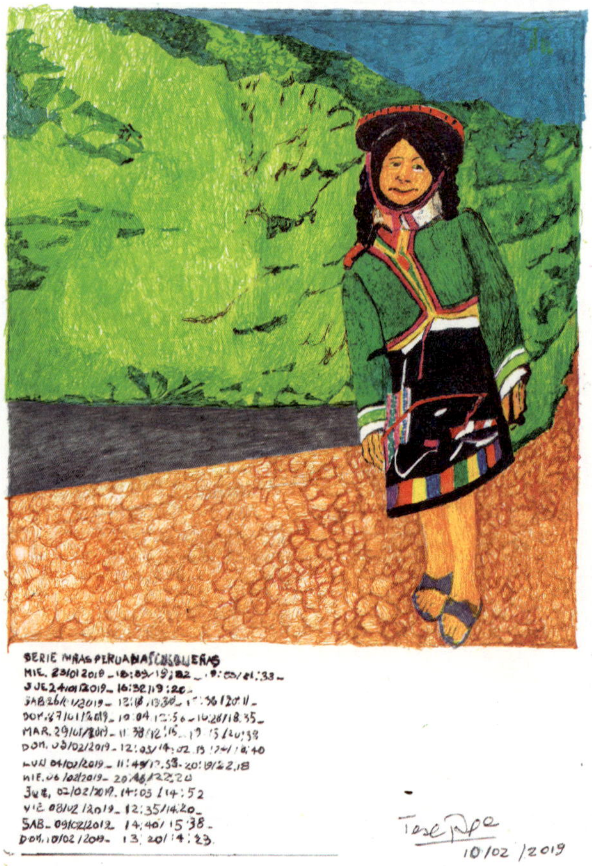

2.

Born 1935, Iquitos, Peru. Lives and works in Lima, Peru.

1. *05 / Abril / 2019*, 2019, mixed media on paper, 29.7 × 21.1 cm (11 ⅝ × 8 ¼ in)
2. *10 / Febrero / 2019*, 2019, mixed media on paper, 29.7 × 21.1 cm (11 ⅝ × 8 ¼ in)

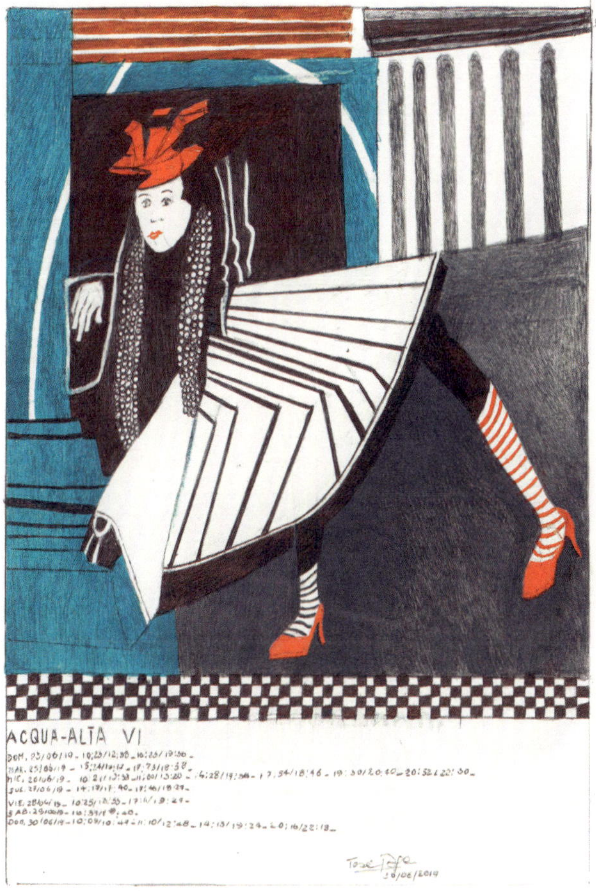

3.

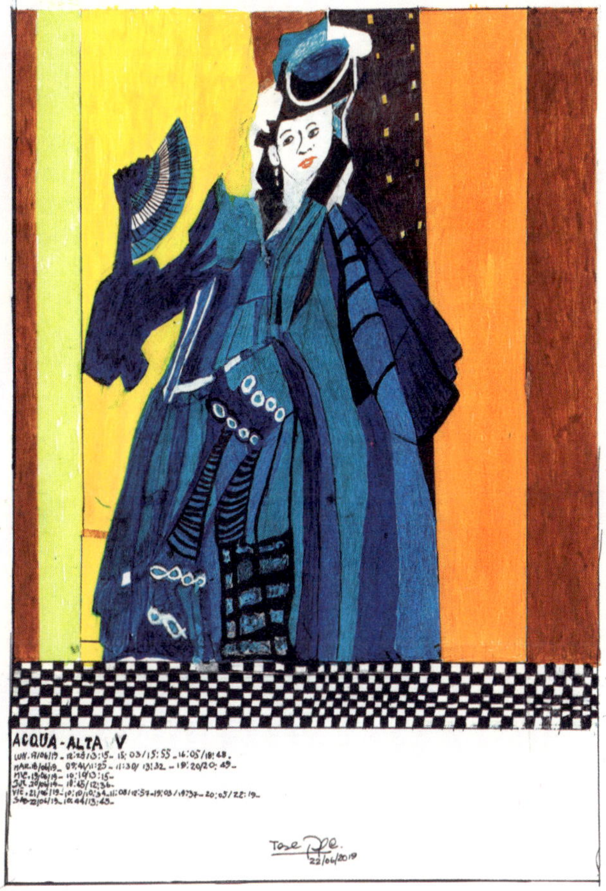

4.

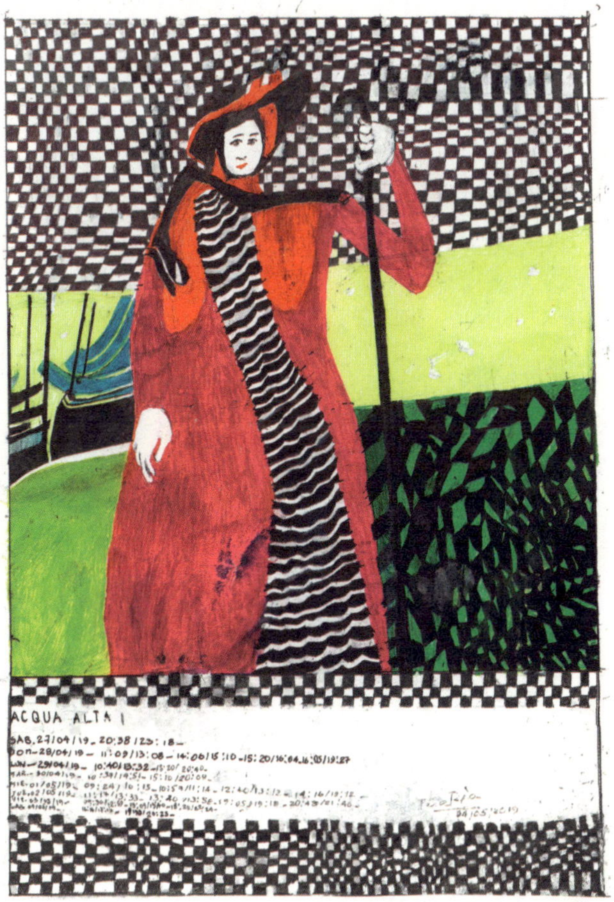

5.

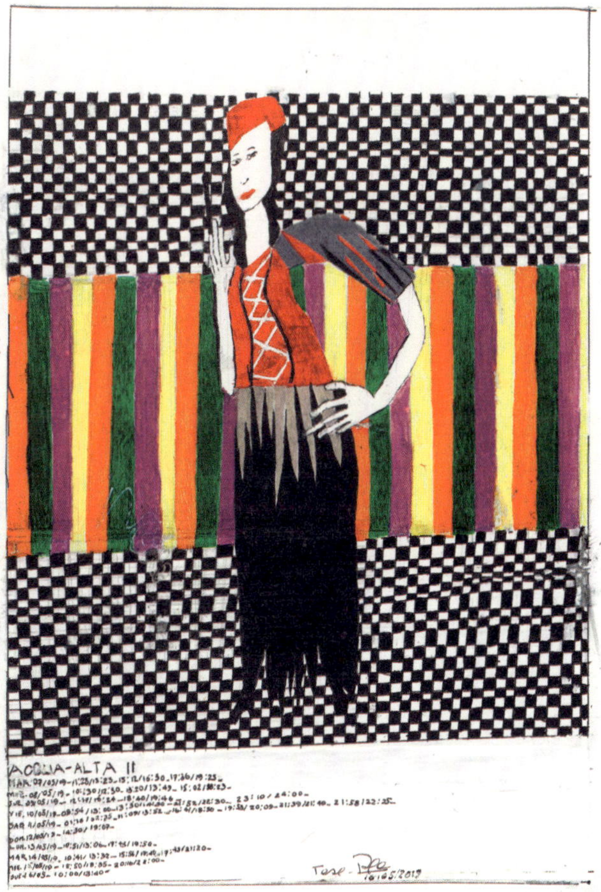

6.

3. *Untitled (Acqua Alta VI)*, 2019, mixed media on collaged paper, 41.9 × 29.2 cm (16 ½ × 11 ½ in)
4. *Untitled (Acqua Alta V)*, 2019, mixed media on collaged paper, 41.9 × 29.2 cm (16 ½ × 11 ½ in)
5. *Untitled (Acqua Alta I)*, 2019, mixed media on collaged paper, 41.9 × 29.2 cm (16 ½ × 11 ½ in)
6. *Untitled (Acqua Alta II)*, 2019, mixed media on collaged paper, 41.9 × 29.2 cm (16 ½ × 11 ½ in)

A D R I A N A   B U S T O S .... Adriana Bustos employs the medium of drawing as if it were a weapon with the potential to remake Western world order. Her true-to-life depictions fabricate systems that suspend or counter the flow of the traditional narratives of history and science. In *Venus Planisphere* (2018), from the 'Vision Machine' series, Bustos sets forth a web of agents, territories, stories and concepts: under-recognized women who were social leaders, together with the flora that was once considered evidence of witchcraft, converge around a map of the constellations. Dotted with notations that can be used as a guide to read the piece, the map is common in its design and yet radical in its proposition. It invites us to reread and retrace alternative paradigms – in this case, a feminine history of society. .... Her methods are also incisive. She employs figurative, precise imagery alongside informative text in what could be taken, at face value, for a standard pedagogical resource. *Nasa* (2016) exemplifies such compositions, in which visuals and language comply by Western epistemologies and channel a message from sender to receiver. Yet the series title, 'Who Says What To Whom', helps us fathom a more complex strategy behind Bustos's method. She upsets linear narratives and disregards scientific fact-checking so that her educational diagrams confer authority to ideas that bend the hegemonic, substituting it with free and imaginative cosmoses. Her slightly sarcastic approach to pedagogy may point to an exhaustion of Western knowledge, and is certainly a much needed call for hybrids – of the likes of the centaur that appears in the work's lower right-hand corner. .... The archive is another institution that Burgos aptly reconfigures. The aforementioned 'Who Says What To Whom?' also includes a series of impossible bookshelves, crowded with titles from different eras that have at some point been banned from circulation. The intersection of drawing and the impossible is also present in other recent works by women, notably that of Ariella Aïsha Azoulay (b.1962), who created a collection of 'drawn photographs' when the Red Cross Archive refused copyright authorization to show images alongside her own interpretative captions. Similarly, Bustos's *Burning Books I* (2017) gives material presence to books rendered otherwise invisible. Her archive brings together different volumes according to themes – those forbidden by political regimes, by religious organizations or because of their sexual content – so that geographic origins and times intermingle. One shelf is devoted to photographic images of the events that made such books disappear, and the realism of the images reinforces that of the carefully drawn, coloured-pencil covers. The ecosystems of Bustos's output exist precisely at that juncture: the one where the 'real' and the 'fake' blur.
.... Catalina Imizcoz

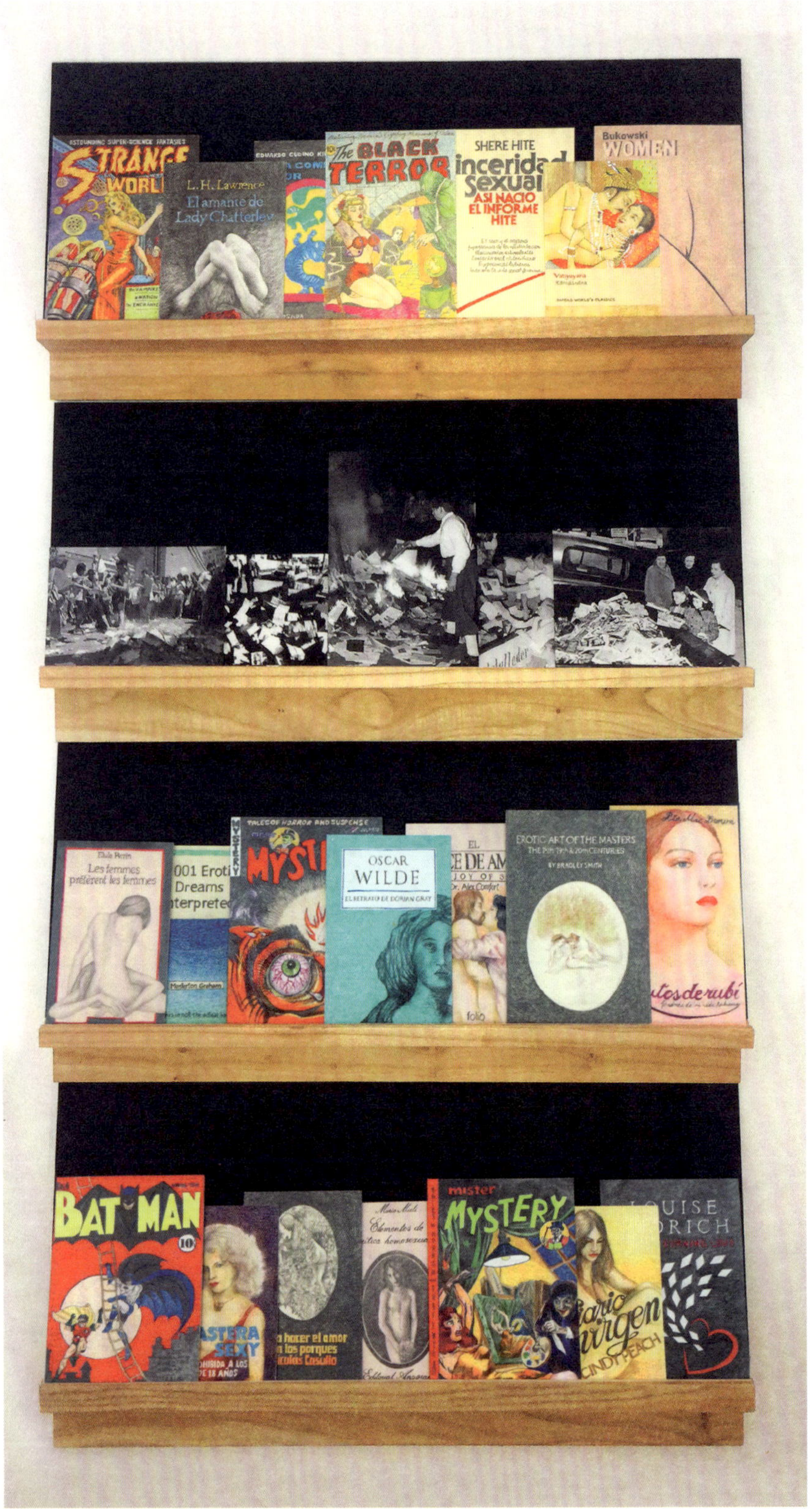

1.

Born 1965, Bahía Blanca, Argentina. Lives and works in Buenos Aires.

1. *Burning Books I* from 'Who Says What To Whom' series, 2017, graphite, coloured pencil and photography on passe-partout, wood and glass, 155 × 78 cm (61 × 30 ¾ in)
2. *Nasa* from 'Who Says What To Whom' series, 2016, graphite, coloured pencil and gold sheets on canvas, 105 × 181 cm (41 ⅜ × 71 ¼ in)
3. *Venus Planisphere* from 'Vision Machine' series, 2018, acrylic, graphite and silver and gold sheets on canvas, 200 × 200 cm (78 ¾ × 73 ¾ in)

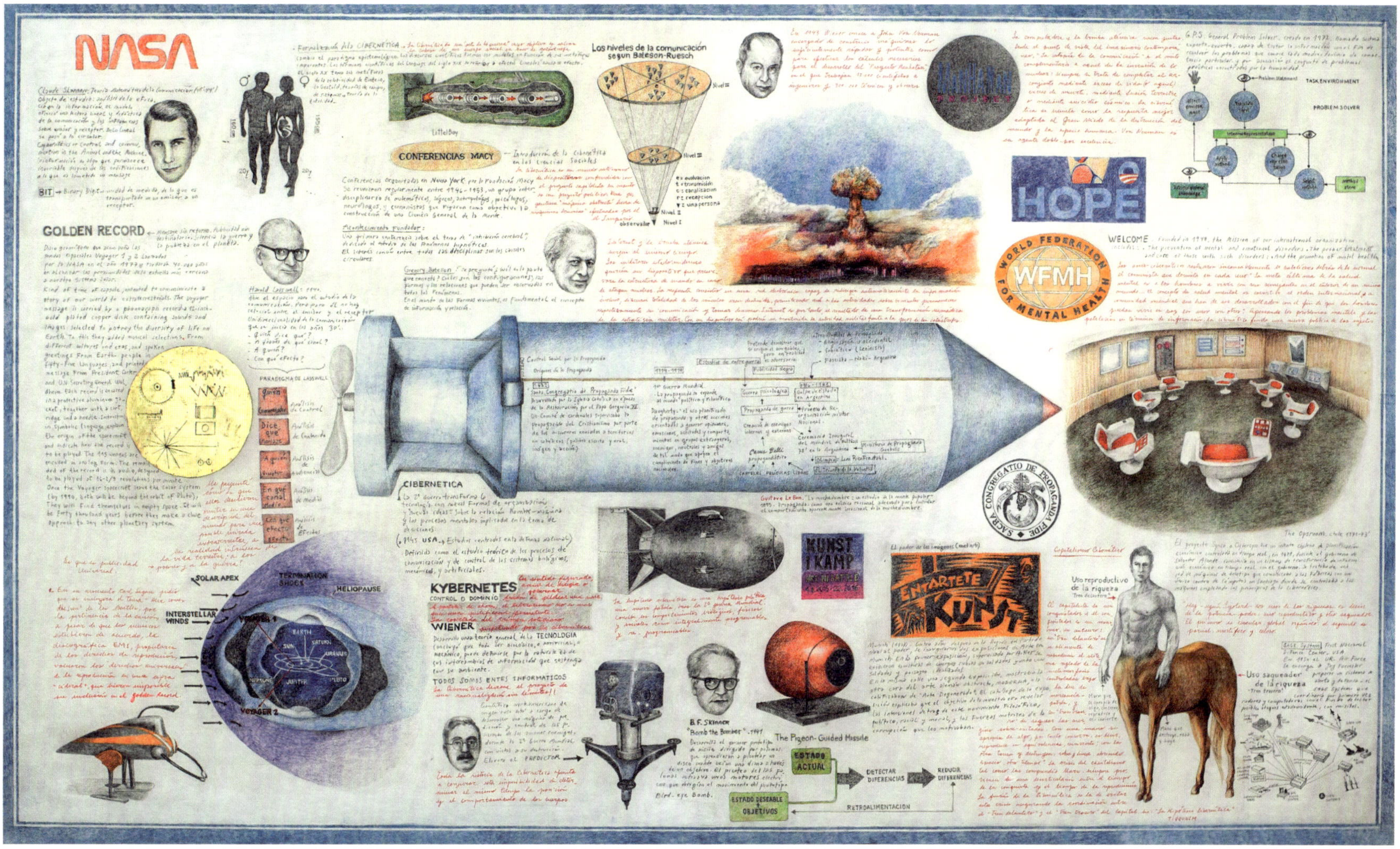
NASA
GOLDEN RECORD
Little Boy
CONFERENCIAS MACY
Los niveles de la comunicación según Bateson-Ruesch
HOPE
WORLD FEDERATION FOR MENTAL HEALTH
WFMH
WELCOME
TASK ENVIRONMENT
PROBLEM SOLVER
CIBERNETICA
KYBERNETES
WIENER
SOLAR APEX
TERMINATION SHOCK
HELIOPAUSE
INTERSTELLAR WINDS
VOYAGER 2
KUNST I KAMP
ENTARTETE KUNST
SACRA CONGREGATIO DE PROPAGANDA FIDE
B.F. Skinner
The Pigeon-Guided Missile
ESTADO ACTUAL
DETECTAR DIFERENCIAS
REDUCIR DIFERENCIAS
ESTADO DESEABLE U OBJETIVOS
RETROALIMENTACION
Uso reproductivo de la riqueza
Uso saqueador de la riqueza

2.

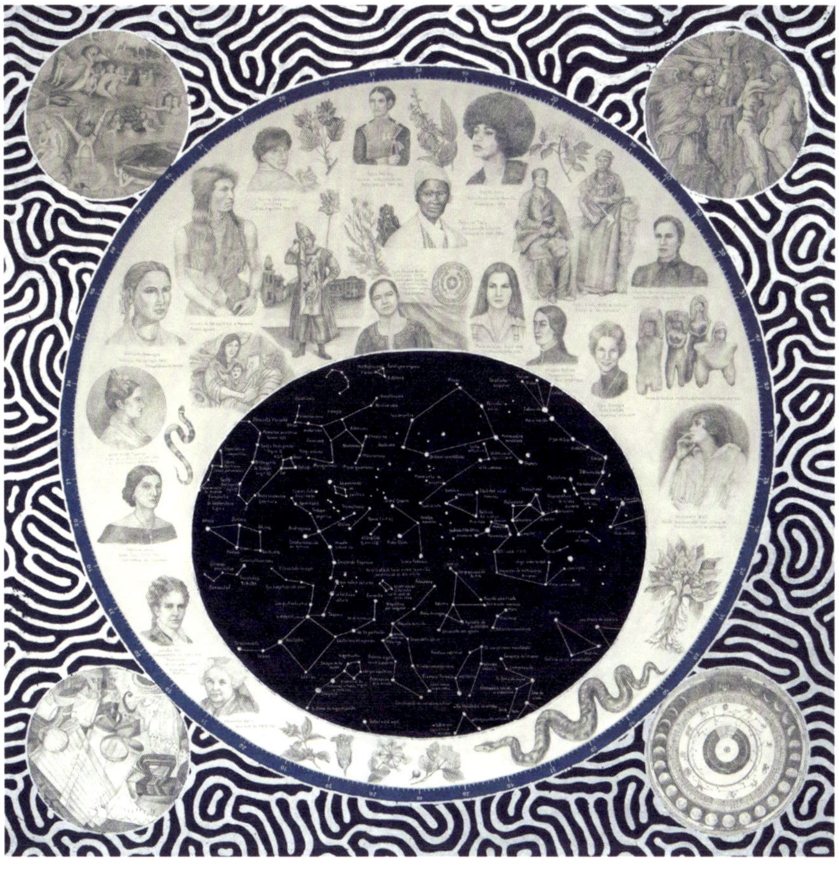

3.

M I R I A M   C A H N .... Rendered in Miriam Cahn's shrill fluorescents, humanity appears at its most primordial, yet most poetic. She lines up one body after the other, neither male nor female, but beyond or before gender, in drawings and paintings that are often larger than life. These are bodies completely saturated with violence as well as desire and tenderness. It would be difficult to look at a work of Cahn's and not feel a simultaneous rush of recognition and repulsion. We know these people, intimately, but the brutality with which they are imbued is one that we would prefer to remain strangers to. .... The artist, born in Basel in 1949, started working with large-format black and white drawings in the late 1970s. With this decision she took a deliberate stance 'against oil painting as "big artwork"', she told Peter Burri on the occasion of her exhibition at Madrid's Fundación "La Caixa" in 2003. Performance was another way that many female artists at the time chose to depart from the male-dominated sphere of painting. Cahn, however, did not want to enact a performance herself, but rather chose to draw as a performative act. She explained to Burri, '[Drawing] always had the character of a performance, both on the floor and on the table... I draw lying down, crawling, crouched.' As a result, whether or not her pictures represent a body, there is something corporeal and fleshy to them. .... *tischchen* (*little table*) (2014/17), for instance, a dark take on the traditional still life, shows a selection of rifles and guns, bleeding colour. This is not an innocent image – there was clearly a body at work here, and with a body comes agency, will and responsibility. Cahn does not shy away from controversial subjects in the name of being politically correct. Rather, her pictures always take a head-on approach, asking us to think and to feel. In *MARE NOSTRUM (Henry Moore)* (2015), she depicts a row of corpse-like figures on a beach. The title, the ancient Roman designation for the Mediterranean Sea, is one that Cahn gave to several works and exhibitions during the height of the refugee crisis. She is a firm believer in the power of imagination and figurative representation during times of crisis. .... Her stance against the 'big artwork', then, is not one against powerful expression, but rather against stasis and conventional monumentality. For Cahn, drawing has the capacity to capture a brief moment of concentration that cannot be tampered with or improved – it is honest. That the artist has since turned to painting on canvas would suggest that drawing is not just a medium, but constitutes something like an attitude. And this attitude is one of confrontational maximalism; Cahn's drawings are massive, numerous and unflinching.
.... Kristian Vistrup Madsen

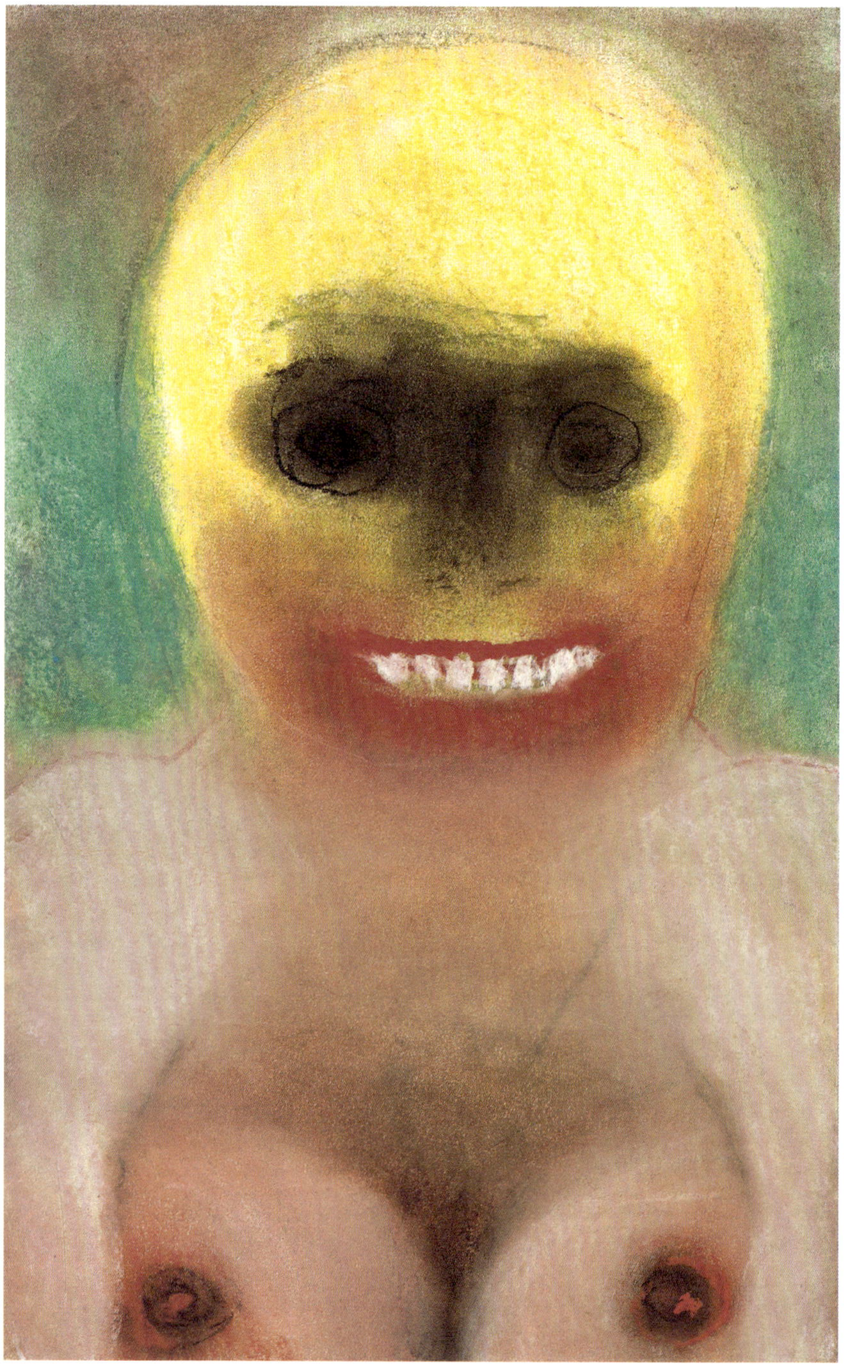

1.

Born 1949, Basel, Switzerland. Lives and works in Stampa, Switzerland.

1. *o.t.*, 2017, pastel on paper, 43 × 27 cm (17 × 10 ⅝ in)
2. *tischchen* (*little table*), 2014/17, watercolour and pencil on paper, 65 × 91 cm (25 ⅝ × 35 ⅞ in)
3. *MARE NOSTRUM (Henry Moore)*, 2015, pencil on paper, 65 × 100 cm (25 ⅝ × 39 ⅜ in)
4. *zurückweichend*, 2012, watercolour and oil stick on paper, 35 × 26 cm (13 ¾ × 10 ¼ in)

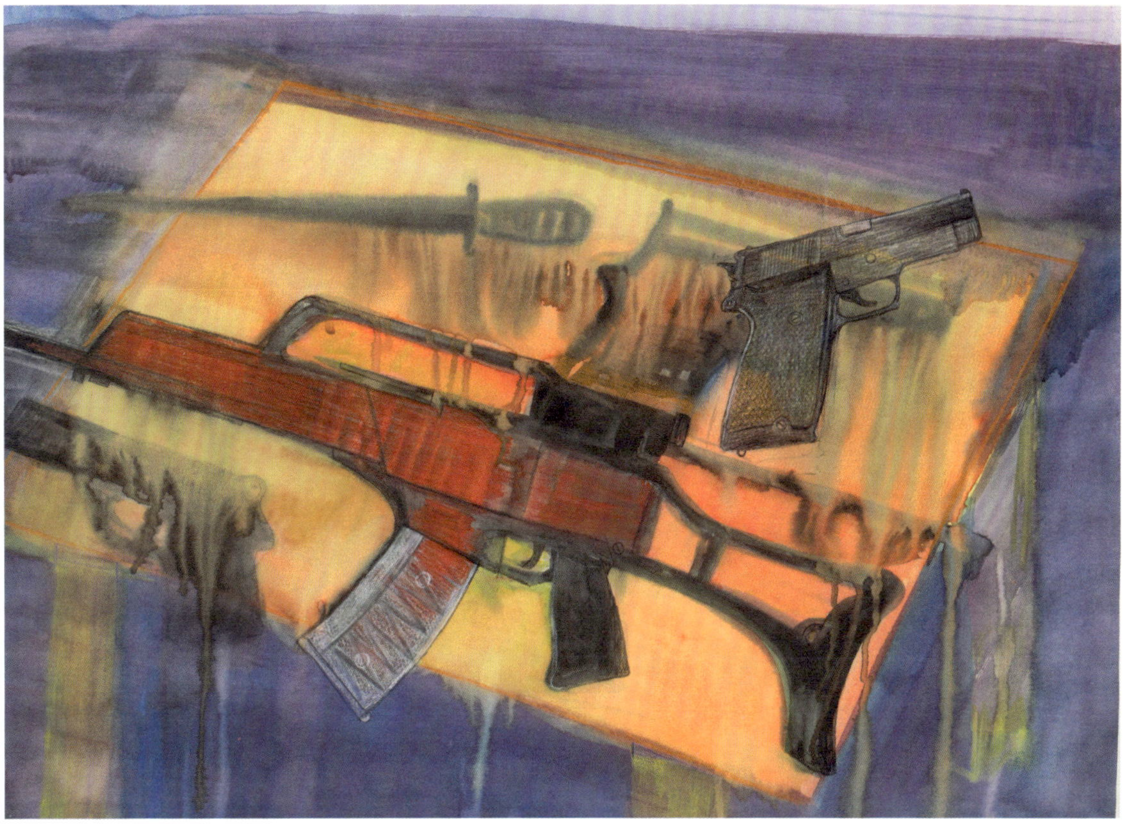

2.

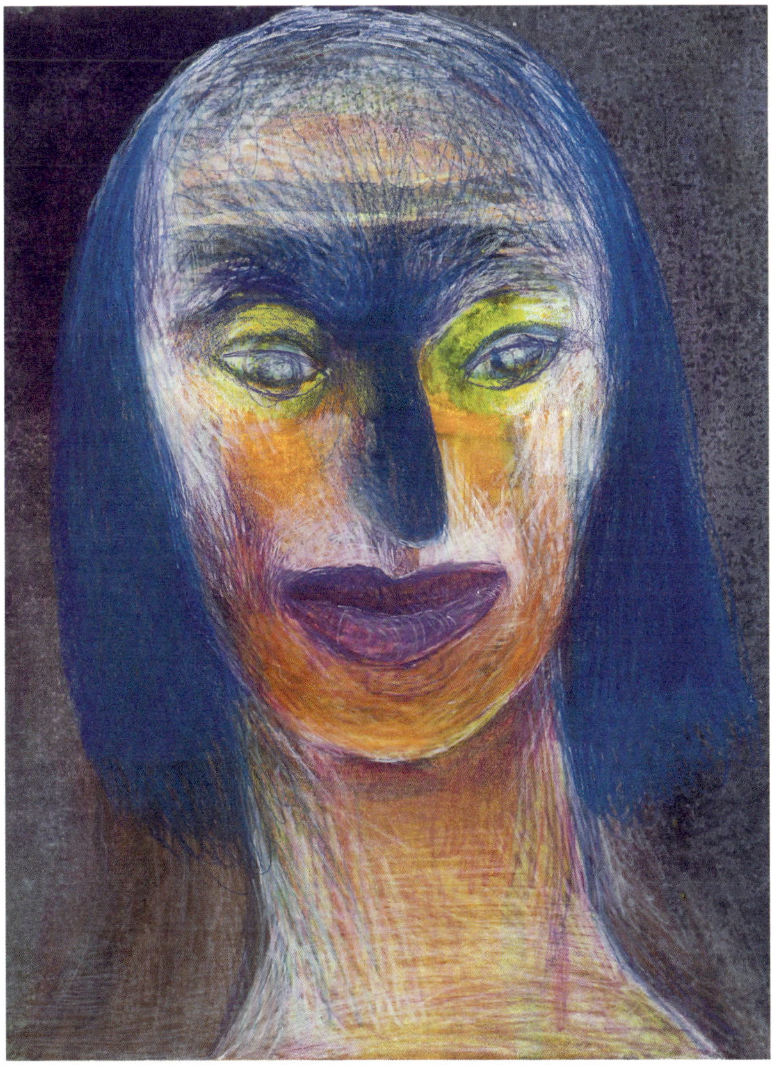

4.

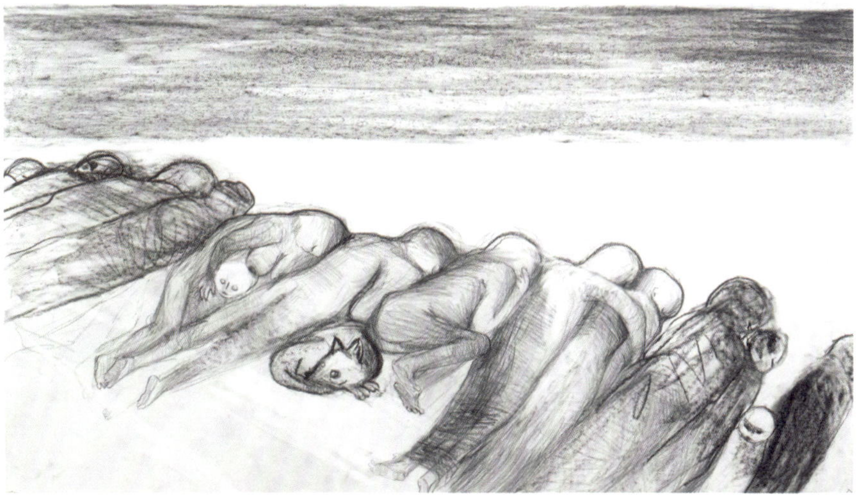

3.

N I D H A L   C H A M E K H .... A single one of Nidhal Chamekh's works might contain Mickey Mouse, precise anatomical depictions of the bone structure of a hand, a hand surreally turned into a burning candle, and a friendly pair of eyes, dissipating like steam into the distance. But this is not juxtaposition, not a matter of staging friction or incongruity, but the opposite. The work in question, *Mémoire Promise 1. (Promise Memory 1.)* (2016), is a memory account – the closest we can get to the truth of something that has already passed, pieced together from scraps and partial visions. In such works poetry, desire and humour sit alongside scientific attempts to comprehend and control, because that is how life registers in humans: all at once. In Chamekh's works we see a deconstruction of testimony that results in the only testimony possible – a question posed as to what memory even is. .... Given the messiness of experience, memory – or to use a broader term, history – is suspiciously tidy. 'Nos Visages' (Our Faces) (2019) is a series of montages based on portraits of soldiers from the French Colonial Empire; Chamekh, born in Tunisia, now also living in Paris, often puts his pen to probing the subjects of colonialism and migration. The already anonymous soldiers are rendered further unrecognizable, their faces, like in a game of exquisite corpse, split and mismatched. The artist explains this gesture as an act against 'coercive representation'. .... In Chamekh's oeuvre history is challenged both for its characters, the story that is told and the progressive linearity imposed upon it. In *The Anti-Clock Project* (2015) a row of sober black and white drawings give equal exposure to an impact crater, millions of years old, the dismantling of the Vendôme Column during the Paris commune in 1871, a beetle rolling a ball of dung, and an obelisk dragged across Cairo's Tahrir Square in 2012. Not only does this line of motifs eclipse distinction between big and small, it also crumbles any fantasy of temporal order. That the installation itself is so very orderly – so neatly framed, and all in white – serves both to exacerbate fraught Enlightenment logic and to lend Chamekh's different and eclectic version an air of self-evidence. .... *Calais, Études et Fragments de Mémoires* (*Calais, Studies and Fragments of Memories*) (2017) likewise folds time up like a map. With great technical precision, Chamekh drew the tents, tools and entrapment infrastructures employed in the migrant camp known as the Calais Jungle from 2015 to 2016. His drawings were accompanied by nineteenth-century illustrations of French soldiers landing on the coast of North Africa and photos from Calais following the destruction wreaked by the First World War. Chamekh shows history as looped and layered, and as black and white only in literal terms.

.... Kristian Vistrup Madsen

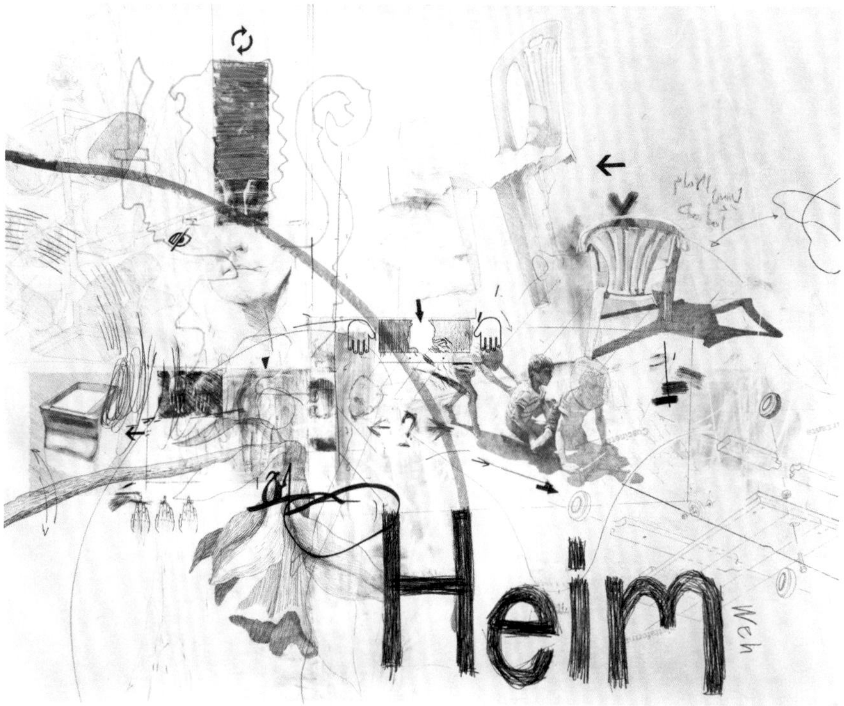

1.

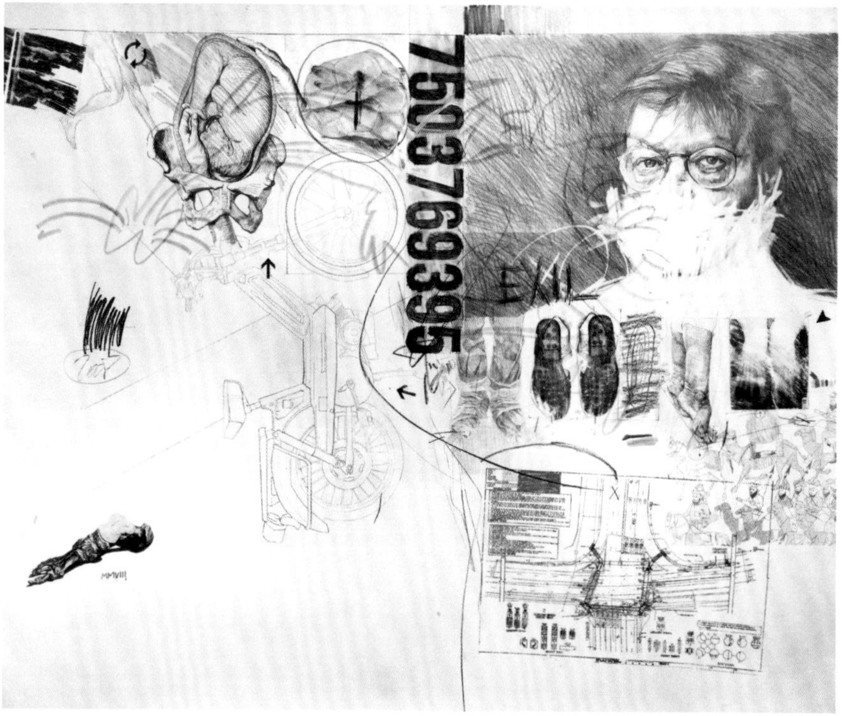

2.

Born 1985, Dahmani, Tunisia. Lives and works in Tunis and Paris.

1. *Exile 1*, 2018, graphite, ink and transfer on cotton paper, 200 × 240 cm (78 ¾ × 94 ⅜ in)
2. *Exile 2*, 2018, graphite, ink and transfer on cotton paper, 200 × 240 cm (78 ¾ × 94 ⅜ in)
3. 'Nos Visages' (Our Faces) series, 2019, ink and nails on cotton paper, 11 drawings, each 30.5 × 23 cm (11 ⅞ × 9 in), installation view, 'Nos Visages', Selma Feriani Gallery, London
4. *Calais, Études et Fragments de Mémoires* (*Calais, Studies and Fragments of Memories*), 2017, ink, graphite and transfer on cotton paper and vintage lithograph, drawing: 100 × 140 cm (39 ⅜ × 55 ⅛ in), installation view, 'Marcher Dans le Rêve d'un Autre', Orléans 1st Architecture Biennial, France

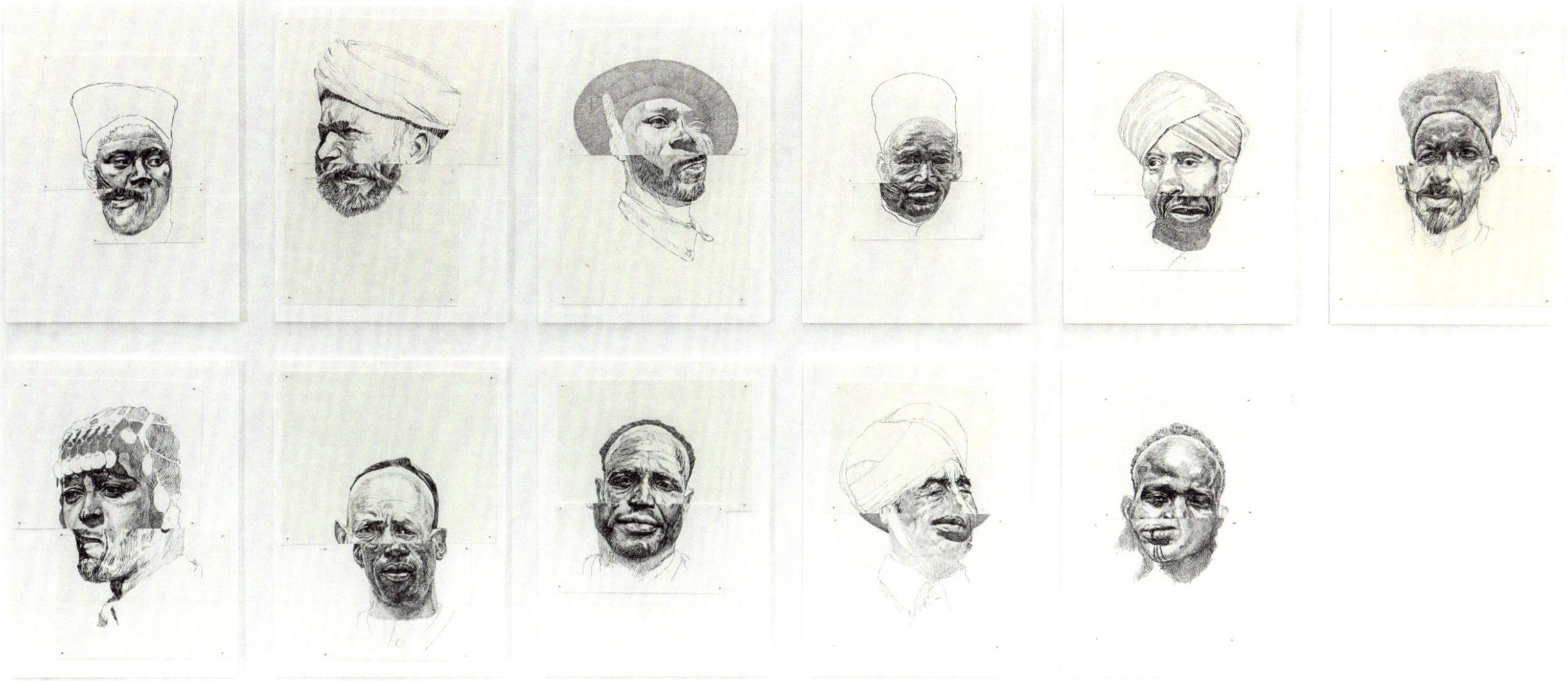

3.

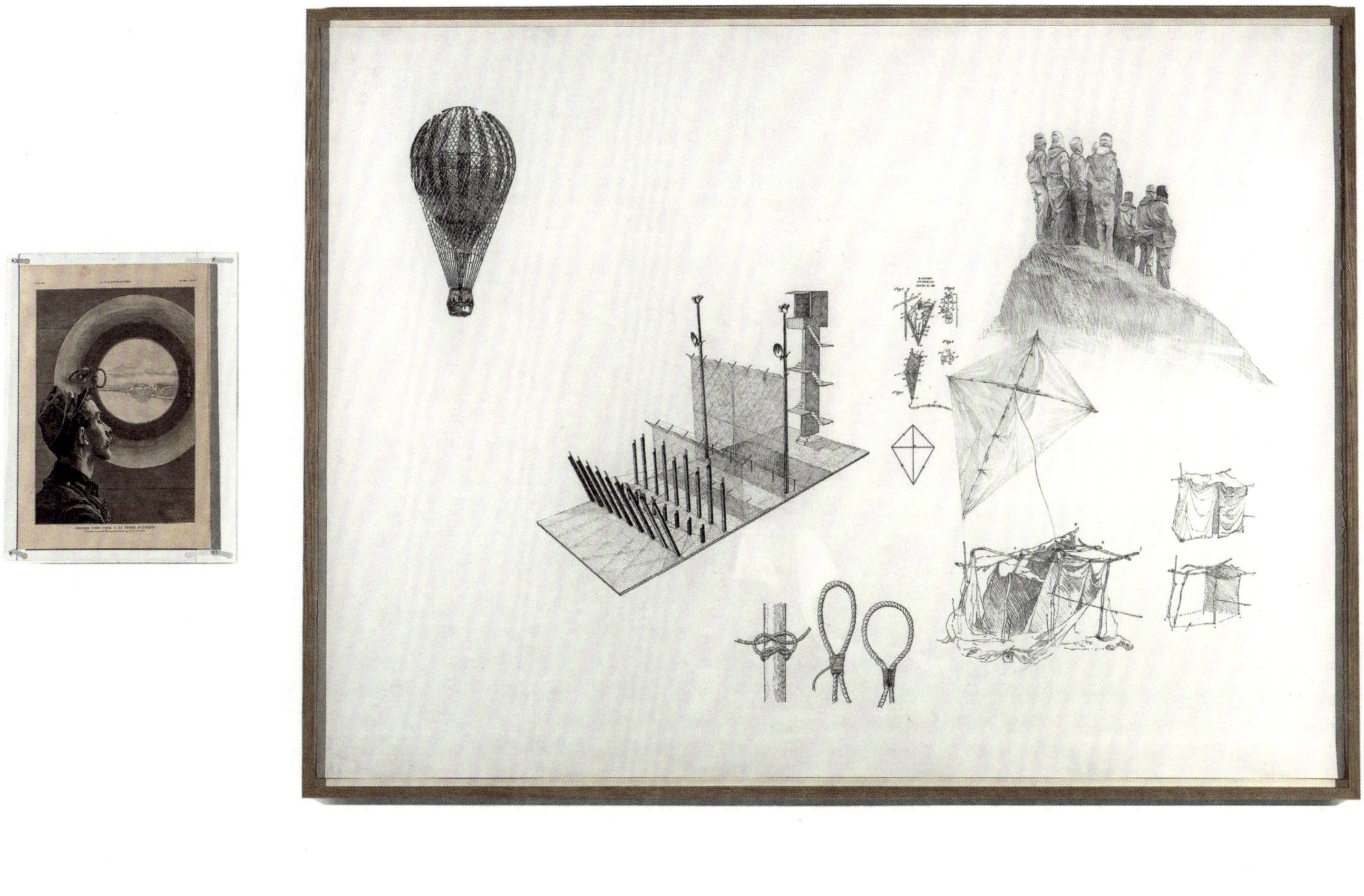

4.

M I L A N O C H O W .... Milano Chow's drawings are populated by elegant women lounging around in grandiose houses. The buildings they inhabit are made to be looked at as much as lived in, with balustrades, mantels and columns depicted with fastidious attention. Seen through windows, behind curtains and partially obscured by blinds, the women are protagonists in their own enigmatic narrative. They portray frozen choreographies painstakingly drawn in pencil on paper. Chow's images are like pages torn from a book, moments in a narrative that remains unresolved. .... What is going on behind these walls and closed doors? The figures look like they have just stepped off the pages of *Vogue* magazine. They wear chic clothes few people can afford with heads full of thoughts we'll never know. *Night Scene with Silhouettes* (2019) is characteristic. The facade of an ornate Neo-Classical townhouse frames the activity of a group of women. We remain bystanders, looking in but locked out on the street outside. Various female characters are glimpsed through windows as another woman appears lost in a moment of reverie peering into the middle distance. The shallow depth of field and even light source, typical of Chow's work, recall a theatre set, enhancing the fictional and dramatic tone. There is a lucidity to the work that feels dreamlike, as if untouched by the vagaries of modern life. .... In *Room 1* (2019) themes of revelation and concealment are further developed. The drawing is expanded sculpturally and folded into a small model-like display. We encounter a female figure partially hidden behind a decorative folding screen. A door behind the figure is open halfway, revealing a monochromatic expanse denoting another room. Art, like theatre, is full of these optical illusions. Symbols that simultaneously direct us to the world and call attention to what is right in front of us. Chow's work asks us to mobilize our imagination and tasks our mind with the work our feet normally do – transporting us into new locations and experiences. .... Chow's preference for Neo-Classicism is crucial. As an architectural style, it was immensely popular across Europe and North America in the nineteenth century. With its evocation of ancient Greek motifs, it remains an aspirational design favoured by governments and financial institutions as a way of denoting power and authority. It is ostentation as a form of camouflage. Like Chow's drawings, it fixes our attention while evading our gaze. Much remains out of sight in these works; as they pirouette between revelation and obfuscation, they dramatize a sense of an anticipation that can never be fully resolved. .... George Vasey

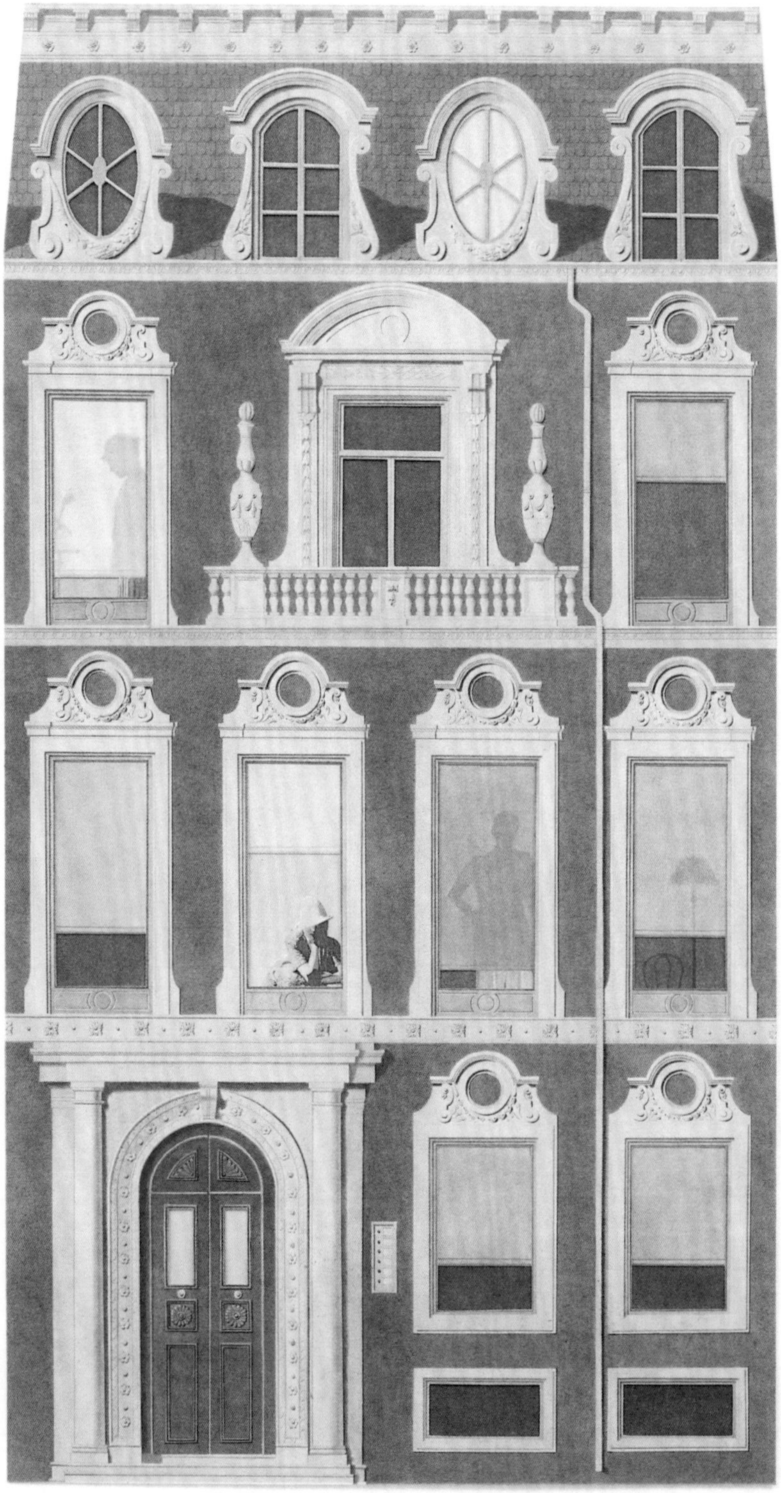

1.

Born 1987, Los Angeles. Lives and works in Los Angeles.

1. *Night Scene with Silhouettes*, 2019, graphite, ink, vinyl paint and photo transfer on paper, 71.1 × 38.1 cm (28 × 15 in)
2. *Mirror (Individualist)*, 2017, graphite, ink, Flashe and photo transfer on paper, 30.5 × 22.9 cm (12 × 9 in)
3. *Portal II*, 2019, graphite, ink, Flashe and photo transfer on paper, 50.8 × 38.1 cm (20 × 15 in)
4. *Horizontal Exterior II*, 2017, graphite, ink, Flashe and photo transfer on paper, 50.8 × 81.3 cm (20 × 32 in)

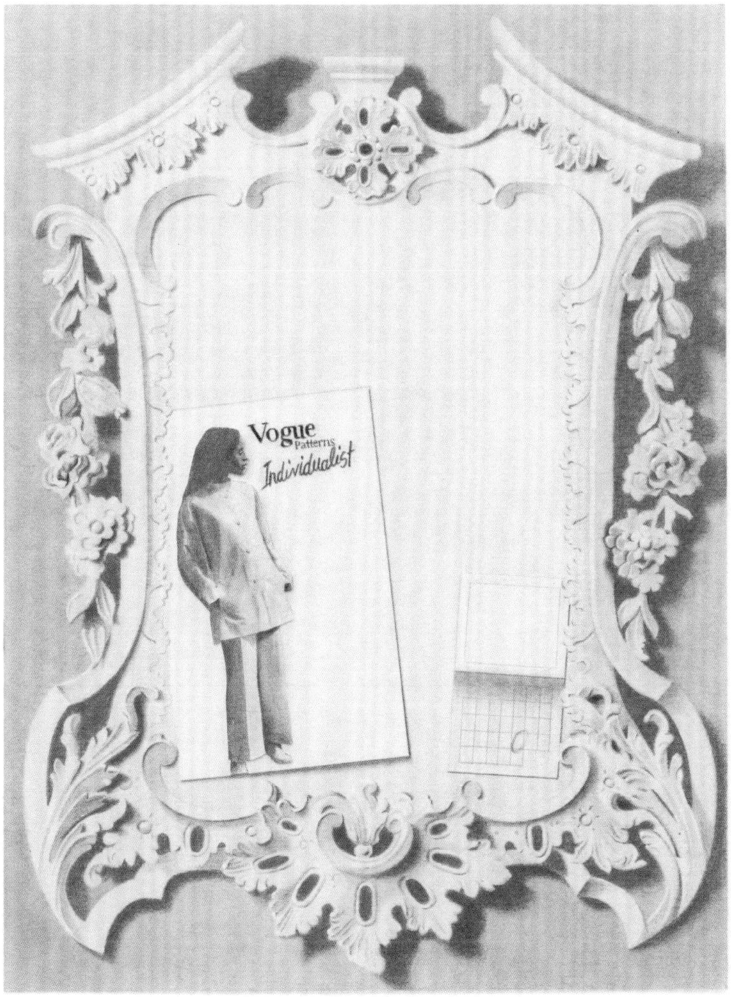

2.

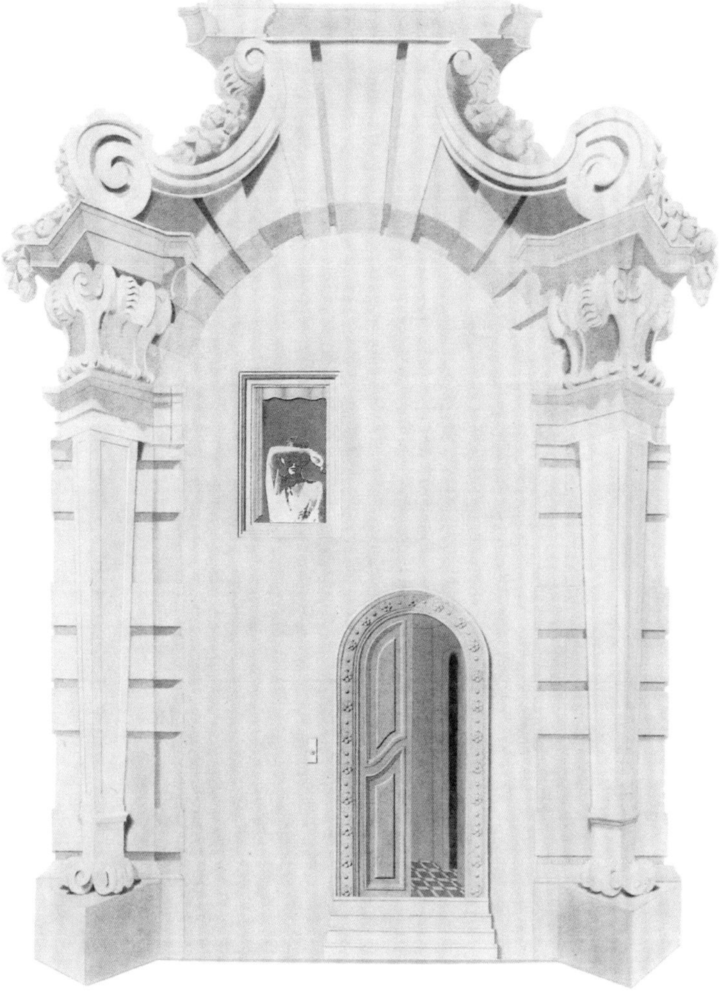

3.

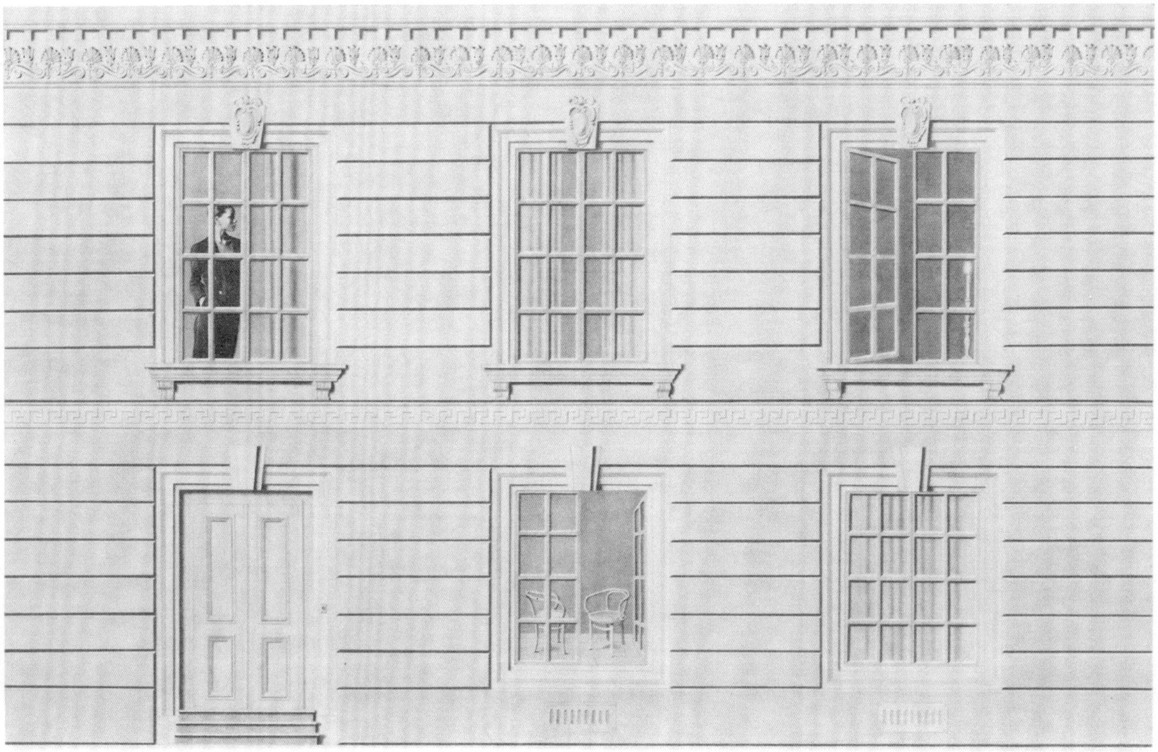

4.

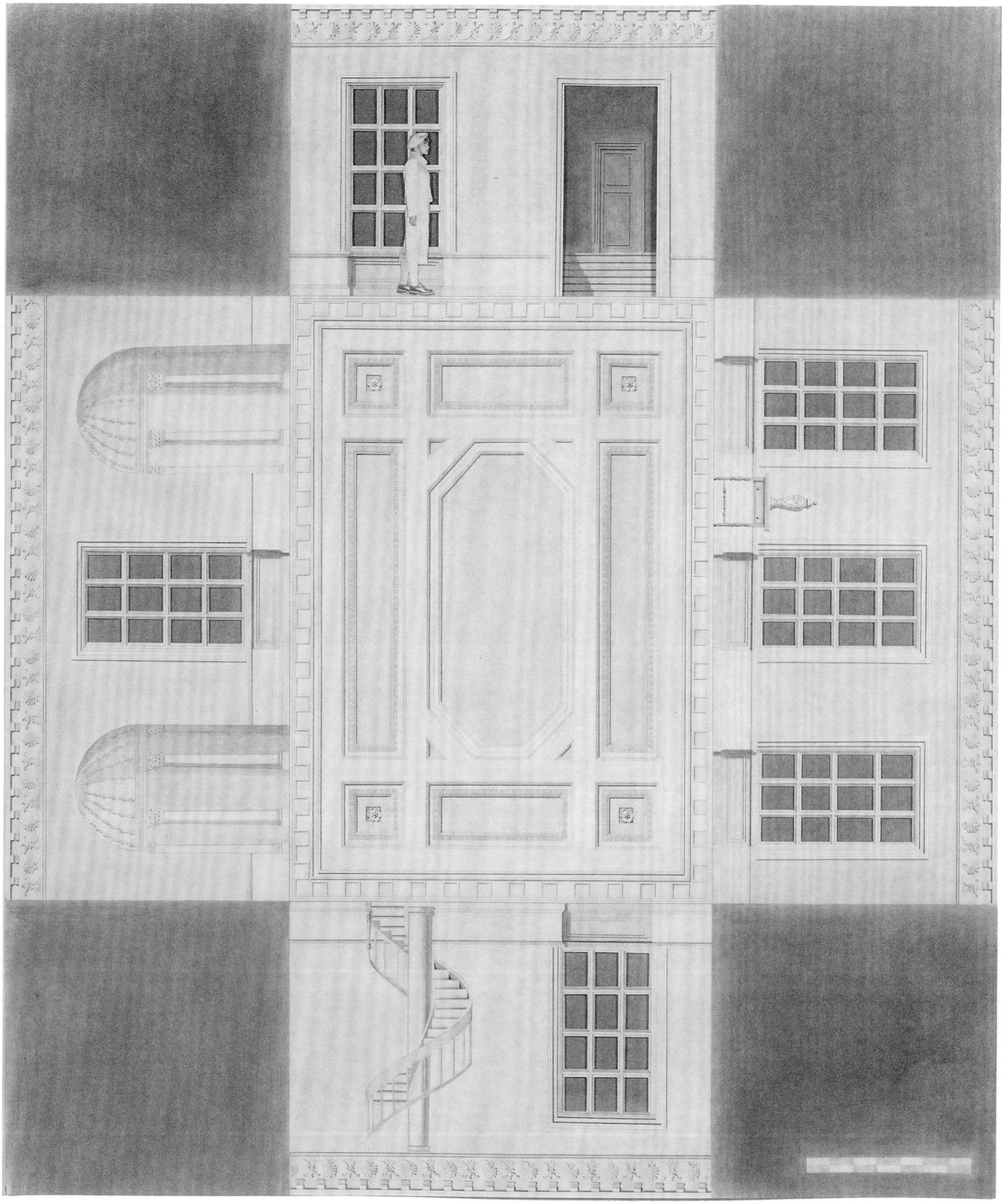

5.

5. *Floor Plan II*, 2019, graphite, ink, vinyl paint and photo transfer on paper, 77.5 × 66.7 cm (30 ½ × 26 ¼ in)
6. *Room I*, 2019, graphite, ink, Flashe and photo transfer on paper mounted to board and fabric, 25.4 × 19.1 × 19.1 cm (10 × 7 ½ × 7 ½ in)

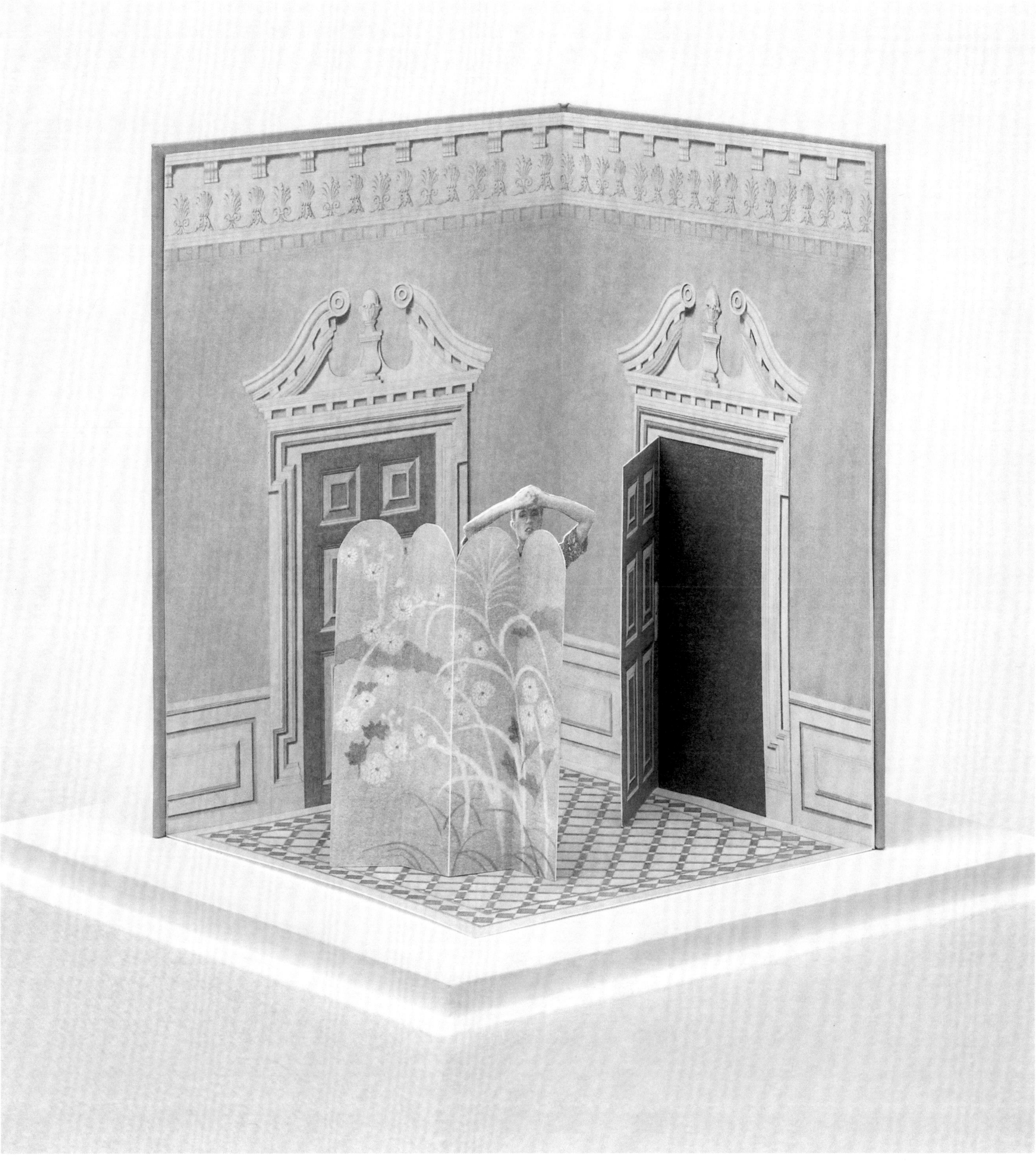

6.

SUSAN COLLIS .... Susan Collis is best known for her deceptive sculptures that explore notions of value, labour and craft. Using various techniques and strategies, she produces objects that initially appear inconsequential but, on closer inspection, are revealed to be replete with value and meaning. Wooden stepladders apparently splattered with paint are, in fact, meticulously inlaid with mother of pearl and semi-precious stones, while the marks on ostensibly stained overalls are all embroidered with painstaking detail. Drawing, which was previously an ancillary activity for Collis, is now central to her practice and, although still working primarily in three dimensions, she considers all her work to be fundamentally concerned with it. .... Were they not displayed in a gallery, the individual drawings comprising Collis's 'The Centre Cannot Hold' series (2018) would certainly be mistaken for scraps of frayed tarpaulin. Each tatty blue fragment is meticulously woven from thin strips of hand-coloured paper. Pinned up high at London's Seventeen Gallery in Collis's 2018 exhibition 'All This Falling', they appeared as the remnants of a larger sheet that was once suspended across the space. Their construction recalls the bag drawings that Collis began making in 2007, which mimic in Fabriano paper and biro the ubiquitous woven plastic laundry bags found in abundance at street markets. Those intricately patterned works similarly hovered between drawing and sculpture, but while they were concerned with issues of labour and production, her shredded tarpaulins represent a new interest in decay and deterioration. .... Many of Collis's works rely on the shift in perception that occurs when viewers realize they are observing elaborate fabrications. Conversely, her recent graphite drawings do not hide their status as artworks. Easily mistaken for simple monochromes, each one is a rubbing, or *frottage*, taken from the interior walls of derelict buildings. The untitled series, which was inspired by the redevelopment of Collis's own studio building, ponders the contemporary wisdom of levelling old structures and replacing years of history with often inferior, characterless structures. The largest of these drawings is *Remainder* (2017), an unframed work comprising two long, wide paper strips suspended from ceiling to floor. Up close, the drawing's densely textured surface reveals a variety of domestic details, including brickwork, tiles and even embossed wallpaper. Collis's use of a dark 5B pencil combines with the drawing's monumental appearance to imbue it with a sense of mourning and loss. Asserting a substantial physical presence, it is a record of a structure that once seemed permanent but has now vanished. In a culture of increasing obsolescence and unnecessary waste, Collis encourages a consideration of the processes by which certain objects are deemed worthy of preservation and others discarded. Value, like beauty, she suggests, is in the eye of the beholder. .... David Trigg

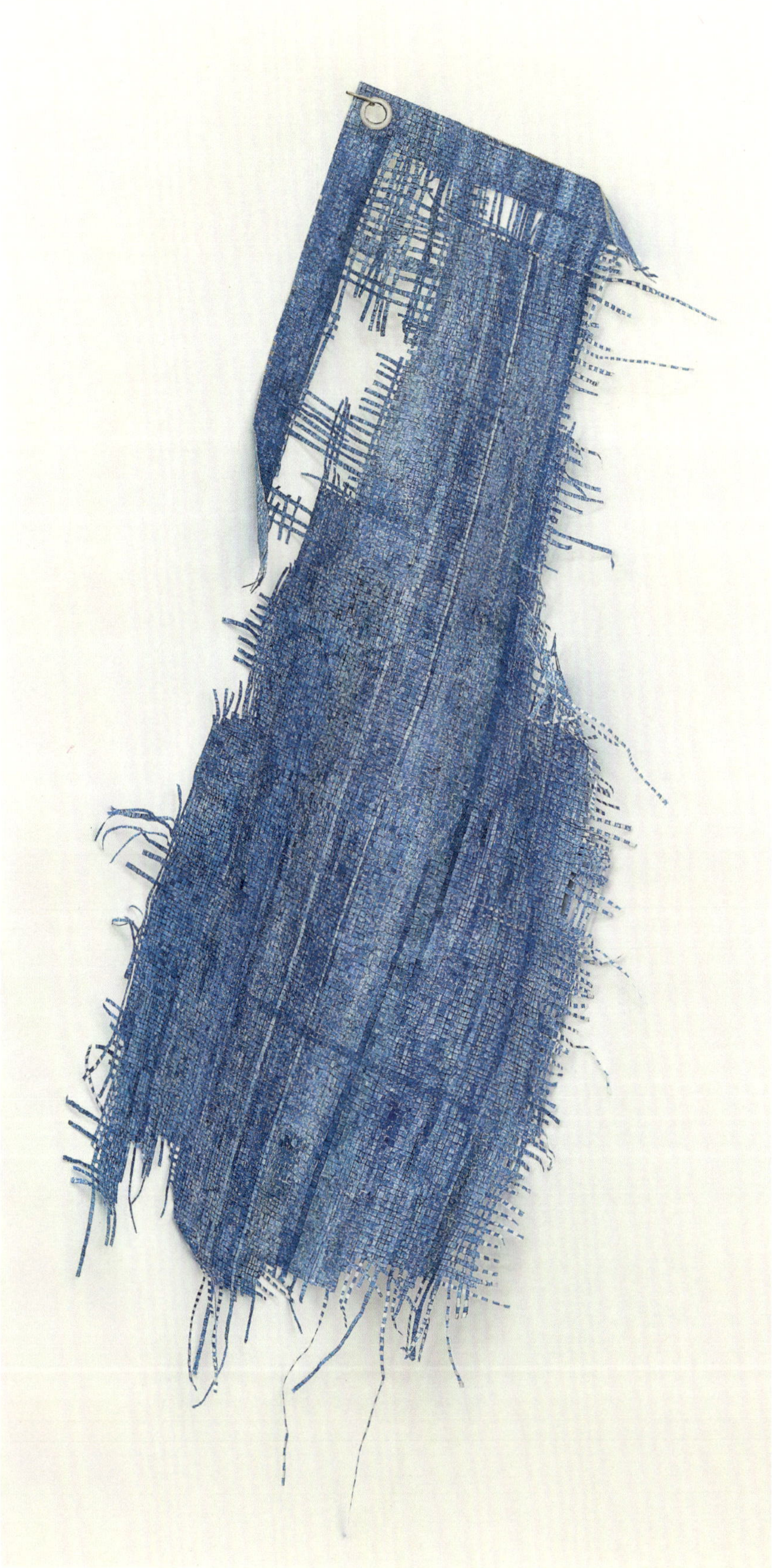

1.

Born 1956, Edinburgh. Lives and works in London.

1. *The Centre Cannot Hold (Brought to Light)*, 2018, ink and pencil on paper and platinum (hallmarked), 96 × 46 × 10 cm (37 ⅞ × 18 ⅛ × 4 in)
2. *Remainder*, 2017, pencil on paper, graphite rubbing of derelict building on white paper, 303 × 300 × 24 cm (119 ¼ × 118 × 9 ½ in)

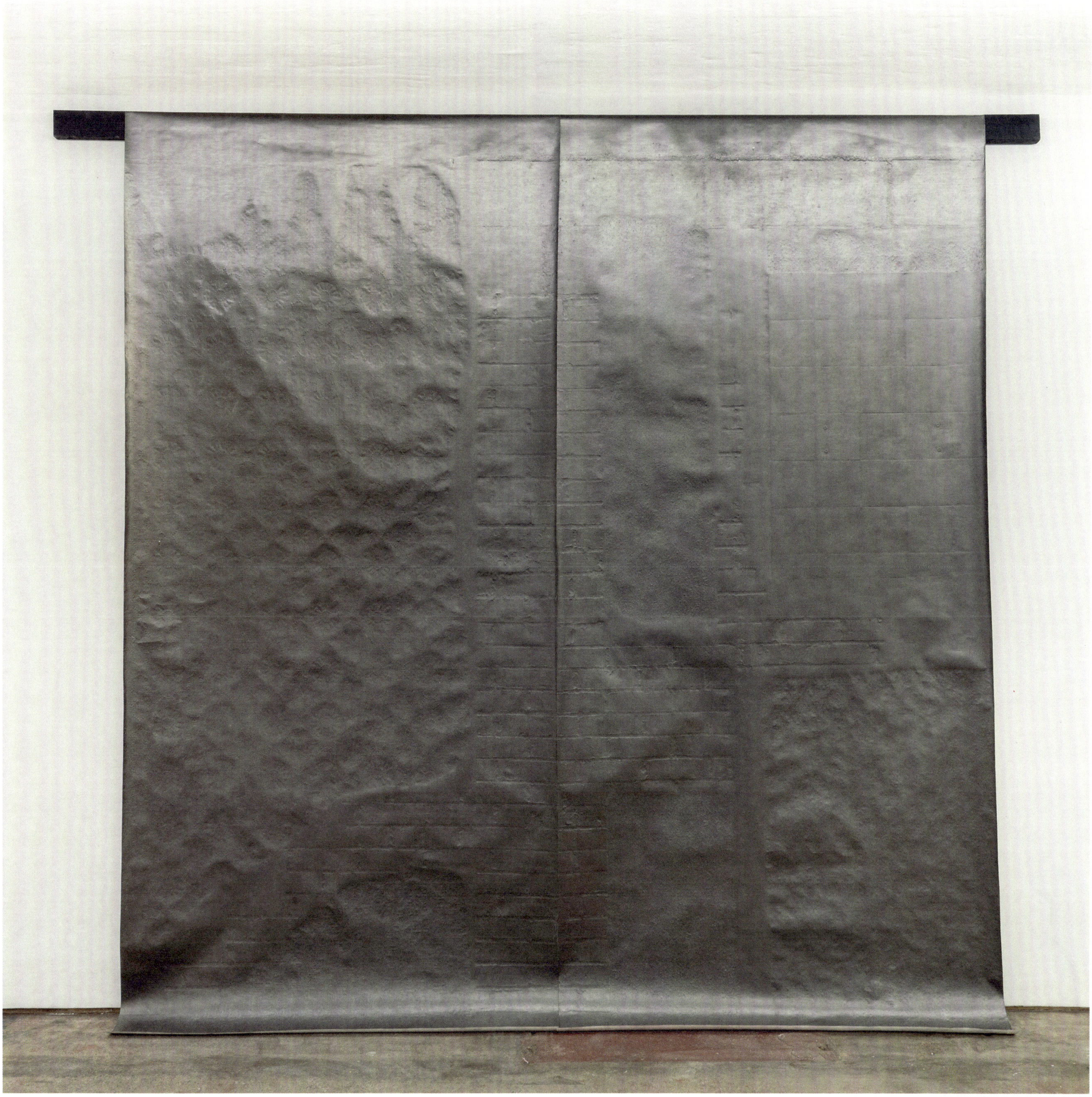

2.

ROBERT CRUMB .... In 1967 Robert Crumb left his job designing greeting cards in Cleveland, Ohio and made his way to the hippie revolution in San Francisco to become a pioneer of the underground comics scene. After taking LSD, a transformative experience that revealed the one-dimensionality of the world he lived in, Crumb began creating more far-out characters, such as Fritz the Cat and the cynical guru-cum-conman Mr. Natural, which were featured in the pre-eminent comic book series, *Zap Comix*. Exaggeration, vulgarity and titillation are the hallmarks of Crumb's style, which pooh-poohs the taboos of modern America's sanitized culture. Revelling in the shift between the sublime and the sordid aspects of life, Crumb often features himself as a character in his own work, embodying the outsider and anti-hero type, an antidote to the saccharine world of Walt Disney. Throughout the decades, his work has ironized the human condition, exposing vanity and insecurity. Like the great caricaturists of the eighteenth and nineteenth centuries – James Gillray (1756–1815), Honoré Daumier (1808–79), for example – he depicts human foibles with a combination of affection and derision. .... Over the years, Crumb has drawn countless portraits of powerful women with strong limbs – Amazonian pin-ups whose clothes strain at the seams. First published in 1996, Crumb's 'Art & Beauty Magazine' is a collection of drawings of women depicted with varying degrees of sexualization, paired with quotations from artists including Leonardo da Vinci (1452–1519) and the cartoonist Harvey Kurtzman (1924–93), famous for his work writing and editing *MAD* magazine. 'Art & Beauty' pays tribute to, and parodies, soft-porn periodicals, while simultaneously contextualizing Crumb's work within an inclusive history of art. Crumb uses the traditional format of the comic book to make deeply unconventional statements about topics such as psychosis, violence and sexual desire. Earlier in his career, he drew from life as well as from photographs; more recently he has based his drawings on photographs, as in his 2019 portrait of Stormy Daniels, the porn star who told the world about her affair with Donald Trump. While Crumb's work is intended for print, his original drawings display the intricacies of his creative process: the white fluid he uses to correct lines, and the textures that are lost in the printing process. .... Crumb's subjects cover a wide spectrum from celebrity figures to the 'Book of Genesis', which he illustrated in 2009. His drawings admit the complexities and contradictions of human nature, providing crude, unromantic portrayals of desire, sex and human relationships – including those in the Bible. His comics are all the more compelling for the truthfulness of this warts-and-all approach. In 2019 he told the *Guardian* newspaper: 'I only feel "misunderstood" when people react to my work as if I were advocating the things I drew; the crazy, violent sex images, the racist images.'
.... Ellen Mara De Wachter

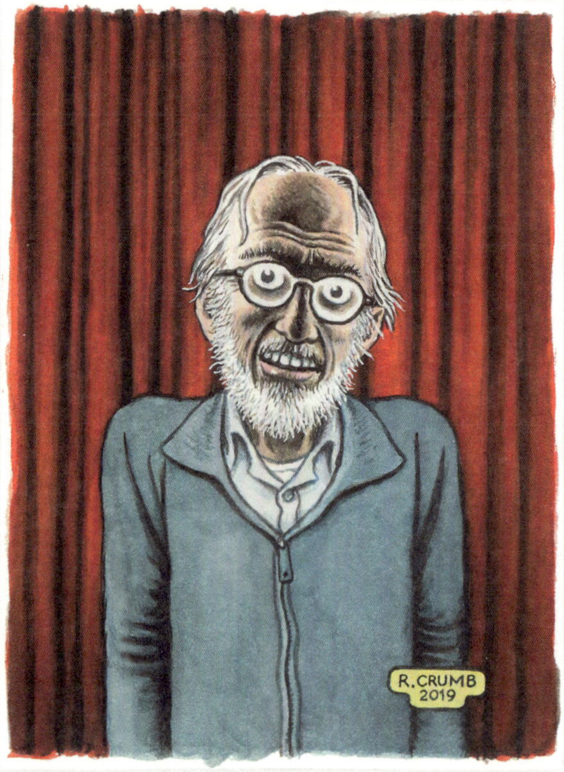

1.

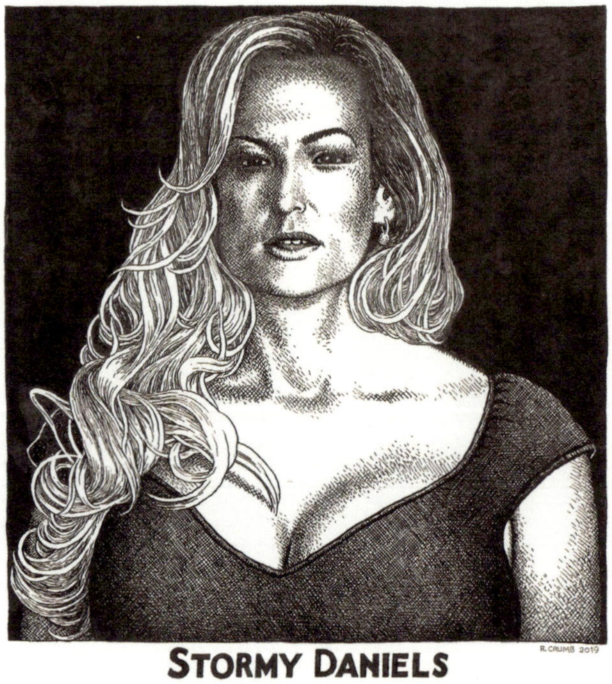

2.

Born 1943, Philadelphia. Lives and works in the South of France.

1. *Untitled (Self portrait)*, 2019, gouache on paper, 24.1 × 17.8 cm (9 ½ × 7 in)
2. *Stormy Daniels*, 2019, ink, correction fluid and graphite on paper, 41.6 × 34.3 cm (16 ¾ × 13 ½ in)

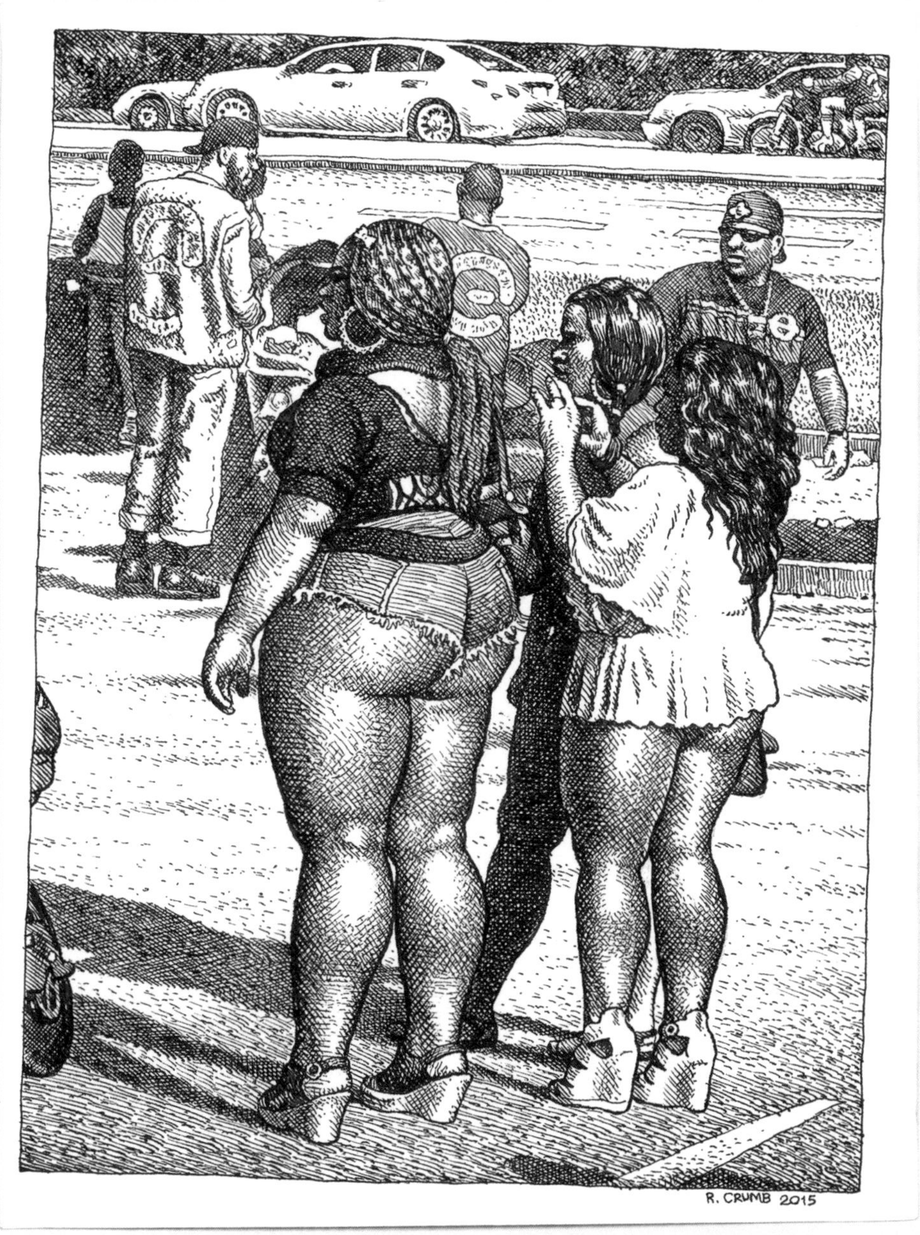

3.

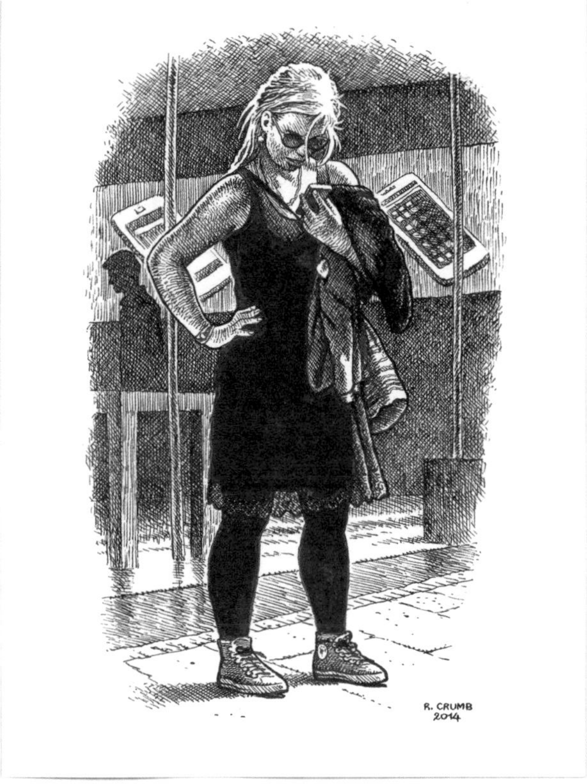

4.

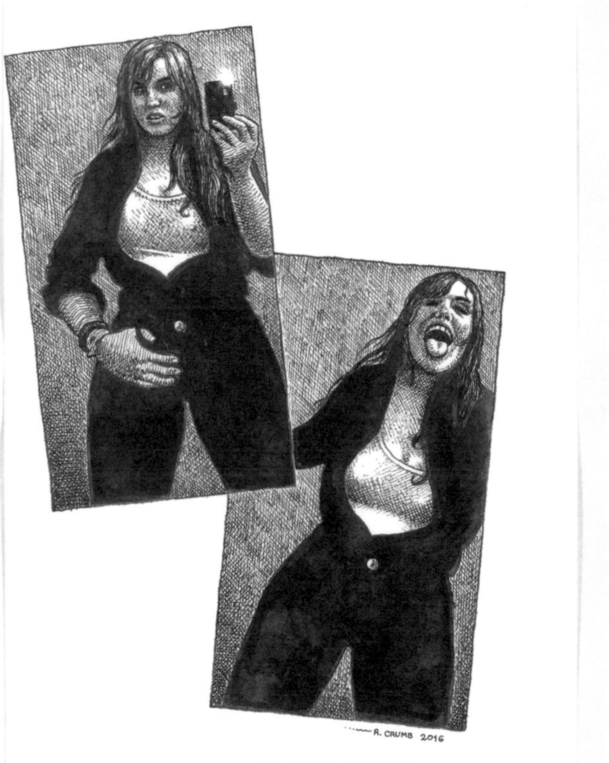

5.

3. *Untitled*, 2015, page from 'Art & Beauty Magazine, Number 3', 2016, ink and correction fluid on paper, 32.5 × 24.8 cm (12 ⅞ × 9 ¾ in)
4. *Untitled*, 2014, page from 'Art & Beauty Magazine, Number 3', 2016, ink and correction fluid on paper, 31.9 × 24.2 cm (12 ⅝ × 9 ½ in)
5. *Untitled*, 2016, page from 'Art & Beauty Magazine, Number 3', 2016, ink and correction fluid on paper, 32.2 × 24.4 cm (12 ¾ × 9 ⅝ in)

DARREN CULLEN .... Sparkling with caustic wit, Darren Cullen's lively cartoons subvert the visual language of advertising to lampoon society's ills. Taking critical aim at consumerism, corporate greed, tabloid culture, corrupt politicians and modern warfare, his drawing practice belongs to a long tradition of British political and social satire that flows from William Hogarth (1697–1764) and James Gillray (1756–1815) all the way to Banksy (b. 1974). As an enthusiastic proponent of subvertising (an underground movement that protests advertising's negative effects on society by removing, defacing and replacing existing adverts), Cullen has hijacked billboards, infiltrated bus shelters and invaded London Underground trains in his pursuit to undermine and derail corporate control of public space. Surprisingly, Cullen once imagined that advertising would become his career and he even studied the subject at art school in Leeds. Yet the more he learned about the dark art of selling and its insidious techniques, the more unsettled he became. As he later noted on his website, 'manipulating the desires and aspirations of the public, and especially children, using an arsenal of sophisticated and emotionally damaging psychological techniques is an appalling way to make a living and an even worse way to sustain an economy'. .... Addressing the mechanics of marketing directly, *Advertising* (2015) shows a doting mother clutching her beaming child next to images of cleaning products and a stark statement: 'Advertising takes a mother's love for her child and uses it to sell bleach'. These words, drawn in bold capital letters against a strong red background, highlight the emotional manipulation and appeals to fear that advertisers regularly use to sell products. Inserted into advertising panels on London Underground trains, the poster greeted travellers on their morning commute. But contrary to the slick graphic design normally found in such spaces, Cullen favours a homespun, comic-book-style aesthetic with bright colours, graphic lines and hand-drawn typography. .... Although Cullen's work addresses serious issues, humour and incongruity play a significant role. Take the absurd police propaganda poster *Police – Community Service* (2017), which ridicules police community outreach schemes by depicting a riot officer serving tea to an elderly pensioner. Heavier subject matter is tackled with similar irreverence in *Nuke Powder* (2017), which transforms the cliched format of washing powder adverts into a stark anti-nuclear message. The dynamic drawing was featured in Cullen's *Mini Daily Mail* (2018), a hand-drawn miniature edition of the British tabloid newspaper filled with mock advertisements and stories such as 'How I lost 3.3lbs in one day by having my brain removed'. The paper was given away to bemused passers-by from a fake newsstand in Liverpool city centre and, though it could later be purchased online, the stunt illustrated that Cullen's work is at its most potent when inadvertently encountered in the public realm.

.... David Trigg

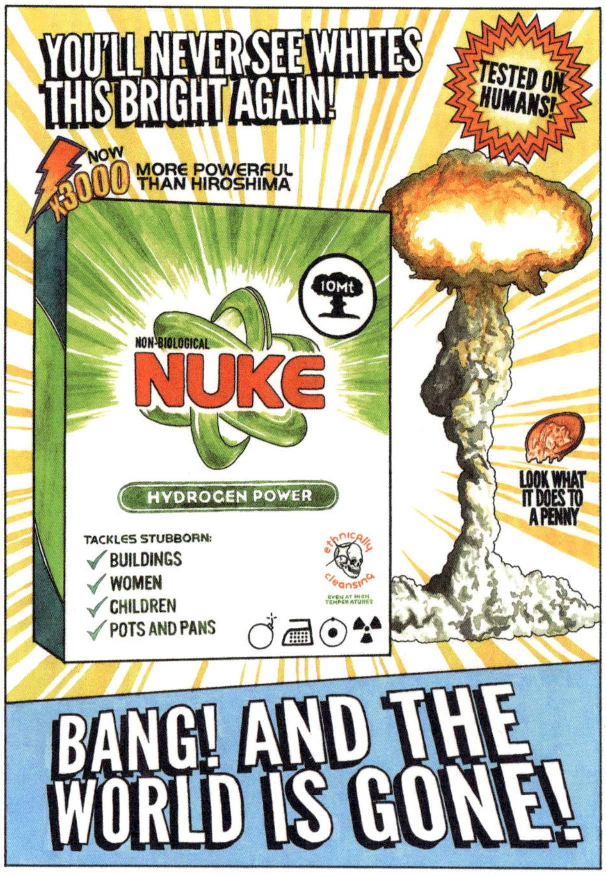

1.

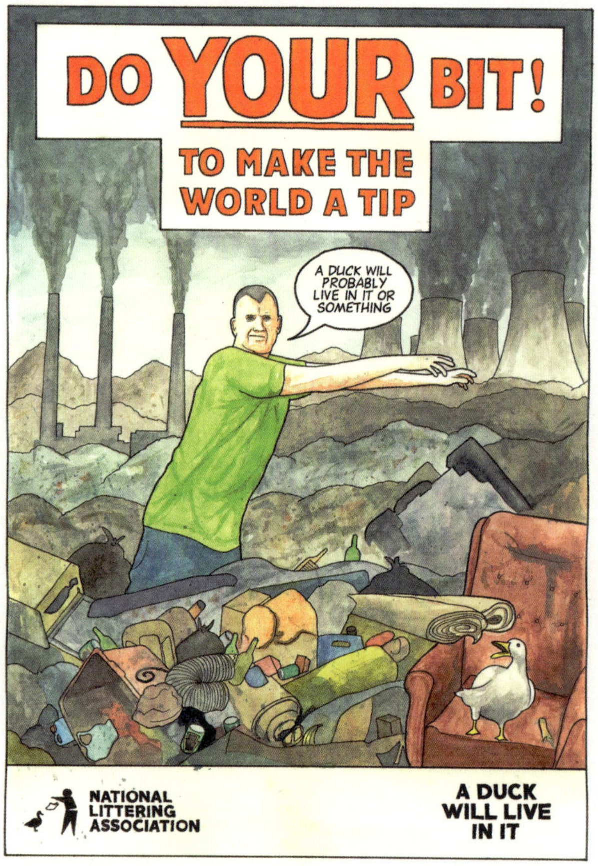

2.

Born 1983, Leeds, UK. Lives and works in London.

1. *Nuke Powder*, 2017, watercolour on cartridge paper, 42 × 29.7 cm (16 ½ × 11 ⅝ in)
2. *A Duck Will Live In It*, 2017, watercolour on cartridge paper, 42 × 29.7 cm (16 ½ × 11 ⅝ in)

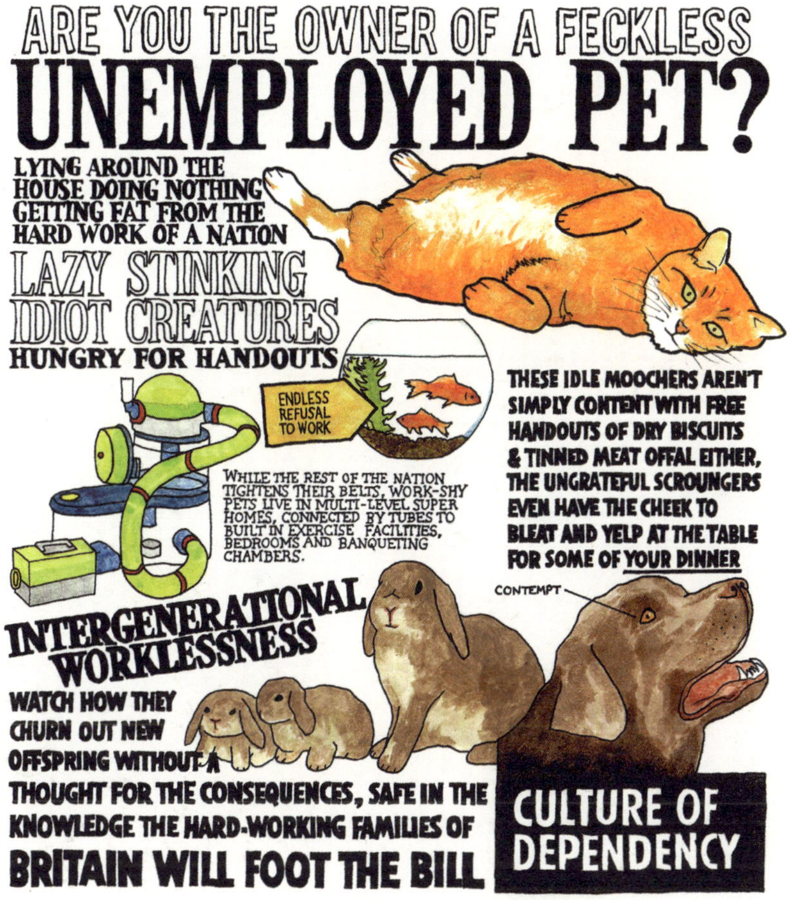

3.

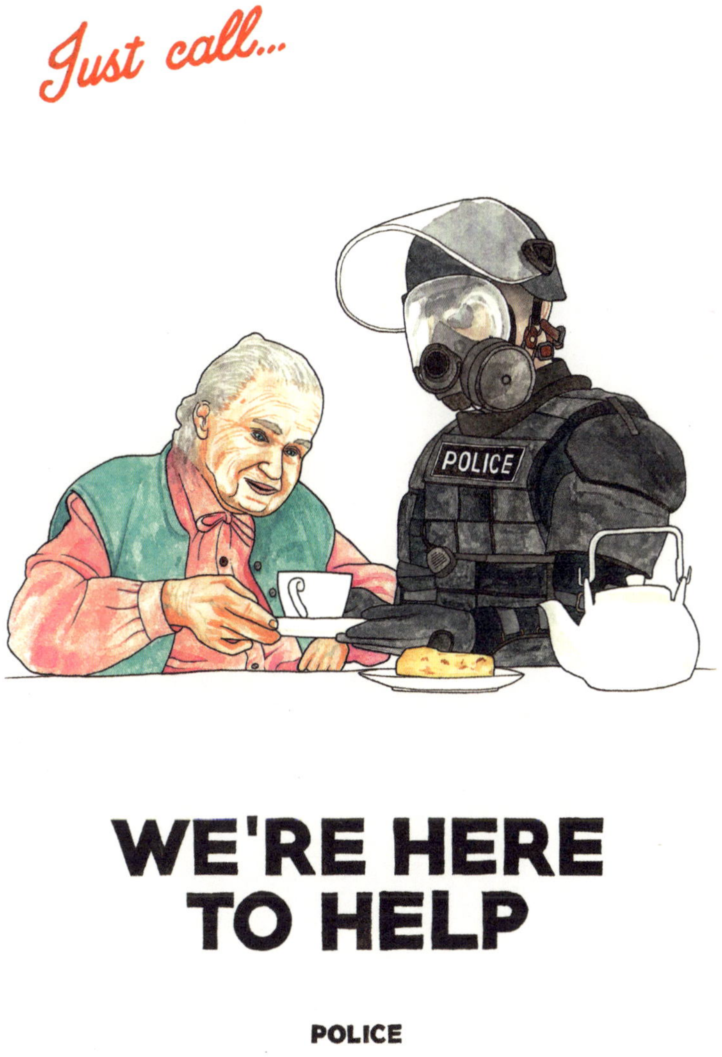

4.

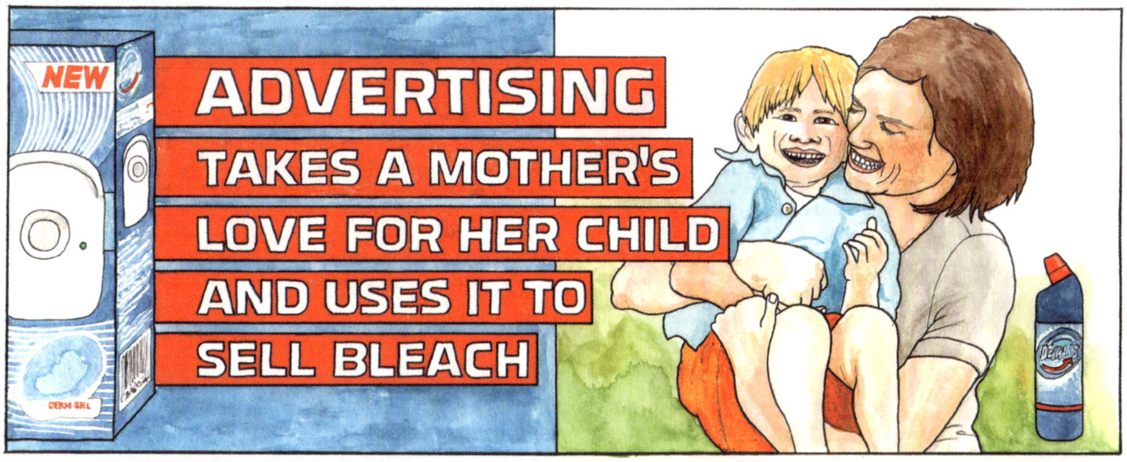

5.

3. *Unemployed Pets*, 2013, watercolour on cartridge paper, 42 × 29.7 cm (16 ½ × 11 ⅝ in)
4. *Police – Community Service*, 2017, watercolour on cartridge paper, 42 × 29.7 cm (16 ½ × 11 ⅝ in)
5. *Advertising*, 2015, acrylic on cartridge paper, 29.7 × 42 cm (11 ⅝ × 16 ½ in)

KENTURAH DAVIS .... Kenturah Davis might be something of a linguistic determinist. This school of thought believes that language fundamentally structures the world around us: not just thought, but perception itself. Davis builds upon this concept to also consider how we use language to construct our – and other people's – identities. Her large-scale, loosely photorealistic portraiture primarily depicts Black women. A closer look reveals that the drawings are made up of text drawn from the work of Toni Morrison and Fred Moten as well as the artist's own songs, poems and other writings. There is a collapse here between writing and other forms of mark-making, but the result is always legible as writing and rarely asemic, or lacking meaning. .... Over time, Davis's practice – which includes forays into sculpture, performance and textiles – has mirrored the historical arc of the written word and its dissemination. Her earliest experiments with text drew upon her research into penmanship and representations of Blackness, and were hand-printed or handwritten in cursive and layered through repetition. More recent work uses rubber stamp letters inked with oil paint, suggesting typesetting, the printing press and other mechanical forms of distribution. *In Praise of Shadows* (2019), which takes its name from Jun'ichirō Tanizaki's 1933 treatise on Japanese aesthetics, uses this technique to create a striking chiaroscuro portrait of a woman. Cobweb-like traceries across her face give her a lovely, paradoxically almost frangible kind of strength. The incorporation of printmaking techniques like monoprinting or *chine collé* further links her works to a tradition of mass media. The latter involves gluing paper to another, thicker support paper and then running both through a printing press. Embossing and debossing provide further texture. .... Of course, the history of printed images is also one of whitewashing. Language, too, is often used to demarcate, define and, in the case of marginalized populations, to discriminate and to disempower. Davis's emphasis on representation and her choice principally to depict Black subjects work as a rejoinder to that. Her subjects are vulnerable yet self-possessed and, above all, non-commodifiable. Her use of doubling and blurring – a Motenian strategy of resistance – reminds us that identity is too varied, too multi-faceted to be captured unidimensionally. The result is a bristling sense of contained motion. Meanwhile, repetitions of grids, usually faintly rendered in graphite, nod to the history of modernism. Occasionally the drawings are spread across multiple frames, as in *A Symphony of Truths* (2019), which is split across four large panels like a picture window. A three-quarter profile of a woman is seen in triplicate, with ghostly traces on each side. Past and present selves, perhaps, or just afterimages from staring at the sun too long.
.... Rahel Aima

1. 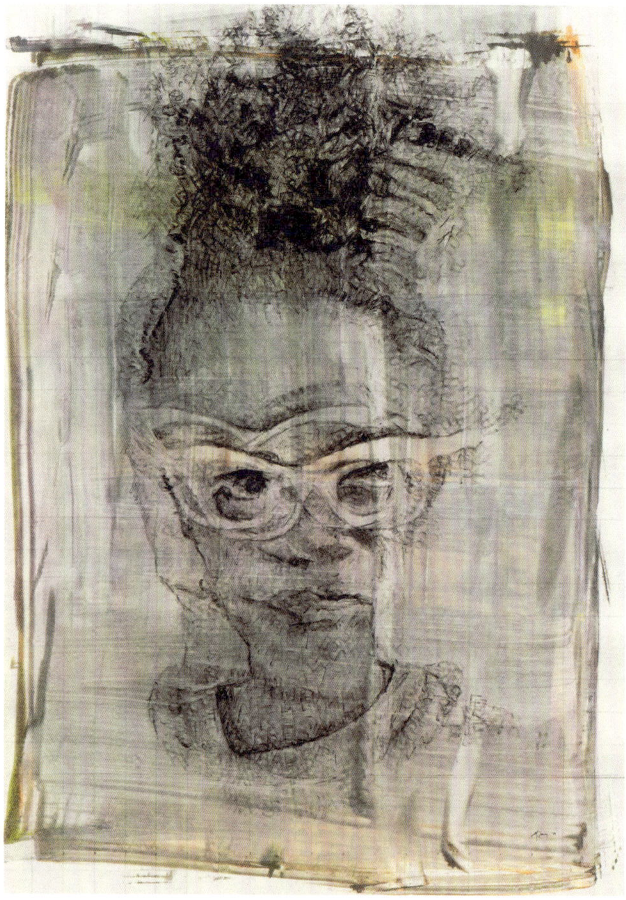

2. 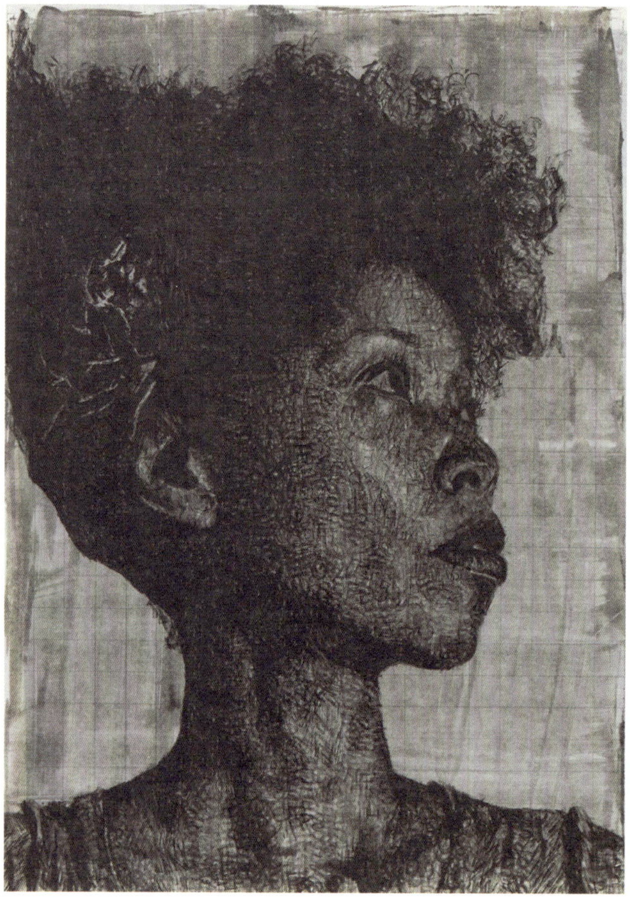

Born 1980, Los Angeles. Lives and works in Los Angeles.

1. *A Sharp Whisper*, 2019, oil paint applied with rubber stamp letters and *Chine-collé* on monoprinted paper with graphite grid, 71.1 × 50.8 cm (28 × 20 in)
2. *In Praise of Shadows*, 2019, oil paint applied with rubber stamp letters on monoprinted paper with graphite grid, 71.1 × 50.8 cm (28 × 20 in)

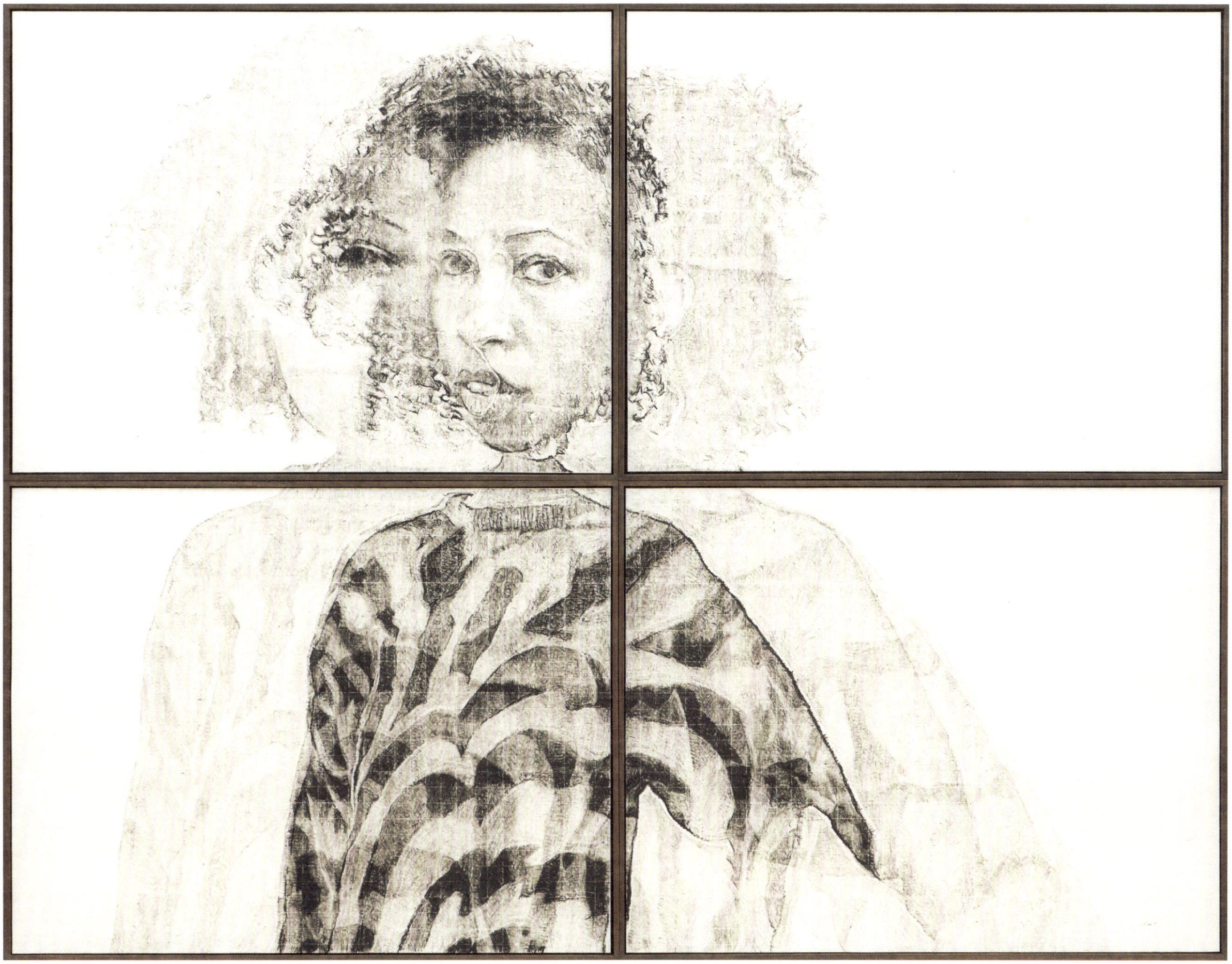

3.

3. *A Symphony of Truths*, 2019, oil paint applied with rubber stamp letters on embossed and debossed Igarashi Kozo paper, overall: 149.9 × 200.7 cm (59 × 79 in)

MIRIAM DE BÚRCA .... If the soil beneath our feet could speak, what dark secrets might it disclose? This is the tacit question underpinning Miriam de Búrca's meticulous drawings, which dominate a practice also including painting and video. Born in Germany but raised in Ireland, the artist explores in her work some of the bleakest episodes of Irish history. Her closely observed studies of lonely waste grounds and earthen sods, replete with verdant grasses, flowers and weeds, address the ways in which Ireland's landscape has for centuries been shaped by socio-political power dynamics and dogmatic belief systems. De Búrca's 'Anatomy of Chaos' series (2018) saw her travel to remote burial grounds across Ireland. These unofficial cemeteries, or *cillíní*, are the final resting place of unbaptized infants, the mentally ill and disabled, vagrants, criminals and anyone else on society's fringes whom the Catholic Church deemed unworthy of burial in consecrated graveyards. Incensed by the cruelty of such injustices, de Búrca responded with large ink drawings depicting clods of earth collected from the graves. *Anatomy of Chaos I: What Remains?* (2018) precisely renders every inch of crumbling soil, unruly vegetation and tangled roots. Despite working for hours with a botanical illustrator's eye, de Búrca is not interested in plant identification; each species remains as anonymous as the person from whose grave it sprouted. While the cemeteries are a sad testament to centuries of religious prejudice, de Búrca's drawings poignantly memorialize those abandoned by the Church. .... Her earlier drawings were similarly exacting. *Deconstructing the North V: Dirt and Roots* (2014) is one of several examining the cultural, religious and political divisions that persist in Irish society. It shows in great detail a clump of earth from the Crom Estate, a conservation area in County Fermanagh, Northern Ireland, whose rural beauty hides a fractious past. While the soil holds memories of colonial rule, further research unearthed sinister stories of hanging and drowning, folkloric myths and class tensions. Isolated and floating in a field of white space, the carefully drawn clod recalls John Donne's famous words 'no man is an island' from *Devotions upon Emergent Occasions* (1624), which speaks to the importance of community. .... Among de Búrca's most harrowing works are those alluding to Ireland's notorious mother and baby homes – institutions run by the Church where unmarried women were sent to give birth, shrouded in secrecy and shame. The small ink drawing *Cluster II: 1961* (2018) depicts a huddle of empty, skeletal cots in reference to the horrifying discovery of an unmarked mass grave at one such home in County Galway, where bodies of deceased infants were callously discarded. Irish society still has many ghosts to confront; de Búrca's drawings are a call for transparency and justice. .... David Trigg

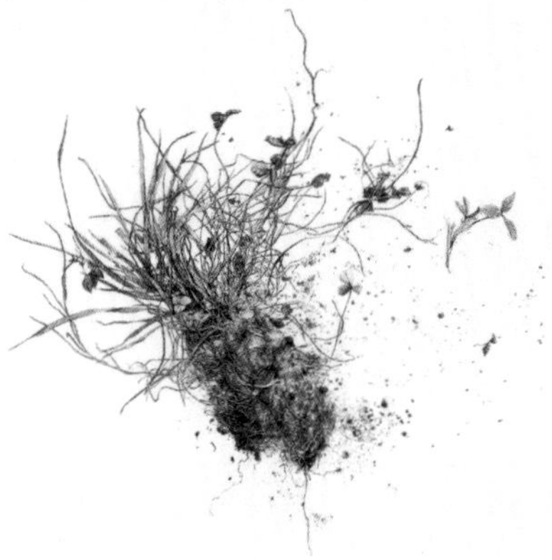

1.

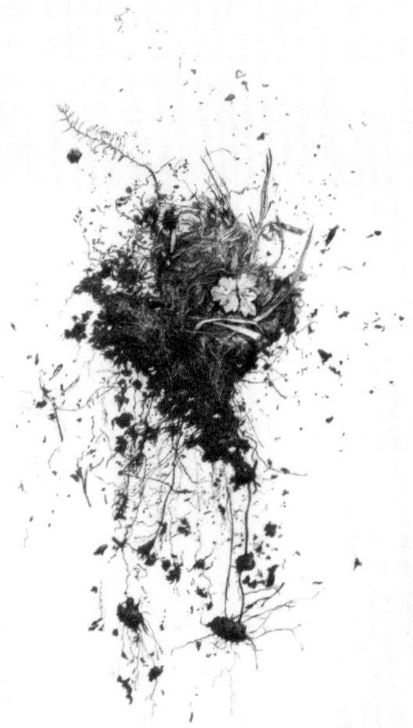

2.

1. *Deconstructing the North III: Grass*, 2013, ink on paper vellum, 50.5 × 34.5 cm (20 × 13 ¾ in)
2. *Deconstructing the North V: Dirt and Roots*, 2014, ink on paper vellum, 50.5 × 34.5 cm (20 × 13 ¾ in)
3. *Anatomy of Chaos I: What Remains?*, 2018, ink on man-made vellum, 50 × 66 cm (19 ⅝ × 26 in)
4. *Anatomy of Chaos III: Forensics as Memorial*, 2018, ink on man-made vellum, 51 × 66 cm (20 × 26 in)
5. *Cluster II: 1961*, 2018, ink on man-made vellum, 25.5 × 32 cm (10 ¼ × 12 ⅝ in)

Born 1972, Munich. Lives and works in Galway, Ireland.

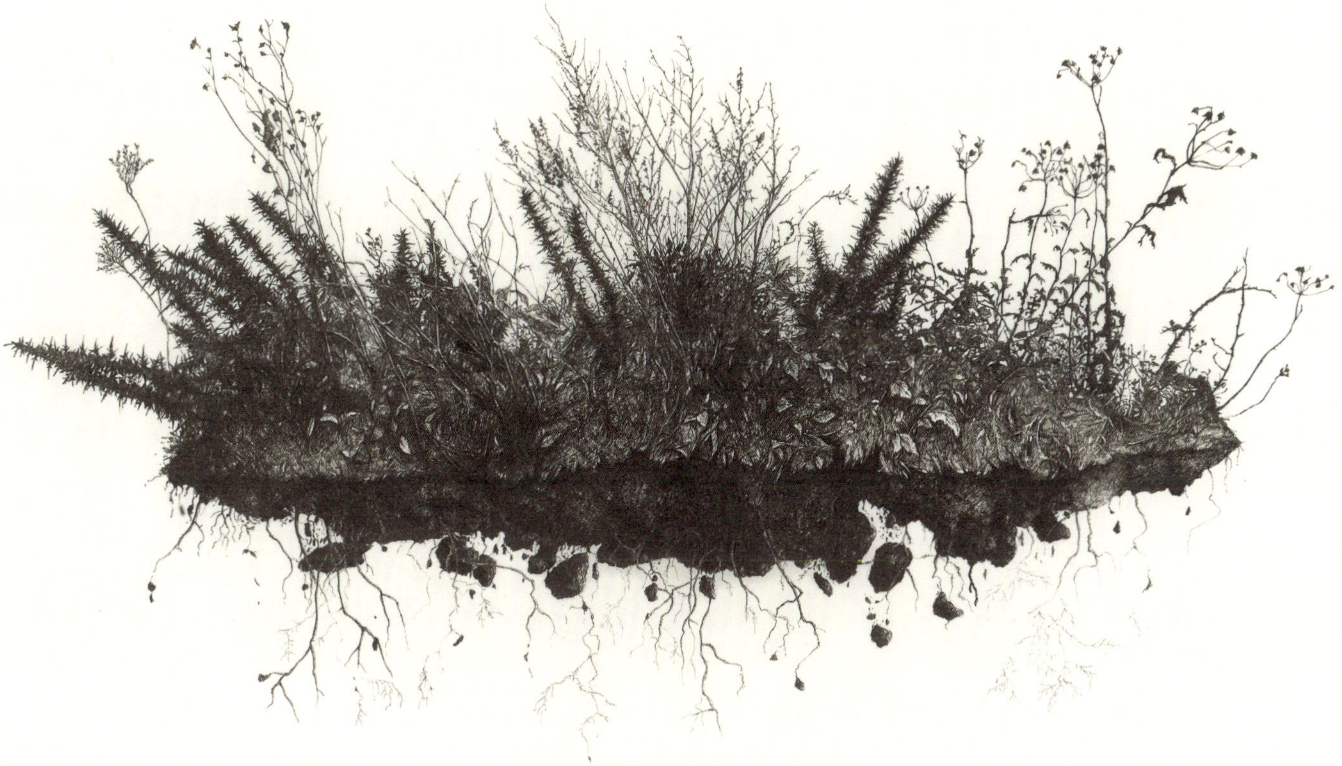

3.

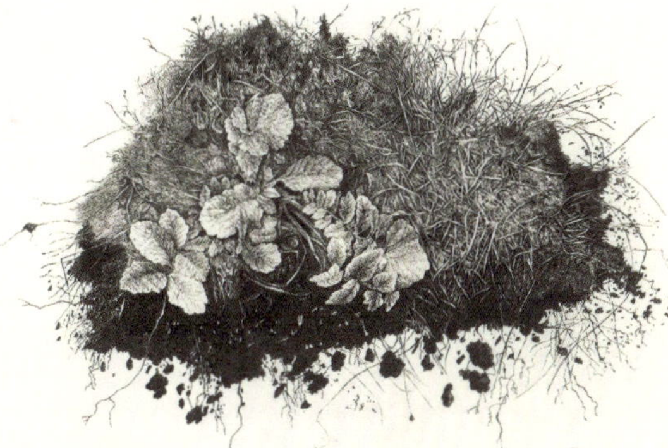

4.

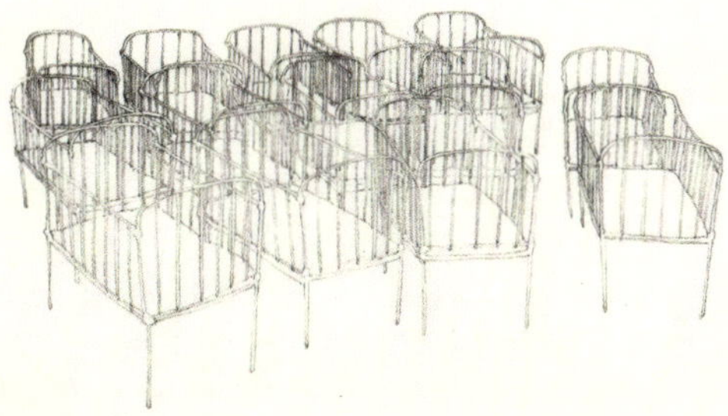

5.

IBRAHIM EL-SALAHI .... In a remarkable career that spans over five decades, Ibrahim El-Salahi has created a unique visual vocabulary that reflects his complex personal history as well as his undying passion for freedom and human dignity. The question of identity, a fundamental notion in most people's lives, in El-Salahi's work has been the subject of constant revisions and investigations, starting from his native Sudan, a country at the crossroads between the Arab and the African worlds, to his time in England, where he had to come to terms with the predominant traits of Western culture. El-Salahi's time at the Slade School of Fine Art in London gave him a set of tools that had the dual effect of perfecting his technical skills while bringing him to the realization that they would have never enabled him to express his true self. What followed was a process of deconstruction, eventually resulting in the signature language El-Salahi is globally known for. One of the main adjustments El-Salahi had to make during his time in Europe was the way he responded to light. In the bright, sun-lit landscape of Omdurman, where he grew up, his eyes had to be half shut to work out the details of his immediate surroundings. Conversely, England's gloomy and crisp colours would force him to keep his eyes constantly wide open. This fact had to be taken in and fully absorbed before being successfully formulated in his work. This is also true for his recurrent use of the square and the circle, and his predilection for black and white tones so as to better capture their structural quality. .... Although art has been the principal driving force in El-Salahi's life, it was not always his main occupation. In the 1970s he held a string of administrative posts, including being Undersecretary for the Sudanese Ministry of Culture. The job took place at a time of political turmoil and was drastically cut short by a period of wrongful incarceration. While in captivity, El-Salahi was banned from drawing or writing, but he bravely fought this restriction by secretly drawing on minuscule pieces of paper cut from cement bags, which he would then hide under the sandy soil of the prison courtyard. These drawings have been lost forever, but the experience would resurface later in El-Salahi's *Prison Notebook* (1976) and the 'Pain Relief' series, a body of work that had cathartic ramifications for his persona and his practice. This also partially accounts for El-Salahi's tendency to favour fragmentation, even when he works on a large scale. Large-format works like *Reborn Sounds of Childhood Dreams III* (2015), the final chapter of a trilogy initiated in the early 1960s about the artist's early influences and memories, grow in a visibly organic fashion, following the inspiration and improvisational talent of their maker. .... Michele Robecchi

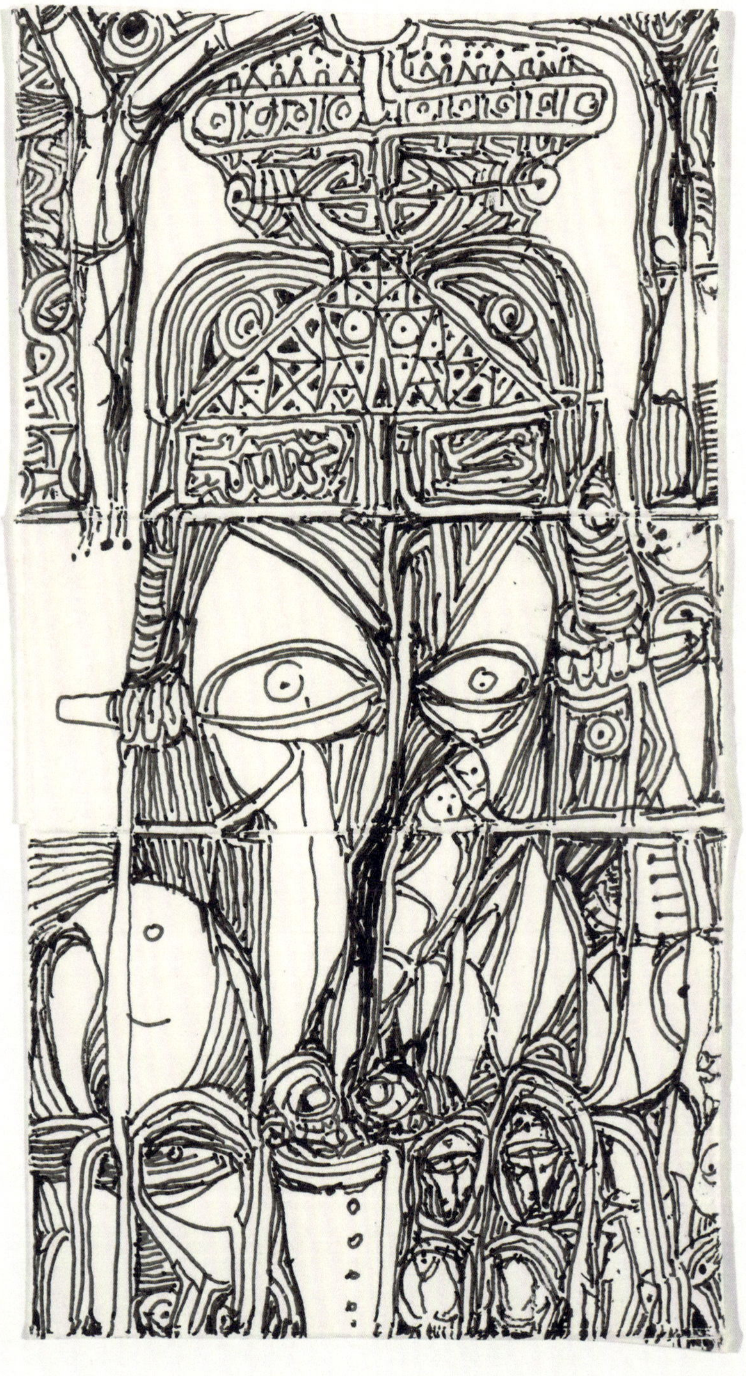

1.

Born 1930, Omdurman, Sudan. Lives and works in Oxford, UK

1. *Pain Relief Drawing*, 2016–18, pen and ink on the back of a medicine packet, 13 × 7 cm (5 ⅛ × 2 ¾ in)
2. *Reborn Sounds of Childhood Dreams III*, 2015, pen and ink on paper mounted on canvas, 122 × 308 cm (48 ⅛ × 121 ¼ in)
3. *Flamenco Dancers*, 2012, ink on paper mounted on canvas, 156 × 372 cm (61 ⅜ × 146 ½ in)

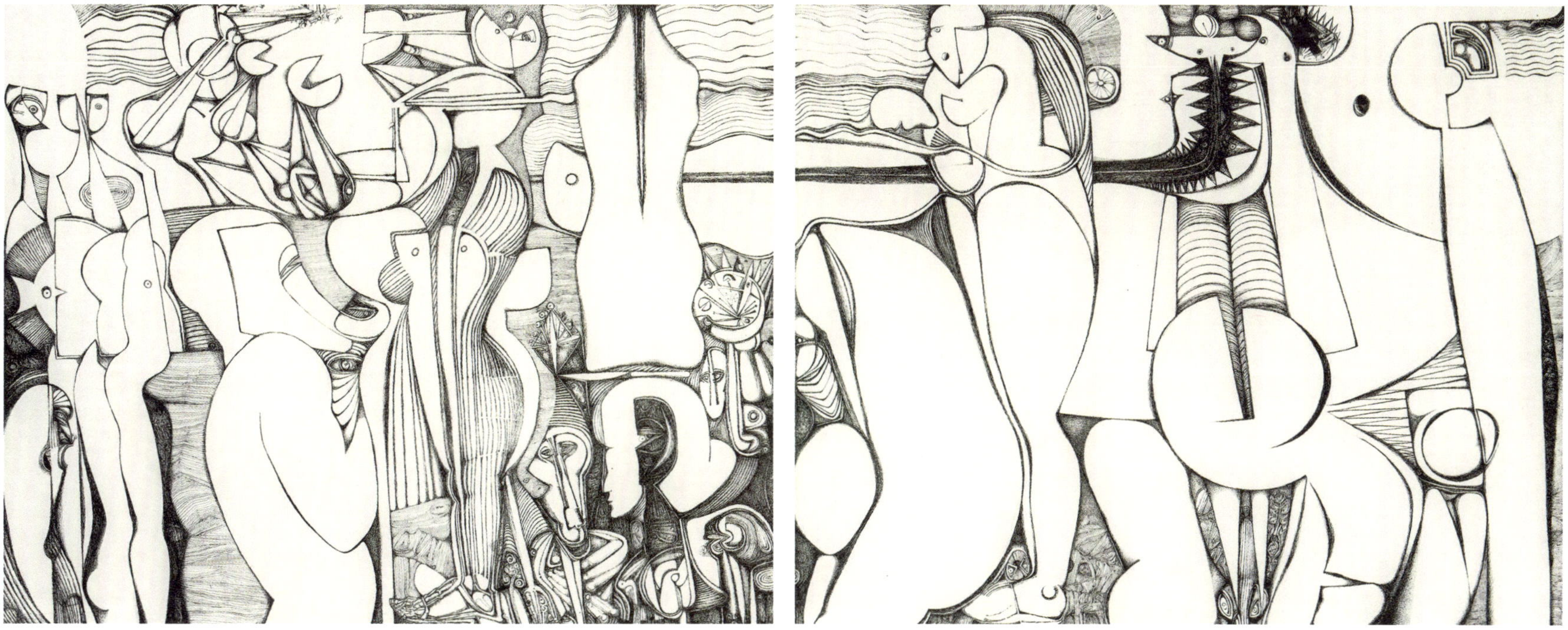

2.

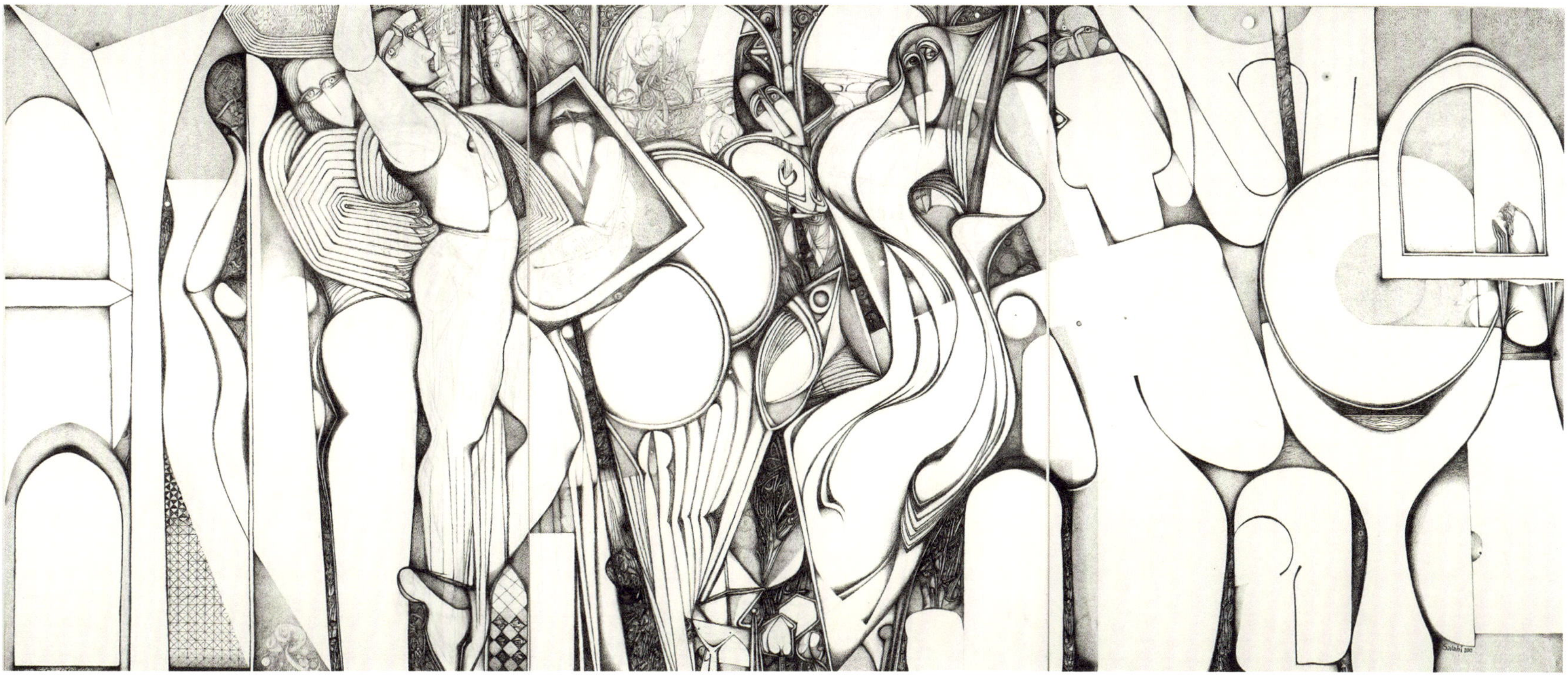

3.

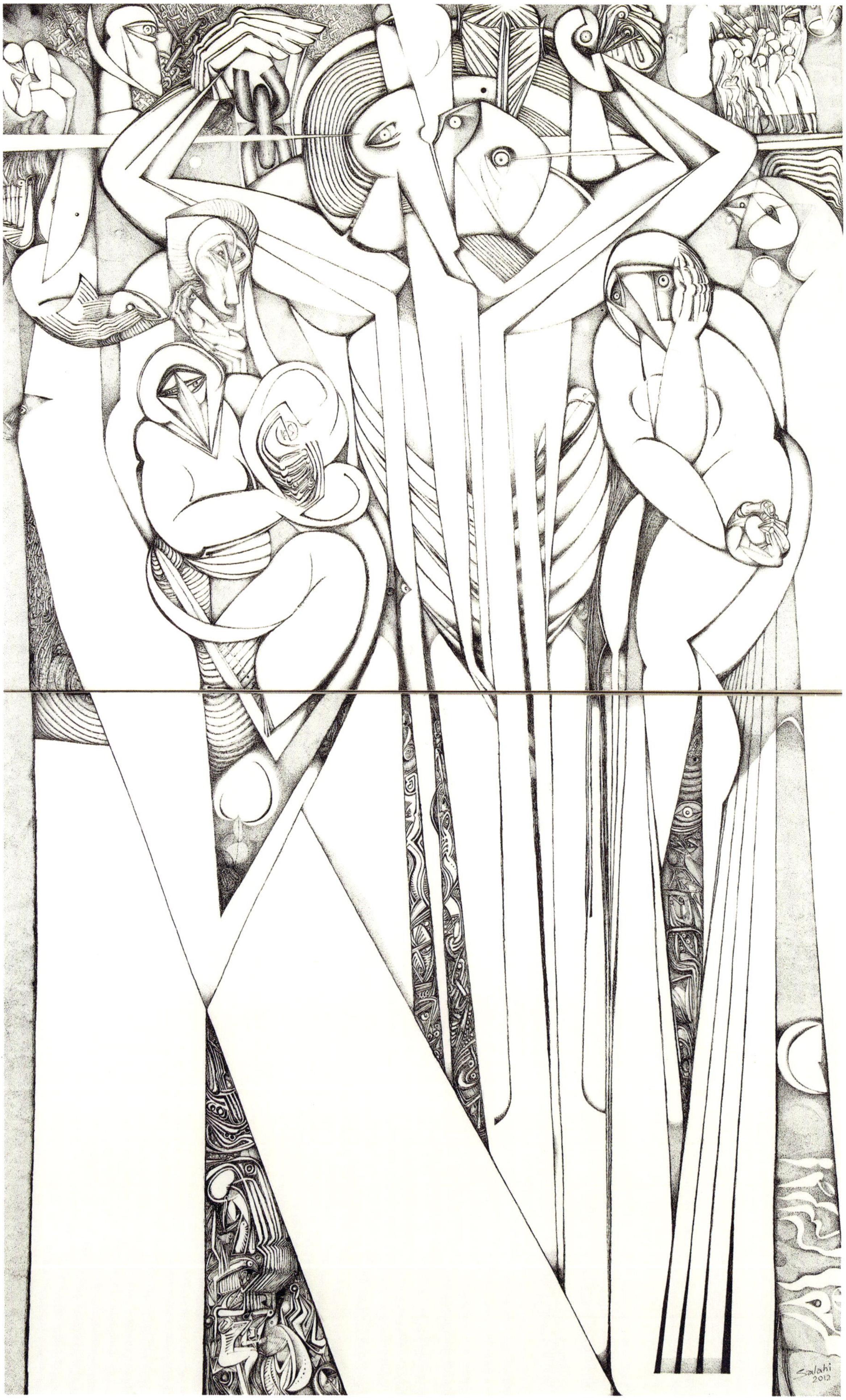

4.

4. *The Tree*, 2012–13, ink on paper mounted on canvas, 2 panels, each 122 × 155 cm (48 ⅛ × 61 ⅛ in)

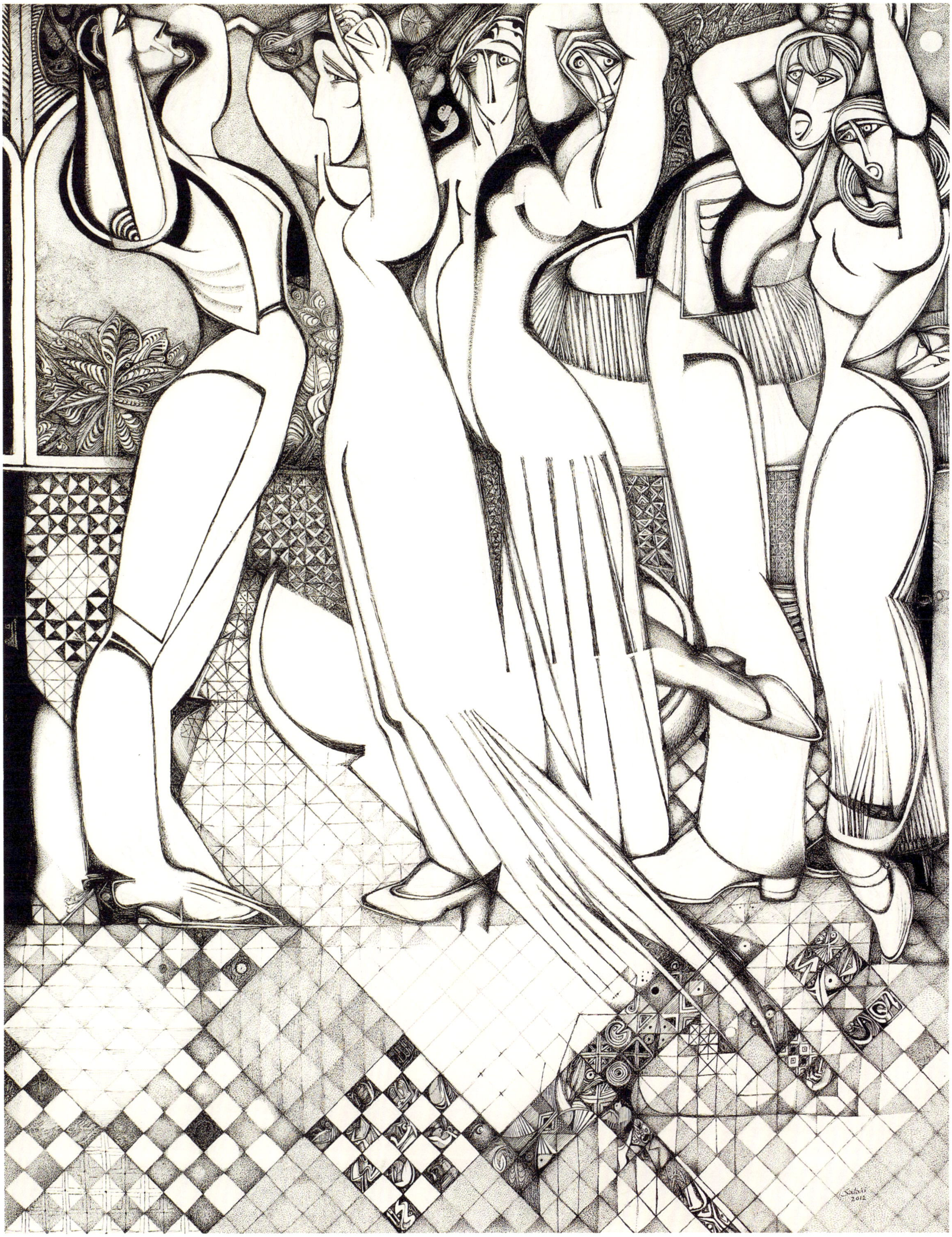

5.

 5. *Flamenco Dancers*, 2012, ink on paper mounted on canvas, 155 × 123 cm (61 ⅛ × 48 ¼ in)

İNCİ EVİNER....... In İnci Eviner's work drawing extends far beyond the page. It is a line that materializes in space as an architectural structure, a line that bleeds out, begins to move and reconfigure in animated films. Drawing, here, is a feeling of transmutation and instability, an image of the change that inevitably occurs in the meeting between figure, time and space. In the four-channel video *Reenactment of Heaven* (2018), female performers in black and white outfits squirm, jump and wiggle among ink splotches in a choreography that functions more like calligraphy, or illustration. The artist conceived the work as an invitation for women to disobey authority, rather taking an active role in performing the 'dark spots in their languages and bodies'....... The relationship of drawing to language and identity was key also to Eviner's immersive installation for the Turkish Pavilion at the Venice Biennale in 2019. Titled *We, Elsewhere*, it consisted of a large ascending stage for a fence of metal rods, which, dramatically lit, drew striped shadows on to the floor and the walls. Big film projections showed bodies posing as shapes, a gesture Eviner extended into the space by having performers slither through the set-up in black clothes. *We, Elsewhere* presented the explosion of an identity, even a collective one, into a myriad of differently mediated fragments. Amid this shattered subjectivity, Eviner wrote in the text that accompanied the exhibition, 'I try to both include and exclude myself...in order to bear witness. The responsibility of being a witness requires the questioning of being us.' Drawing, then, is both a way of witnessing, of being on the outside, and of actively participating in the construction of our shared language. Eviner is interested in the constitution of the 'we', 'us' and 'I' that looks and speaks....... In her smaller works on paper we see this approach applied to the scale of an individual. *Human Index xx* (2019), an ink drawing of little more than A4-size, has the sharp contours of a linocut. It shows a crouched, likely female, figure with long hair and a mouth, somehow about to burst. Like *Mindfulness* (2019), a human silhouette whose face has slipped off on to the ground, there is a nightmarish intensity to it – a dark trace of the subconscious that points to a self at its most fractured and confused. The 'Birdmind' series (2017) follows what looks like a set of striped pyjamas, inhabited in turn by humans and birds; beaks and feathers come out from under the shirt, like a child escaping the womb, wings flapping out of the captivity of an elastic waistband. In Eviner's work we find our deepest anxieties wrought in lines of running ink and, sometimes, running bodies. .... Kristian Vistrup Madsen

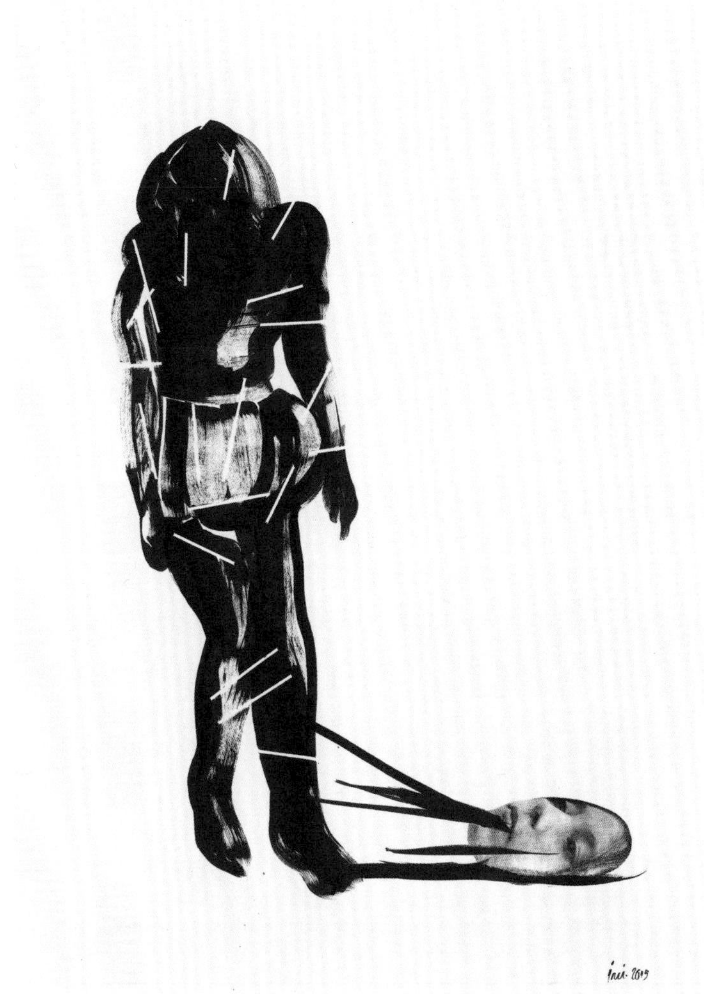

1.

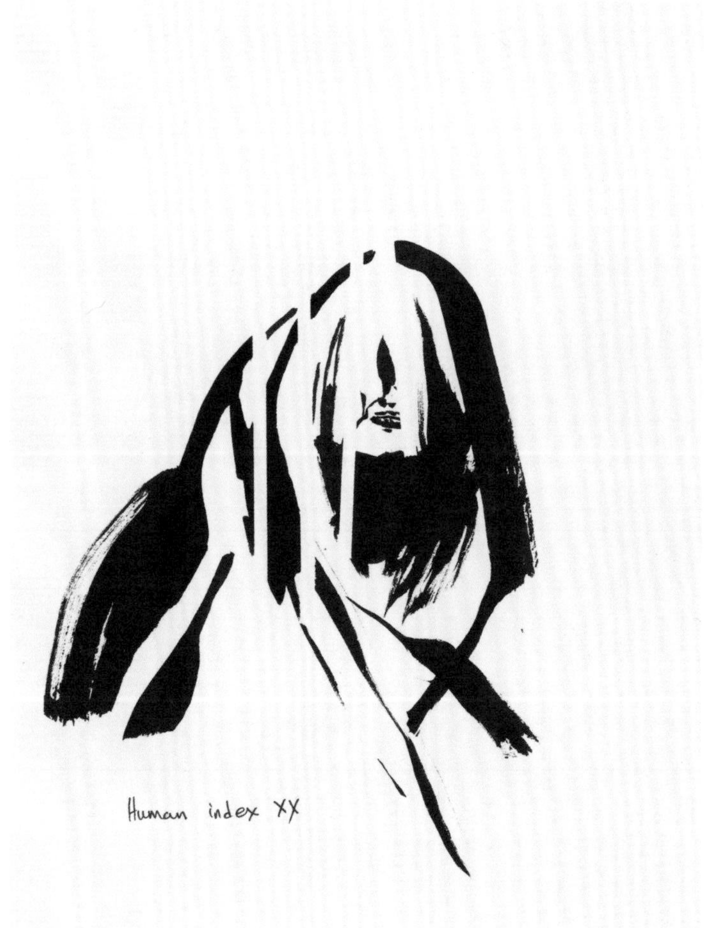

2.

Born 1956, Ankara, Turkey. Lives and works in Istanbul.

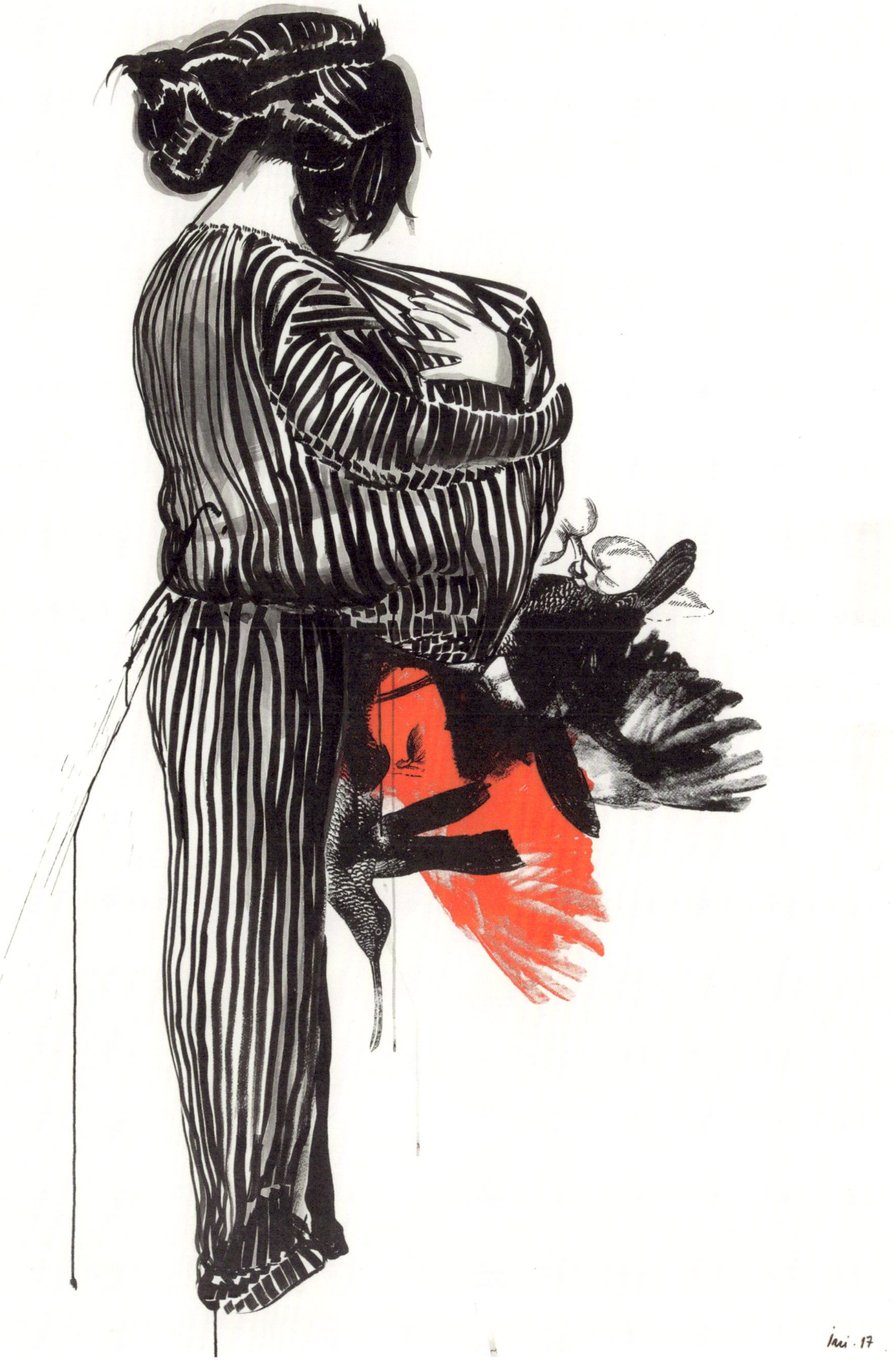

3.

1. *Mindfulness*, 2019, ink and silk screen on paper, 140 × 100 cm (55 ⅛ × 39 ⅜ in)
2. *Human Index xx*, 2019, ink on paper, 30 × 22.5 cm (11 ¾ × 8 ⅞ in)
3. *Bird Mind III*, 2017, ink and silk screen on paper, 140 × 107 cm (55 ⅛ × 42 ⅛ in)

E D I E   F A K E .... Edie Fake draws dazzling compositions that fluidly remap the built environment, tracking the evolution of architecture and design based on use-value and changing aesthetics. Flat bright areas of colour are contained within unifying black lines and expanses of space. The spectrum is a translation of the rainbow Pride flag into a broader intersecting palette. Different historical eras are blended here – bold Art Deco geometric patterns merge with brash disco-era paint shades, colliding with Egyptian lotus or Buddhist mandala shapes – invoking real and fantasy places. In *Personal Business* (2015) evidence of different eras is synthesized to reveal Fake's concerns about display and formal expression; the urban landscape is created over time, becoming a fusion of socially coded messages, evocative of how culture is communally signified and encrypted. As an LGBTQ+ activist and trans artist, Fake is interested in coded messages, covert signs that have historically been interpreted by different communities based on legal, social and sexual conventions that shape meaning and identity. Taking the architectural structures of buildings, doorways, pediments and other ornaments of decoration to represent cultural shifts and evolving sensibilities of queer space, Fake explores visibility, signals of gender, allusions to social exchanges and non-binary taxonomies. .... In most of Fake's work, the spectator is situated on the outside; the buildings function as a membrane between inside and outside, mediating between body and constructed space. There are no people, doors are closed, while windows obstruct interior activity. Implied is an active social scene for the initiated who seem to have access to more intimate areas. *The Stick It Inn* (2016) may be based on a historical San Francisco bar, or perhaps it is pure conjecture, a joyous invention to dream about what may have transpired there. The eccentric tessellation includes pulsating arrows and an elevated triangulated structure, possibly a repurposed cinema marquee, with a porthole orifice on what may be a swinging door, studded with a flurry of stars. We sense an ethos of adaptation, manufactured interventions, authorless yet communal traces, an invisible infrastructure that one must learn to navigate. The arrangement of interlocking shapes and complex repeated patterns resonates with the vernacular of advertisements and urban signage, forming a barrage of embellishment synonymous with commodity culture, imploring us to look. Such overexaggerated, highly stylized details may reflect on drag culture, presenting as one thing while being ultimately something else, unclassifiable, ambiguous. In a world where appearances are complex and unfixed, and the notion of a singular definition is misleading, Fake's work reflects on how the built landscape is part of a continuum that we all innately know is constantly in flux.
.... Kathleen Madden

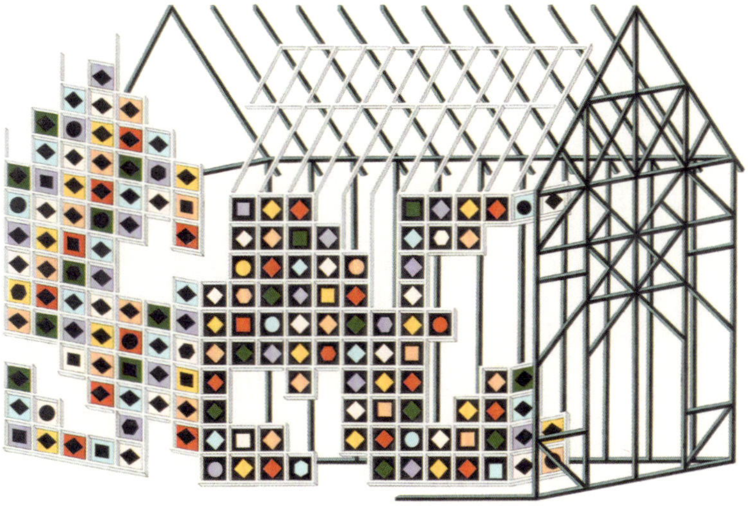

1.

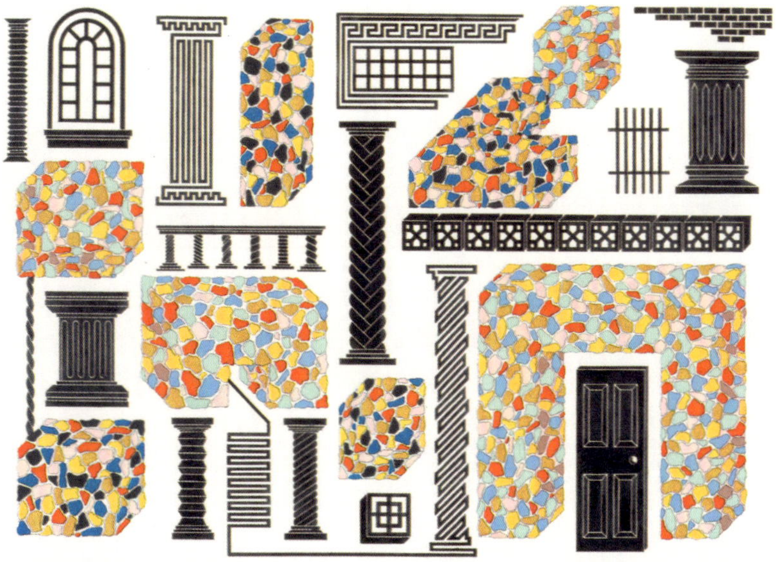

2.

Born 1980, Evanston, IL. Lives and works just outside of Los Angeles.

1. *Fronts*, 2016, gouache and ink on paper, 64.5 × 84.1 cm (25 ⅜ × 33 ⅛ in)
2. *Before Stonewall*, 2015, gouache and ink on paper, 64.5 × 84.1 cm (25 ⅜ × 33 ⅛ in)
3. *The Stick It Inn*, 2016, gouache and ink on paper, 84.1 × 64.5 cm (33 ⅛ × 25 ⅜ in)

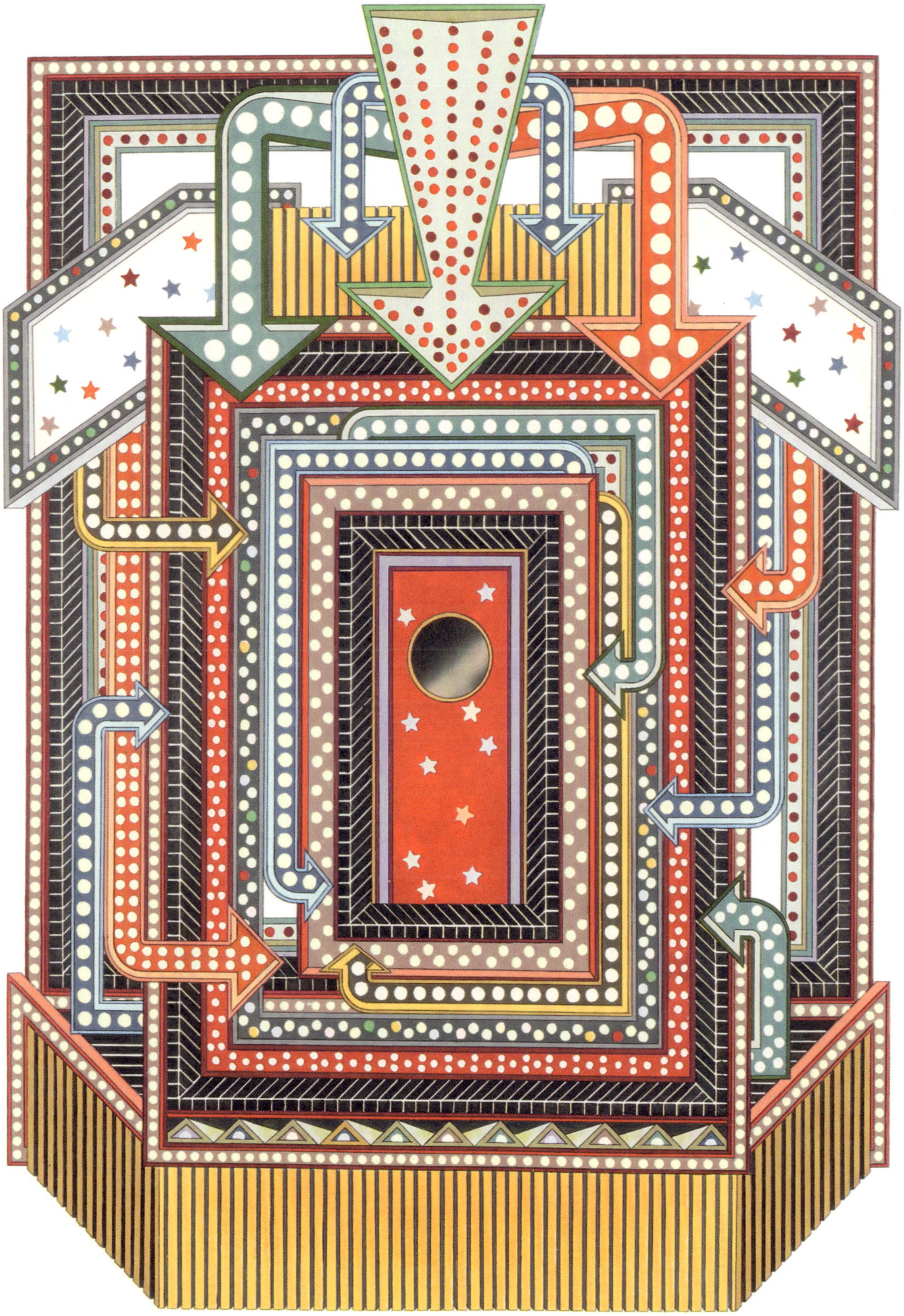

3.

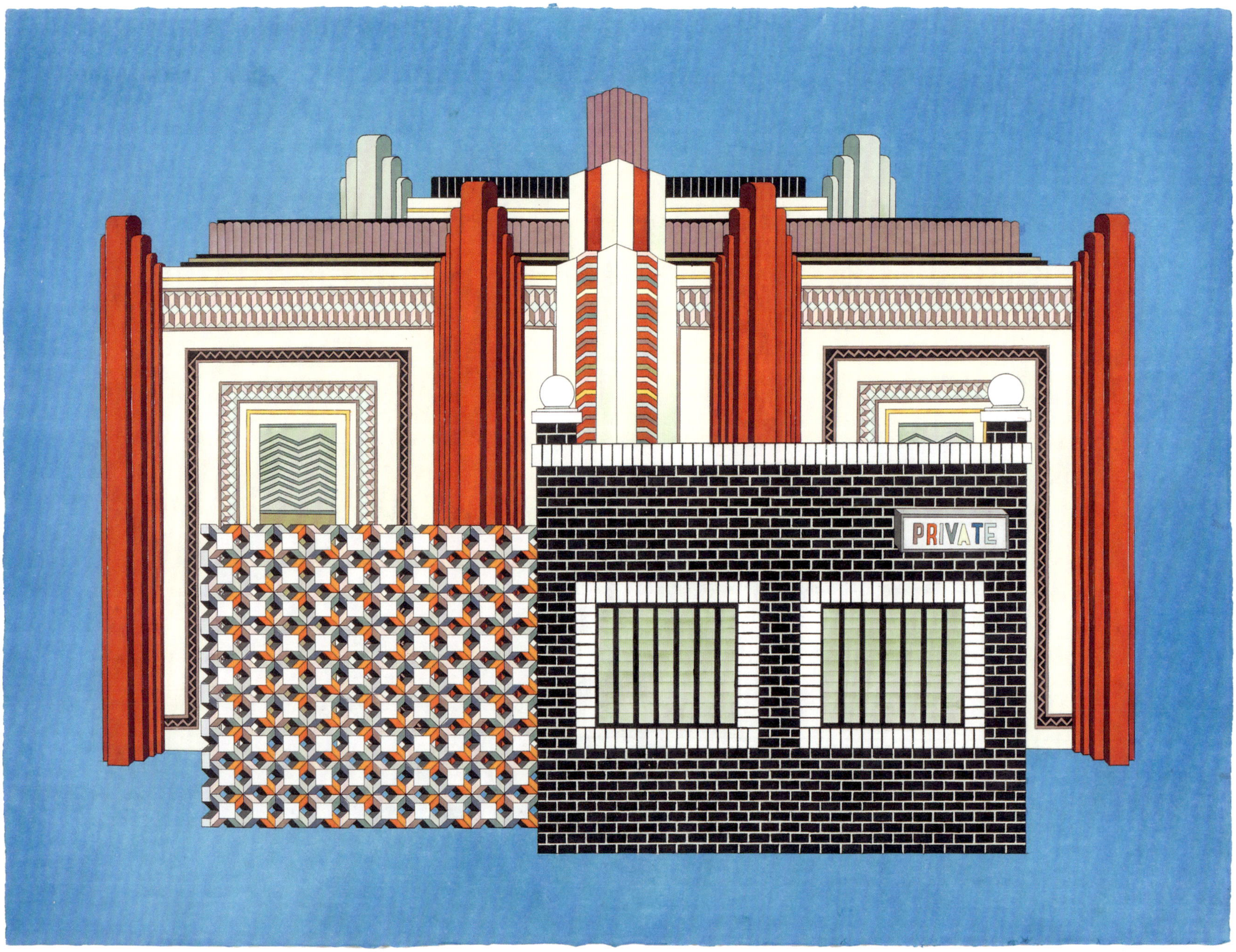

4.

4. *Personal Business*, 2015, gouache and ink on paper, 64.5 × 84.1 cm (25 ⅜ × 33 ⅛ in)
5. *Spinsters*, 2015, gouache and ink on paper, 84.1 × 64.5 cm (33 ⅛ × 25 ⅜ in)

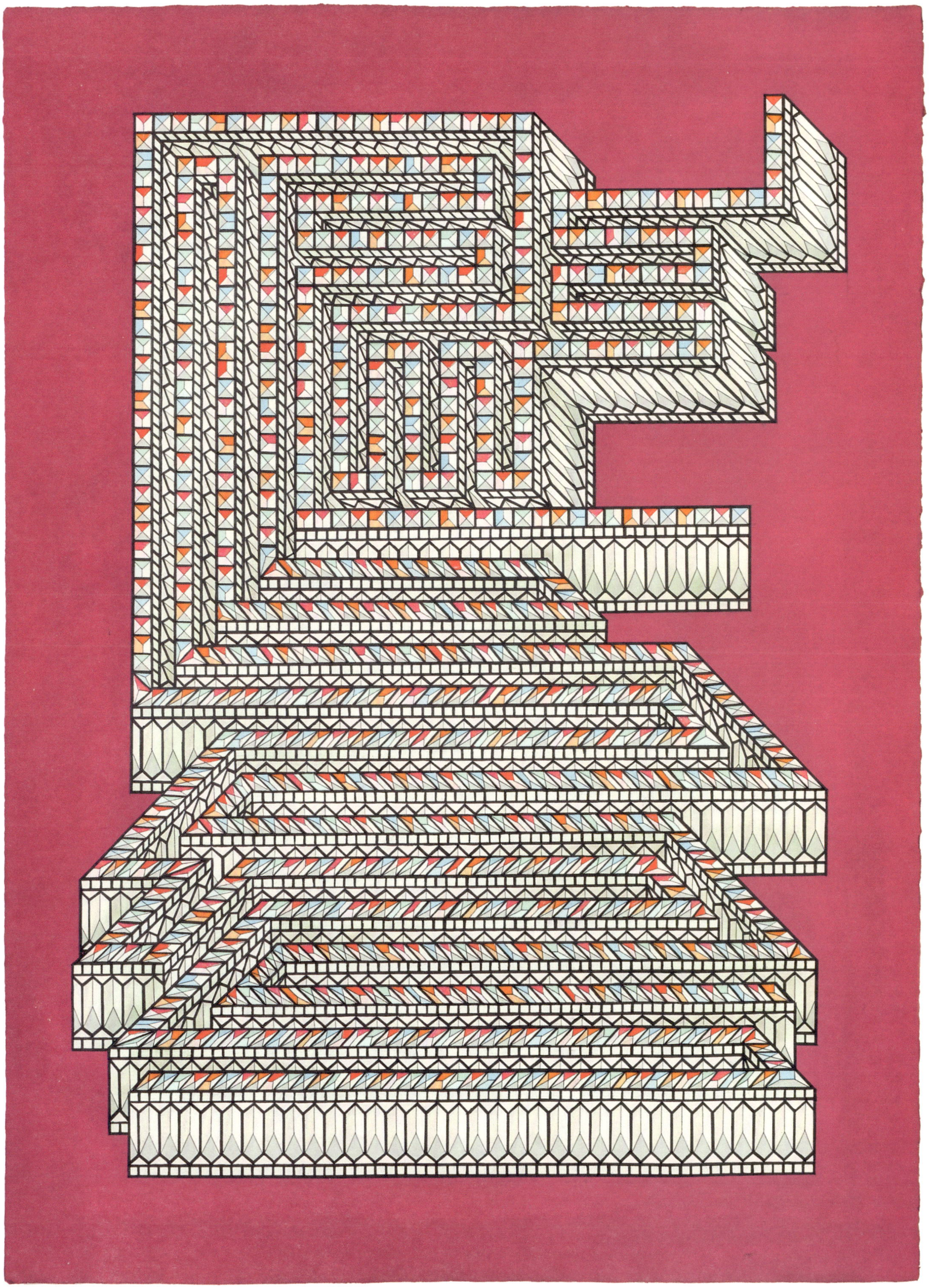

5.

HONDARTZA FRAGA .... Every day throughout 2015 Hondartza Fraga made an intricate pencil drawing of a blank globe on A5 paper. Some sit on a pile of old books, others are mounted on to outmoded astrological equipment. But all are somehow out of time as if belonging to a fictional past that points to a different future from the one we are living. 'I drew each globe blank,' she explained, to suggest 'an unexplored or post-apocalyptic world.' This is a fantasy of reversing discovery and reinventing the void. With these works, Fraga asks poignant questions about the incessant mapping and rationalization of the world. What good has come of it? What are the limits to what we can understand? .... From Da Vinci's Vitruvian Man (1490) to the technical depictions of flora and fauna of the Enlightenment, drawing was always used in the service of science. The more of the world, or even the universe, that we can see, the logic goes, the better we can know it – and knowledge is power. 'Saturn Incognito' (2019–) is an ongoing series of drawings based on raw images from NASA's Cassini space mission to Saturn, which began in 1997. Raw images can be understood as pure data, lacking the materiality, temporality and aura of traditional photography. But, of course, along with flowers, outer space remains the perfect metaphor for anything beautiful or sad. By rendering partial views of the mammoth planet in ultra-fine lines on antique paper, Fraga reintroduces poetry and melancholy to images whose expressed aim is to uncover, to communicate discovery. In these works, speckles on the paper become part of star formations, and dust from the pencil makes a halo on the rings of Saturn. .... The artist's gaze turns the other way in the ongoing 'Specimen' series, started in 2018, with its atmospheric graphite drawings of space shuttles and submarines emerging from chiaroscuro. Fraga is interested in extreme remoteness and our relationship as humans to the dark and inaccessible. In the deep sea or far-away orbits, Enlightenment logic fails; the more we see, the more likely we are to be dumbfounded by what is out there. Previous works in other media suggest that she does not employ drawing for its capacity to document truthfully, but rather as an opportunity to undermine our expectations of reality. A series of photographs, 'Seaward Bound' (2013), for instance, shows the ocean and the horizon, but somehow much too sharply, from too close or too far away, rendering the familiar scene almost unrecognizable. Likewise, the animation *Sway* (2012) shows X-rays of bodies, but with a jellyfish in the lungs or a butterfly in the brain. The visual, in Fraga's work, is not a means of comprehension but of mystification.
.... Kristian Vistrup Madsen

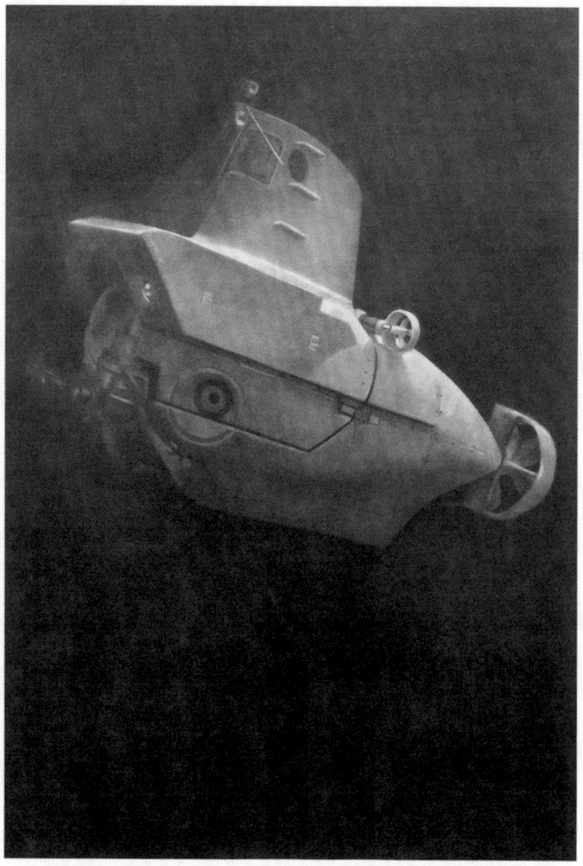
1.

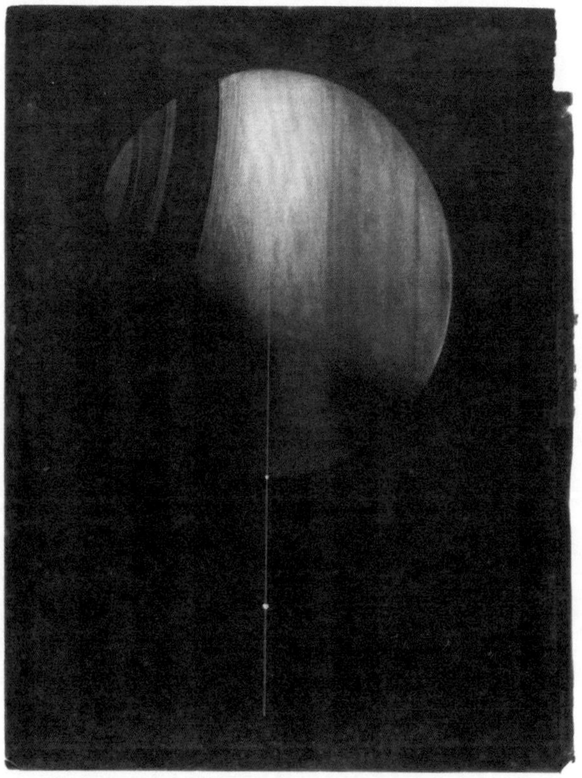
2.

Born 1982, A Coruña, Spain. Lives in Leeds, UK.

1. *Specimens I*, 2018, graphite on paper, 100 × 70 cm (39 ⅜ × 27 ½ in)
2. *Saturn Incognito II (Positive Prints)*, 2019, digital print of inverted original drawings (pencil on antique paper), 59 × 42 cm (23 ¼ × 16 ½ in)
3. *365 Globes*, 2015, (selection of 12 out of 365), pencil on paper, each 21 × 15 cm (8 ¼ × 5 ⅞ in)

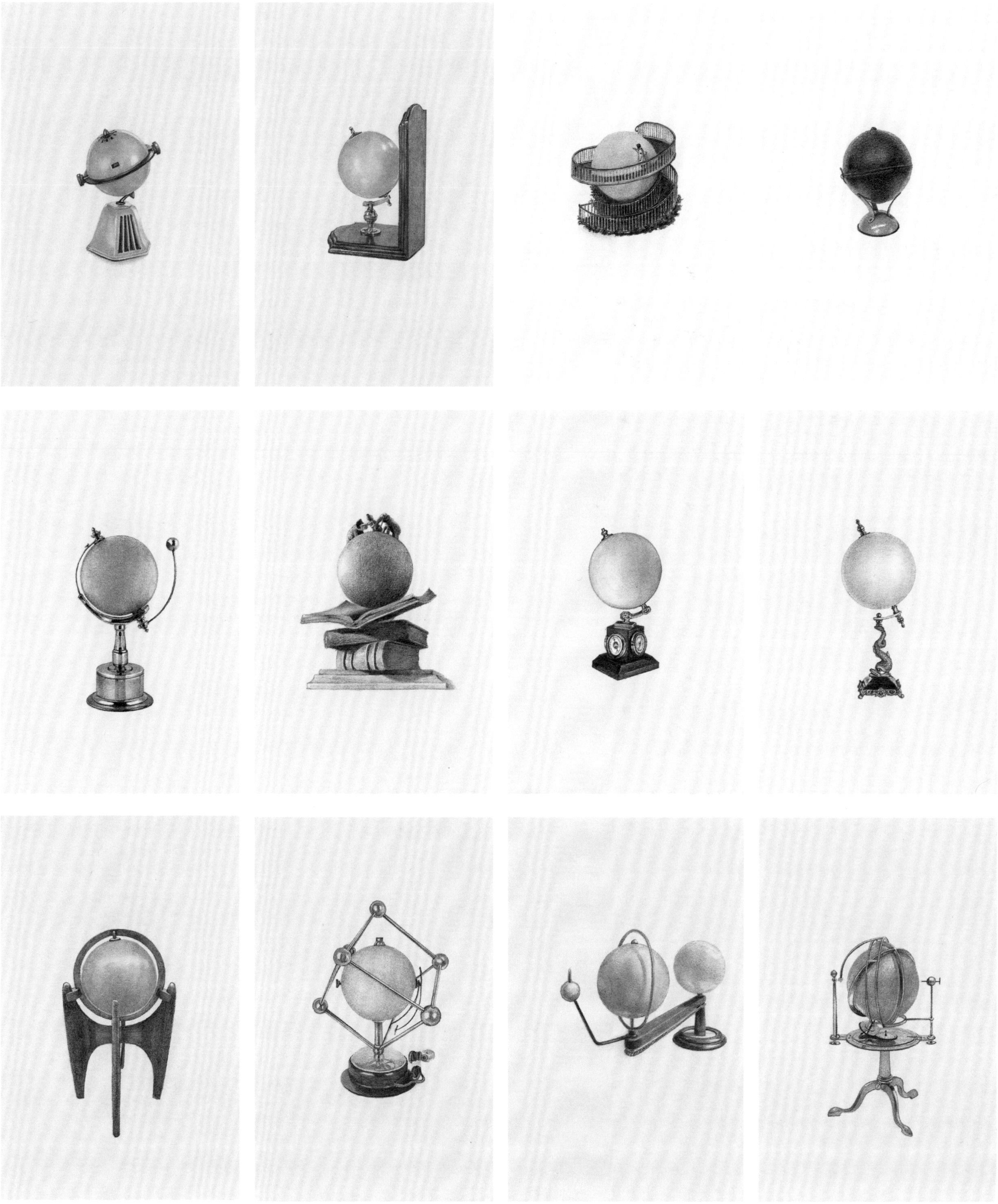

3.

TOM FRIEDMAN .... Appearances can be deceiving, and the art of Tom Friedman cheerfully admits this. While he may be best known as a sculptor of meticulously rendered ordinariness made surreal through strategies of unexpected scale or recombination – a basic caricature of a man lazily staring up at the sky, but built up to ten metres (thirty-three feet) high in stainless steel, or whole grain cereal boxes cut into tiny squares and added back together to make just one box – the artist's drawings likewise assume a modest stance with subtle hints of odd pathos. .... With *Happy Cyclops* (2012), a coloured pencil drawing where multiple rings of saturated, variegated colour seemingly ripple outwards from a white core anchored by a black dot at its centre, one might be forgiven for assuming this is a purely abstract image on first glance. A sustained view might give a clue as to the subject matter implied by the title, but surely without consulting it one might just be able to clock this image and move on with false confidence. The artist frequently plays with viewers' assumptions that they can know anything at face value. .... *Big Bang* (2018), another coloured pencil on paper work, also leans into the ambiguous stakes of attempting to represent any particular phenomenon, situation or even artistic intention, thereby slyly undercutting romantic clichés about art's capability to convey truth, as if that were a singular, consensus-driven standard. The piece is a fairly large drawing – over two metres (six and a half feet) wide – and its Prussian blue lines shooting out towards every edge of the paper emit from a centre, but it remains opaque and flat. There is nothing exceptionally grand about this birth of the universe, and that perhaps is the work's point, though not cynically so. Rather, it implies that to strive for the perception of accuracy, by way of a breathless imaginary, might simply be insincere. Even its scale, large enough to be impressive to a human eye but not big enough to patronize by pretending imitation, would seem to take into account the absurdity of reaching for hyperbole via an ornate vision. By avoiding spectacle, it becomes relatable. .... In a similarly understated style, *Mom Watching Shoa* (2018) is a contour drawing of a casual scene: the artist's mother watching television. The title implies she is watching an important Holocaust documentary, but nothing in the picture points to this. Her TV screen is a puff of powder blue, and what really fizzes are the rainbow of candies in a dish near her feet and the riot of pattern in the cushion next to her. Perhaps real tragedy is always present, but so is the will to imagine decorative furnishings – a pathetic fact and delightful fancy all in one.
.... Paige K. Bradley

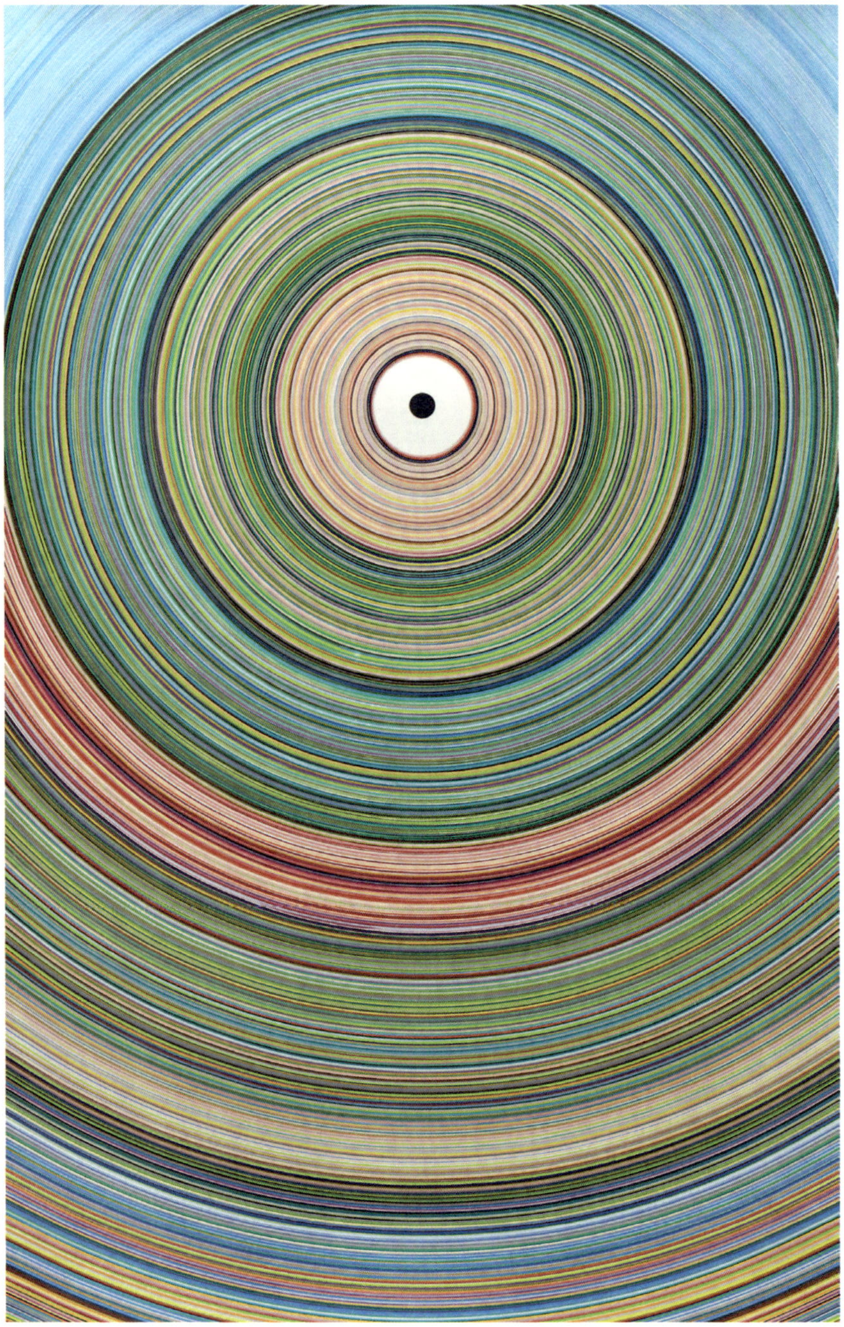

1.

Born 1965, St. Louis, MO. Lives and works in Northampton, MA.

1. *Happy Cyclops*, 2012, coloured pencil on paper, 133 × 87.5 cm (52 ⅜ × 34 ⅜ in)
2. *Big Bang*, 2018, coloured pencil on paper, 114 × 205.5 cm (44 ⅞ × 80 ⅞ in)
3. *Untitled (Genealogies)*, 2012, coloured pencil on paper, 61 × 48.3 cm (21 × 19 in)

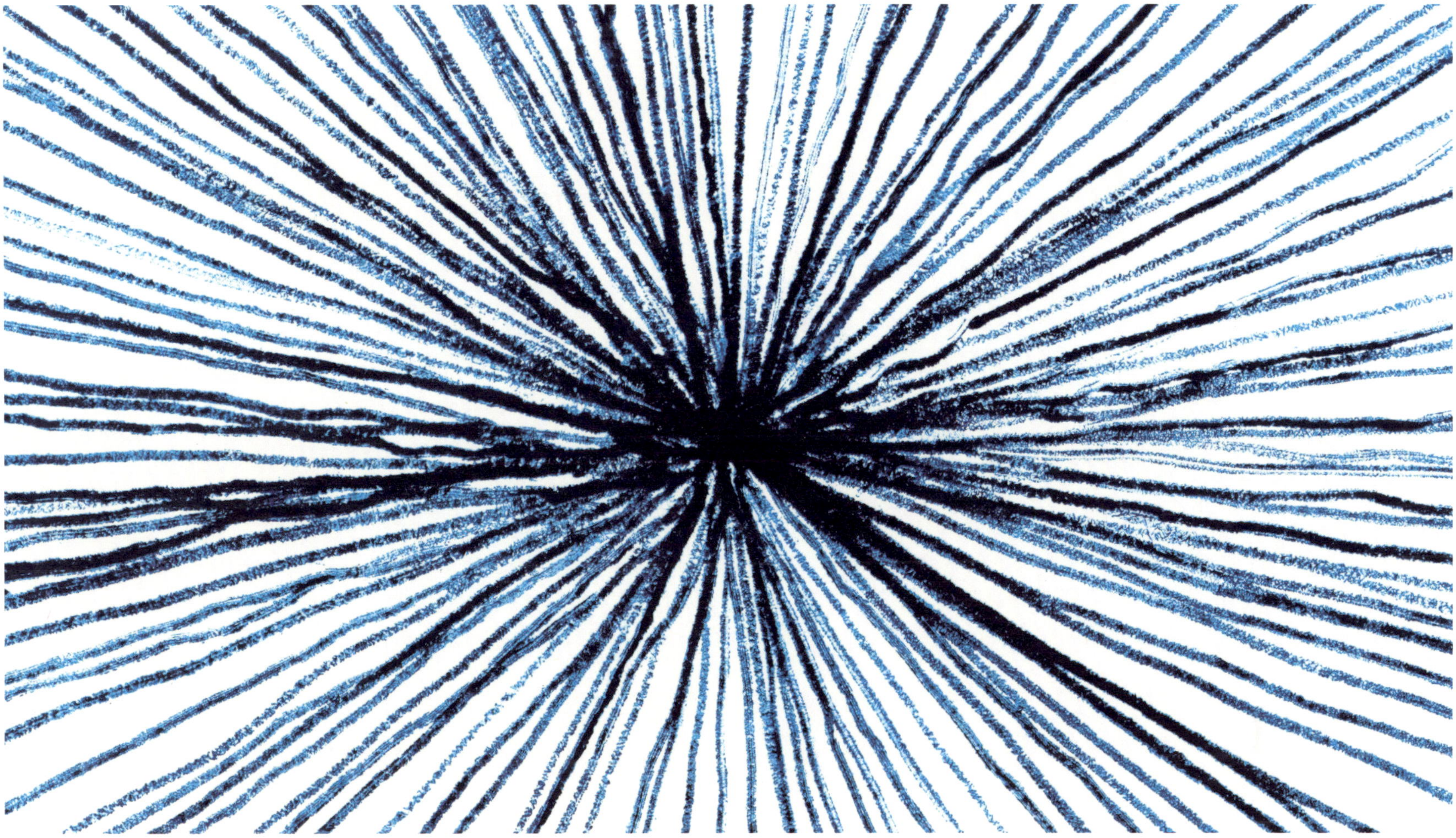

2.

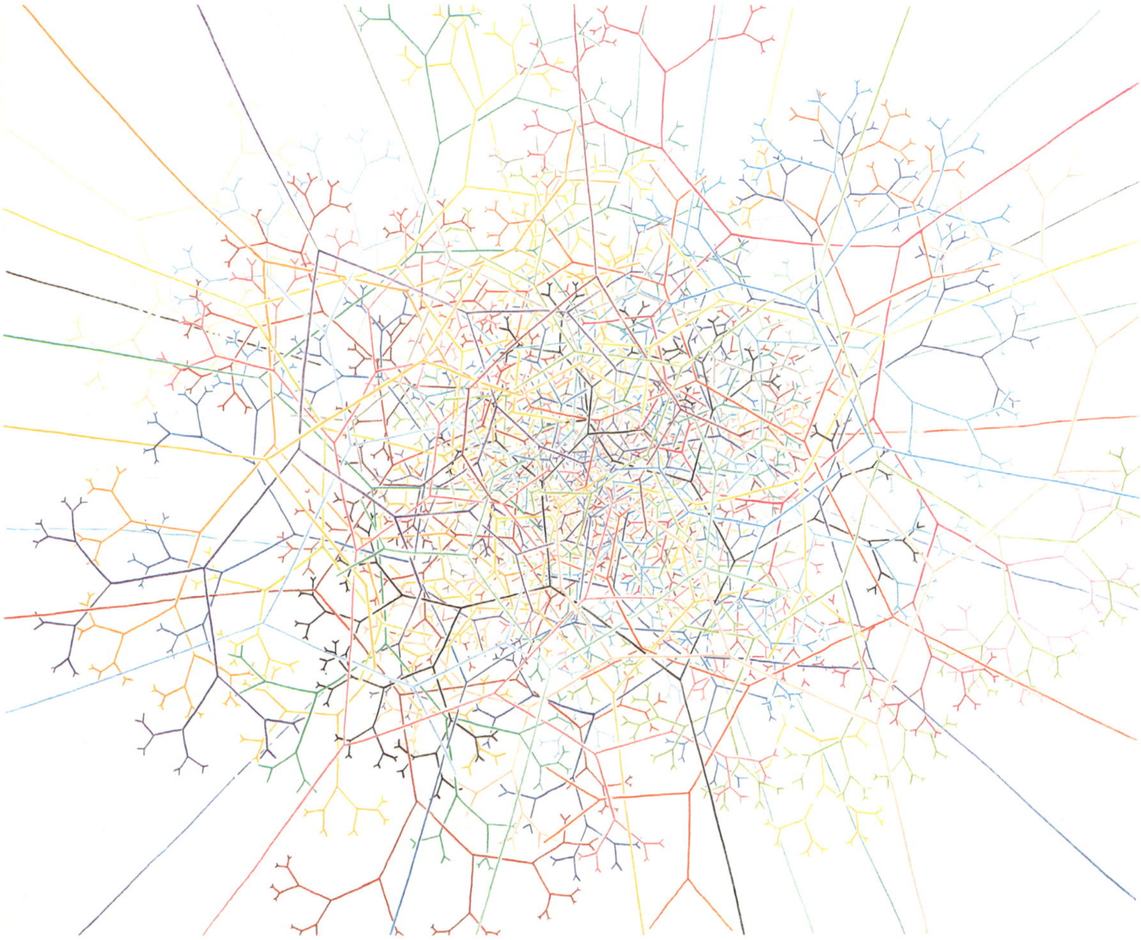

3.

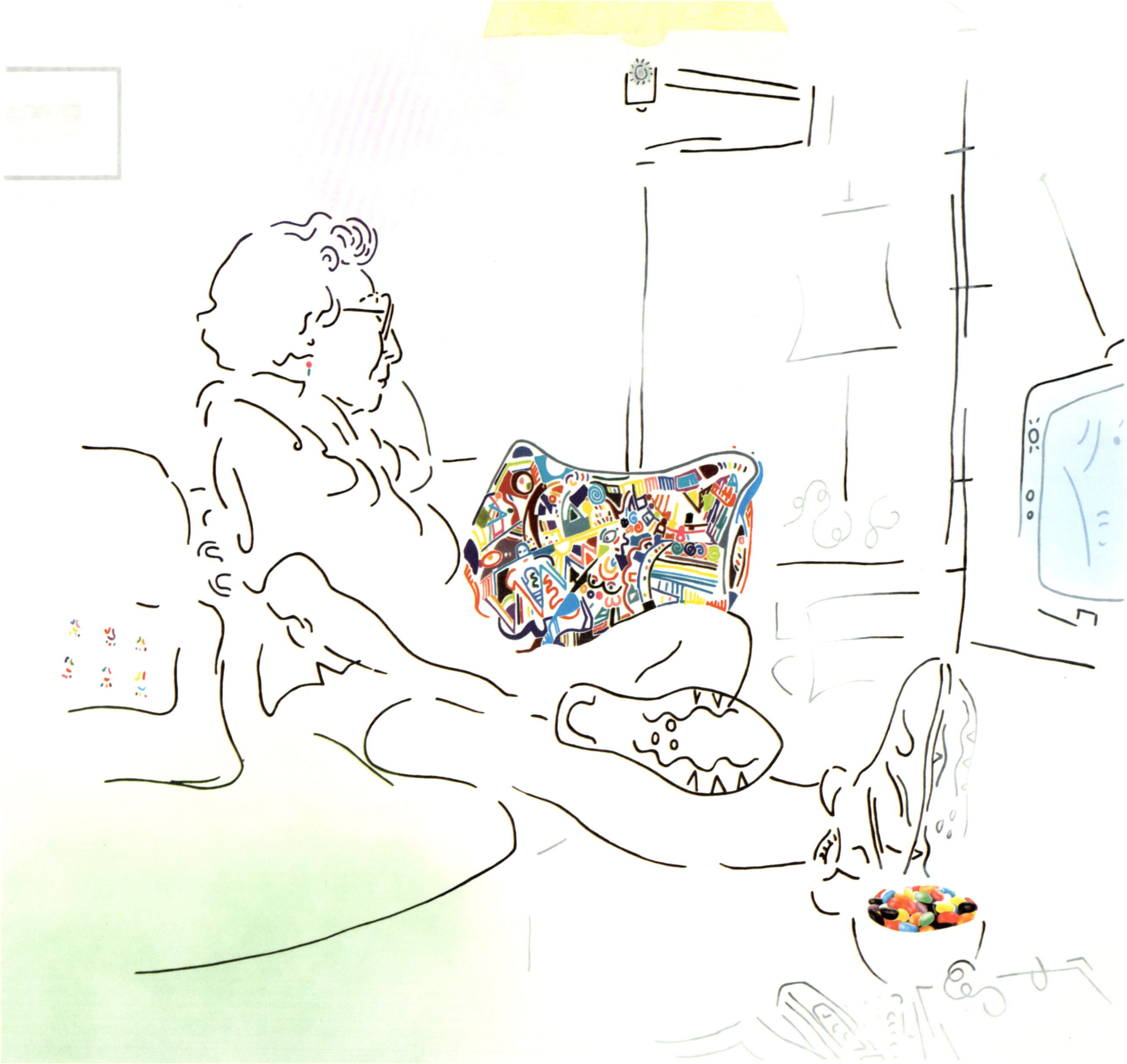

4.

4. *Mom Watching Shoa*, 2018, coloured pencil and watercolour on paper, 104 × 113.5 cm (40 ⅞ × 44 ⅝ in)
5. *Self Portrait for Sugar Cubes Figure*, 2018, coloured pencil on paper, 144.4 × 110.6 cm (56 ⅞ × 43 ½ in)

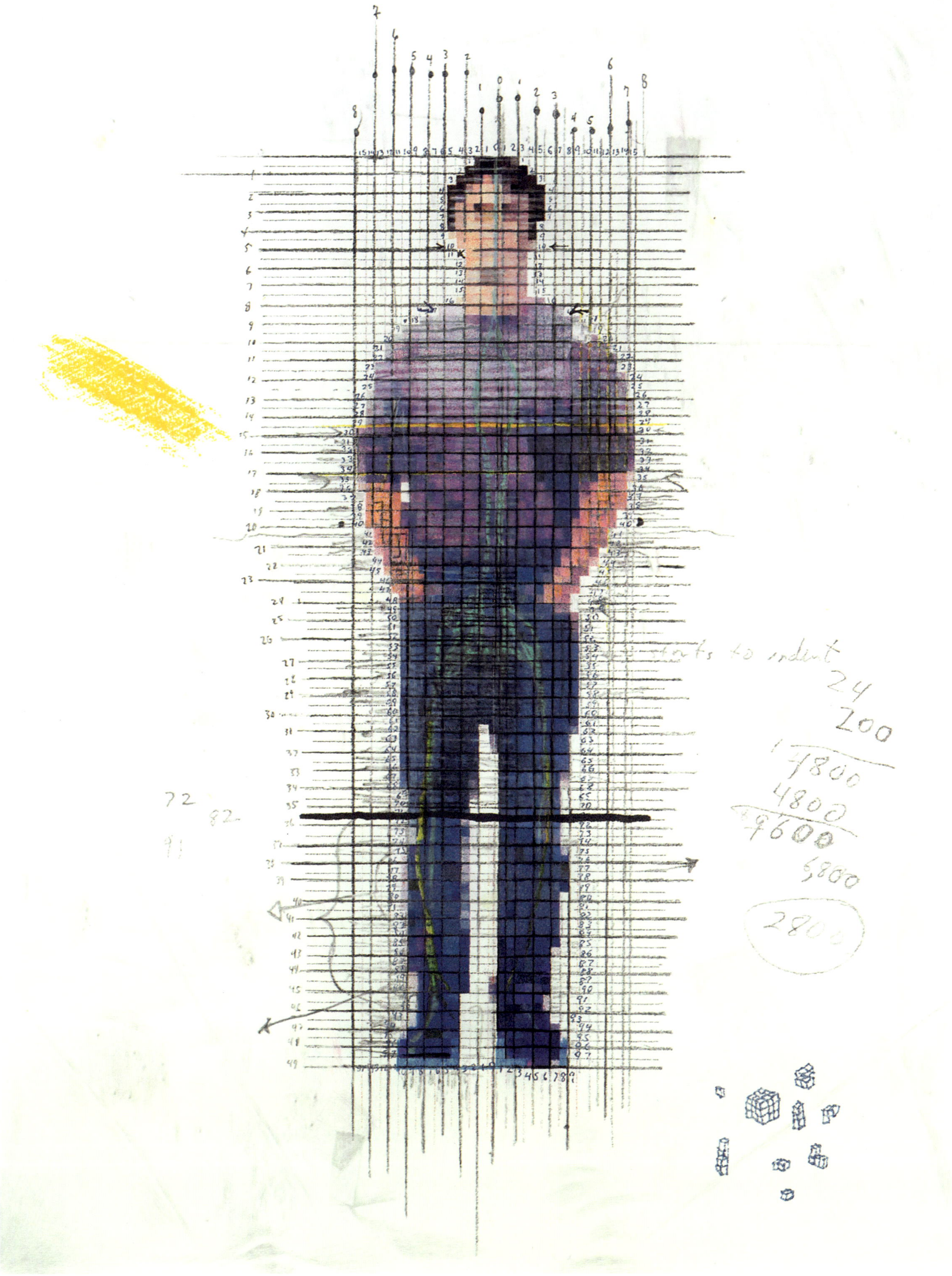

5.

CHITRA GANESH .... Artificial hair, fake fur, gold leaf, Styrofoam, marbles and textiles; the materials list for Chitra Ganesh's multi-media works is long and varied. Ganesh is an archaeologist as much as an artist, excavating a wide variety of media, ideas and images and transforming them afresh. Her practice weaves together surrealism, comic books, science fiction and Hindu and Buddhist imagery to create complex mythologies. The lush tone of Ganesh's work conceals a deep political engagement exploring themes of gender, colonialism and technology. .... The female protagonist in *Night Vision* (2016) is depicted with the stylistic economy of Japanese anime. Her eyes are closed and there is a contraption on her head assembled out of sequins, beads, jewellery and beetle wings. It seems to be reading or, perhaps, wiping her memory. An apparition depicting a woman filming on an old-fashioned video camera appears underneath. The image conflates nostalgic and futuristic forms of looking and recording. Are we viewing an imagined future or remembering the recent past? Time becomes jumbled in these images. Seeing for these characters is temporal as much as it is spatial – looking becomes a form of time travel. .... *Eyes of Time: Universal Eye* and *Eyes of Time: Gear Girl* (both 2014–15) belong to a wall mural made for the Brooklyn Museum in New York. Inspired by the gallery's rich collection, the painting updates the iconography of Kali, the Hindu goddess of destruction and rebirth. Ganesh rewires historical imagery to create contemporary representations of empowered female protagonists. The figure in *Universal Eye* grasps a piece of the universe that obscures one of her eyes as she looks out of the other. Surrounded by totemic items, her body appears to be morphing into a crab-like form. Ganesh's heroes are hybrid beings that merge technological, human and natural elements. This is a world of affinities expressed between species, eras and cultures. *Gear Girl* presents a futuristic vision with the body merging into machine parts, ligaments and muscles becoming cogs and gears. The body is porous and continually invaded by non-human elements. .... Ganesh's protagonists have inner visions. They possess the power to look even when their eyes are firmly shut. This sense of heightened awareness, pervaded by histories and potential futures, puts the characters in charge of their own destinies. If, historically, the universal subject was encoded as white and male, Ganesh extends this privilege. She centres the experience of women of colour, furnishing them with the power of representation, recognition and vision. They have the capacity of storytellers, outside of the imagination of men, to imagine a future inhabited by broader communities.

.... George Vasey

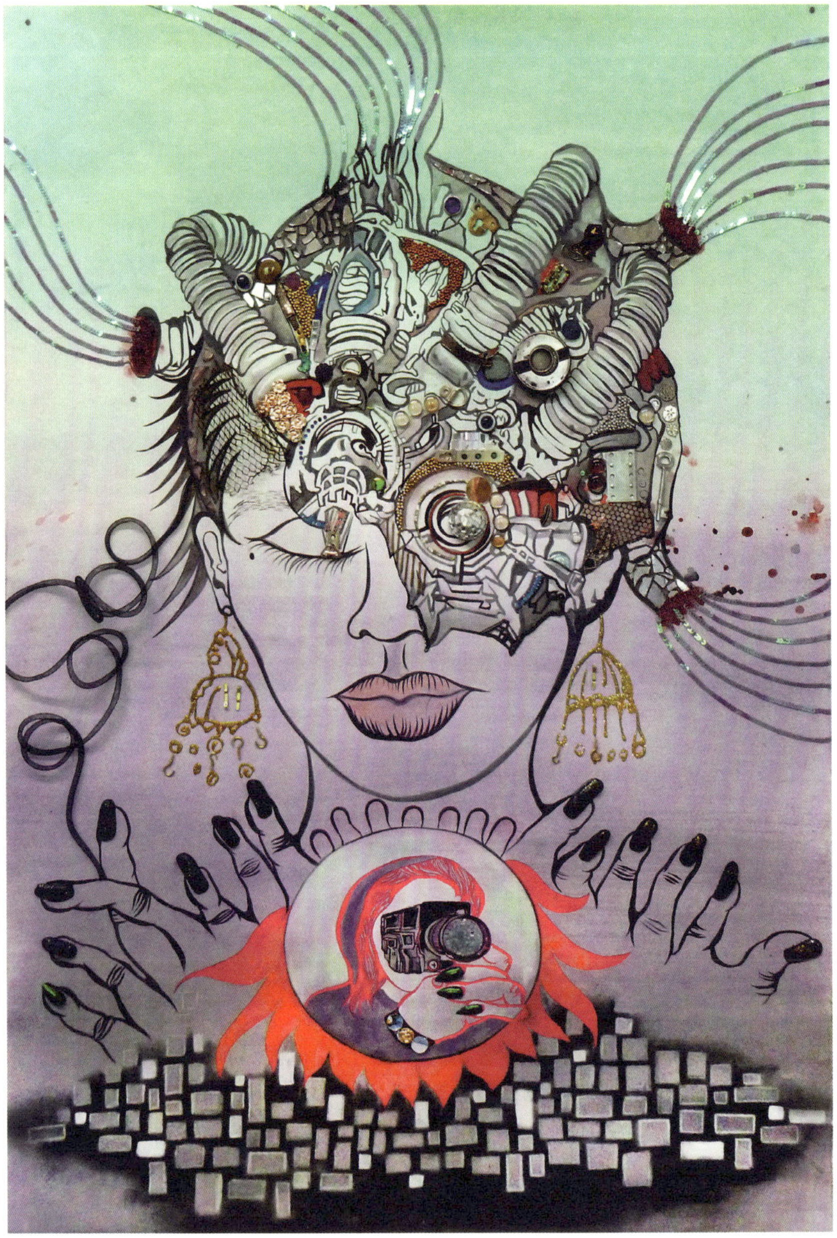

1.

Born 1975, Brooklyn, New York. Lives and works in Brooklyn.

1. *Night Vision*, 2016, mixed media on paper including beads, marbles, sequins, washers, screws and other hardware, metal grating, plastic tubes, costume jewellery crushed glass, mica flakes, shredded tyre rubber, beetle wings, glitter and mirror, 152.4 × 101.6 cm (60 × 40 in)
2. *Eyes of Time: Universal Eye*, 2014–15, (detail), mixed media on wall including brass, resin, foam, artificial hair, speakers, electronic fragments, fake fur, disco balls, wire, shredded tyre rubber, Styrofoam, vintage Indian glass, gold leaf, marbles, textile and silkscreen, 4.6 × 14.3 m (15 × 47 ft), installation view of a site-specific commission at the Brooklyn Museum, Elizabeth A. Sackler Center for Feminist Art, New York
3. *Eyes of Time: Gear Girl*, 2014–15, (detail), mixed media on wall including brass, resin, foam, artificial hair, speakers, electronic fragments, fake fur, disco balls, wire, shredded tyre rubber, Styrofoam, vintage Indian glass, gold leaf, marbles, textiles and silkscreen, 4.6 × 14.3 m (15 × 47 ft), installation view as above

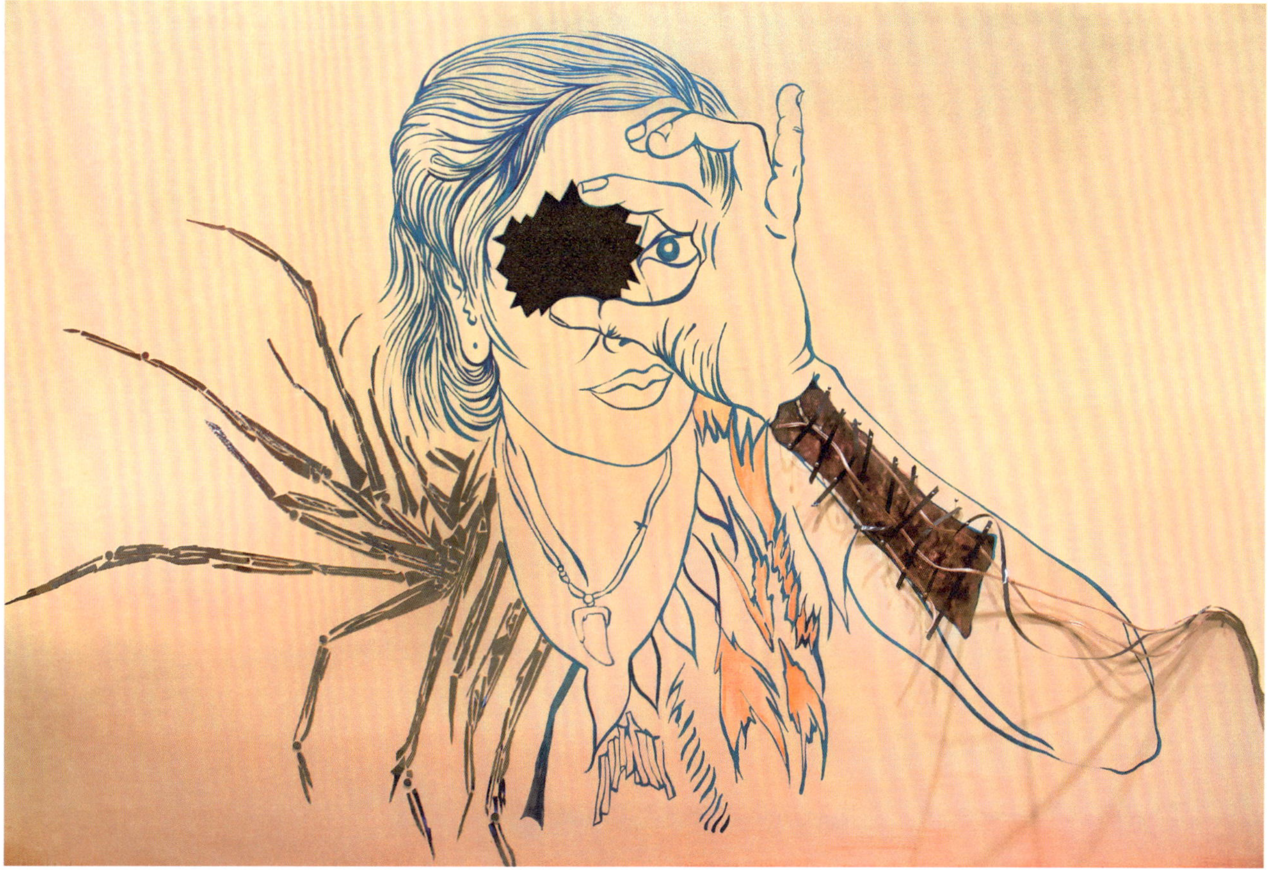

2.

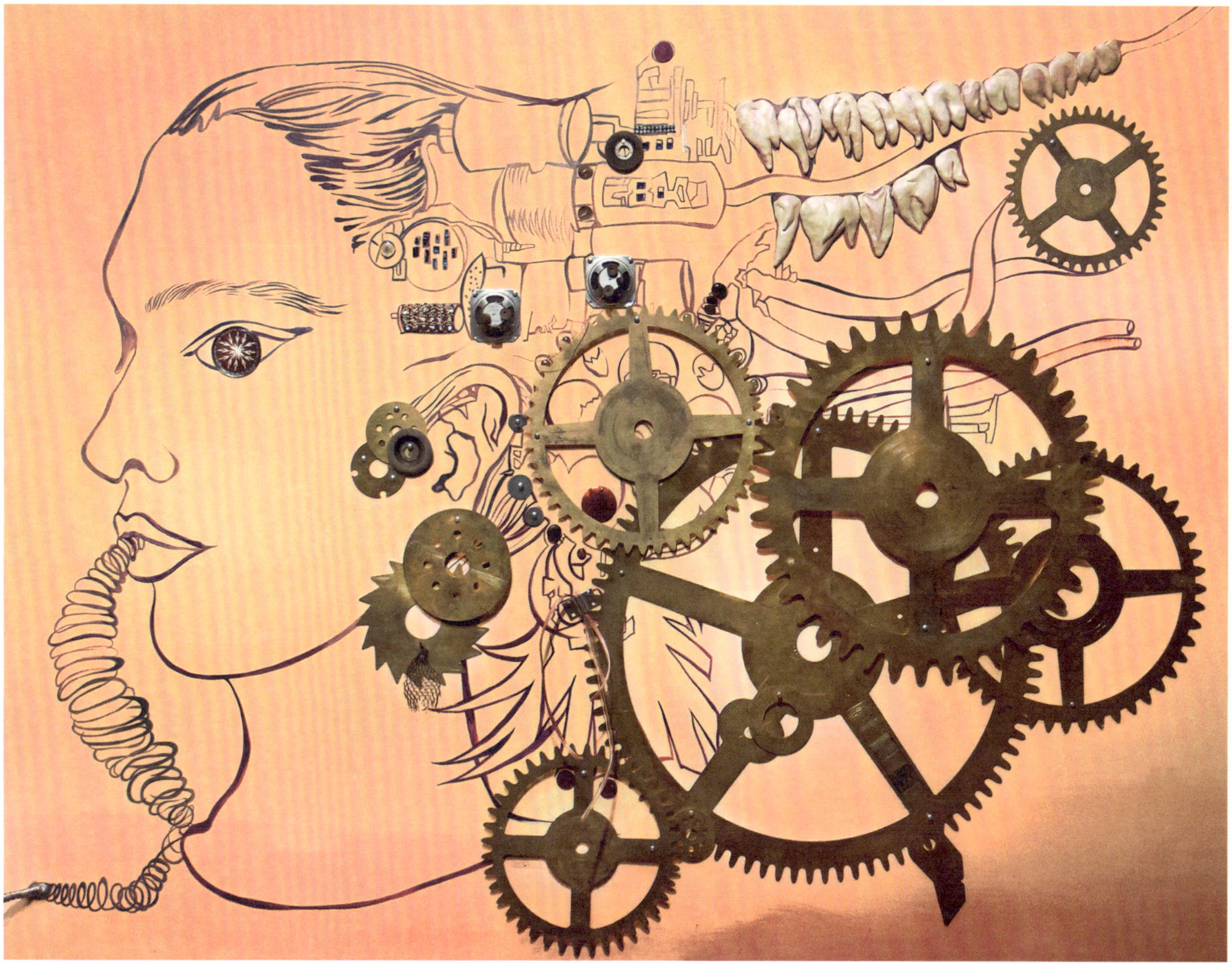

3.

N I K O L A U S G A N S T E R E R Viennese artist, performer and researcher Nikolaus Gansterer produces intricate drawings that resemble scientific networks and structures. He incorporates performance, blackboard assemblages and large banners or maps of what he terms 'bodying' as part of a practice that investigates micro and macro systems. Drawing, thinking and action are intertwined in dynamic astrophysical markings and diagrams, as evident in *Choreographic Figures Diagrams, Figure of Vibrating Affinity II* (2017). Here flourishes and entangled lines sweep across black paper: the effect is cosmological. Gansterer's compositions are not literal; rather each drawing is sensory and dynamic, alluding to different states and interrelationships. In a studio conversation with Florian Langhammer for *Collectors Agenda* in 2017, Gansterer remarked on his preoccupation with drawing: 'For me personally, an extended drawing practice plays a central role, not so much in order to mimetically depict and explain the world, thus making it more controllable, but rather to make phenomena – things and the relationships between them that are not initially obvious – visible, and as precisely as possible, for both myself, and others.' His notation systems suggest dimensions, experience and space. Using mind maps and memory of places he has been, Gansterer deploys drawing as an experimental mode across time, space and movement. Not surprisingly, travel and residencies are occasions when he conceptualizes new work and hypotheses. Previously, he spent over a year charting the psychogeography of airports and drew his own recollections of the city of Damascus. For Gansterer, drawing has an immediacy that requires little technical proficiency yet allows for an exploration of the sensory. For example, his 'Translectures' are ad hoc performative diagrams and recordings, made using a variety of materials including pencil, chalk, ink, stone and paper. He writes with chalk on a blackboard, where words like 'thinking' and 'drawing' are accompanied by diagrams with coordinates, dotted lines, measurements and notations, props, rubbings and cartoon outlines that infer a quasi-mathematical language. Ideas are rehearsed, rubbed out and reinstated. By co-opting the lecture format in a transdisciplinary way, Gansterer conjugates drawing, improvisation, choreography and performance. In 1998 he co-founded the Institute for Transacoustic Research, an organization that uses methodologies from the arts and science to host events, hearings, performances, workshops and installations. The series 'Maps of Bodying' uses marker, pencil and crayon on canvas to evoke action and ideas in motion, indicated in graphic notations across large-scale wall hangings that resemble banners. Exhibited in a number of shows, including a solo presentation 'Drawing as Thinking in Action' at the Drawing Lab in Paris (2019) and 'Con-notations' at Villa Arson in Nice, France (2018), Gansterer's notations and visual algorithms use drawing as a way to think schematically: a method to find an atmosphere with its own vocabulary, circuits and configurations.
.... Natalie King

Born 1974, Klosterneuburg, Austria. Lives and works in Vienna.

1. *Translecture Untertagüberbau*, 2017, drawing performance, pencil, chalk, ink, stones, paper and various objects on blackboard, 70 × 100 cm (27 ½ × 39 ⅜ in)
2. *Translecture on Con-notations*, 2018, drawing performance, pencil, chalk, ink, stones, paper and various objects on blackboard, 70 × 100 cm (27 ½ × 39 ⅜ in), installation view, 'Con-notations', Villa Arson Centre d'Art Contemporain, Nice, France
3. *Choreo-graphic Figures Diagrams, Figure of Vibrating Affinity II*, 2017, pencil and crayon on black paper, 31 × 40 cm (12 ⅛ × 15 ¾ in)
4. *Maps of Bodying (IV)*, 2018, marker, pencil and crayon on canvas, 222 × 144 cm (87 ⅜ × 56 ⅝ in)
5. *Maps of Bodying (VI)*, 2019, marker, pencil and crayon on canvas, 222 × 144 cm (87 ⅜ × 56 ⅝ in)

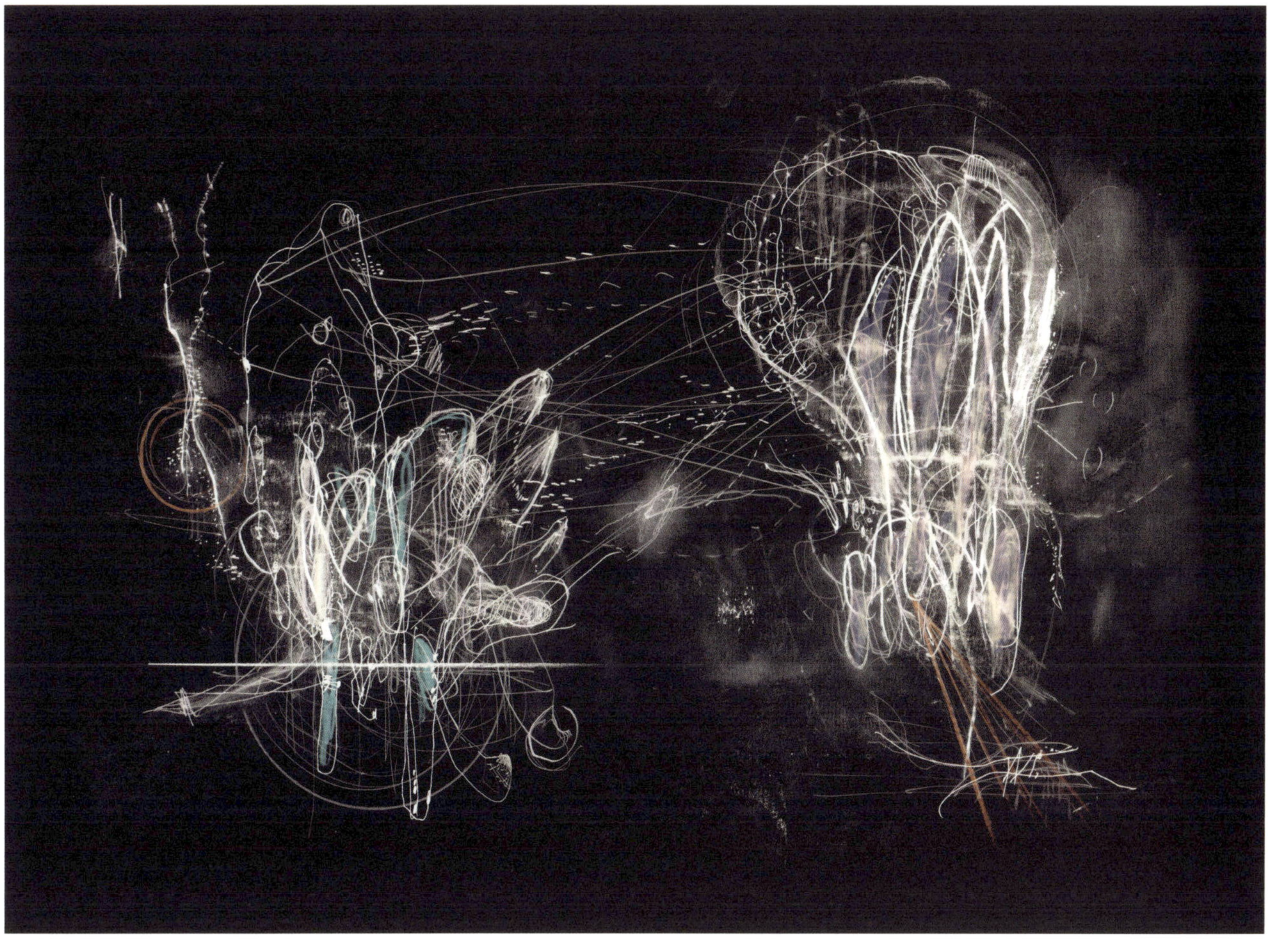

3.

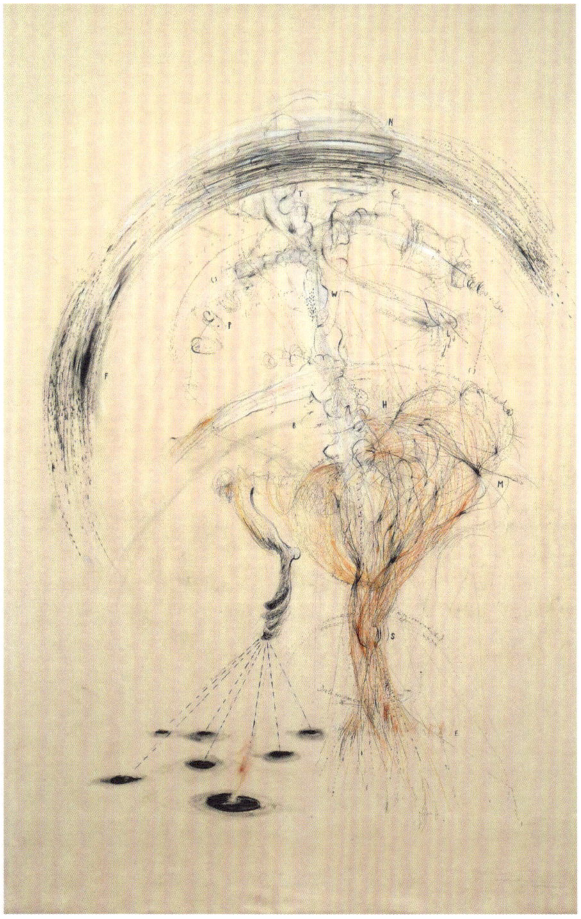

4.

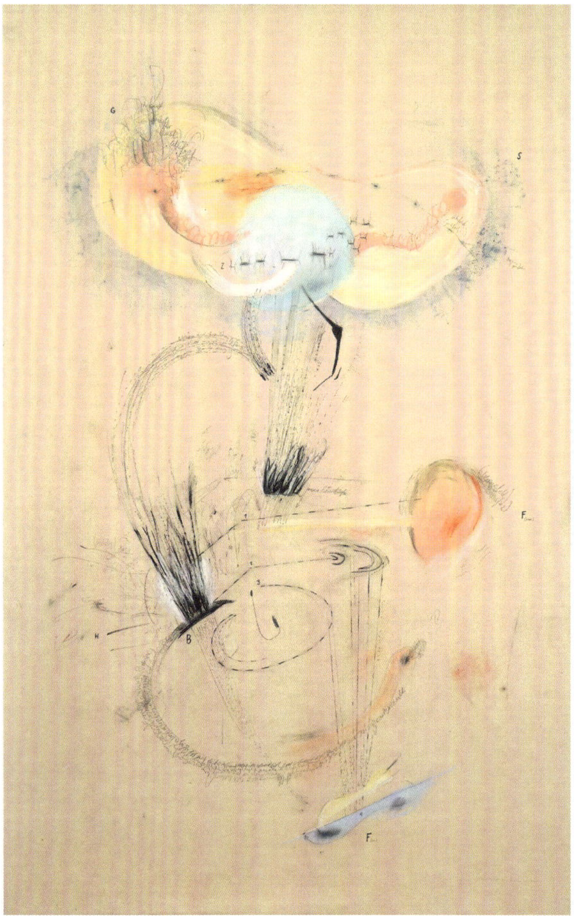

5.

CLAIRE GAVRONSKY .... The figure is a constant in Claire Gavronsky's wide-ranging practice. 'It is primary, the absolute entry into the work,' insists the artist. Over the past decade, alongside her printmaking, painting and sculpture, Gavronsky has produced drawings in various media depicting human and animal subjects, sometimes rendered in stoic isolation, but just as often presented in gregarious assemblies. An artist capable of virtuoso description, naturalism is a secondary concern: Gavronsky is compelled by the 'possibility and semantics' of the line and mark, and resolutely believes that the 'precision of observation' required when drawing offers a means to access, as well as to convey, empathy. Ethics is an enduring theme in the artist's drawings and represents a way of seeing that is strongly informed by her South African upbringing. Born into a family of Jewish Lithuanian émigrés who settled in Johannesburg, her father was briefly married to writer Nadine Gordimer. As a teenager she attended extramural art classes with artist William Kentridge (b. 1955), whose legal family formed part of this politically involved circle; the two artists remain friends and collaborators. It was Gordimer's second husband, dealer Reinhold Cassirer, who in the 1980s first exhibited Gavronsky's Neo-Expressionist drawings. .... In 1985, together with her partner and long-time collaborator, artist Rosemarie Shakinovsky (b. 1953), Gavronsky settled in Florence. The classical setting cultivated a deeper appreciation for European art history and her drawings reference various classical Mediterranean traditions. For instance, *The Theorist's Blind Spots* (2012) is part of a suite of poised ink drawings depicting collapsed figures that directly allude to Francisco Goya's (1746–1828) print series, 'The Disasters of War' (1810–20), although Eugène Delacroix's (1798–1863) many stricken figures are also palpable. .... Gavronsky rarely, if ever, works with a reference in front of her, a fact that astonished the German painter Jörg Immendorff (1945–2007) and prompted him to invite her to work in his studio in the late 1980s. Drawing is a fully contained practice for Gavronsky, not a preparatory activity, and as such demands full engagement with the weight and volume of a subject, rather than its outline. She describes it as a sculptural method of drawing, one that enables her to explore laden subjects. For example, the limpid drawing *Sanguine* (2013) forms part of a trio of works exploring race shaming and quotes the 'brown paper bag test' used by African-American elites to grant lighter-skinned compatriots privileges to associations and churches. Compassion, rather than judgement, informs this and others works, including a more recent suite of six drawings exploring the possibility of repentance within a framework of toxic masculinity. A remorseful hunter embraces his former prey in *The Deer Forgives the Hunter* (2017). This tender description of apology and mutuality was realized on already primed paper that allowed no erasure or makeover.

.... Sean O'Toole

1.

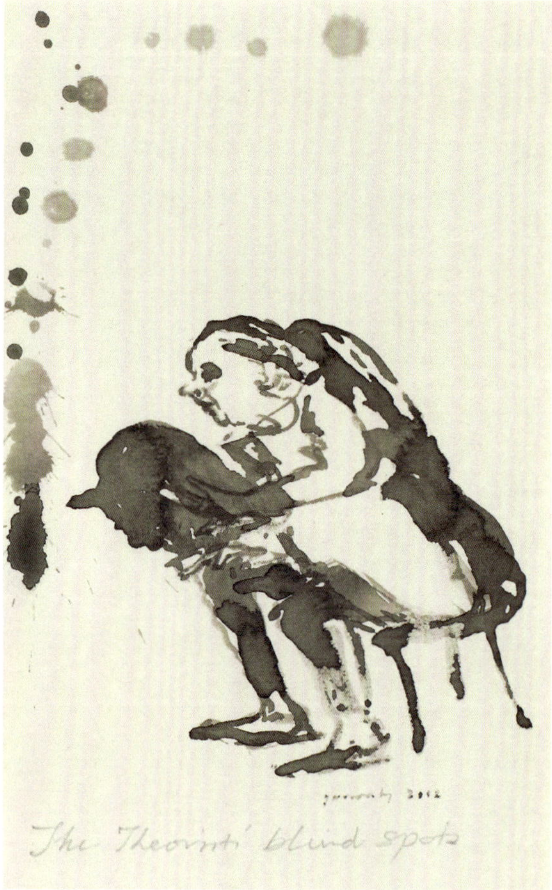

2.

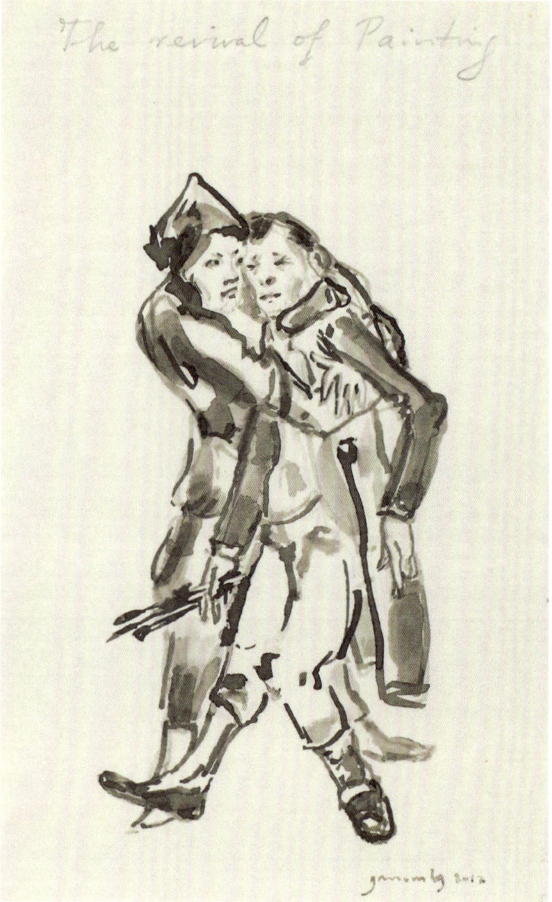

Born 1957, Johannesburg. Lives and works in Florence.

1. *The Theorist's Blind Spots*, 2012, ink on vintage paper, 17 × 11 cm (6 ⅝ × 4 ¼ in)
2. *The Revival of Painting*, 2012, ink on vintage paper, 17 × 11 cm (6 ⅝ × 4 ¼ in)

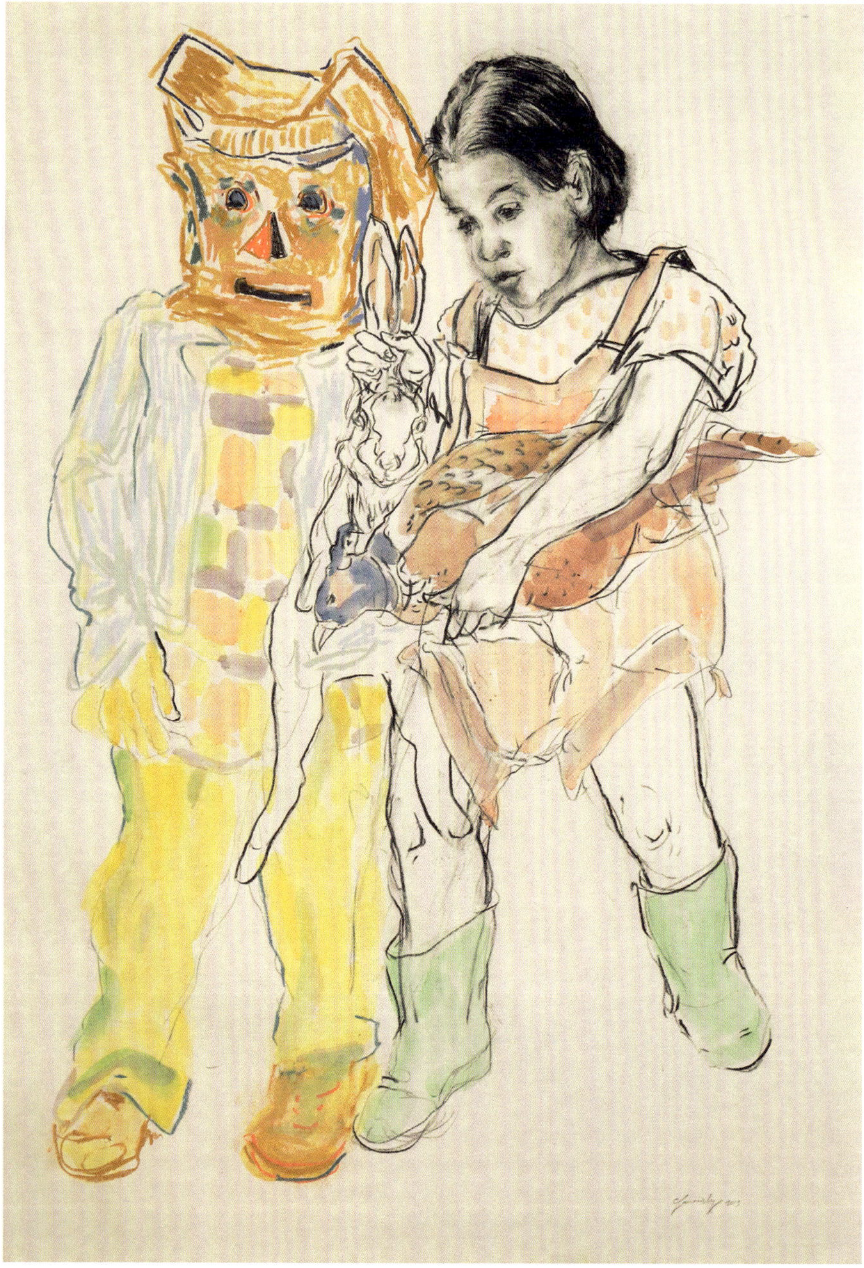

3.

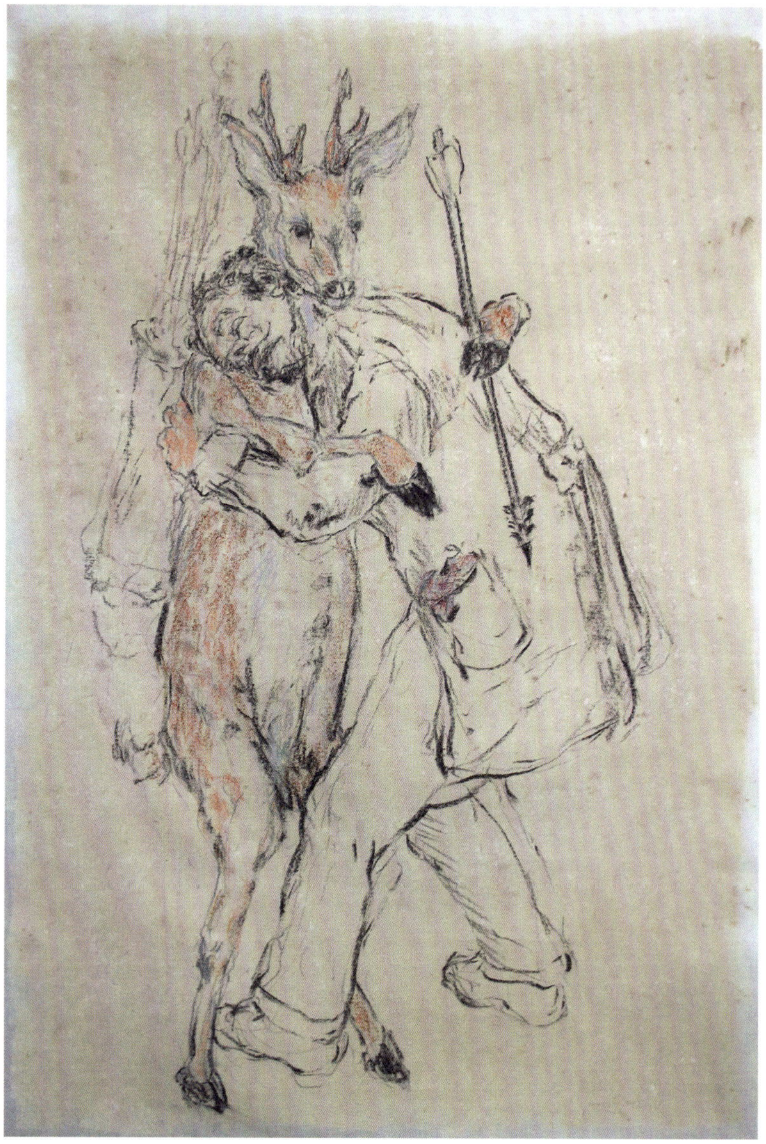

4.

3. *Sanguine*, 2013, charcoal and pastel on paper, 100 × 70 cm (39 ⅜ × 27 ½ in)

4. *The Deer Forgives the Hunter*, 2017, pastel on TNT spun fibre, 130 × 90 cm (51 ⅛ × 35 ⅜ in)

MAURO GIACONI .... The fact that Mauro Giaconi studied to become an architect for three years before completing his degree in painting is telling. His drawings and the space they occupy are both as carefully configured as each other, so that the viewer's experience of them is unavoidably physical. .... For his performative exhibition 'Felicidad' at Ruth Benzacar in Buenos Aires in 2017, Giaconi presented a two-part piece. The first half was the original iteration of what then became *Línea Necia* (*Foolish Line*) (2017) at Galeria Vermelho in São Paulo – where the performance lasted four hours. On both occasions, the artist started off facing a clean wall, armed with a hammer and backpack full of pencils. As he violently tried to nail these to the white surface, both the pencils and the wall cracked, generating a noisy and frustrating scenario. The second section of the performance began when the artist and his audience left the destruction behind and moved on to the main space, where handmade concrete cubes coated with thick graphite dotted the floor. The artist grabbed hold of one such block and hurled it against the wall, gesturing for the audience to join in and repeat the action. As the cubes shattered, the graphite dust sprinkled the white wall, revealing a pre-drawn yet up to that point invisible wire-netting pattern. .... Populating the floor with graphite-covered objects is a recurrent feature of Giaconi's work; he staged a similar scenario for *Desde el fondo del tiempo* (*From the Depth of Time*) (2016) at the Museo Universitario del Chopo in Mexico City. The installation consisted of recycled plastic bags covered in lead, scattered over the floor but also forming a big pile of black garbage, which faced a wall drawing depicting a more elaborate metal fence, complete with spikes and bundles of barbed wire. Time played a role in this seemingly static installation: the pile was activated by a performer hidden inside it, who would move it around almost imperceptibly. Likewise, the mural was put together through daily exercises that consisted of sketching and then erasing the image – the final one resulting from the collaged leftovers of all the previous ones. .... *Mazúrquica Modérnica* (2019) epitomizes the deceitful proposition that underlies Giaconi's art. Upon careful examination, we discover that the supporting sheets of paper are being resized by drawn, fictional ones – their limits blurred. Conceptually, Giaconi is not only interested in physical presences but also in absences; in the way these linger, and how the binary systems that oppose the present to the absent succumb at that precise instant when the graphite explodes and the cube and the dust coexist, or real and fake sheets overlap.
.... Catalina Imizcoz

1.

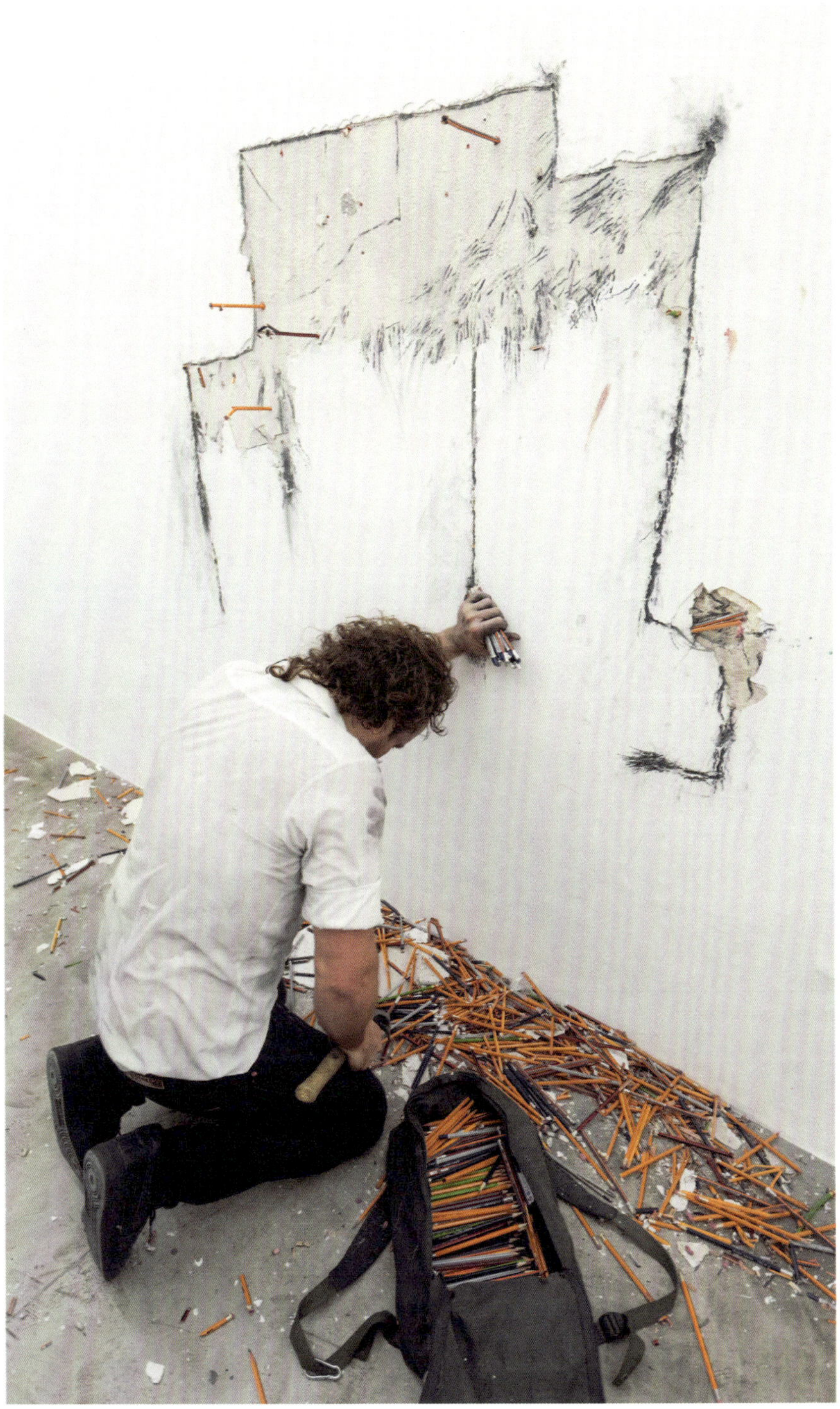

Born 1977, Buenos Aires. Lives in Mexico City.

1. *Línea Necia* (*Foolish Line*), 2017, performance: drawing carved on the wall using a hammer and 1,000 graphite pencils against the wall, duration 4 hrs, 'VERBO 2017: Festival of Performance Art', Galeria Vermelho, São Paulo
2. *Mazúrquica Modérnica*, 2019, graphite powder, pigments and eraser on 60 mixed pages (Violeta Parra cover, history books, recycled plastics, Uruguayan Modern Painting, Giaconi's old drawings, envelopes, etc., 160 × 200 cm (63 × 78 ¾ in)
3. *Consignas* (*Slogans*), 2019, graphite powder, pigments and eraser on 80 mixed pages (athletics books, old earthquake magazines, anarchist newspapers, political flyers, Giaconi's old drawings, recycled plastic bags, etc., 160 × 201 cm (63 × 79 ⅛ in)

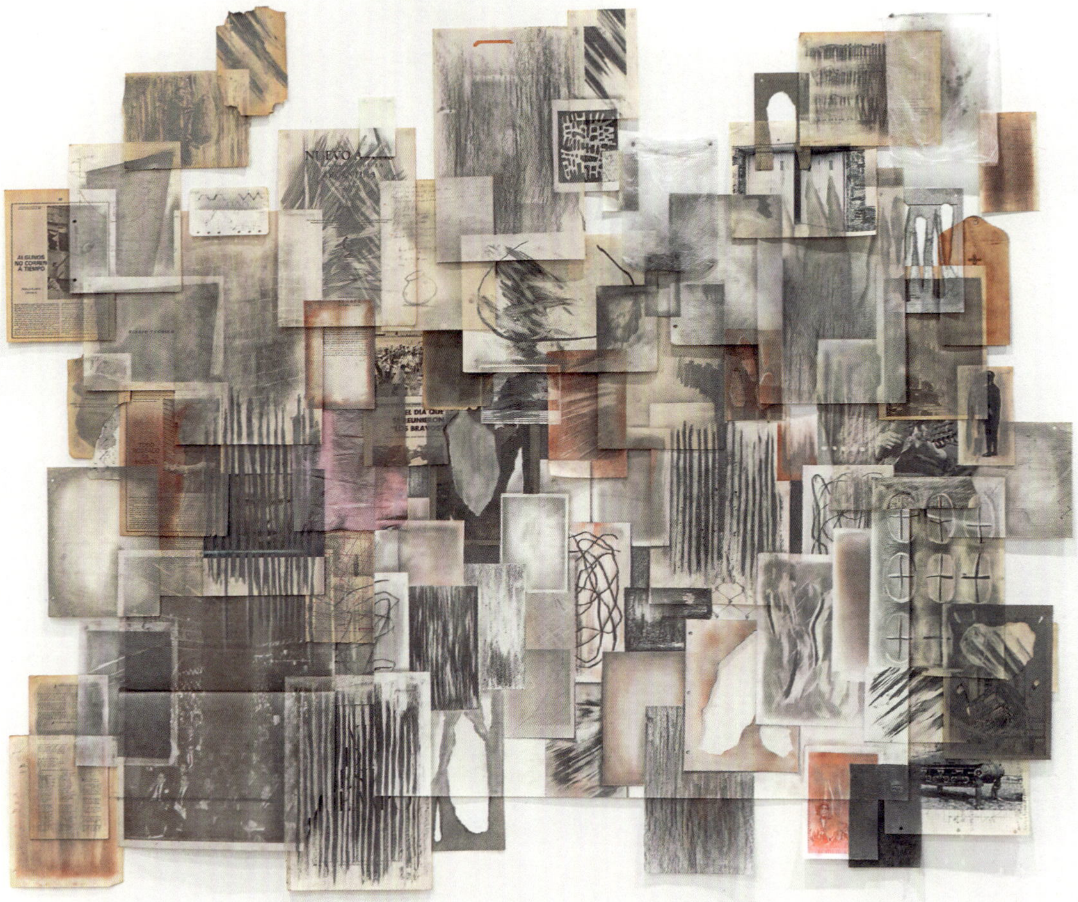

2.

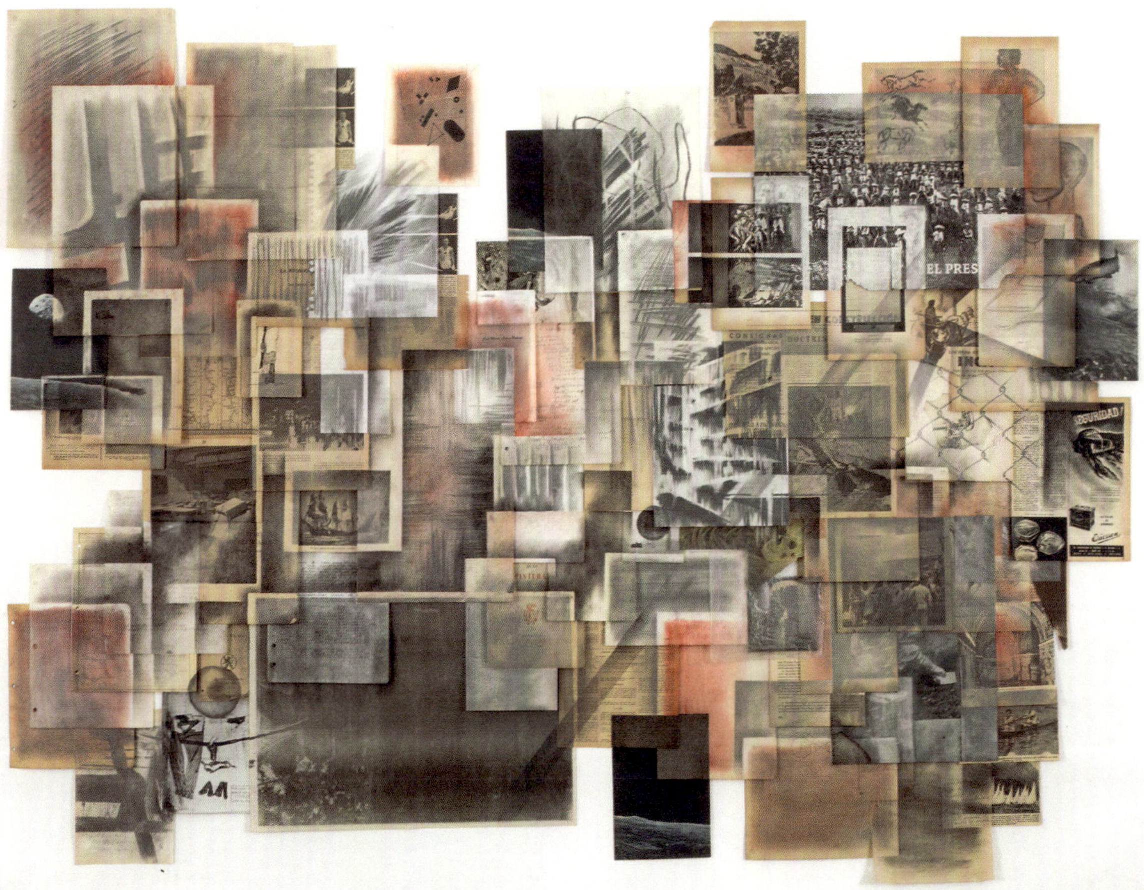

3.

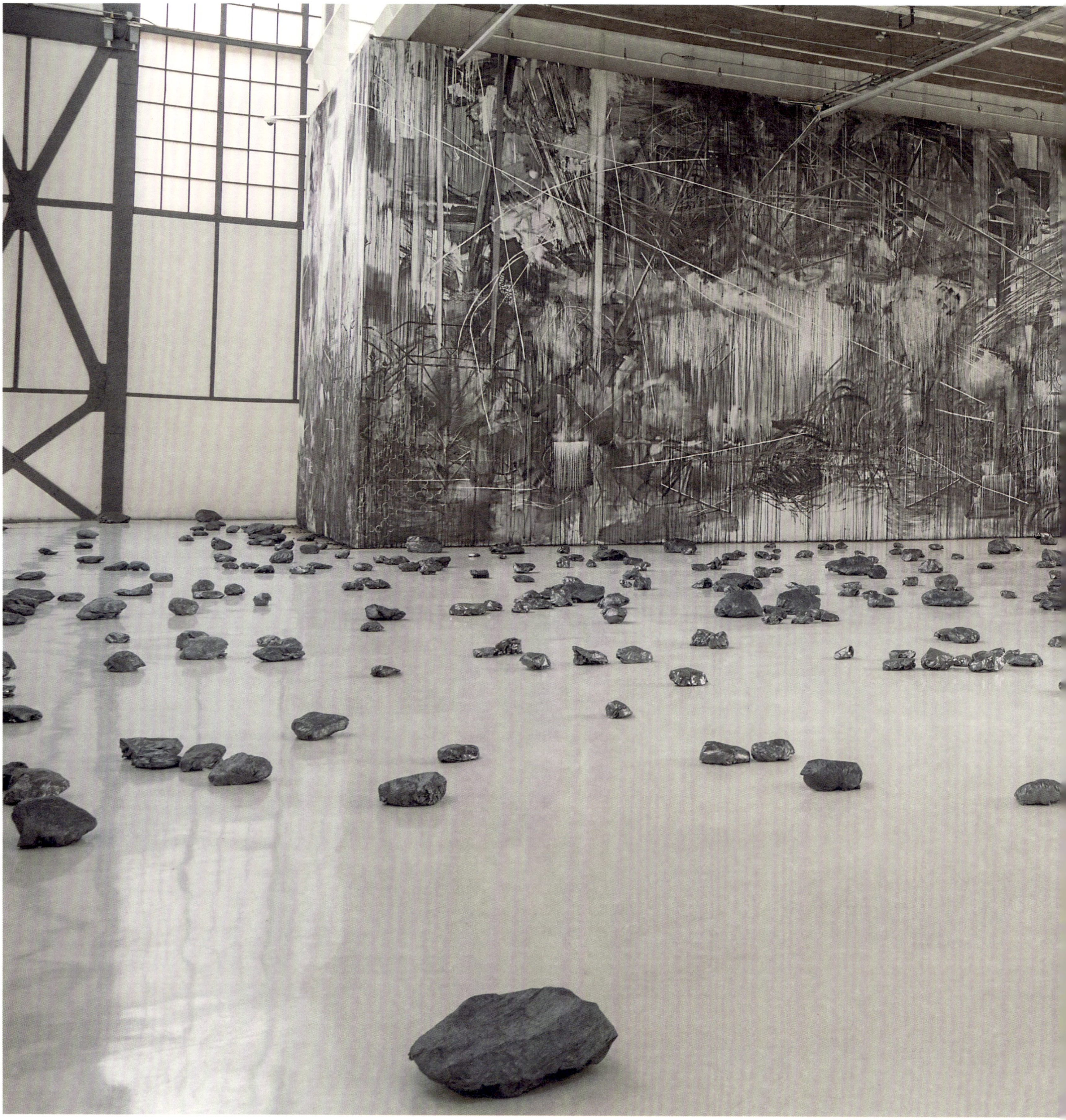

4.

4. *Desde el fondo del tiempo* (*From the Depth of Time*), 2016, installation made with empty recycled plastic bags covered with graphite powder and wall drawing interventions made with graphite and eraser, dimensions variable, installation view at Museo Universitario del Chopo, Mexico City

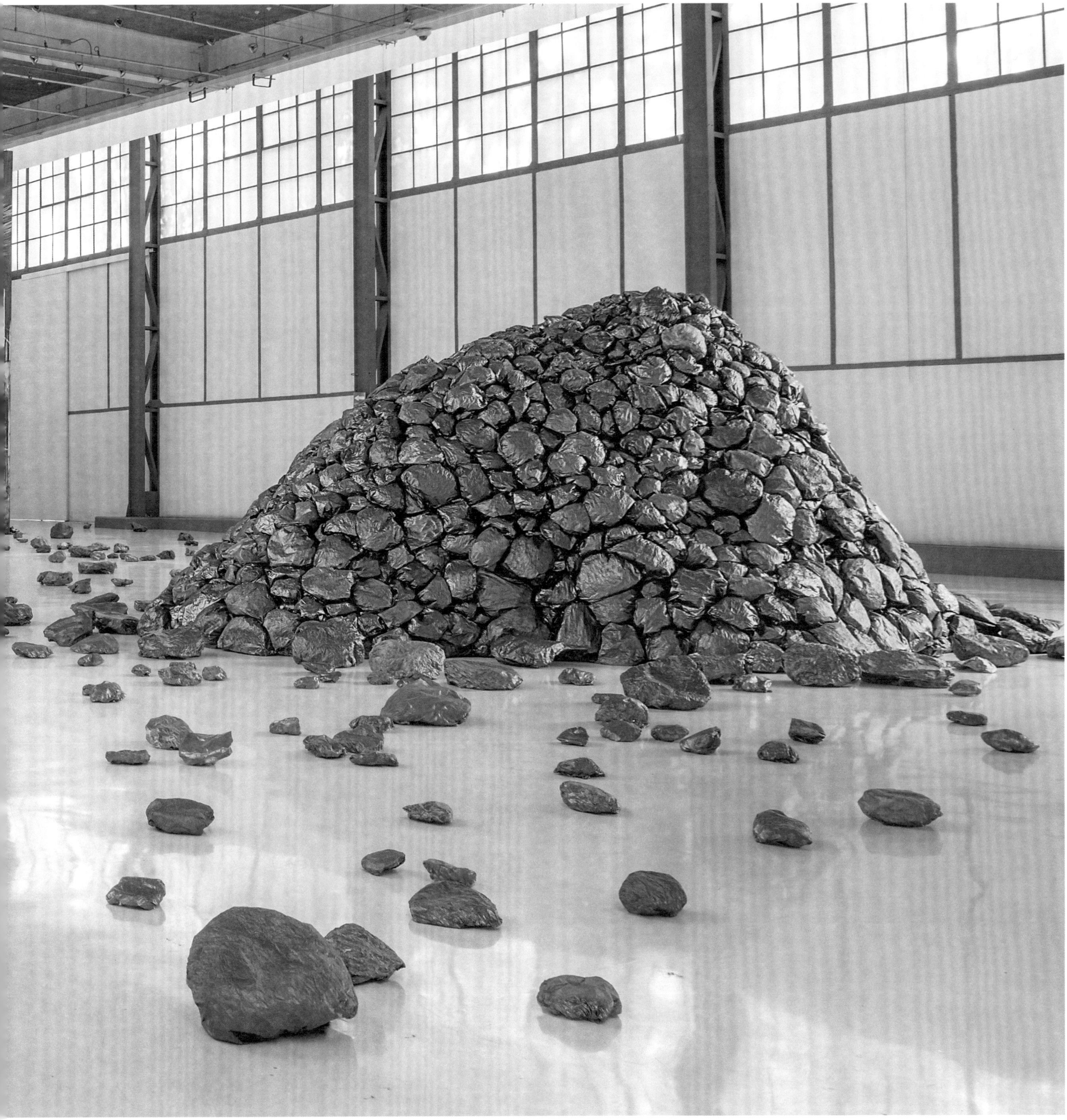

RACHEL GOODYEAR .... Rachel Goodyear's drawings – and her wider practice – invite us to be swept away, led, with childlike innocence, to a world of celestial mystery, psychological abstraction and curious dark rituals. In her intimate and delicate works on paper – small enough to necessitate close-up viewing – we find an ensemble of different characters, contexts, situations and actions. In works such as *Balancing* (2019), we see a woman of roughly middle age rendered in soft, almost brush-like lines of pencil and pencil crayon so that her outline is hazy. She has been contorted into a near-impossible pose. This is not a yoga posture, nor a torturer's 'stress position'; rather with two silver eggs balanced on the figure's upturned heels, this is something operating entirely by its own set of rules. Giving it a basic reading, perhaps this could be seen as a comment on the notion of female fertility? The eggs standing in for ovaries, the female body constricted biologically by their presence, her back turned trying to ignore them yet all the time shaped by their presence? However, in Goodyear's practice things are not that simple and no one image stands alone, each one linking to the next. One must move on to find clues to her larger thoughts. ....
In *Molehills* (2012), drawn in a more graphic style, we find a single female character (Goodyear's subjects are mostly but not always women) repeated seven times in something of a lunar landscape where she performs a series of actions. They are directed towards a nameless black beast who lives in a crater; he strokes her leg in one scene, while she dances for him provocatively in another. It is when we assemble Goodyear's pictures together in our minds that we start to see her broader interests, namely interior psychological conditions for which she is not trying to portray a static illustration but rather a dynamic state that one might come in and out of. This is seen in *Feeder* (2019), where we find a young girl drawn in fine detail. She seems lost in a different world, ignoring the viewer but also the nine red sparrows, highlighted in red watercolour, that dance and flap around her. As the title suggests, this girl has become an object, stripped of her own agency and put on display in the world. Her psychological state is expressed, not through her lowered gaze, but through the grotesque neck manacle that she has been made to wear; covered in breadcrumbs, like some Greek mythical character, she is forced to endure the insistent company of birds who return again and again to flap and peck in her face.
.......James Smith

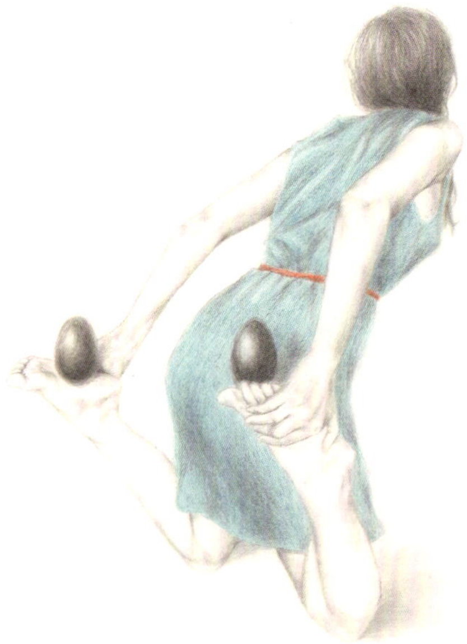

1.

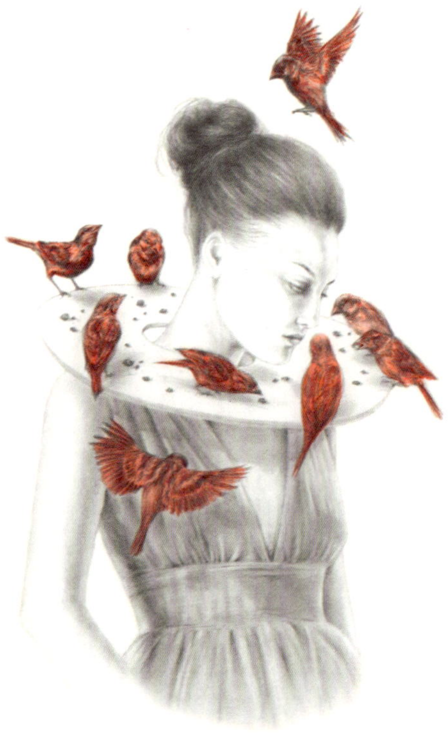

2.

Born 1978, Oldham, Lancashire, UK. Lives and works in Manchester, UK.

1. *Balancing*, 2019, pencil and pencil crayon on paper, 42 × 30 cm (16 ½ × 11 ¾ in)
2. *Feeder*, 2019, pencil and watercolour on paper, 60 × 42 cm (23 ⅝ × 16 ½ in)
3. *Bathing*, 2018, pencil and watercolour on paper, 49.5 × 33 cm (19 ½ × 12 ⅞ in)

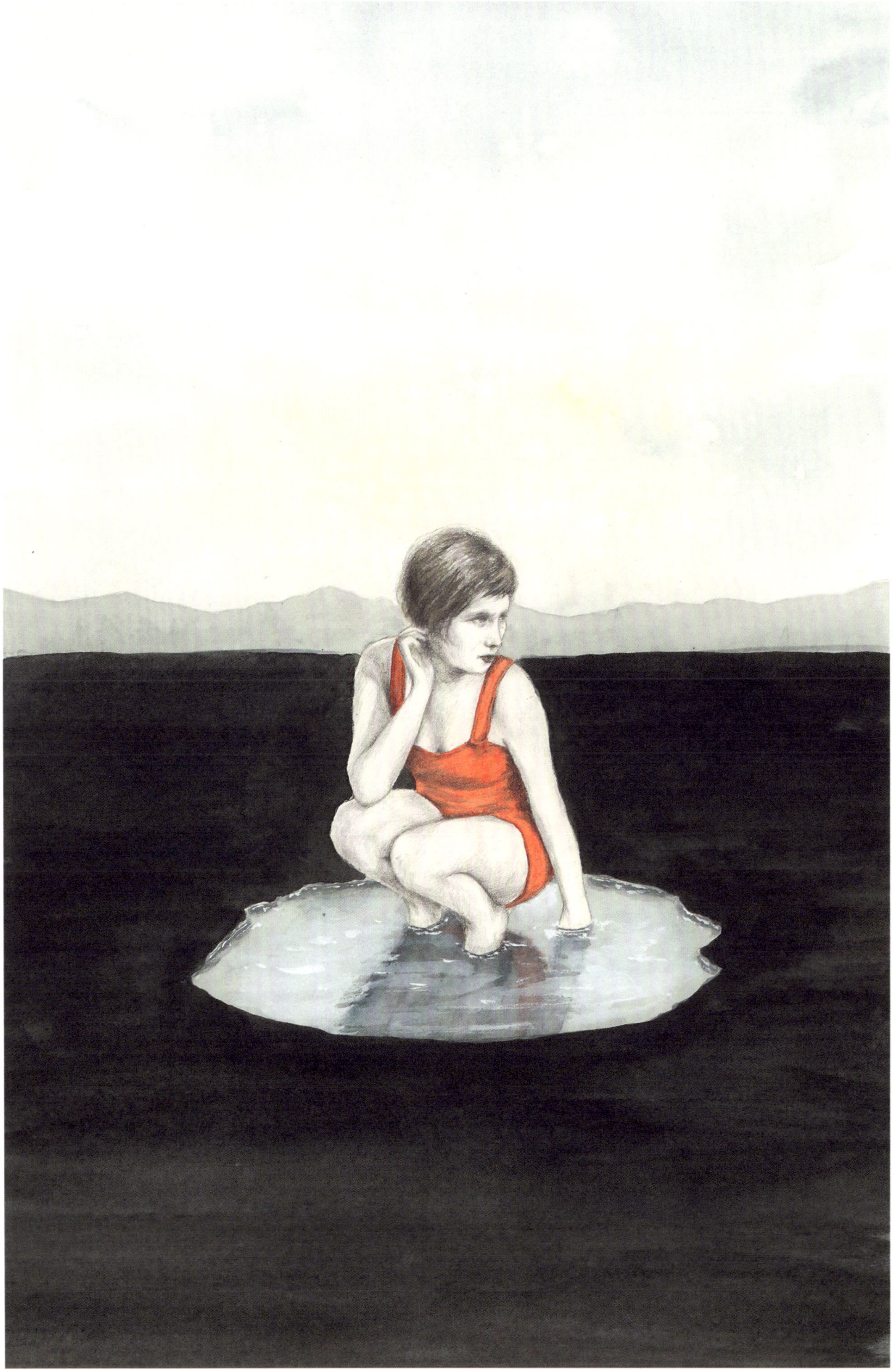

3.

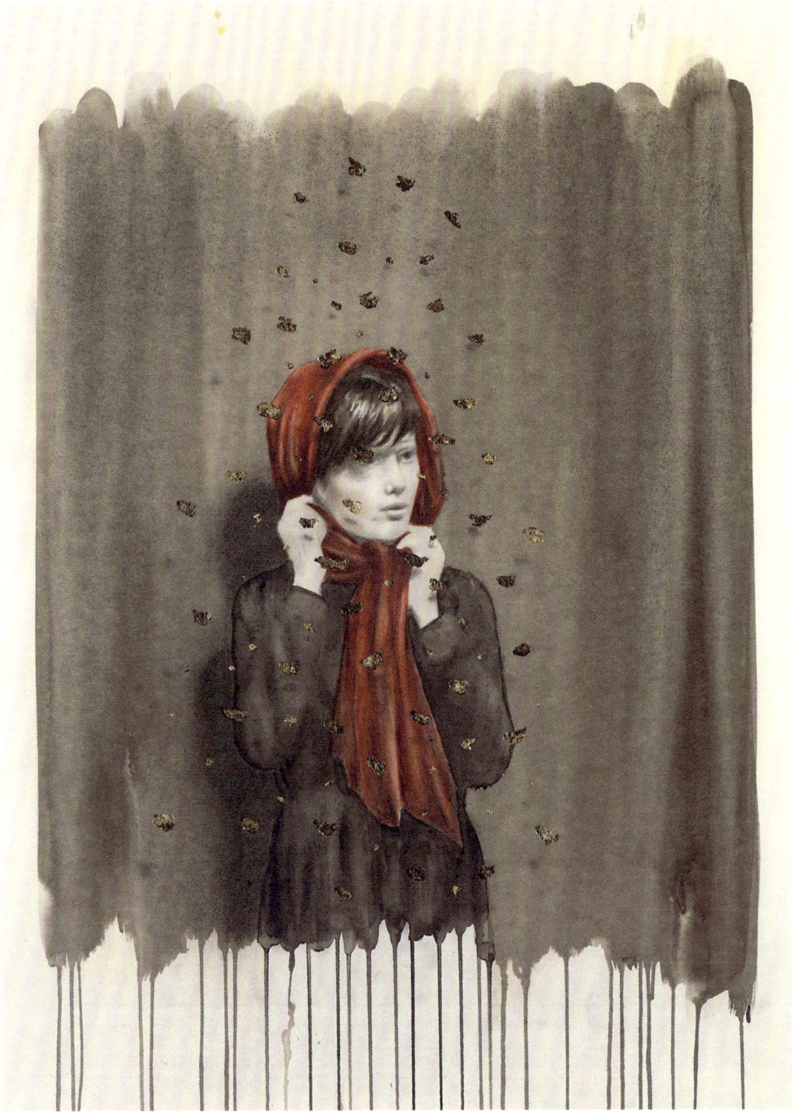

4.

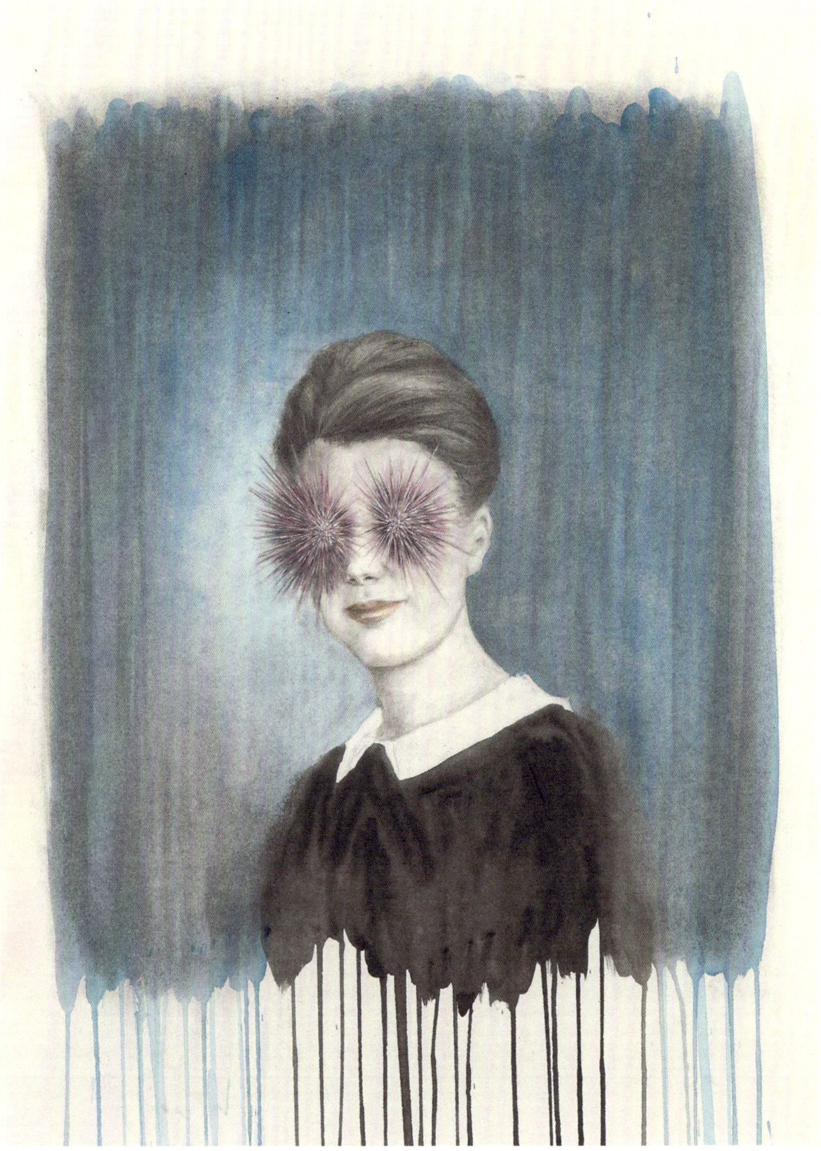

5.

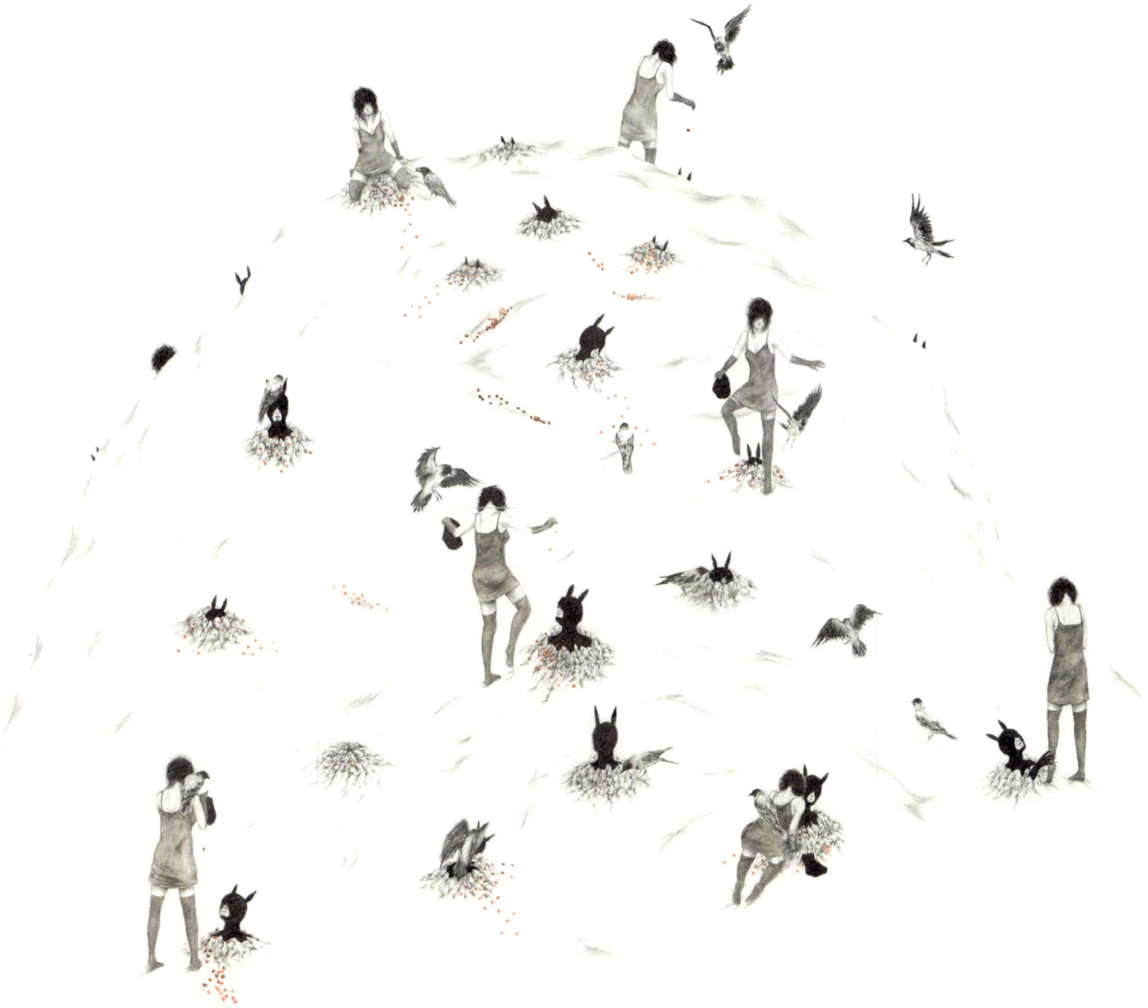

6.

4. *Red Scarf*, 2016, pencil, watercolour, charcoal, ink and gold leaf on paper, 72 × 53 cm (28 ¼ × 20 ⅞ in)
5. *Urchins 2*, 2016, pencil, watercolour and charcoal on paper, 72 × 53 cm (28 ¼ × 20 ⅞ in)
6. *Molehills*, 2012, pencil and watercolour on paper, 120 × 126 cm (47 ¼ × 49 ⅝ in)

MONIKA GRZYMALA....... Much in the way that a lapsed Catholic who is baptized remains a Catholic according to canon law, a residue of faith in sculpture informs Monika Grzymala's space-transforming drawing installations. Best known for her works made from various adhesive tapes, Grzymala's spatial drawings (*Raumzeichnung* in German) are informed by her training. After apprenticing as a stonemason and restorer in the early 1990s, Grzymala, who lives in Berlin, went on to study at art schools in Karlsruhe, Kassel and Hamburg. A supportive professor, recognizing her struggles with sculpture, suggested drawing. It prompted the first of many evolutions in her practice. 'I started with line drawing on paper in a sketchbook,' Grzymala explained in 2010 while producing a commission for 'On Line: Drawing Through the Twentieth Century', an important group show of applied drawing at the Museum of Modern Art, New York. 'Very quickly,' she added, 'my line left the page and continued on the wall.' Two early works, *loop 01* and *loop 02* (2000), were made with gaffer tape in profuse colours that Grzymala flatly applied to the interiors of a Hamburg building. She shortly liberated her line from a two-dimensional plane and began making works – mostly with tape or handmade paper – that spilled from nooks, connected opposing planes and sometimes even partitioned space....... The installation *Raumzeichnung (compass/the mirror)* (*Spatial drawing compass/the mirror*) (2016), made from clear adhesive tape and silver-reflecting tape, is emblematic. The work's central feature was a cross, created by an intersection of tape strung from four pillars in a museum in Reykjavík, Iceland, and offered a true in-situ reading of the four main geographical coordinates on a compass. The work appeared in Grzymala's 2016 exhibition 'Envoi', named for an obscure poem by Octavio Paz. The poem is also the epigraph to Marxist sociologist Henri Lefebvre's book, *The Production of Space* (1974), in which he argues that space 'is neither subject nor object' but a 'social reality' and 'a set of relations and forms'....... These abstruse propositions inform Grzymala's constructions, many of which are ephemeral, but also capable of being repurposed. Composed of 1.5 km of black paper tape, *Raumzeichnung (shifting) (Spatial drawing shifting)* appeared in a 2015 exhibition in Berlin that included sculptural mounds of rolled-up tape from past installations. The integrity of personal labour is central to Grzymala's temporary drawings, as is the agency of her throwaway materials. The artist meticulously records the length of tape she uses in each of her installations. *Raumzeichnung (rhizome) (Spatial drawing rhizome)*, a three-part installation exhibited in the Polish city of Katowice in 2019, appears relatively compact in photographs but in fact utilized 10.8 km of black-paper and silver-mirroring tapes. The fractional lines that make up Grzymala's voluminous works, when properly audited, are considerable, both in length and ambition.
.... Sean O'Toole

1.
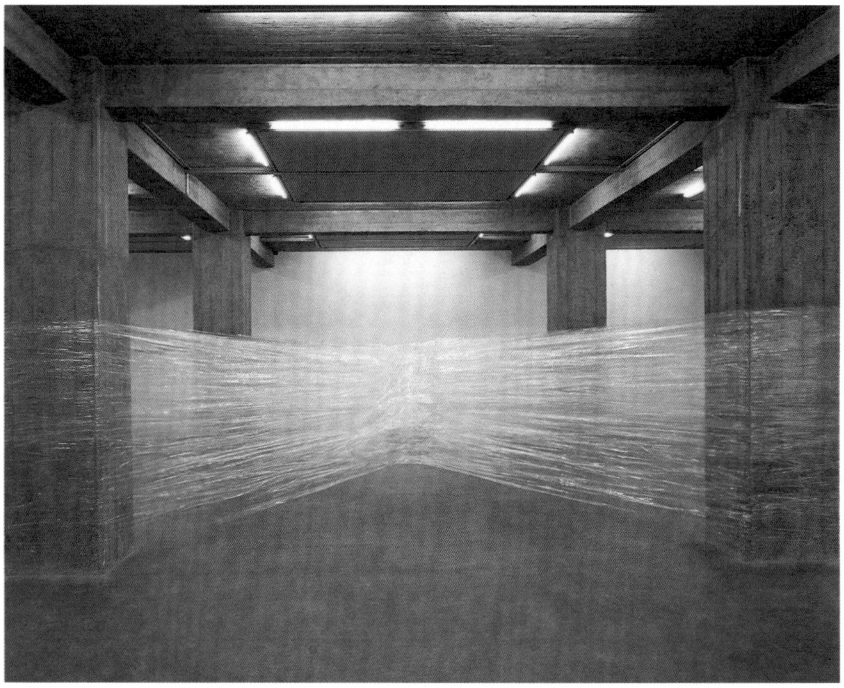

2.
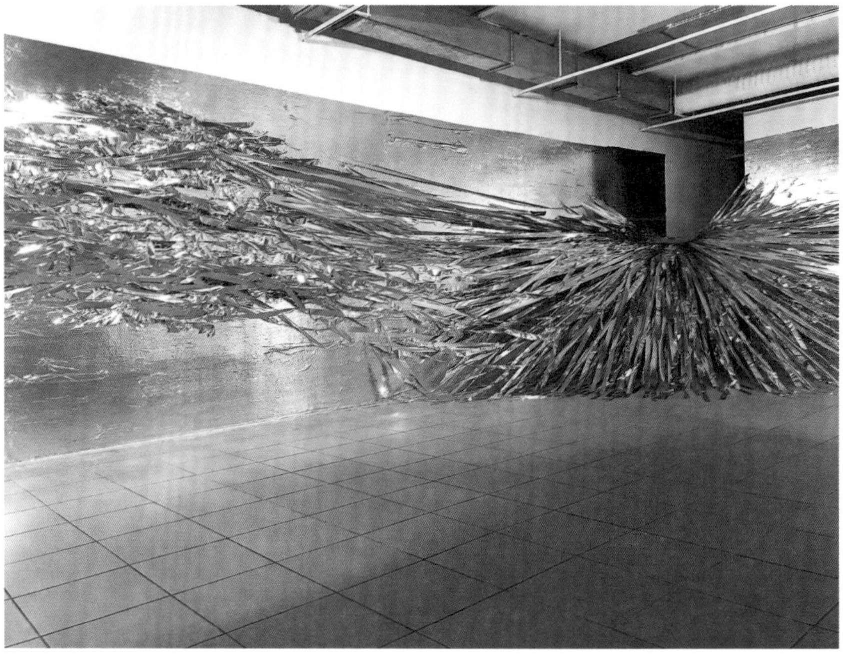

Born 1970, Zabrze, Poland. Lives and works in Berlin.

1. *Raumzeichnung (compass/the mirror)* (*Spatial drawing compass/the mirror*), 2016, (detail), site-specific installation of 10 km (6.2 miles) of clear adhesive tape and 1.4 km (0.9 miles) of silver reflective tape, installation view, 'Monika Grzymala: Envoi' at Reykjavík Art Museum Hafnarhus, Iceland
2. *Raumzeichnung (Rhizome)* (*Spatial drawing rhizome*), 2019, (detail), site-specific installation of 10.8 km (6.7 miles) of black paper tape and silver mirroring tape, installation view, 'Monika Grzymala & Damien Deroubaix: On the Nature of the World', BWA Contemporary Art Gallery, Kattowitz, Poland
3. *Raumzeichnung (Shifting)* (*Spatial drawing shifting*), 2015, (detail), site-specific installation of 1.5 km (0.9 miles) of black paper tape, installation view, 'Monika Grzymala: The Making Of Forming Something New', Galerie Crone, Berlin

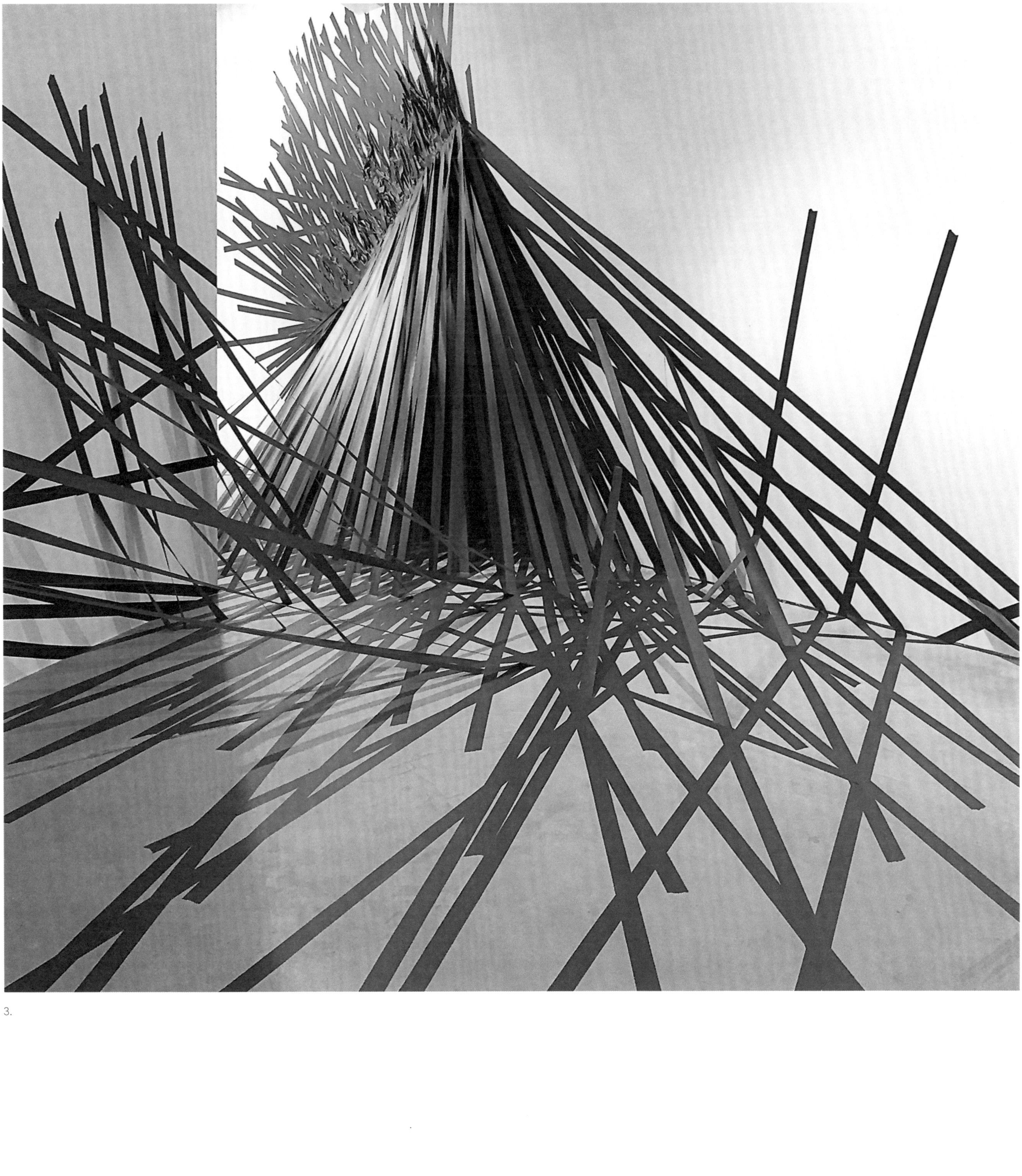

3.

E N V E R   H A D Z I J A J .... Enver Hadzijaj's tender pencil and crayon portraits share an economy of line often found in fashion sketches, while also operating as windows on to wistful narratives. In the small drawing *Lonelydays Q.e.d.* (2018), Hadzijaj depicts a figure with their back turned. Smoke from the cigarette they are nonchalantly holding meanders to the top of the composition. The head is shaved close to the skull – an effect Hadzijaj approximates with little grey dots produced with the sharpened tip of the pencil – and they are wearing an off-the-shoulder jumper. Fabric billows around the arms and torso, a motion represented by simple wavy lines. A mark on a bare shoulder captures the attention. The artist has burned the paper, creating the impression of a wound. Around this dark, painful-looking mark smoke stains and smudged charcoal mingle. The presence of physical harm is also indicated by Hadzijaj's choice of colours. A heavy outline of black and red is used to delineate the flesh – colours reminiscent of blood and bruising. .... *Lonelydays Q.e.d.* captures the harsh glamour of youth – its hedonism, angst and vulnerability. These themes are also present in the drawing *Perfect Lineage* (2018), in which a figure stands, eyes closed, before a mirror. The shape of their raised middle finger is echoed by a graffiti-style penis scrawled across their cheek. For the exhibition 'Cruise Collection' (2020) at Fragile in Berlin, Hadzijaj produced a text linking his work to a childhood relationship with an older sister. 'There was a petrol station near our house to which she would send me to buy red Gauloises for her and sweets for myself,' he wrote. 'In those mornings we would talk and wonder why things had turned out to be that difficult.' In the same text, Hadzijaj also describes watching his sister apply her makeup. This activity is the subject of *Contouring Tutorial* (2019), a monochrome drawing made using red crayon on paper in which the face of a young woman fills the page. Hadzijaj has coloured the background with vertical red strokes, using the white space left on the page to represent the figure's skin. Lines are marked out down either side of her nose and on her cheek – a technique used for 'contouring', where makeup is applied to dramatically accentuate the bone structure. The mood of the drawing is calm, perhaps even devotional. Her eyes are closed and a pale stream of smoke emerges from her nostril like a cartoon cloud. *Contouring Tutorial* is the product of a familial gaze – the kind of awed, curious looking often reserved for observing older siblings, figures who appear, for a short while, to hold the answers to the mysteries of adulthood.
.... Rosanna Mclaughlin

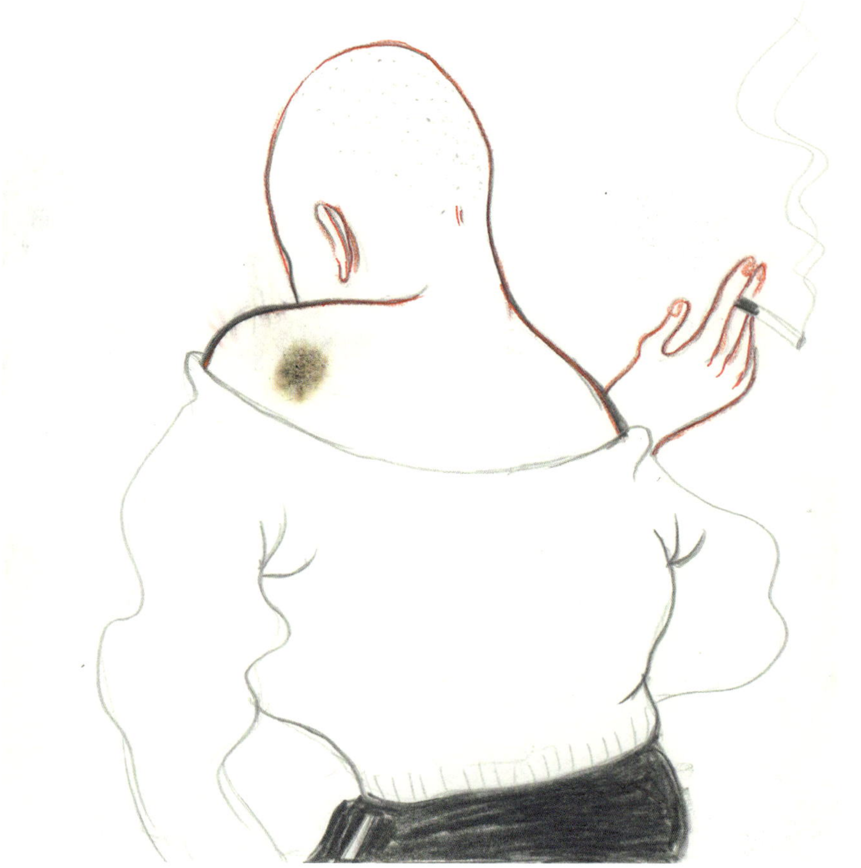
1.

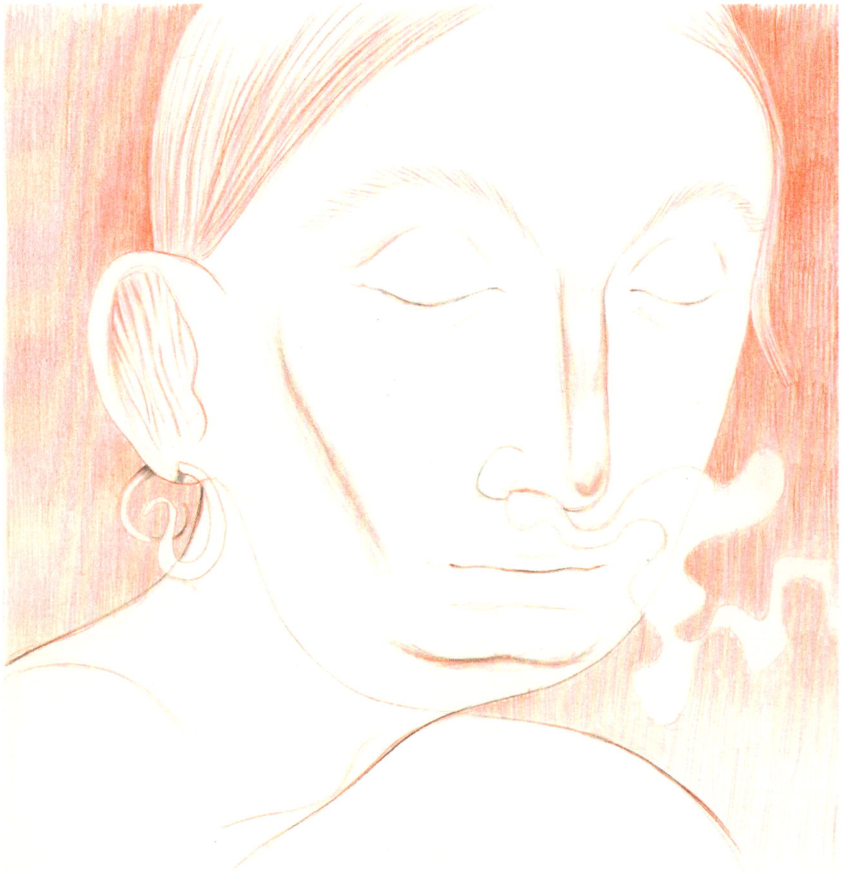
2.

Born 1980, Frankfurt. Lives and works in Berlin.

1. *Lonelydays Q.e.d.*, 2018, crayon and pencil on paper with burn mark, 21 × 21 cm (8 ¼ × 8 ¼ in)
2. *Contouring Tutorial*, 2019, crayon on paper, 21 × 21 cm (8 ¼ × 8 ¼ in)
3. *Perfect Lineage*, 2018, pencil on paper, 29.7 × 21 cm (11 ¾ × 8 ¼ in)

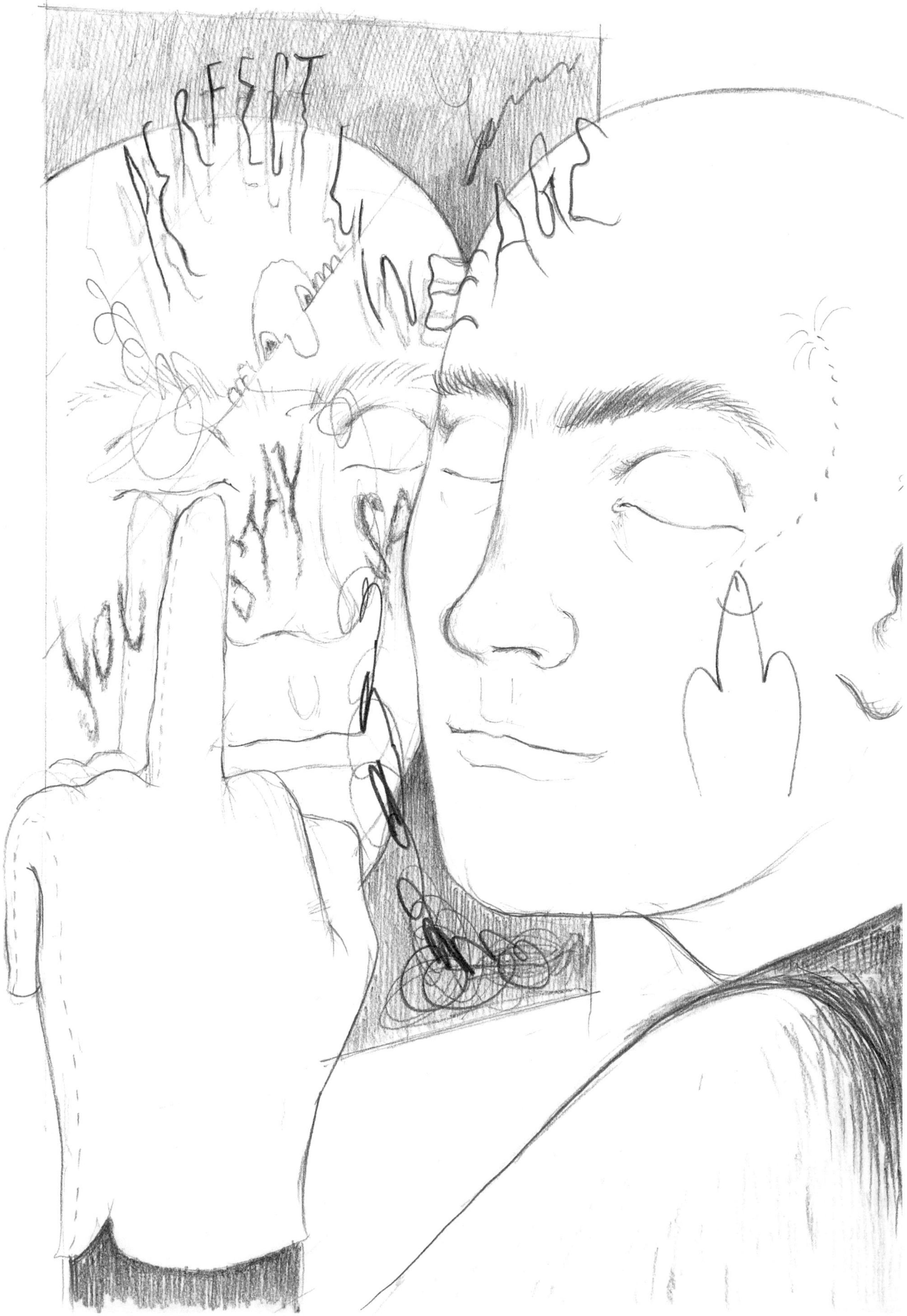

3.

SHEROANAWE HAKIHIIWE .... Sheroanawe Hakihiiwe uses materials sourced in the Amazon to express the philosophy and mythology of the Yanomami people. Hakihiiwe is a member of an indigenous community named the Pori Pori that live in the Venezuelan rainforest. Inspired by natural forms significant to Yanomami spiritualism, his work has a distinctive graphic style, favouring bold, minimal shapes and contrasting colours. *Yaro Shinaki (Parrot's Feather)* (2018), for which Hakihiiwe painted acrylic onto paper covered in sugar cane fibre, depicts a bird's feather: one of approximately thirty species of parrot that live in the Amazon region. Half red and half black and scaled-up in size to almost half a metre (nineteen and a half inches) tall, the feather has the appearance of a shield. The Yanomami believe all animate and inanimate forms contain a spirit, and the parrot feather has a specific importance. Spirits known as *xapiripë* are believed to wear their plumage. .... While *Yaro Shinaki* is loosely figurative, many of Hakihiiwe's artworks abstract and distil their subject to the point at which it is no longer immediately recognizable. To the unfamiliar eye, *Tipikwe (Dots)* (2019) looks like a hand-painted grid, constructed from separate rectangles of black dots. The pattern is marked by inconsistency, each dot evading mathematic stricture to instead recall the aerial view of a landscape, reduced to its most essential form. *Huwe Moshi #34 (Coral Serpent #34)* (2018), a monotype print on paper made from the mulberry tree, also takes a grid-like form. This time, the grid is constructed from lines broken down into red, black and white sections, the vibrant colours of the coral snake that lives in the Orinoco river, a strikingly beautiful animal with a powerful venom. The expansion of the lines across the page into a symmetrical network suggests an omnipresent force – the shape of once-colourful scales transformed into linear geometries as if shed to reveal a new life. .... During the early 1990s Hakihiiwe began producing handmade paper using natural fibres. Wishing to share the techniques he had learned, he established the Yanomami Owëmamotima (The Yanomami art of producing paper), a collective community publishing project, in collaboration with the artist Laura Anderson Barbata (b. 1958). Over the previous century, when the Yanomami first came into sustained contact with outsiders, they have faced an existential threat. Protecting themselves and their way of life from epidemics, deforestation, mining, climate disaster and other encroachments and attacks upon their home is a continuing struggle. Hakihiiwe's drawings, handmade paper and the collective ethos of Yanomami Owëmamotima are each testament to a culture with a profound knowledge of, and respect for, the ecosystem in which they live and the principles of sustainability. .... Rosanna Mclaughlin

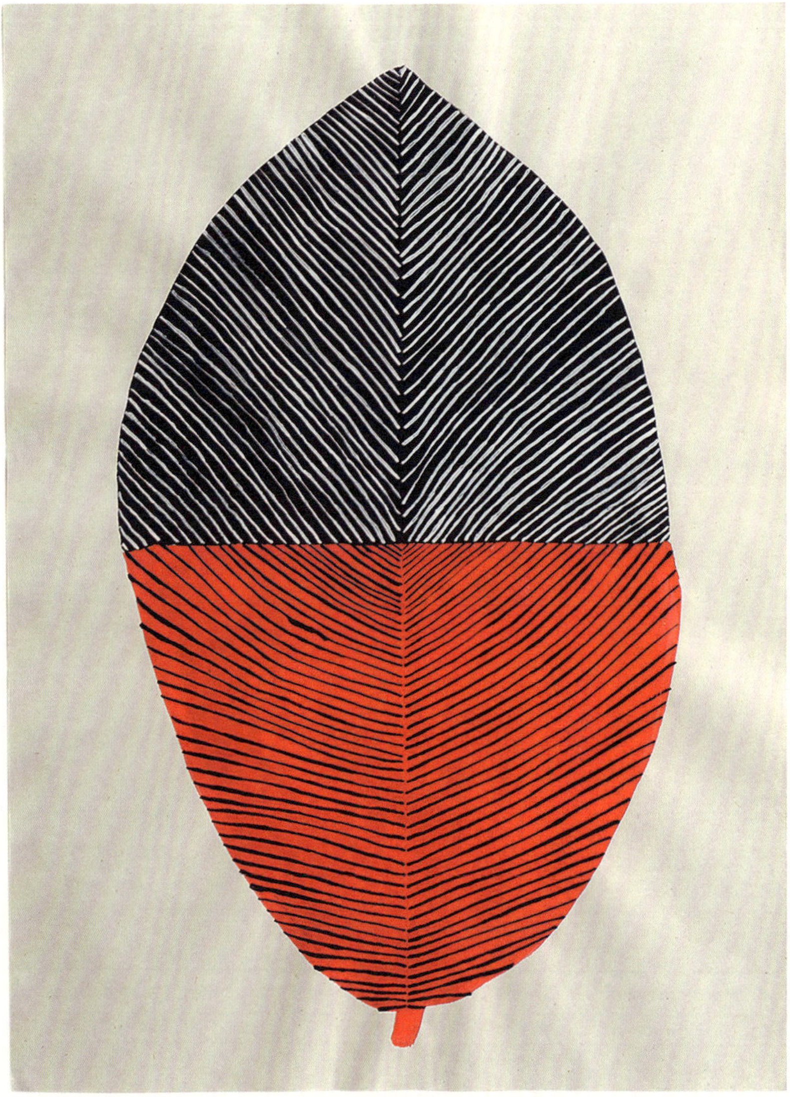

1.

Born 1971, Sheroana, Amazonas, Venezuela. Lives and works in Caracas and Platanal, Alto Orinoco, Amazonas, Venezuela.

1. *Yaro Shinaki* (*Parrot's Feather*), 2018, acrylic on sugar cane fibre-coated paper, 70 × 50 cm (27 ½ × 19 ⅝ in)
2. *Tipikiwe* (*Dots*), 2019, monotype print on mulberry paper, 75 × 144 cm (29 ½ × 56 ⅝ in)
3. *Huwe Moshi #34* (*Coral Serpent #34*), 2018, acrylic on sugar cane fibre- coated paper, 50 × 70 cm (19 ⅝ × 27 ½ in)

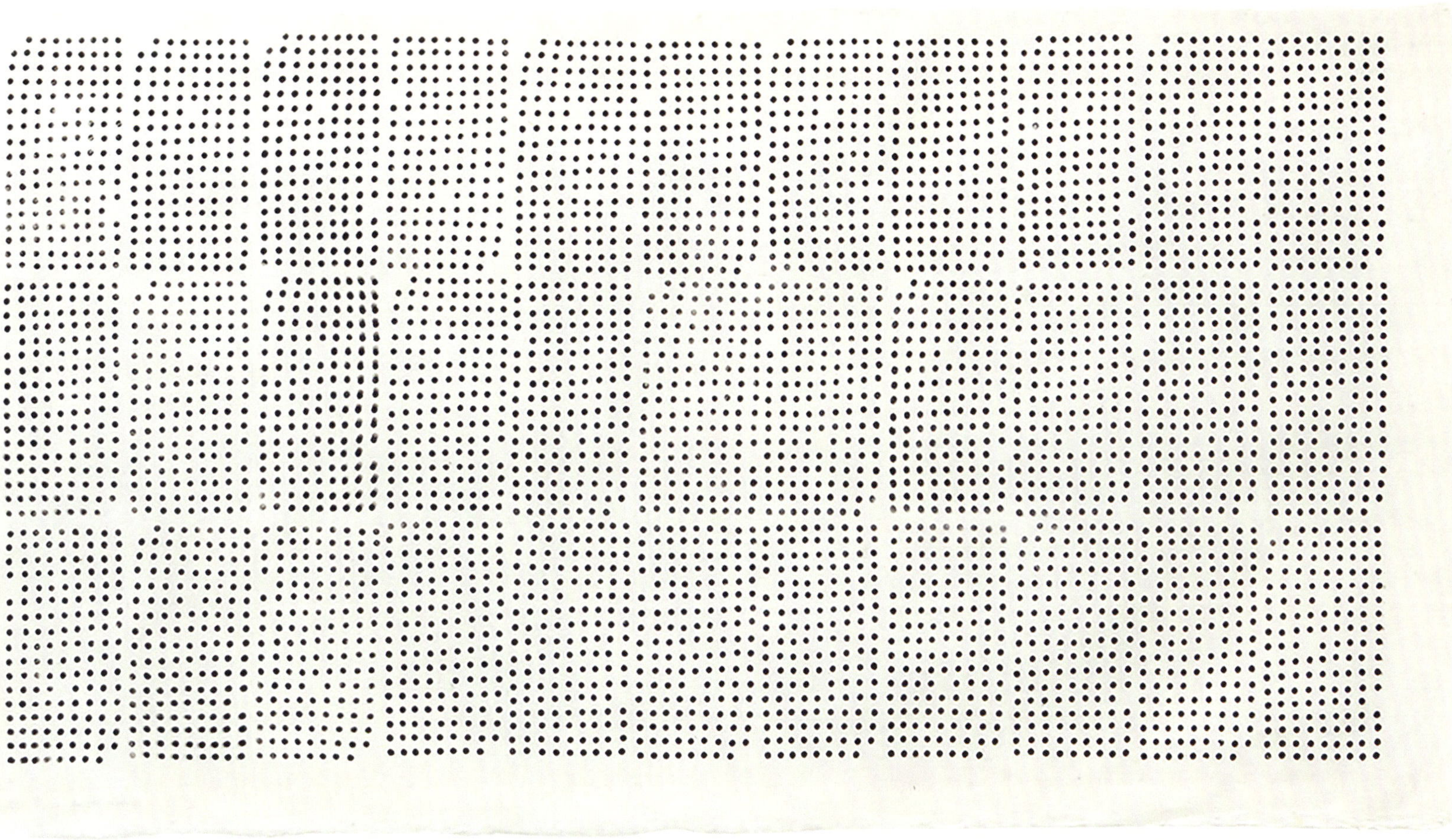

2.

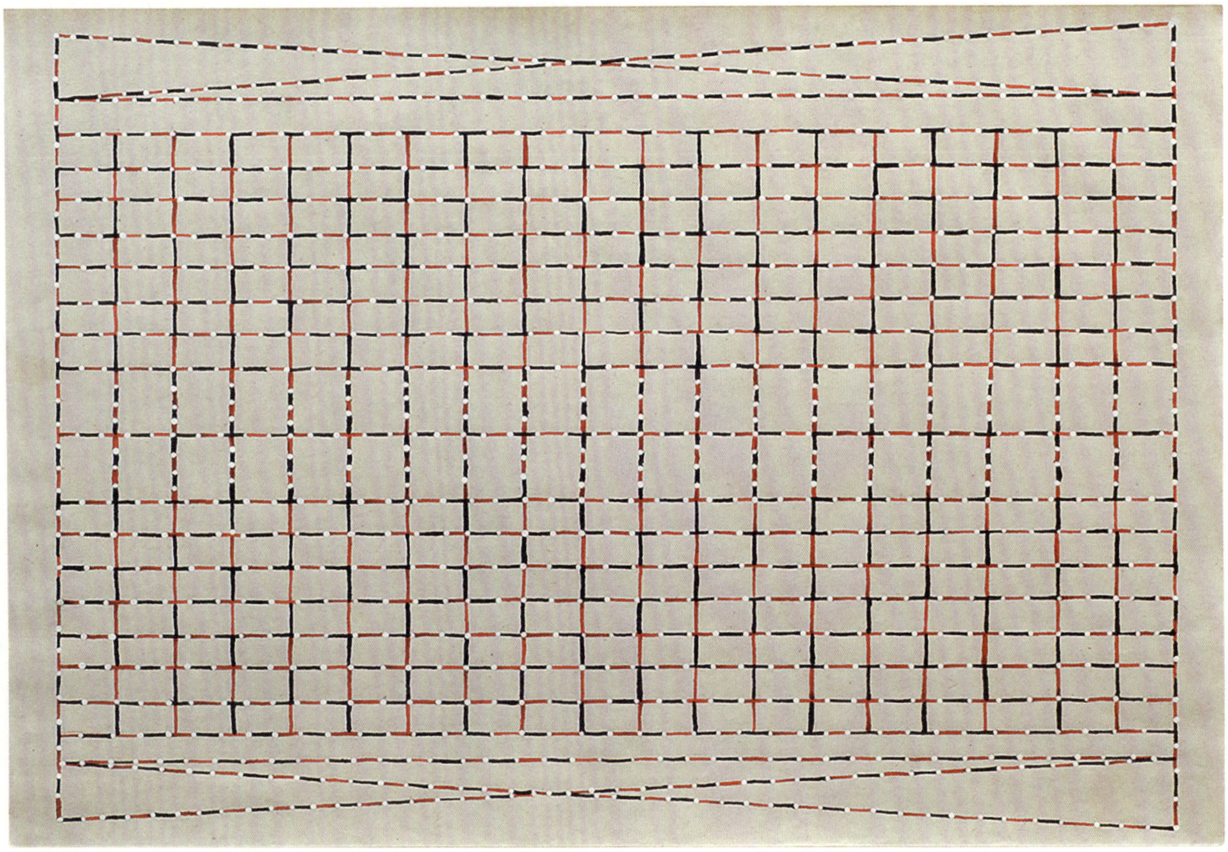

3.

MASANORI HANDA....... Masanori Handa's extravagantly eccentric drawings are a network of overpainted and underpainted landscapes: palimpsests of plants, contour lines, mountain ranges, cartoonish abysses, collaged fragments and flower-like patterns. As they sprawl towards his drawings' edges, these agglomerations are only marginally contained by borders. The bright vegetable shapes might spill on forever. For all that Handa's meticulously painted, semi-abstract drawings look at first sight as if they have been carelessly assembled from a catalogue of zombie abstraction's neo-modernist tricks, in fact they are made by an artist whose large installations are precise, careful and inflected by mathematics, for instance *Art House Project*, which Handa presented for the 2019 Setouchi Triennale at Inujima, Japan....... It would be quite convenient to imagine that *toononefurino* (2015) is a mind map and its watercolour and oil-pastel-outlined plant tendrils are the notations of an over-relaxed self. However, born in 1979, Handa is a so-called 'Xennial', wedged between Generation X and Millennial. His childhood was analogue and his adulthood has been digital. If Xennials are said to embody generational fuzziness, so this ambiguity encapsulates the dialogue between Handa's drawings and his extremely disciplined but elaborate sculptural contributions to exhibitions and biennials around the world. One way to decode Handa's drawings is to imagine a messy, menacing id (his squishy, spreading, indeterminately erotic shapes) regulated by the sharp, multiple perspectives and cleanly receding spaces of the ego (the dark recessions that dominate *Onjiki Ni Kaete* (2017), for example). Equally, *Onjiki Ni Kaete*'s black and white, perky swirls and floating crisp lozenges attract any number of memories of souls adrift across the sea reaching for the safe shores of post-painterly abstraction....... And yet the idea of autobiography proves to be no way to understand Handa's drawings, aleatory and improvised though they seem. The patterning in his drawings both attracts attention and draws the eye away from his main game. It would be more correct to conclude that *Onjiki Ni Kaete*'s multiple spaces, like *toononefurino*'s nestling plants and interlocking cascades, are like sand thrown in our eyes. This apparent parading of himself in his drawings is, more likely, a form of unexpected artistic humility. His titles point to his desire that we consume his pretending without too many questions. Handa's drawing method is only apparently random, since from edge of paper to edge of paper his semi-figurative chaos consistently touches the edges of geometric order. And, therefore, *Onjiki Ni Kaete* requires that we remember our art history, including the notoriously trippy prints and late 1960s record covers of Tadanori Yokoo (b. 1936). Handa updates that Baby Boomer era. So, despite their visual unlikeness, his drawings meld seamlessly with his larger sculptural assemblages. The faux-genuine delicacy of Handa's drawings masks the same accumulative compositional method.
.... Charles Green

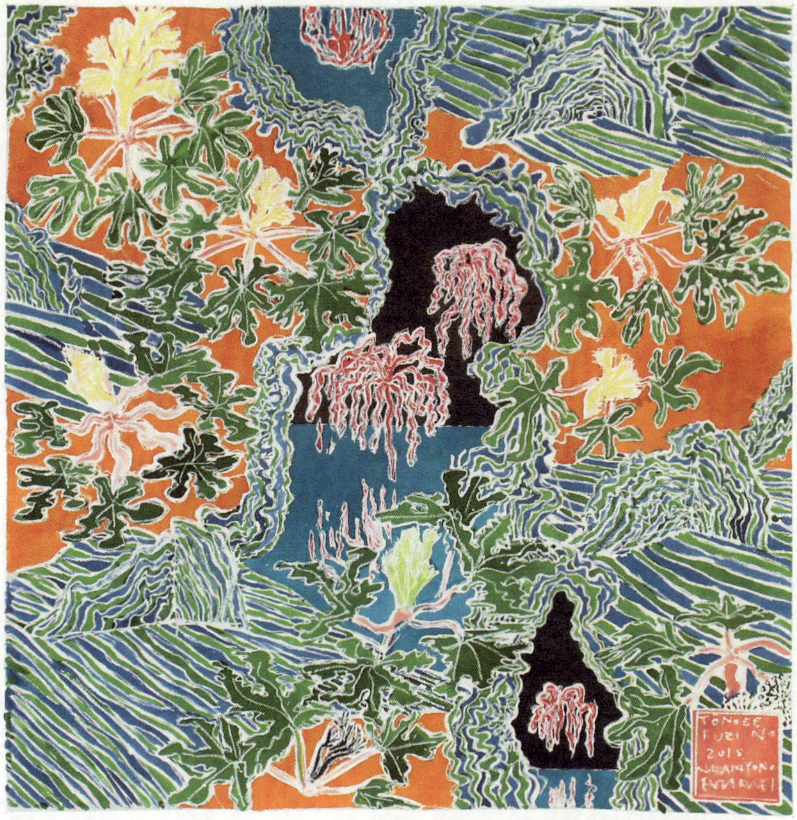
1.

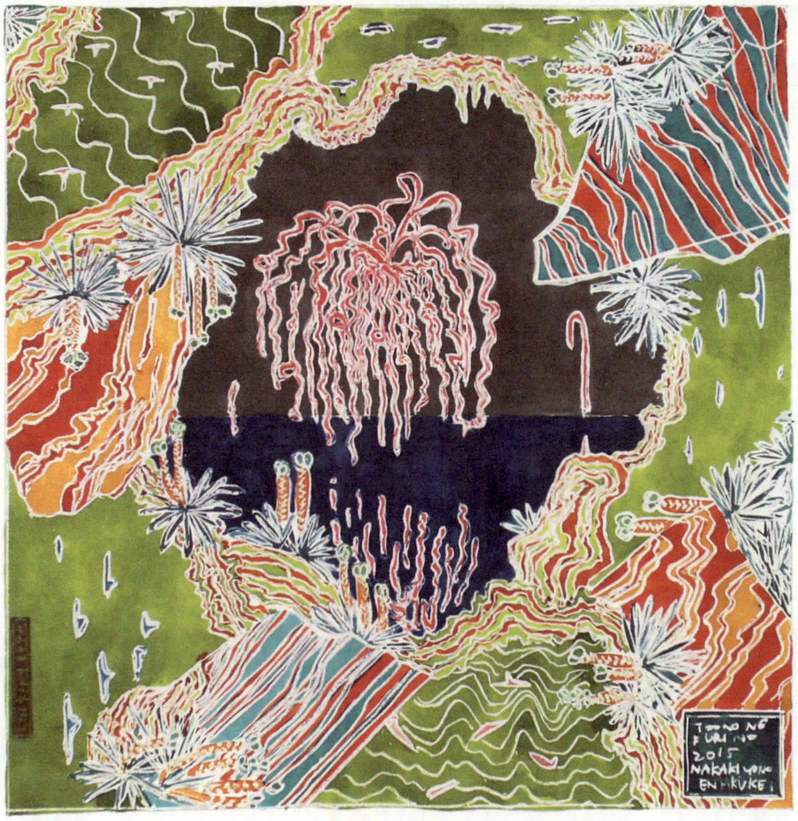
2.

Born 1979, Kanagawa, Japan. Lives and works in Tokyo.

1. *toononefurino*, 2015, watercolour and oil pastel on paper, 74.5 × 74.5 cm (29 ½ × 29 ½ in)
2. *toononefurino*, 2015, watercolour and oil pastel on paper, 73.5 × 73.3 cm (29 ⅛ × 28 ⅞ in)
3. *Onjiki Ni Kaete*, 2017, watercolour and oil pastel on paper, 108 × 108 cm (42 ½ × 42 ½ in)

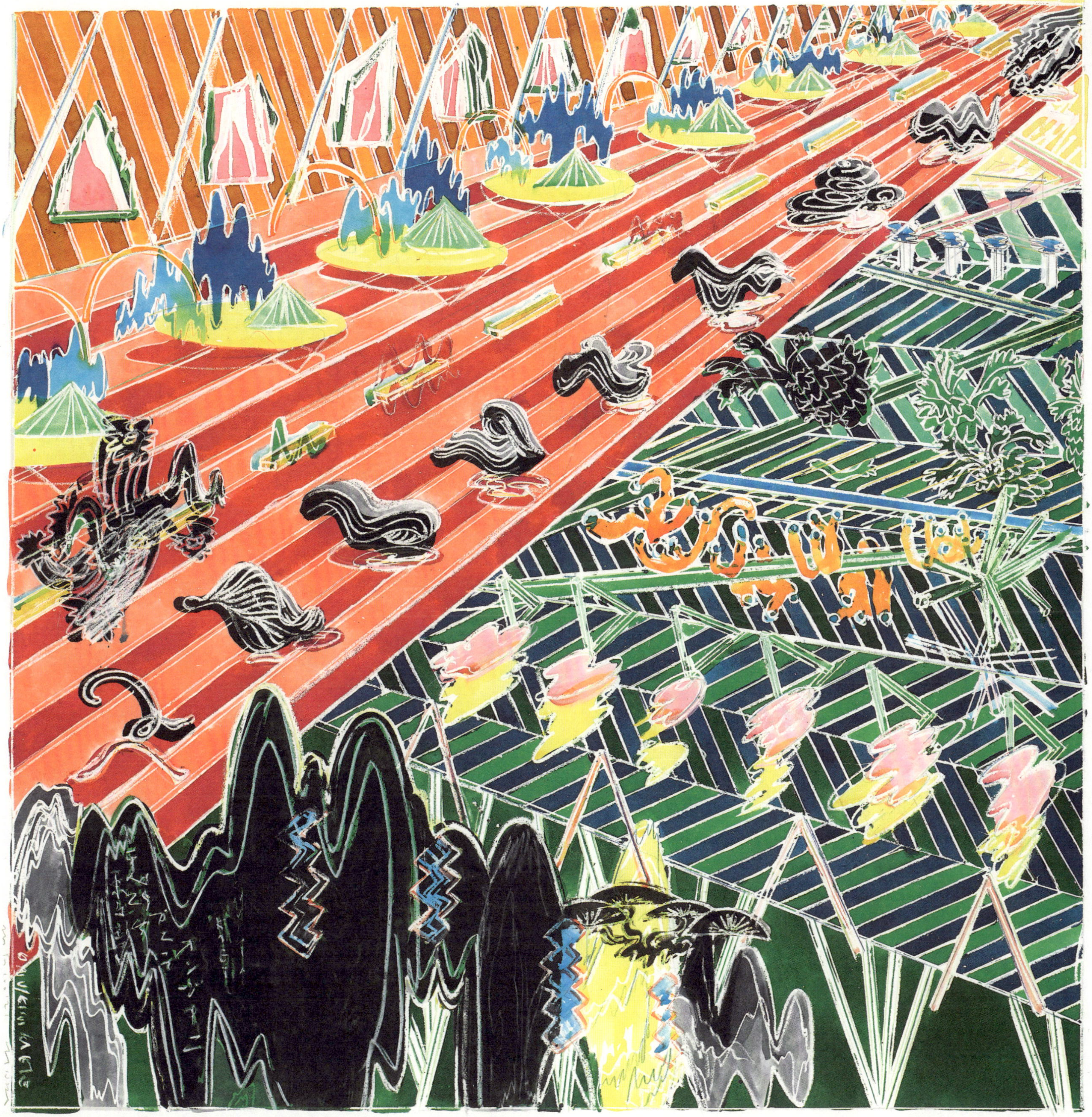

3.

NAOTAKA HIRO .... The corporeal human self, particularly as it is explored in Naotaka Hiro's drawings, sculptures and films that document his performances, is an unknowable place. This 'dilemma of the unknowability,' as Hiro put it in a 2015 interview, of not being able to see all of his body without optical or mechanical aids, has been the fulcrum for the artist's relentlessly personal practice of documenting his body. Hiro's atomized self-portraiture, while emblematic of a post-Freudian conception of a fractured self, cleaves more closely to radical traditions in performance art, from Viennese Actionism to the early work of Bruce Nauman (b. 1941). .... After graduating from the California Institute of the Arts in 2000, Hiro initially worked in performance, as well as its accessory media, film and sculpture. His earliest works expressionistically analyzed and reconfigured the skull, intestines and anus. Skulls were a particular point of focus, justifiably given that this locus of sentience and speech has for millennia enjoyed preferential treatment in sacred rites and, later, art. His visceral performances, which explored abjection and the macabre, recalled an earlier generation of body artists, notably Paul McCarthy (b. 1945), with whom Hiro later collaborated on drawings in 2014–15. .... The artist's 2013 New York solo show, 'Pit & Log', marked a turning point in his practice. The exhibition engaged a figure from Japanese folklore, the *futakuchi-onna*, a woman with two mouths, one located at the back of her head beneath a tangle of hair. Hiro produced a wearable latex sculpture, *Two Mouths* (2013), depicting this woman of myth, as well as three pencil and acrylic drawings. The circular absences in *Untitled (Pinnacle)*, a 2017 drawing on cut and folded paper acquired by the Museum of Modern Art, New York, and *Untitled (Pose)*, from the artist's 2016 New York exhibition 'Big Question', trace their form back to these earlier drawings. They also invite consideration of playwright Antonin Artaud's notion of 'a body without organs', a provocation investigated by radical philosopher Gilles Deleuze. ...... The artist has credited the birth of his son in the early 2010s as prompting a more determined engagement with drawing. Working from his garage-studio late at night, Hiro would produce fifteen to twenty drawings per day. He continues to be compelled by the idea of figuring his body in his drawings, which vary from abstracted action events to confident figural statements, all rendered in a scale approximating the artist's height. His suite of twelve drawings shown in 'Big Question' included, at bottom right, a seated orange figure rendered in graphite and acrylic. The sinuous figure in *Untitled (Reaching)* recalls the gambolling forms of Henri Matisse's (1869–1954) painting *The Dance* (1910), a not unlikely reference given Hiro's appreciation for art-historical sources such as the enigmatic figurative watercolours of William Blake (1757–1827) and translucent female nudes by Auguste Rodin (1840–1917). .... Sean O'Toole

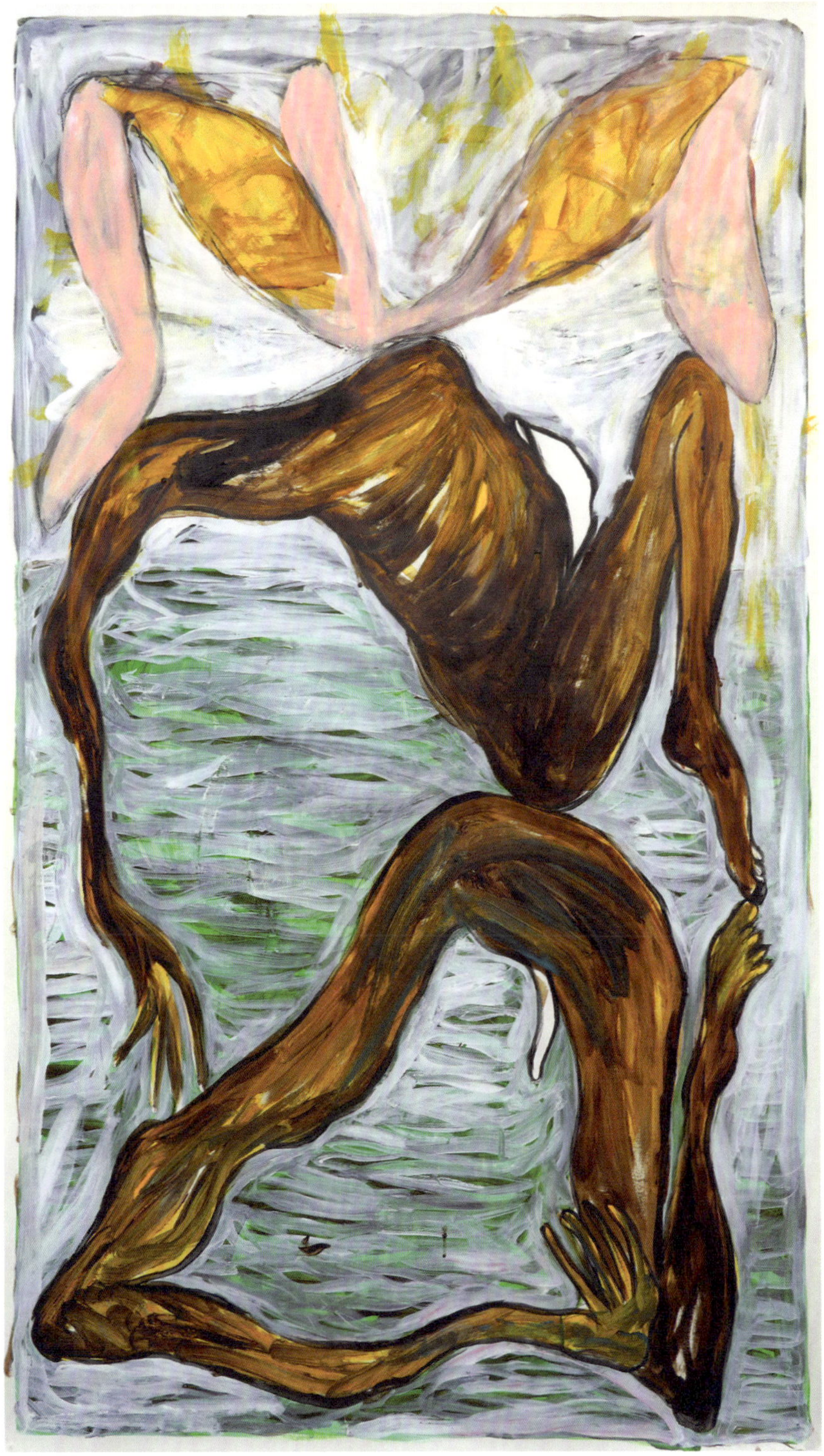

1.

Born 1972, Osaka, Japan. Lives and works in Los Angeles.

1. *Untitled*, 2014, acrylic, graphite and grease pencil on paper, 182.9 × 106.7 cm (72 × 42 in)
2. *Untitled (Pinnacle)*, 2017, acrylic, graphite and grease pencil on paper, 106.7 × 81.3 cm (42 × 32 in)

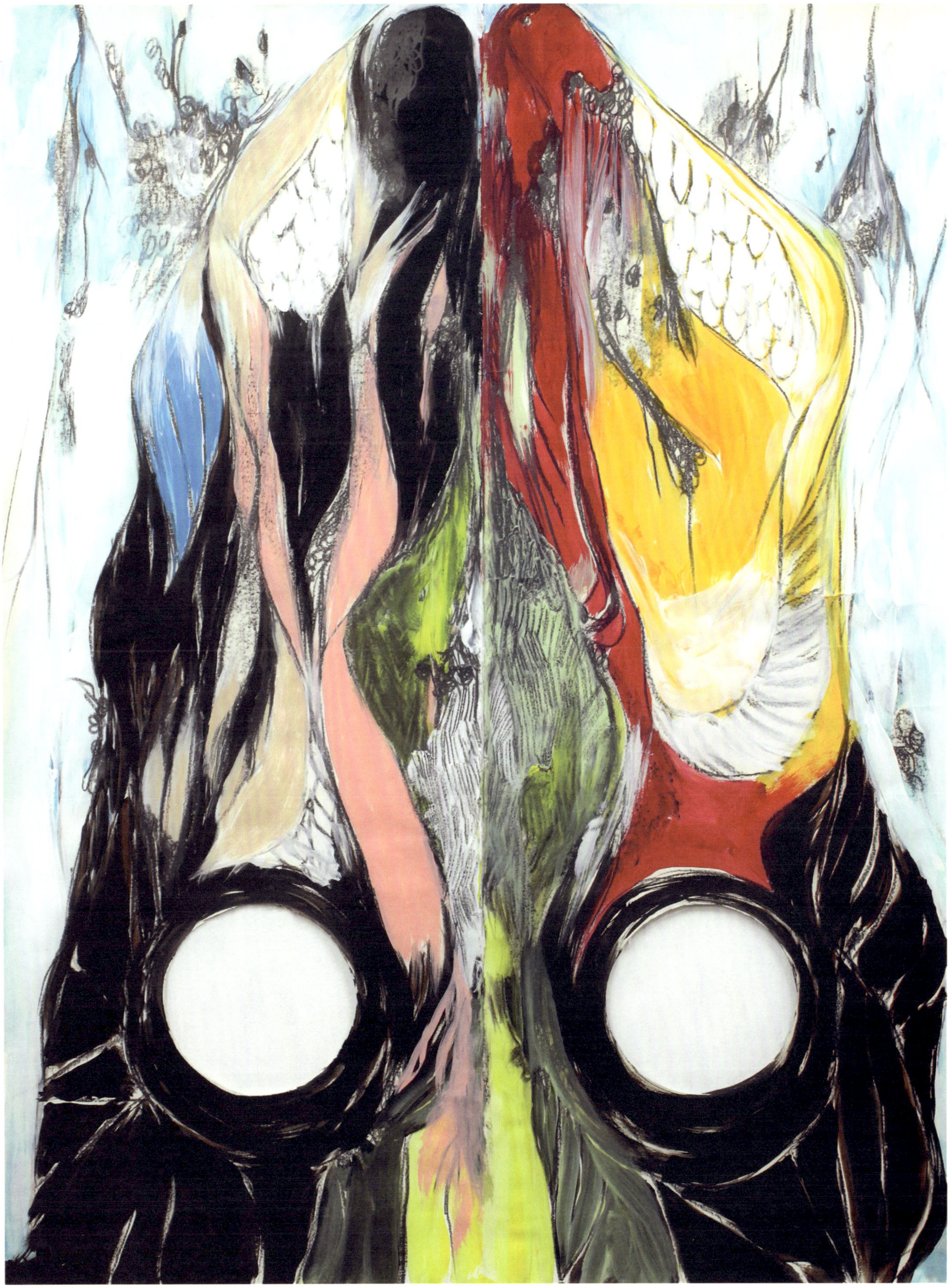

2.

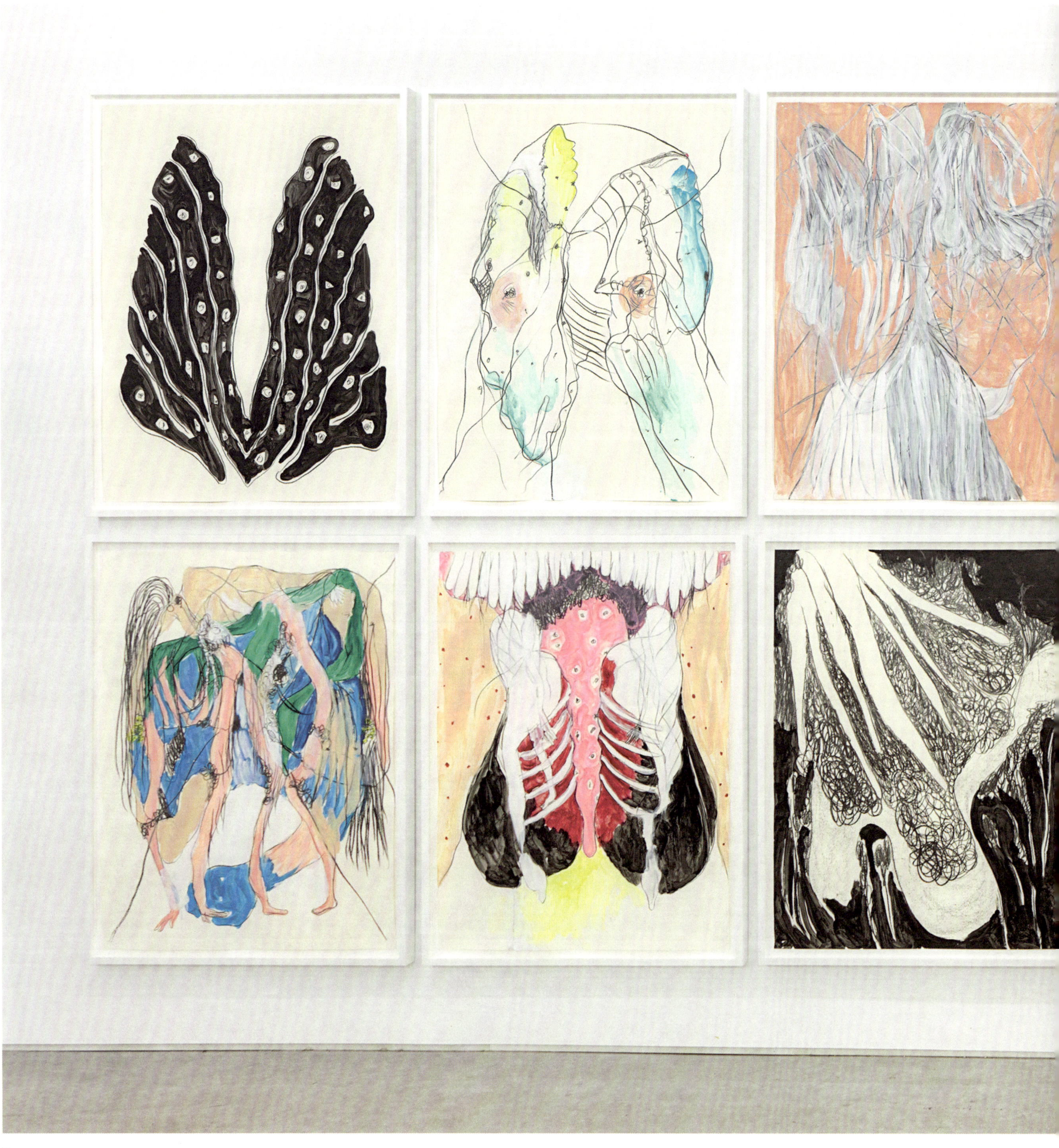

3.

3. Installation view, 'Big Question', Brennan & Griffin, New York, 2016

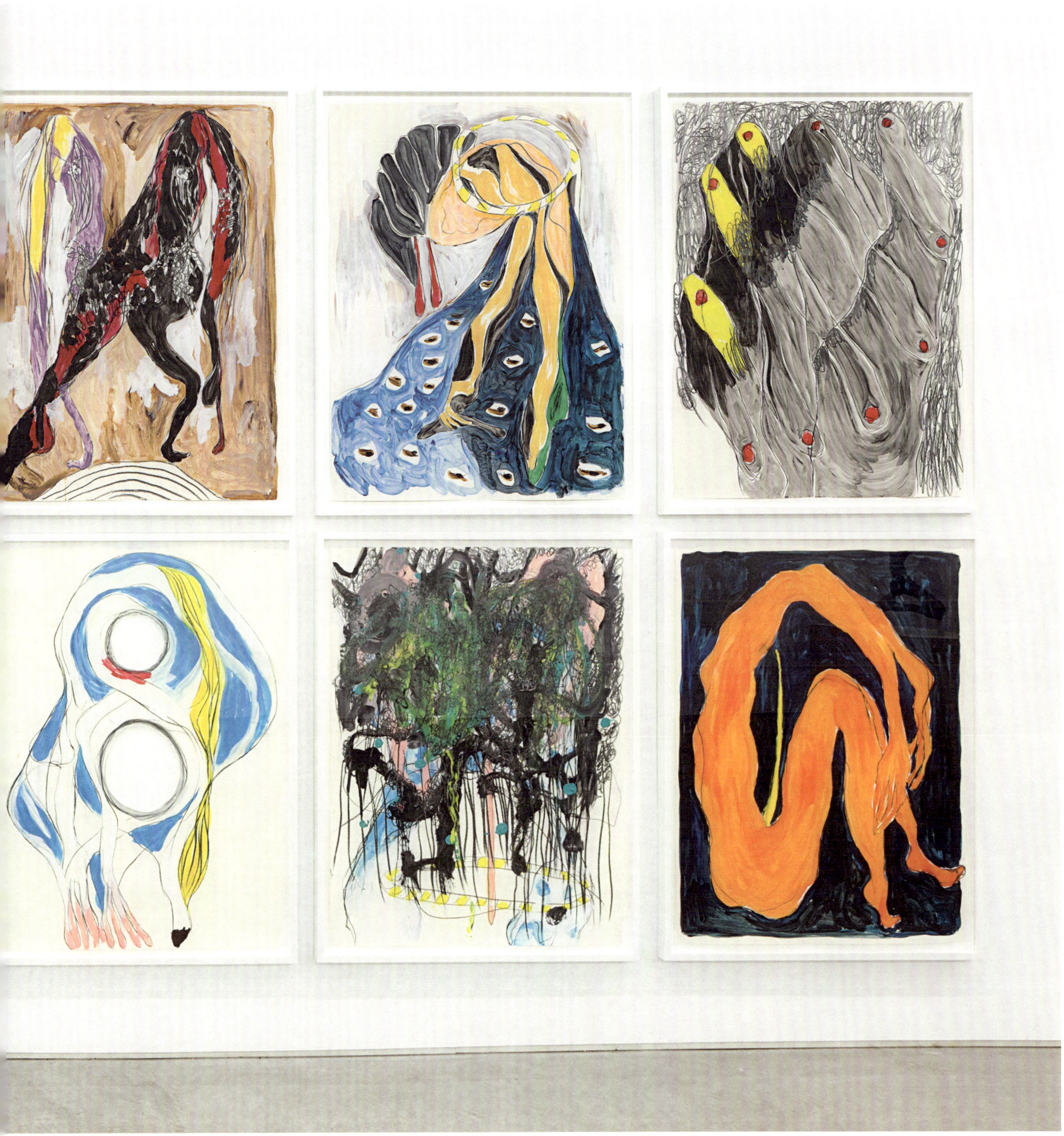

AHMET DOĞU İPEK....... Ahmet Doğu İpek's epic drawings combine mathematical precision with dystopian atmospherics. For *Construction Regime* (2014), part of the series 'Building Porn', he created a succession of coiling towers, painted in minute detail in ink and watercolour. Look once, and you may see rolls of metal mesh. Look again, and a ghostly city appears. At the top of the drawing, spikes rise into the blank white of the paper: a sign that more architectural levels could yet be constructed, perhaps, but also a warning....... *Construction Regime* may read like a nightmarish vision of global capitalism – an inhospitable city that threatens to grow in size until the entire planet is covered in steel skyscrapers – but it could just as easily be a phenomenon viewed through the lens of a microscope. An ambiguous relationship to scale is characteristic of İpek's work. For the drawing *Second Harvest VII* (2015), he tackles a near-impossible task: representing a twisted and knotted material, in appearance like a ball of fabric or rope, contained within a perfect circle. Placed in the middle of a white sheet of paper, it could equally represent something planetoid or cellular in size. The suggestion of infinite growth or reduction is reminiscent of mathematical forms such as the fractal – in which each part has the same structure as the whole – as well as traditional Islamic arts in which abstract geometric patterns are used to represent the religious sublime. .... Perhaps surprisingly, given his precise draughtsmanship, İpek describes his drawings as developing organically of their own accord. 'After a certain stage, the picture decides itself how to progress,' he said in a 2015 interview with Box In A Box Idea. Once the initial pattern is determined, the drawing begins to unfold across the paper like a 'game'. Games, puzzles and architectural systems are key to İpek's methods, placing him in a tradition of graphic art that includes the surreal tessellation of M.C. Escher (1898–1972), the nightmarish science-fictions of H.R. Geiger (1940–2014) and open-ended video game series such as SimCity, where players are invited to construct their own metropoles....... Despite the extraordinary range of possibilities İpek's works suggest, he typically limits himself to using paper, watercolour and pencil and restricts himself to the use of greyscale tones. His monochrome palette gives his drawings an immersive and foreboding atmosphere, redolent of the claustrophobia and anxiety typical of dystopian fiction, and the gloomy, nocturnal landscapes of crime noir graphic novels and films. Rooted in carefully planned mathematical logic, İpek's drawings grow to propose the beginnings of many worlds and many stories.
.... Rosanna Mclaughlin

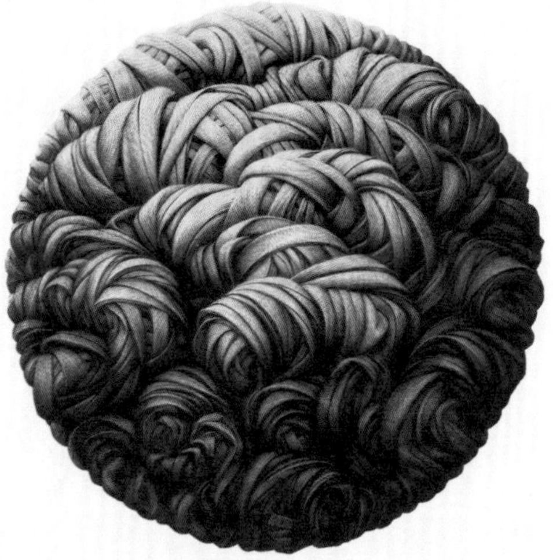

1.

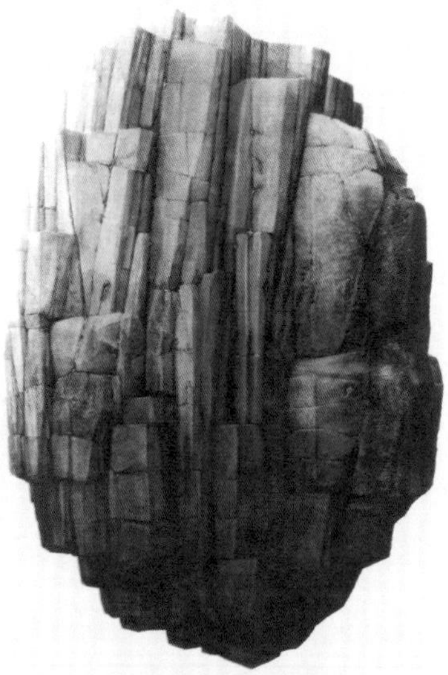

2.

Born 1983, Adıyaman, Turkey. Lives and works in Istanbul, Turkey.

1. *Second Harvest VII*, 2015, pencil on paper, 130 × 100 cm (51 ⅛ × 39 ⅜ in)
2. *Repair III*, 2017, watercolour and gold on paper, 145 × 110 cm (57 × 43 ⅜ in)
3. *Construction Regime*, 2014, watercolour on paper, 120 × 110 cm (47 ¼ × 43 ⅜ in)

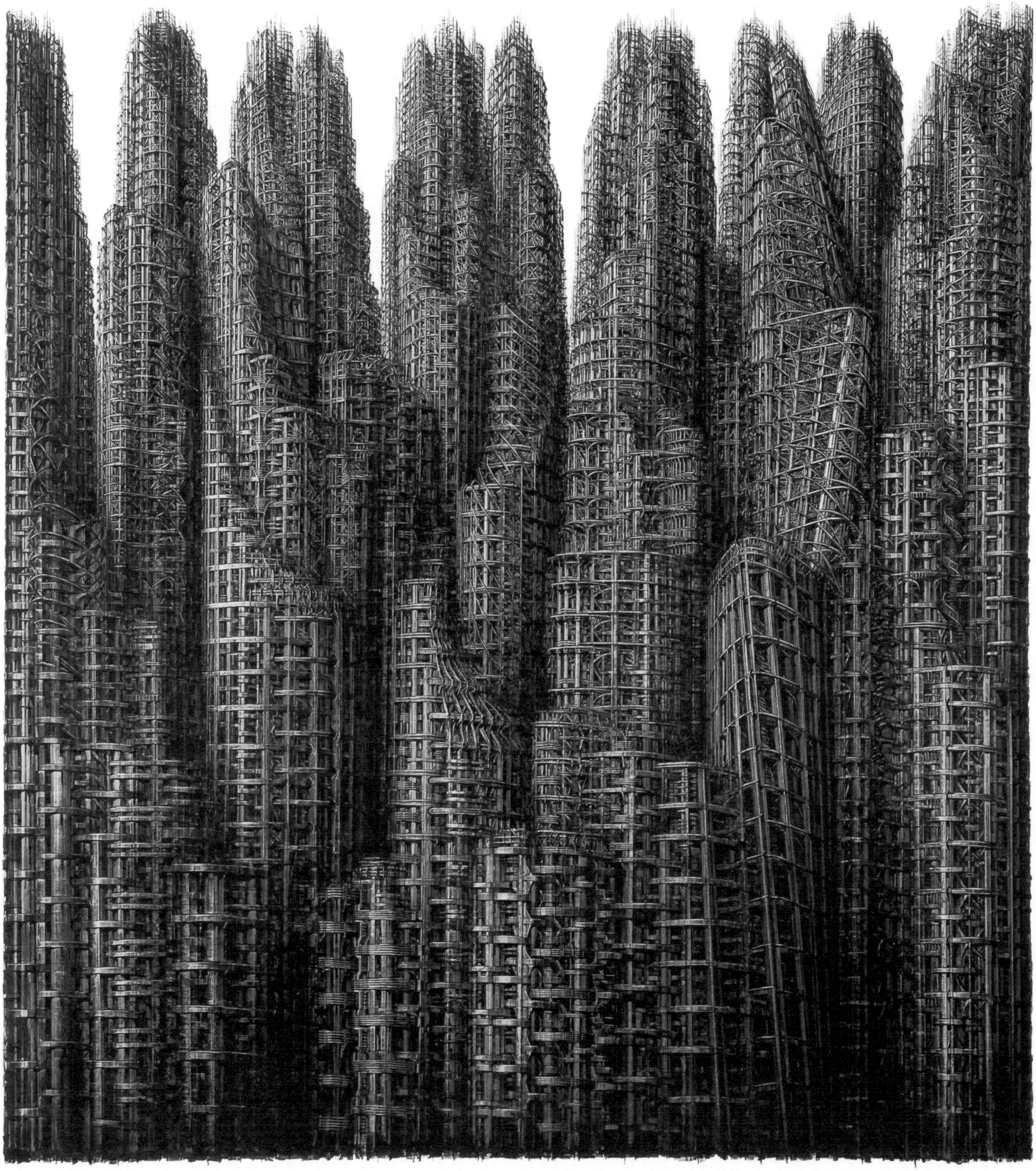

3.

MARIE JACOTEY .... Marie Jacotey turns each of us into voyeurs. Her drawings are like a window into the intimate lives of others – one that reveals only selected fragments as opposed to the whole. *À dieu* (2018), a work in dry pastel on Japanese paper, could be a close-up still from a film: the scene severs the head of a woman at the neck, while decapitating the man altogether, his truncated torso filling the frame. Hands fondling zipper, this is seemingly a moment of coolness in the aftermath of... what exactly? Would we say passion, or abuse, or something else altogether? Turning away from one another, the female's eyes are nearly closed. Jacotey keeps us guessing about what has come to pass. A muted palette of mottled peaches and greys colour the man's skin, echoed on the walls behind. Emphasizing the surface plane, there is an intensity to this uneasy ambiguity. In the top right-hand corner the eponymous words 'À dieu' are repeated over and over, perhaps what the figures whisper to one another. .... It is this compressed perspective, this zooming in, the captioned snippets of words that render Jacotey's compositions more akin to the self-selected (collaged) reveals of an Instagram feed. As she said in a 2016 video directed by Olivia Beasley, 'I use social media as a reference in my work... I think it's interesting and intriguing to see how everyone is storytelling their own life.' So it is human relationships that are at the heart of her drawings: their difficulties and entanglements; dark eroticism and sensuality. Indeed, her series 'Morning Defeats' (2017), exhibited at Hannah Barry Gallery in London, explored what remains hidden in relationships; the sadness that may simmer under the surface. A giant curtain with comic-book-style drawings was pulled across the centre of the exhibition, perhaps symbolic of what might be revealed when the curtains are drawn. .... Graduating from an MA in Printmaking at London's Royal College of Art in 2013, Jacotey originally used coloured pencils, wax crayons and felt-tip pens because of their immediacy, introducing the medium of dry pastel into her repertoire later, as well as paintings on plaster and digital prints on velvet. In a 2020 interview with *Elephant Magazine* she described how, 'Drawing is my instinctively chosen tool... in many ways, I find it very comparable to writing, to taking notes.' Notes are snippets, they hint at the whole. Such is Jacotey's world: one that is partially revealed, partially veiled. As with *The gold room* (2018) – a work nearing a traditional still life with ornate vase and white rag; it is, in fact, the Polaroid image (window or mirror?) revealing lovers entwined on an office chair, legs spread, that piques our interest. Life is sometimes dignified, sometime messy; the trick is knowing which moments to reveal, and when. .... Louisa Elderton

1.
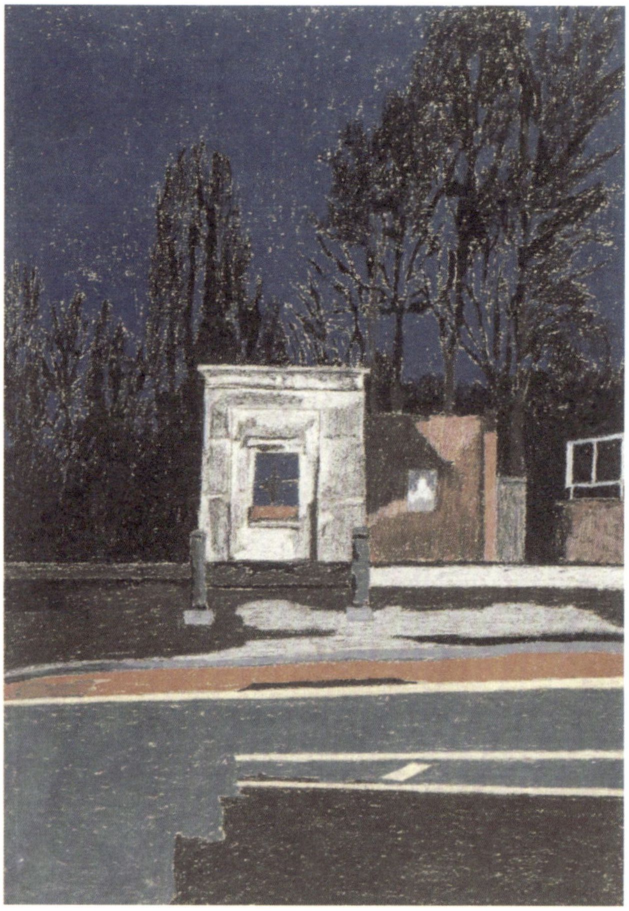

2.
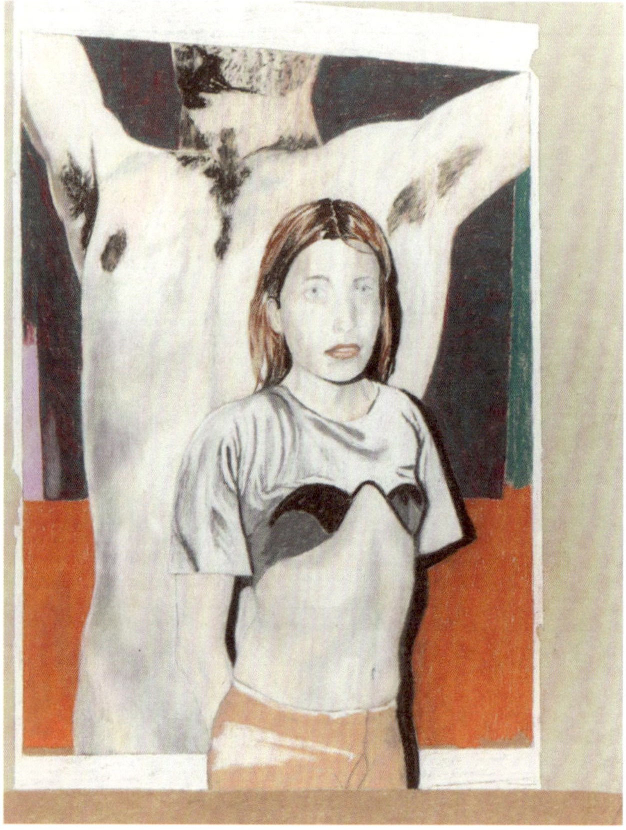

Born 1988, Paris. Lives and works in Athens and London.

1. *Abney cemetery at night*, 2018, dry pastel on cardboard, 51 × 36 cm (20 ⅛ × 14 ¼ in)
2. *La cosa*, 2018, dry pastel on Japanese paper, 69 × 54 cm (27 ⅛ × 21 ¼ in)

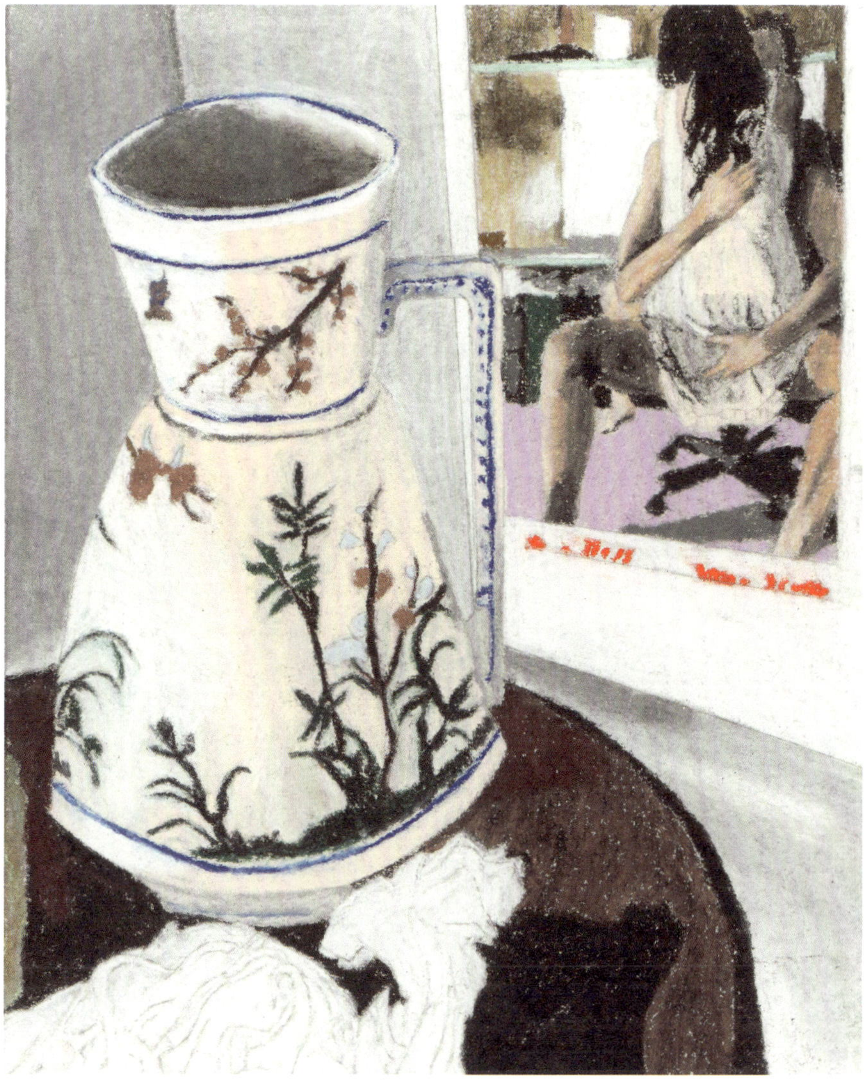

3.

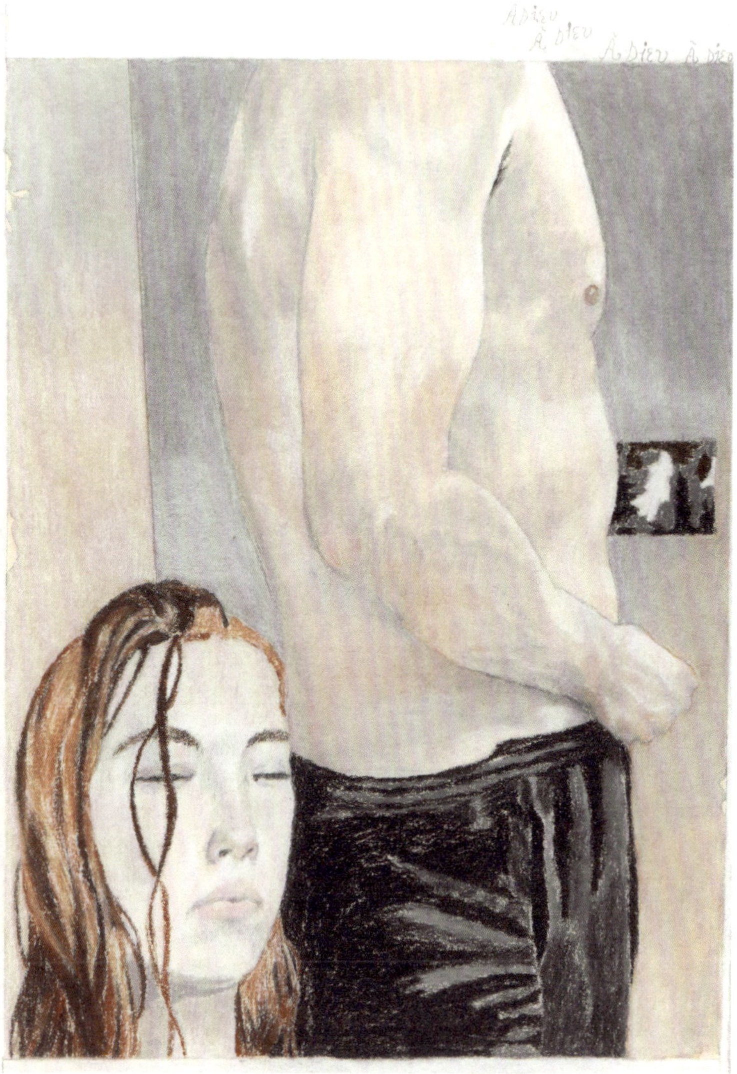

4.

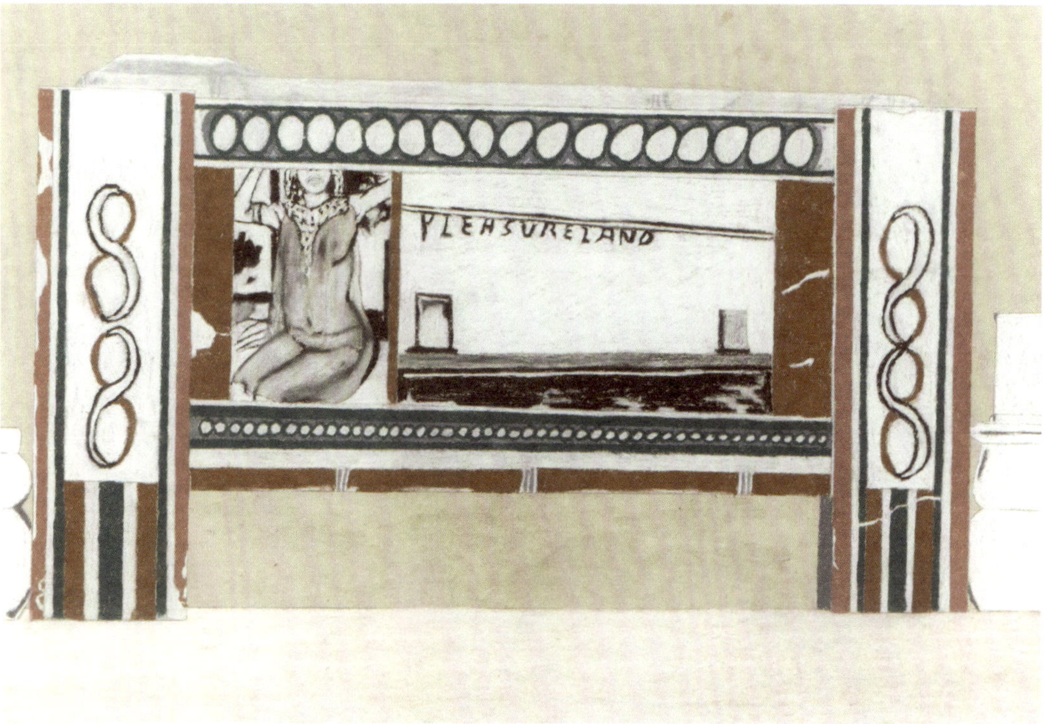

5.

3. *The gold room*, 2018, dry pastel on Japanese paper, 27 × 22 cm (10 ⅝ × 8 ⅝ in)
4. *À dieu*, 2018, dry pastel on Japanese paper, 46.5 × 34 cm (18 ¼ × 13 ⅜ in)
5. *Sarcophagus bed*, 2018, dry pastel on Japanese paper, 46 × 69 cm (18 ⅛ × 27 ⅛ in)

CLAUDETTE JOHNSON .... To encounter Claudette Johnson's work is to contemplate what it means to stand in direct relationship to another human being – albeit one that is drawn and painted but in many ways no less real than the sitter who spent time with the artist having their body and personality rendered. Johnson's pictures are deliberately large-scale and bold; she fills each work with her subjects so that they touch, or come close to touching, the edges of the ground, as if straining against a type of confinement. This is wonderfully illustrated by *Reclining Figure* (2017) where the figure of a large woman lies horizontally, her gaze turned in towards herself, her eyes half closed: sleepy, yet thoughtful. Johnson's focus is primarily the sitter's face and arms, which are detailed in pastel and constructed through a complex gradient of different marks, speaking to the pressure applied and the shape made by the artist's hand as she converses with her muse. The effect is incredibly intimate, not least because the clothed body of the figure is only a simple pencil outline held in by block colours of red and blue. This forces our eyes repeatedly back to her face; again and again we are made to encounter her and join her in deep thought. .... None of Johnson's sitters are named, nor does she give many clues to their lives. Whereas in traditional portraits, a sitter might have commissioned a work to emphasize a particular characteristic they wanted to communicate, Johnson refutes this idea almost entirely. Yet the question of identity in portraiture remains deeply rooted in her work and, indeed, her wider practice. In a 2019 interview with the *Financial Times* she explained: 'They are portraits because they are women I know. They are not portraits because they explore aspects of race and sexuality that stand outside of this tradition.' This statement acts as an assertion of equivalence, a demand or rather an axiomatic fact – that, as an artist who draws and paints portraits, she stands as an equal to all those (mostly white men) who have thus far been admitted into the artistic canon because, very simply, of her body of work. In *Untitled (Yellow Blocks)* (2019) we find the embodiment of this idea. An almost sculptural and evocative portrait rendered in ochre and bounded by yellow squares, the figure is brought to life with the simplest of touches, smudges and lines of pastel. Johnson's work lives the very idea of why we produce portraits: to encounter and discover each other and, at the same time, ourselves.
.... James Smith

1.
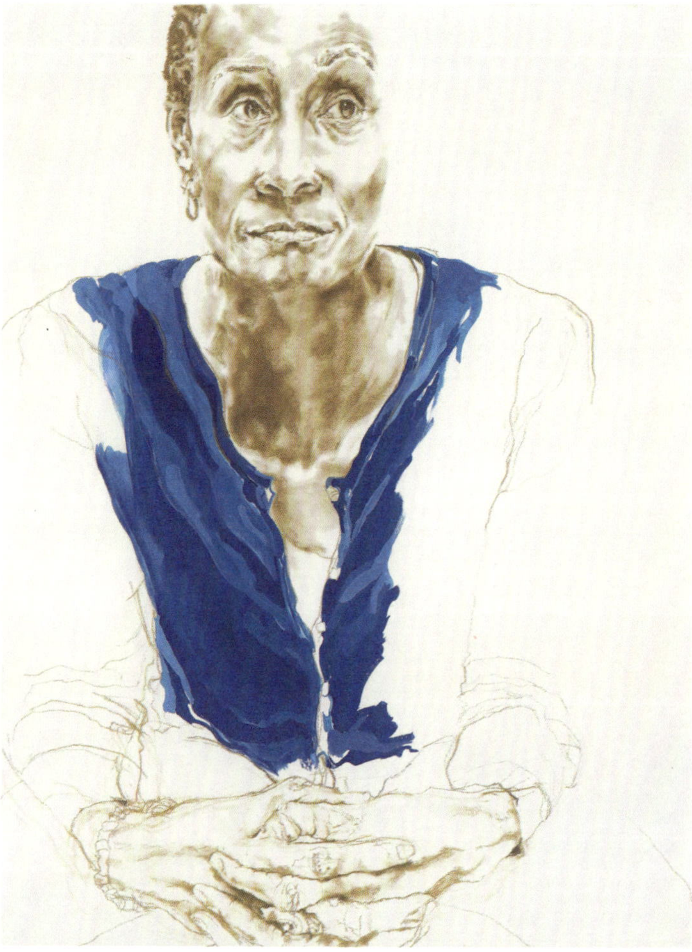

2.
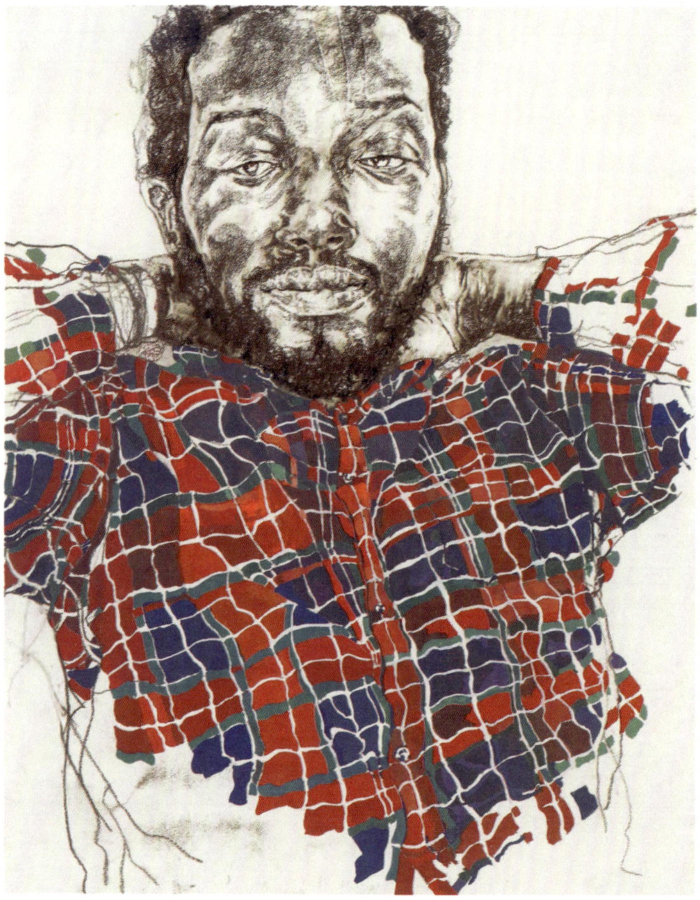

Born 1959, Manchester, UK. Lives and works in London.

1. *Seated Figure II*, 2017, gouache and pastel on paper, 161 × 124 cm (63 ⅜ × 48 ⅞ in)
2. *Figure with Raised Arms*, 2017, gouache and pastel on paper, 163 × 132 cm (64 ⅛ × 52 in)

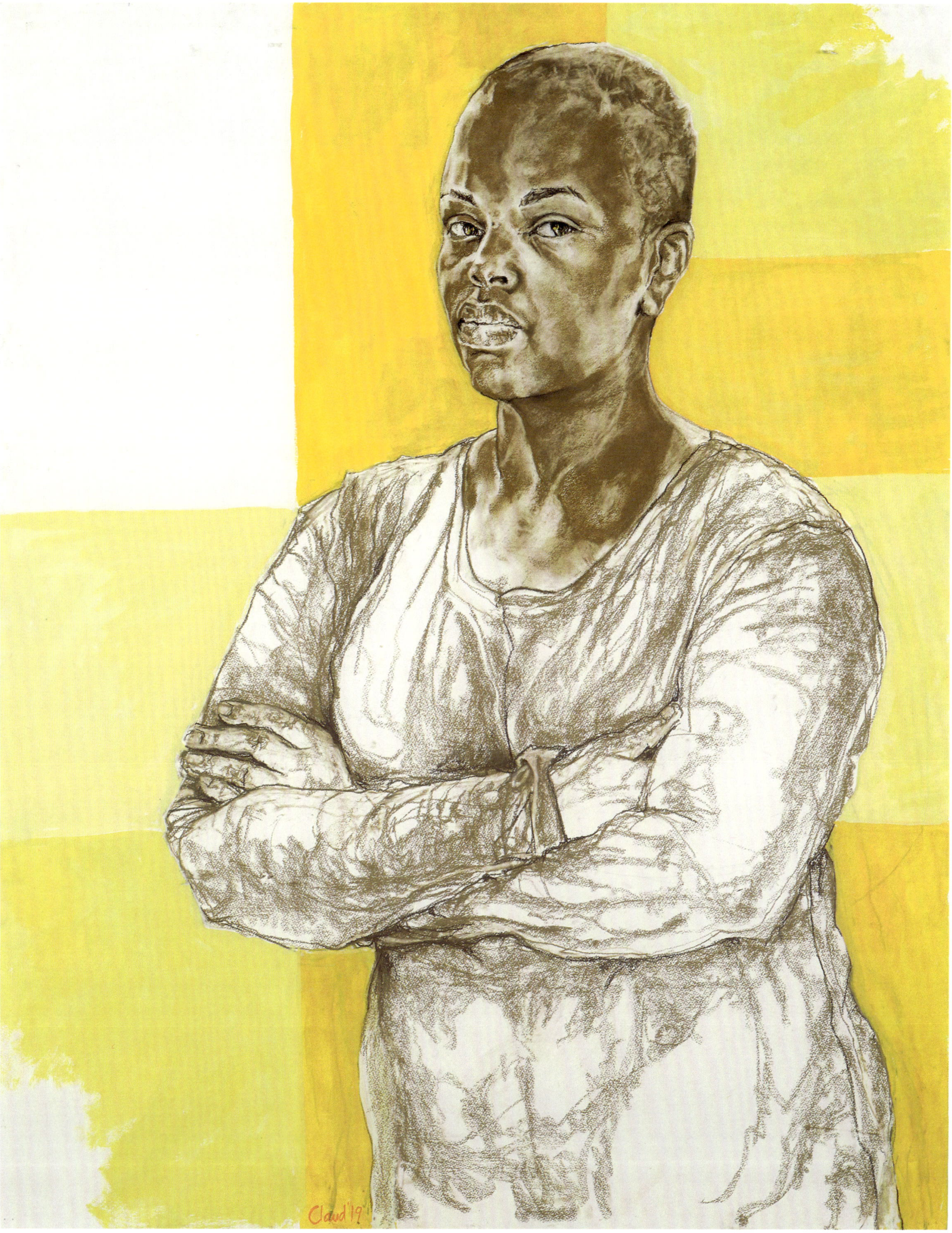

3.

3. *Untitled (Yellow Blocks)*, 2019, gouache and pastel on paper, 152.4 × 121.9 cm (60 × 48 in)

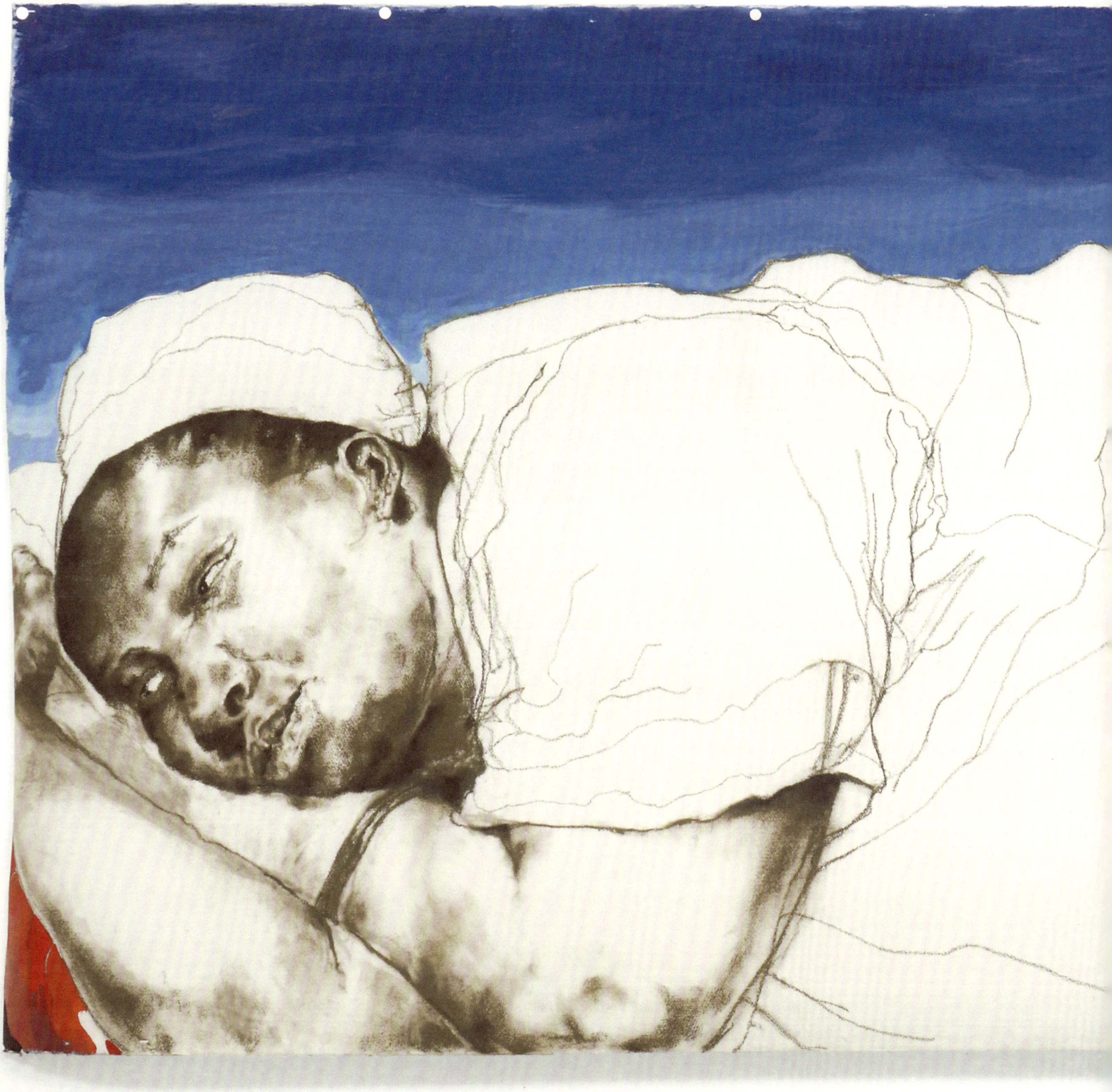

4.

4. *Reclining Figure*, 2017, gouache and pastel on paper, 113 × 257 cm (44 ½ × 101 ⅛ in)

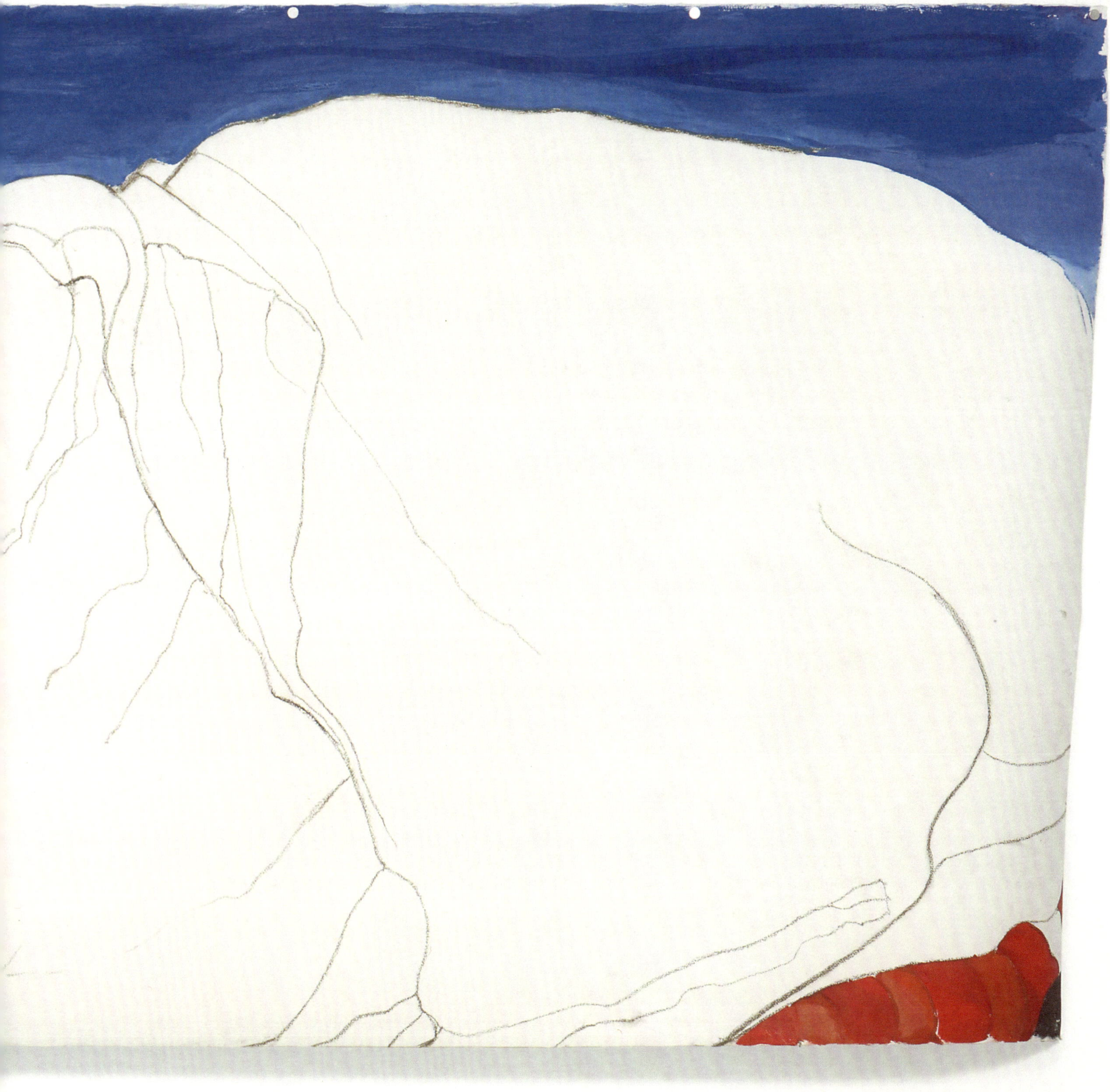

RASHID JOHNSON .... Rashid Johnson's multivalent practice originated in conceptual photography but has since expanded to include painting, drawing, installation and film. He came to prominence as the youngest artist in Thelma Golden's influential 'Freestyle' exhibition at Harlem's Studio Museum in 2001, as part of the generation that would, for a time, be called 'post-black' art. His wall-based mixed-media sculptures include materials from Black cultural identity and intellectual life, like shea butter and black soap – made from the ashes of plants like plantains, cocoa pods and palm leaves – both of which unspool the relationship between being African and African American. They are joined with found books and records alongside other materials like wood, wax, live palms and other tropical plants, and several metals. .... Often, Johnson plays with racial stereotypes, as in his controversial 2001 series 'Chickenbones and Watermelon Seeds', in which he placed the titular bones and seeds, along with cotton seeds and black-eyed peas, on photographic paper to create ghostly images. Other bodies of work speak to the generalized tension – and statistical death sentence – of being Black in America, as with his 'Anxious Men' and 'Anxious Audiences' series of drawings begun in 2015 and 2016, respectively. These monumental works primarily involve black soap and wax smeared on ceramic tile, in an extension of the great American tradition of gestural abstraction. The use of tile pays homage to a storeyed Russian bathhouse in Chicago, which Johnson began frequenting in graduate school, even as it further invokes the monochromes and grids of American Minimalism and Conceptualism. Years later, he would pay further tribute by restaging Amiri Baraka's 1964 play *Dutchman* there, following a run at a New York bathhouse as part of Performa 13. .... The faces of Johnson's anxious men are scratched into the splattered black sludge using a subtractive *sgraffito* method. They are heavily stylized, almost like cartoon robots, with rectangular faces, big oval eyes, small suggestions of a nose and grimacing rectangular rictuses for a mouth. The two works entitled *Untitled Anxious Drawing* (2017, 2018) both reprise the same face and monochromatic palette, but transpose it on to black oil on white cotton rag paper. Sometimes they appear alone, as in the 2017 drawing, and at other times crammed into unbroken grids, with occasional red or yellow daubs about the mouth in the 2018 work. While Johnson has generally been more interested in individual experiences of negotiating race, culture and history, these works speak to the broader currents and collective unease of the United States today. En masse, the faces do not just worry but also witness together: police brutality, climate change and environmental racism, disproportionate access to healthcare and other resources, and an increasingly incendiary political climate.

.... Rahel Aima

1.

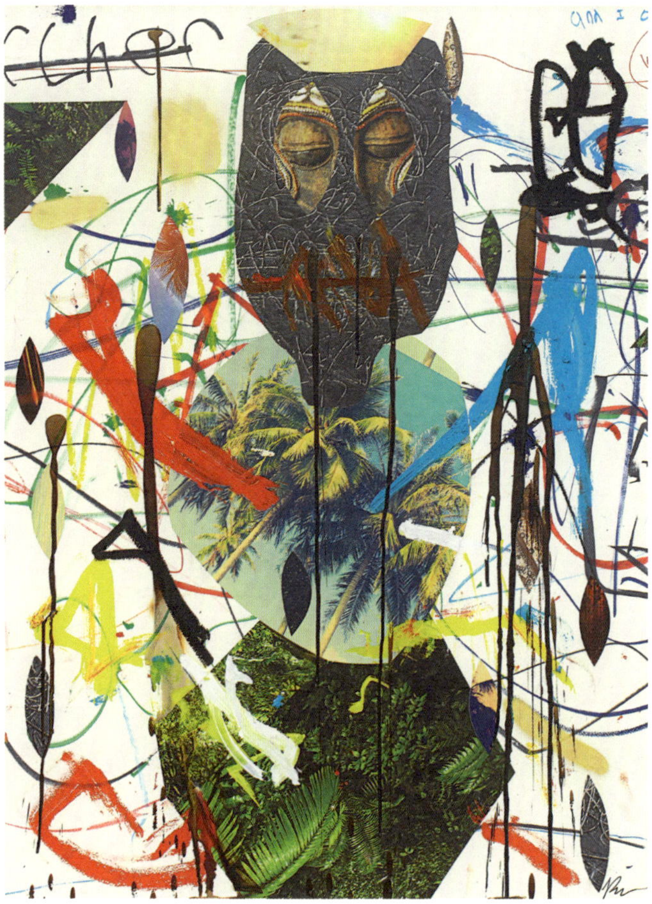

2.

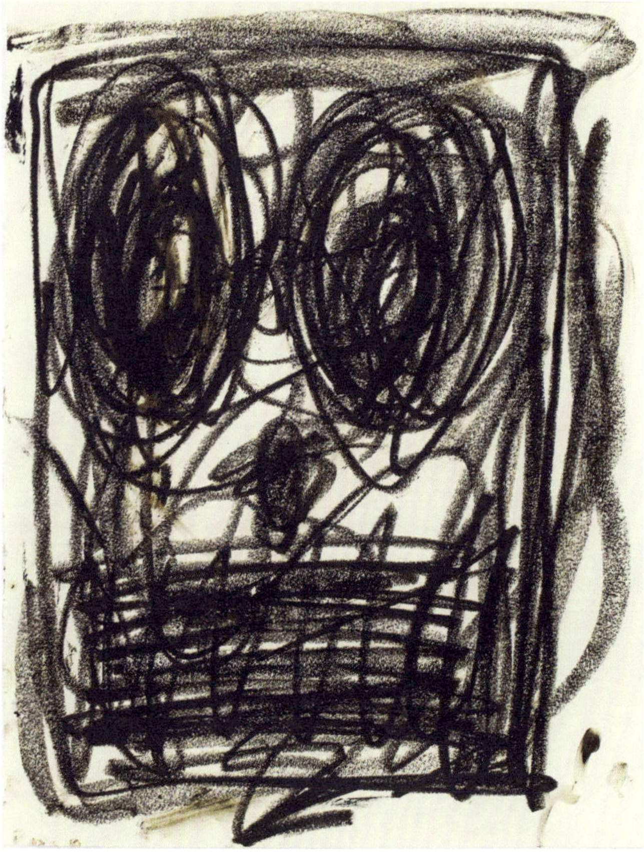

Born 1977, Chicago, IL. Lives and works in New York.

1. *Escape Men 'Bangers'*, 2019, vinyl, spray enamel, felt-tip pen and oil stick on cotton rag, 108.6 × 83.2 cm (42 ¾ × 32 ¾ in)
2. *Untitled Anxious Drawing*, 2017, oil on cotton rag, 82.8 × 63.5 cm (32 ½ × 25 in)
3. *Untitled Anxious Drawing*, 2018, oil on cotton rag, 168.4 × 230.4 cm (66 ⅜ × 90 ¾ in)

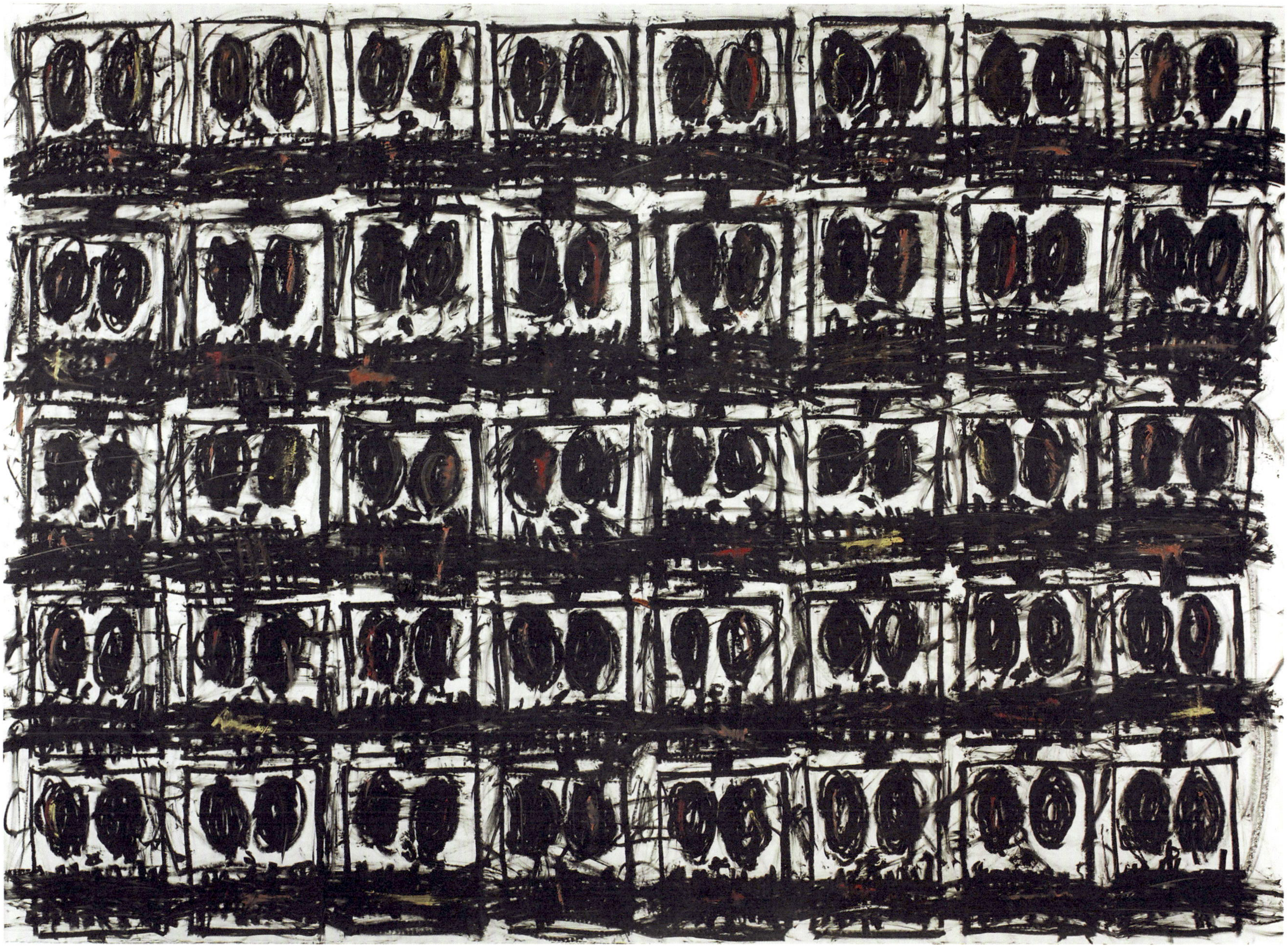

3.

JASMINE NILANI JOSEPH....... The Sri Lankan civil war, a ruinous ethnic conflict between majority Sinhalese Buddhists and minority Tamils that ended in 2009, remains fixed in the cultural imaginary of this South Asian island nation. Contemporary novelists and artists continue to dwell on this defining postcolonial trauma, which started in 1983, a decade after independence. Jasmine Nilani Joseph's meticulous architectural renderings of derelict homes and boundary markers offer a measure of the physical ruins and psychic ravages of this war. The artist's pen drawings are informed by her first-hand experience of the conflict. .... Born in Jaffna, a northern citadel of Tamil resistance, the artist and her family were expelled from their coastal village in 1995 by Sinhalese military establishing a military cordon, and fled to Vavuniya, a regional city that housed many internally displaced Sri Lankans. 'There, I was surrounded by several kinds of fences,' recounted Joseph in an essay accompanying a 2017 exhibition of six drawings from her 'Fence' series (2016–18). 'Every day I was kept waiting for many hours with my family, in front of a police station fence, for the renewal of our temporary residential pass to live in Vavuniya.' She also observed how, once settled in encampments, refugees used roofing material to build small barriers to protect their gardens and create privacy around wells for bathing. These fence-making activities continued when displaced families were resettled in government-housing schemes. .... Joseph studied art in Jaffna. Returning to her homeland, she was struck by the aggressive barriers erected by the Sinhalese military. Military land seizures during and after the civil war were commonplace, and often resulted in domestic fences being removed and boundaries erased. Following the wholesale return of land, displaced settlers have tried to re-inscribe old boundaries, typically using barbed wire and palmyra leaves. Boundary disputes, especially among Tamils, endure. Joseph's drawings of fences key into a larger body of work descriptive of Sri Lanka's post-conflict landscapes. Her output includes a suite of thirty drawings describing Jaffna's many abandoned homes, works characterized by their cool objectivity, sweeping horizontality and the artist's method of 'floating' her architectural descriptions on paper. .... While informed by Sri Lanka's recent conflicts, Joseph's drawings also offer a *longue-durée* sense of Sri Lankan political and cultural history. In 1707 Dutch colonizers codified traditional Tamil law to facilitate the administration of the Jaffna peninsula, inaugurating a long history of boundary disputes among neighbours and relatives. Her unpeopled landscapes also highlight the status of women in Sri Lanka's patriarchal society. The Tamil word *veli* refers to a fence but is also traditionally associated with the propriety and boundaries observed by respectable woman.
.... Sean O'Toole

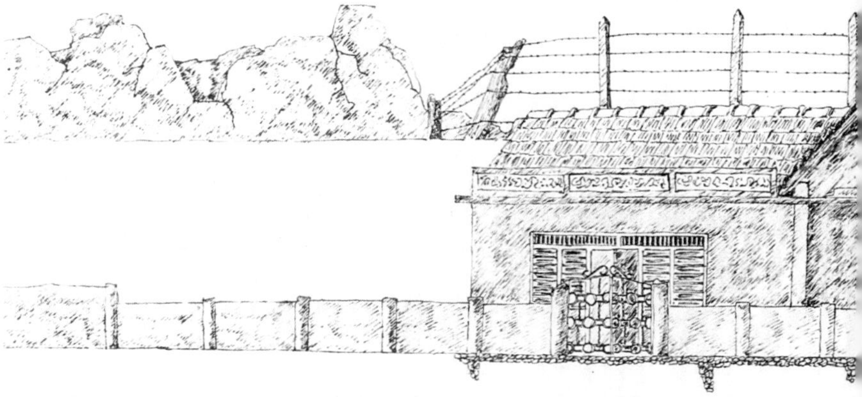

1.

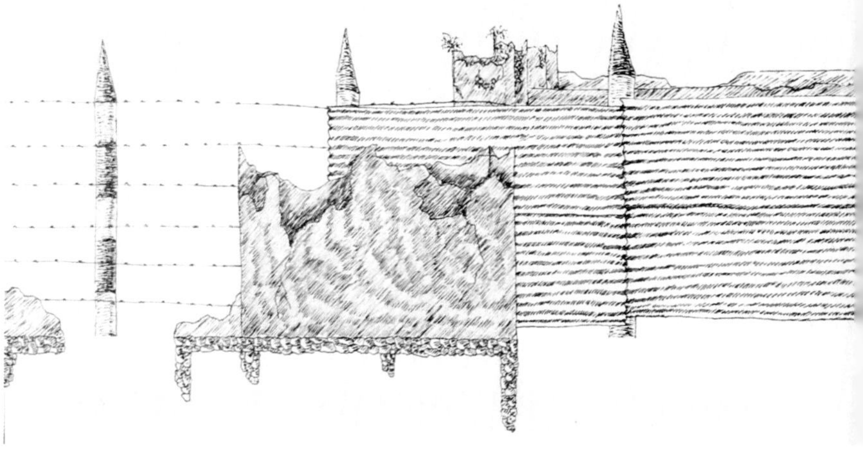

2.

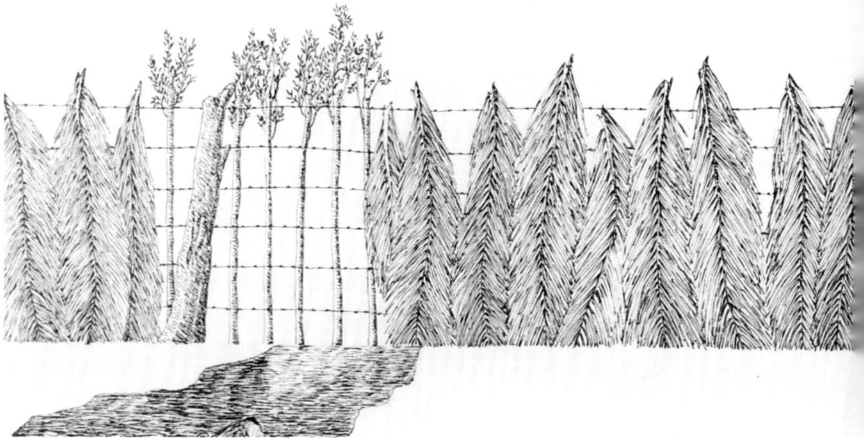

3.

Born 1990, Jaffna, Sri Lanka. Lives and works in Jaffna.

1. *Address of Residence I*, 2018, pen on paper, 14.5 × 76 cm (5 ¾ × 30 in)
2. *Fence VII*, 2018, pen on paper, 14.5 × 76 cm (5 ¾ × 30 in)
3. *Fence VIII*, 2018, pen on paper, 14.5 × 76 cm (5 ¾ × 30 in)

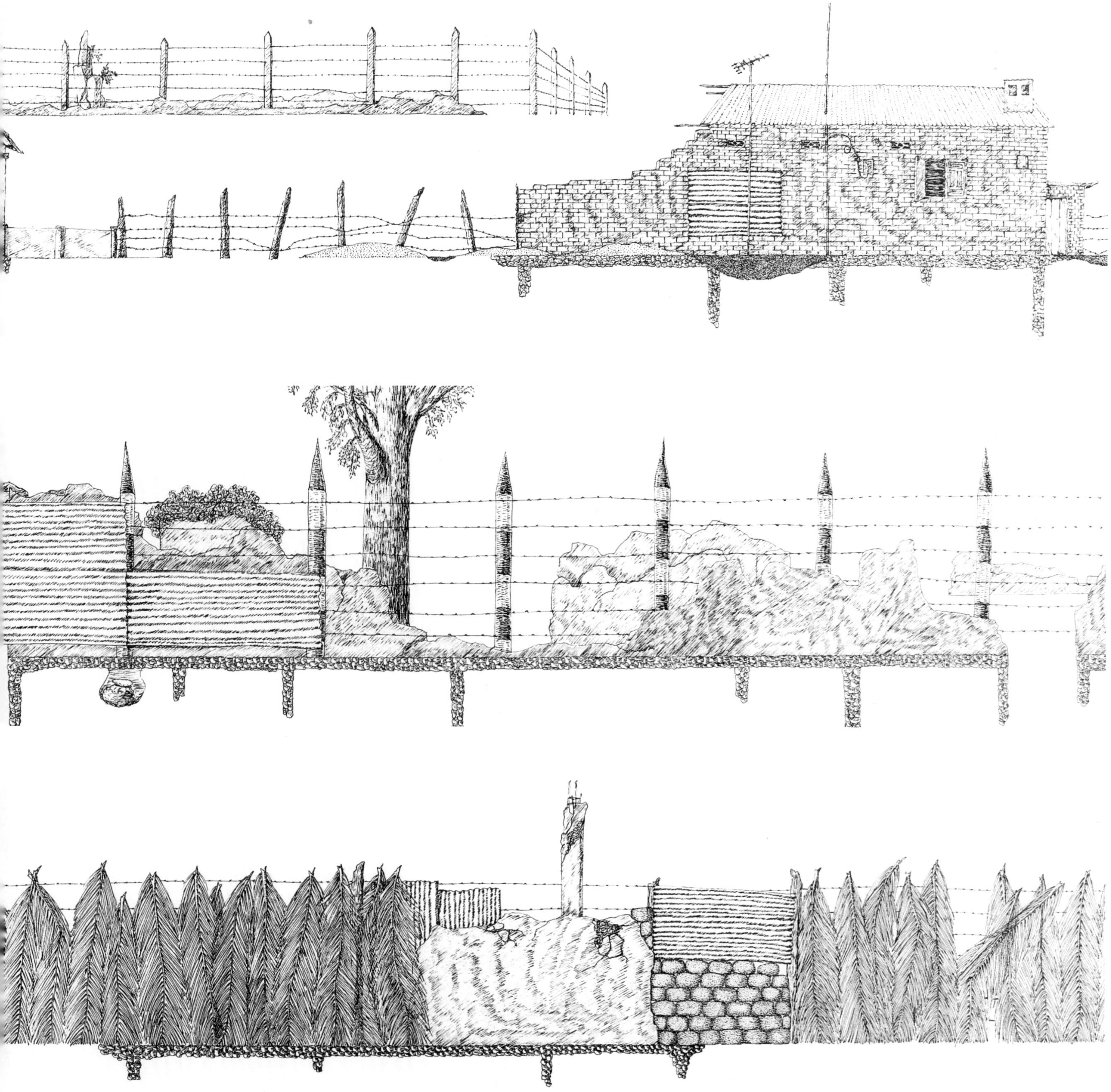

A N T O N K A N N E M E Y E R....... In 1995, a year after
South Africa's transition to non-racial democracy, Anton
Kannemeyer published an autobiographical story in the fifth
issue of *Bitterkomix*, an ongoing comic book he co-founded
with Conrad Botes (p.50) three years earlier. Titled 'Boetie'
('Sonny') and credited to Joe Dog, Kannemeyer's occasional
pen name, the cartoon strip opened with two panels depicting
the artist – a frequent character in his work – bemoaning his
inability to conjure fantasies in his drawings. Rendered in the
spry clear-line style of Tintin creator, Georges 'Hergé' Remi
(1907–83), the ensuing tale recounted the sexual abuse meted
out by the artist's father, J.C. Kannemeyer, a renowned
Afrikaans literary scholar. The story was an important template
for the artist, suggesting a way to communicate difficult and
traumatic subject matter plainly........ Kannemeyer is not the
first artist to subvert Tintin for seditious ends, but the consis-
tency of his return to the racist tropes visualized in *Tintin in
the Congo* (1931) highlight the importance of identity and its
associated politics in his *détournements*. Some critics, however, have labelled Kannemeyer racist for reiterating debased
tropes of Blackness in his work. His many realistic portrayals
of Black political leaders, among them Nelson Mandela and
Barack Obama, rebut this criticism. A 2014 drawing of writer
Chimamanda Ngozi Adichie that quotes her 2009 TED Talk on
race and stereotyping forms part of a large body of drawings
depicting figures of interest whose opinions either chime
with his own – philosopher Slavoj Žižek, for example – or merit
opprobrium........ Hergé aside, Kannemeyer has credited
comics artists Jacques Tardi (b. 1946), Chantal Montellier (b.
1947) and Charles Burns (b. 1955) as influences. Art Spiegelman
and Françoise Mouly's *RAW* (1980–91) informed *Bitterkomix*'s
amalgam of muckraking and literary ambition, while *RAW*
contributor Gary Panter's (b. 1950) sketchbooks offered a model
of process unbridled from narrative or decorum. Kannemeyer's
sketchbooks, many of which have been exhibited in the past,
track the evolution of his style from jagged and angry, to
precise, analytic and elegiac. Kannemeyer's anger – at his
father, and the sham values his vanquished class once represented – hasn't entirely dissipated and serves as the fulcrum
for much of his practice. His output includes mocking satires
of social manners. Initially aimed at religious conservatives,
works like *Compelling Backstory* (2019) form part of a growing
corpus skewering the mendacity and equivocation of liberals.
His ongoing 'Alphabet of Democracy' series is an epigrammatic
archive of post-apartheid follies. Rendered in diverse styles,
the series is linked by Kannemeyer's fidelity to statement or
event. Started in 2005, the earliest works in this series included
a plaintive study of a dog lying next to a murdered farmer
covered with a blue blanket (*J is for Jack Russell*). The series is
now stocked with dancing ministers, crony capitalists, aspirant
presidents and repentant sports cheats.
.... Sean O'Toole

Born 1967, Cape Town. Lives and works in Cape Town.

1.

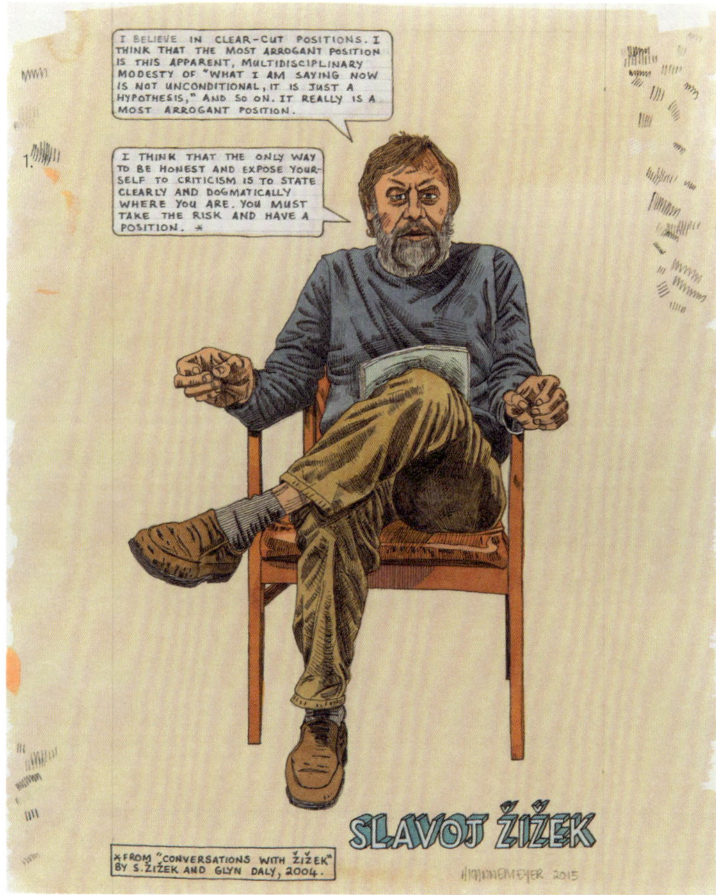

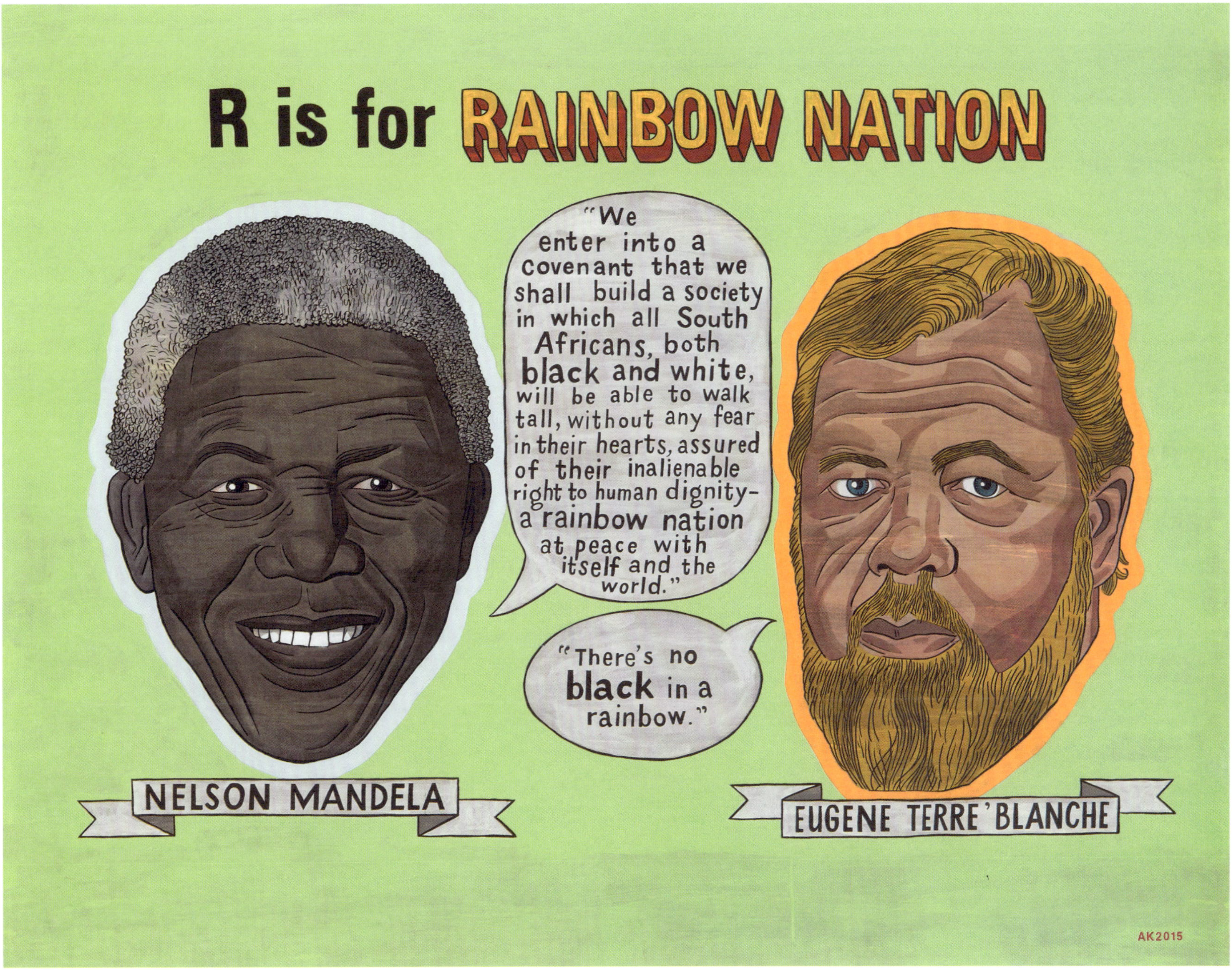
R is for RAINBOW NATION
"We enter into a covenant that we shall build a society in which all South Africans, both black and white, will be able to walk tall, without any fear in their hearts, assured of their inalienable right to human dignity- a rainbow nation at peace with itself and the world."
"There's no black in a rainbow."
NELSON MANDELA
EUGENE TERRE'BLANCHE
AK2015

3.

1. *Compelling Backstory*, 2019, acrylic on paper, 210 × 150 cm (82 ⅝ × 59 in)
2. *Zizek*, 2015, black ink and acrylic on paper, 29.7 × 21 cm (11 ⅝ × 8 ¼ in)
3. *R is for Rainbow Nation* from the series 'Alphabet of Democracy', 2015, black ink and acrylic on paper, 150 × 215 cm (59 × 84 ⅝ in)

NICK KENNEDY .... Analogous to a Zen thought experiment, Nick Kennedy's work – and wider practice – uses an altered notion of drawing to explore two seemingly incompatible dichotomies: the subatomic and the infinite. Whereas traditionally the artist's presence would be communicated by the transformative touch of the pencil or brush on a surface, Kennedy seeks to delete the hand of the artist altogether, replacing it with a number of intricate devices that serve to produce the work in his stead so that it becomes cyclically auto-generated. This is beautifully illustrated in *Timecasting* (2013), an installation of eighty-one delicately balanced drawing mechanisms. Laid out on the floor in a nine by nine grid, each one has its own generative capacity. A central mechanism is built around a quartz clock movement; built on to this are two appendage-like arms, on to which the artist has attached two sets of protuberant, leg-like pieces of graphite (no different from an ordinary pencil drawing set). As they turn on their axis, they give a feather-light touch to the paper below, forming, in most cases, and over a period of time, a densely packed and finely woven piece of drawn circular tracery. In theory, as each machine is identical, each drawing should be the same. However, each one is totally and distinctly unique, illuminating Kennedy's interest in the forces of chaos and order. .... These interests are found and replicated elsewhere in Kennedy's practice. It is almost as if he uses drawing in a scientific sense, as a way of questioning theories about his chosen material, and to stretch and expand its utility, thereby seeking a deeper substance. In *Truthplotter II* (2019) we are presented with another device, this time in the context of a wall drawing. This work also has a dynamic motor at its core that, once set up and primed by the artist, precisely renders a fine line drawing that is almost incised into the wall as it repetitively tracks its previous mark. In this instance the machine loops around to create the infinity symbol – or indeed perhaps it is rendering a kind of Möbius strip, a surface that only has one side and loops back in on itself, so if it was followed there would be no beginning and no end. What we are left with is the drawn equivalent of the solidifying of time, a sedimentation of marks that are the end product of the artist's machine, but that also articulate analogously his exploration of scale, from the infinitesimally small to the endlessly infinite.

.... James Smith

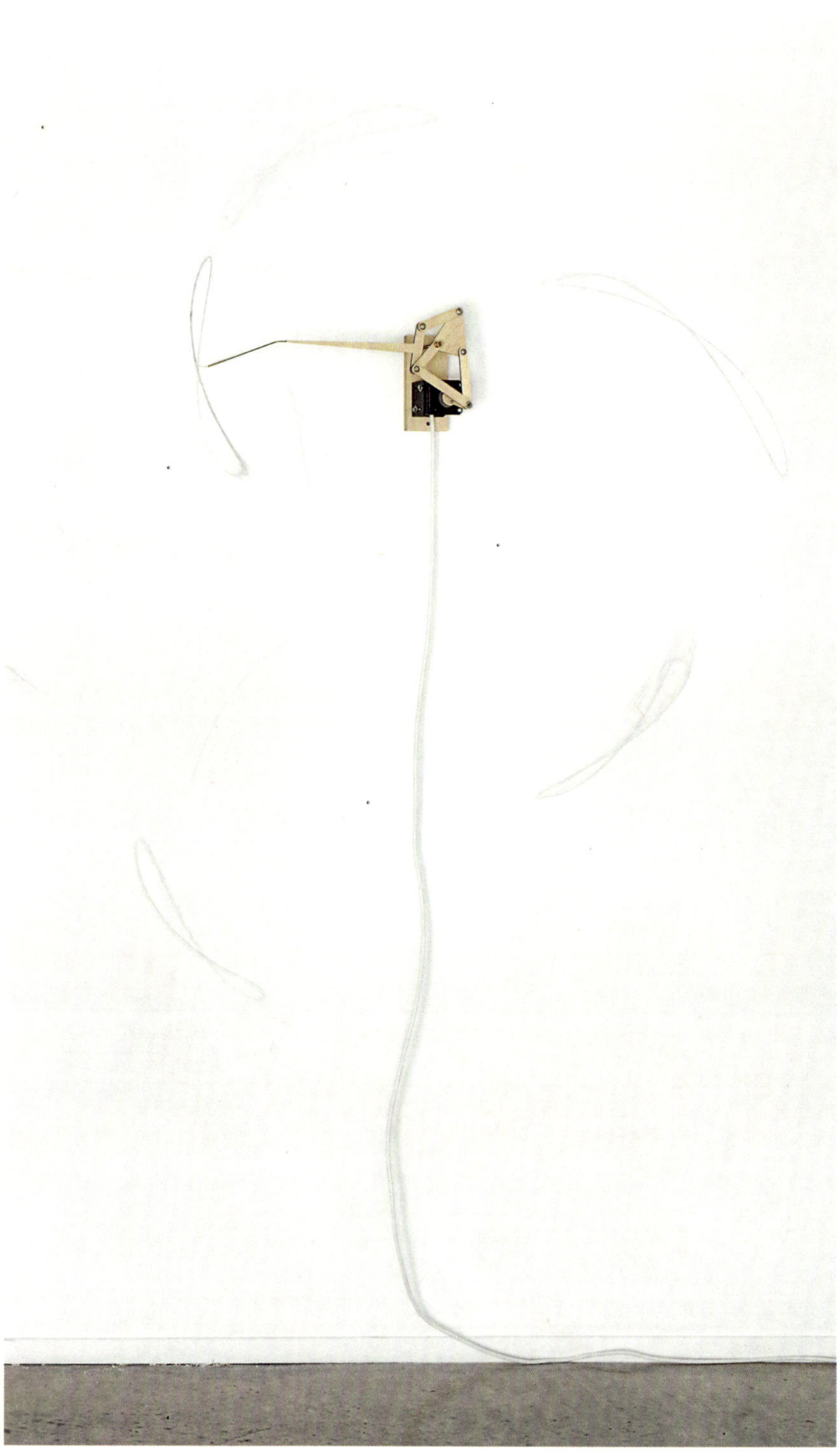

1.

1. *Truthplotter II*, 2019, (detail), motor, Arduino, driver, power supply, cables, bearings, brass, birch plywood, adhesives, silver and wall, 250 × 400 × 20 cm (98 ⅜ × 157 ⅜ × 7 ⅞ in)
2. *Timecasting*, 2013, quartz clock movements, batteries, brass, steel, adhesives, graphite and paper, 500 × 500 × 5 cm (196 ⅞ × 196 ⅞ × 2 in)
3. *Timecaster V*, 2014–present, quartz clock movement, battery, gold, white gold, silver, brass, steel, gesso, MDF, glass, felt, adhesives and screws, 26.9 × 26.9 × 23.5 cm (10 ½ × 10 ½ × 9 ¼ in)

Born 1983, Middlesbrough, UK. Lives and works in Newcastle upon Tyne, UK.

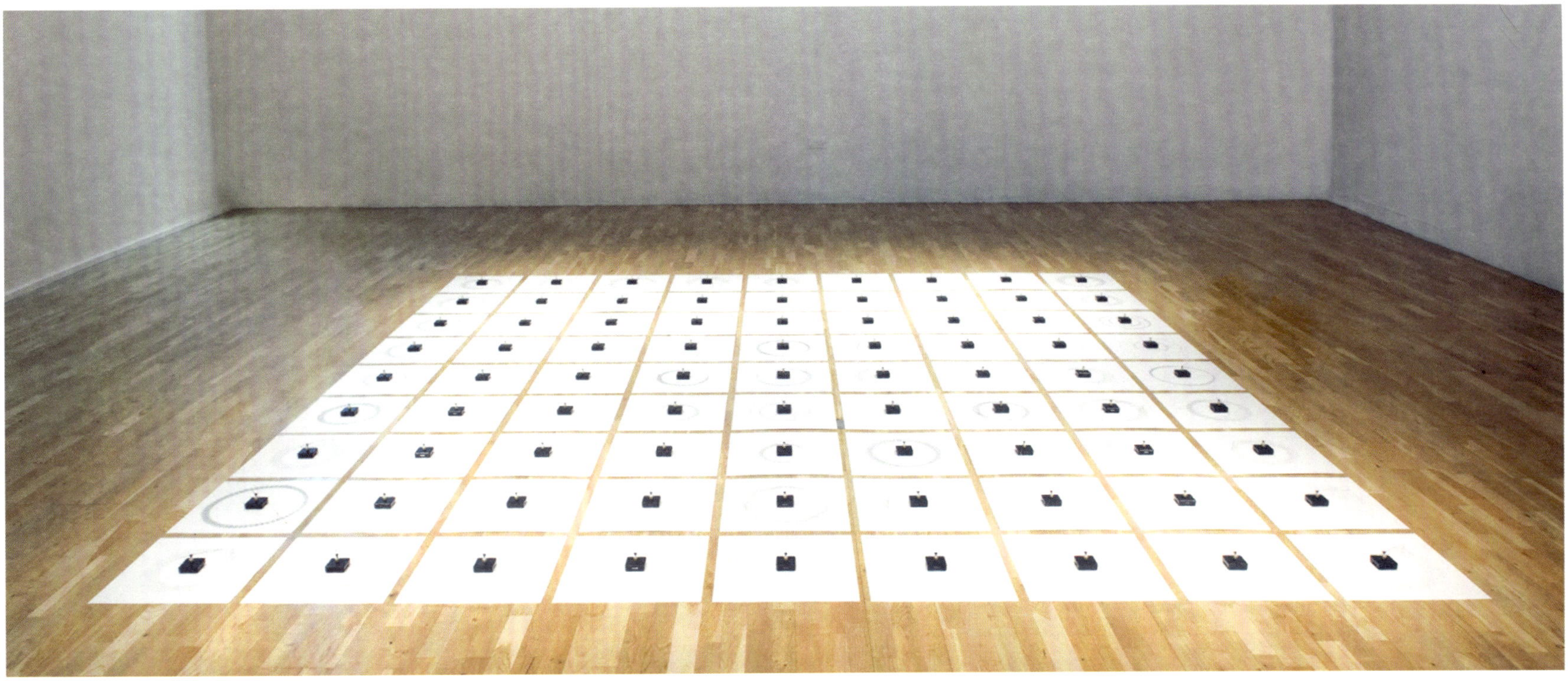

2.

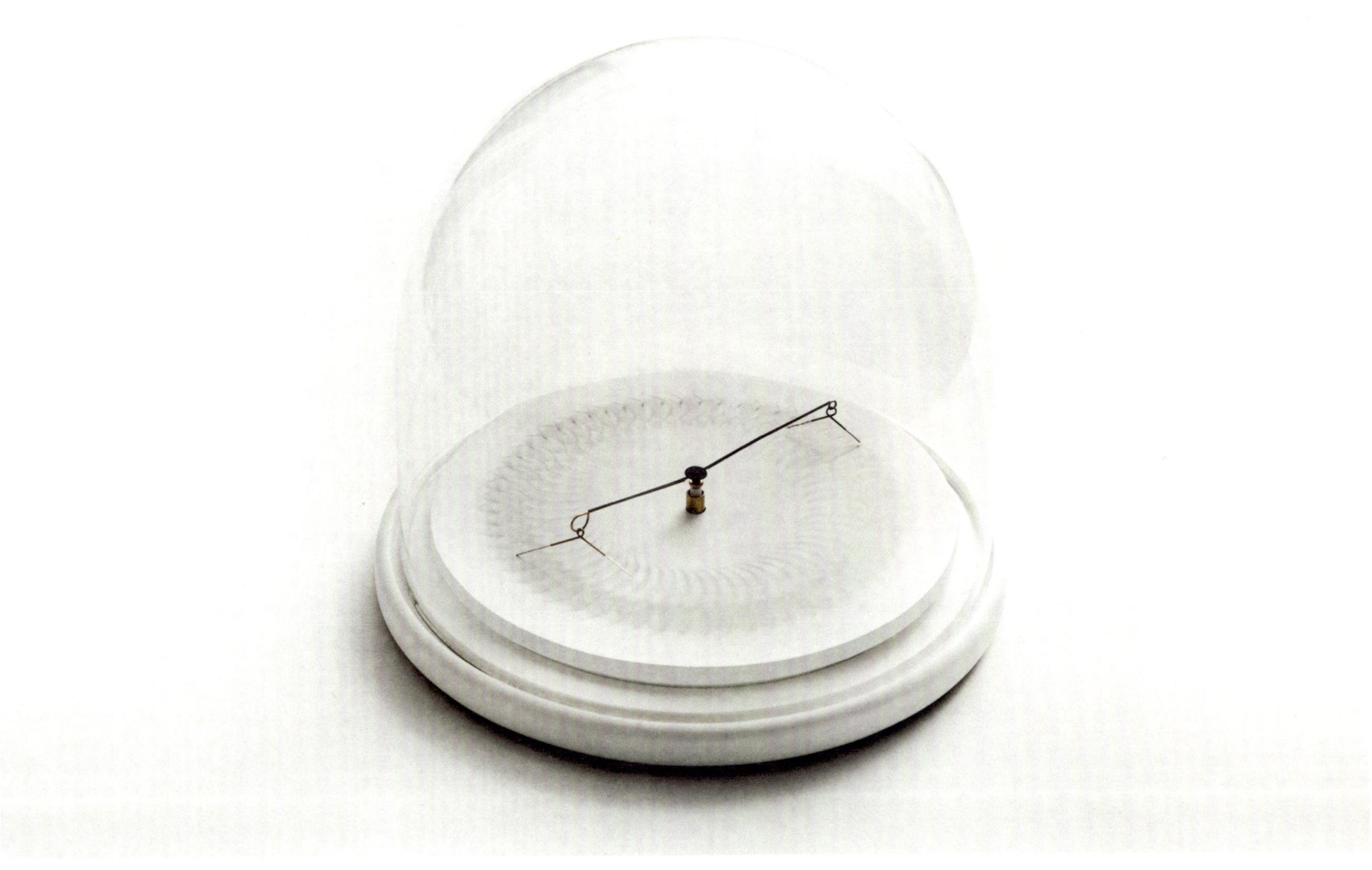

3.

CHRISTINE SUN KIM .... Many people may have first encountered Christine Sun Kim's boldly declarative style over the course of a flashy few seconds of television broadcast when she performed the US national anthem, as well as 'America the Beautiful', in American Sign Language (ASL) for the fifty-fourth Super Bowl's opening ceremony in 2020. The artist, though, had been making work largely about her own experience for nearly two decades prior to the momentous occasion. While culturally identifying as Deaf, to oppose the associations of a medical condition that the lowercase phrasing has signified, Kim has established an artistic practice that engages mediums such as sound, performance, public art and drawing. Often plainly rendered in charcoal and black oil pastel on expansive sheets of white paper, her pieces utilize the graphic signalling of diagrams, pie charts and musical notation, as well as the vocabulary of her first language – ASL – for compositions with elliptical sentences and meditative repetitions describing some of the situations Deaf people encounter in everyday life. .... In a deadpan style referencing the visual appearance of statistical evidence, drawings such as *Degrees of My Deaf Rage in the Art World* (2018) represent varying strengths of anger the artist holds against agents or institutions of power in the professional field of art – ranging from museums with no programming for Deaf people (a full and opaque black circle bisected by a single terse line indicating 'full on rage') to the accessibility manager at a branch of the Guggenheim museums (an acute angle compressed by two lines into a searing point resembling a freshly sharpened pencil head and showing 'acute rage'). Reducing her articulation of a supposedly negative or unproductive emotion to a bluntly scribbled schematic, and then exhibiting it in a prestigious venue such as the Whitney Museum of American Art's 2019 Biennial exhibition in New York, was a tautly passive-aggressive countering of her industry's expectation that artists be perpetually grateful and acquiescent, regardless of the insults and degradations borne along the way to success. .... Anger is an energy and it can be self-sustaining, like any source of intense focus. For a charcoal drawing from 2017, reproduced on printed vinyl for a large-scale mural in the artist's 2020 exhibition at the MIT List Visual Arts Center in Cambridge, Massachusetts, Kim addresses another kind of sustenance: obsession. Titled *The Sound of Obsessing*, it depicts a small letter 'p', the symbol in sheet music instructing one to play more quietly. By visualizing that prompt but blurring its legibility through repetitions drawn too close together, the artist engages an aural medium, which she often utilizes as a conceptual vehicle for her deafness.

.... Paige K. Bradley

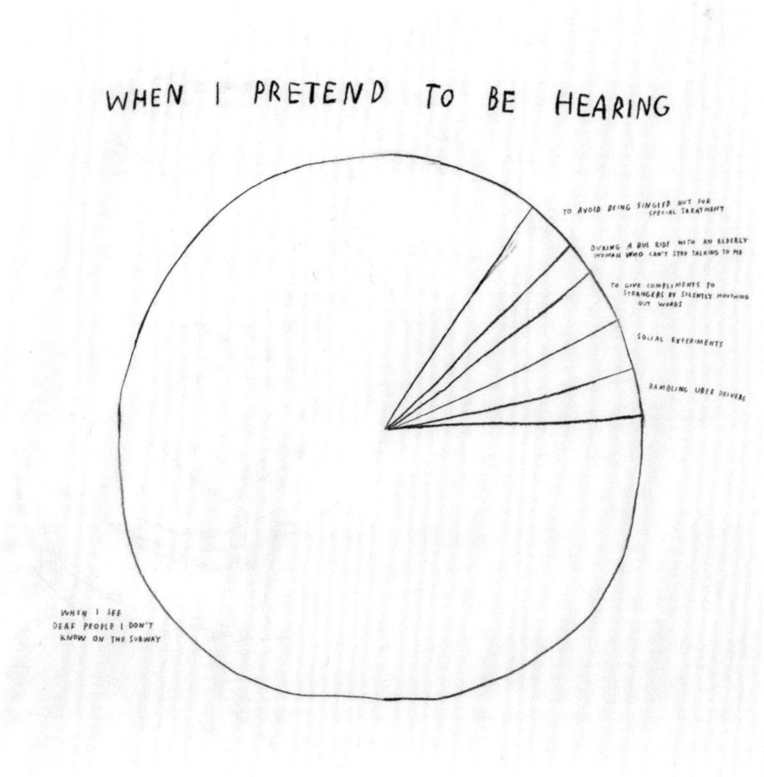

1.

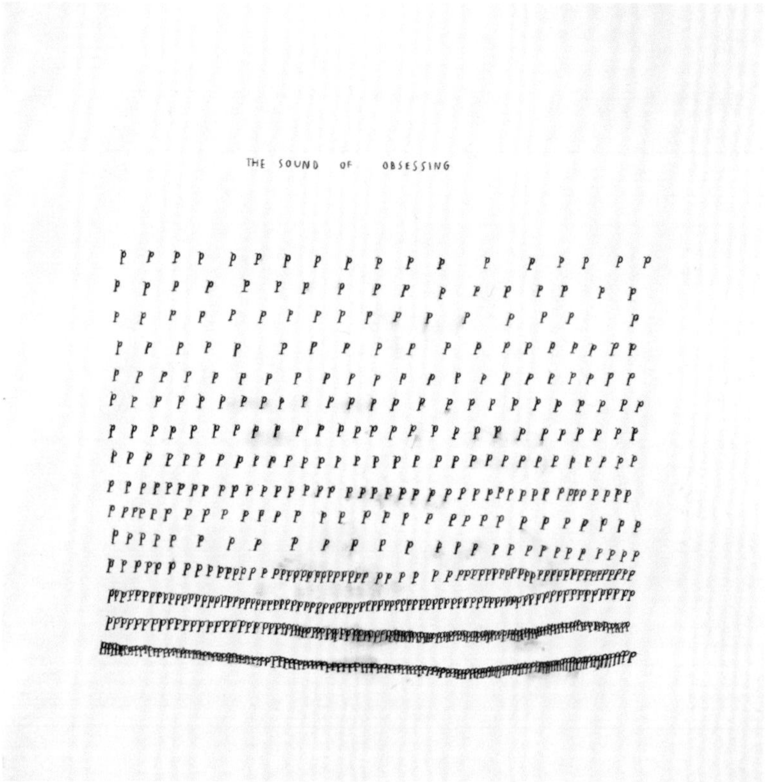

2.

Born 1980, Orange County, CA. Lives and works in Berlin.

1. *When I Pretend To Be Hearing*, 2019, charcoal and oil pastel on paper, 125 × 125 cm (49 ⅛ × 49 ⅛ in)
2. *The Sound of Obsessing*, 2017, charcoal on paper, 125 × 125 cm (49 ⅛ × 49 ⅛ in)
3. *Suggested Amount of Talking on Phone in the Presence of a Deaf Person*, 2018, charcoal on paper, 42 × 29.7 cm (16 ½ × 11 ¾ in)
4. *Degrees of My Deaf Rage in the Art World*, 2018, charcoal and oil pastel on paper, 125 × 125 cm (49 ⅛ × 49 ⅛ in)

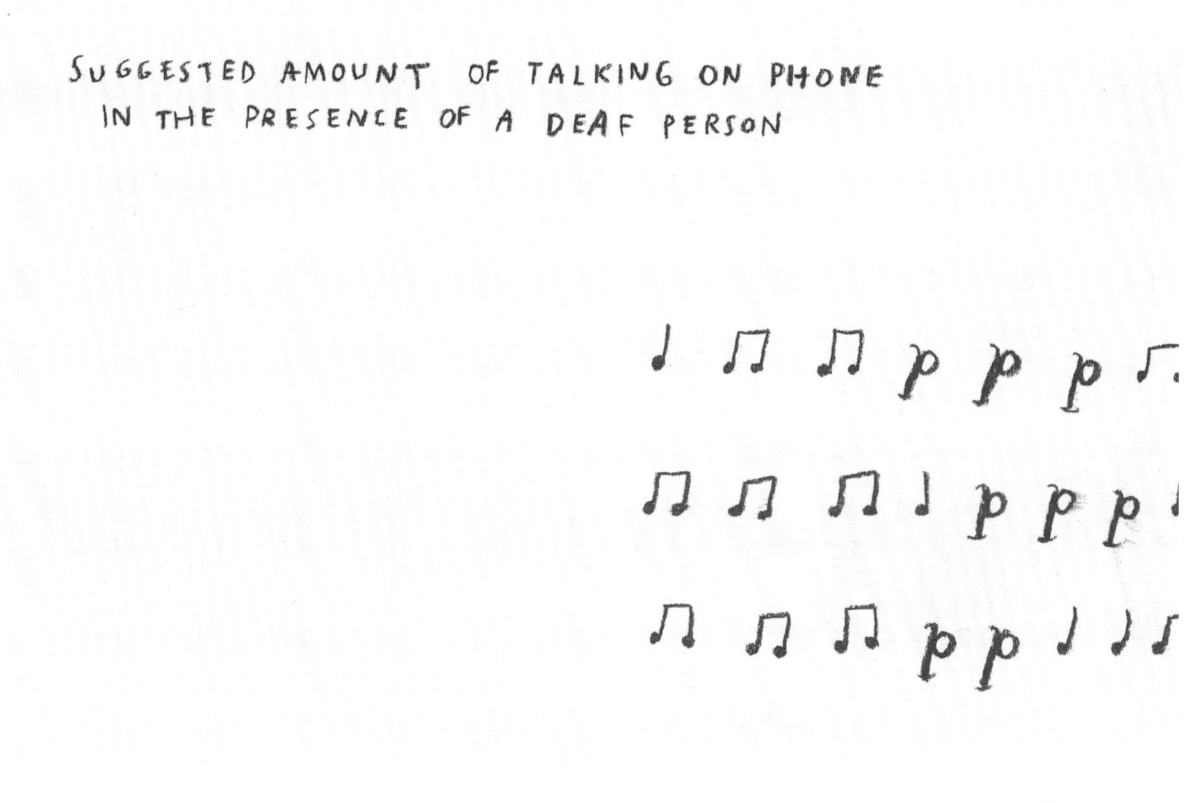
SUGGESTED AMOUNT OF TALKING ON PHONE
IN THE PRESENCE OF A DEAF PERSON

3.

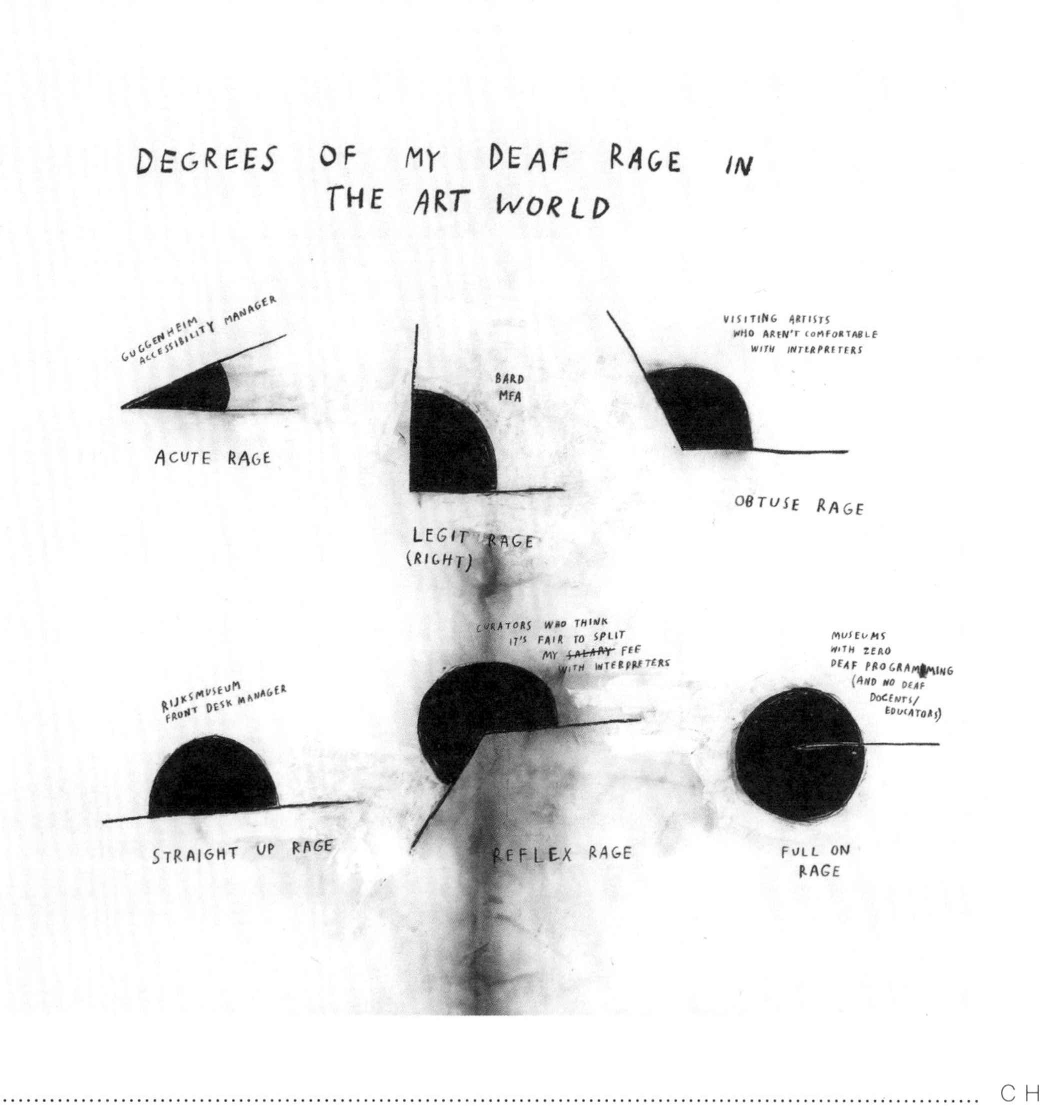
DEGREES OF MY DEAF RAGE IN
THE ART WORLD
GUGGENHEIM
ACCESSIBILITY MANAGER
ACUTE RAGE
BARD
MFA
LEGIT RAGE
(RIGHT)
VISITING ARTISTS
WHO AREN'T COMFORTABLE
WITH INTERPRETERS
OBTUSE RAGE
RIJKSMUSEUM
FRONT DESK MANAGER
STRAIGHT UP RAGE
CURATORS WHO THINK
IT'S FAIR TO SPLIT
MY ~~SALARY~~ FEE
WITH INTERPRETERS
REFLEX RAGE
MUSEUMS
WITH ZERO
DEAF PROGRAMMING
(AND NO DEAF
DOCENTS/
EDUCATORS)
FULL ON
RAGE

4.

MINJUNG KIM .... Minjung Kim's minimal and meditative collages are object-lessons in patience and control. She began honing her craft in South Korea at a young age – she studied under the renowned watercolourist Yeongyun Kang (b. 1941), and learned the traditional art of calligraphy for over a decade – influences visible in her acute understanding of the properties of shadow, weight, colour and volume. *The Room* (2007) gives the impression of looking into a light-filled architectural space: a place of ethereal calmness. Kim made the work by cutting thin strips of paper, singeing their edges with incense and collaging the pieces so that the charred borders function like drawn likes, directing the eye inwards. .... The process of layering burnt paper is typical of her practice, which is largely restricted to the use of three materials: fire, ink and Hanji paper, made from the bark of the paper mulberry tree native to Korea. Kim also spends days alone in her studio, and as a result an atmosphere of deep quietude pervades the things she makes; following calligraphic practices, she works on the floor. The 'rules' of her practice place her in a lineage of artists and writers who choose to liberate their creativity by setting themselves limitations. Included among them are French writer George Perec, whose 1969 novel *La Disparition* (*A Void*) was written using only words that do not contain the letter 'e'. .... When Kim moved to Milan in 1991, she became interested in the mark-making and interior worlds manifested in the work of modern Western artists. *Phasing* (2017) is a compelling combination of East Asian graphic traditions and European explorations of artistic subjectivity. Deep, black stripes on the paper appear like perfectly formed expressive marks, as if brushstrokcs have been frozen in time, their every contour painstakingly explored. For *Insight* (2017) Kim used a series of paper discs to give a flat sheet of paper the appearance of an open book. The two halves of the composition seem to arc into a central cavity. In order to enhance the impression of depth and motion, Kim applied various gradations of off-white to the discs, as well as singeing their edges. The careful manipulation of shape and colour, and the astonishing spatial illusion it produces, is reminiscent of the Op art movement of the 1960s – in particular the abstract canvases of Bridget Riley (b. 1931) – albeit Kim's limited palette is muted by comparison. In her work, space is as much a formal property as it is a means of expressing emotional states of being. To follow the undulations of light and depth is to find oneself immersed in silent contemplation.
.... Rosanna Mclaughlin

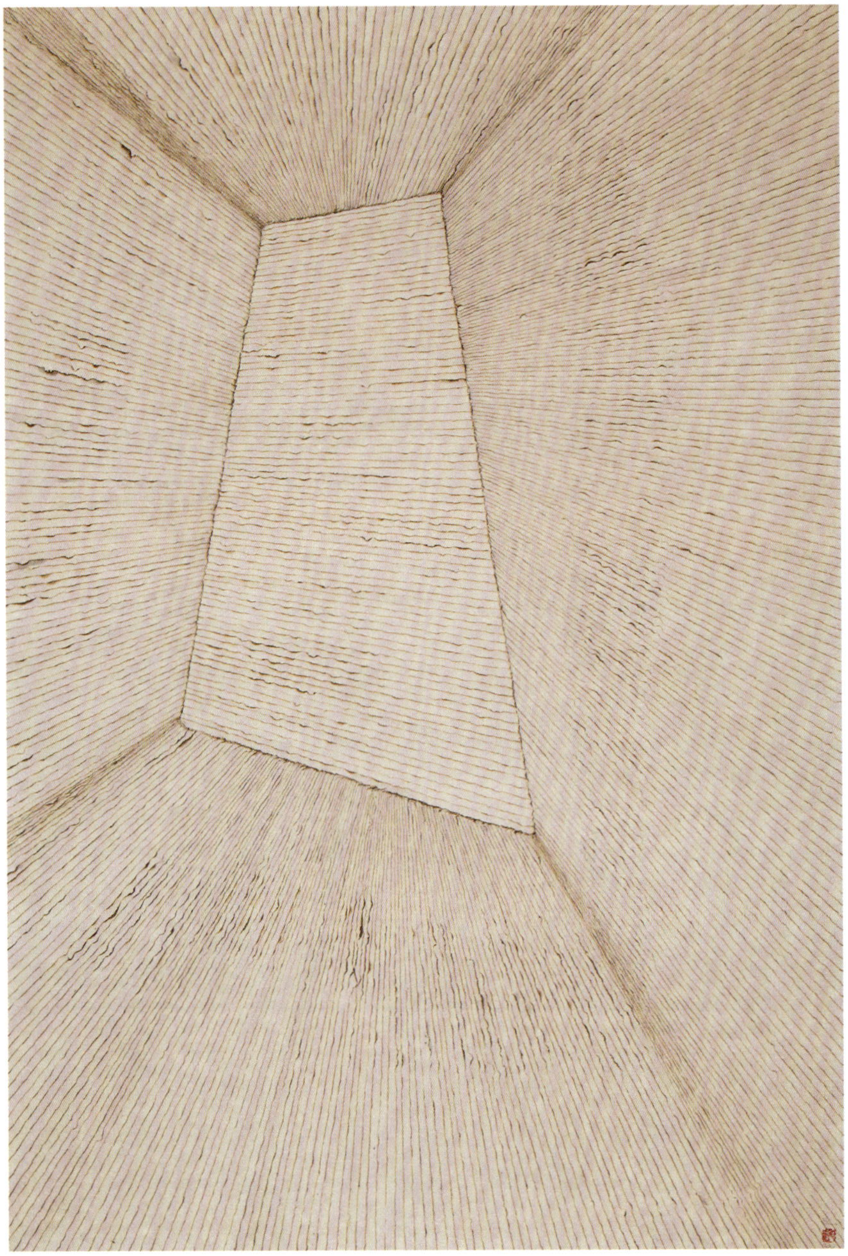
1.

Born 1962, Gwangju, South Korea. Lives and works in Saint Paul de Vence, France, and New York.

1. *The Room*, 2007, burnt Hanji collage on mulberry Hanji paper, 202 × 142 cm (79 ½ × 56 in)
2. *Mountain*, 2016, ink on mulberry Hanji paper, 159 × 130 cm (62 ⅝ × 51 ⅛ in)
3. *Phasing*, 2017, ink and burnt Hanji collage on mulberry Hanji paper, 100 × 80 cm (39 ⅜ × 31 ½ in)
4. *Insight*, 2017, burnt Hanji collage on mulberry Hanji paper, 142 × 206 cm (56 × 81 in)

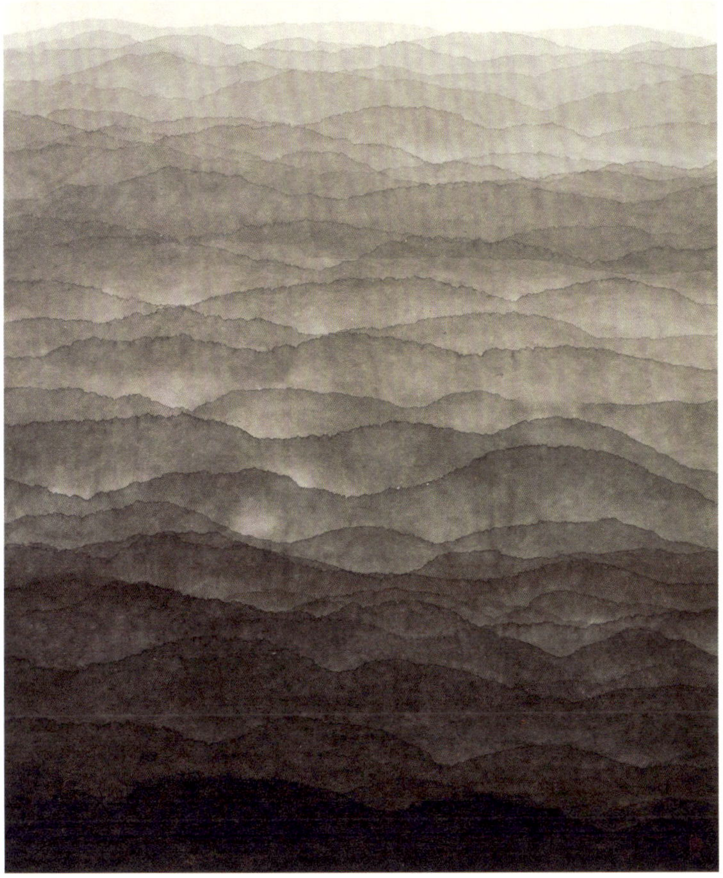
2.

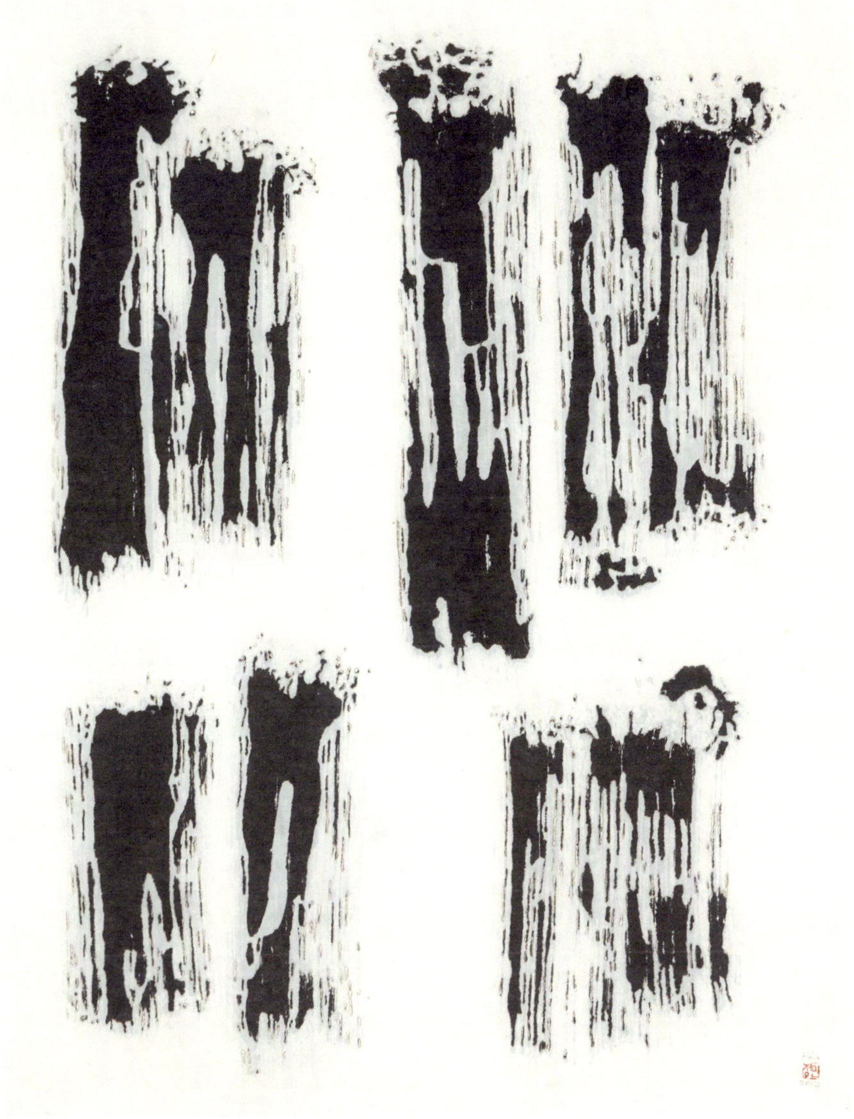
3.

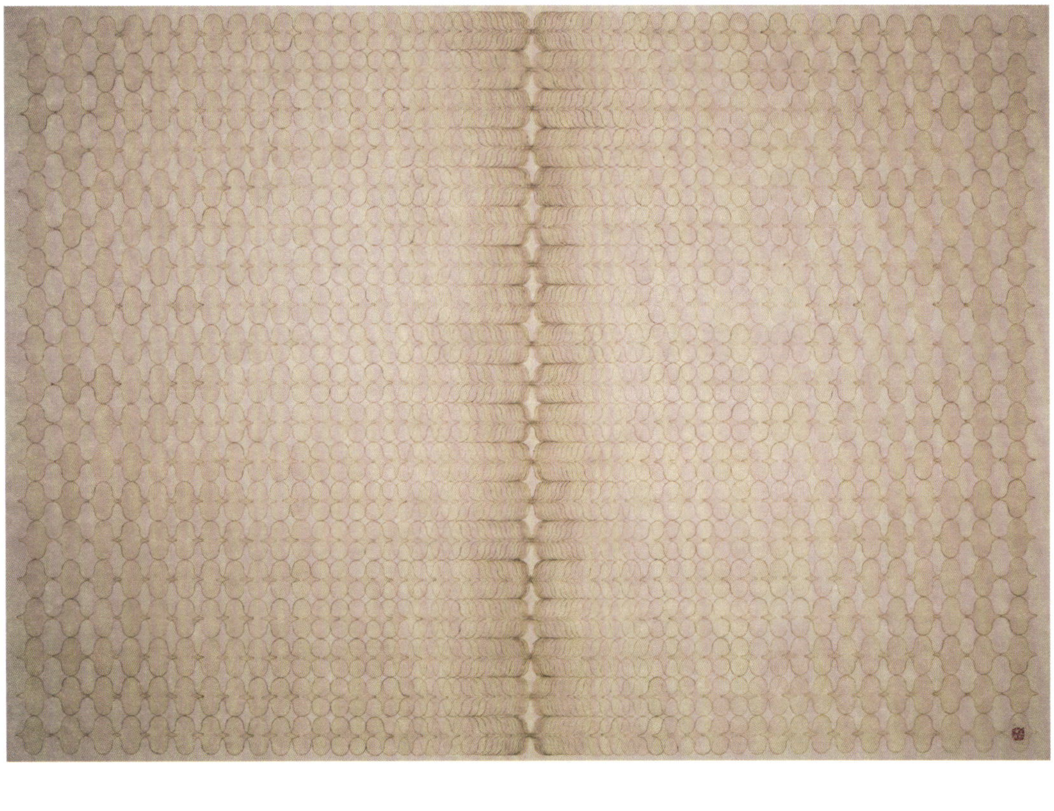
4.

TANIA KOVATS .... The world can be contained – or at least mapped – in drawings, so Tania Kovats believes. Her extraordinarily complex works on paper show how an artist emerging in an age of often anti-visual conceptualism grapples with images, not words, in order to construct memory systems that encompass the world, while at the same time admitting the tenuous relationship of intention to the finished work of art. *All the Islands of All the Seas* (2017), a collection of thirty-two framed drawings in which Kovats superimposes island upon island on transparent Mylar film, is not a critique of theories of memory nor of mapping, but rather extracts memory-substitutes from a particular description of the world – the atlas. In effect, *All the Islands of All the Seas* is a new, quite systematic atlas of the world's islands. In contrast, her large drawing *Rain* (2015) arrives at its composition by indexicality: different-sized drops of ink landing on blotting paper produce smaller or larger 'raindrops'. Given such precision, framed (here, literally) by a transparent process, what are we offered by way of meaning? .... That is the underlying question across all this artist's environmentally oriented drawings and installations. In her highly individual version of Land art, she assembles, reassembles and overlays land, water or air, always making lists. These lists, in turn, make the things that they contain relative. Her lists give perspective, and might therefore be considered ethical in themselves, because they relativize the individual, self-centred subjectivity that is, as we have seen over the last few years, a poor guide as to how to act geographically. Kovats made *Only Blue (UK)* in 2015, before Brexit. Presciently obliterating 'Little England', Kovats overpainted maps depicting different parts of the United Kingdom with white gesso, leaving only the sea in its different shades of eggshell blue untouched. According to pre-modern writers on memory, the commemorative process transpiring from the act of reading is an ethical one because reading a book resembles a meeting of minds, a way of making others present, reaching beyond the confines of an egoistic 'I'. Kovats's recapitulations of islands, or of the United Kingdom, or of greater- or lesser-sized drops of water, offer us the performance of our own reading. Reducing the United Kingdom to a collection of pure shapes, white on blue, is a simple visual method of grasping a complex abstraction – the federation of unlike peoples and places – without it becoming overwhelming. Philosopher Elizabeth Grosz once paraphrased Nietzsche as arguing that 'a counterforgetfulness needs to be instituted', so Kovats institutes collections, establishing drawing as an aid to counterforgetfulness. .... Charles Green

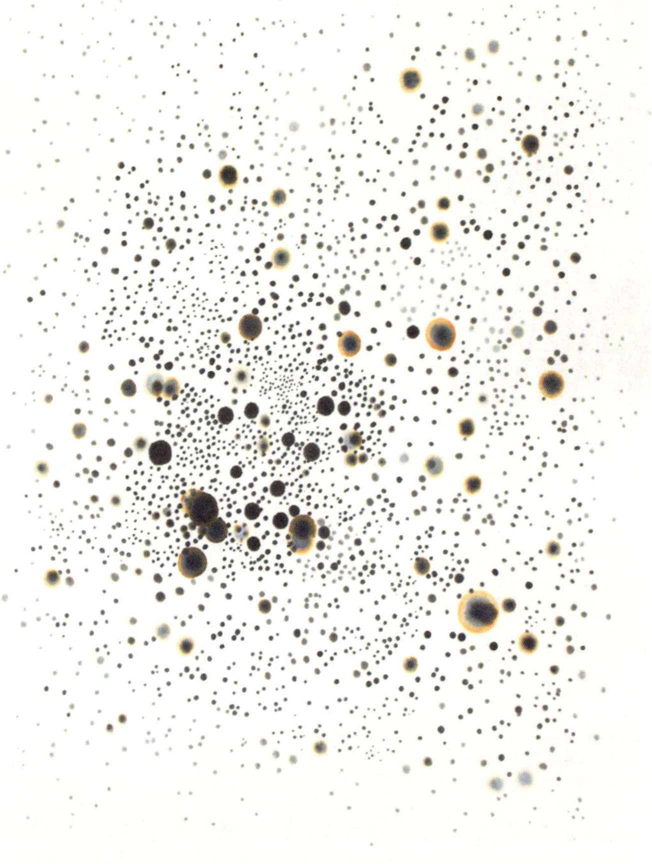

1.

2.

Born 1966, Brighton, UK. Lives and works in Devon, UK.

1. *Rain*, 2015, ink and blotting paper, 70 × 60 cm (27 ½ × 23 ⅝ in)
2. *Evaporation (Black No. 31)*, 2015, ink, salt and blotting paper, 25 × 25 cm (9 ⅞ × 9 ⅞ in)
3. *Sea Mark (Payne's Grey)*, 2015, Paynes Grey gouache and paper, 100 × 125 cm (39 ⅜ × 49 ¼ in)

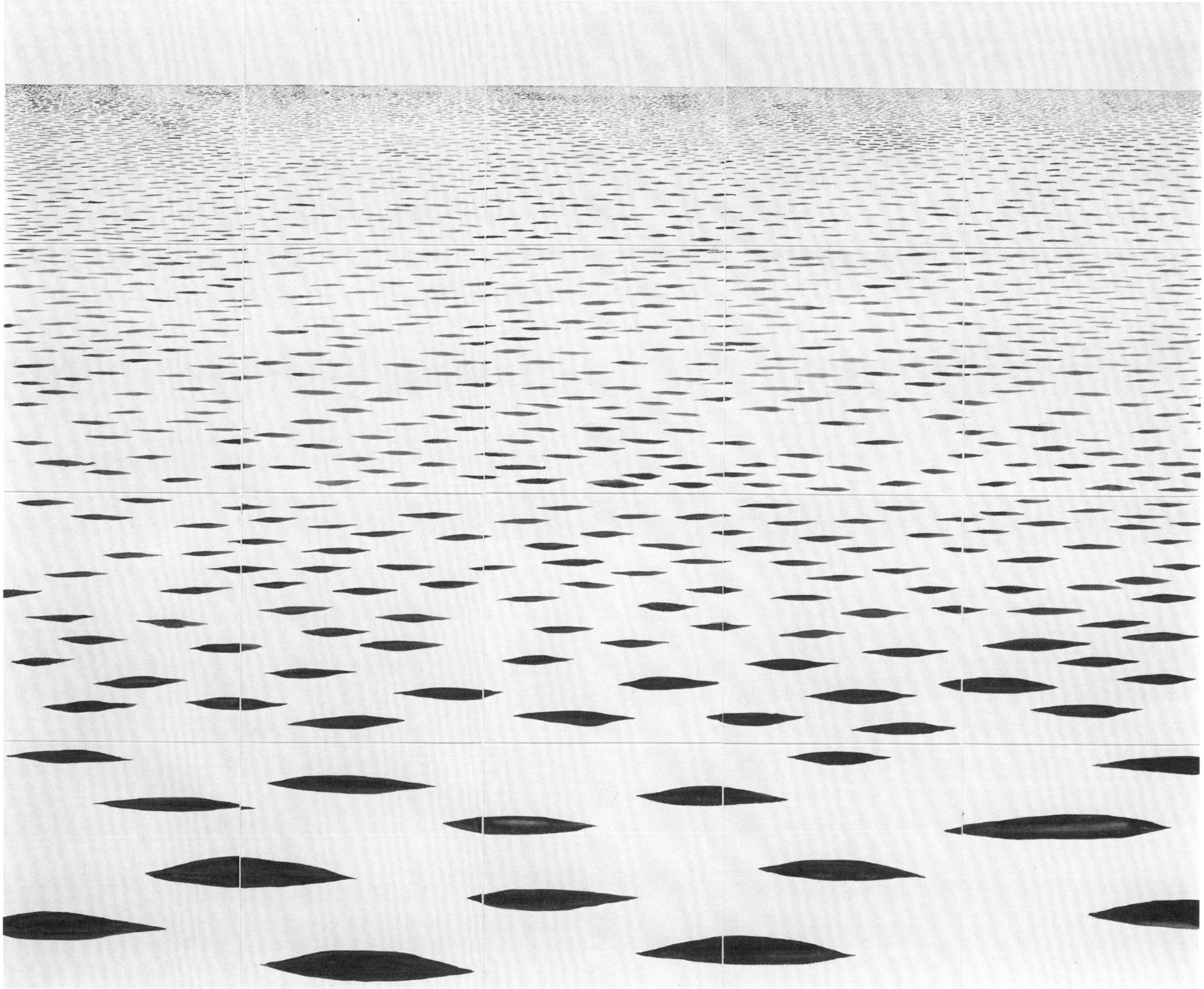

3.

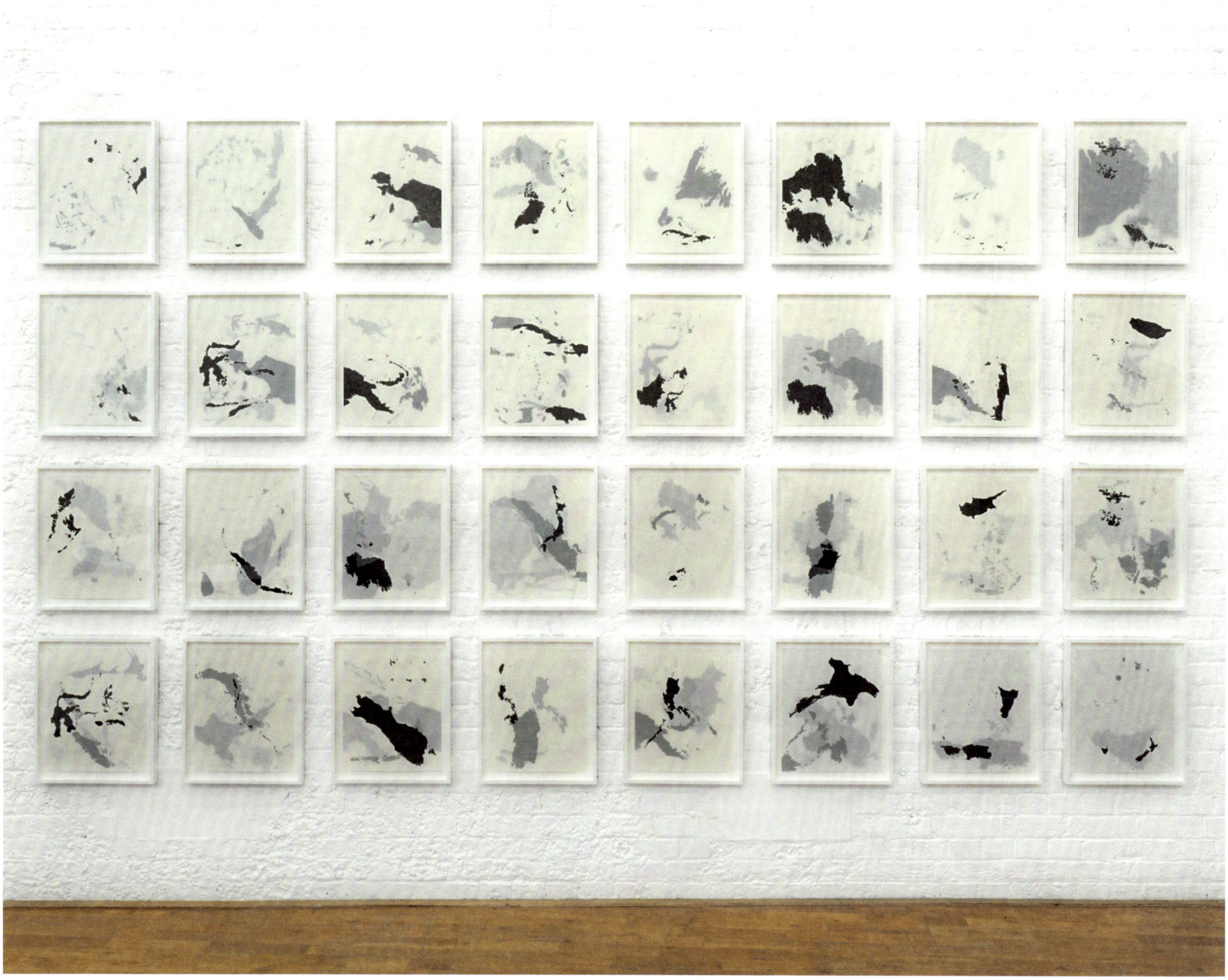

4.

4. *All the Islands of All the Seas*, 2017, ink on Mylar paper and pins, 32-part framed work, each frame 55 × 48 cm (22 × 19 in)
5. *Only Blue (UK)*, 2015, white gesso and various atlases, 150 × 130 cm (59 × 51 in)

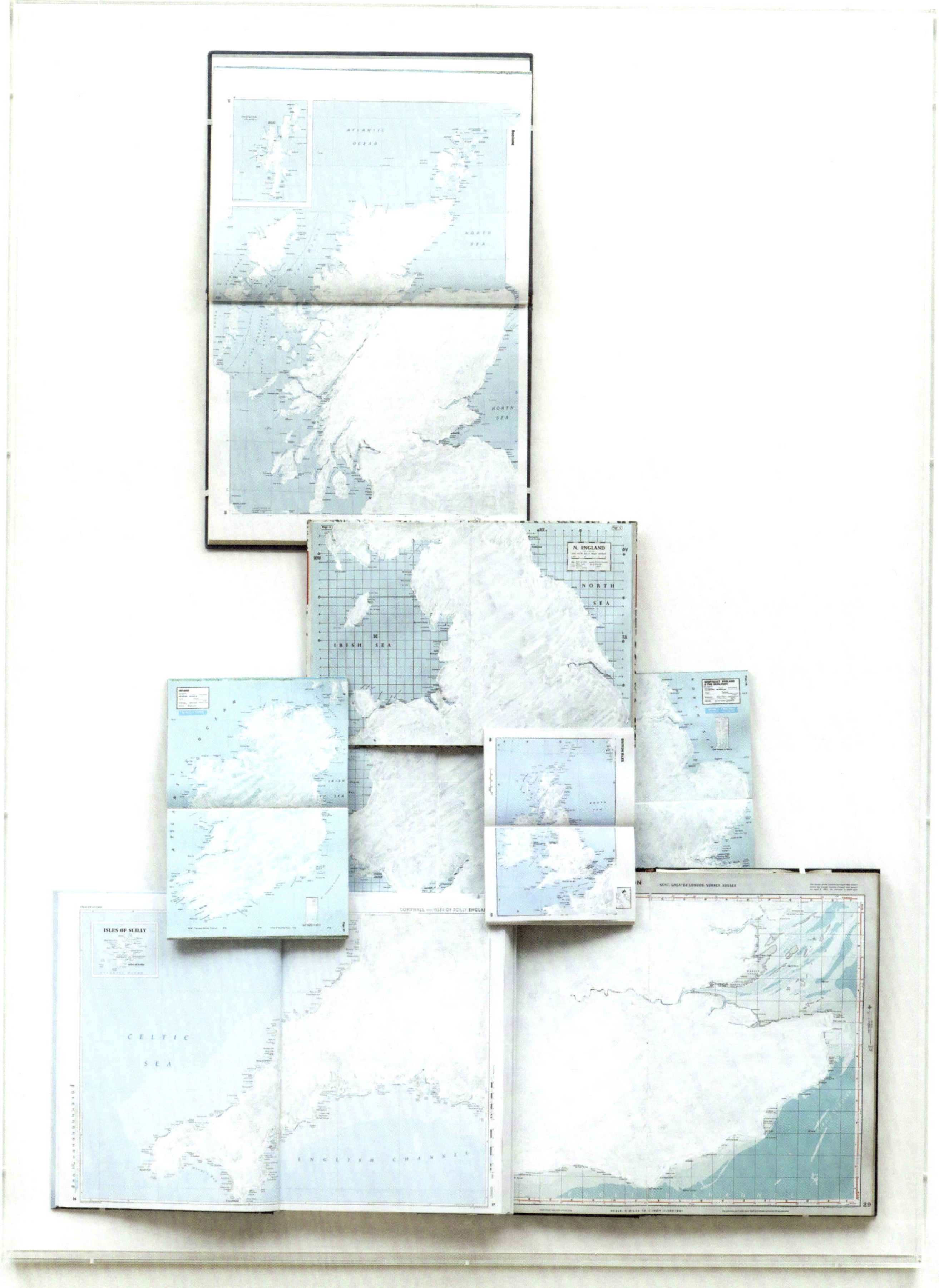
N. ENGLAND
NORTH SEA
IRISH SEA
ISLES OF SCILLY
CELTIC SEA
ENGLISH CHANNEL

5.

MAIJA KURŠEVA .... Maija Kurševa's wide-ranging artistic output includes drawing, silk-screening, printmaking, sculpture, installations and animation. But beyond her art-making, she is also a publisher, an educator and co-founder of an artist-run space in Riga, Latvia. An iridescent web of humour connects her multifaceted practice, which can alternate, with sumptuous ease, between brazen or illustrative pronunciations and minimalist or conceptual gestures. .... Language plays an important role in the development of her work, although it is usually only featured in its most abstracted form in finished pieces. Several letters of the Roman and Latvian alphabet can be identified in the collection of drawings on paper that form the work *Untitled* (2018), alongside less discernible characters that resemble bulbous markings or cartoonish doodles. The piece, along with other similar drawings, as well as sculptural installations, formed the core of the 2018 exhibition 'Investigation' (at Kim? Contemporary Art Center in Riga), which was based on the artist's poetry. Kurševa removed words from one of her own poems in the process of transferring it into drawings, subtracting the language such that the resulting works only feature fragmented, oblique signs that together form a visual riddle. Rather than attempt to read or decipher it, the viewer can find poetry in the rhythm and melody of the forms, in their sequences and repetition. 'I hope it works like a Hugo Ball poem,' the artist told *Artforum*, referencing the German Dada poet, 'just from the sounds that sound like words but that don't actually mean anything.' .... The works in the series 'Black Lines' (2019) have undergone an even greater process of subtraction and removal: only the traces left by the brush where it had touched the surface of the paper make up the individual artworks. These thick lines have been cut out and carefully attached to the wall using small dabs of acrylic to create only minimal points of contact. The gouache-on-paper pieces draw the focus to the intuitive movement of the lines, as if pointing towards a stream of thoughts untethered by the need for explanation. The eye begins to trace the snaking of curves and loops, and while they don't signify anything concrete, they trigger the viewer to rely on recognition and associations for interpretation. Resembling black nets, nooses or twine, some of them gain an unexpected solemnity. And although they are, technically, works on paper, these artworks straddle the line between soft sculptures and drawings. 'When you put the pen to paper, you aren't always thinking about the outcome – you are in a constant moment of the present, of now,' the artist said in the *Artforum* interview. 'The most exciting instant is when the brush touches the surface, and what it leaves behind is already the past.'
.... Hili Perlson

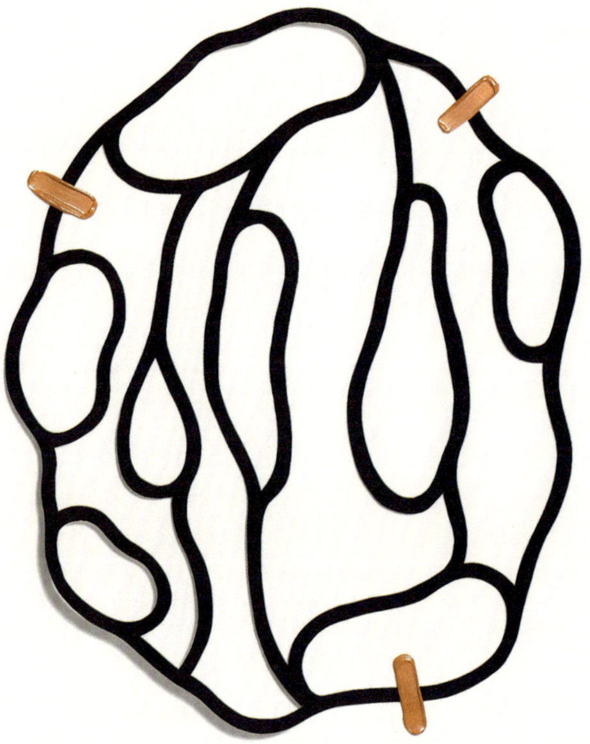

1.

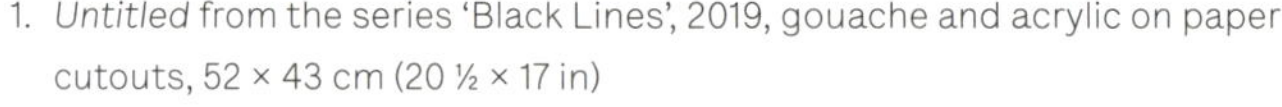

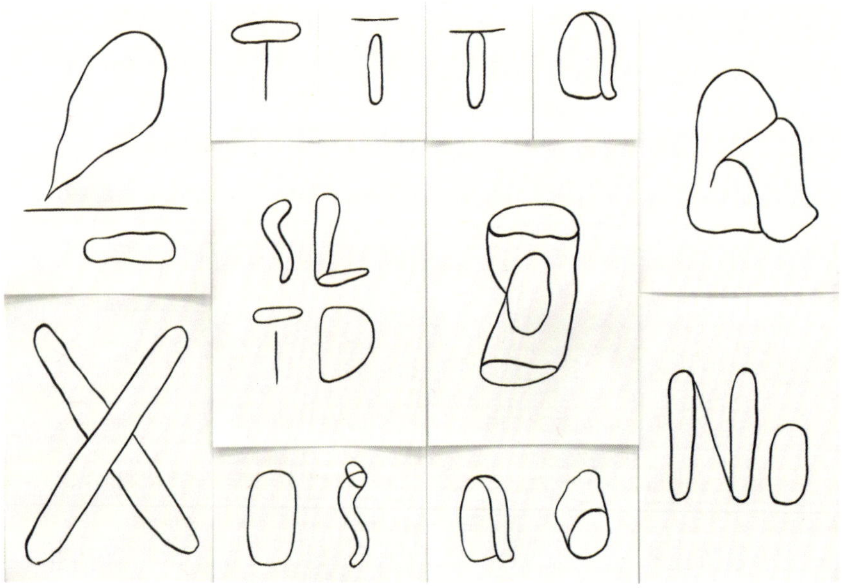

2.

Born 1981 Lielplatone, Latvia. Lives and works in Riga, Latvia.

1. *Untitled* from the series 'Black Lines', 2019, gouache and acrylic on paper cutouts, 52 × 43 cm (20 ½ × 17 in)
2. *Untitled*, 2018, gouache on paper, 6 drawings each 42 × 29.7 cm (16 ½ × 11 ¾ in); 2 drawings each 29.7 × 21 cm (11 ¾ × 8 ¼ in); 4 drawings each 21 × 14.8 cm (8 ¼ 5 ⅞ in), installation view 'Investigation', Kim? Contemporary Art Center, Riga
3. *Untitled* from the series 'Black Lines', 2019, gouache and acrylic on paper cutouts, 140 × 13 cm (55 ⅛ × 5 ⅛ in); 52 × 43 cm (20 ½ × 17 in); 140 × 13 cm (55 ⅛ × 5 ⅛ in); 130 × 60 cm (51 ⅛ × 23 ⅝ in); 120 × 21 cm (47 ¼ × 8 ¼ in)

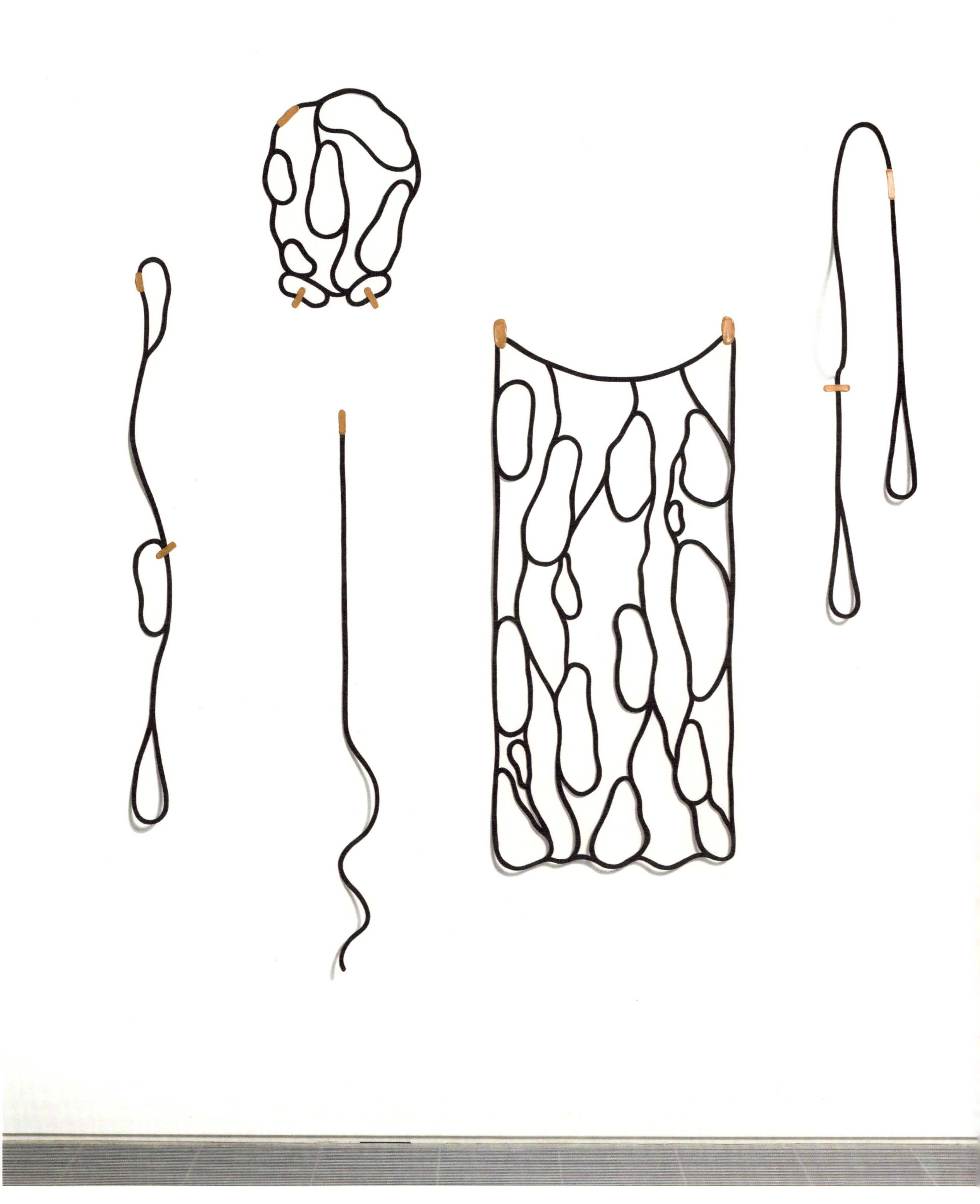
3.

GLENDA LEÓN....... Cuban-born artist Glenda León uses simple forms to convey wonderment at natural phenomena and hope for a more harmonious world. Whether working with installation, photography, video or drawing, humble materials are often bestowed with unexpected significance. Appearances can be deceiving. A cloud might reveal itself to be a piece of chewed-up gum, a drawn line a human hair. *Cuerpos Celestes: Supernova* (*Celestial Bodies: Supernova*) (2019) may look like a pastel drawing of an astronomical event. In fact it is made from ground-up butterfly wings dispersed over black velvet. The white, blue and gold pigment of the wings creates the impression of a distant burst of colour in the night sky, as in the explosion of a star....... León's work is suffused with a belief that the natural world contains within it the key to intellectual and spiritual awakenings – both for the individual and for the wider population. For *Formas de Salvar el Mundo: N.4 (Rocear con Ayahuasca el Mundo Entero Ena Vez Cada 21 Días por 3 Años)* (*Ways to Save the World: N.4 (To Spread Ayahuasca Over the Whole World Once Every 21 Days During 3 Years)*) (2012) she applied blue and purple crayon to vellum, producing a childlike drawing of a helicopter flying over the world. The work makes a fantastical suggestion for improved global wellbeing: dispensing the psychedelic drug Ayahuasca over the citizens of planet Earth. For centuries this powerful hallucinogenic concoction, made from a vine that grows in the South American rainforest, has been used as a psychic medicine and educational tool by indigenous peoples of the Amazon. The drawing belongs to 'Formas de Salvar el Mundo' (2012), a series of solutions for planetary salvation. In addition to distributing other naturally occurring hallucinogens, including mescaline, works in the series suggest erasing national borders, and learning to accept others and ourselves....... León's interest in the stars, and her visions for a kinder Earth, may have romantic and surreal tendencies, but her work also bears a strong political message. In *La Internacional (Serie IV, N.1)* (*The International (Series IV, N.1)*) (2016) she attached tiny scraps of torn up money, collected from countries across the world, to a musical score. The scraps have been placed to mark out the tune of 'The Internationale', a global anthem for labour movements. Written in 1888 by Pierre Degeyter, the music accompanies lyrics by Eugène Pottier encouraging the downtrodden to unite and overthrow their oppressors. By exchanging musical notes with ripped up bank notes, León suggests a radical redistribution of global economic wealth that reflects the song's core message – a belief that together we can unite to create a fairer world.
.... Rosanna Mclaughlin

1.

Born 1976, Havana. Lives and works in Havana and Madrid.

1. *Entre el Instante y la Eternidad (Serie I, N. 1)* (*Between Instant and Eternity (Series I, N. 1)*), 2018, ink, graphite and watercolour on cardboard, 76 × 57.5 cm (30 × 22 ⅝ in)
2. *Formas de Salvar el Mundo: N.4 (Rocear con Ayahuasca el Mundo Entero Ena Vez Cada 21 Días por 3 Años)* (*Ways to Save the World: N.4 (To Spread Ayahuasca Over the Whole World Once Every 21 Days During 3 Years)*), 2012, ink and crayon on vellum paper, 21 × 29.7 cm (8 ¼ × 11 ¾ in)
3. *Todo Está en tu Cabeza (Cerebro)* (*It's All in Your Head (Brain)*), 2018, hair and graphite on cardboard, 64 × 91 cm (25 ⅛ × 35 ⅞ in)
4. *La Internacional (Serie IV, N.1)* (*The Internationale (Series IV, N.1)*), 2016, pieces of bills from different parts of the world and inkjet print on cotton paper, 100 × 150 cm (39 ⅜ × 59 in)

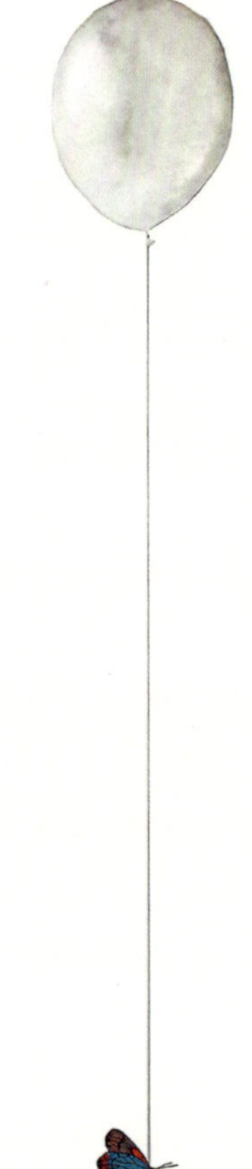

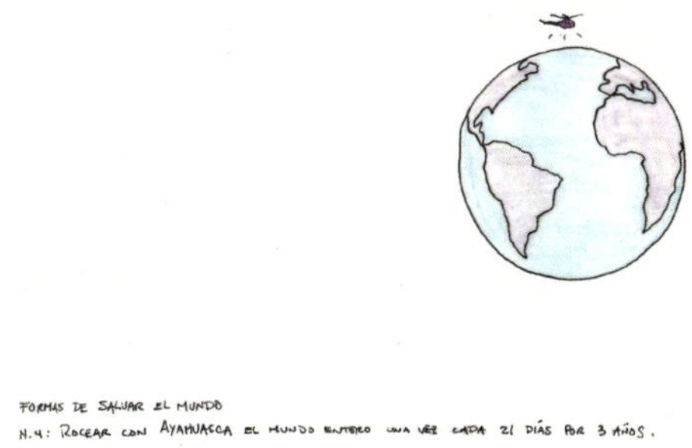
FORMAS DE SALVAR EL MUNDO
N.4: ROCEAR CON AYAHUASCA EL MUNDO ENTERO UNA VEZ CADA 21 DÍAS POR 3 AÑOS.

2.

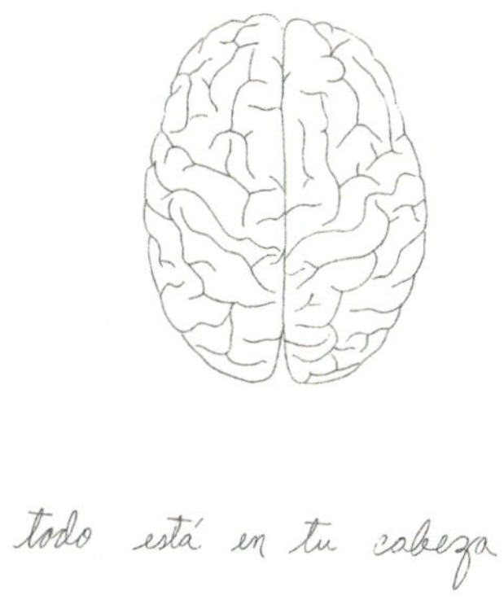
todo está en tu cabeza

3.

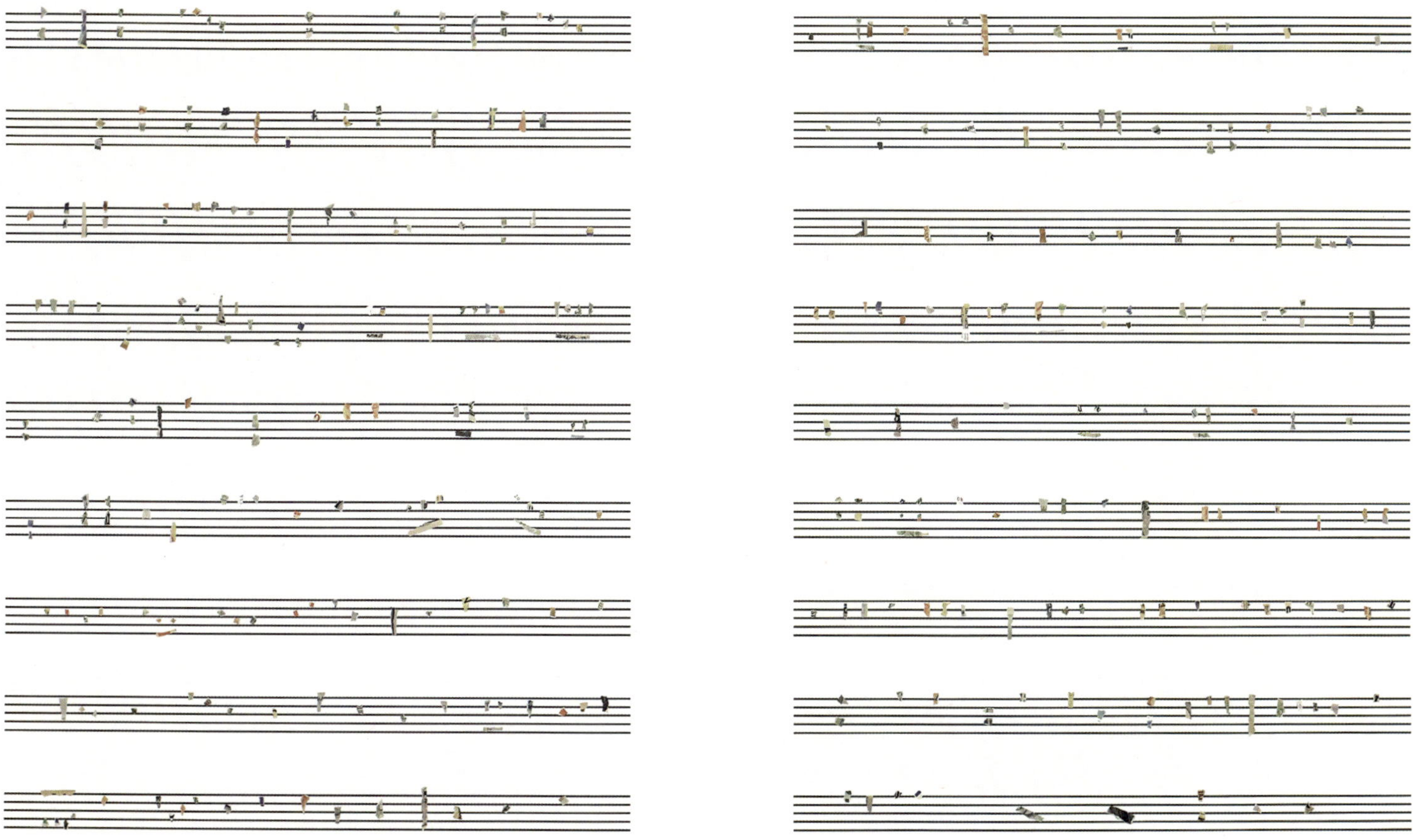

4.

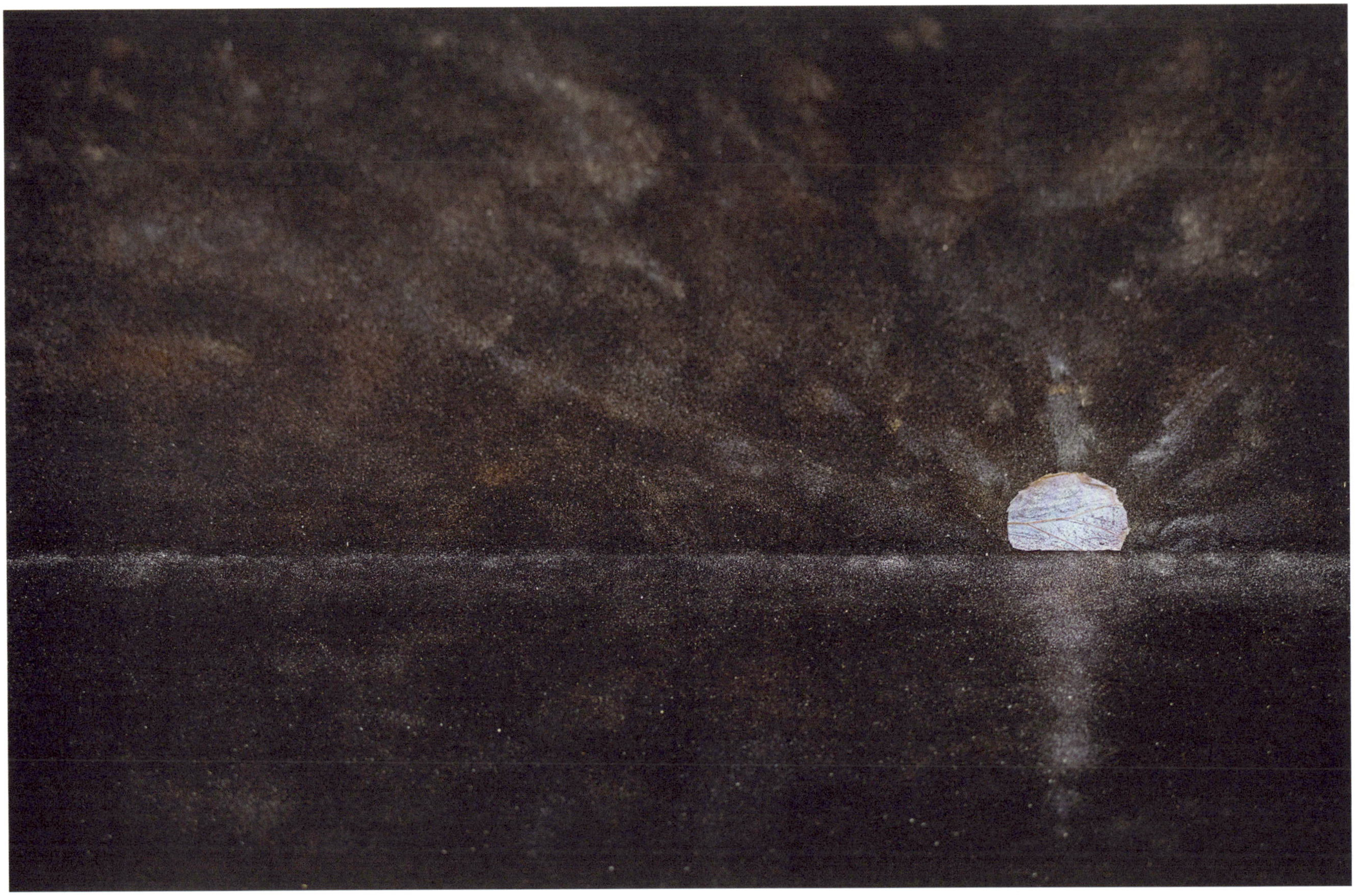

5.

5. *Cuerpos Celestes: El Nacimiento de un Sol Azul* (*Celestial Bodies: Birth of a Blue Sun*), 2019, powder of butterfly wings and fragment of butterfly wing on velvet, 24 × 32.5 cm (9 ½ × 12 ¾ in)
6. *Cuerpos Celestes: Supernova* (*Celestial Bodies: Supernova*), 2019, powder of butterfly wings on velvet, 24 × 32.5 cm (9 ½ × 12 ¾ in)

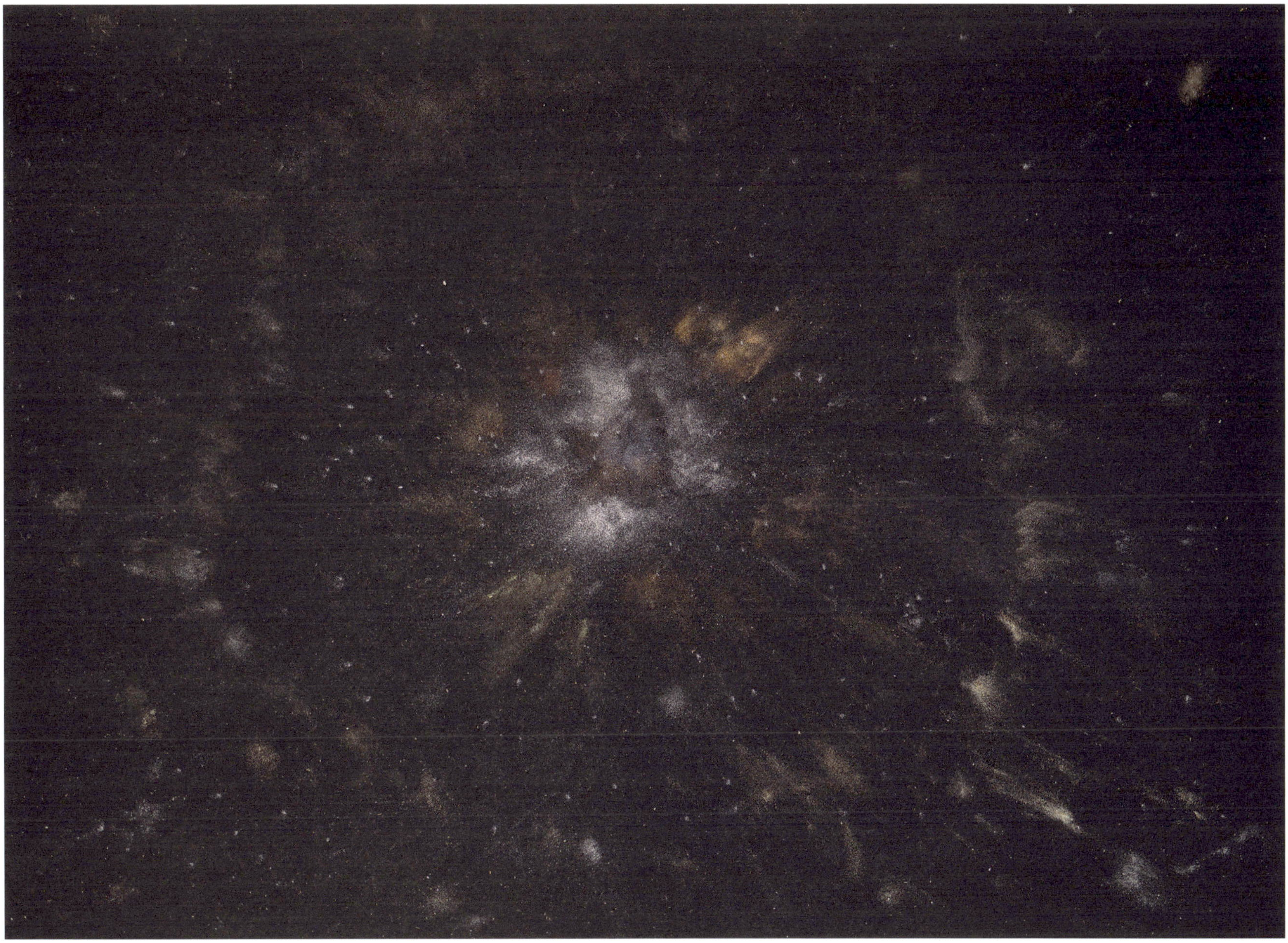

6.

ZILLA LEUTENEGGER .... At the core of Zilla Leutenegger's art sit three tightly interrelated concepts: persistence, as a form of dedication and desire to constantly explore new formal and theoretical possibilities; dreams, as the ideal place where aspirations can lead; and failure, as a tangible form of vulnerability that no one should be ashamed of due to its intrinsic honesty. All three are to be understood in the broadest terms within her work, filtered through a remarkably poetic sensibility designed to elevate mundane activities to episodes of significance. It is hardly surprising, then, that drawing claims a central role in Leutenegger's practice. The gestural immediacy of the medium is the perfect vehicle to capture the fleeting moments she is interested in, while expressing the sincerity of her intent. This is borne out by her hand style, which is stripped down to essential but well-marked lines and flat colours. The latter are strategically deployed to emphasize specific areas or to achieve particular effects. This can be seen in *Panties 4* (2015), the description of an ordinary and very identifiable activity like dressing, where patches of acrylic paint serve to dye the pieces of clothing in an otherwise monochromatic composition. In another sartorially driven work, the 2017 diptych *Gonna Genovese* (*Genoan Skirt*), a light beam acts as a *trait d'union* between two different moments in the same room, timidly originating in one and blasting into the other, covering everything in its way with a pastel-yellow tinge. .... Leutenegger's minimal aesthetic is the result of a somewhat elaborate process. Her drawings often part ways from the paper on which they originated to become digital animations, interacting with found objects, sculptures and other drawings. At times their role is functional, like the whirl of smoke from a girl's cigarette or the halo of a swinging light bulb. Other times they contribute an additional element to the story without betraying the circular narrative that defines it. Leutenegger has labelled this technique, which she started mastering in 1999, as 'video drawing'. One of the most representative examples, *Corridor* (2004), is a black and white stairway painted on the wall that turns three-dimensional to spill on to the floor, acting as a shelter for an animated self-portrait of the artist. The transition from wall sketch to trompe l'oeil and sculpture generates multiple layers of reality that happily coexist, calling into question the boundaries between fact and fiction. In the self-descriptive *Ein Hut, ein Stock, ein Regenschirn* (*A Hat, A Stick, An Umbrella*) (2018) the group of hats, sticks and umbrellas arranged in a hallway people a scene that on close inspection reveals itself to be empty, with the stand at the bottom complying with its designated task only when viewed as a reflected entity in the mirror. Conversely, the rack above supports an actual fedora along with a drawn candle lit via a spotlight.
.... Michele Robecchi

1.
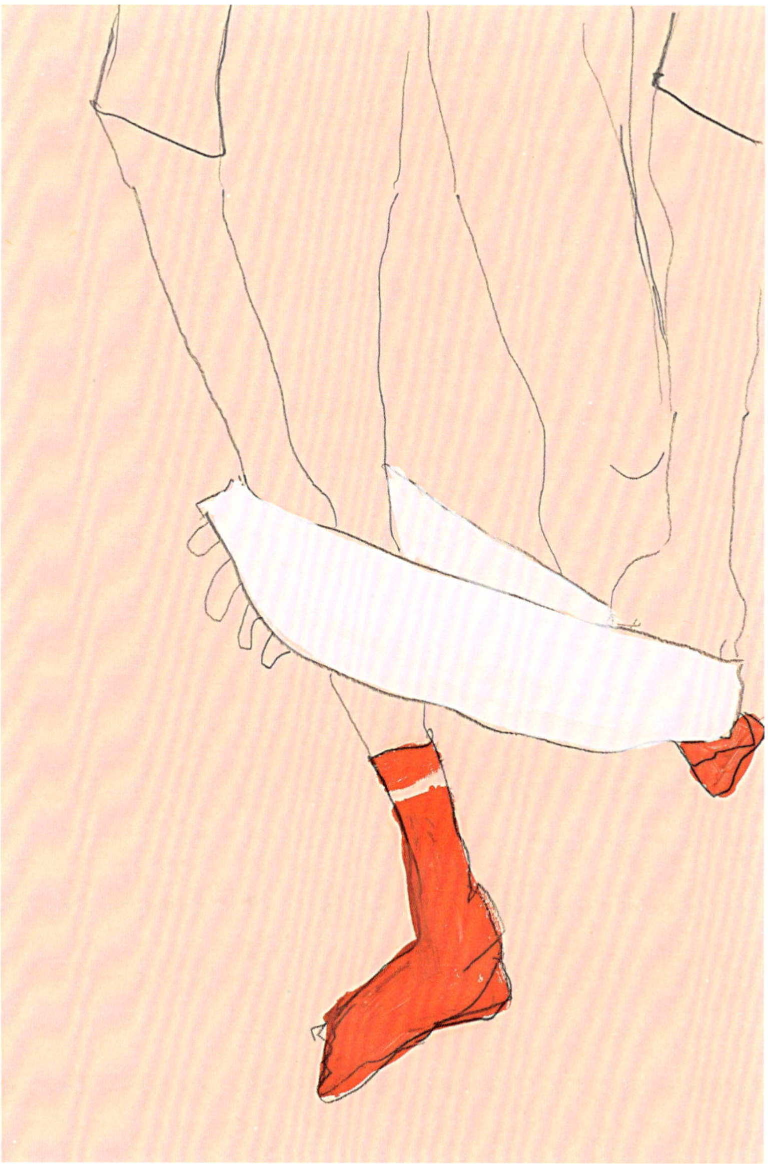

2.
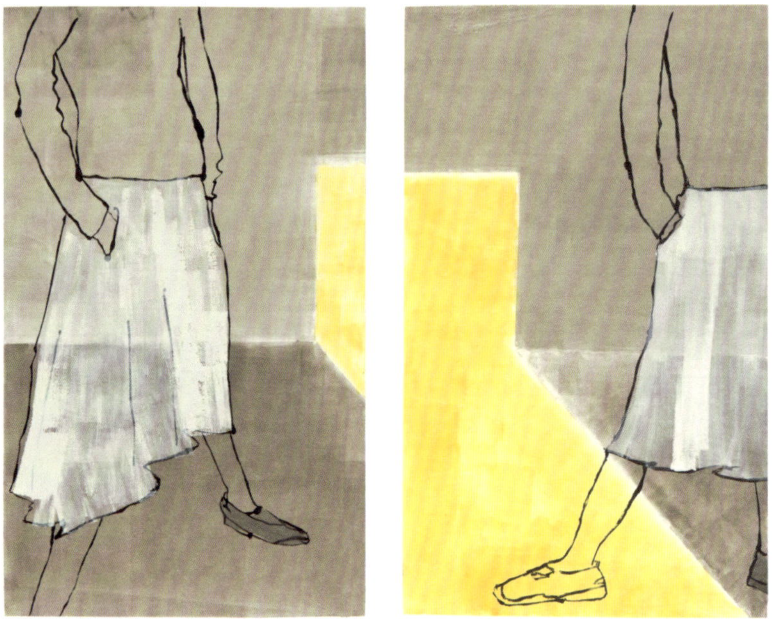

Born 1968, Zurich. Lives and works in Zurich.

1. *Panties 4*, 2015, pencil and acrylic on paper, 48.2 × 32.9 cm (19 × 16 in)
2. *Gonna Genovese* (*Genoan Skirt*), 2017, diptych, oil on cotton paper (monotype), each 92 × 56.5 cm (36 ¼ × 22 ¼ in)

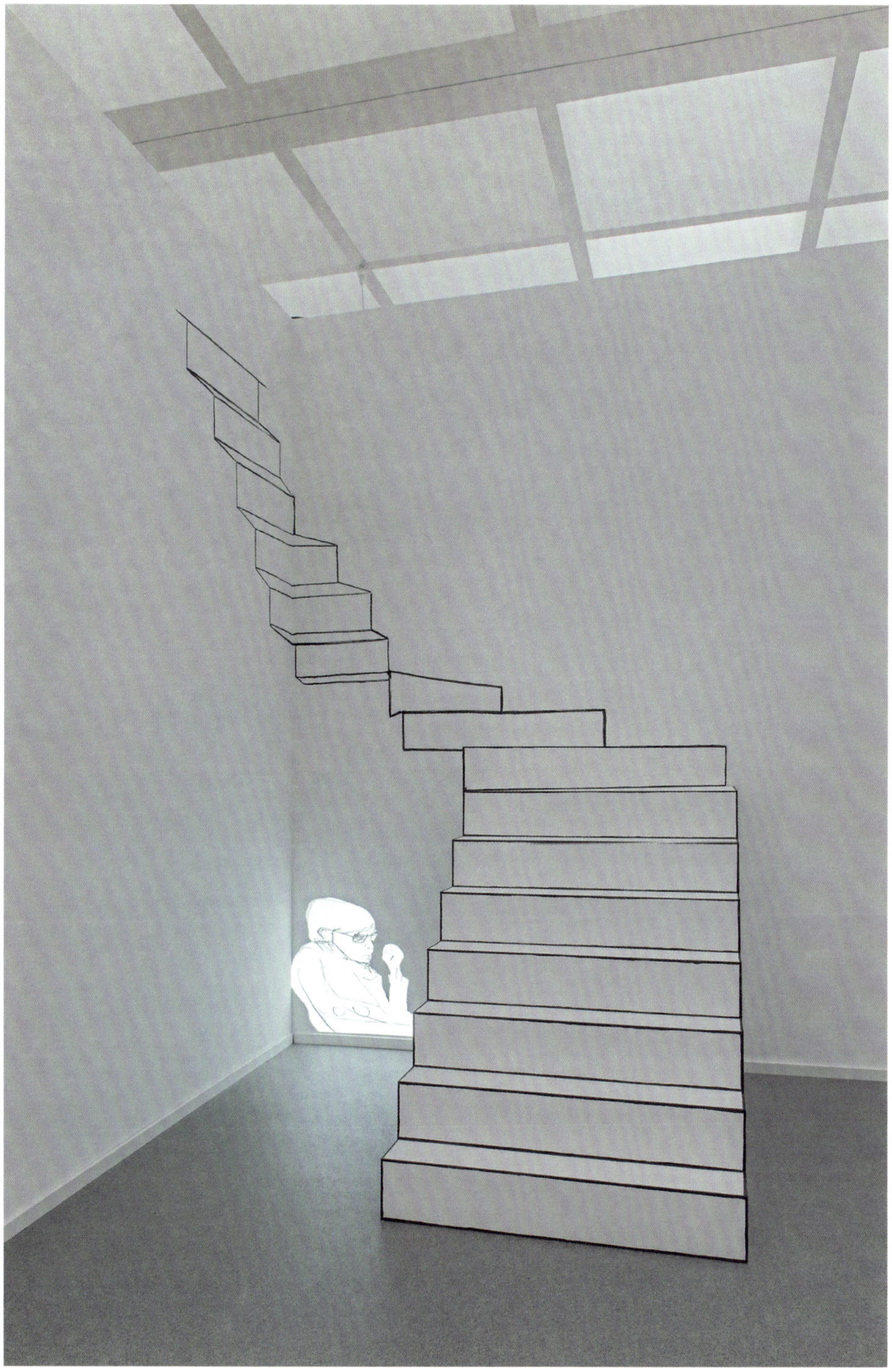

3.

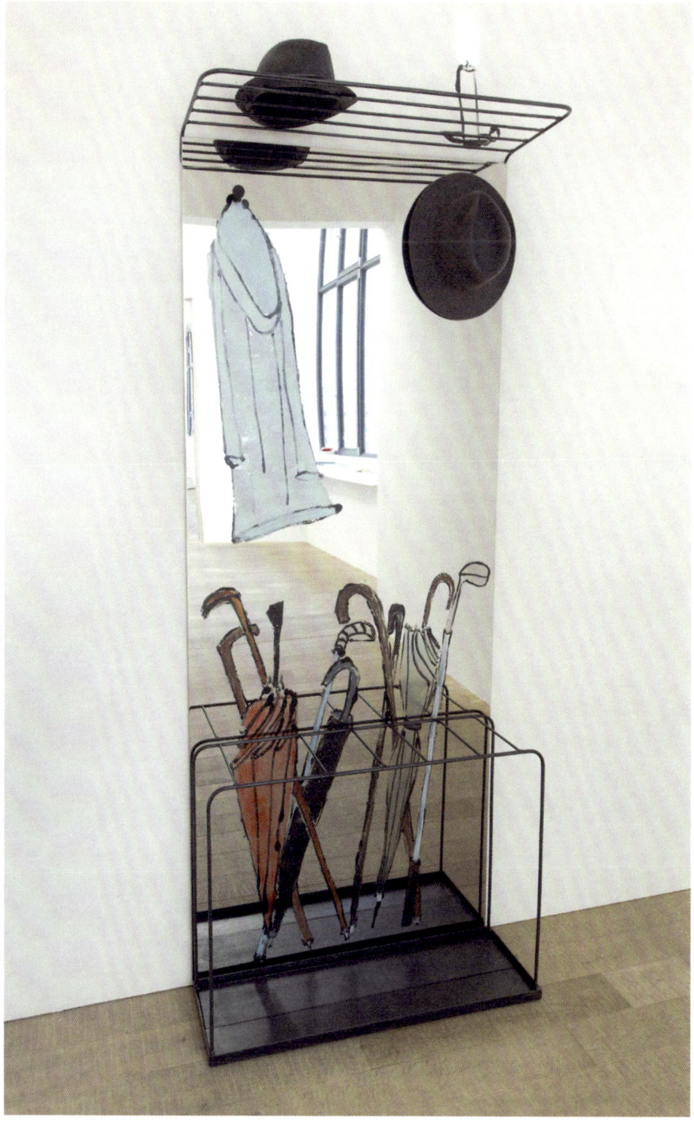

4.

3. *Corridor*, 2004, video installation with wall drawing, 320 × 200 × 250 cm (126 × 78 ¾ × 98 ½ in), installation view at Pinakothek der Moderne, Munich
4. *Ein Hut, ein Stock, ein Regenschirm (A Hat, A Stick, An Umbrella)*, 2018, monotype (oil on polished chrome steel), wall drawing, video projection (colour, no sound, 60-sec. loop), 2 hats and metal structure, 193 × 80 × 23 cm (76 × 31 ½ × 9 in)

TONY LEWIS .... Tony Lewis works with drawing in its expanded forms, which include not only mark-making and abstraction on paper, but also the very materiality of graphite powder. Smudges and imprints in the loose, hard-to-control substance have become a sort of signature, reappearing throughout his body of work. Lewis's drawings often highlight the medium's strong links to language. The social and political themes that contextualize his practice – which confronts race relations, labour and power structures in the United States – are often revealed through his aptly carving space for meaning through redactions and omissions. In *Man* (2018), Lewis collaged eight panels of a newspaper comic strip (he often culls from Bill Watterson's *Calvin and Hobbes*) on transparent foil, obliterating text segments in the speech bubbles and obfuscating or drawing over the panels' imagery. He leaves only disconnected abstract elements visible, adding bright colours that pop out. The effect is that of a visual poem, in which each panel's dimensions, together with its colours and remaining language, would correspond to, or dictate, the musicality, rhythm and tonality of the words. In *Predator* (2019) the bright red print letters spelling out the titular danger are scattered in disarray across the paper, which has been folded and unfolded, crumpled and distressed. A thin pencilled line threads from letter to letter, as if attempting to trick the viewer into putting them together in the wrong order, and so miss the warning, the proverbial 'writing on the wall', in the process. .... The artist switches seamlessly between small- and large-scale artworks. His site-specific floor drawings are created through a labour-intensive process in which an exhibition space's floor is covered in paper, which is then painted over and subsequently strewn with graphite powder. 'We literally pour the material out; we dance, we rub, we scrub,' he explains in a 2015 video interview produced by the Museum of Contemporary Art Cleveland, Ohio. 'It can be exhausting, constantly rubbing...the entire floor.' The drawing, folded and removed, is then exhibited again and again, becoming a sort of living sculpture that shape-shifts with each installation and shipment. 'Wrestling with the work – the poking and the prodding, the pulling and the ripping – it's very physical,' Lewis adds. .... *Plunder* (2017), a domineering mural at the Rose Art Museum in Waltham, Massachusetts, is rendered in another technique that recurs in Lewis's practice. Thousands of rubber bands dipped in graphite are stretched on screws to generate a smudgy line drawing. Though it may seem like a mere squiggle, in fact it spells out the titular word notated in Gregg shorthand, a popular stenographic script similar to abbreviated cursive. Lewis's use of words as objects, and of the abstracted shorthand as icons, harks back to his unrelenting investigation of language as material.
.... Hili Perlson

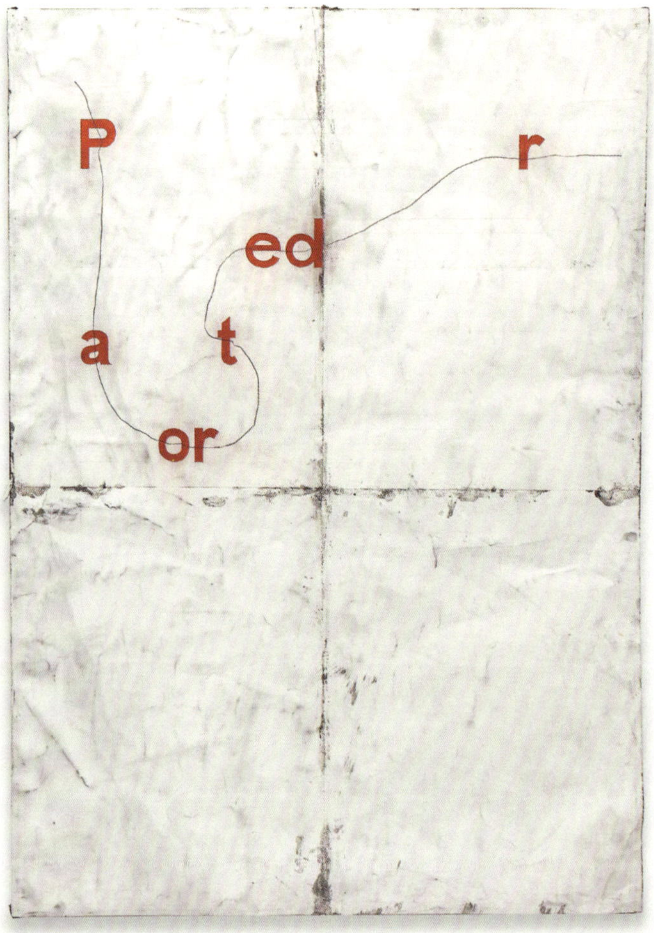

1.

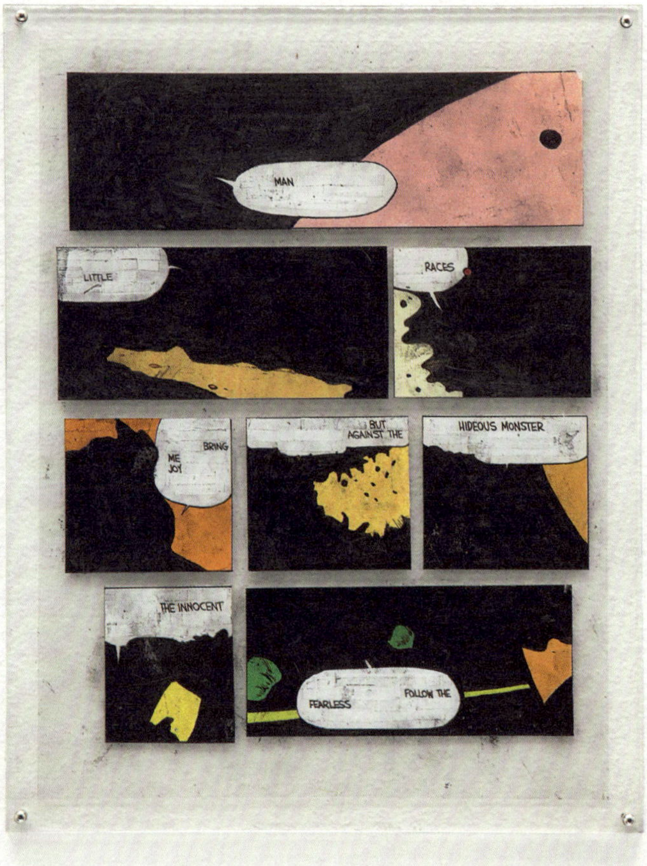

2.

Born 1986, Los Angeles. Lives and works in Chicago.

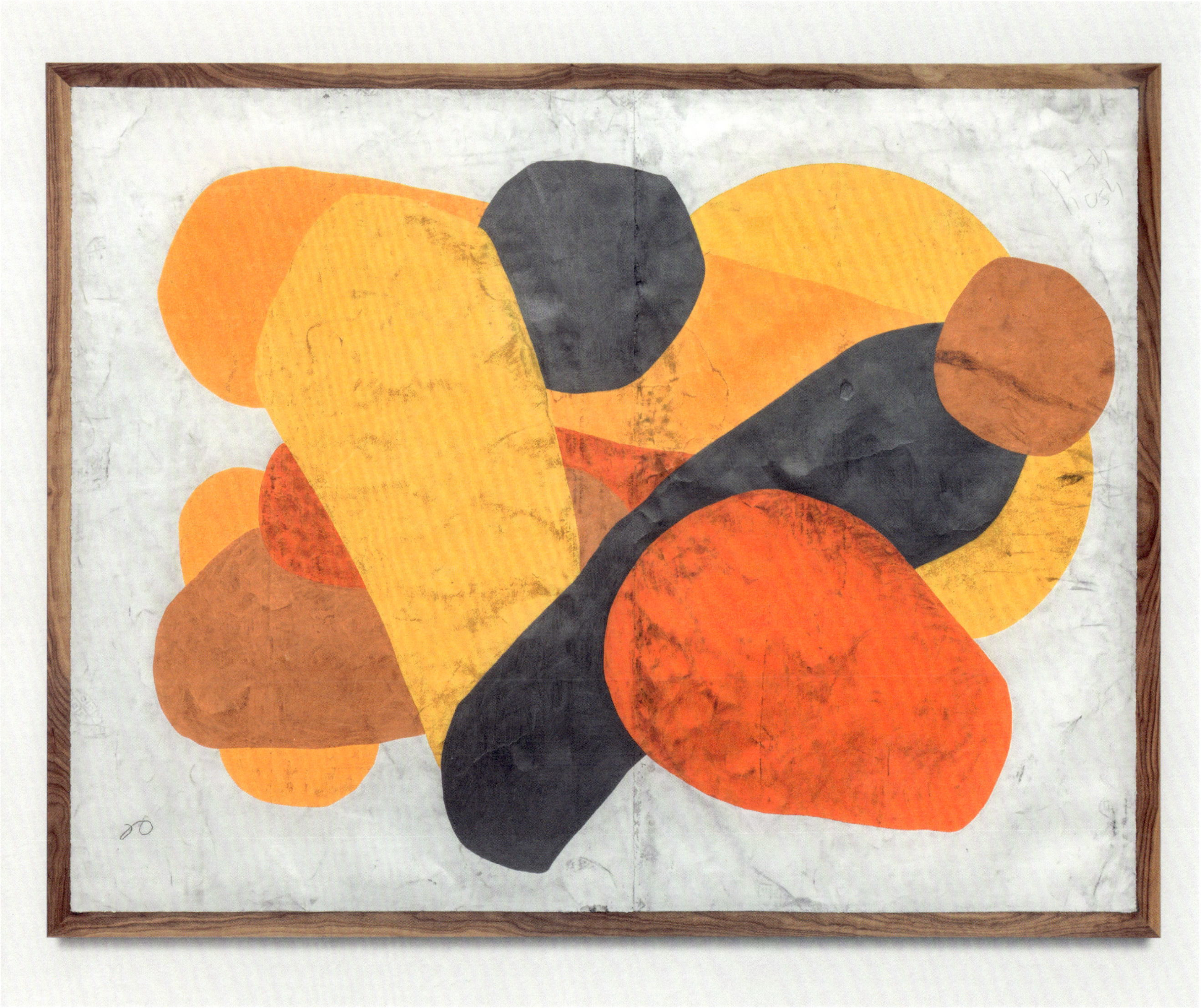

3.

1. *Predator*, 2019, pencil, coloured pencil and graphite powder on paper, 213.4 × 152.4 cm (84 × 60 in)
2. *Man*, 2018, pencil, graphite powder and correction tape on paper and transparency, 30.5 × 24.1 cm (12 × 9 ½ in)
3. *Arizona*, 2017, graphite, pencil and coloured pencil on paper mounted on wood, 194.3 × 255.3 cm (76 ½ × 100 ½ in)

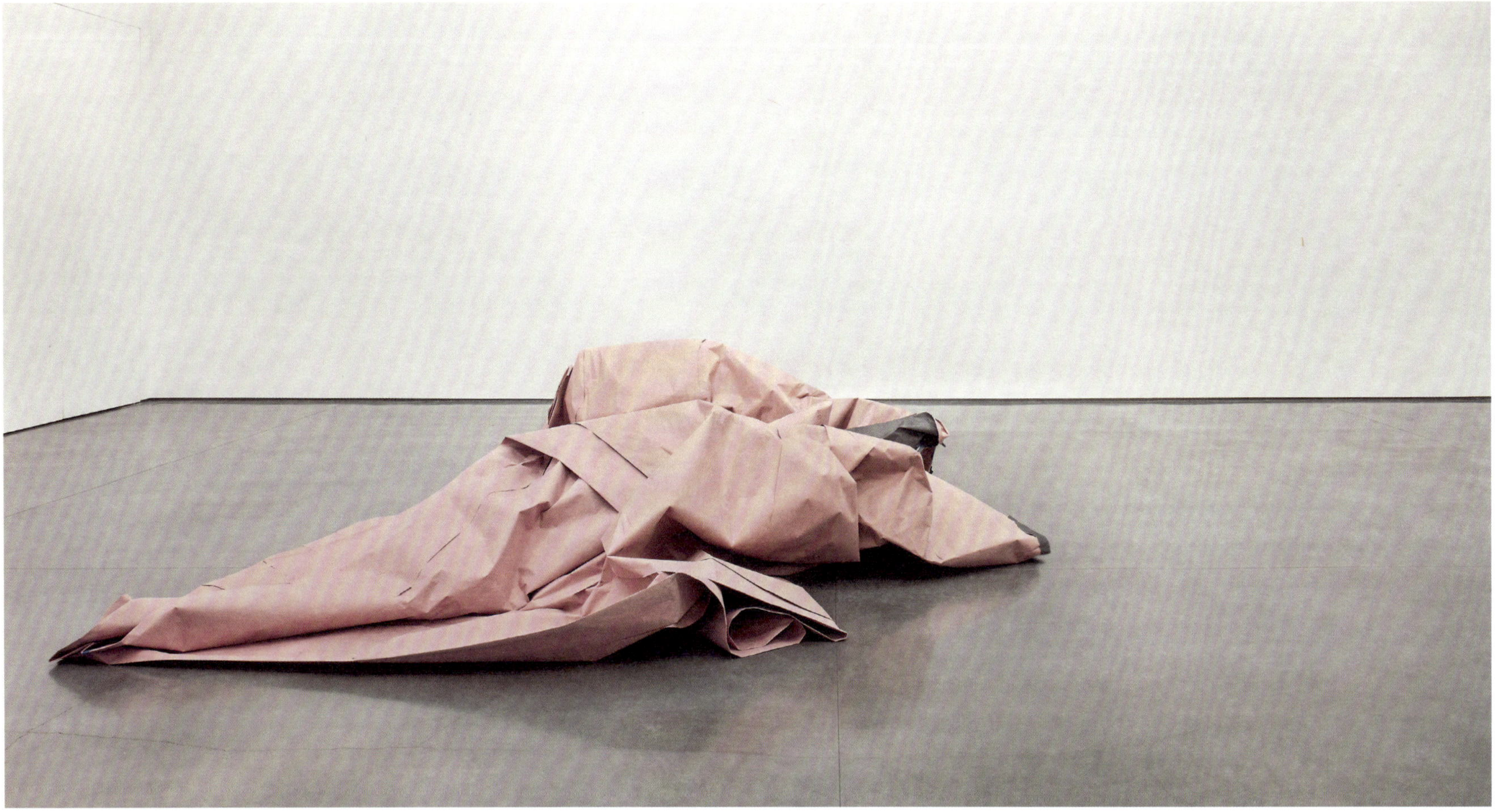

4.

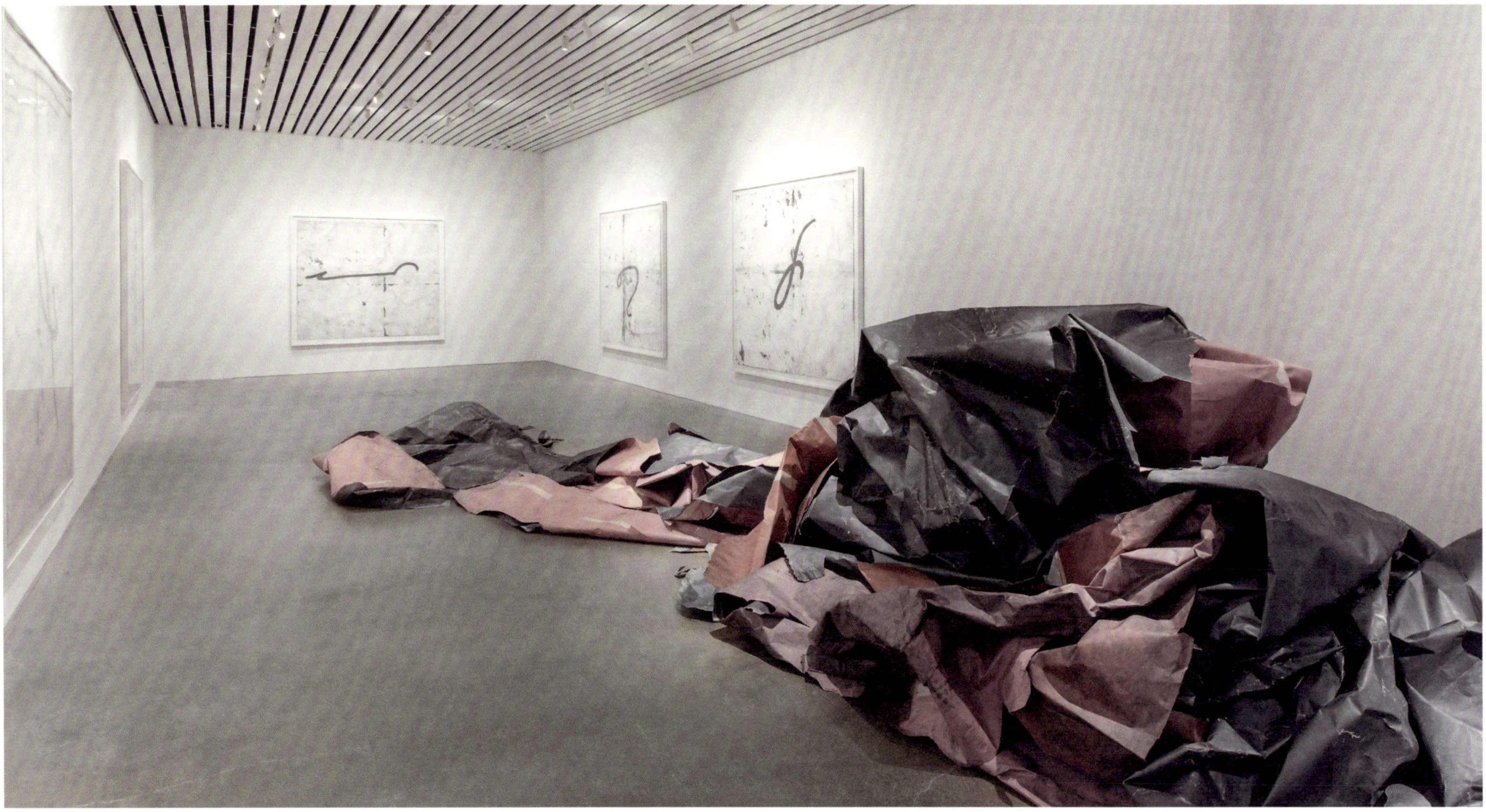

5.

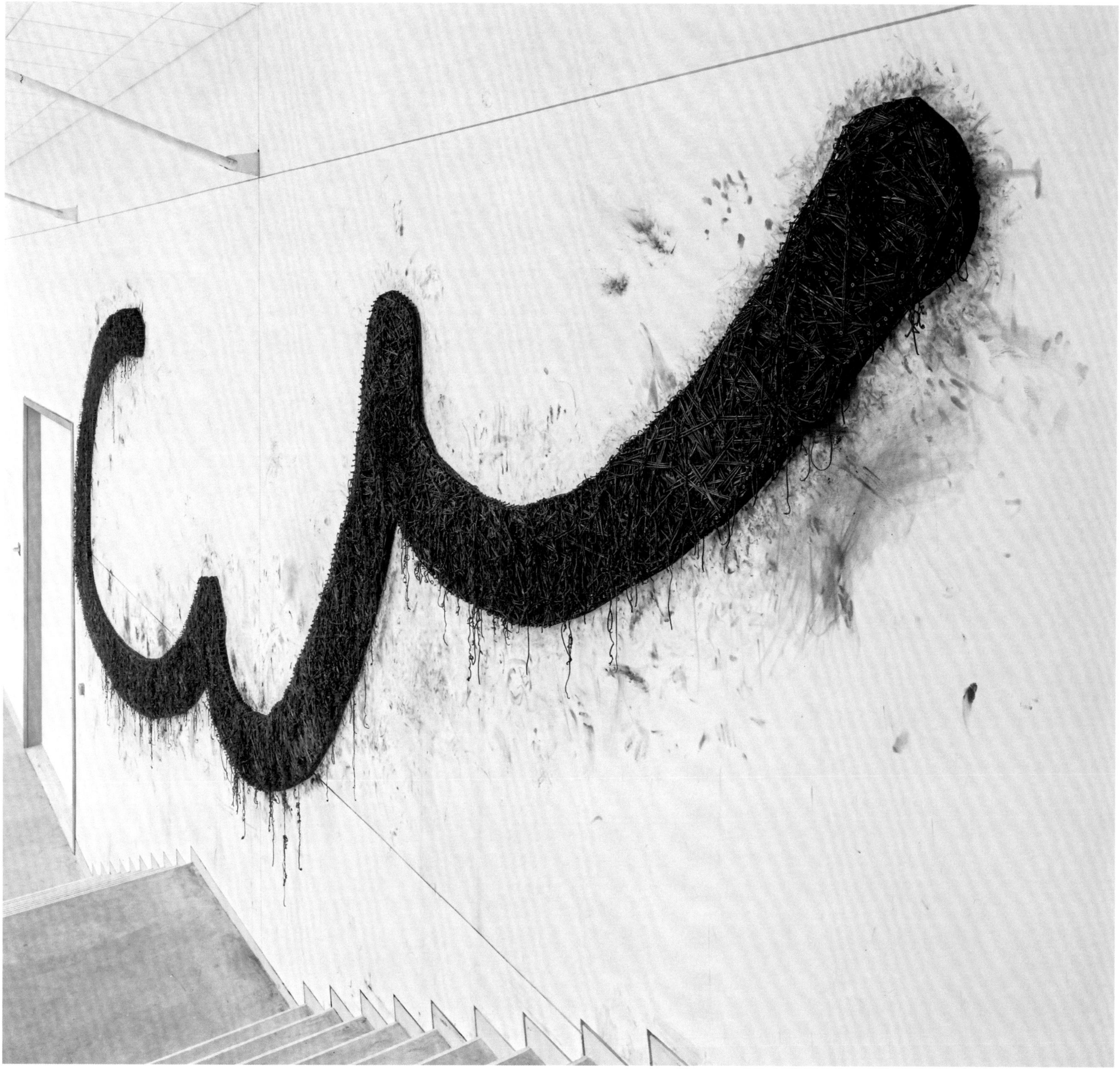

6.

4. *Untitled 5*, 2015, graphite powder, paint and tape on paper, installed dimensions variable, installation view, 'The Revolution Will Not Be Gray', Aspen Art Museum, Colorado, 2016
5. Floor: *Untitled 5* (2015-), 2015, graphite powder, paint and tape on paper, installed dimensions variable. Visible drawings on wall (L-R): *nomenclature*, 2015, pencil and graphite powder on paper, 181.61 x 212.73 cm (71 ½ x 83 ¾ in); *free*, 2015, pencil and graphite powder on paper, 181.61 x 212.73 cm (71 ½ x 83 ¾ in); *power*, 2015, pencil and graphite powder on paper, 181.61 x 212.73 cm (71 ½ x 83 ¾ in), installation view, 'Tony Lewis: Free Movement Power Nomenclature Pressure Weight', Museum of Contemporary Art, Cleveland, Ohio, 2015
6. *Plunder*, 2017, graphite powder, screws and rubber bands, installation view, Rose Art Museum, Brandeis University, Waltham, Massachusetts

ATEF MAATALLAH .... The magnificent remains of ancient Roman buildings, with their glorious mosaics and statues, are to be found at the archaeological site of Thuburbo Majus near El Fahs in Tunisia, birthplace of the artist Atef Maatallah. Many of his drawings are set against a background of ruined temples and pillars, or intricate mosaics, objects that are as integral to his country's heritage as they are to his art. His work is multi-layered; with the softest of graphite marks and an unmistakable degree of compassion, he embraces the past, the present and the future hopes of his country. .... In *Chambre 6* (*Room 6*), a diptych from 2017, three images of the same man's head face in different directions, masterfully drawn with graphite pencil on cotton paper. Two of the faces are turned towards a television screen on which the sacred Islamic site of Kaaba, at the centre of the Great Mosque of Mecca, is represented. The head in the right foreground faces downwards, shoulders hunched in a melancholic posture. This man's hair, moustache and beard are depicted with layer upon layer of the finest of pencil lines. The expression in his averted eyes is haunting and poignant. Cockroaches dot the wall behind, close to the man's head and below the television screen. These prehistoric insects symbolize endurance and the ability to overcome disaster – a metaphor perhaps for survival and hope, contributing to the mood of the drawing. ...... In *Le Rêveur des Muses* (*The Dreamer of the Muses*) of 2019, another man, wearing sneakers, jeans, a quilted jacket and a hat, lies on a traditional mosaic floor. Maatallah instils tremendous empathy in his depiction of the figure's curled-up posture, his hands folded and eyes closed, capturing a sense of desperation. The drawing embraces daily life as well as the historical elements of the city; this merging of the timelessness of history and images of contemporary Tunisian society is a recurrent feature in the artist's meticulous drawings. .... In the work *Sans Titre* (*Untitled*) (2014), Maatallah depicts the gaunt fragile figure of a man sitting on a chair. His thin legs are crossed and with fingers interlocked he grips his upper knee. Dressed in a hospital gown, cap on his head, intravenous tubes run from his arms in an upwards direction. He stares at the viewer while the two tubes cross beneath his left eye. The expression is haunting and perplexed: for what is he waiting? As with so many of his images, Maatallah skilfully reveals the psyche of the figure, one seemingly marred with a haunting sense of anticipation.
.... Elbé Coetsee

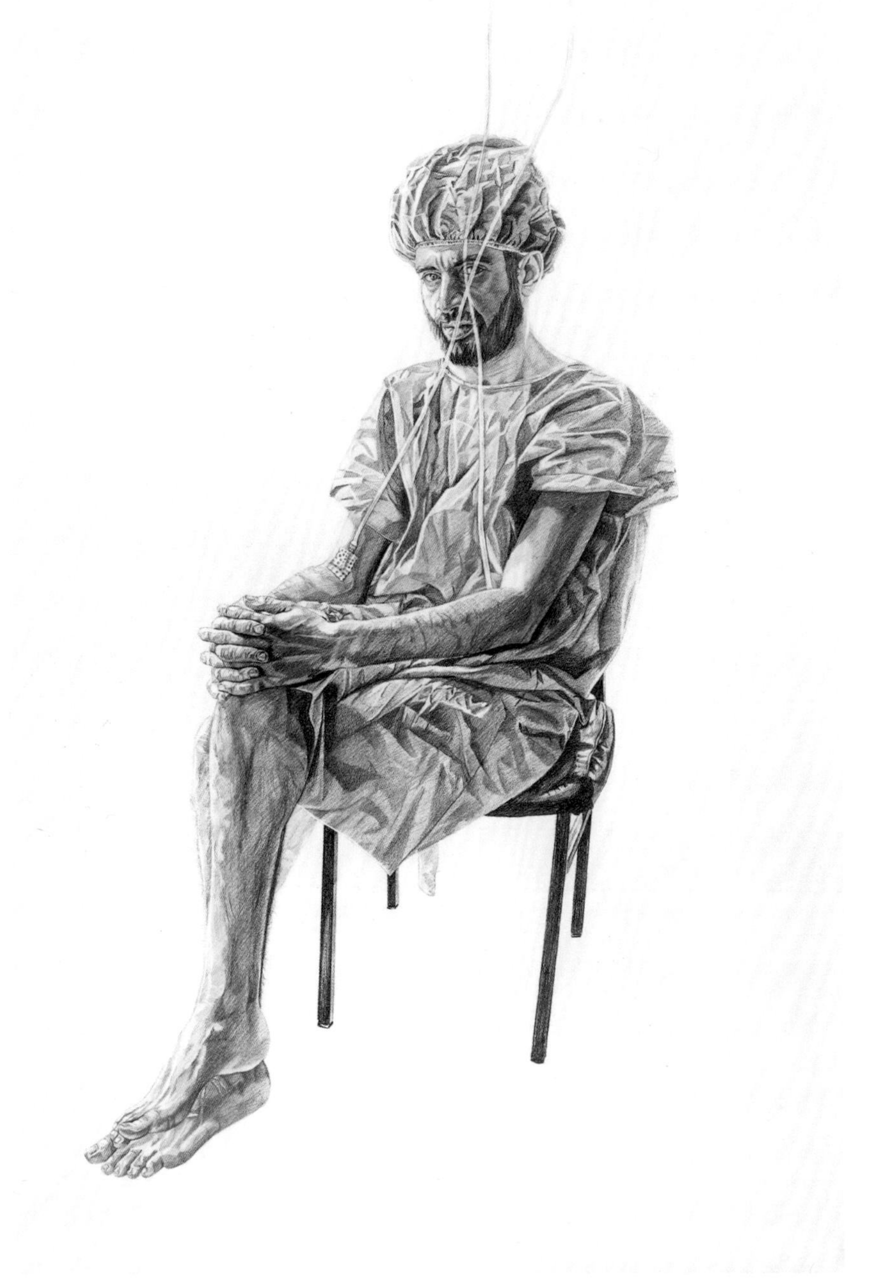

1.

Born 1981, Al Fahs, Tunisia. Lives and works in Tunis.

1. *Sans Titre* (*Untitled*), 2014, graphite on Canson paper, 240 × 150 cm (94 ½ × 59 in)
2. *Chambre 6* (*Room 6*), 2017, diptych, graphite on cotton paper, 57 × 153 cm (22 ⅜ × 60 in)
3. *Le Rêveur des Muses* (*The Dreamer of the Muses*), 2019, graphite on fine art paper, 100 × 146.6 cm (39 × 57 in)

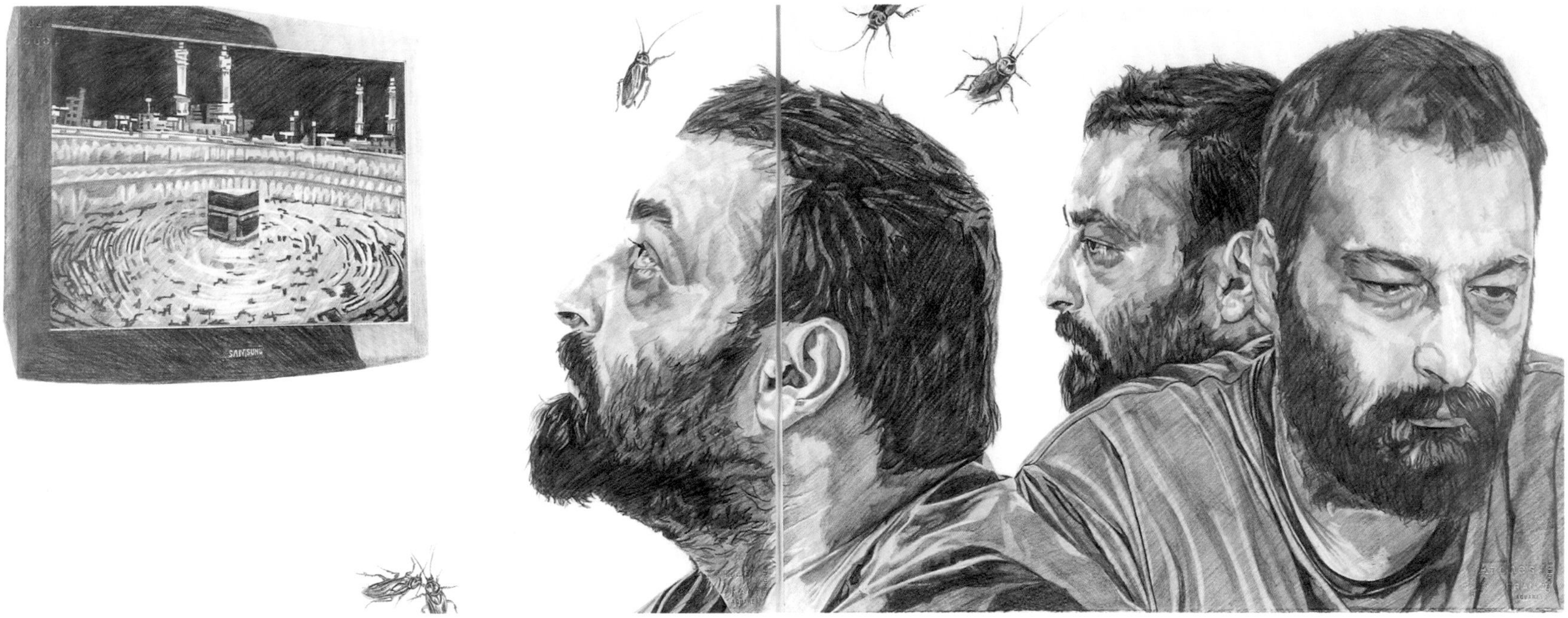

2.

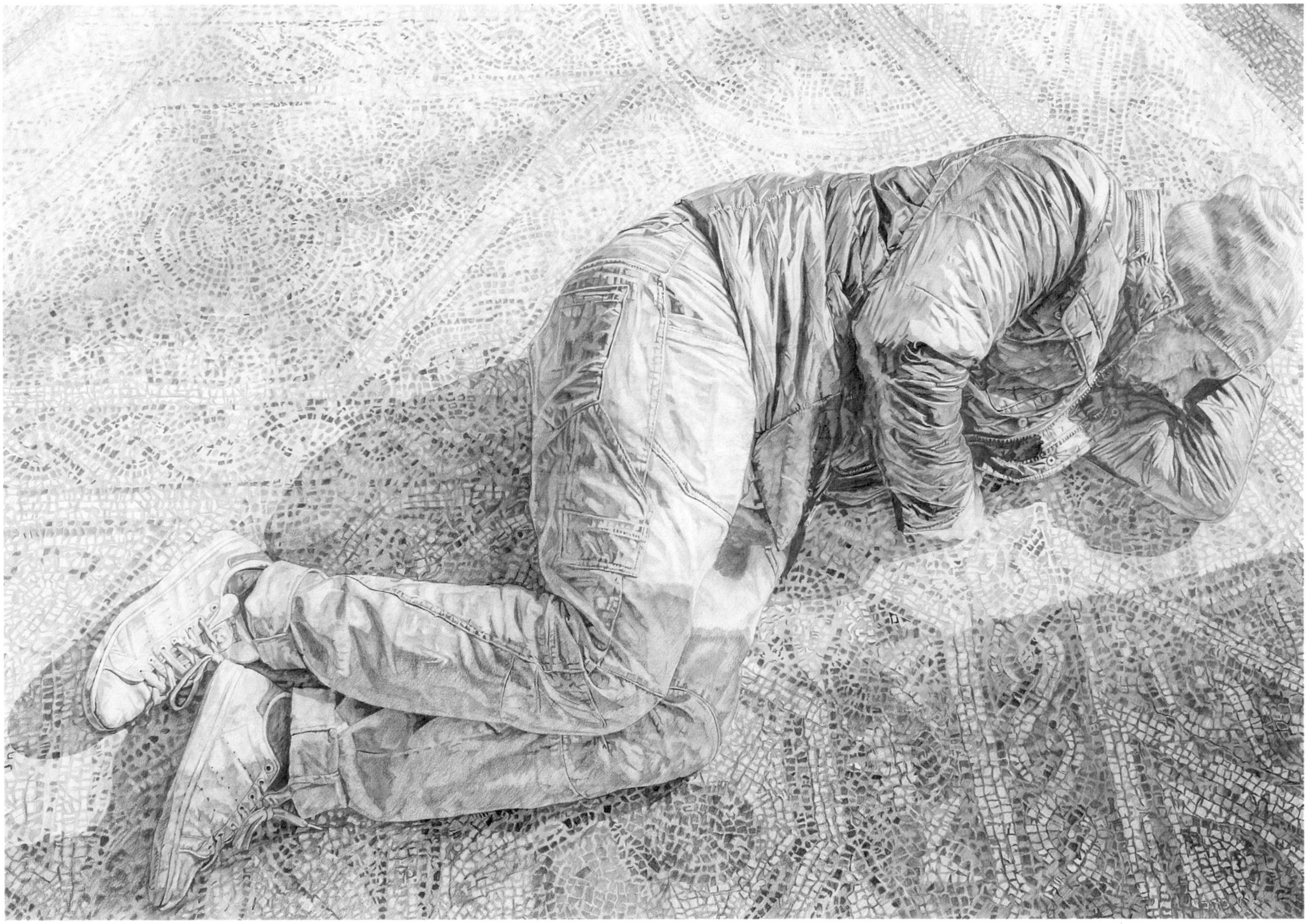

3.

JESSIE MAKINSON....... To look at Jessie Makinson's drawings and paintings is to be pulled, with a quick jerk, into an intense colour-filled world, full of characters, myths, moods and surreal curiosities. Hers is a place of chance encounters that draws subtly from our own historical myths, storytelling and art histories, albeit in landscapes where she dictates the rules of the location. In the somewhat riotous picture *Dearest Creature* (2019) we find a jungle-like episode with streaked and camouflaged characters dancing among the dense vegetation. None of them are idle, each playing out a role like actors on a stage at the key moment of their character's journey. In the centre we find a female archer embracing another person, who, like the two-faced Janus (the Roman god of beginnings, transitions, duality, doorways and endings) is removing her mask. Following her body down, we find her legs entwined by the entrails of a third, contentedly disembowelled character. Makinson asks us to cast traditional symbolic interpretation aside and, instead of thinking too hard about known classical myths, to interpret the narrative with our own subjective interpretation, thereby possibly fashioning a new contemporary mythology....... Watching Makinson work one understands a lot more about how she generates her worlds and characters: in reality, her starting point is more lyrical and random than the final works might suggest. Standing in front of an empty wall or piece of drawing paper, she allows her material and the idea of random gesture to 'speak' to her as she starts intuitively to make marks in front of her. In her wall drawings she then covers these marks with a thin wash of diluted primer, as seen in *Dearest Creature*, so that the painting hung on top jumps further forward. This random mark-making, however, is for her a protean moment that acts as a new dialogue from which to unfurl unknown moments. This is seen in *Lashes thickly II* (2018) where the random marks are seen as inspiration for the characters and the whole narrative that is taking place. Here, in the top right-hand corner, we see what could once be described as a splotch of red fashioned, using careful red structural lines, into a Quasimodo-esque alien form with a smiling and cheeky face, which is, unexpectedly, having its nose sucked by what could be an angel. Elsewhere 'noses' form something of a trope in this work, sometimes elephantine, sometimes phallic. By these means Makinson takes the seemingly random possibilities of mark-making and drawing and fashions them into the very reason for the artwork to exist and tell its own story.
.... James Smith

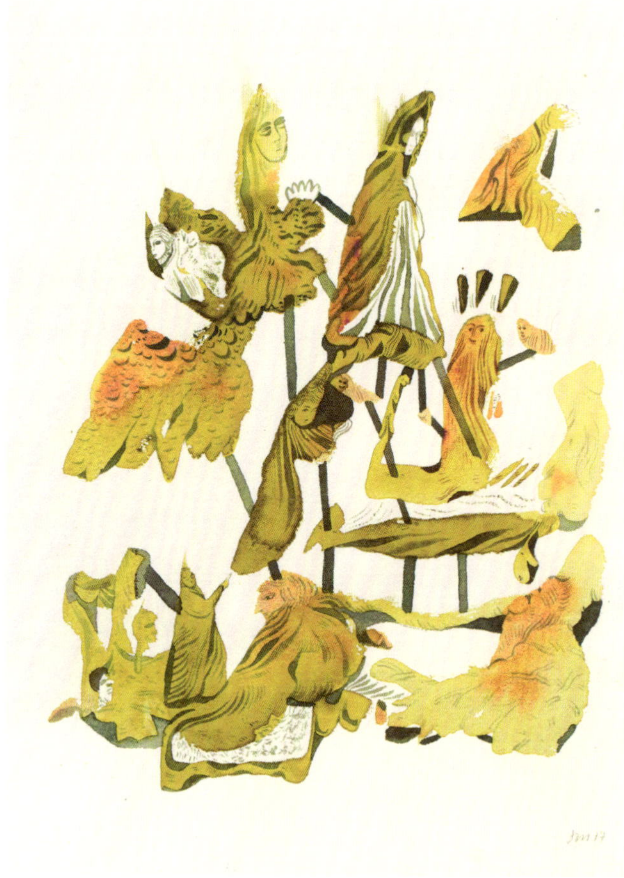

1.

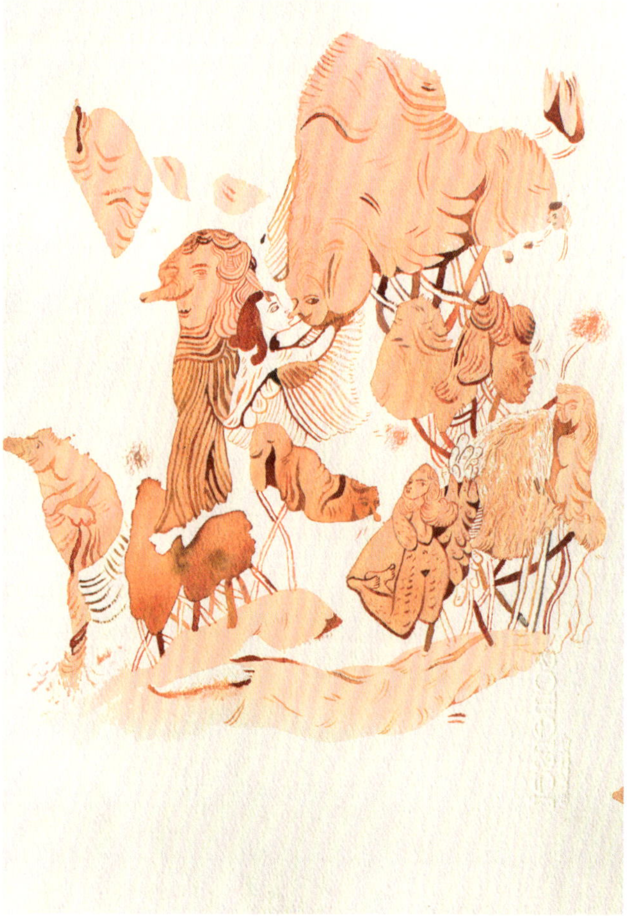

2.

Born 1985, London. Lives and works in London.

1. *Rag was*, 2017, watercolour and shellac on paper, 38 × 28 cm (15 × 11 in)
2. *Lashes thickly II*, 2018, watercolour on paper, 38 × 28 cm (15 × 11 in)
3. *Courtly Bee*, 2018, wall drawing and acrylic, installation view, 'Breaking Shells', The Koppel Project, London

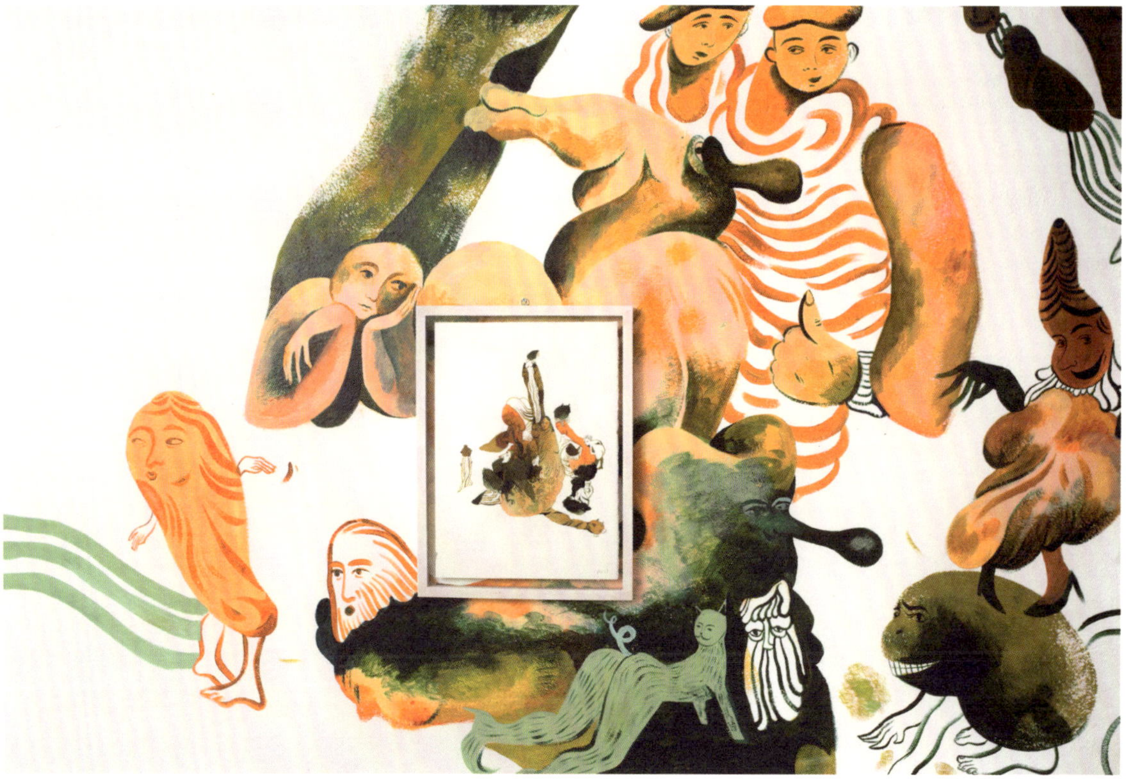

3.

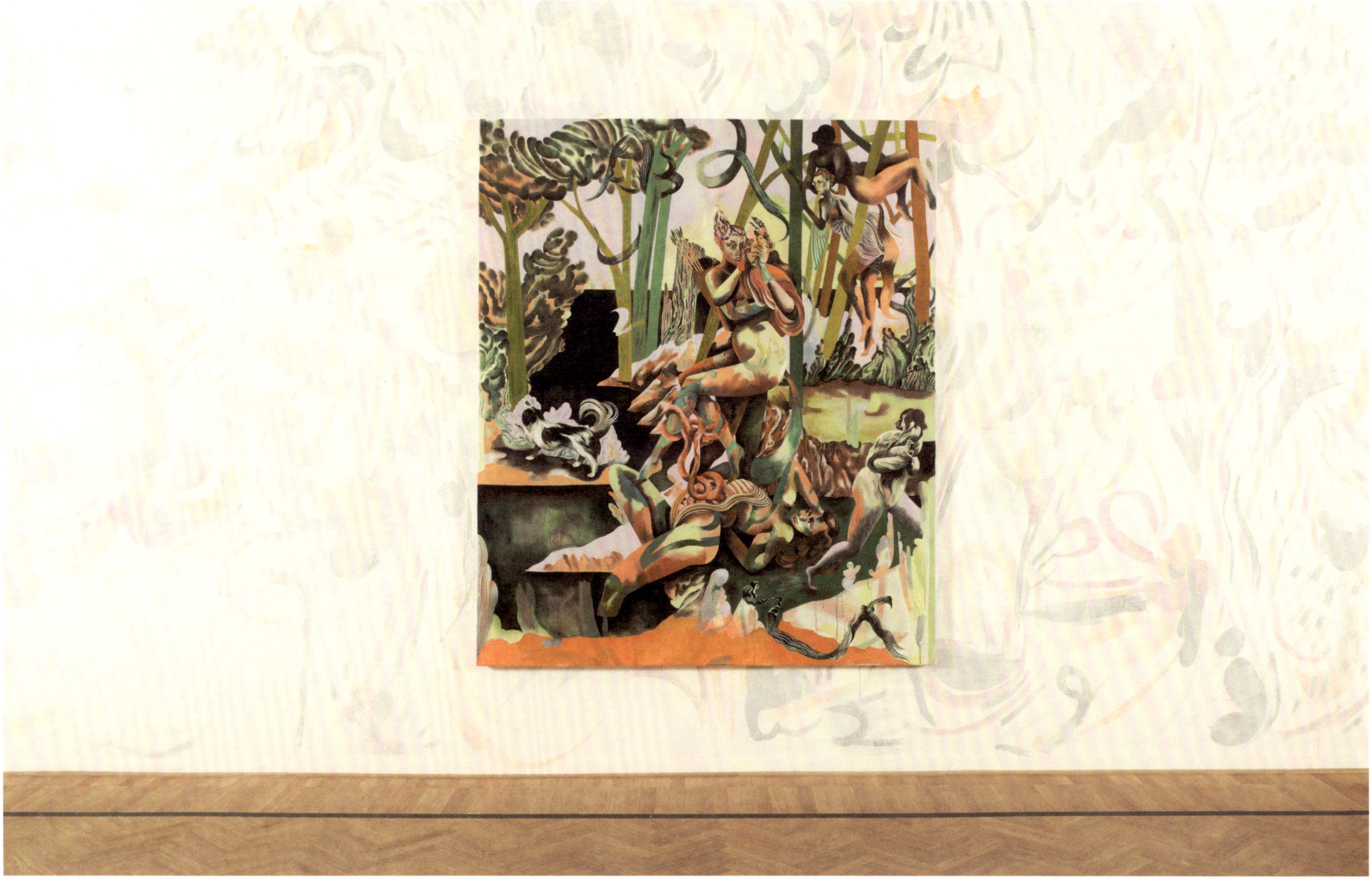

4.

4. *Dearest Creature*, 2019, painting on top of wall drawing, drawing: pigment and acrylic dispersant, painting: oil on canvas, 190 × 165 cm (75 × 65 in), installation view, 'Nobody Axed You To', Fabian Lang Gallery, Zurich

NICK MAUSS……. In 2012, when multi-disciplinary German-American artist Nick Mauss participated in the Whitney Biennial, he covered the rectangular entrance to his allocated gallery with appliqué on velvet to resemble a sketchily painted Neo-Classical interior, the museum's plain doors transformed into the illusion of a grandiose panelled doorway. Based on a Parisian Guerlain spa from 1939, it was like the stage-set for a play or an opera, and became a backdrop against which to present various works of art. The theatricality of Mauss's exhibition craft did not end there, with two-sided drawings mounted on glass presented in black frames on plinths, as if sculptures, that could be viewed from either side. ……. This presentation set the stage, some six years later in 2018, for Mauss's first museum solo exhibition, 'Transmissions', also at the Whitney Museum of American Art. Only this time he literally used the exhibition as a stage, inviting sixteen professional ballet dancers into the space in groups of four. Mauss presented his own works alongside pieces by others, including photographs by Carl Van Vechten (1880–1964) and George Platt Lynes (1907–55) of ballet dancers from the early to mid-twentieth century. With numerous works mounted on glass walls, the live performers could be seen beyond, enacting Mauss's vision for an exhibition referencing the mid-century heyday of modernist ballet and the avant-garde in New York. ……. Mauss's own drawings are often preoccupied with themes and motifs relating to the human body, ballet, choreography, performance, acting and physical gesture. In *Banderole* (2019) a small group of young men gathers around a scroll or ribbon as if acting out a scene from fiction or history. The pencil and ink lines are slight, like a sketch or under-drawing; indeed, Mauss's works are often described as looking as if they are 'in process' or provisional. An untitled charcoal work from 2016 depicts a young man in a dark top, viewed up-close from below, his hand covering half of his face. His thoughts are elsewhere. In the foreground, perhaps the source of his distraction, is the back of a letter, with a small black heart on the flap. Emerging through him, a figure can be seen faintly in the middle distance, an arm raised, perhaps dancing. As with his approach to exhibitions, Mauss's drawings are regularly multi-layered, employing devices such as juxtaposition, superimposition, inversion, reflection and mirroring. Breaking free of two-dimensions, Mauss takes his drawing practice out into the world by means of glazed ceramics or reversed glass paintings on mirror. In the twelve-panelled *or a net* (2015) viewers follow an outline, life-size figure into their own reflection, a prancing green silhouette above a harlequin pattern on one panel marking the interface between the here and now and the other side of the looking glass.
……. Matt Price

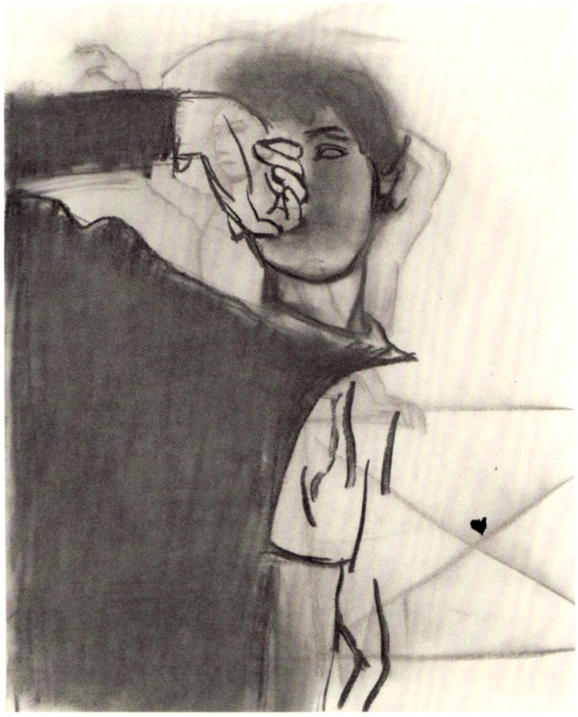
1.

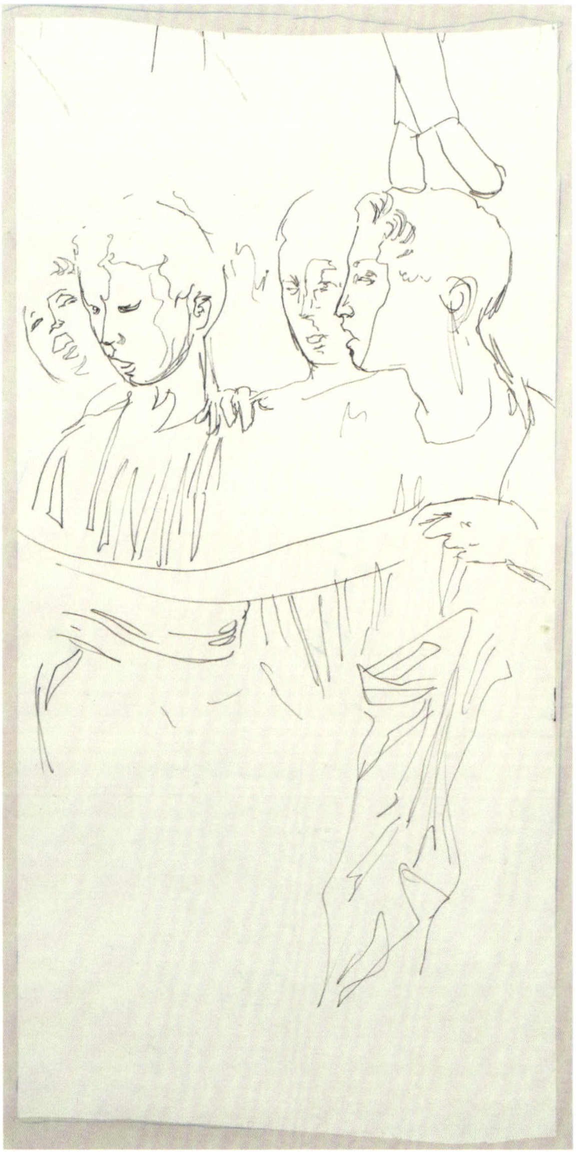
2.

Born 1980, New York. Lives and works in New York.

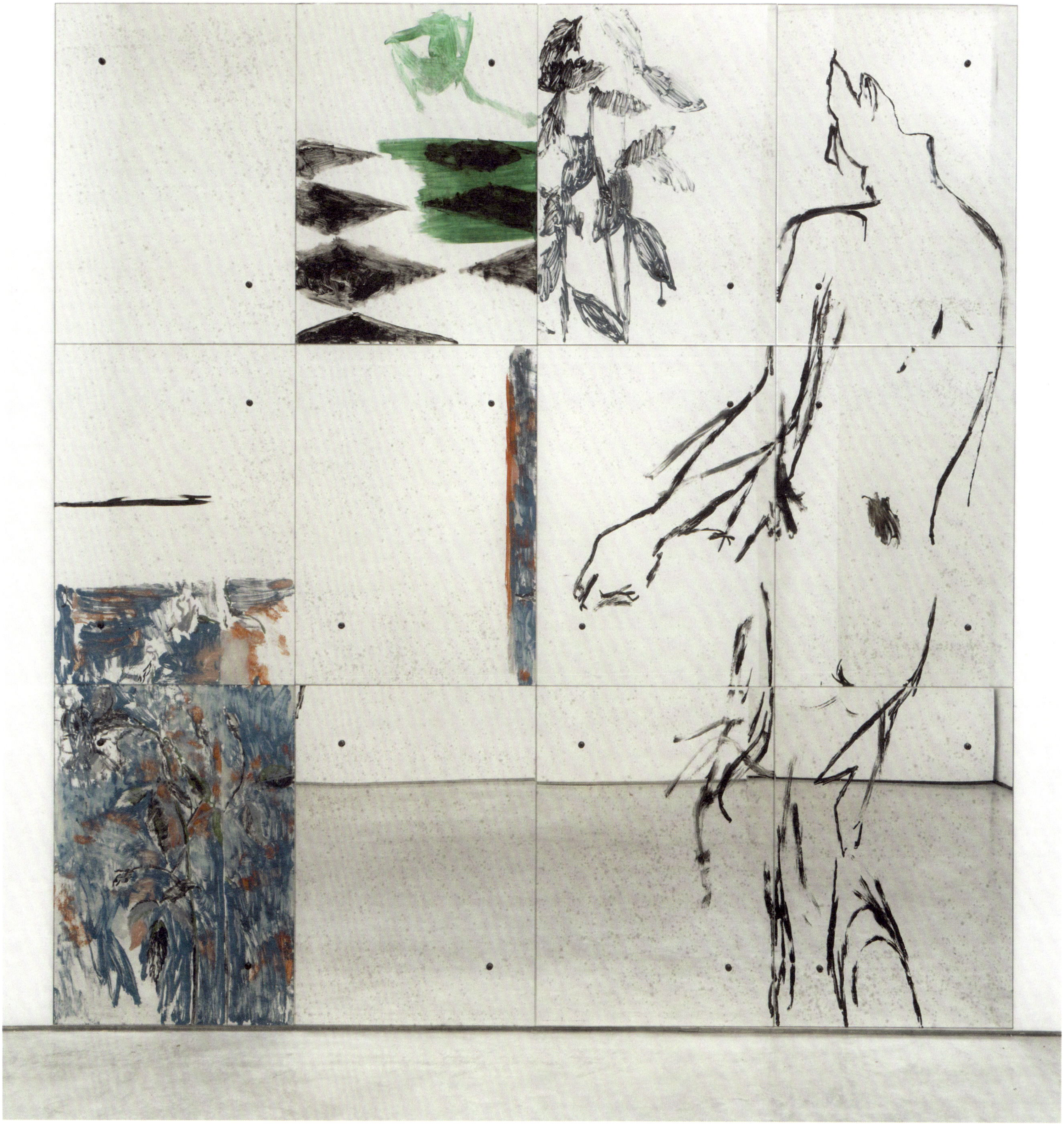

3.

1. *Untitled*, 2016, charcoal on paper, 43.2 × 35.6 cm (17 × 14 in)
2. *Banderole*, 2019, pencil, ink and paper on canvas, 191.8 × 97.8 cm (75 ½ × 38 ½ in)
3. *or a net*, 2015, 12 panels with reverse glass painting, mirrored, 213.4 × 221 cm (84 × 87 in)

EMMA MCNALLY .... The often large-scale graphite and charcoal drawings of Emma McNally are regularly likened to maps and charts, and while this is only part of the story, the comparison provides a useful point of entry into her intricate practice. A work such as *Scratches Traces Spaces* (2015) – a digital inversion of a drawing – resembles an aerial diagram or annotated satellite view of some unknown site of great significance, like a vast military base, covered with layer upon layer of data, the cartographer's callipers, compass and ruling pen evoked through the myriad marks, lines, dots and dashes that the artist painstakingly employs. The imagination is allowed plenty of scope to interpret what the eyes see; whether flight paths or walking routes, telecommunication signals or bombing targets, the topography is defined, demarcated, catalogued. Graphic boxes and strips function as de facto labels, simulating text, adding to the sense that reconnaissance and data analysis are the primary objectives. While warfare, power and control in the digital era spring to mind, this could just as easily be a chart mapping distant galaxies or the results of some deep-sea survey. .... The ambiguously titled SG (2019) looks like the kind of image found in a book about urban planning, charting how a village grew into a town and then a city, or revealing something about the demographics in specific geographical areas. McNally is a magician of infographics, creating the illusion of visual systems for storing and communicating information while actually giving us rich, open-ended abstractions that evoke thoughts on both macro and micro levels, from atoms to nebulae, individuals to civilizations, milliseconds to millennia. .... While some works are strikingly graphic, others are elemental verging on the sublime. The dark and brooding *Choral Field 9* (2016), from a series of twelve imposing graphite works, triggers thoughts of landscapes and harsh weather, such as desert storms or forest fires seen from ground level, volcanic eruptions or storm clouds viewed from the air. The drama and power of the natural world can be keenly sensed. This body of work was made in McNally's studio in West India Dock on the bank of the Thames in London, not only inviting analogies to water – waves crashing or powerful currents – but to other, often invisible forces, such as magnetic fields, electrical currents or sound waves. The musical reference in the title suggests that the polyphony of a choir is akin to the symphony of sound in the natural world, and the artist's complex visual vocabularies orchestrate this idea with both gusto and finesse. A self-taught artist whose interest and passion for drawing developed along-side her academic studies in the field of philosophy, McNally takes the viewer along on her exploration of the universe – of waves, particles and beyond.

.... Matt Price

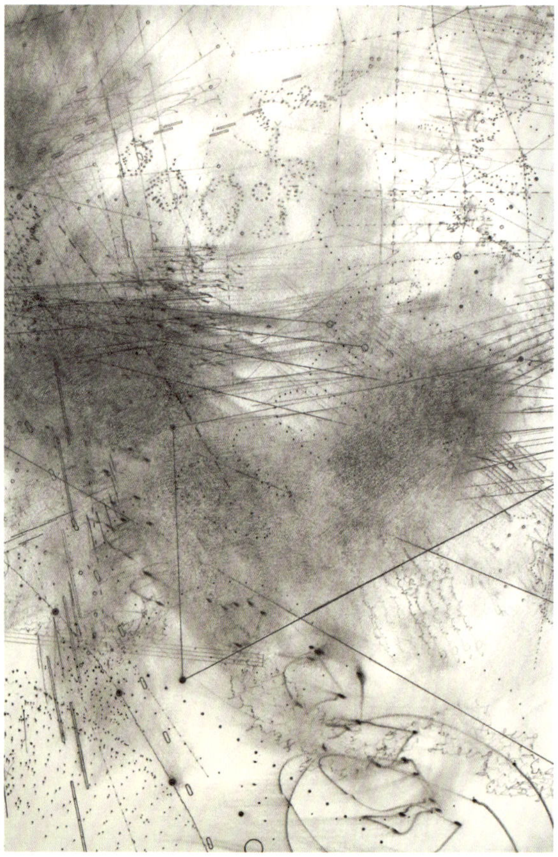

1.

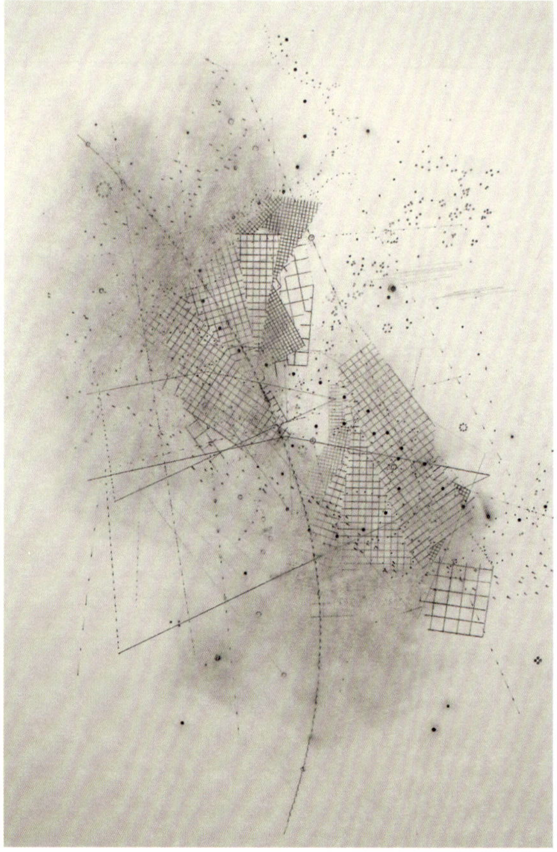

2.

Born 1969, Hoddesdon, UK. Lives and works in London.

1. *SG*, 2019, graphite on paper, 140 × 100 cm (55 ⅛ × 30 ⅜ in)
2. *TS1*, 2019, graphite on paper, 140 × 100 cm (55 ⅛ × 30 ⅜ in)
3. *Scratches Traces Spaces*, 2015, digital inversion of drawing, graphite on paper, 75 ×100 cm (29 ½ × 39 ⅜ in)
4. *Choral Field 9*, 2016, graphite on paper, 215 × 305 cm (84 ⅝ × 120 in)

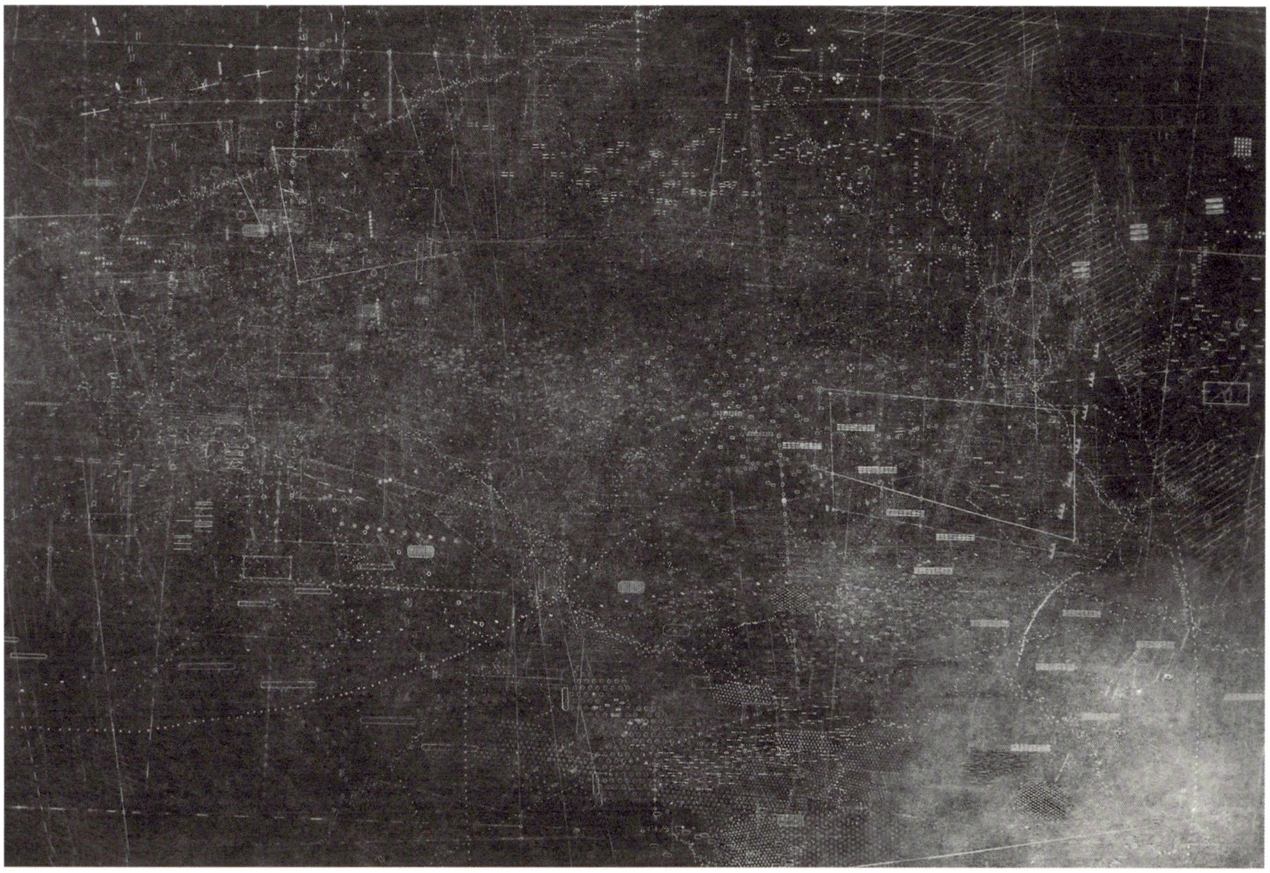
3.

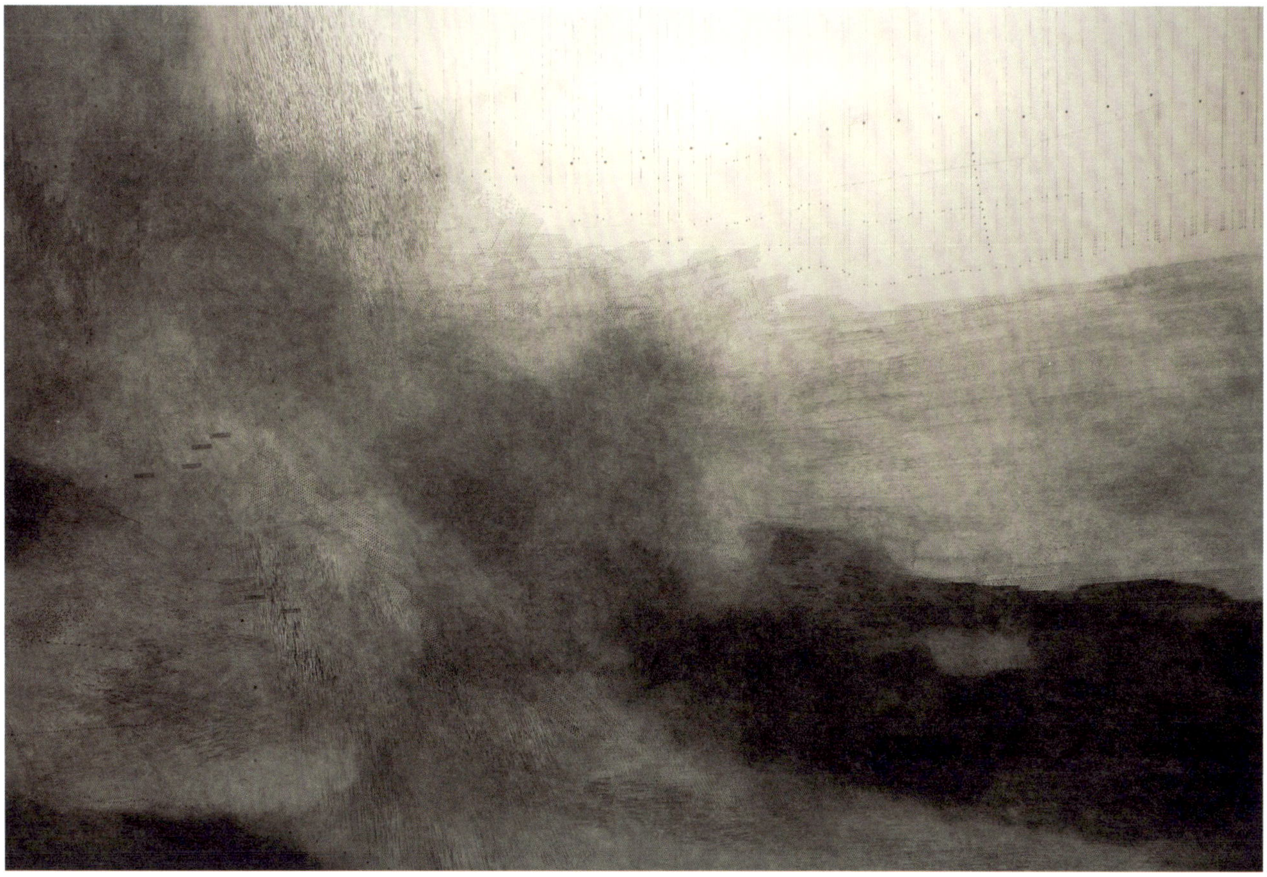
4.

JADE MONTSERRAT .... Jade Montserrat uses drawing as a means to reflect on personal and historical events, as well as to define and occupy space. She considers her work to be a combination of art and activism: informed by her own mixed-race heritage, her art aims to challenge society's embedded racism and inequalities related to gender, age, ability, religion and other characteristics. Montserrat is especially attuned to what happens when situations intersect to cause more complex forms of discrimination, and she weaves academic research into her visual art to reframe questions around the representation of Black bodies and women's bodies in terms of care, protection and preservation. .... A figure of particular significance in Montserrat's life and work is the entertainer, French Resistance agent and civil rights activist Josephine Baker. In the 1950s Baker began creating a 'Rainbow Tribe', eventually adopting twelve ethnically diverse children in an attempt to create an ideal mixed-race family as an emblem of a post-racial world. Montserrat's ongoing 'Rainbow Tribe' project was inspired by Baker's, and tackles the idealism and naivety of such attempts to sweep racism off the table without grappling with its profound insidiousness. The rainbow recurs in Montserrat's work as a visual motif too: in *Necessarily Pass Through* (2017), a blood-red ribbon intricately woven through afro-textured hair is passed over by a radiant multi-coloured arc. Montserrat's work seeks to reveal detrimental lacunae in popular, political and academic uses of language, in particular in relation to institutionalized and casual racism, both historically and today. A recurring concern in her work is the body's capacity to be both resilient and vulnerable, and the effect social injustice can have on people's bodies. Earlier in her career, Montserrat explored this issue by creating endurance performances for which she recruited her physical energy and skill up to the point where her body gave up. In *Revue* (2018) she re-enacted Baker's dance routines from 'La Revue Nègre' as part of a twenty-four-hour live performance. .... Montserrat's drawings frequently use language to powerful effect, her statements impressive on the level of both scale and meaning. In her 2018 exhibition 'Instituting Care', vast wall drawings extended from floor to ceiling, displaying quotations from influential Black thinkers and writers including Frantz Fanon, Audre Lorde and Stuart Hall. Their words, drawn and shaded in charcoal, seem to curl around one another. Some of the drawings feature statements by artists on the topic of education, the role of art and individual or collective creativity. Set against text-images rendered at such a large scale, the body of the viewer appears immersed in words; Montserrat's hope is that they will also be marked by their message.
.... Ellen Mara De Wachter

1.

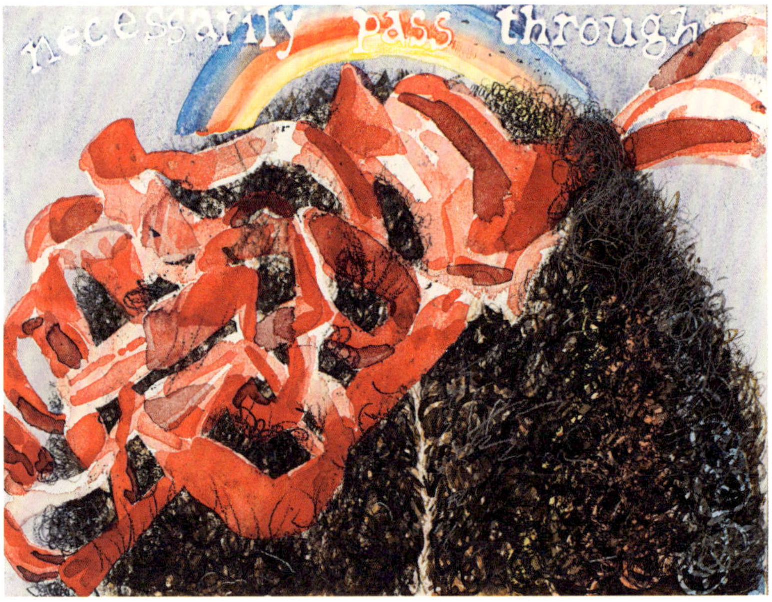

2.

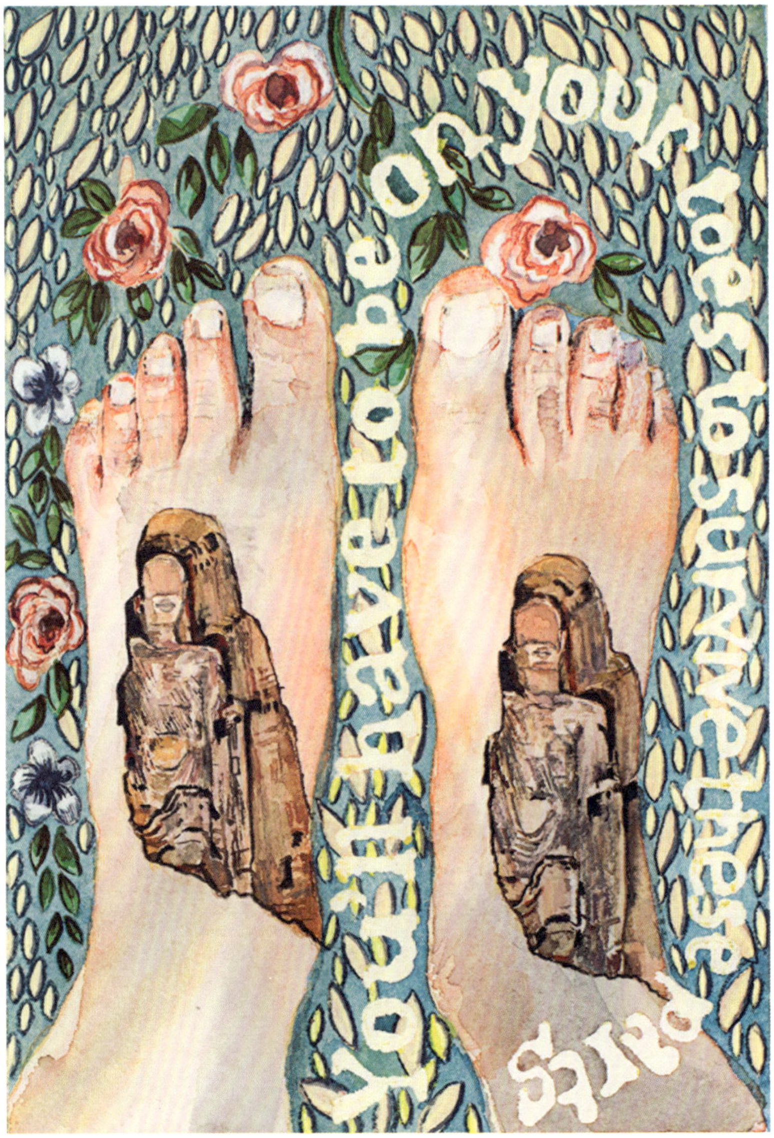

Born 1981, London. Lives and works in Scarborough, UK.

1. *Necessarily Pass Through*, 2017, watercolour, Indian ink, gouache, pencil, charcoal and pen on paper, 36.5 × 48 cm (14 ⅜ × 18 ⅞ in)
2. *You'll Have To Be On Your Toes*, 2015, watercolour, gouache, pencil and pencil crayon on paper, 25 × 17.7 cm (9 ⅞ × 7 in)
3. *Instituting Care*, 2018, charcoal drawing, installation view, Bluecoat, Liverpool, UK

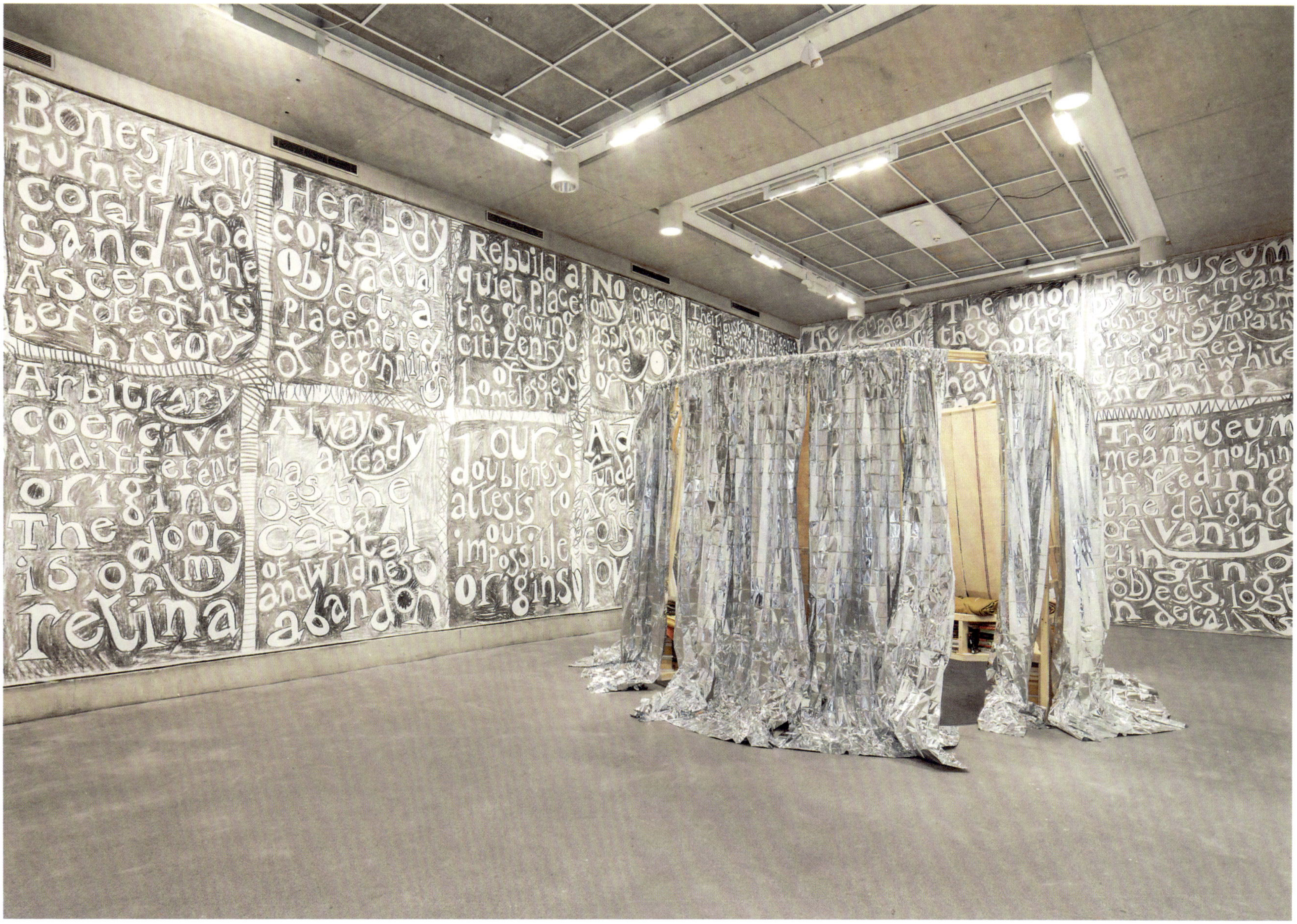
Arbitrary coercive indifferent origins The door is on my retina
Always already has the sexual capital of wildness and abandon
Rebuild a quiet place the growing citizenry of homelessness
Our doubleness attests to our impossible origins

3.

ALICE MOREY....... Calcium in our bones. Iron swimming around our bloodstream. The average human is home to millions of minerals and bacteria that are as likely to be found in the soil as in our gut. These non-human cells live on and inside us, regulating activity in our brains and bodies. Alice Morey's artworks explore biological and ecological entanglements. Her unprimed canvases are typically smeared, splattered and stained with pigment mixed with yoghurt, merging probiotics with painting. Drawings of flora and fauna jostle for attention next to moments of abstraction. In later works, the canvases are marked with stratified areas of distinct imagery that recall geological maps depicting rocks and minerals. *Voodoo Sketch* (2018) exemplifies these interests. Through a transparent green wash, sketched forms suggest organisms that are supported by harnesses. They recall medical equipment evoking injury and vulnerability. At the top of the picture, pigment appears as though blown on to the bare canvas. At the bottom, plant-like forms float and sprout upwards, partially obscuring what look like human eyes or cells. While the imagery is disparate, there is a sense of an interspecies communion with animals, humans and plants involved in some complex cohabitation.

.......Alongside her works on canvas, Morey has also produced performances and installations that further explore the relationship between natural and chemical processes. There is a digestive quality to much of this work, with images secreted as much as drawn. We are reminded that art, eating and ecological processes all produce their own forms of material transformation. In *Wafts* (2018) disparate images coexist in the same picture. An elemental drawing of leaves in the top part of the composition sits above blue, green and red pigment smeared to suggest water. The paint frames a drawing of what looks like an underground pipe or top hat. Incidental marks sit alongside deliberate ones, moments of activity situated next to empty and bare canvas.

.... Light and shade, excess and blankness; these images derive their pictorial drama from a collagist's flair for dynamic incongruities. They trade on a tension between figuration and something more reticent. Images are held back, and the gaps left in. These works zoom in and out of monumental and microscopic processes: the transformation of a mountain range by tectonic plates; the imprint of teeth on a bitten apple; the composition of a flower drawn by a pencil. The artist's translation of materials into images is another transformation among many. Pictures contain their own formal logic, but Morey reminds us that ultimately art – despite its symbols and codes conceived and decoded by humans over thousands of years – remains as unknown as the world it inhabits.

.... George Vasey

Born 1986, London. Lives and works in Berlin.

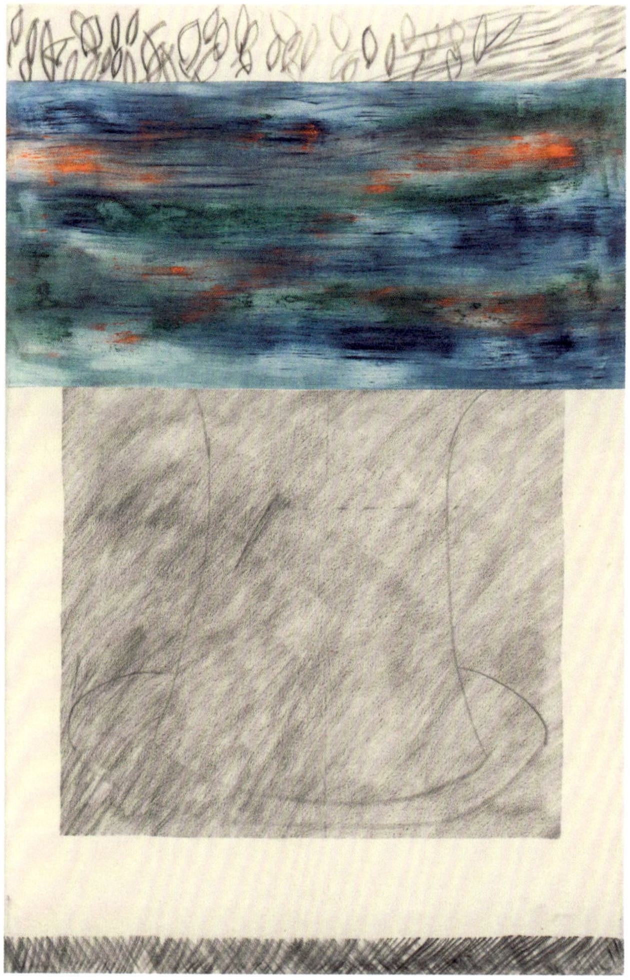

1.

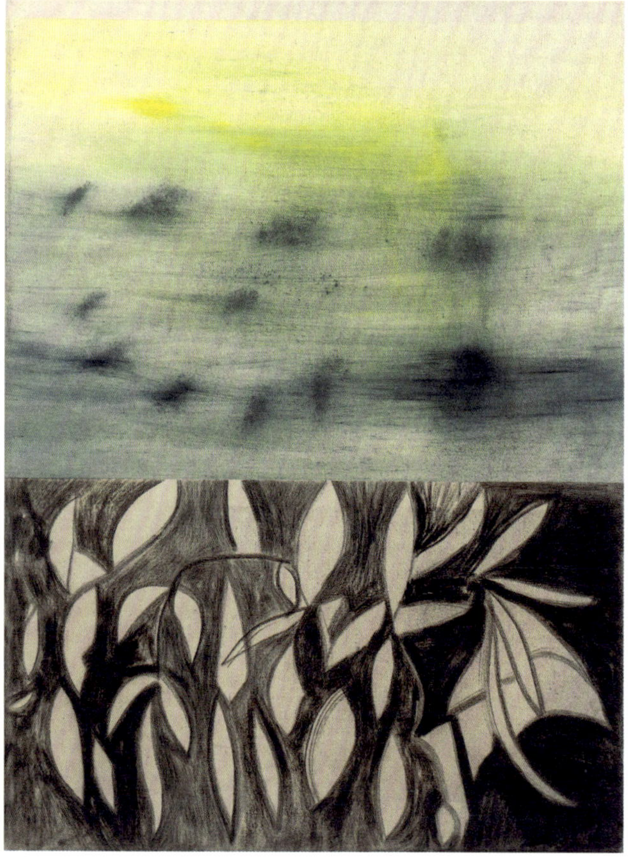

2.

1. *Wafts*, 2018, charcoal, pigment and yoghurt on unprimed canvas, 120 × 80 cm (47 ¼ × 31 ½ in)
2. *Beneath, beckons, beyond*, 2019, charcoal, pigment, iron oxide, cadmium and yoghurt on unprimed canvas, 80 × 60 cm (31 ½ × 23 ⅝ in)

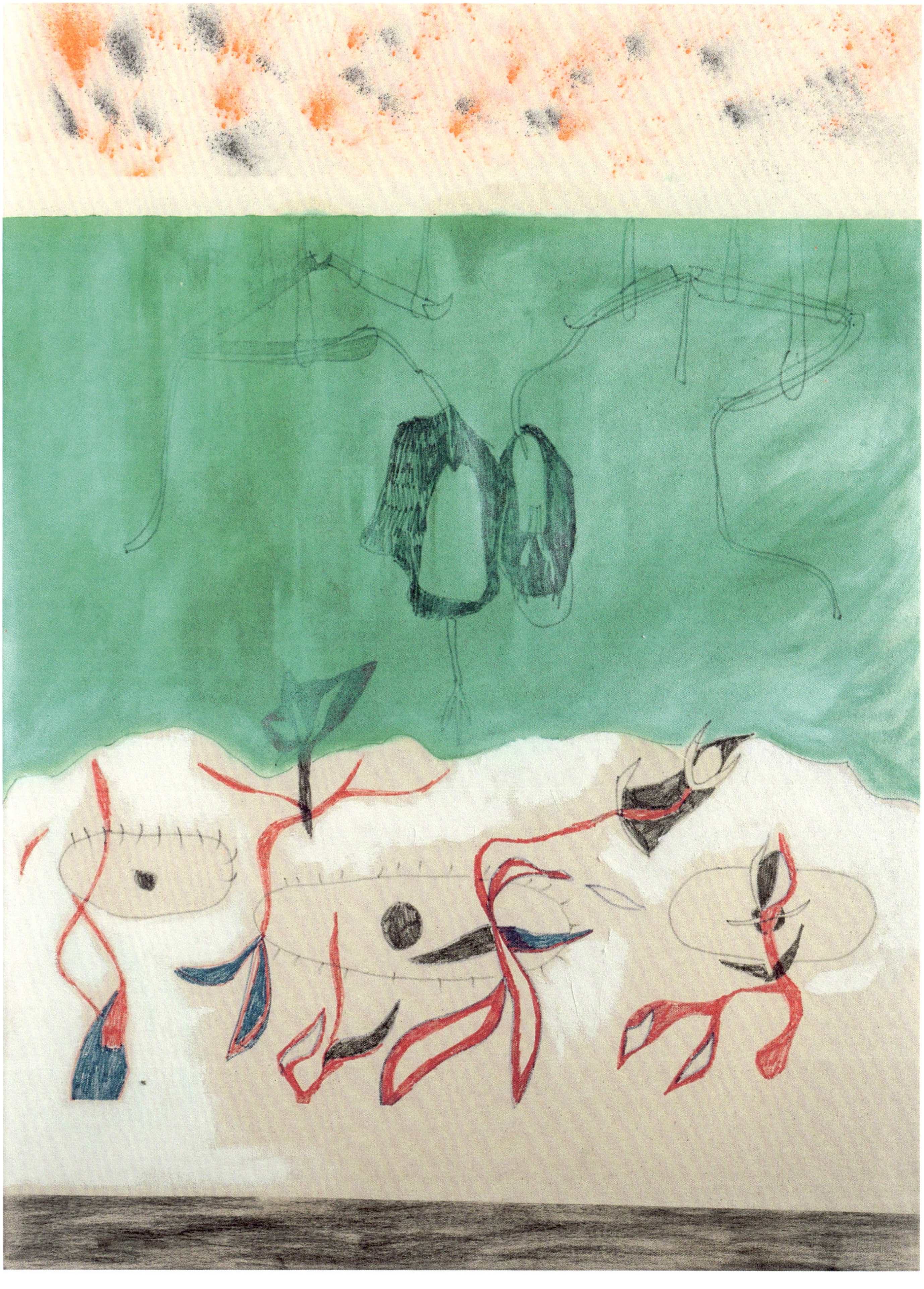

3.

3. *Voodoo Sketch*, 2018, pen, pencil, oil and pigment on unprimed canvas,
80 × 60 cm (31 ½ × 23 ⅝ in)

P I E R R E M U K E B A .... In Pierre Mukeba's four-metre- (thirteen-foot-) long painting *Ride to Church* (2019), three adults and three children are squeezed together, seated on a single motorcycle. First, the artist has drawn out the figures and the machine in black and red ink, before intermittently filling the drawings up with layers of paint and collaged swatches of patterned fabric. The painting depicts a memory from the part of the artist's childhood spent in Zimbabwe. Mukeba was born in the Democratic Republic of the Congo but his family was forced to flee to a refugee camp in Zambia during the civil war in Bukavu, Eastern Congo, when he was very young. Soon they moved to Zimbabwe to join his older brother. When Robert Mugabe commanded the expulsion of all immigrants from the country, the family had to relocate once again and, in 2006, was granted asylum in Australia. .... Mukeba was eleven years old when he began his adolescence in Adelaide. In his art, he draws from the recollections of a boyhood of displacement and travel – experiences that lend his work a raw authenticity and a heady determination. *Ride to Church* is a striking example of Mukeba's characteristic use of synthetic polymer paint, brush pens and fabric appliqué on canvas. As a child, Mukeba would watch his uncle sculpt and draw, and began to imitate him. 'He taught me how to draw farms, trees and people, the basics,' he explained in a 2017 interview with *Art Collector*. Indeed, Mukeba continues this tradition of staying with the basics: he pays deep attention to his figures, each of which is animated by special idiosyncrasies. They hold their own in Mukeba's elaborate tableaux. When he is not mixing media on canvas, he draws portraits in pen and acrylic on paper. These are sometimes diptychs and, as seen in two untitled 'drawings from sketchbook 3' (2019), present simple but powerful juxtapositions of characters. Mukeba first began drawing on bed sheets with pencil and pen, and fabric has always been integral to his practice. He gradually moved onto thin, unstretched canvas. He sometimes stitches over his drawn lines, while leaving other parts raw, or he collages drawing and painting with brightly coloured, vivid fabrics sourced from Southern Africa. Something about the way Mukeba layers up paint and fabric on to his drawings makes his figures jump and dance, as though they are chasing after themselves. They are curiously animated and, more often than not, make direct eye contact with their viewers, as in *Transgression* (2017), where a woman dressed in navy blue fabric locks us in her steely gaze. Like things that are hazily remembered, Mukeba's lines take on an unstable charge; they flail and disperse, as though his characters are about to come to life. .... Skye Arundhati Thomas

1.

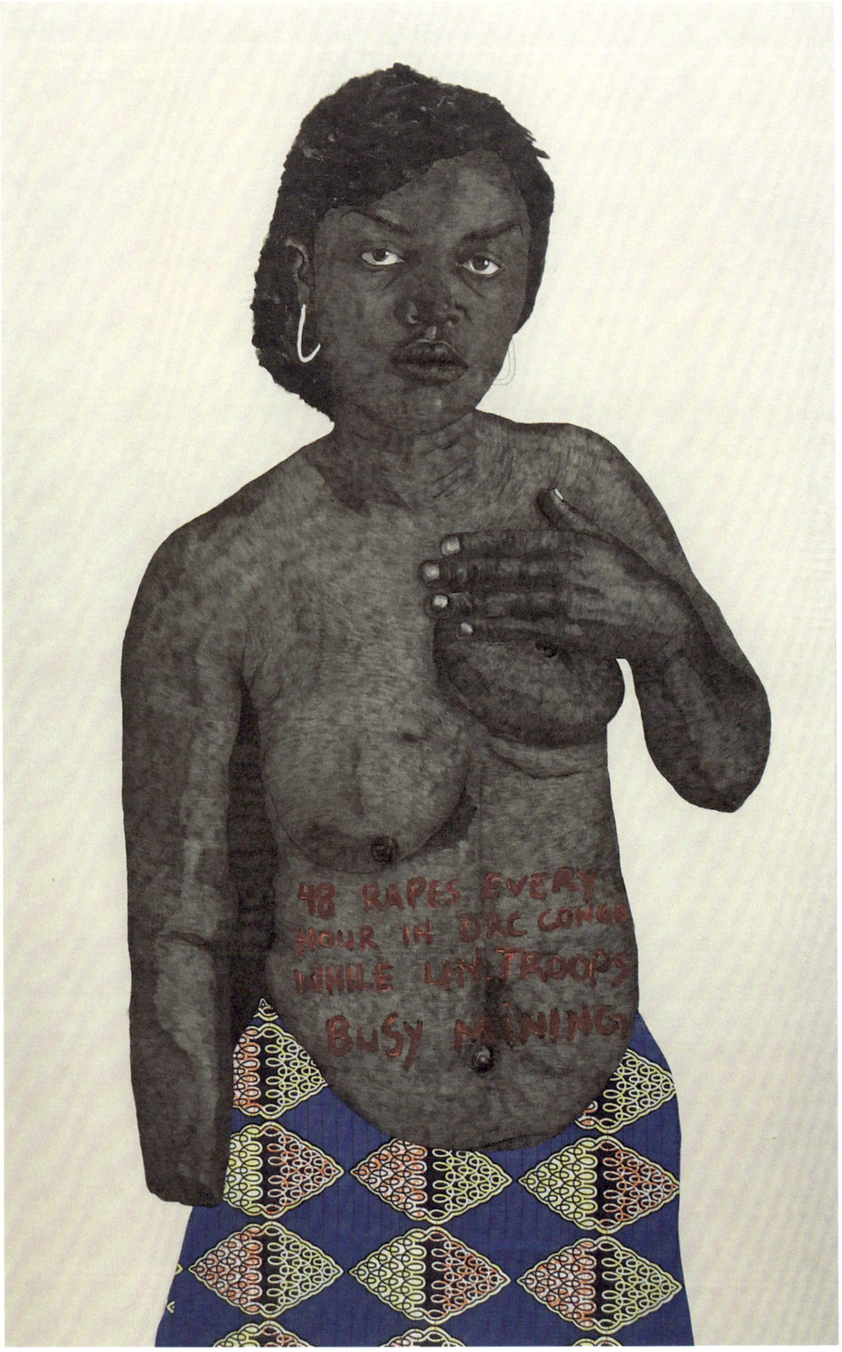

Born 1995, Bukavu, Democratic Republic of the Congo. Lives and works in Adelaide, Australia.

1. *Transgression*, 2017, brush, pen and fabric appliqué on cotton, 280 × 180 cm (110 ¼ × 70 ⅞ in)
2. *Untitled (drawing from sketchbook 3)*, 2019, brush, pen and acrylic on paper, 52 × 21 cm (20 ½ × 8 ¼ in)
3. *Untitled (drawing from sketchbook 3)*, 2019, brush, pen and acrylic on paper, 52 × 21 cm (20 ½ × 8 ¼ in)

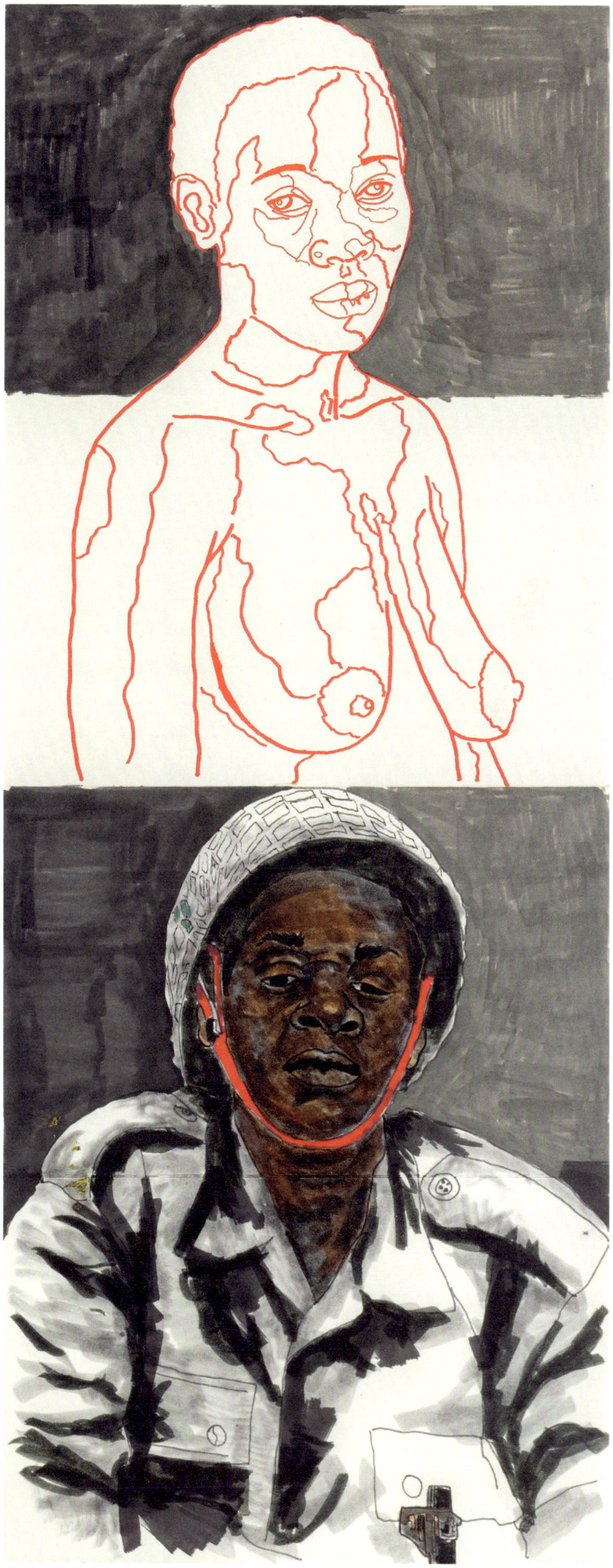

2.

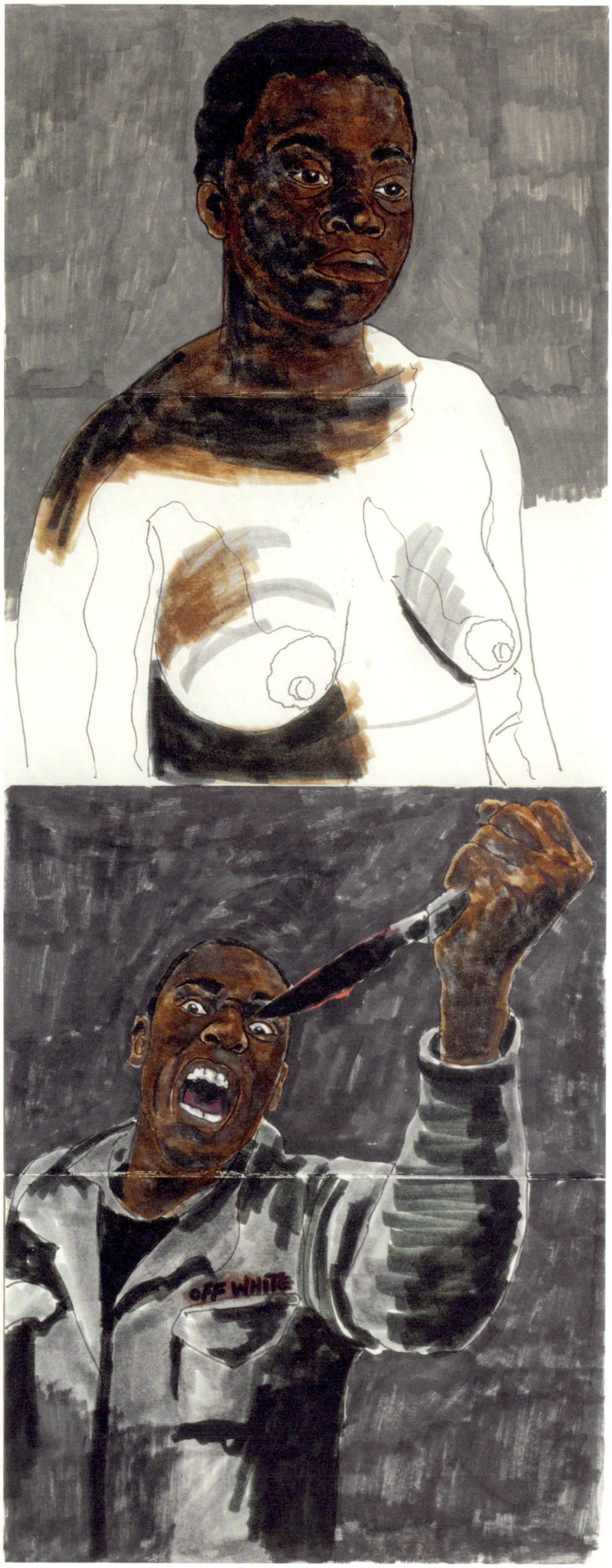

3.

OSCAR MUÑOZ....... 'I've always thought that drawing is not a medium. It's something that is constantly present in our lives and in our minds, it is part of the structure of our idea of things,' reflected Oscar Muñoz on the occasion of his retrospective exhibition 'Protographs', which toured Latin America and Europe from 2012 to 2014. Beginning in the 1970s, in the culturally bourgeoning city of Cali in Colombia, Muñoz's approach to drawing was at that time a hyper-realist one, centred on the contrast of light and shadow and depicting a range of social motifs. In a practice that has, over four decades, shown itself to be technically inventive, the 1980s saw Muñoz turn to unconventional supports such as in his famous *Cortinas de baño* (*Shower Curtains*) (1985–6), where elusive figures loom from everyday shower curtains....... Dematerialization, with its origins in Latin American practices of the 1960s, is one of the artist's ongoing concerns. Traversed by the violent socio-political landscape of his country's decades-long civil war, his body of work sits at the intersection of memory and reality, between that which is stable and fixed and that which exists only as an illusion or evocation. The piece *Narcisos* (*Narcissi*), begun in 1995, epitomizes the ephemerality of life in a three-stage technical process that ultimately involves something as transient as printing on water. Carbon dust is applied as the slimmest of films on the water's surface – this is the moment of creation. It progresses as the water evaporates – akin to the development of life – and finally sediments unpredictably at the bottom of the receptacle, indicating the moment of death. In the self-portrait motif, the viewer is reminded of their own fragile existence....... In order to explore further the notion of time and the transformation of images, Muñoz has also developed a practice in video. Pieces like *Narciso* (*Narcissus*) (2001) and *Re/trato* (*Portrait/I Try Again*) (2004) show the evolution of other self-portraits. The presence of water becomes not only a reminder of the slippery nature of our own bodies, faces and identities, but also of the randomness that takes control over the outcome and drains any illusion of power. The overlapping images – the floating carbon one and its shadow in *Narciso* and the one formed by relentless water brushstrokes on hot stone in *Re/trato* – once again question the truthfulness of recollections and representations, and hint towards the impossibility of making memory match reality. The play on words that makes up the title *Re/trato* – 'retrato' means 'portrait' but can be split into the prefix 're' and the word 'trato', 'to try' – is a clue to the artist having resigned himself to the impossibility of fixing images or identity. .... Catalina Imizcoz

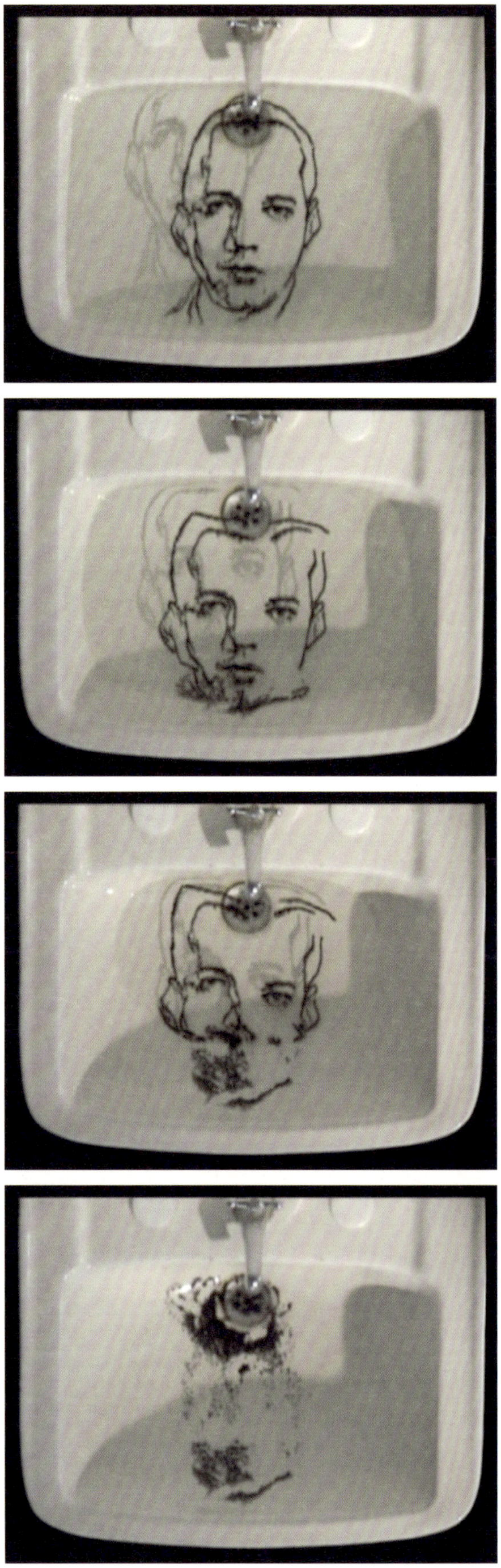

1.

Born 1951, Popayán, Colombia. Lives in Cali, Colombia.

1. *Narciso* (*Narcissus*), 2001, stills from single-channel video, 4:3, 3 mins, sound
2. *Narcisos* (*Narcissi*), 1995–2011, coal dust on paper on water in acrylic containers, 50 × 50 × 10 cm (19 ⅝ × 19 ⅝ × 4 in)
3. *Re/trato* (*Portrait/I Try Again*), 2004, stills from single-channel video projection, 4:3, 28 mins, no sound

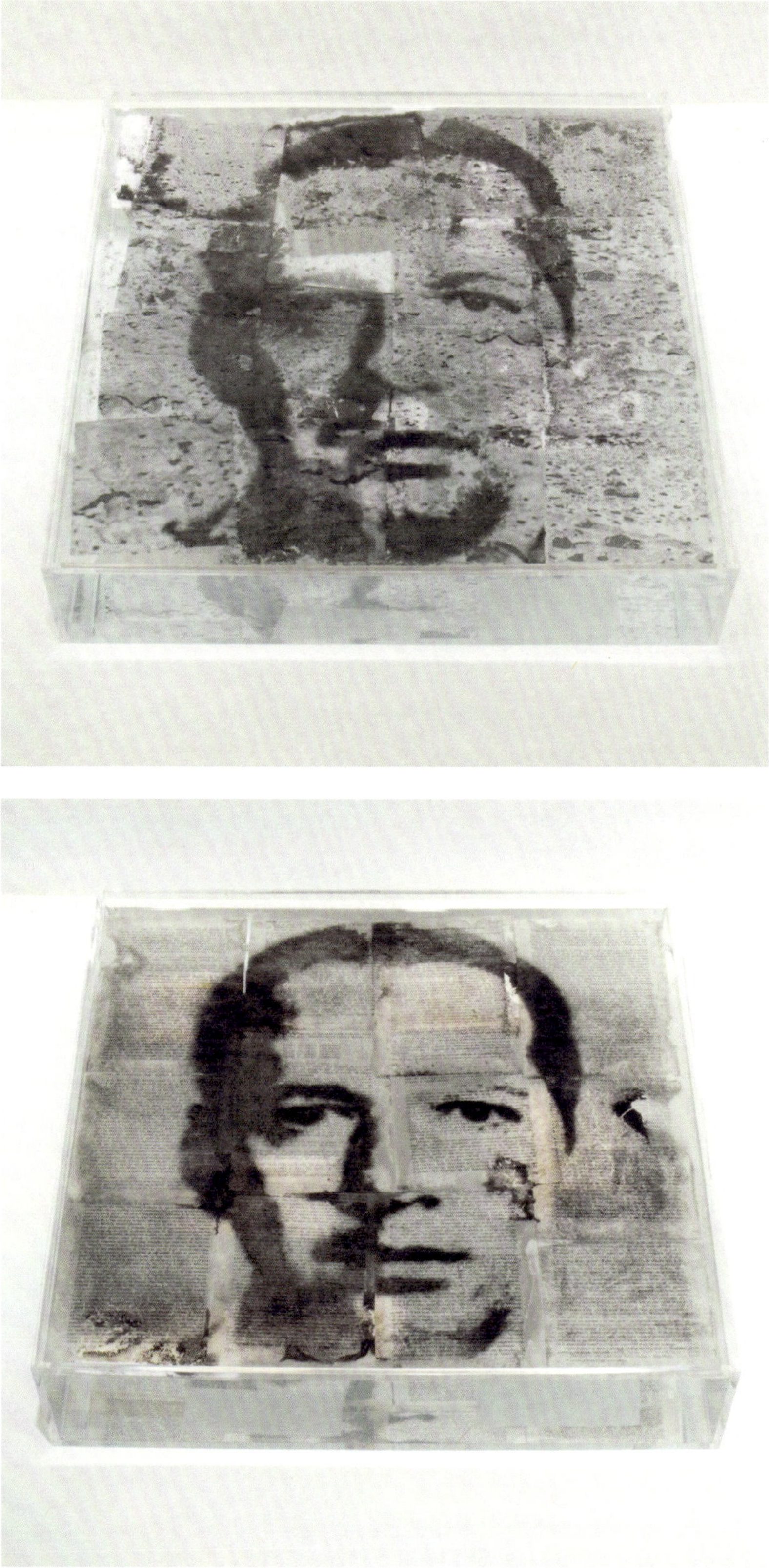

2.

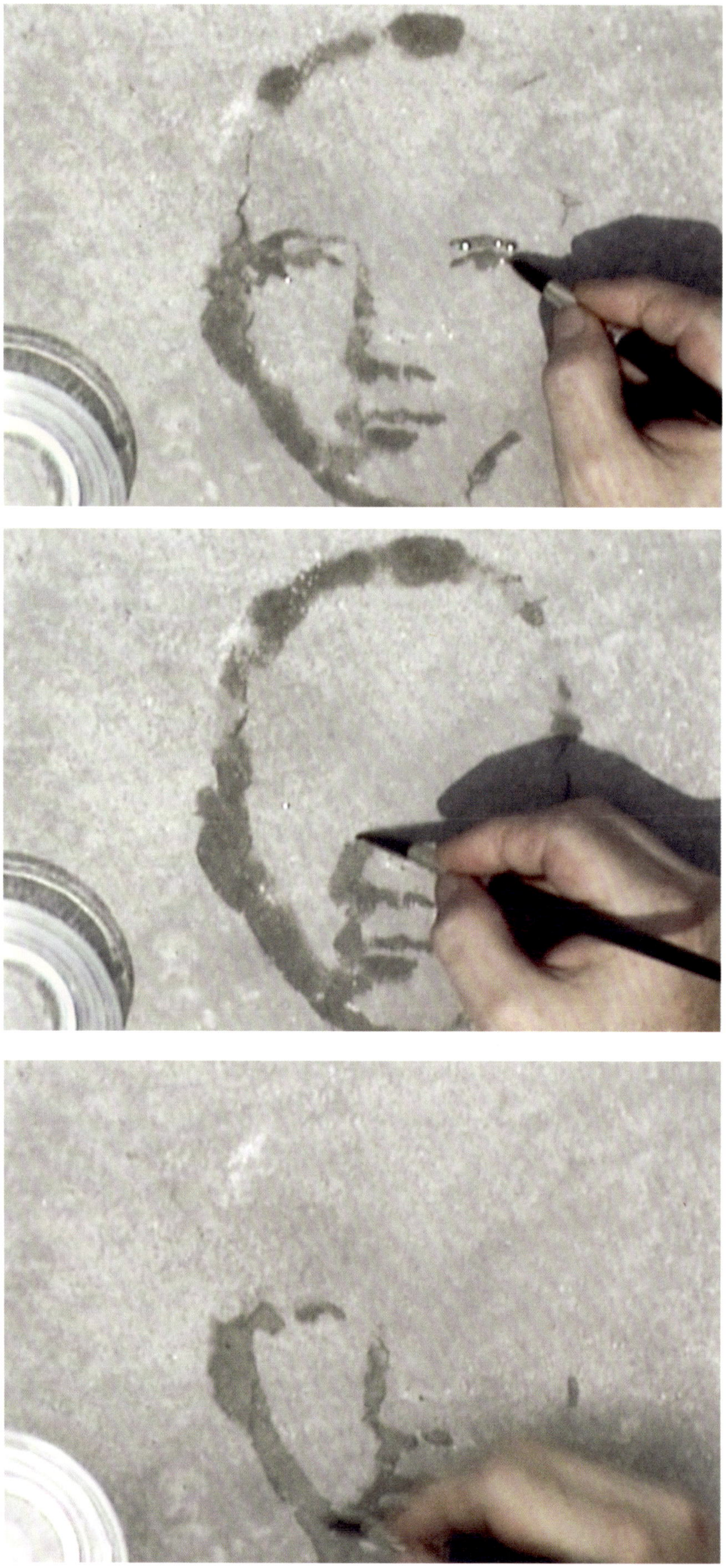

3.

E B E C H O M U S L I M O V A .... When Ebecho Muslimova began making drawings of a zaftig, beguiling and audacious alter-ego she dubbed Fatebe, she was still a student in the sculpture department at Cooper Union in New York. Having felt intimidated in a male-dominated studio environment, Fatebe materialized as Muslimova's bold survival strategy. The artist established ground rules for drawing the insouciant character: Fatebe would always be depicted alone, often looking directly at the viewer (as a nod to Édouard Manet's *Olympia* (1863)), always maniacally grinning and naked. Drawn in incisive black ink, Fatebe is calligraphic, her larger-than-life figure serially placed in difficult, ridiculous situations that mirror the angst of modern life. Muslimova has asserted that Fatebe's size is not about body image or shaming but rather is about malleability and projecting expansive capacity, using the bodacious physique of her alter-ego to her advantage and to reflect on the desire to shape and control life through surrendering to absurdity. .... In *Fatebe Ceiling Fan* (2016) the figure is shown hanging from an overhead fixture, suspended by her toes from two fan blades, with her arms gripping another one while two other blades perform anal penetration, expanding her orifice to an impossible size. Through it all Fatebe smiles broadly with her raven-black hair flowing and breasts flopping. It is an abject image in the age of #MeToo, facing the anxieties of the world through comic satire. .... *Fatebe Shadow Bunny* (2019) references both the simple game of making shadow puppets out of fingers and Ludwig Wittgenstein's use of the rabbit-duck illusion to describe the power of subjective ambiguity when interpreting information. As a model of equivocality, Fatebe is depicted by Muslimova as both herself – as a cast bunny shadow – and, by extension, a projection of ourselves. Muslimova liberates our libidinal fantasies and social conditioning. In another drawing, *Fatebe Arms Display* (2017), the voluptuous body is pierced with seventeen sabres, demonstrating terror in the form of military precision. But has Fatebe sprung a trap? Or is she a victim of assassination? Nobody is to blame, nobody else is visible, so the violence inflicted on the character of Fatebe is relatively blameless, yet we see she is visibly penetrated, by our gaze as well as the knife blades. .... Fatebe is an avatar for Muslimova's comedic insolence and wit, which is visualized in her drawings as prurient, scatological, even sensual. Fatebe's conspicuous corpulent abundance subverts expectations; Muslimova's intent is less about depicting an ideal image of the female and more about being unapologetic, uninhibited and indomitable. The drawings of Fatebe embody naked truth, because she is an assertive, unrestrained feminist, tackling misogynist cultural attitudes about the female form.
.... Kathleen Madden

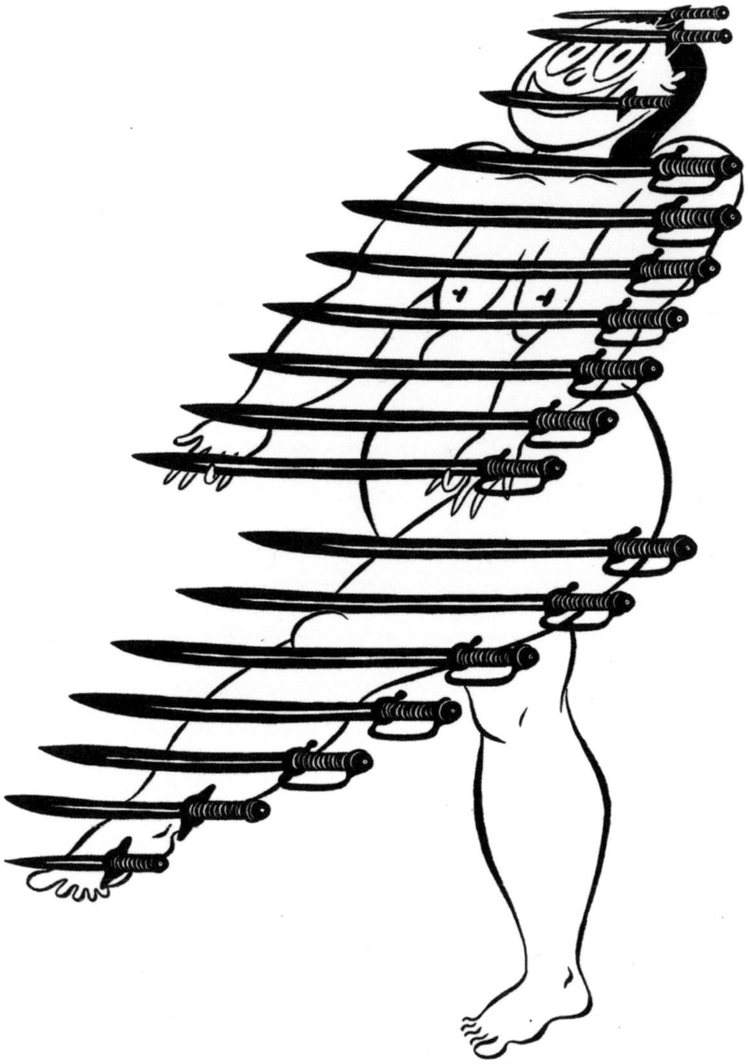

1.

Born 1984, Makhachkala, Republic of Dagestan, Russia. Lives and works in Brooklyn, New York.

1. *Fatebe Arms Display*, 2017, sumi ink on paper, 30.5 22.9 cm (12 × 9 in)
2. *Fatebe Ceiling Fan*, 2016, sumi ink on paper, 22.9 × 30.5 cm (9 × 12 in)
3. *Fatebe Shadow Bunny*, 2019, sumi ink on paper, 30.5 × 22.9 cm (12 × 9 in)
4. *Fatebe Pendulum*, 2018, sumi ink on paper, 25.4 × 25.4 cm (10 × 10 in)

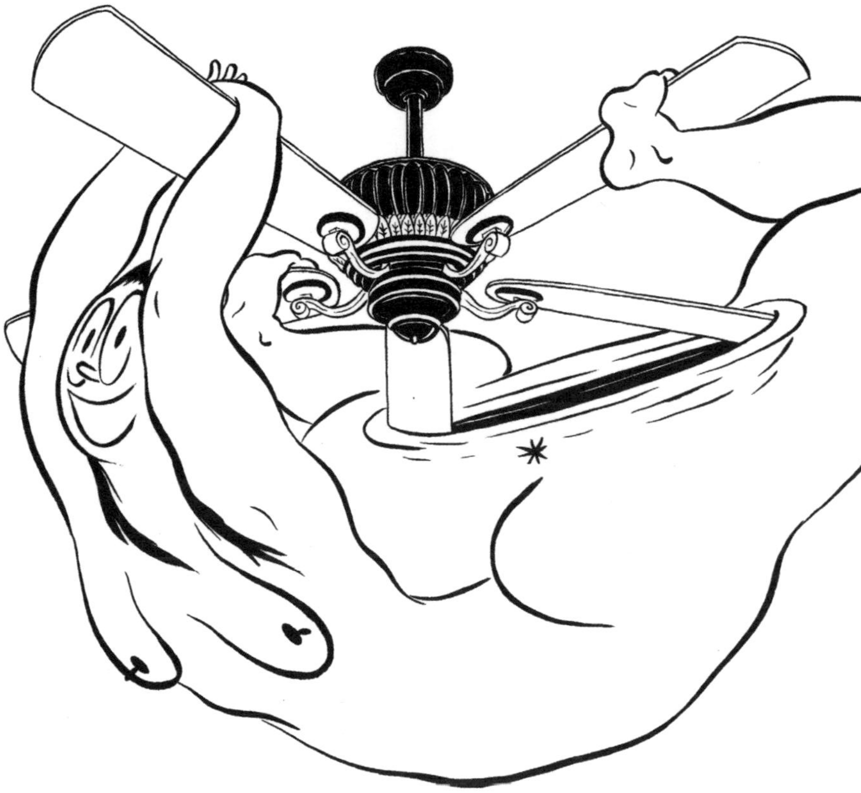

2.

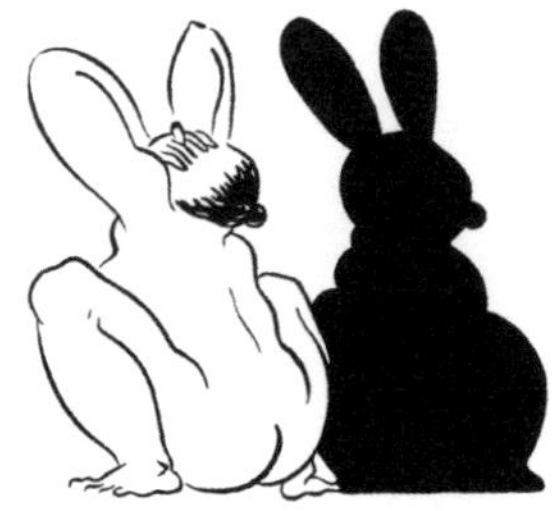

3.

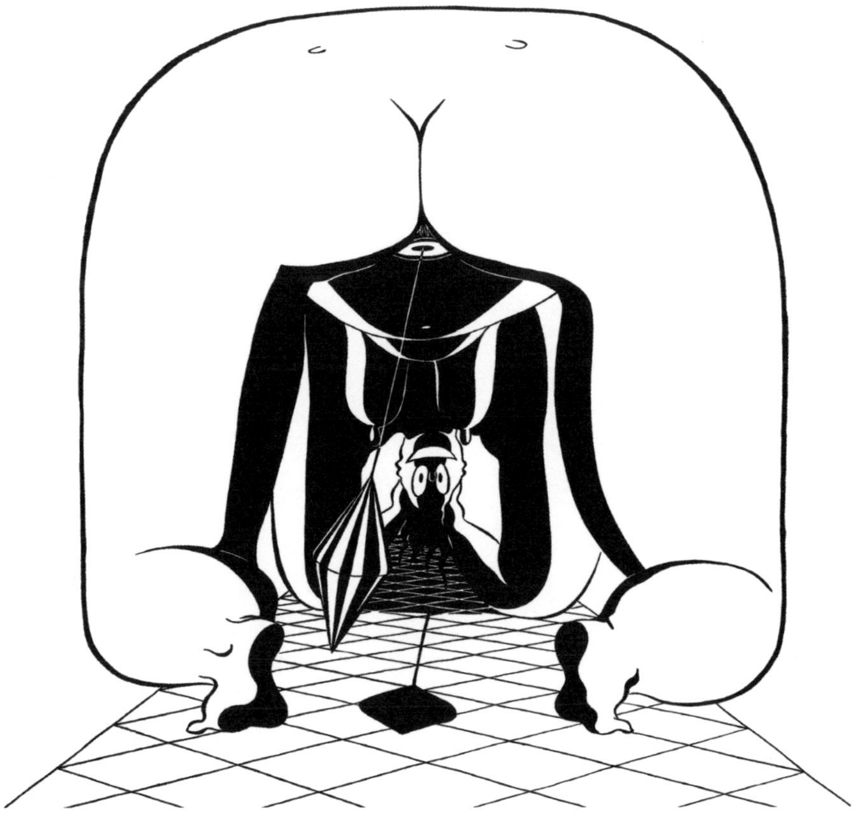

4.

IVÁN NAVARRO .... 'Love turns, with little indulgence, to indifference or disgust,' the early nineteenth-century essayist William Hazlitt wrote in 'On the Pleasure of Hating' (c.1826), 'hatred alone is immortal.' .... Nearly two centuries after the publication of Hazlitt's acid-tinctured essay, few contemporary artists channel their inner misanthrope like the Colombian Iván Navarro. Satire, often of the cruellest kind, is Navarro's métier. A master caricaturist, he has perfected a methodology familiar to those who binge-watch Jason Statham action movies: kicking ass and asking questions later. The fact that he does so with ink, pencil and pastel on paper and largely within the precincts of Colombia's cultural politics renders his achievement no less vigorous. His is the lusty spirit of artist William Hogarth (1697–1764) and the French satirical magazine *Charlie Hebdo*. When attacked in public – as he has been by personages he has caricatured directly – he doubles down rather than turn the other cheek. .... Navarro has been likened by one Colombian critic – the quick-witted Elkin Rubiano – to Alan, a bearded, pot-bellied, timid character in *The Hangover* movies. A gadfly-like figure whose actions provoke conniptions in others, his drawings have ruthlessly ridiculed important figures belonging to his country's cultural and economic elite: among them, major artists, galleries and cultural institutions (one drawing features the Bogotá Museum of Modern Art as Fort Knox). As more than one commentator has written: satire is a weapon harnessed by the powerless against the powerful. .... Starting with his 2014 book *Feo* (*Ugly*), Navarro focused on the warts and all aspects of his country's flora and fauna. If the charcoal drawings included in that volume featured wrinkles, moles, scars, blotches, humps and oversized probosces, the artist more recently moved to record the uglier character defects hidden beneath the faces of well-known figures as they turn towards the warm glow of the public. The effect can be revelatory. Just as Hans Christian Andersen's tale relied on childhood bravery to declare the emperor naked, Navarro's illustrated victims freely, even naively, flout their myopia, arrogance, corruption and bad language for all the world to see. .... Several of Navarro's drawings from his 2014 'Crush Series' call out the secret mashings of Colombia's better-known artists. 'Nailed: Pablo Adarme is Diego Medina's crush' reads one pastel on paper portrait; 'Osiris Ramires is Sebastían Herrera's crush' another. A larger drawing from 2011 titled *Culebrones: Síntomas* (*Soap Operas: Symptoms*) proposes a constellation of faces familiar to Bogotá's art scene: one likeness sports a party-going smile and has blood running from both nostrils. But it is a smaller 2019 ink and typewriter on paper work titled *Memorias quebrantadas (Broken Memories)* that significantly raises the satirical stakes: a drawing whose subject is a monument for the victims of Colombia's runaway violence, it pictures a famous artist and patron colluding to sanitize its meaning. Cruel to be kind, indeed.
.... Christian Viveros-Fauné

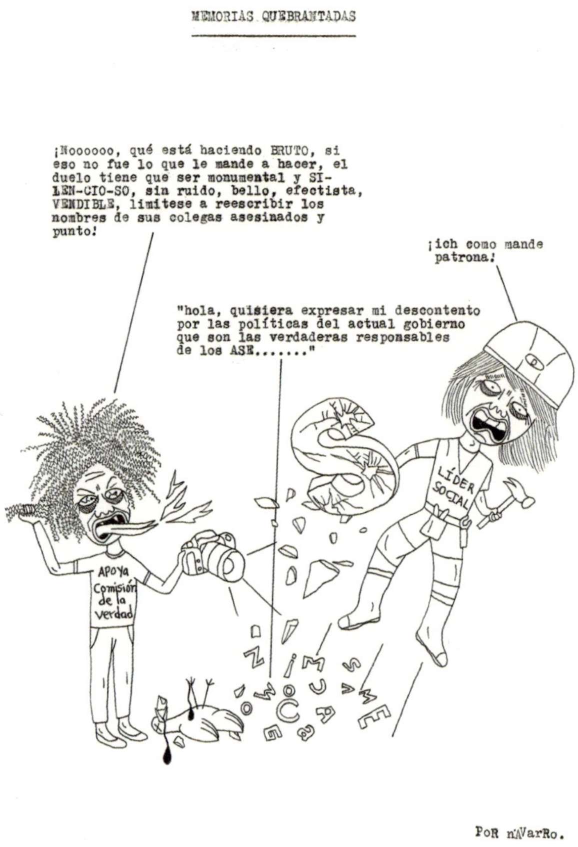

1.

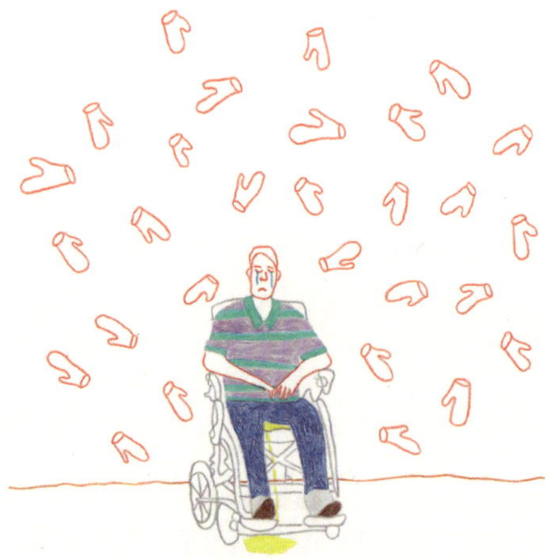

2.

....

Born 1984, Bogotá. Lives and works in Bogotá.

....

1. *Memorias quebrantadas*, (*Broken Memories*), 2019, ink on paper and typewriter text, 28 × 21 cm (11 × 8 ¼ in)
2. *Culebrones: Mordiendo Polvo* (*Soap Operas: Bite the Dust*), 2011, coloured pencil on paper, 27.9 × 21.6 cm (11 × 8 ½ in) ....

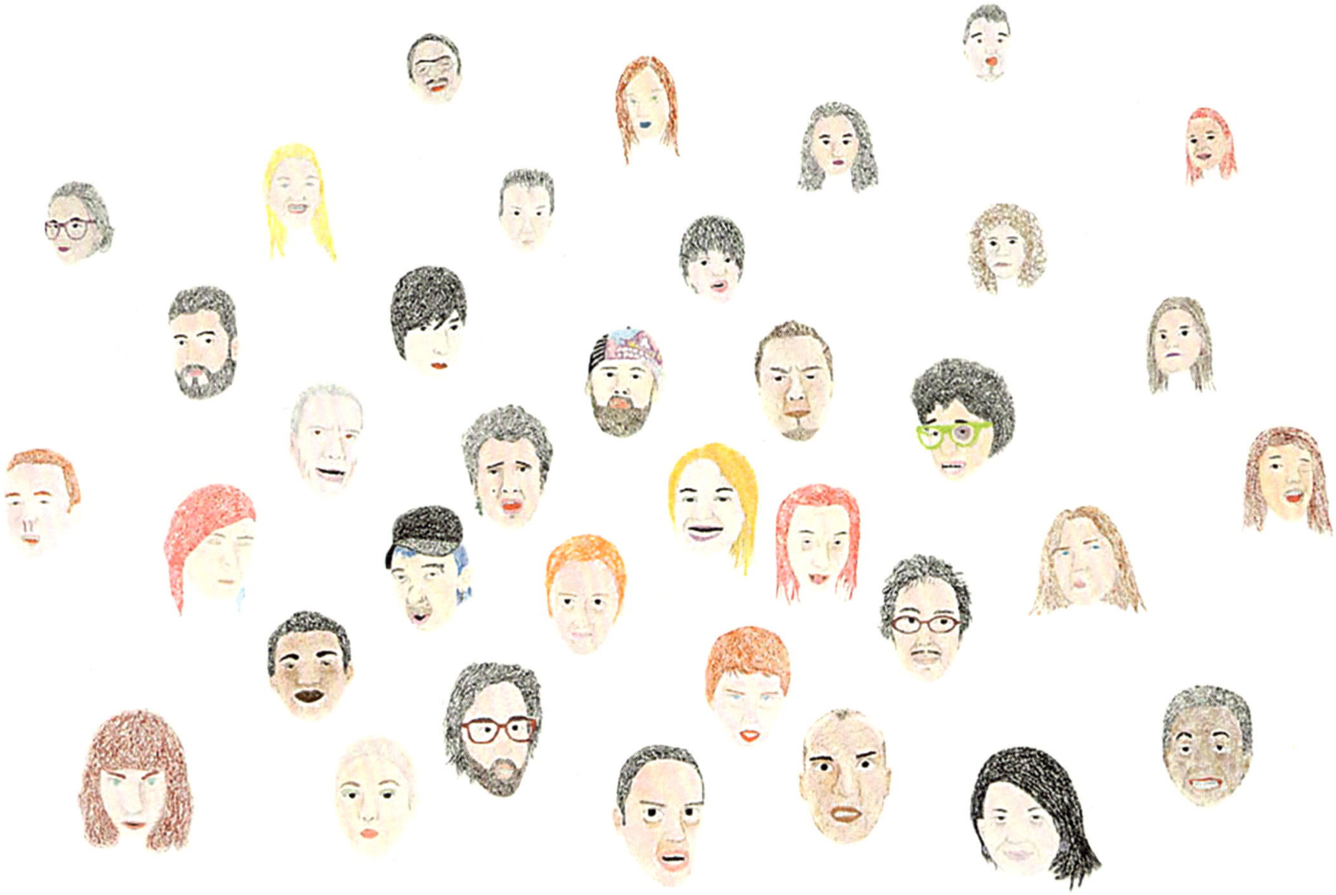

3.

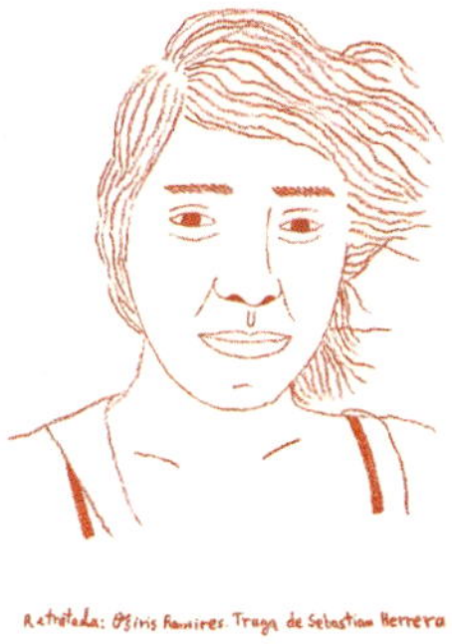

4.

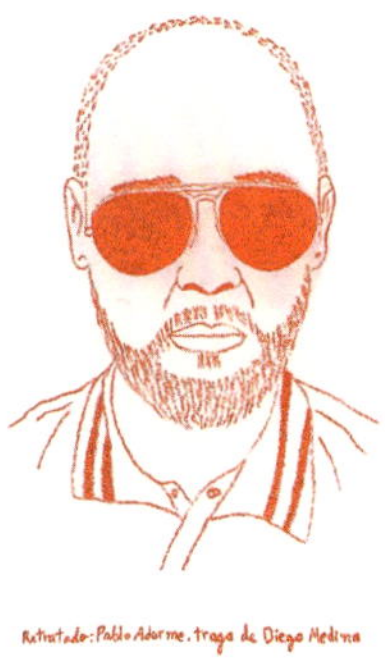

5.

3. *Culebrones: Síntomas* (*Soap Operas: Symptoms*), 2011, coloured pencil on wall, 100 × 149.9 cm (39⅜ × 59 in)
4. *Osiris Ramires. Crush of Sebastían Herrera* from 'Crush Series', 2014, pastel on paper, 30 × 27.9 cm (8¼ × 11 in)
5. *Diego Medina. Crush of Pablo Adarme* from 'Crush Series', 2014, pastel on paper, 30 × 27.9 cm (8¼ × 11 in)

TOM NICHOLSON .... Tom Nicholson's conceptual practice spans a variety of disciplines, yet a formal training in drawing lies at the heart of his approach to art-making. With research-based projects that often culminate in multi-part artworks accompanied by artist books, Nicholson seeks to shift the viewer's attention to the visual traces of politics and identity-building in their surroundings, which are as easily overlooked as they are ubiquitous. Monuments and public art are particular examples of the ways in which historical processes solidify; with conceptual proposals for unrealized structures, Nicholson attempts to challenge the fixedness of how such processes are perceived. 'If you look at a drawing you can usually see every single mark that is made on that sheet of paper, whereas a monument is always seeking to efface its own processes,' he explained in a 2019 video interview for the Australian Centre For Contemporary Art, Melbourne. 'So there's something about those two polar opposites and what happens when you draw them into a relationship.' .... In the suite of charcoal drawings titled *Gorge Photograph, 13 September 1939* (2017–18), Nicholson revisits the artistic exchange between Victorian watercolourist Rex Battarbee (1893–1973) and the Western Arrernte artist Albert Namatjira (1902–59) who, in 1939, were on a painting expedition at the Ormiston Gorge in Australia's Northern Territory as news of the outbreak of the Second World War reached them. The two artists took many photographs on the expedition, some of which formed the basis of several watercolours, but Nicholson's dark drawings imagine negatives that do not exist, which might have been taken in the tumultuous moment when Battarbee, who was deeply impacted by the First World War, learned that another war had begun. The resulting abstract works also connect the act of drawing with charcoal – in which the material disaggregates on to the paper as the image takes shape – with photography, the act of drawing with light. .... The work *Cartoons for Joseph Selleny* has so far been created in three iterations, with the first one produced in 2014. It consists of abstract wall drawings that entirely cover three walls of an exhibition space. Facing them, a sequence of twelve near-black works on paper is installed. These are in fact the 'cartoons', or preparatory drawings, for the wall drawings. Here, Nicholson uses the Renaissance technique of outlining frescos by perforating large-scale sketches and then beating them with cheesecloth filled with charcoal to trace the images onto the areas where the fresco would be painted. The titular Joseph Selleny (1824–75) refers to the official artist aboard the Austrian ship, *Novara*, which reached the Sydney Harbour in 1858. Aboriginal objects taken during its stay there are still on view in Vienna's Ethnographic Museum. Through the medium of drawing Nicholson connects his work to wider cultural histories, actions and their traces.

.... Hili Perlson

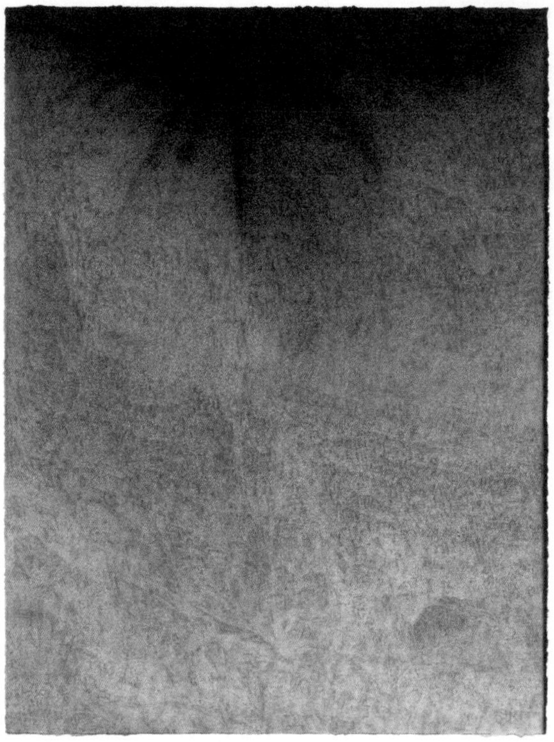

1.

2.

Born 1973, Melbourne, Australia. Lives and works in Melbourne.

1. & 2. *Gorge Photograph, 13 September 1939 2*, 2017–18, willow charcoal and compressed charcoal on paper, each 130 × 100 cm (51 ¼ × 39 ½ in)
3. *Cartoons for Joseph Selleny*, 2014, (detail), wall drawing in 6 parts, created through pouncing cartoons with cheesecloth full of ground charcoal, overall: 5 × 32.5 m (16 ⅜ × 106 ½ ft), installation view at TarraWarra Museum of Art, Australia
4. *Cartoons for Joseph Selleny*, 2014, (detail), fragment of a perforated and pounced cartoon, two sheets, each 108 × 155 cm (42 ½ × 61 in)
5. *Cartoons for Joseph Selleny*, 2014, 12 perforated and pounced cartoons, dimensions variable, installation view at Institute of Modern Art, Brisbane, 2018

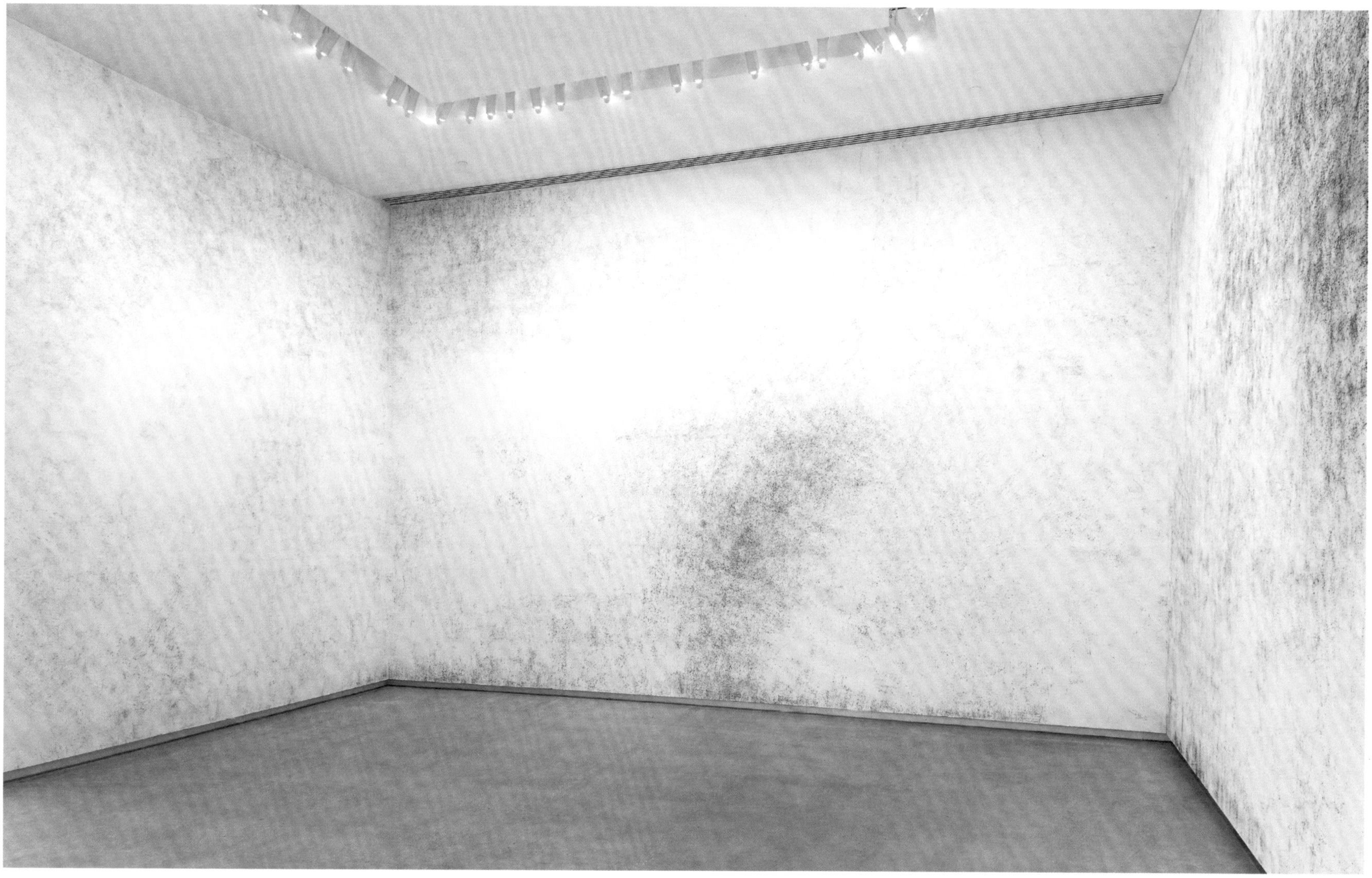

3.

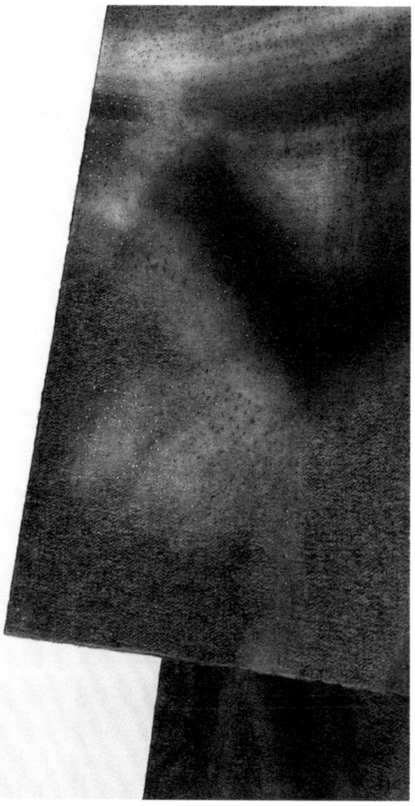

4.

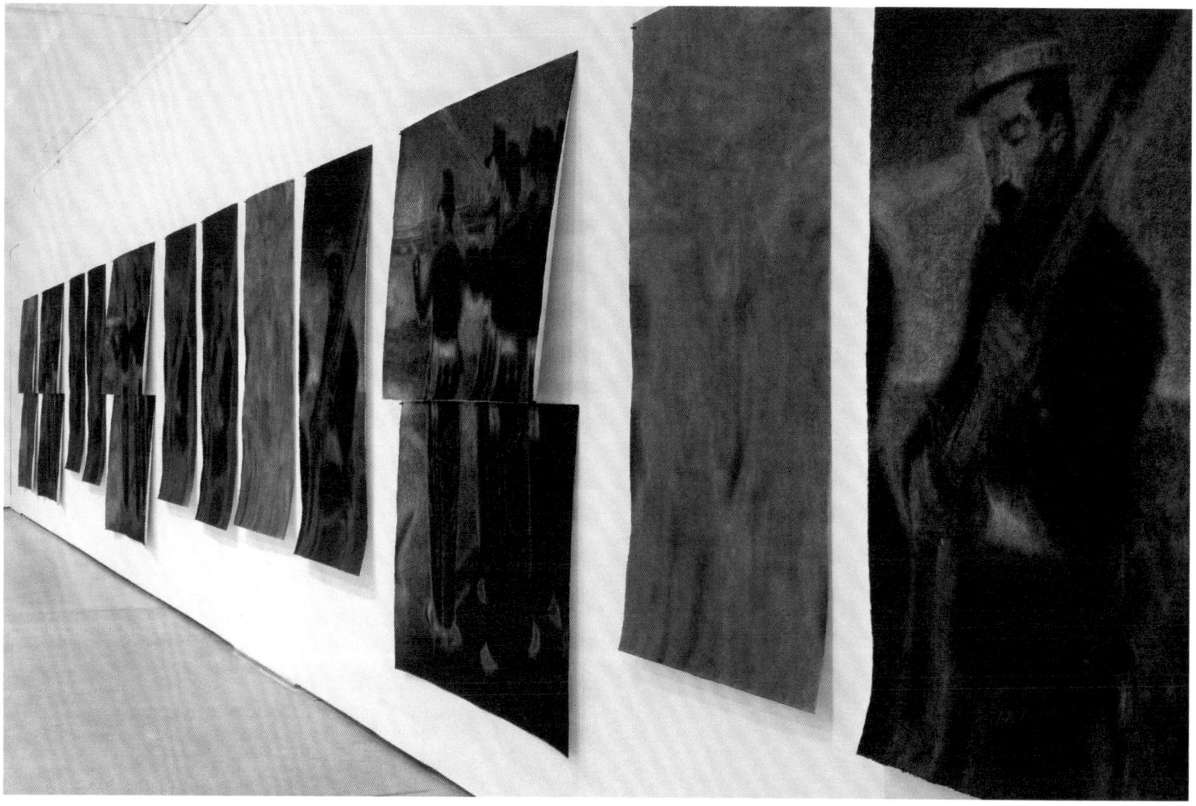

5.

OTOBONG NKANGA .... Nigerian-born, Antwerp-based artist Otobong Nkanga practises a form of memory alchemy. Interested in the emotional resonances and histories that attach to seemingly ordinary things, many of them tangentially linked to her youth in Lagos, the artist has in the past staged multisensory encounters with medicinal plants, soaps, metalware and stones of various origin and preciousness. Nkanga's strikingly materialist and haptic practice draws on her deep knowledge of plants and minerals. It is also framed by formal and affect-driven research trajectories that she orientates towards recovering, as she put it in 2013, 'hidden secrets, altered histories and forgotten stories'. A cultural nomad, Nkanga's research has seen her visit stone quarries in Italy, a botanical garden in South Africa and an ethnographic museum in Germany. While prone to exploring tangents and manifesting her findings in a multiplicity of media – including installation, sculpture, tapestry, photography, performance and drawing – Nkanga's art is characterized by its search for intersections and convergence. In all of this, drawing is foundational. 'Many of my ideas start with drawings,' she told *Flash Art* in 2019. 'They are the first place that allows the brain to reflect on things.' .... Her drawings encompass both private expressions (sketchbooks) and public works (on paper and walls). They often recycle the same motifs, key among them plants, stones and mannequin-like female figures, presented either whole or in part. The multi-armed figure with one leg in *Scaffolding – Loss* (2018), her upper body obscured by plates of stone, was specifically created for a 2019 drawing exhibition at The Hunterian in Glasgow. The work rehearses many key ideas in Nkanga's drawing practice, most notably her interest in landscape and its relation to the body. Two early works, *Awaiting Pleasures* (2002) and *Delta Stories* (2005–6), suggest the evolution of Nkanga's drawing. Produced during her 2002–3 residency at Rijksakademie in Amsterdam, *Awaiting Pleasures* incorporates root-like tendrils emerging from the beatific female figure, a trope further explored in *Flint* (2019). The patchwork mosaic in *Masterplan* (2018) cycles back to camouflage-like aerial topographies in *Delta Stories*, a suite of eighteen ink and acrylic works loosely based on the oil-rich Delta region of Nigeria and characterized by its environmental consciousness. .... The billowing plumes of smoke that appear in *Delta Stories* recur in *Scaffolding – Loss* (2018), albeit here they gesture to a more intimate trauma. Both the artist's parents died when she was young. A fire also destroyed all but two photographs from her Nigerian childhood. Memory has come to play an important role in directing the artist's research and also informs her interest in engaging a full spectrum of senses, rather than just sight. 'The photographic image is evidence, but it's not necessarily the truth,' she told *The White Review* in 2014.

.... Sean O'Toole

1.

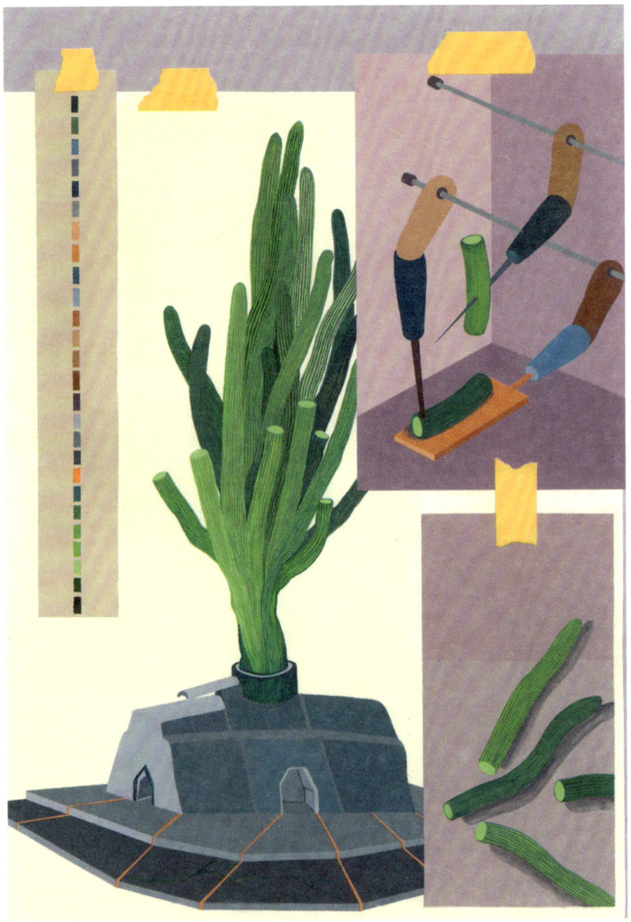

2.

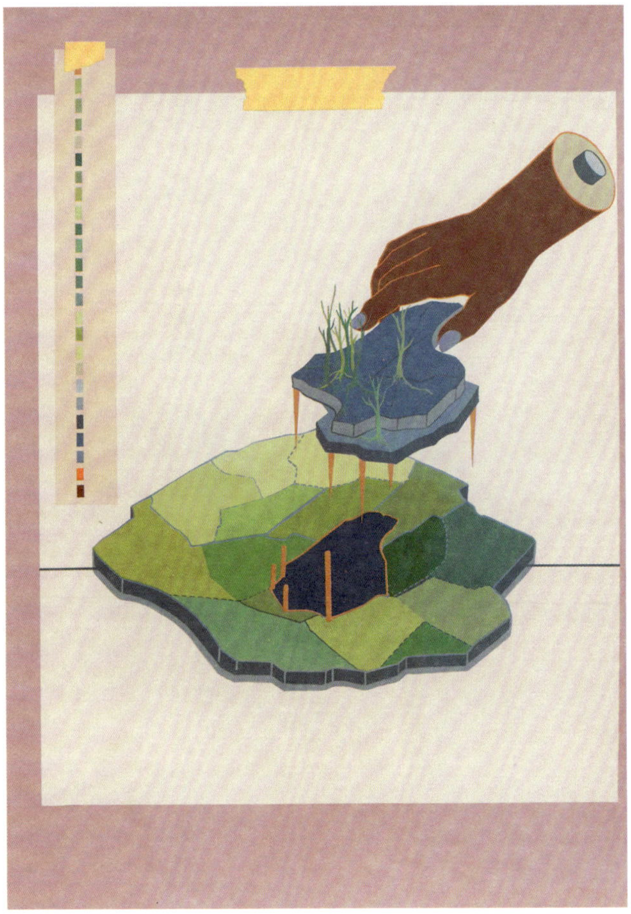

Born 1974 Kano, Nigeria. Lives and works in Antwerp, Belgium.

1. *Extraction*, 2019, acrylic on paper, 42 × 29.7 cm (16 ½ × 11 ¾ in)
2. *Masterplan*, 2018, acrylic on paper, 42 × 29.7 cm (16 ½ × 11 ¾ in)
3. *Flint*, 2019, acrylic on paper, 42 × 29.7 cm (16 ½ × 11 ¾ in)

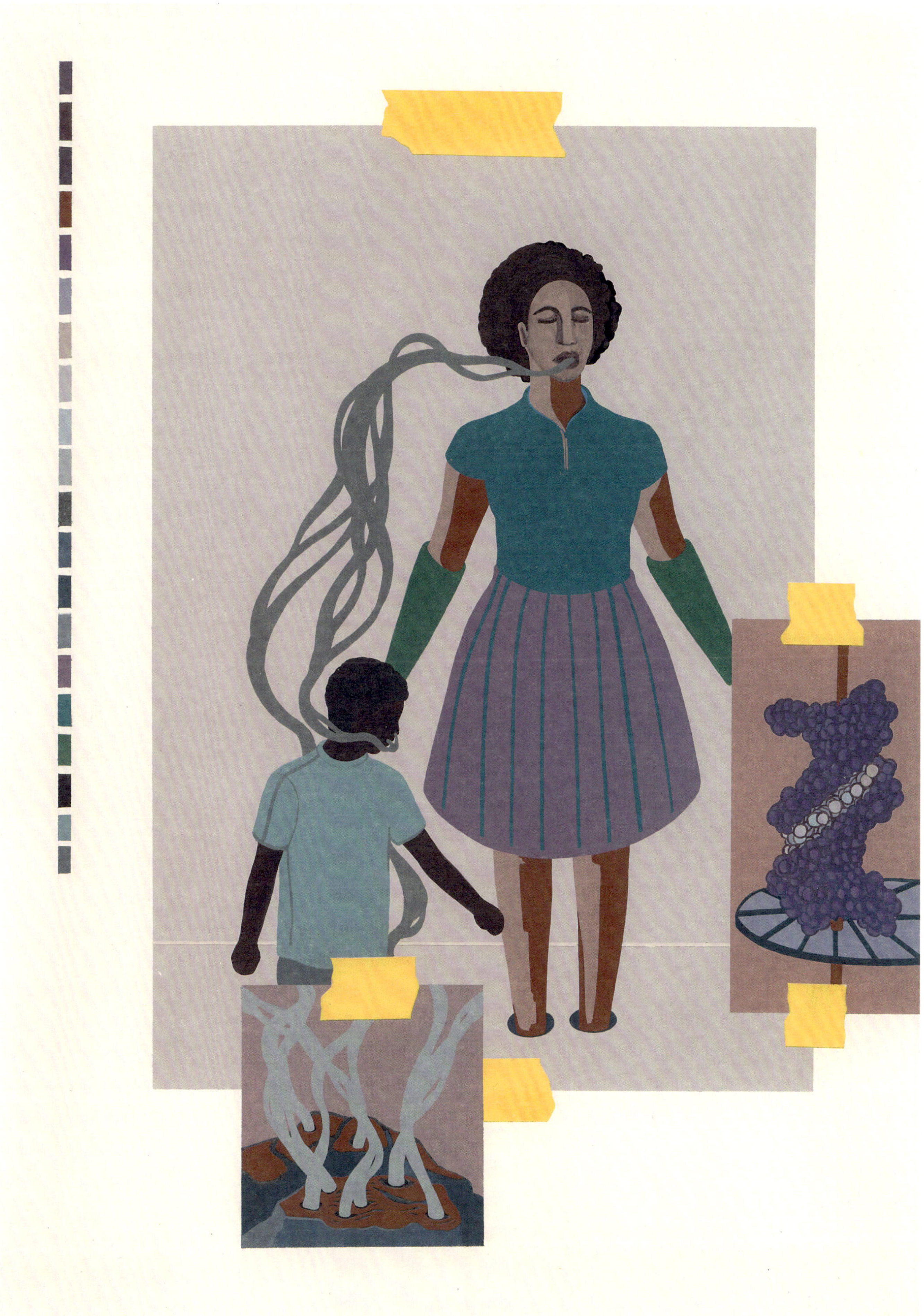

3.

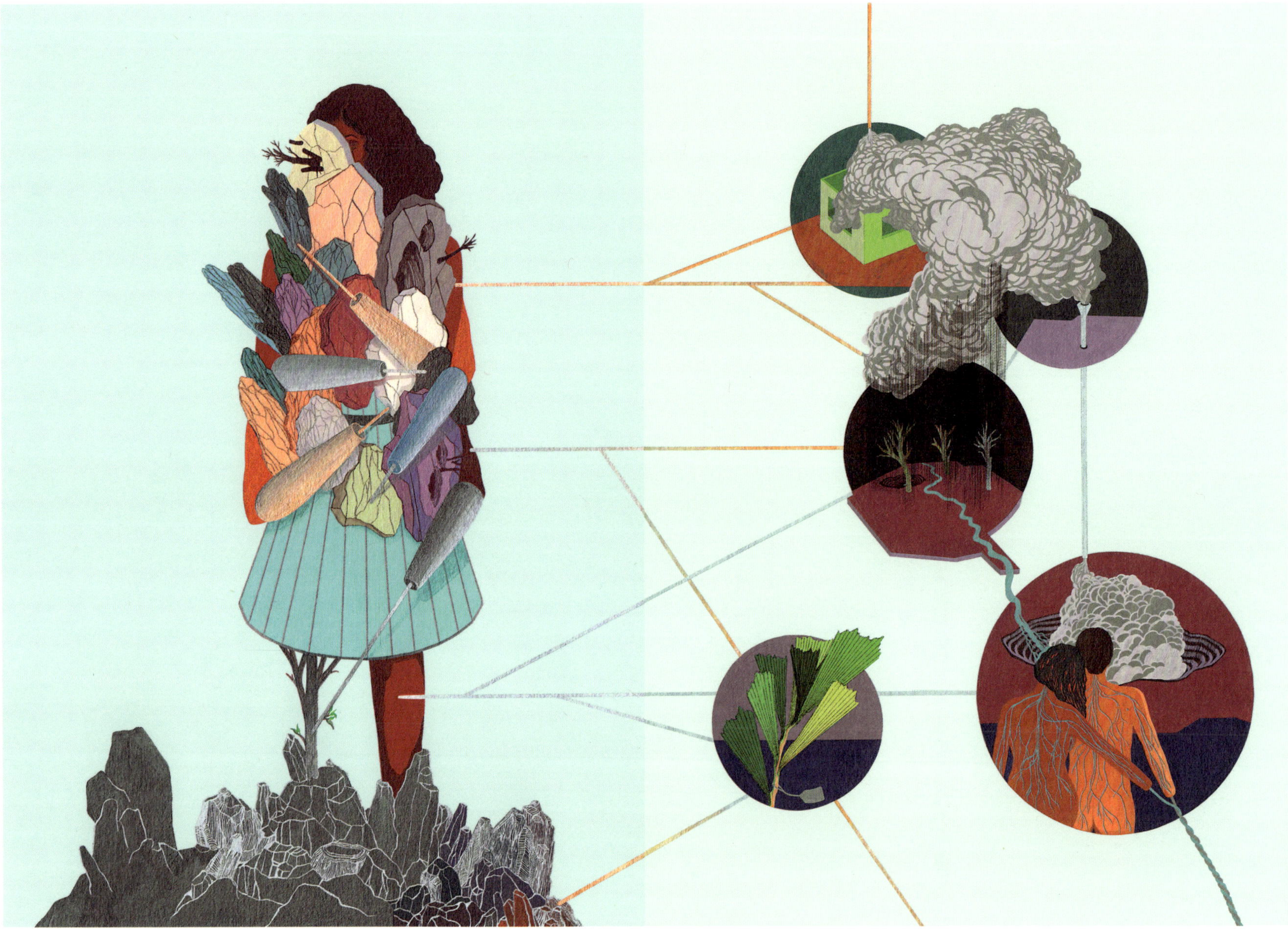

4.

4. *Scaffolding – Loss*, 2018, acrylic and carbon on paper, each 56.5 × 40.5 cm (22 ¼ × 16 in)
5. *Scaffolding – The Beginning*, 2018, acrylic and carbon on paper, 56.5 × 40.5 cm (22 ¼ × 16 in)

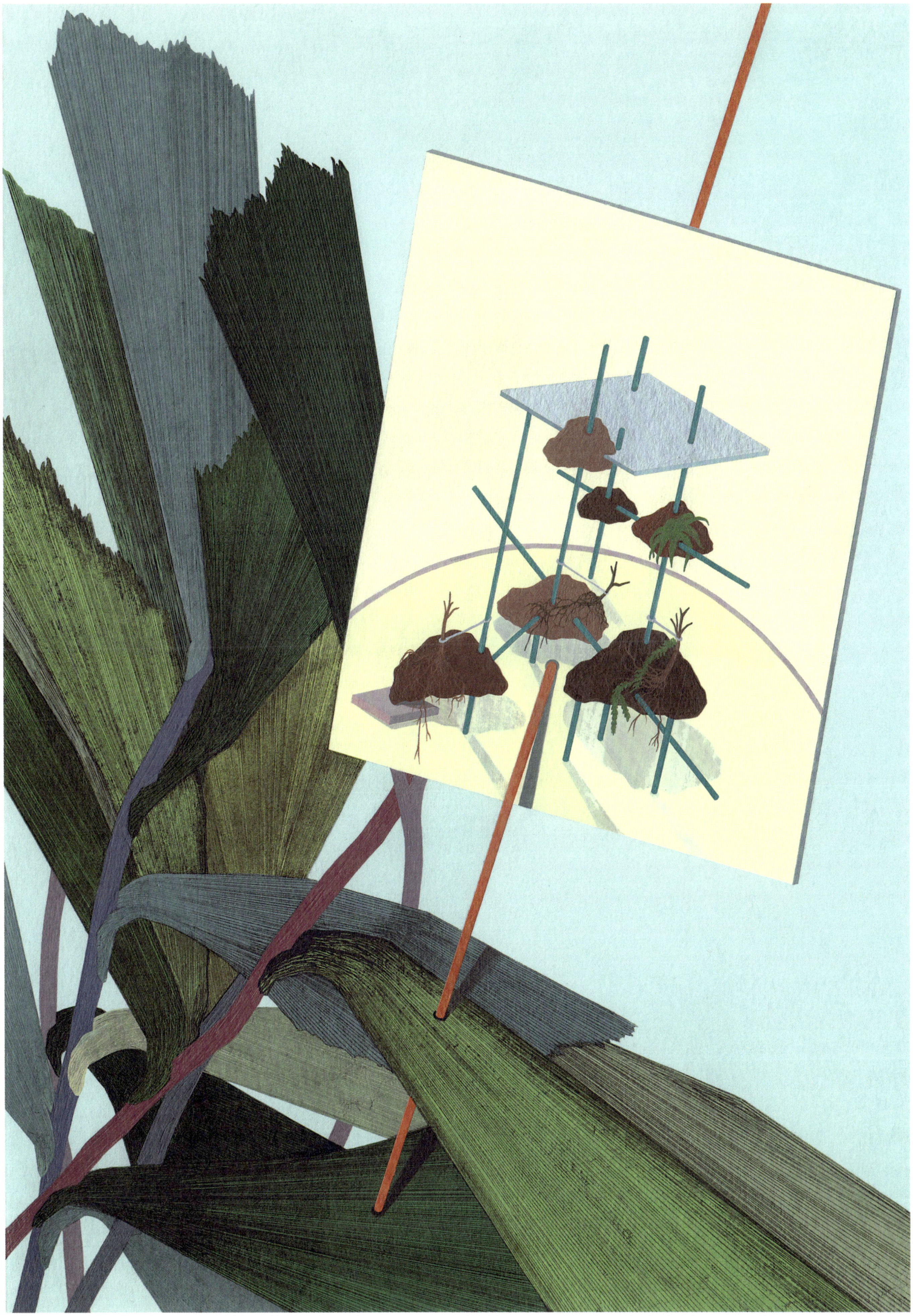

5.

GARETH NYANDORO .... Gareth Nyandoro's large-scale drawings chronicle the myriad little transactions of daily life, whether social or commercial. He seems to take the adage that reality is stranger than fiction and apply it to his art. In his drawings, the quotidian is resurfaced anew. He is best known for his scenes of daily life in his native Zimbabwe, but even when showing abroad his approach emphasizes local economies of circulation. For his first French solo show, he presented an installation inspired by the Parisian *bouquinistes*, or antiquarian booksellers, who line the banks of the River Seine. .... With a background in printmaking, Nyandoro employs a signature multimedia décollage-like technique that he calls *kucheka-cheka*, a term that combines two conjugations of the Shona verb 'to cut.' He begins by thickly layering many pieces of paper on to canvas before lacerating them, surgeon-like, with multiple cuts. Crosshatching is especially common, giving the final work a sketchy look. He then sponges ink on to the surface and uses tape to remove the top layers, leaving ink only where he made the cuts. The technique produces little strips and coils of cut-paper detritus, some of which is layered back on to the work or otherwise presented alongside the drawing, discarded like litter on the gallery floor. Essentially, Nyandoro draws with a knife. Sometimes this takes figurative form as in *Legal Hustle II* (2019), where a man is seen in profile, under the words LEGAL HUSTLE in 1980s horror-movie-type font. The effect suggests both a movie poster and the legal grey area of circulating compilation DVDs of movies. Elsewhere, the figure is not detailed so much as intimated with blocky swathes of black. .... There is a horizontality to Nyandoro's choice of subjects, which range from African cultural figures and celebrity footballers to the ordinary everyman on the street. Phone charger or broom vendors, and customers alike, are granted equal space and dignity. His primary subject, however, is the explosive rise of informal economies in an otherwise predominantly agrarian country. Often, this results in a profusion of temporary architecture as growth exceeds local infrastructure's ability to keep apace. The history of this rapid-fire development – one of persistence and struggle as opposed to lubricated neoliberal commerce – is writ large on the hand-painted signposts-cum-advertisements that are ubiquitous in Harare, and which make their way into Nyandoro's drawings too. In *Jedza Welders* (2019) we see a person clad in a blue and yellow-striped boiler suit, an equally ubiquitous choice of workwear. A red, white and blue sign – primary colours dominate – advertises the titular welding shop and its services on offer: window frames, screens and all manner of metal repairs.

.... Rahel Aima

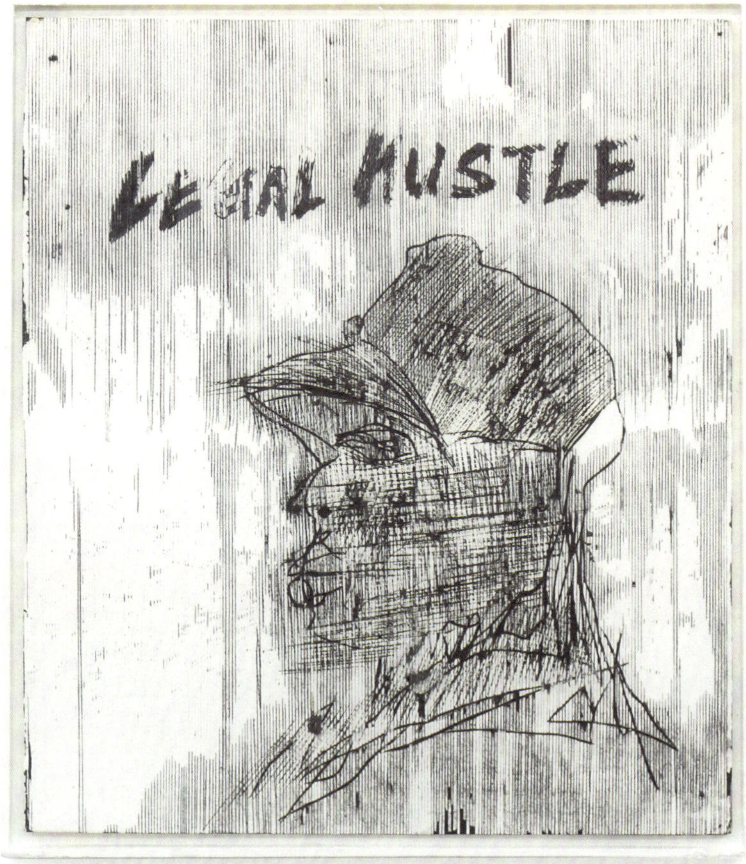

1.

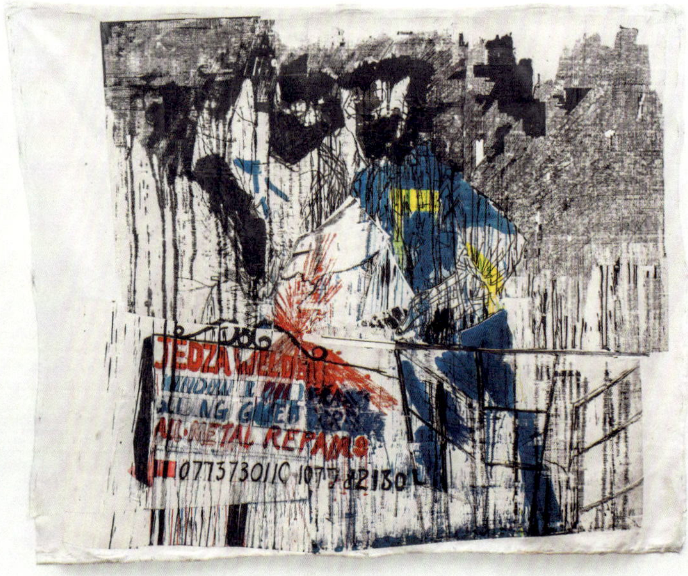

2.

Born 1982, Bikita, Zimbabwe. Lives and works in Harare, Zimbabwe.

1. *Legal Hustle II*, 2019, ink on paper mounted on board, 54 × 61 cm (21 ¼ × 24 in)
2. *Jedza Welders*, 2019, ink on paper mounted on canvas, 140 × 196 cm (55 ⅛ × 77 ⅛ in)
3. *Boot Seller*, 2016, ink on paper mounted on canvas, 253 × 253 cm (99 ½ × 99 ½ in)

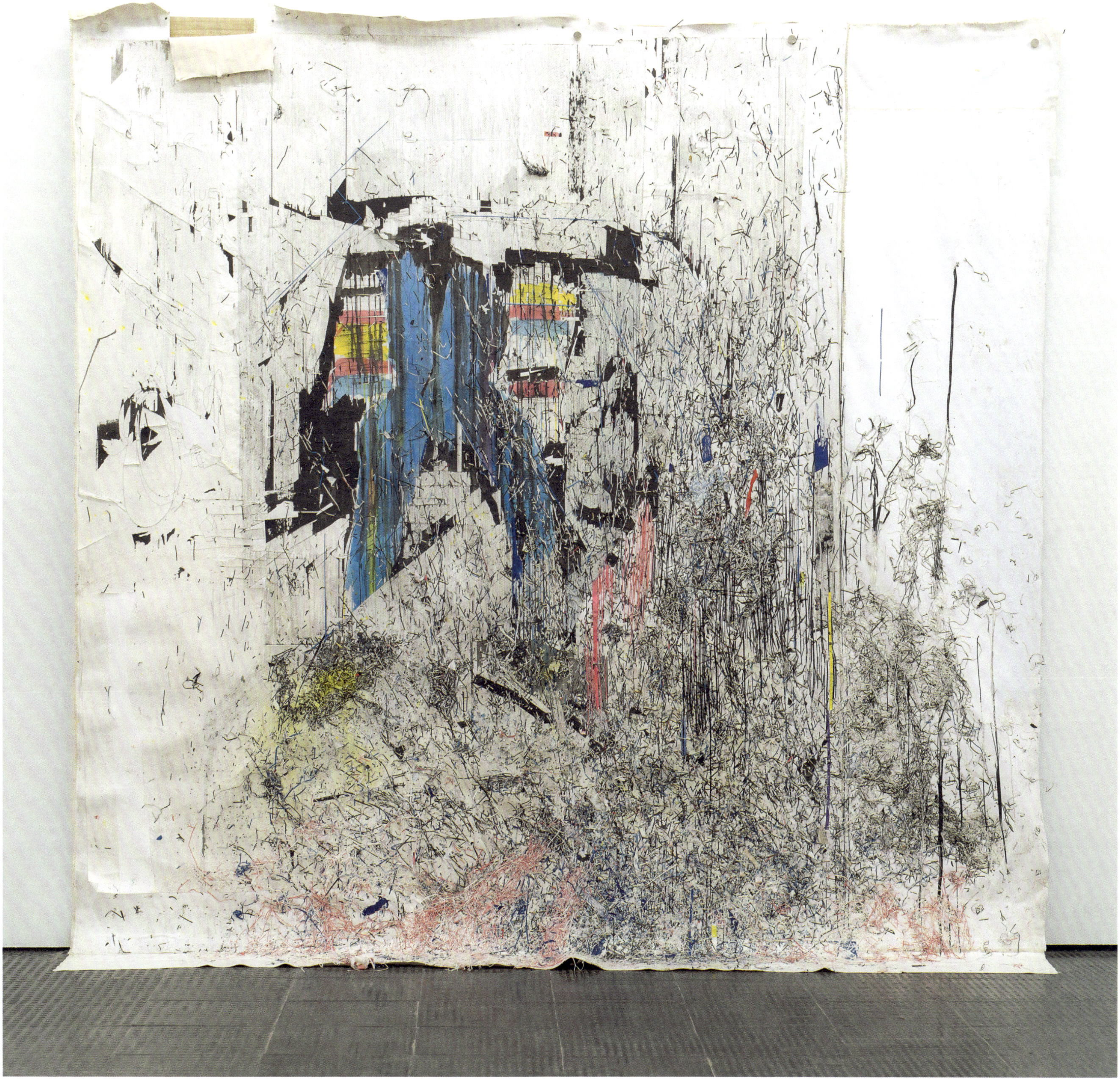

3.

TOYIN OJIH ODUTOLA....... The drawings of Toyin Ojih Odutola are layered with fascinating narratives. Her 2018 exhibition 'When Legends Die' showcased a selection of works based on her storytelling, featuring figures from fictional noble clans in Nigeria, where Odutola was born. In her hometown of Ife, oral tradition is embedded in the culture. The artist integrates an enormous amount of research into her work that involves a diversity of inspirational concepts ranging from comic strips, animation, fashion and art-historical references to the work of artists such as Kerry James Marshall (b.1955), Romare Bearden (1911–88), Lynette Yiadom-Boakye (b.1977), Jacob Lawrence (1917–2000), Elizabeth Catlett (1915–2012), John Singer Sargent (1856–1925), Daidō Moriyama (b.1938), Edward Hopper (1882–1967) and Lucian Freud (1922–2011). .... Although her drawings are inspired by portraiture traditions, Odutola assertively pushes the boundaries of the genre. Her subject matter is the human figure and the remarkable representation of black skin colour through intricate layers of lines to create tonal gradations and density. Her figures are often enigmatic and placed in unexpected surroundings that grasp the viewer's imagination. In the charcoal, pastel and pencil drawing *Anchor* (2018), for example, the placement of the female figure on a balcony, staring down with a fixed gaze, certainly invites a storyline. Her position in the centre of the composition relates to how the spirit of women is portrayed in Odutola's work – composed, confident and daring. Here, the slender Black woman is fashionably dressed in a beautiful white garment with folds indicating a luxurious fabric such as satin or silk. Her gold jewellery emphasizes her standing. .... Another drawing, *The Privilege of Placement* (2017), depicts a detailed domestic interior with a standing mirror placed in the centre. A Black man's head is reflected in the mirror and a carved black bust hangs against the wall to the left of the mirror, so that the two profiles face each other. The focus is on the reflection in the mirror and the black carving, both positioned in the centre of the work. Surrounding them, a suite of significant objects – the luxurious carpet, a vivid blue velvet cushion, a Delft or Ming ceramic vase on the mantelpiece, beautifully bound books – are indicative of wealth and convey the sense of privilege pointed to in the title. This layered, complicated scene invites the viewer to contemplate identity, culture, wealth and status and to complete the visual narrative for themselves.
.... Elbé Coetsee

1.

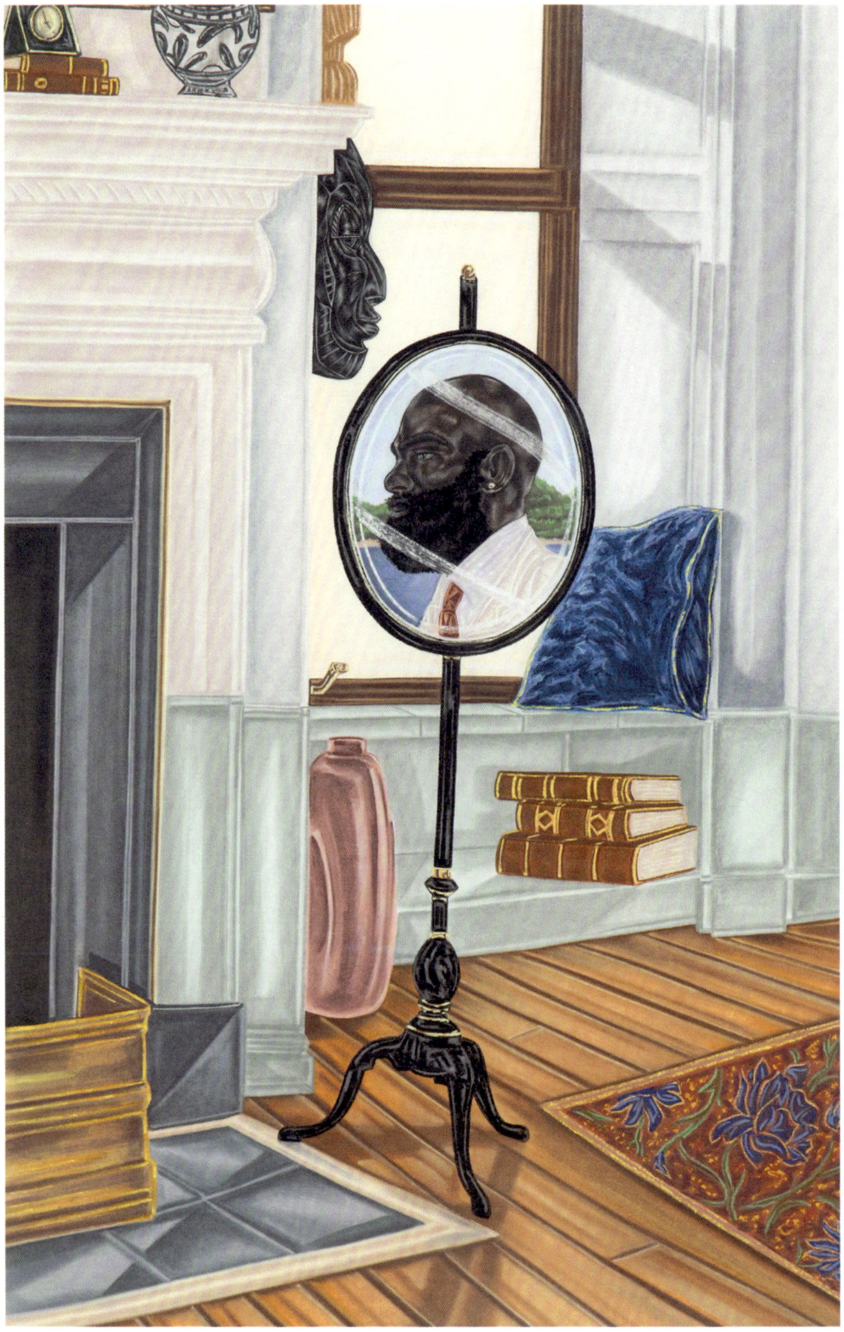

Born 1985, Ife, Nigeria. Lives and works in New York.

1. *The Privilege of Placement*, 2017, pastel, charcoal and pencil on paper, 167 × 107 cm (65 ¾ × 42 ⅛ in)
2. *She Wasn't Warned Odutola*, 2014, mixed media on paper, 74.9 × 108 cm (29 ½ × 42 ½ in)
3. *Mating Ritual*, 2019, triptych, charcoal, pastel and chalk on board, 107.3 × 234 cm (42 ¼ × 92 ⅛ in)

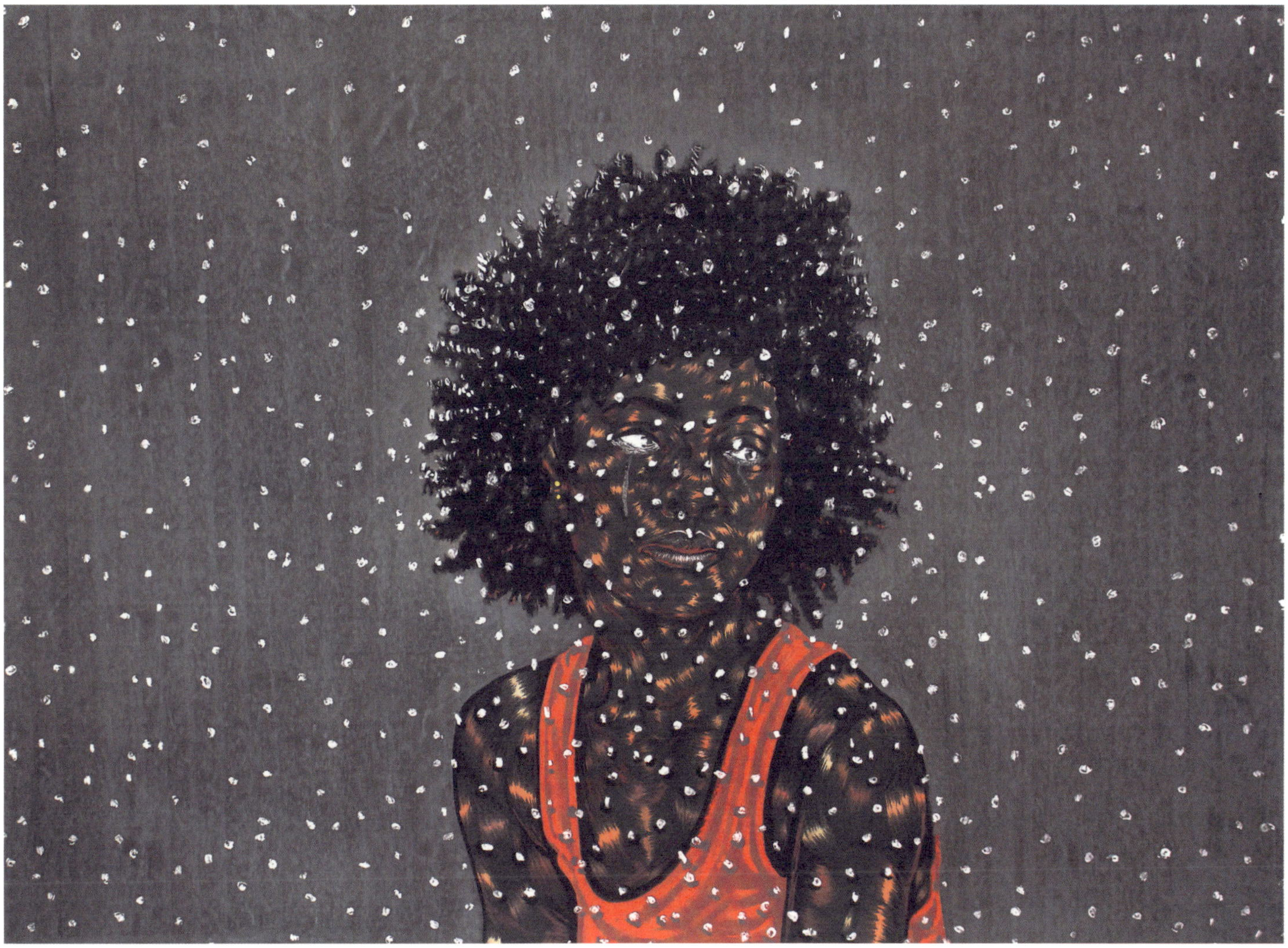

2.

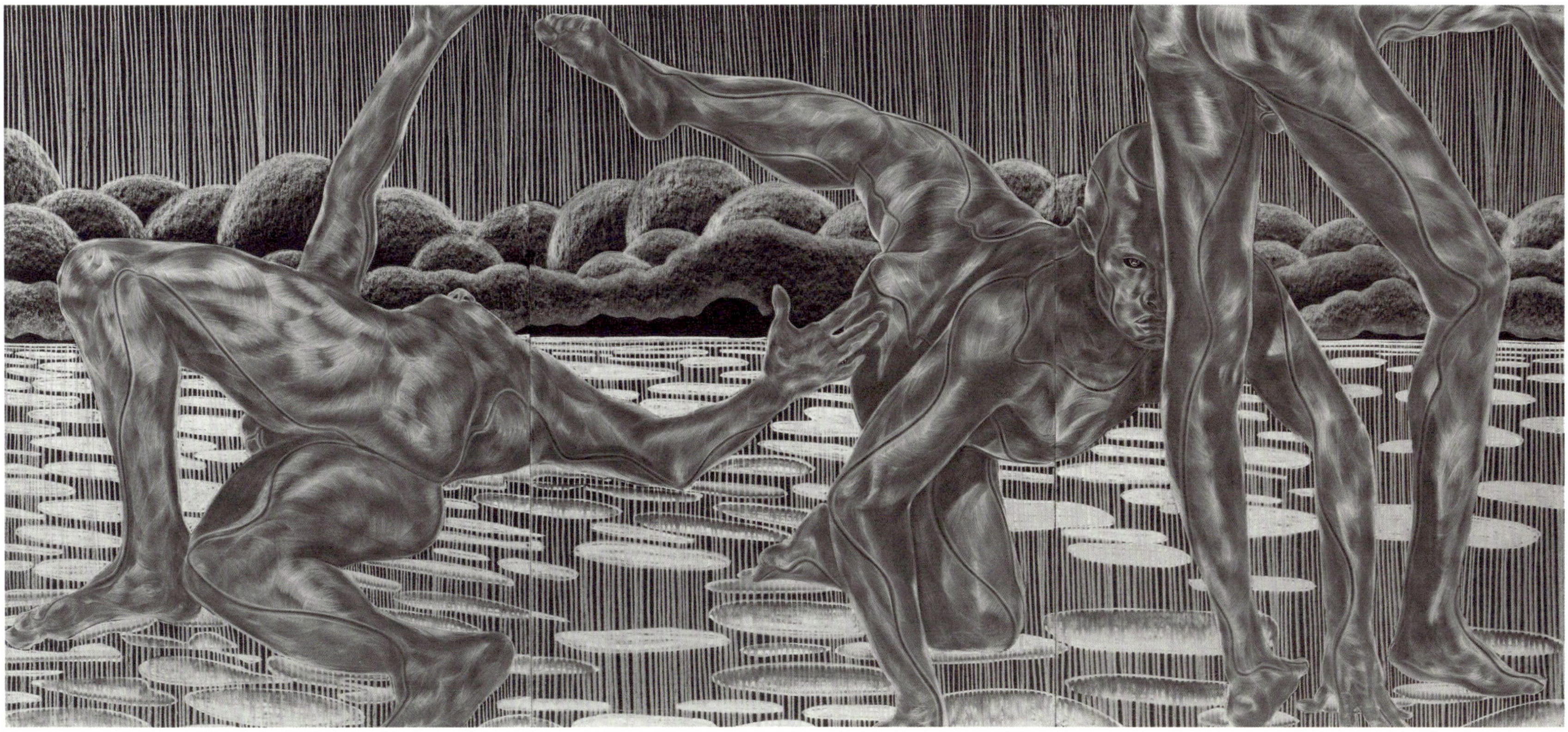

3.

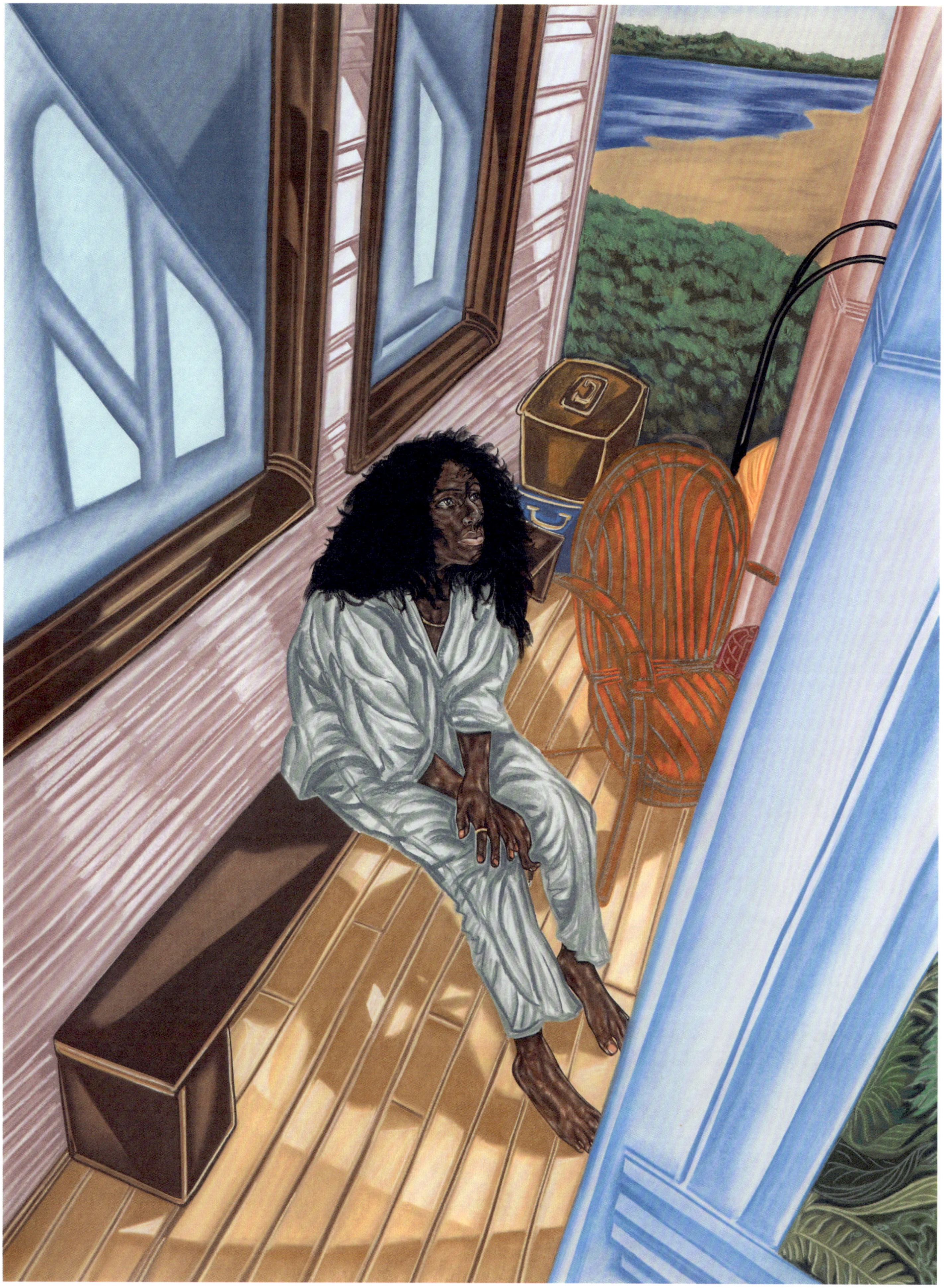

4.

TOYIN OJIH ODUTOLA

4. *Gap Year*, 2017, charcoal, pastel and pencil on paper, 201 × 152.1 cm (79 ⅛ × 59 ⅞ in)
5. *Anchor*, 2018, charcoal, pastel and pencil on paper, 99.1 × 75.6 cm (39 × 29 ¾ in)

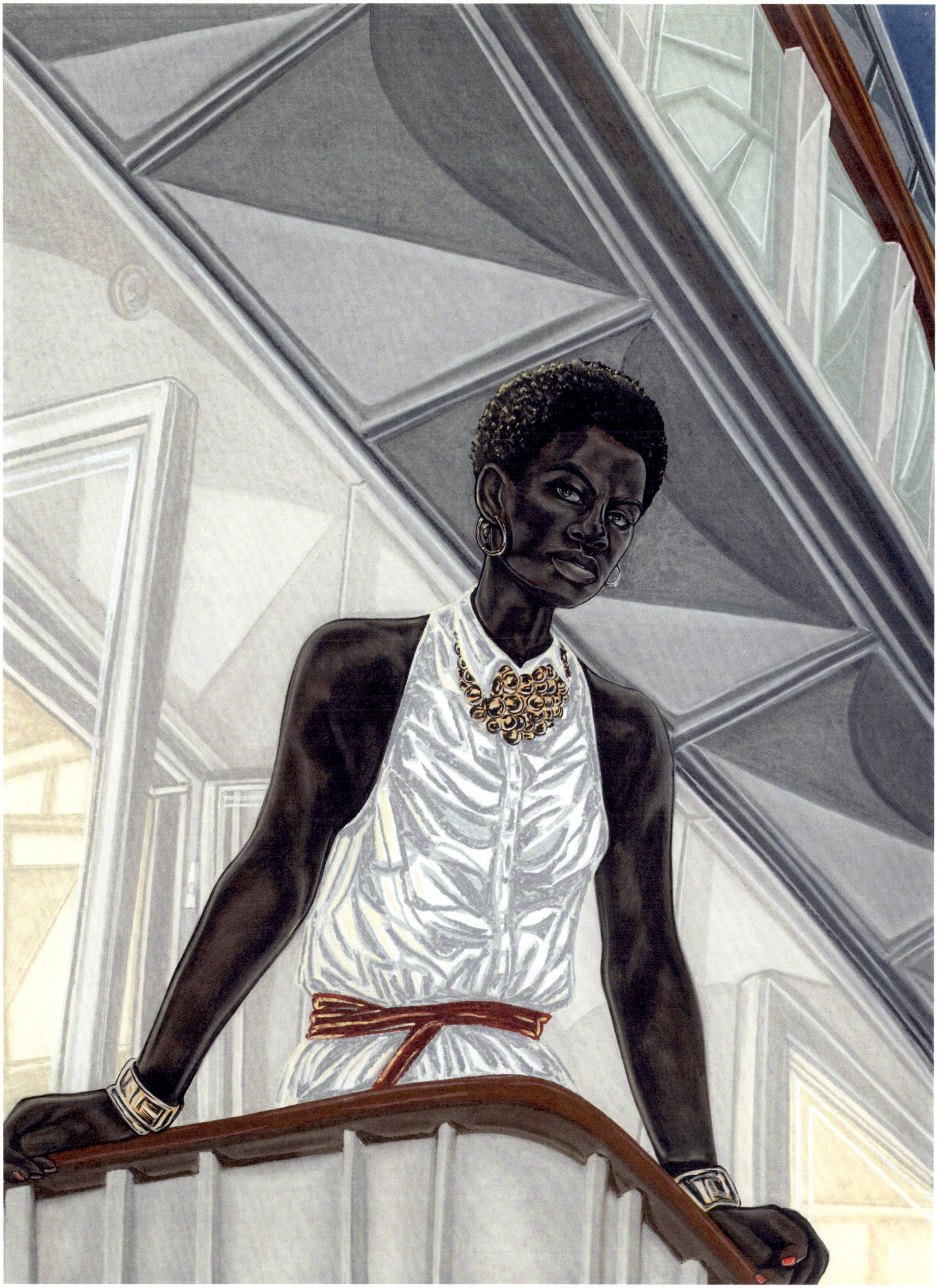
5.

BERNARDO ORTIZ .... In 2018 Colombian artist Bernardo Ortiz participated in two exhibitions that employed drawing as a tool to render visible the passing of time. In his commission for Siobhan Davies Dance studios in London, *Amerikanische Lieder* (*American Songs*), the artist presented a drawing-cum-score that was performed by three dancers. A computer-generated algorithmic pattern resulted from Ortiz's digitalized drawing of lyrics and was offered as the material to which the dancers were invited to respond. The exercise involved multiple stages: the poetics of song became abstracted into drawing, which in turn was mechanized into a rhythmic design, itself then embodied and transformed into the dancers' movements. Similarly, for the two-person show 'Tipología del Espejo' (Mirror Typology) that took place in Bogotá, artist Erick Beltrán (b.1974) and Ortiz engaged in conversation for eight hours on the opening day. This dialogical material provided both content and context for the remaining elements of the exhibition, which were all geared towards sharpening the viewer's perception of how drawing intercepts space, how one discipline shares the discourses of the other and how time generates layers of perception. Ortiz's practice is one of constantly delving into the component elements of images, asking the public to take the time to appreciate the structures that support them. ...... Stripped bare and vulnerable, Ortiz's drawings are left unframed when exhibited. Instead, they exist as part of architectural forms or are suspended on slim wooden rails, allowing their materiality to become the focal point. The thick Japanese kozo paper of *Untitled* (2017), for example, appears to be rippled by the subtle strokes of black sumi ink. Likewise, the capital letters of the titular words in *Untitled (Best Western)* (2019) produce a hair-splitting, geometric sequence that is but a detail on the carefully stretched surface. When Ortiz draws intricate grids on to tracing paper for works such as *Untitled (Friction)* (2017) – shown at Galería Luisa Strina in São Paulo as part of an installation that zigzagged for metres across the space – the repetitious strokes are as much pointing to the tension between the support and the medium, as they are to the anachronistic and yet atemporal process that brought such images into existence. He has spoken about drawing being an outdated technique, one that he nonetheless continues to resort to, in what has become a decades-long practice centred around the line, as well as the written word, spatial installation and philosophy. Ortiz encourages the viewer to examine what is absent as much as what is present, a minimalistic outlook succinctly encapsulated by *Untitled* (2018), where it is in the voids left behind by the hole punch that allow the underlying shades of red to find their voice.
.... Catalina Imizcoz

1.

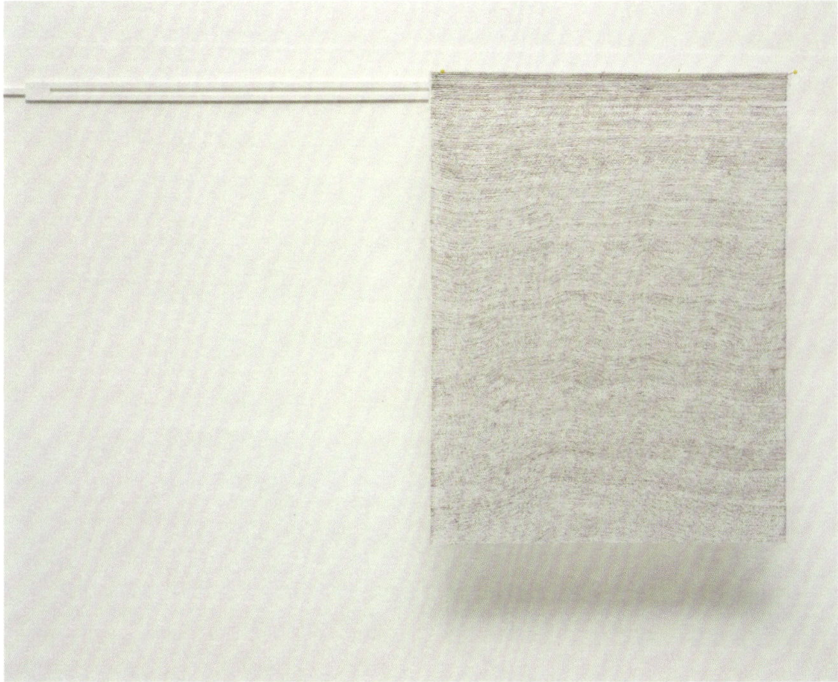

2.

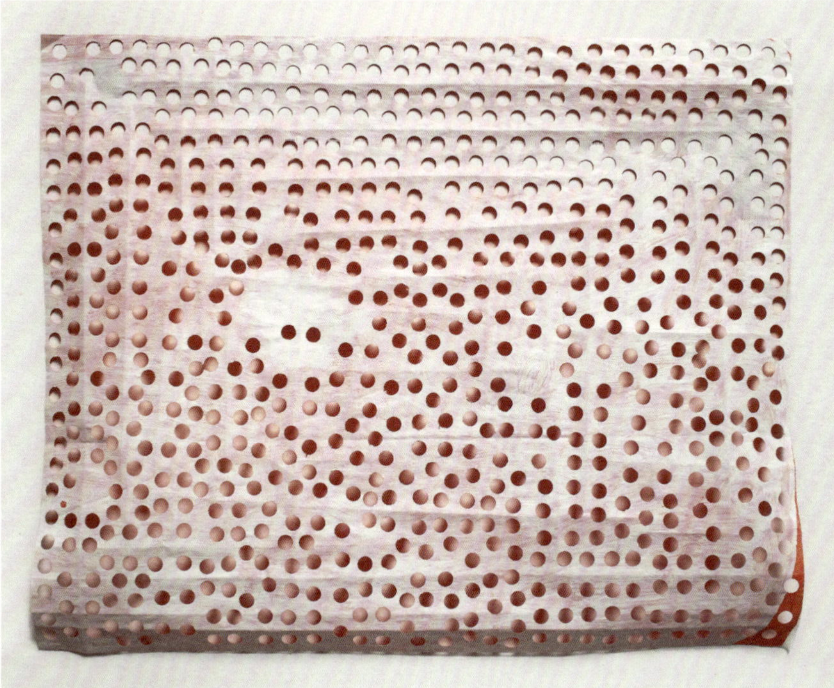

Born 1972, Bogotá. Lives and works in Bogotá.

1. *Untitled*, 2017, sumi ink on kozo paper mounted on painted wooden structure, 30 × 150 × 6 cm (11 ¾ × 59 × 2 ⅜ in)
2. *Untitled*, 2018, oil and hole punch on waxed tracing paper painted on both sides, 25 × 30 cm (9 ⅞ × 11 ⅞ in)
3. *Untitled (Best Western)*, 2019, pencil on rabbit-skin glue and calcium carbonate prepared canvas mounted on wood, 170 × 140 cm (67 × 55 ⅛ in)

3.

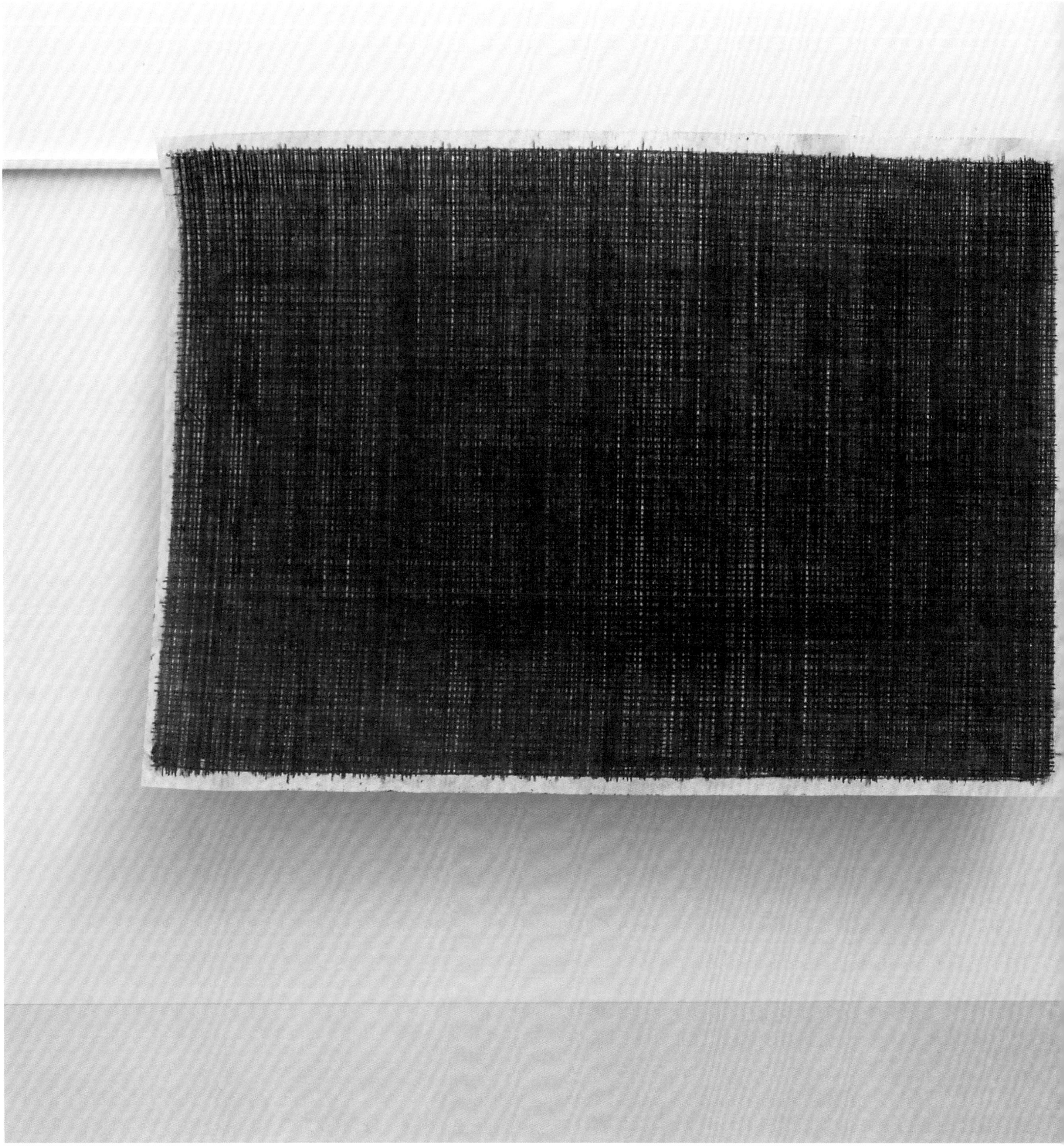

4.

4. *Untitled (Friction)*, 2017, charcoal, pencil, ink and pastel on tracing paper mounted on freestanding wooden structure, 400 × 800 × 250 cm (157 ½ × 315 × 98 ½ in)

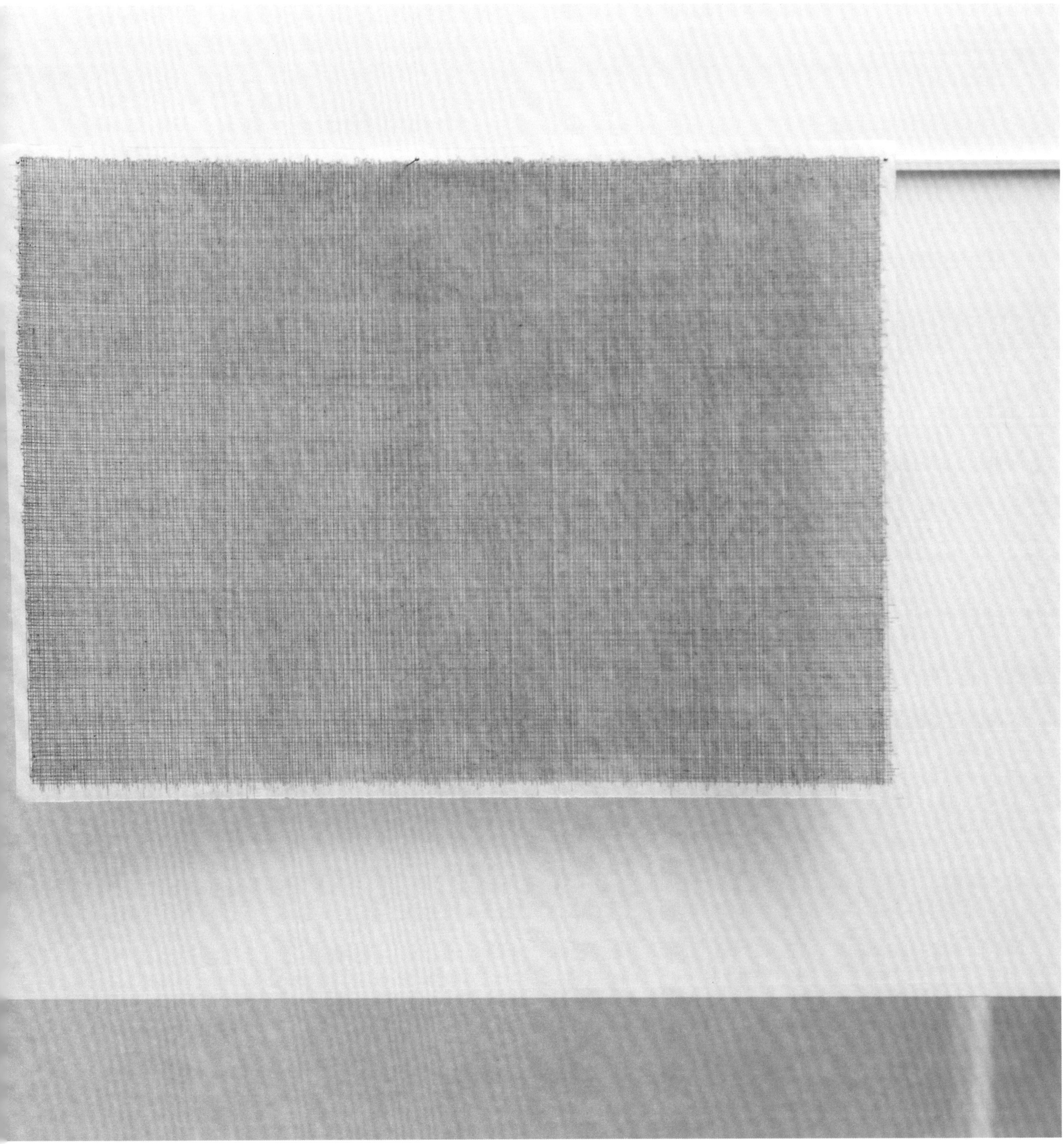

SANOU OUMAR .... An infinity of the finest of fine lines set within circles, rectangles and elongated diamond shapes creates an optical allure and sense of vibration that saturate the sublime works on paper of Sanou Oumar. Using pen, marker and coloured pencil, the artist simply titles his works with the single date on which they were made. In *6/26/19* (2019) a pixelation of tiny black marks forms the contour of three perfect circles, set on a diagonal, while the concentration of brilliant colour towards their centres creates depth. The arrangement and visual order form a placating composition that inspires infinite calm, while the brightly coloured geometric shapes propose an abstract language. Oumar was born and grew up in Burkina Faso before travelling to the United States as an asylum seeker. The physical and emotional turmoil of his past and present situations are communicated within another realm through his kaleidoscopic daily drawings, which he reportedly finds both spiritual and ritualistic, allowing him to heed his lived experiences. .... A continuity in the repetition of shapes and colours holds the eye and encourages meditation, while the absolute symmetry and meticulous detail of his drawings generate a spiritual energy within an alternative dimension. A similar abstract geometric language was explored by the Swiss artist, researcher and natural healer Emma Kunz (1892–1963), while an analogous spirituality can be perceived in the works of Swedish artist and mystic Hilma af Klint (1862–1944). The visual order and balance in Oumar's work invites contemplation and meditation in a process that courts harmony and balance in much the same way as Indian mandalas or prismatic kaleidoscopes. Works such as *5/26/19* (2019) balance simple yet complex shapes – circles, twisted swirls, rectilinear lines – with extraordinary detail and repetitive meticulous mark-making. .... The vibrant colours, intricate patterns and prominent architectural shapes of the artist's home country of Burkina Faso had a profound influence on his creative energy. The bright colours in his drawings are reminiscent of the colourful wax print Vlisco fabrics sold at the marketplaces, and the patterning recalls the repetitive details in Islamic tiles and mosaics. Oumar found the simplicity of forms in the local architecture, such as the circles, rectangles, triangles and pointed shapes of the modern bank building in the country's capital Ouagadougou, fascinating.
.... Elbé Coetsee

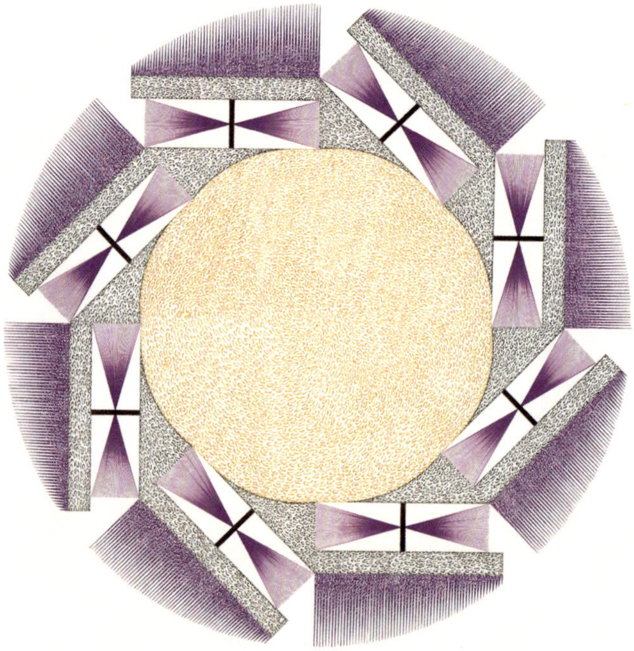

1.

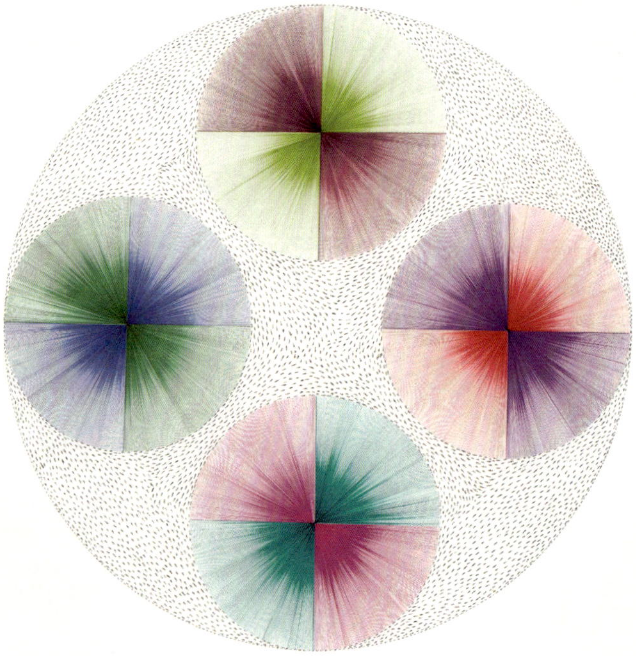

2.

Born Burkina Faso, West Africa. Lives and works in New York.

1. *3/12/19*, 2019, pen on paper board, 101.6 × 81.3 cm (40 × 32 in)
2. *3/14/19*, 2019, pen on paper board, 101.6 × 81.3 cm (40 × 32 in)
3. *6/26/19*, 2019, pen on paper board, 81.3 × 101.6 cm (32 × 40 in)

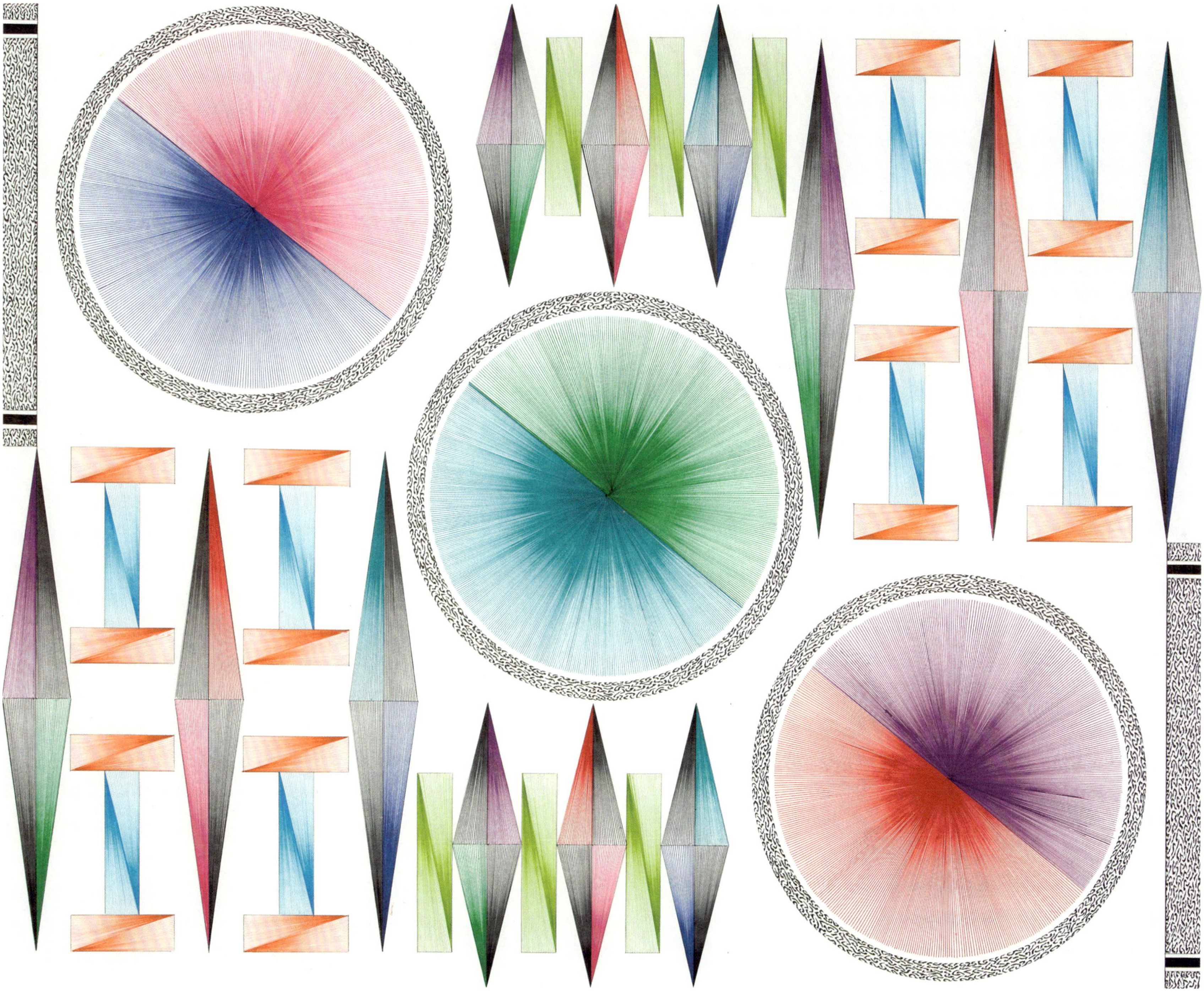

3.

CEREN OYKUT....... Ceren Oykut's practice expands the possibilities of drawing to include a wide range of techniques beyond works on paper. Her detailed drawings have appeared as book illustrations and she has created murals on disused buildings, stop-motion animation, live-drawing performances and site-specific installations featuring metal cutouts of her sketches. The performative aspect of her work is often collaborative, and involves other artists mostly working with light and sound. Oykut's metal cutout pieces are sometimes played by musicians in live performances using percussion mallets....... Oykut's works portray the intricacies of everyday experiences in styles that meld caricature and comics with mark-making and miniature art. Set in dense urban landscapes, the drawings speak of projected internal or mental states. There is often a sense of alienation and isolation in the elaborate scenes, where miscommunication and culture clashes abound. This is particularly present in works she has produced since relocating from Istanbul to Berlin. The pen-on-paper piece *Projection* (2015) consists of three free-floating panels sharing one sheet of paper. Yet each is aligned differently, forcing the viewer to either turn the page upside down or – if the work is hung on a wall – bend their body sideways to decipher the tiny scenes. The top panel shows a theatre-like stage setting in which a building's facade folds like a cardboard prop; two figures stand in front of it, with one of them appearing to operate a projector, casting images on to a scaffolding. The middle panel resembles a cartography drawing of an archipelago, thin strips of land branching out in all directions. The bottom panel again features a scene inside a theatre or concert hall, but a field takes up the space where rows of seats should be. Little figures leisurely strewn across the grass face a screen held up by a giant creature, watching a projection emitted from a projector positioned on a wooden crate. There is a sense of freedom in the scene, of reclaiming abandoned structures and carving out alternative communal spaces....... *Bibliopole* (2015) is a site-specific work executed with marker on a window of the contemporary art space Galata Greek School in Istanbul. The window's glass acts like a transparent foil where, from an imagined structure on a non-existent hill superimposed over the view outside, two figures look out on to the Turkish metropolis. It is part of the larger body of work 'Sketchbooks of Constantinople and Hagia Sophia' that Oykut based on a historical study, published in 1990, which explores the foundation of Constantinople and Hagia Sophia – its cathedral turned mosque – in Turkish traditions. In her series Oykut links architectural elements and the city's outline to connect the descriptions in the study with present-day Istanbul.
.... Hili Perlson

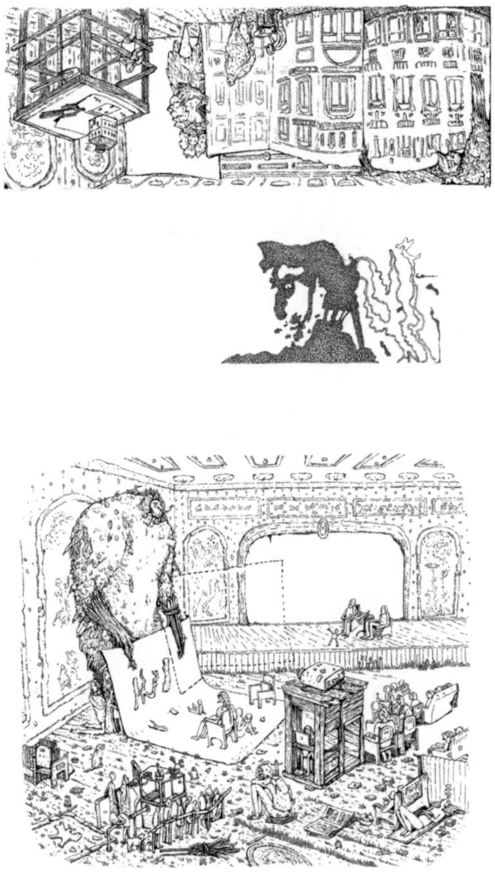

1.

Born 1978, Istanbul, Turkey. Lives and works in Berlin.

1. *Projection*, 2015, pen on paper, 61 × 45.5 cm (24 × 18 in)
2. *Bibliopole*, 2015, (detail), marker on window, 14 × 14.5 cm (5 ½ × 5 ¾ in) installation view, 'Sketchbooks of Constantinople and Hagia Sophia', Galata Greek School, Istanbul
3. *The Sketch*, 2019, metal pieces, 210 × 170 × 90 cm (82 ⅝ × 66 ⅞ × 35 ⅜ in), installation view at the artist's studio, Berlin

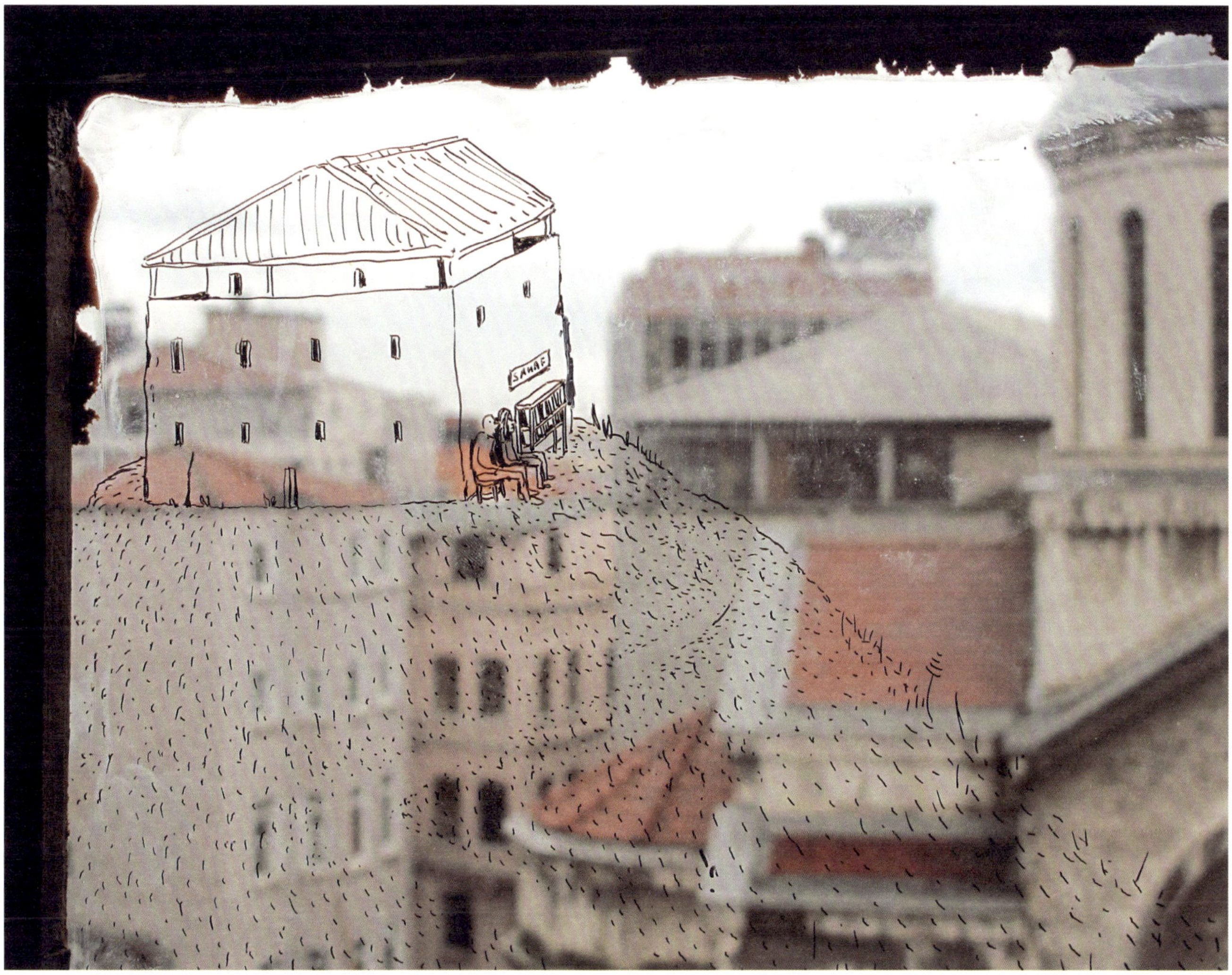

2.

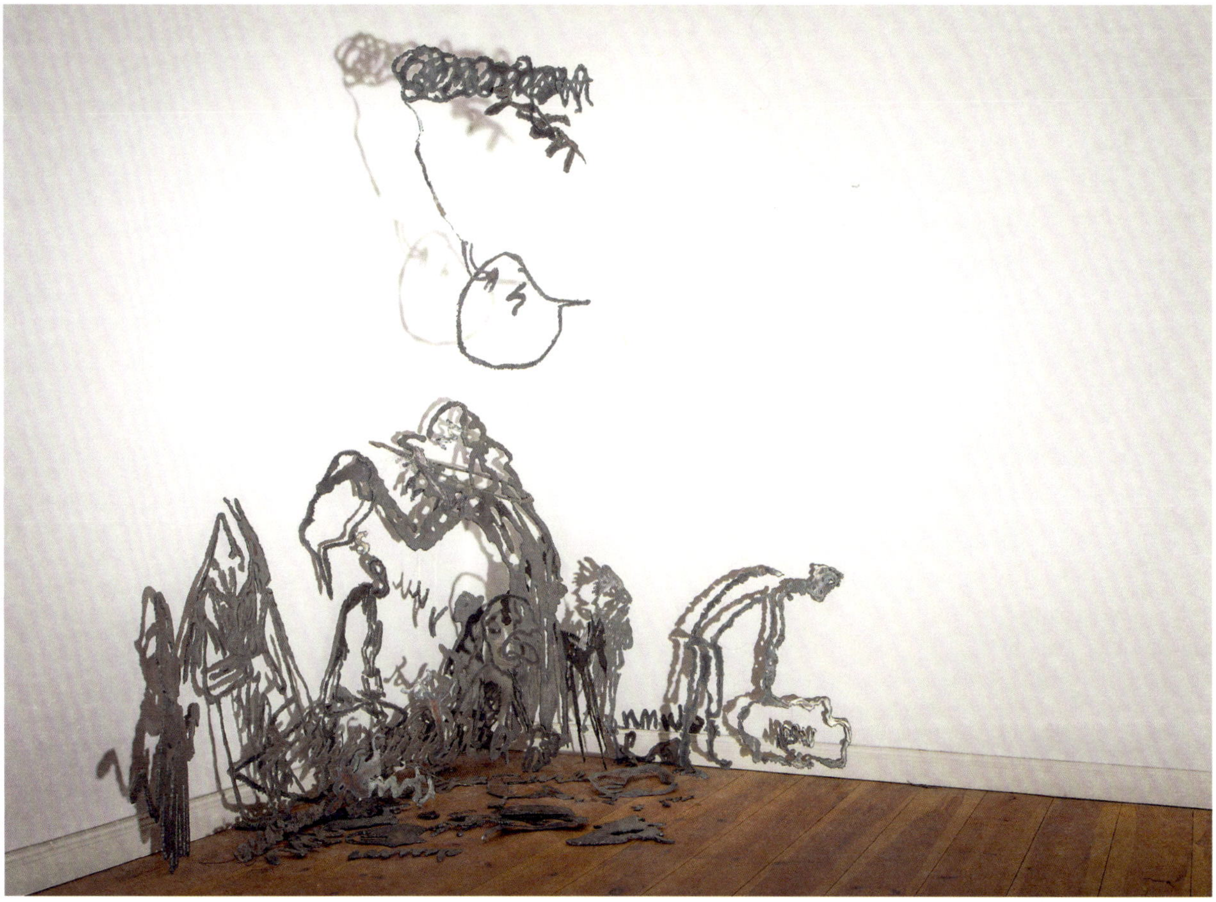

3.

PRABHAKAR PACHPUTE .... For his first solo show, in 2012, at Clark House Initiative in Mumbai, India, Prabhakar Pachpute excluded all light from the gallery space and filled its interior walls with charcoal drawings of all sizes, dripping water and lumps of coal. His intention was to take viewers on a trip down into a coal mine. The drawings were of solitary characters and elongated animal-human-machine hybrids that wandered desolate landscapes. Visitors were cast into a dreamlike interior and given silver torches to run light along the walls and ceilings, chancing upon the drawings. Born in Sasti, a village in the heart of the eastern Indian state of Maharashtra's coal mining belt, Pachpute wrote in his post-graduate thesis, 'The Possibilities of Drawing' (2011), that, 'In my opinion drawing is the only medium that itself tried to become a popular art form.' For him, drawing is an effective and vernacular way to translate the landscapes of his childhood and the experiences of his friends and family, and to deliver them with an almost cinematic quality to his viewers. He works on a grand scale and there is a great pageantry to his drawings, which sometimes spill into installation and sculpture. .... Pachpute builds entire worlds in a single piece. These worlds are populated by a number of individuals, inspired by local anecdotes, poetry and folklore. This cast of characters – full of idiosyncrasies and private passions – are his companions, his totems, as they recur throughout his works. For instance, there is the manager, often seen peering at a map; the inquisitive antenna-men; the wind indicators, with their billowing red and white hoods; the all-knowing owl; the headlamps with human bodies; and plumes of dense black smoke that are infused with their own animated charge. Pachpute's work is deeply rooted in the politics of his region, and as a result, in labour rights and protests across the country. In the charcoal and acrylic on canvas work *The Resistance Movement* (2017), farmers hold on to their land in a tight embrace, to protect it from stormy winds. This reads as a potent metaphor for the indigenous reclaiming of land, afforestation and a return to farming. In other works, Pachpute pays specific attention to Indian farmers' protests against unfair land acquisition by the government and indentured debt cycles. He rarely uses bright colours; instead, a muddy, earthen palette dominates his work. *Broken Varaha* (2016) – a charcoal and dry pastel drawing with acrylic paint and terracotta – is a rare exception. Local histories, proverbs and legends intermingle with global politics in Pachpute's drawings, and he has also travelled to the mines of Chile, Australia and Italy. His is a practice of resistance: drawing as a way of remembering and outlasting the erstwhile erasure of labour histories. .... Skye Arundhati Thomas

1.

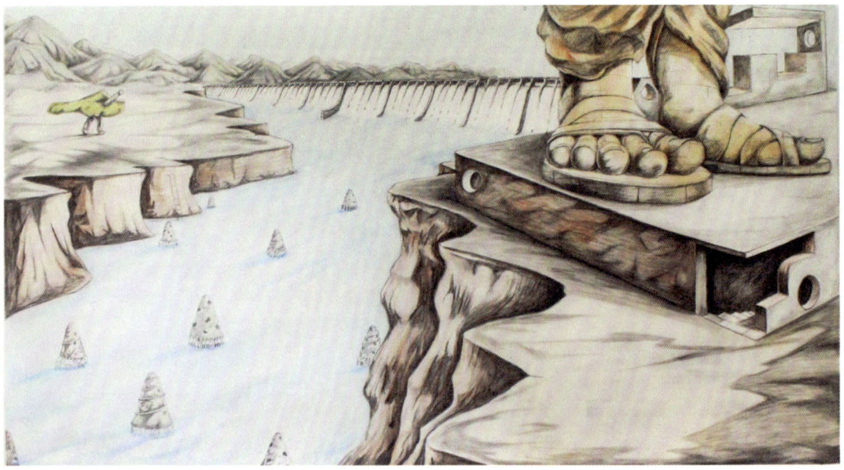

2.

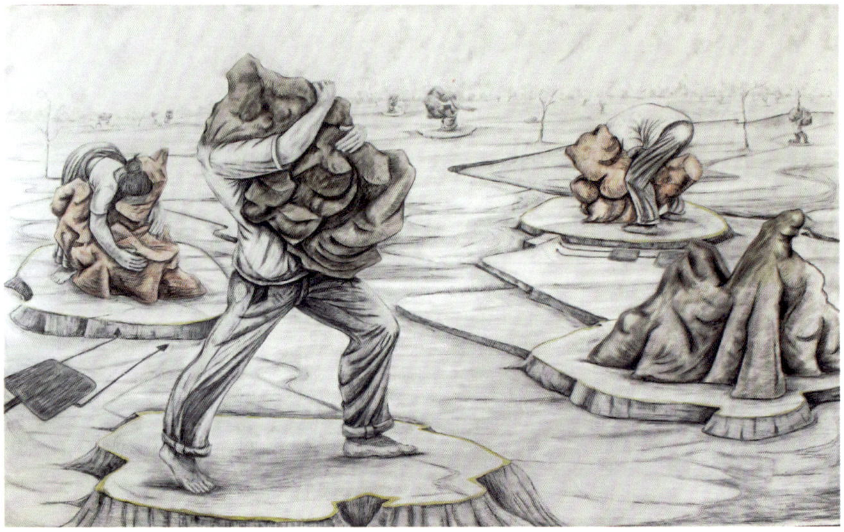

3.

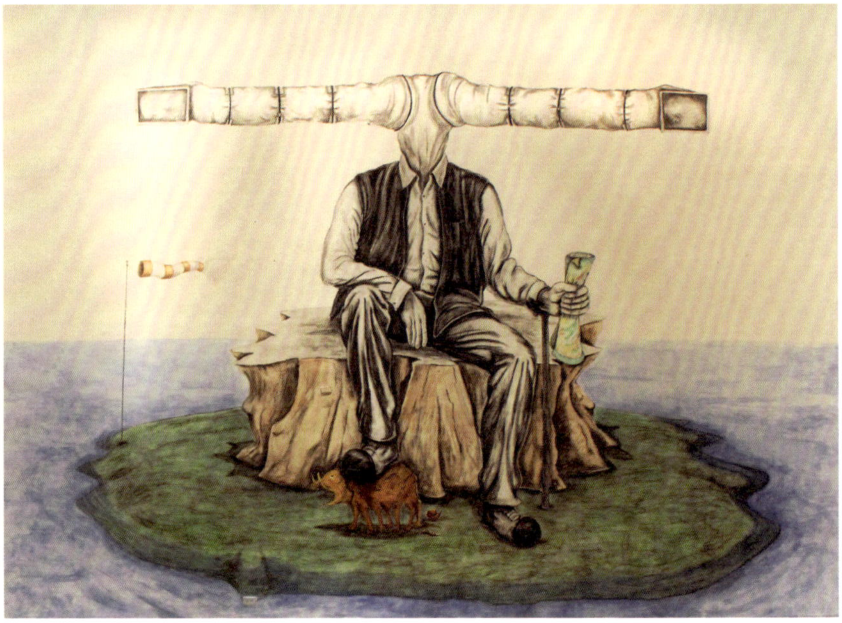

Born 1986, Sasti, Chandrapur, India. Lives and works in Mumbai, India.

1. *The Beast of Burden and Other Promises*, 2019, acrylic, charcoal and graphite on canvas, 137.2 × 259.1 cm (54 × 102 in)
2. *The Resistance Movement*, 2017, charcoal and acrylic on canvas, 91.4 × 243.8 cm (36 × 96 in)
3. *Broken Varaha*, 2016, charcoal, dry pastels, acrylic and terracotta, 762 × 914.4 cm (300 × 360 in), installation view at the Museum of Contemporary Art and Design (MCAD), Manila

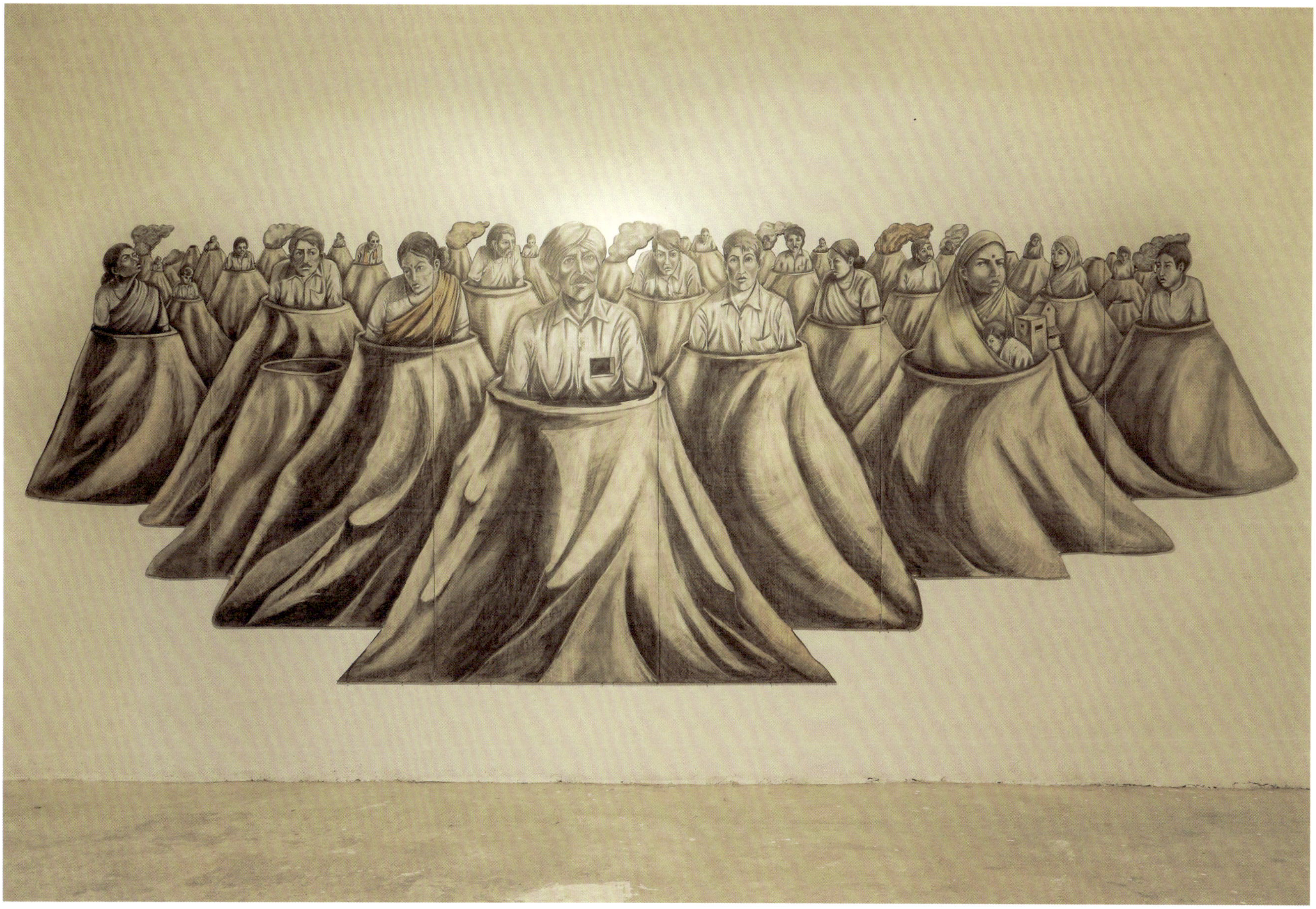

4.

4. *Resilient Bodies in the Era of Resistance*, 2018, charcoal and acrylic on plywood cutouts, 243.8 × 701 cm (96 × 276 in), installation view at the Kochi-Muziris Biennale 2018, India

HARDEEP PANDHAL .... Hardeep Pandhal's confrontationally lurid drawings teem with figures on the boundaries of caricature, and also with scrawled annotations – which he sees as 'a way of claiming an idea'. His practice extends to installation, music and knitted works made collaboratively with his mother, but he is best known for short films that animate the drawings in the style of a fantasy computer game, feeding the words into deadpan rap soundtracks. Both films and drawings feature what Pandhal describes as 'parodic parallel worlds', through which he expresses his frustration at how social structures reinforce injustice and discrimination. He exposes racism and misogyny with an acid humour, which both reveals and ridicules. .... The animations' themes emerge from Pandhal's identity as a second-generation British Sikh, born in Birmingham and based in Glasgow – two cities visibly built on the history of Empire. *BAME of Thrones (trailer)* (2019), for example, shows migrant cultures under surveillance, making punning use of the acronym for 'Black, Asian and minority ethnic' people to imagine 'overlooking my miscegenation nation where every single person looks at least half Asian'. *Pool Party Pilot Episode* (2018) posits a post-patriarchal world in which women thrive after learning to reproduce asexually, leaving the odd surviving man to drift around superfluously. The drawings share their spirit. *I Didn't Dream of Dragons* (2018) suggests someone who did dream, rather, of new races – via an alien taking part in what the scrawled text terms a 'colour blind casting call'. 'If we can have werewolves,' reads one line, 'we can have Black people' – a commonplace reality becomes a sci-fi fantasy. .... Pandhal filters a wide range of historical and literary inspirations. *Notes on Monster Portraits (Samatar)* (2018) refers to Del and Sofia Samatar's book proposing monsters as combinations of things that shouldn't go together, and linking that to their memories as a pair of mixed children growing up in the 1980s. 'Simultaneity is monstrous' is Pandhal's summary notation, while a decapitated head declares that 'creating monsters is an act of faith'. That figure is a recurring motif that Pandhal uses to tap in to us metaphorically losing our heads – indeed, another of his sources is Frances Larson's 2014 book *Severed: A History of Heads Lost and Heads Found*. In *Untitled* (2014) Pandhal's BA degree certificate from Leeds Metropolitan University is overpainted with several Indian heads, apparently unmoored from senior academics' bodies. The certificate forms the body of a splayed figure, presumably Pandhal himself, who declares sardonically that 'you need people like me'. And he's right: not so much to help universities' claims to be promoting racial equality as to nurture a broad range of voices in our art.
.... Paul Carey-Kent

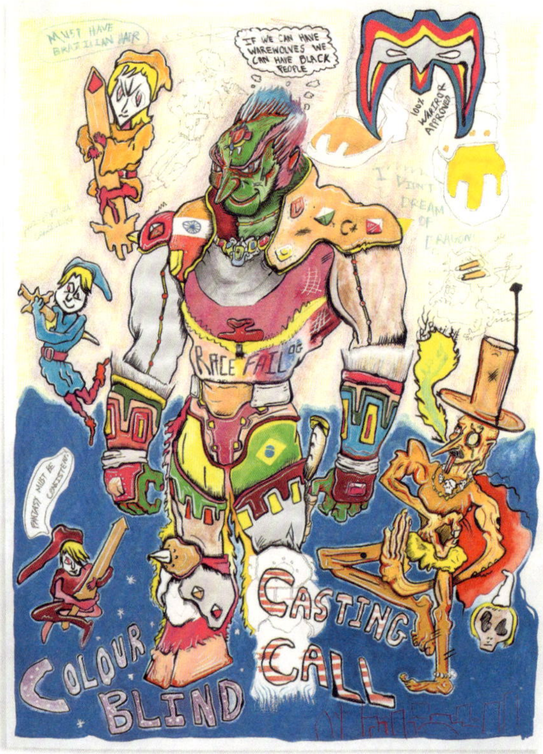

1.

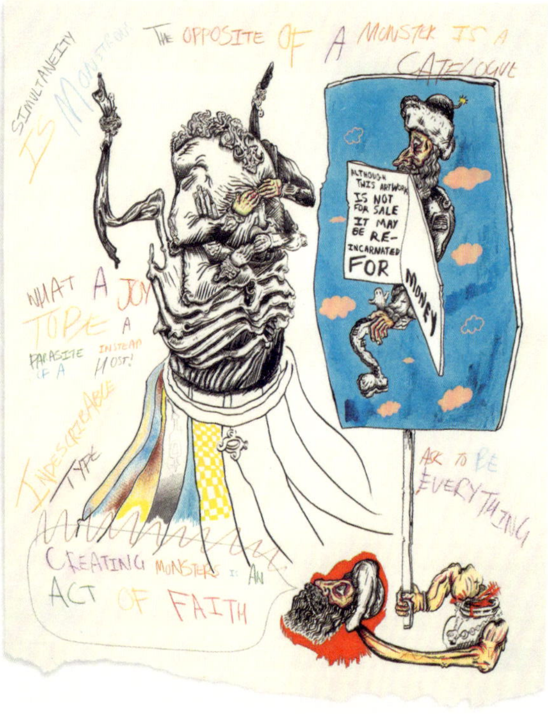

2.

Born 1985, Birmingham, UK. Lives and works in Glasgow.

1. *I Didn't Dream of Dragons*, 2018, India ink, gouache and coloured pencil on paper, 75.5 × 56 cm (29 ¾ × 22 in)
2. *Notes on Monster Portraits (Samatar)*, 2018, India ink, gouache and coloured pencil on paper, 70.5 × 56.2 cm (27 ¾ × 22 ⅛ in)
3. *Untitled*, 2014, India ink, gouache, metal clips and pencil on paper, 42 × 60 cm (16 ½ × 23 ⅝ in)
4. *Untitled*, 2014, India ink, gouache, metal clips and BA (Hons) Fine Art degree on paper, 42 × 60 cm (16 ½ × 23 ⅝ in)

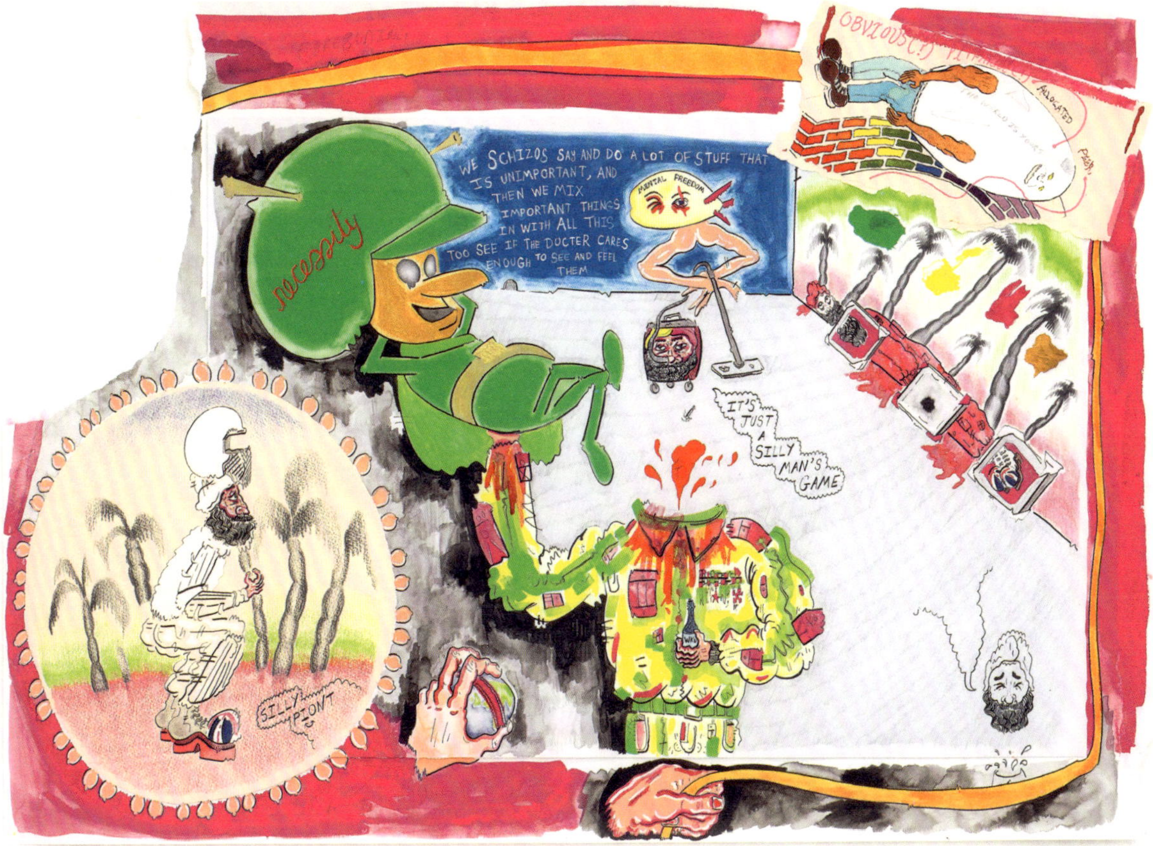
WE SCHIZOS SAY AND DO A LOT OF STUFF THAT IS UNIMPORTANT, AND THEN WE MIX IMPORTANT THINGS IN WITH ALL THIS TOO SEE IF THE DOCTER CARES ENOUGH TO SEE AND FEEL THEM
MENTAL FREEDOM
ALLOCATED
PEER
IT'S JUST A SILLY MAN'S GAME
SILLY PIONT

3.

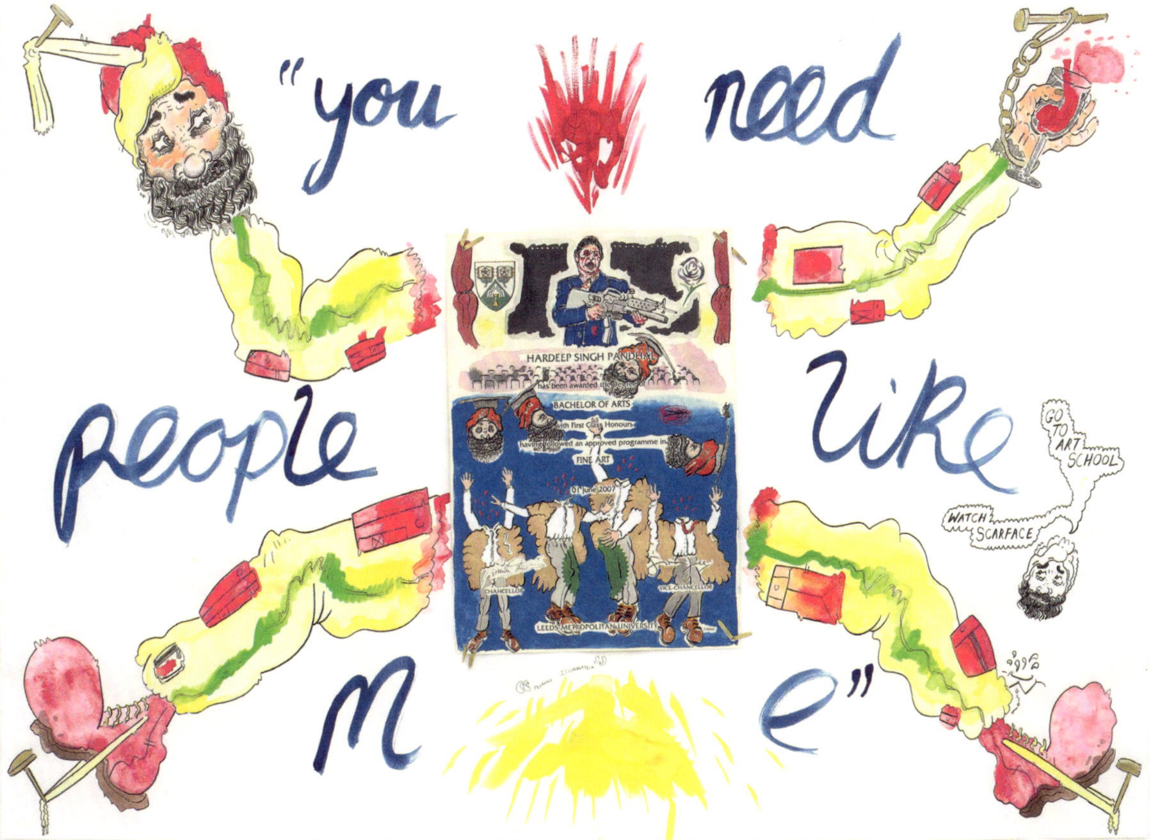
"you need
people like
m e"
HARDEEP SINGH PANDHAL
has been awarded
BACHELOR OF ARTS
with First Class Honours
having followed an approved programme in
FINE ART
01 June 2007
CHANCELLOR
VICE-CHANCELLOR
LEEDS METROPOLITAN UNIVERSITY
GO TO ART SCHOOL
WATCH SCARFACE

4.

Micha Payer and Martin Gabriel started collaborating in 2000. Like many artists fresh out of art school, their initial efforts were characterized by a desire to experiment with different formal solutions, including sculpture, drawing, photography and animation, and although all these media are still very much part of their practice, drawing eventually prevailed. Parallel to this, the equally important question of establishing a way to collaborate effectively had to be investigated. Their response turned out to be the creation of a visual dictionary – an ongoing collection of images that soon reached significant proportions and that the pair regularly tap into with the two-fold objective of unifying their efforts and reinforcing the notion of seeing the diverse facets of their work as a cohesive oeuvre. As a result, every single piece could be conceived as a valid narrative element within multiple contexts. This modus operandi treats repetition as a concept closer to the idea of recurrence, rather than seriality. Evidence of an inclination to explore the possibilities presented by repetition and duality are tangible in some of the duo's early photographs. This is the case in *Im Fall* (2006) from the series 'Nuclear Family', where the two artists and their child are depicted as if flattened by a series of identical panels; or *Kabine* (2005), where a man holding a guitar case stands in front of two identical elevator doors leading to apparently diverse scenarios. When Payer Gabriel are drawing, however, their technique becomes visibly more versatile. The question of 'Who is doing what?' – an interrogative inevitably attached to every collaborative venture – turns out to be superfluous, as drawings are created with no designated areas of expertise and with a great deal of discussion. Some of their drawings express a thinly disguised preference for presenting objects or people as entities in perennial movement and in abundant quantity, with varying degrees of realism. If *Untitled/Drones #15* (2018), for example, offers a reasonably realistic picture of a loose formation of drones flying over a menacing grey sky, the heavy traffic of bikers in *Untitled (homo portans)* (2014) is a scene defined by such perspectival variety and background neutrality as to elude any potential mark of plausibility. Conversely, works like the ink and pencil on paper of the 'doppelgänger' series (2017) and the botanical *The Absence of Nothingness* (2019) suggest a strong encyclopedic feel. Yet their approach to the subject is not entirely acritical. Encyclopedias traditionally bring together the most disparate notions to display them in authoritative fashion. In Payer Gabriel's work, conflicting truths are gathered together to educate and entertain, but also to raise existential dilemmas. Their images are a study in how the human brain works, with the never-ending battle between science as a source of information and philosophy as an interpretational device acting like a giant undertow.
.... Michele Robecchi

Micha Payer: born 1979, Wolfsberg, Austria. Martin Gabriel: born 1976, Linz, Austria. Both artists live and work in Vienna.

1. *doppelgänger*, 2017, series of drawings in pencil and ink on paper, each 29.7 × 63 cm (11 ¾ × 24 ⅞ in)

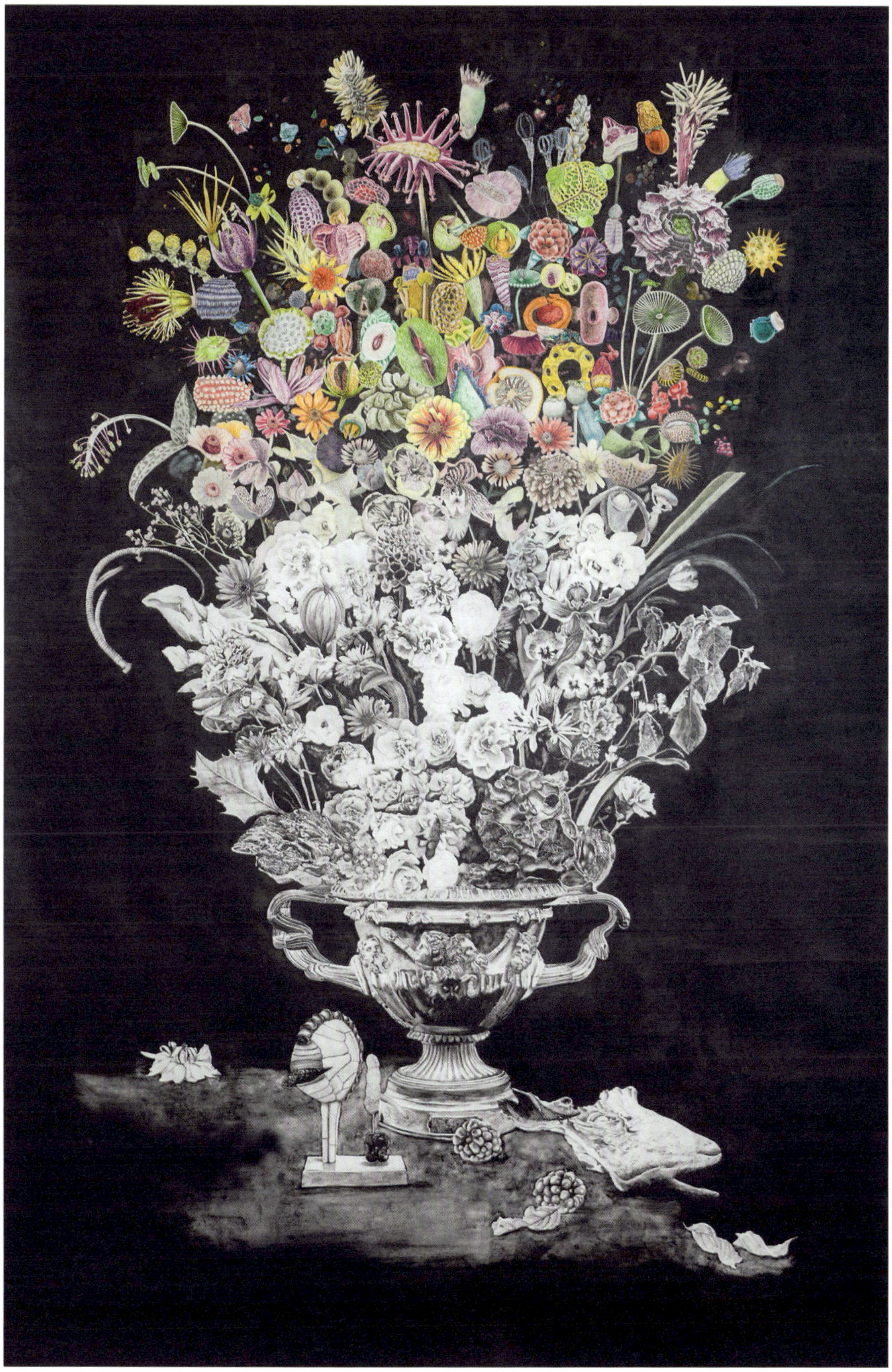

2.

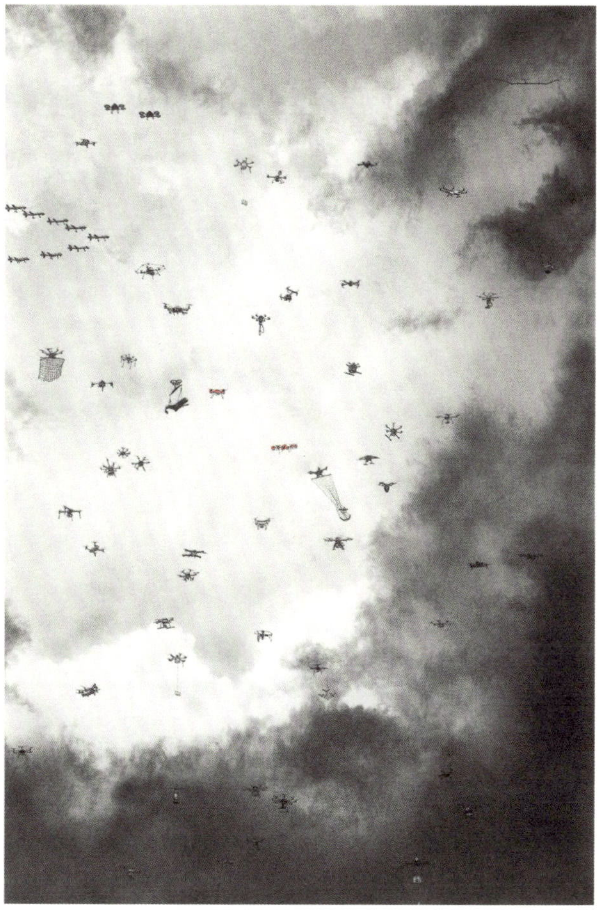

3.

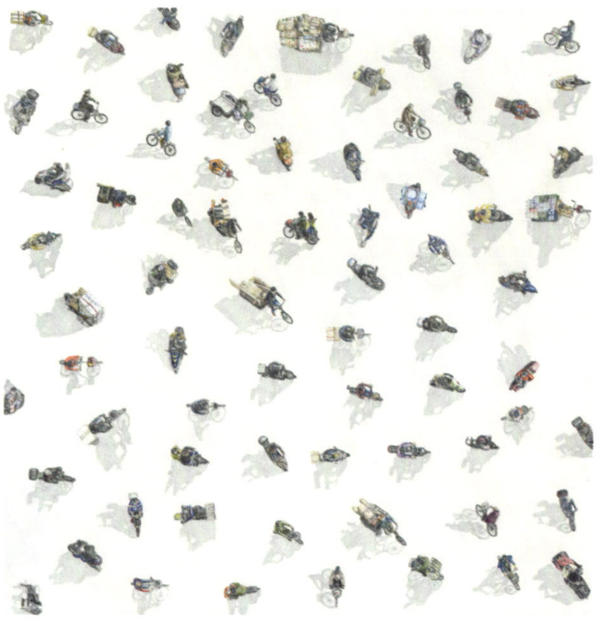

4.

2. *The Absence of Nothingness*, 2019, pencil, crayon and graphite putty on paper, 150 × 100 cm (59 × 39 ⅜ in)
3. *Untitled/Drones #15*, 2018, pencil, crayon and graphite powder on paper, 100 × 70 cm (39 ⅜ × 27 ½ in)
4. *Untitled (homo portans)*, 2014, pencil and crayon on paper, 40 × 40 cm (15 ¾ × 15 ¾ in)

GUSTAVO PÉREZ MONZÓN....... The mythology around Gustavo Pérez Monzón tells a narrative of rediscovery not uncommon for local art movements of the twentieth century taking shape outside the traditional art centres of Europe and the United Sates. Having made a profound and lasting impact, in the early 1980s, on the art scene in his native Cuba, Pérez Monzón, at the height of his success, chose to retreat from the art world and focus on teaching instead. With his work rediscovered by an influential collector nearly four decades later, Pérez Monzón has recently returned to creating art, producing mixed-media works on paper as well as site-specific installations that evince the same formal preoccupation with Minimalism and Conceptualism that had shaped his earlier work. The explorations at the basis of his practice can be described as introspective – spiritual, even; their elegant, pared-down aesthetic is imbued with an interest in coded systems and a fascination with arcane sciences. .... *Untitled* (2018), is reminiscent of a maze with its branching thick black lines and angles. Yet no path can be traced within the drawing; all entrances lead to dead ends. It is as if the geometrical figures created by the lines – which occasionally evoke ancient sacred patterns – were extended to reject the dogma of there being a single thinkable answer. The viewer's gaze, erring to and fro, eventually eases to absorb the work in its entirety, perhaps noticing for the first time that the arrangement is off-centre. The cumulation of grey, black and striped shapes in *Untitled* (2016) resembles an aerial view of farmland, in which the demarcation of the adjacent plots follows an impenetrable logic, while their patterned interiors provide clues to what might be cultivated within. In a 2018 interview in *Studio International*, Pérez Monzón explained he 'was interested in the idea of a world of invisible connections and meanings, as expressed in ancient sciences such as numerology, the Kabbalah and certain esoteric schools...the way in which geometric forms express abstract, philosophical, and even emotional concepts.' Two elongated shapes dominate another untitled work from 2016 – one a yellowish amber, one black – created by staggered repetitions of geometric patterns. The same patterns are repeated across the drawing's entire surface in thin, interconnected lines. The effect of this is multiple overlaid planes, as if the patterns exist all around, floating in the ether, and have coalesced by chance, or intervention, into something resembling totems or pillars. In the Book of Exodus, the Israelites are said to have followed a pillar of fire by night and a pillar of cloud by day to lead them through the desert in their flight from slavery to self-determination. Here, the two pillar-like shapes echo this notion of cosmic divination existing in dualism.
.... Hili Perlson

1.

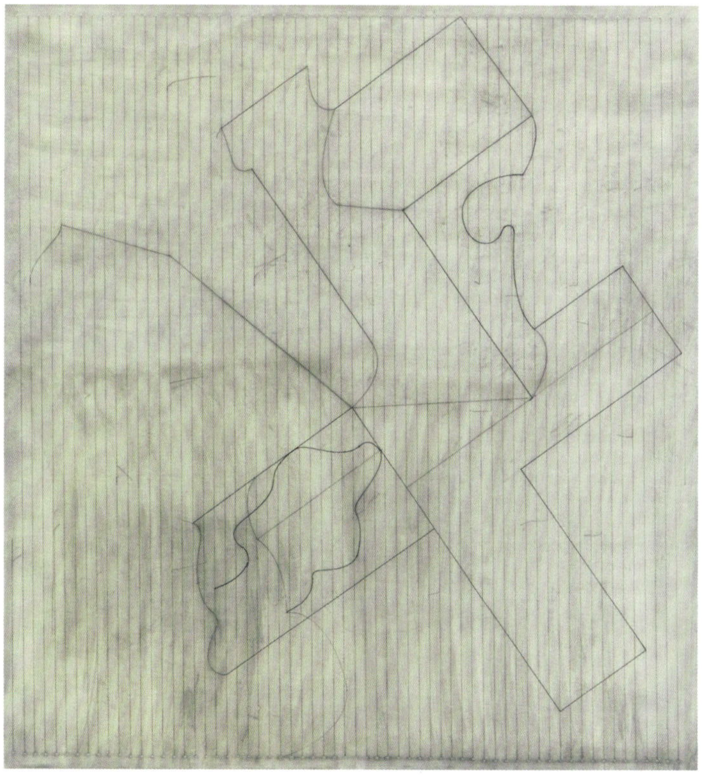
2.

Born 1956, Sancti Spiritus, Cuba. Lives and works in Cuernavaca, Morelos, Mexico.

1. *Untitled*, 2018, mixed media on cromocotex paper, 100 × 70 cm (39 ⅜ × 27 ½ in)
2. *Untitled* 2018, mixed media on cromocotex paper, 75 × 70 cm (29 ½ × 27 ½ in)
3. *Untitled*, 2016, aluminium, ink, graphite and pigment on cromocotex paper, 95 × 70 cm (37 ⅜ × 27 ½ in)
4. *Untitled*, 2018 mixed media on cromocotex paper, 100 × 70 cm (39 ⅜ × 27 ½ in)

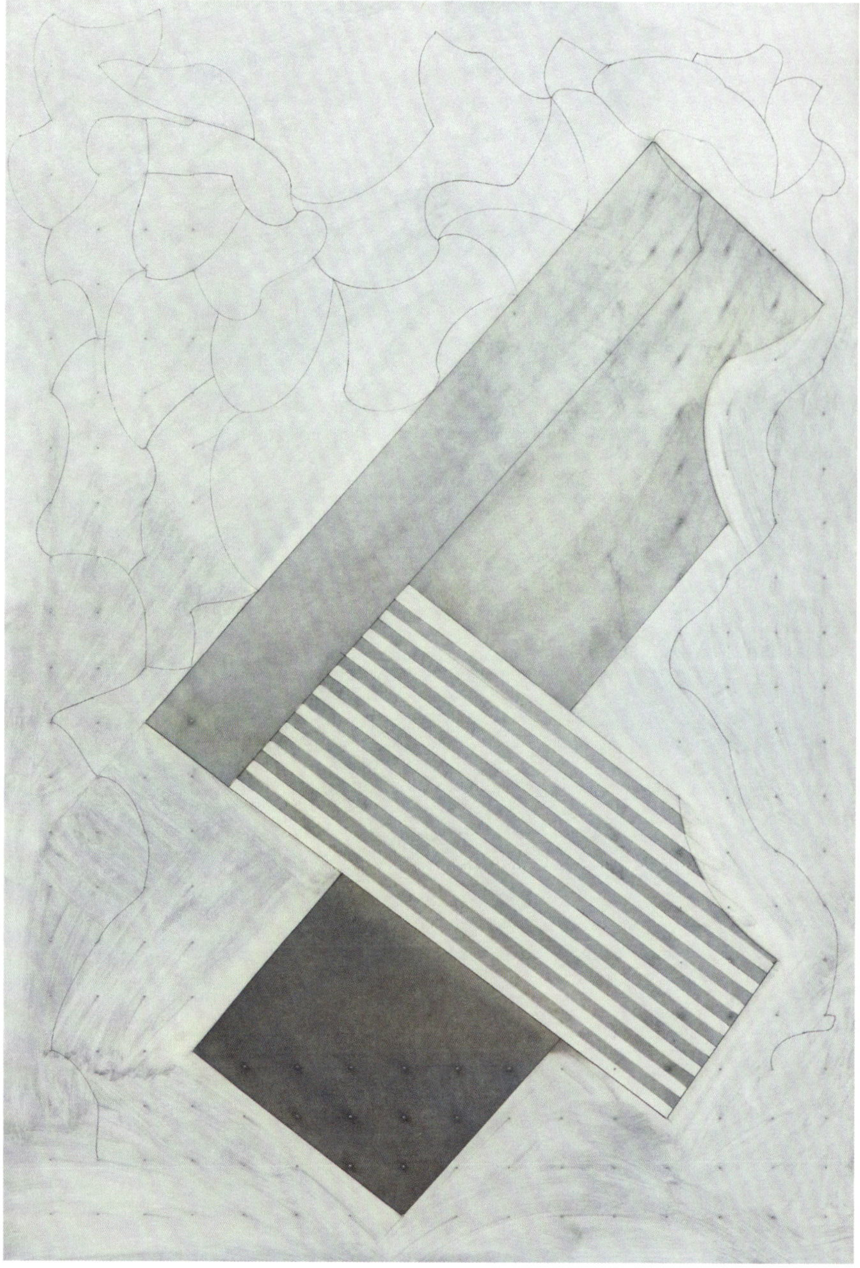

4.

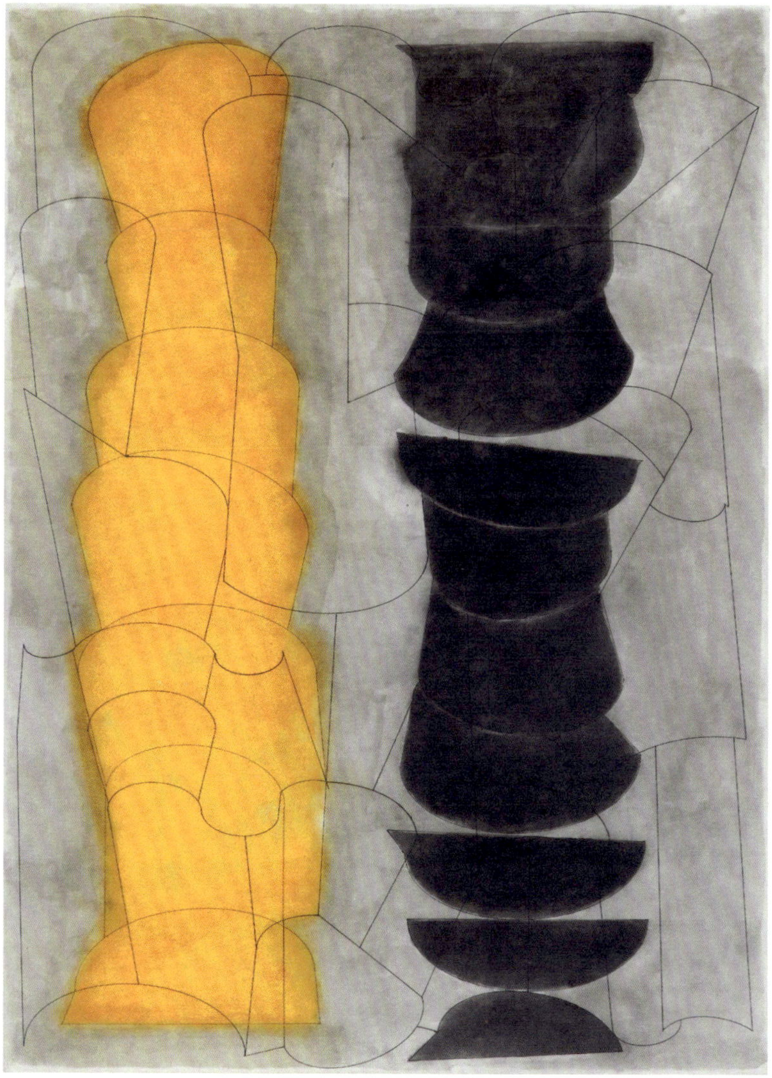

3.

MICK PETER....... Mick Peter's drawings often remain incomplete until they exit the white page. His caricature-like creations on paper are enlarged and remade into flat life-size sculptures in materials such as steel and plywood. The figures in his sketches are in a style gleaned from pre-digital-era graphic design, where little figures and characters were used in branding. The sculptural pieces are exhibited as room-spanning installations that tell witty narratives about the absurdities of everyday life, but also cheekily question symbols of authority and deep-seated conceptions. The sprawling installation *To Me, To You* (2019) was presented on an entire floor of the BALTIC Centre for Contemporary Art in Gateshead, UK. Viewers were invited to walk through the set-up and around the individual pieces, which had been installed in ways that made playful reference to their two-dimensionality. Possibly one of Peter's works that functions most like a comic strip, *To Me, To You* follows the journey of a stone sculpture from production in the artist's studio to public showing at an art institution. In a sequence of comical scenes, replete with visual idioms and recognizable tropes, Peter shows a slapstick-like decision-making process that ends up affecting the sculpture's final shape, completely undermining the artwork's integrity. The sculpture itself is rendered in a modernist abstract style that is sometimes utilized by the media to illustrate the impenetrability and elitism of modern art. Viewers encountered multiple nearly-identical rooms, each indicating a single scene, where small changes in details set forward the narrative. The unglamorous inner workings of an art institution were not spared from the elaborate gag, either; the visitors had to enter the exhibition through a cartoon set that looked like a drab office, cat posters and all. 'It's quite legible, but then you find the subtext in the details,' Peter explains in a video interview. 'For me it's all those things [showing] what it actually feels like to try and make a show.' .... In his 2017 exhibition '110%', Peter took as his starting point signs and symbols used to compose infographics. They are characters in a visual language that stands for hard facts; statistical calculations conveyed in universally recognizable (though, arguably, uninviting) manner. The trompe-l'oeil drawings and sculptures in the show were anthropomorphized – perhaps a reminder that the cold numbers on the graphs represent real impacts on human lives. Man-figures drawn in a style that reflects their neutrality, as mere carriers of statistical information, were filled in with different amounts of red and yellow paint corresponding to the percentage they stand in for. In *55%*, for example, on figure red up to just over half the height of the sculpture, whereas the figure struggling to represent the 110% of the exhibition's title is standing on a deconstructed percentage symbol for extra elevation. .... Hili Perlson

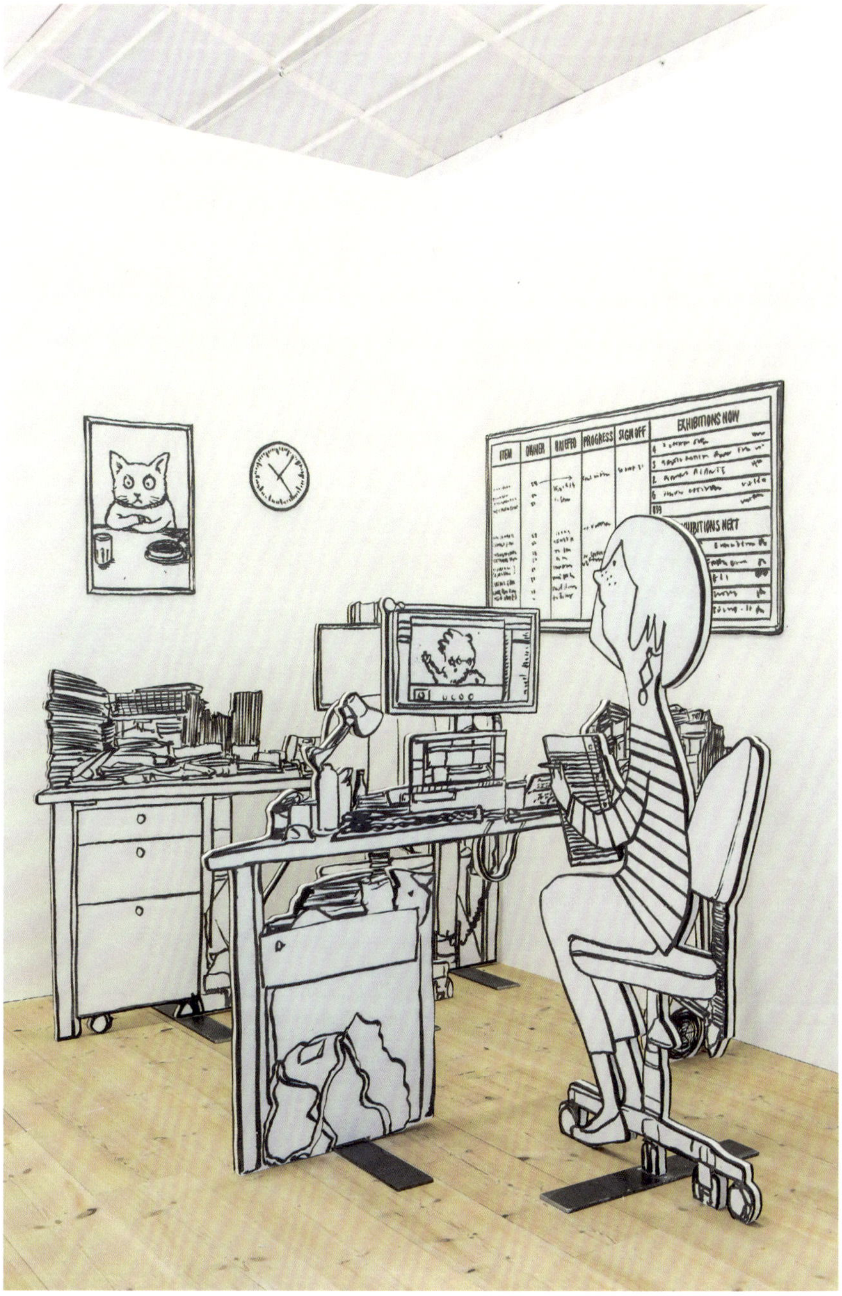

1.

Born 1974, Berlin, Germany . Lives and works in Glasgow.

1. *To Me, To You*, 2019, (detail), digital print, plywood, steel and MDF, seated figure: 148 × 79 × 3 cm (58 ¼ × 31 × 1 ⅛ in), installation view, 'To Me, To You', BALTIC Centre for Contemporary Art, Gateshead, UK
2. *To Me, To You*, 2019, (detail), 2019, blue back poster, digital print, plywood, MDF, steel, acrylic, lights, plastic roofing and timber frame, 'sculpture' shown: 220 × 102 × 3 cm (86 ⅝ × 40 ⅛ × 1 ⅛ in), installation view as above
3. *55%* and *110%*, 2017, acrylic resin, MDF and Jesmonite pigment, 195 × 101 × 61 cm (76 ¾ × 39 ¾ × 24 in) and 201 × 101 × 61 cm (79 ⅛ × 39 ¾ × 24 in), installation view, "110%", Workplace, Gateshead, UK
4. *Untitled (Figure Carrying Zip)*, 2015, acrylic resin, steel, Jesmonite pigment, red paint, polyurethane foam, hessian and MDF, figure: 175 × 75 × 20 cm (69 × 29 ½ × 8 in), zip: 80 × 320 × 25 cm (31 ½ × 126 × 9 ⅞ in), installation view, 'Pyramid Selling', Tramway, Glasgow

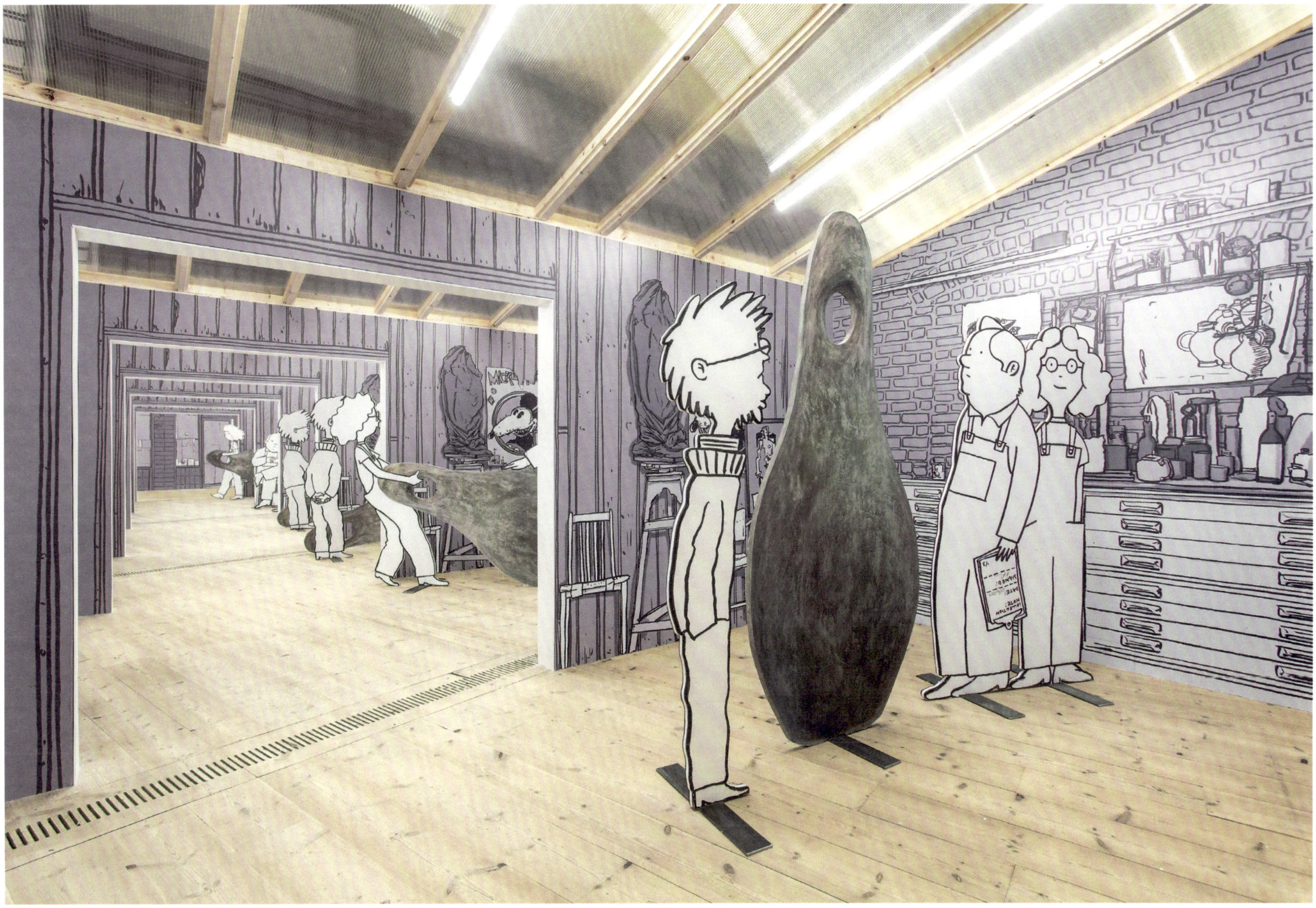

2.

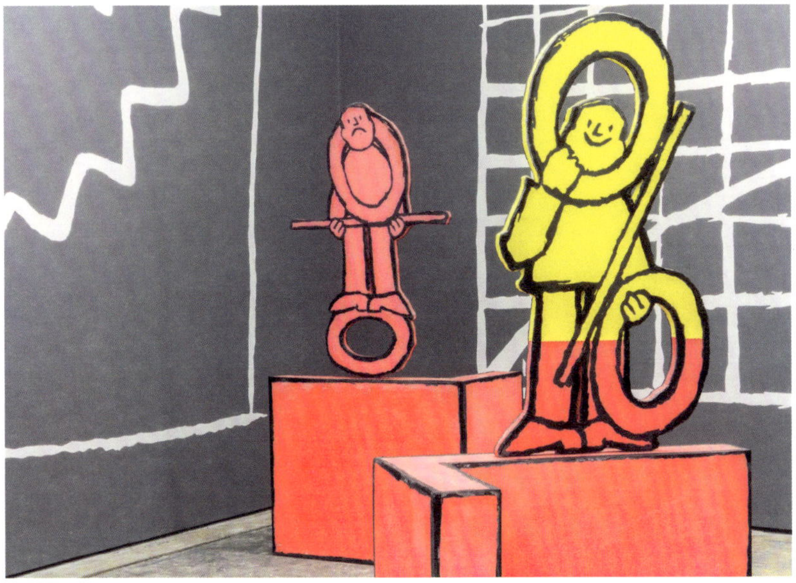

3.

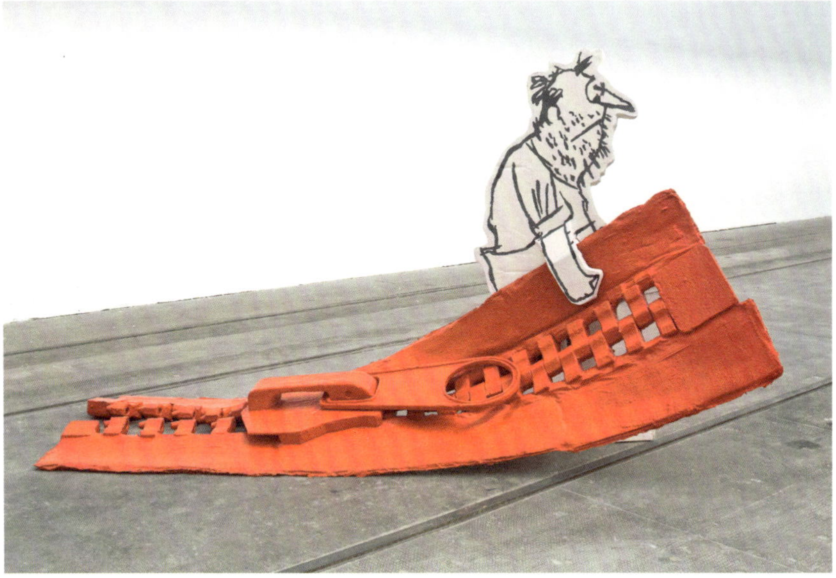

4.

DEANNA PETHERBRIDGE....... Working almost exclusively in monochromatic pen and ink, Deanna Petherbridge has dedicated herself to drawing for over forty years. Her work conflates bold geometries with the imagery of pistons and machines, merging industrial and architectural motifs. More recent large-format pieces feature urban landscapes characterized by vertiginous perspective and dramatic shifts in scale. Everything is untethered from gravity as objects float freely amid constant spatial and perspectival contradictions. The effect of Petherbridge's work is both disorientating and exhilarating....... Alongside her drawings, the artist has made murals and theatre backdrops. She has also written extensively, advocating for the medium as a teacher and public figure. In later works buildings are turned inside out and cities are depicted in cyclical states of construction and carnage. Petherbridge's vision of the metropolis is mediated through the prism of daily news broadcasts and science fiction films. We are reminded of the ubiquity of cranes and building sites in urban spaces and cities unwillingly reshaped by conflict. Wars, natural disasters and economic impulses each shape the city in different ways, leaving behind psychic and physical scars. .... *The Destruction of the City of Homs* (2016) references the ancient Syrian city that was obliterated during the Syrian civil war. Over three large pieces of paper, the dense image portrays high-rises that have been reduced to concrete skeletons with rebar jutting out of crumbling mortar. We view the bombed-out city floating amid the ruins from a drone's eye view. Petherbridge's art is ominous and highly dramatic, her pen and ink picking out the details like an expert cinematographer. Bridges cut across the image suggesting transit, yet the environment has long been evacuated – the city is left as a contemporary ruin ghosted by its previous community. *The Wall* (2019) is similarly claustrophobic. A wall occupies the foreground of the image. Behind it is another barrier. The picture is like a prison and leaves little space for manoeuvre. While much of Petherbridge's work reminds us of the violence of displacement, this image focuses on the aggressive infrastructure of containment. It is impossible to look at it and not think of real and imagined walls around the world and the plight of desperate people trying to climb them to find safer and better lives....... These are tangled drawings that invoke the speed in which urban spaces are made and unmade. Yet, for all their evocation of velocity, Petherbridge asks us to slow down and pay attention to the role of images. She makes drawings with cinematic ambition, situating the discipline alongside filmmaking, music and literature as a cultural form capable of articulating the crises that pervade our current moment.
.... George Vasey

1.
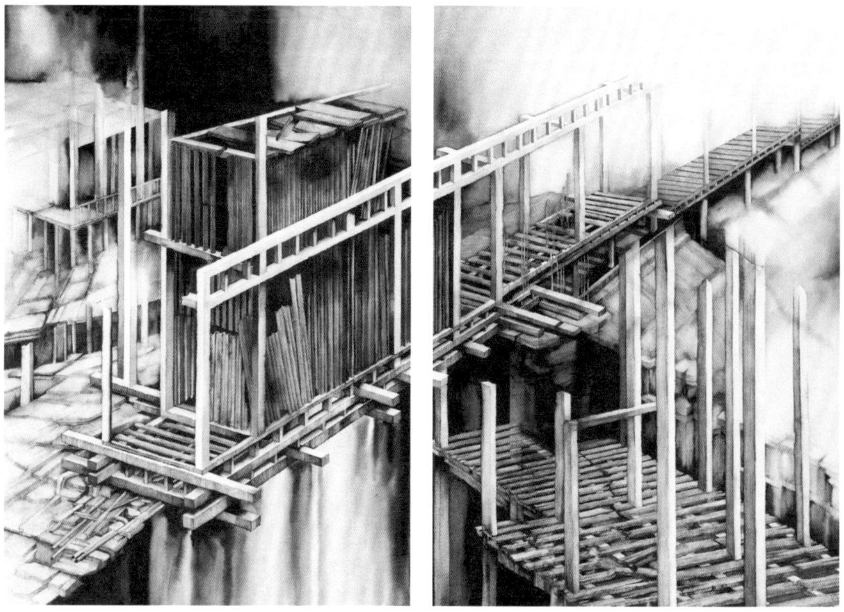

2.
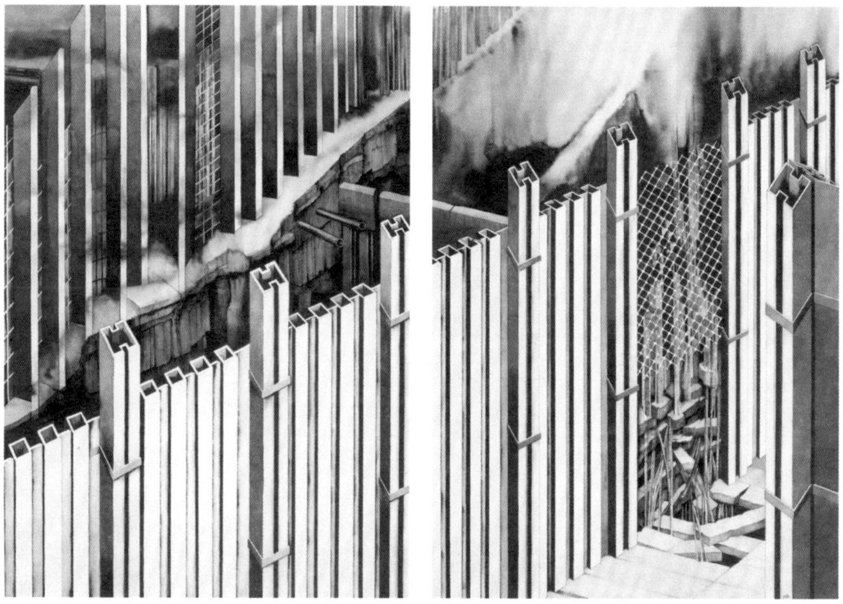

Born 1939, Pretoria, South Africa. Lives and works in London.

1. *Crossing the Abyss*, 2019, diptych, Chinese ink on paper, 105 × 148 cm (41 ¼ × 58 ¼ in)
2. *The Wall*, 2019, diptych, ink and wash on paper, 105 × 148 cm (41 ¼ × 58 ¼ in)
3. *Migration 1*, 2018, diptych, ink and watercolour on paper, 105 × 148 cm (41 ¼ × 58 ¼ in)
4. *The Destruction of the City of Homs*, 2016, triptych, pen, ink and wash on paper, 127.7 × 252 cm (50 ¼ × 99 ¼ in)

3.
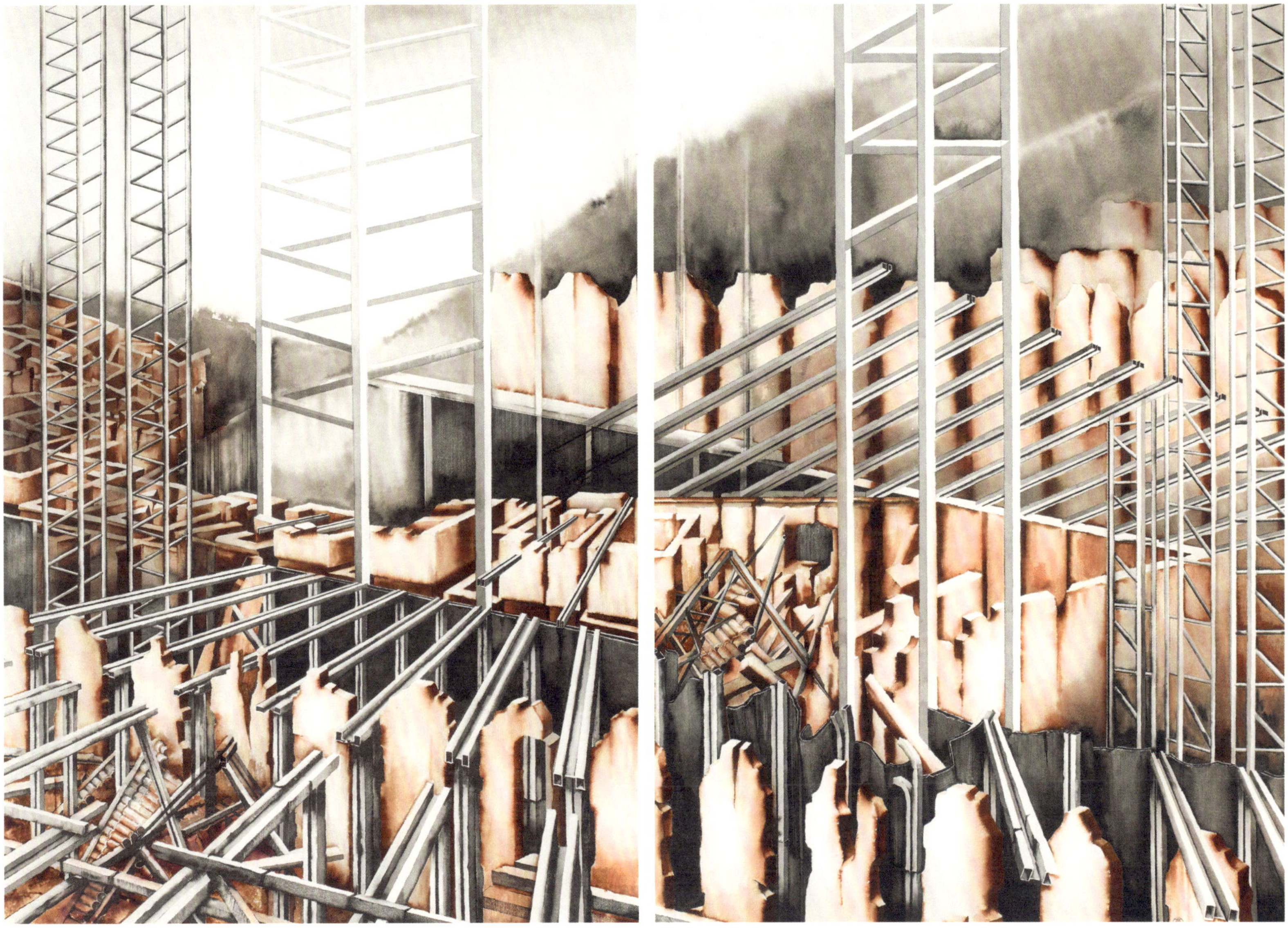

4.
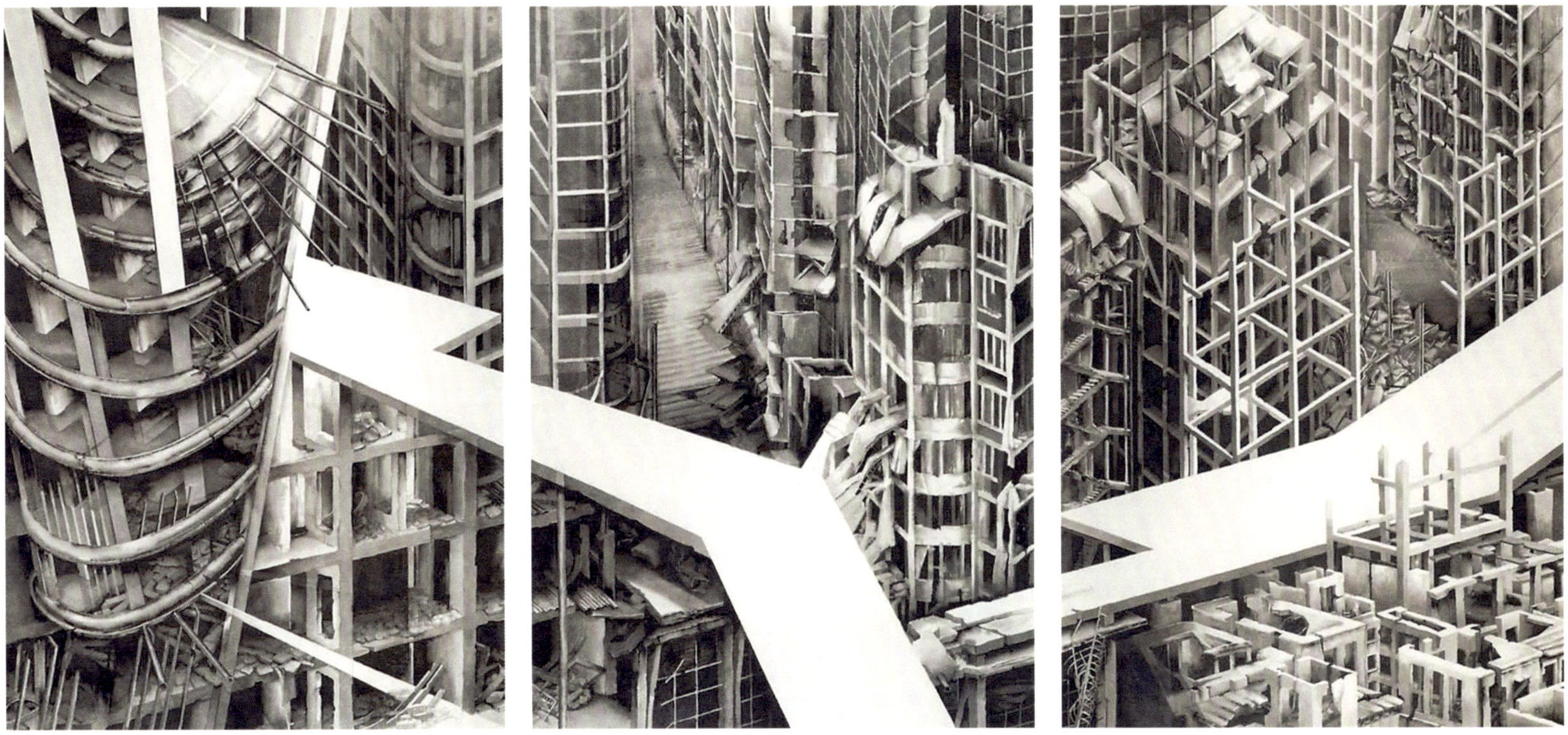

QIU ANXIONG .... Trained as a painter, as well as in animation and film-making, Qiu Anxiong combines all three mediums in his multi-disciplinary practice. Born in China and living in Germany during his five-year study, the cultural differences between the two countries motivated him to reconsider the relevance of Chinese artistic traditions and to work with themes related to Chinese ink-and-brush landscape paintings. During this process, he came to realize that the ancient landscape paintings he admired and emulated were in fact records of the contemporary times and reality of their painters. Since then, his art has been focused on reflecting his own contemporary reality, with painting remaining central even to his work in video, animation and installation. .... 'New Book of Mountains and Seas' is an ongoing series of ink drawings on paper, started in 2004, that takes its inspiration from the ancient Chinese *Classic of Mountains and Seas* (*Shanghaijing*), an encyclopedic compilation containing detailed descriptions of mythical beasts and geographical locations. Each of Qiu's drawings replicates a traditional woodblock-printed text with accompanying illustrations. In the place of the imaginary creatures in his source, Qiu depicts mutated beasts with features of modern machines and weapons, inhabiting settings typical of traditional Chinese paintings. Each black and white image bears a title with the creature's name and an account of its prominent characteristics, written by Qiu. .... These drawings preceded and led to the conception and making of a three-chapter animation project, starting in 2006. The first three-channel video, *New Classic of Mountains and Seas (I)*, is essentially a bleak story of wars and conflict from ancient times to the present, portraying a land overrun by outlandish creatures, with dystopic overtones of technology run amok. It was followed by two sequences, the second looking at contemporary technology and the third at life under surveillance in the information society. Each animation is based on thousands of monochromatic drawings and paintings made with diluted acrylic that evokes traditional Chinese ink painting. Some of these then become stills in Qiu's videos and some exist as independent works on paper. Since 2017 he has begun to use colour in these drawings. *New Book of Mountains and Seas – Moon Walker* and *New Book of Mountains and Seas – Guan Que* (both 2019) are painted in a traditional Chinese line-drawing technique, with washes of ink and colour added layer by layer to achieve a gradated effect. The first of these modern monsters is a two-legged beast roving across the desolate and lifeless environment of Mars. The second is a camera, depicted as a one-eyed yet headless bird. Surveillance is ubiquitous in today's world: self-monitoring has become our default setting. Qiu maps out a gloomy prospect, the consequence of mass urbanization and the environmental degradation inflicted by humans.
.... Carol Yinghua Lu

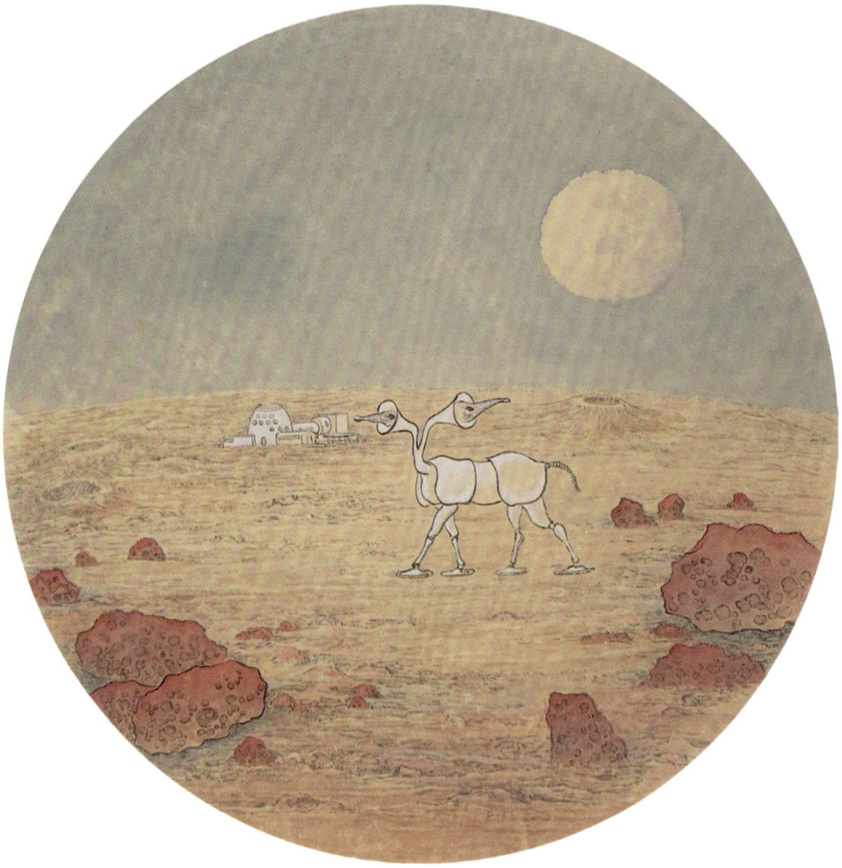

1.

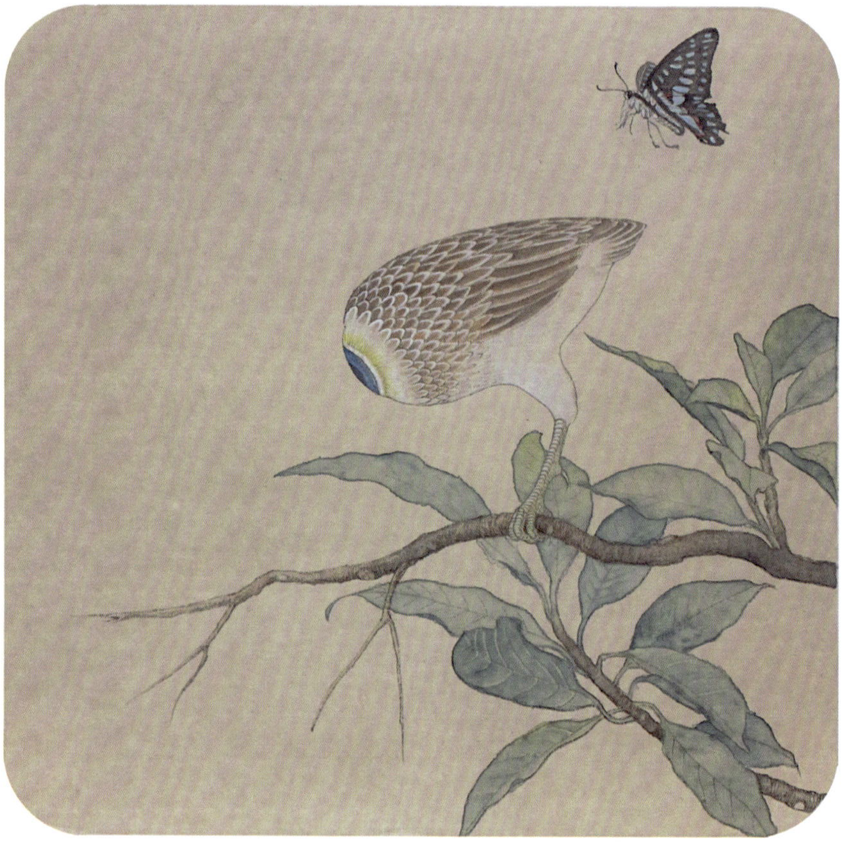

2.

Born 1972, Sichuan, China. Lives and works in Shanghai.

1. *New Book of Mountains and Seas – Moon Walker*, 2019, ink on paper, diam: 32 cm (12 ½ in)
2. *New Book of Mountains and Seas – Guan Que*, 2019, ink on paper, 32 × 32 cm (12 ½ × 12 ½ in)

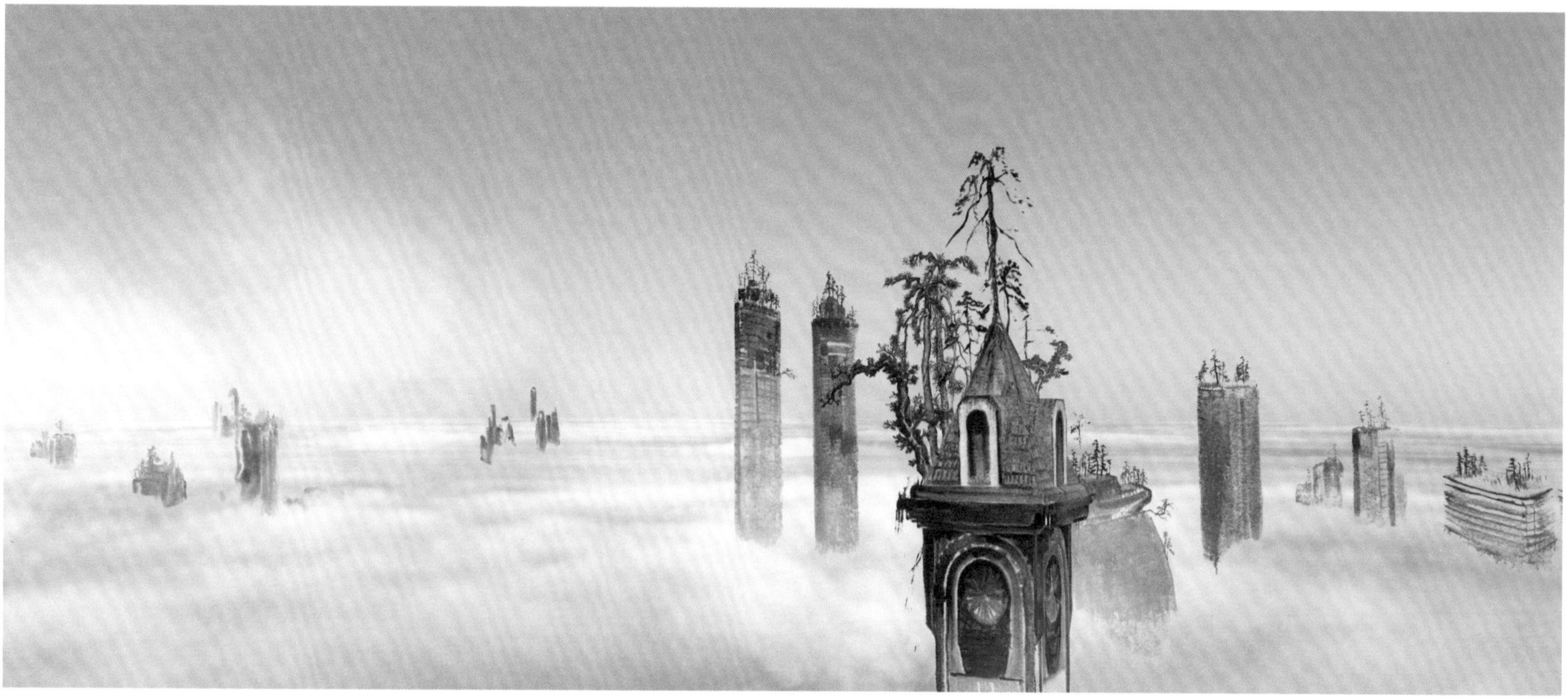

3.

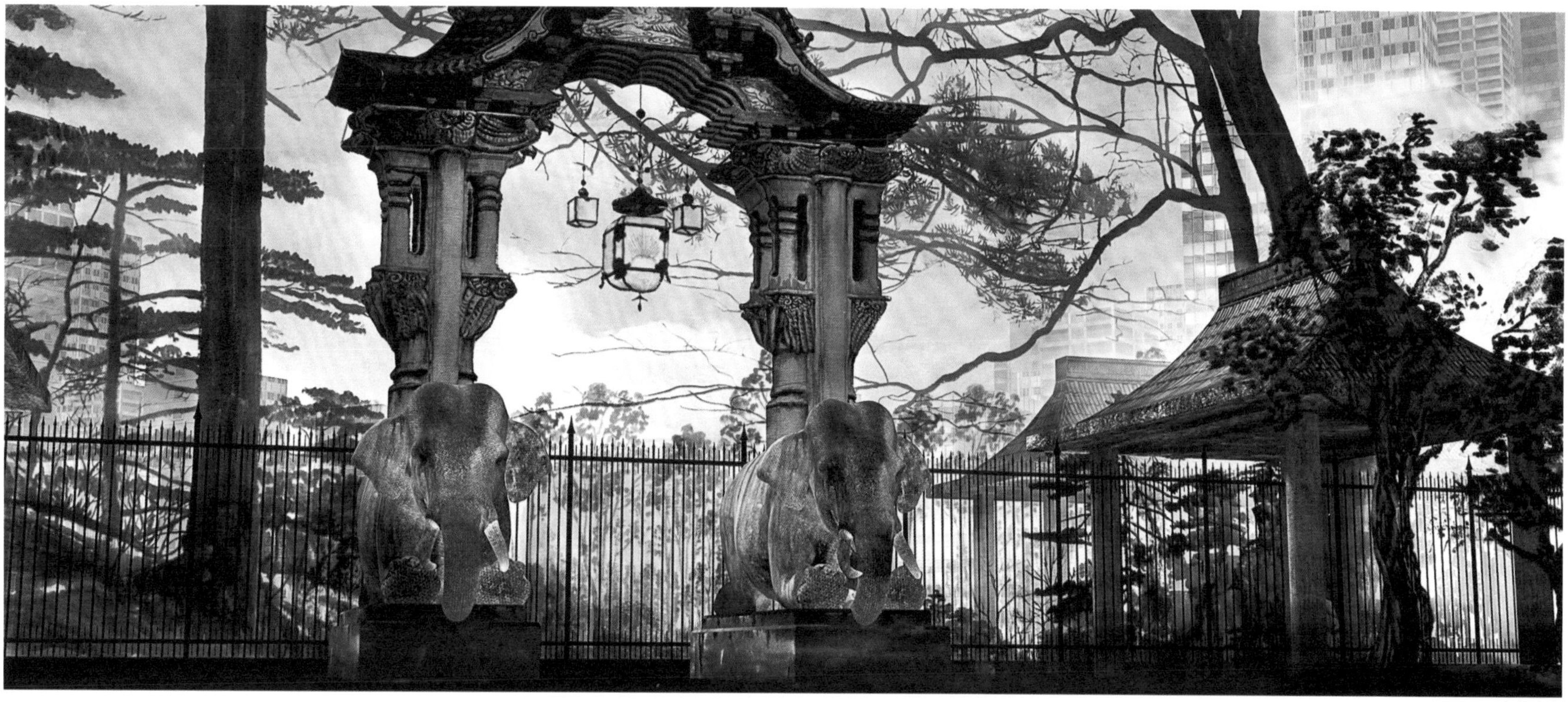

4.

3. *New Book of Mountains and Seas Part 3 – Above the Cloud*, 2013–17, still from animation film of ink drawing
4. *New Book of Mountains and Seas Part 3 – Zoo*, 2013–17, still from animation film of ink drawing

QIU ZHIJIE .... A central figure in contemporary art well beyond his native China, Qiu Zhijie's artistic output takes on a variety of forms – not only as a visual artist, but also as a teacher, producer and curator of major exhibitions. He is also a master of calligraphy, a practice that is at the basis of much of his art-making, which spans a multitude of disciplines including photography, sculpture, room-size installations, works on paper and new media. And although Qiu's work can't be defined by a single style or interest, it is connected nevertheless by an adherence to the concept of 'total art', the idea that new cohesive meanings can be forged by joining a variety of cultural perspectives, a-synchronic systems of thought and diverse philosophies. .... In 2010, after more than two decades of making art, Qiu started drawing maps, a medium through which he fully integrates his interests in research and representation, as well as his strength as a calligrapher. His large-scale hand-drawn map works represent purely conceptual cartographies that reflect the transfer and exchange of ideas rather than actual geographies. 'To me, maps are a source of knowledge… not derived from being on the ground, but from above, giving you a bird's eye view so as to understand the correlations of everything involved there,' he said in a 2017 video interview on the occasion of his solo exhibition at the Van Abbemuseum in Eindhoven, Netherlands. 'Things are not taken on their own but in context, where they are in relation to one another.' In the six-panel work *Map of 'Art and China after 1989: Theater of the World'* (2017) the artist painstakingly mapped out the six sections of the eponymous exhibition at the Guggenheim Museum in New York by charting Chinese and global art movements, ideological currents, political events and market booms and crashes spanning the exhibition's years of focus, from 1989 to 2008. Commissioned especially for this major show, the map's terrain is labelled with topographies such as 'Socialist market economics', the 'Peak of the scientific outlook on development', or the lake of 'Kitsch art' to name but a few. .... Although Qiu's elaborate maps open up the realm of fantasy and ideas, the artist doesn't dispute that maps also represent complicated histories and politics. Territorial disputes, the legacies of colonialism and imperialism, scientific progress – all are inherent to map-making. His work *True Knowledge Should Be Learned Intently, Even If It Could Only Be Found in a Country as Far as China* (2019) takes its title from a Uyghur saying and charts, on six colourful panels, a history of Chinese-Arab relations. 'Maps have real impacts,' Qiu said in 2017. 'Mapping is a modus operandi by which the integrity of the world can be rebuilt as correlations are elucidated.'
.... Hili Perlson

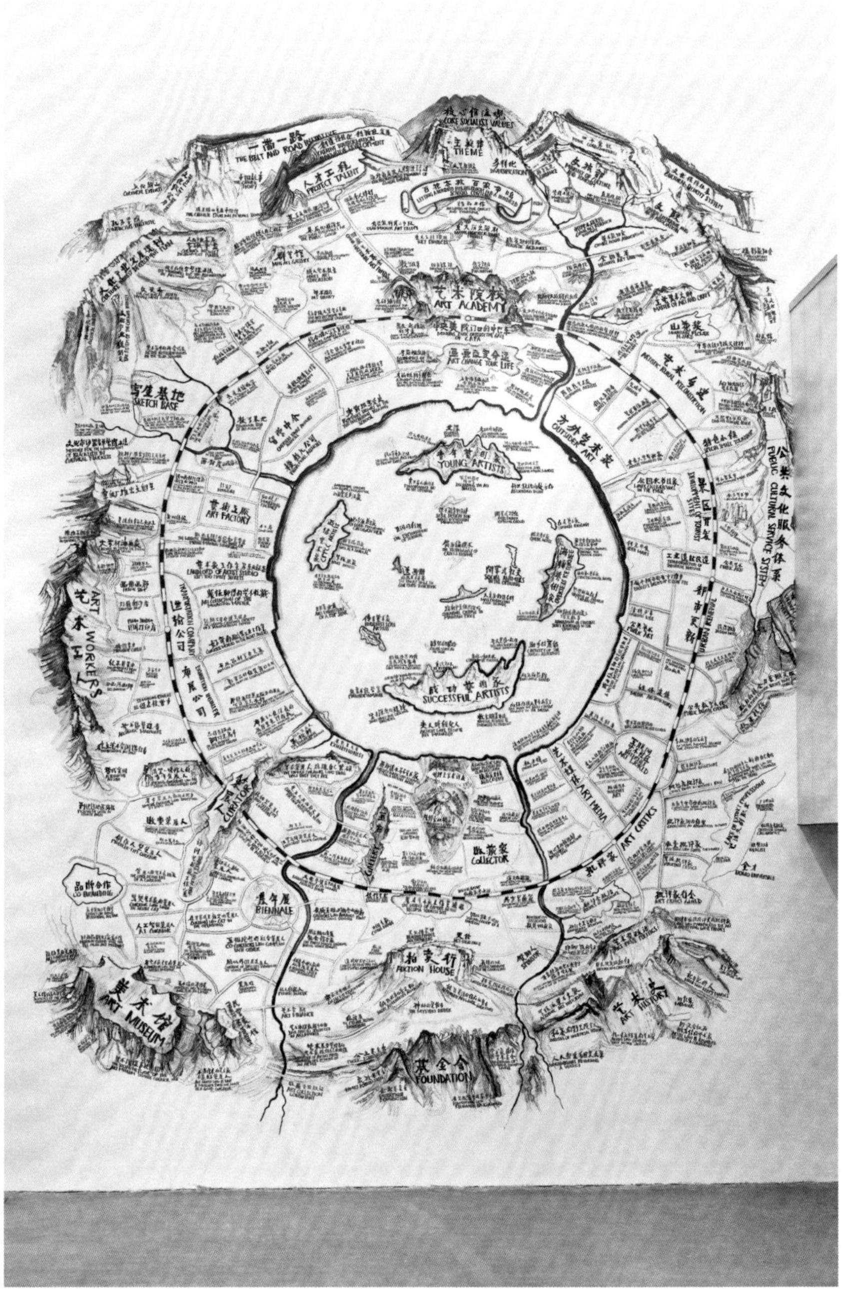

1.

Born 1969, Zhangzhou, Fujian Province, China. Lives and works in Beijing.

1. *Map of the Art World*, 2019, ink mural, 10 × 8 m, (32 ¾ × 26 ¼ ft), installation view 'Mappa Mundi', UCCA Center for Contemporary Art, Beijing
2. *Map of Continuum*, 2017, ink on paper, 3 panels, overall: 240 × 360 cm (94 ½ × 141 ¾ in)
3. *True Knowledge Should Be Learned Intently, Even If It Could Only Be Found in a Country as Far as China*, 2019, ink on paper, 6 panels, overall: 240 × 720 cm (94 ½ × 283 ½ in)

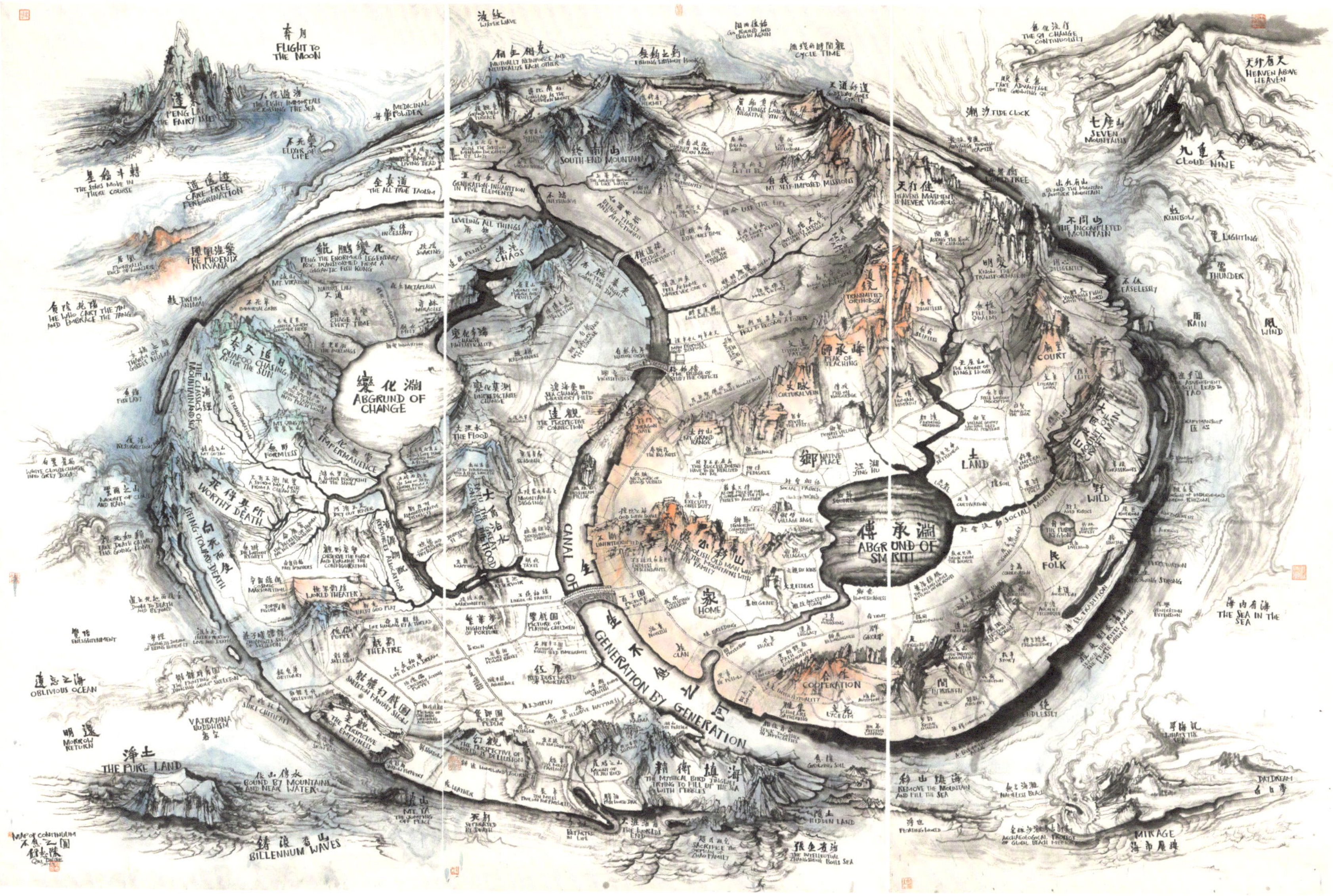
FLIGHT TO THE MOON
變化淵
ABGRUND OF CHANGE
傳承淵
SOUTH END MOUNTAIN
CHAOS
SEVEN MOUNTAINS
CLOUD NINE
THUNDER
RAIN
WIND
LAND
COURT
FOLK
HOME
THEATRE
GENERATION BY GENERATION
THE SEA IN THE SEA
OBLIVIOUS OCEAN
淨土
THE PURE LAND
MIRAGE

2.

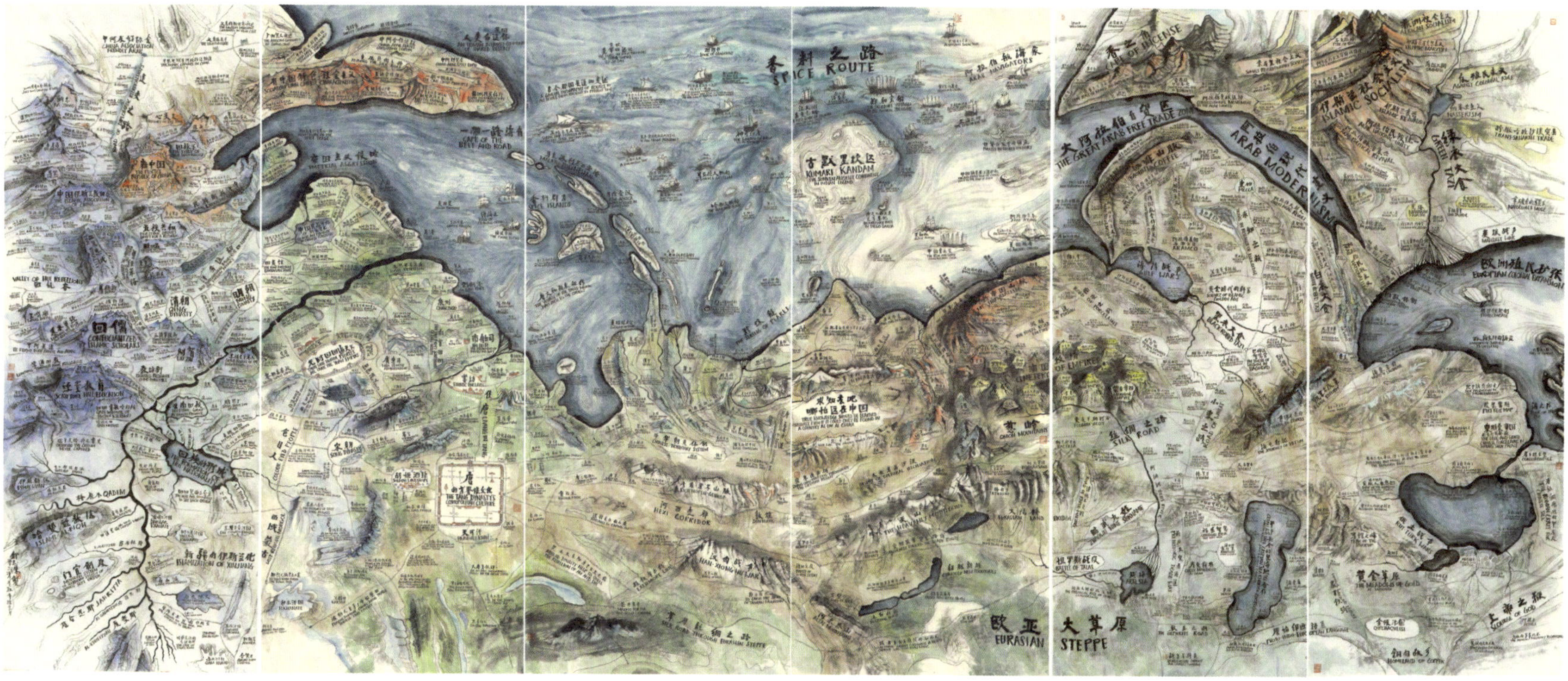
香料之路
SPICE ROUTE
ARAB MODERNISM
欧亚大草原
EURASIAN STEPPE

3.

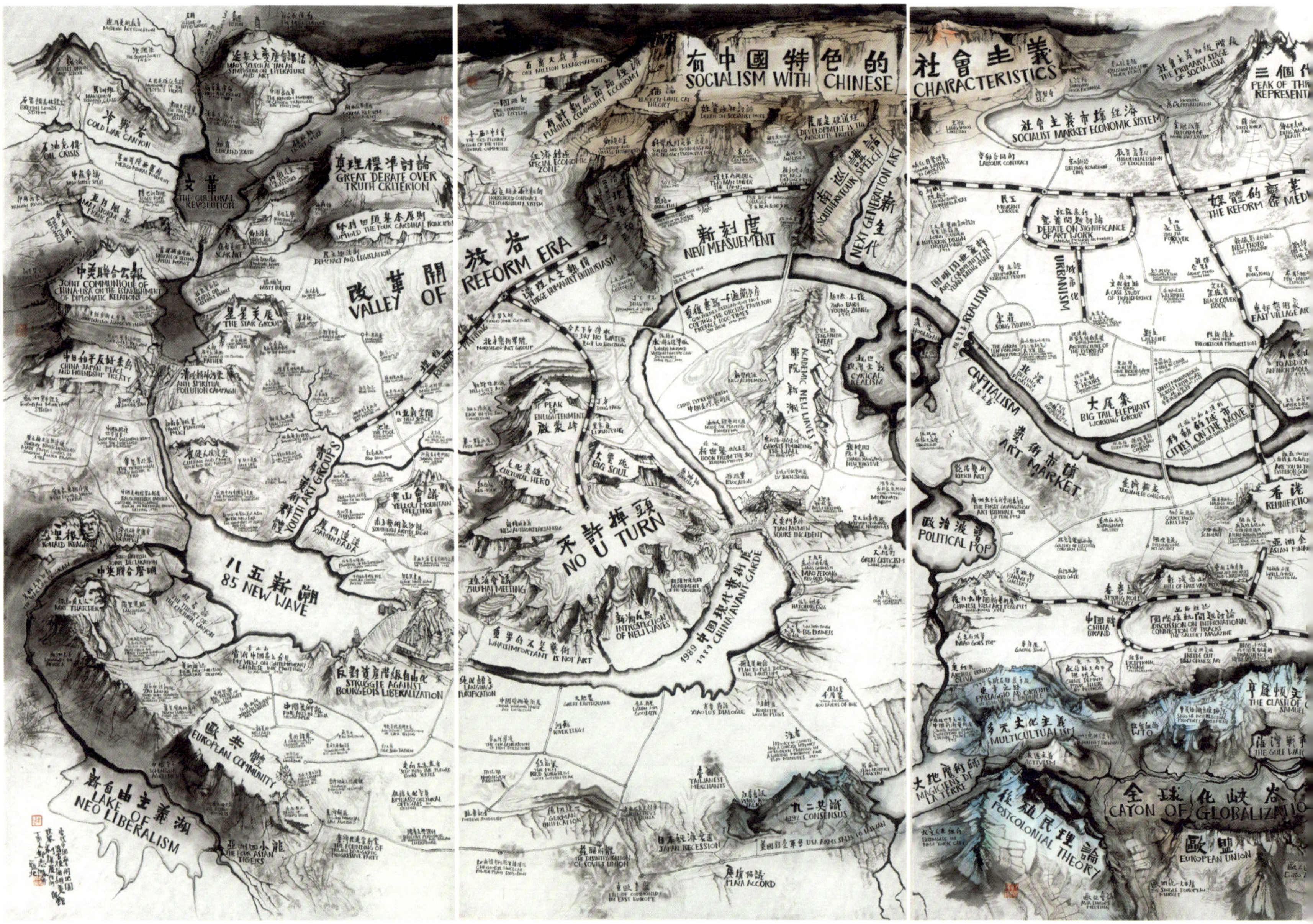

4.

4. *Map of 'Art and China after 1989: Theater of the World'*, 2017, ink on paper, 6 panels, overall: 240 × 720 cm (94 ½ in × 23 ft, 7 7⁄16 in)

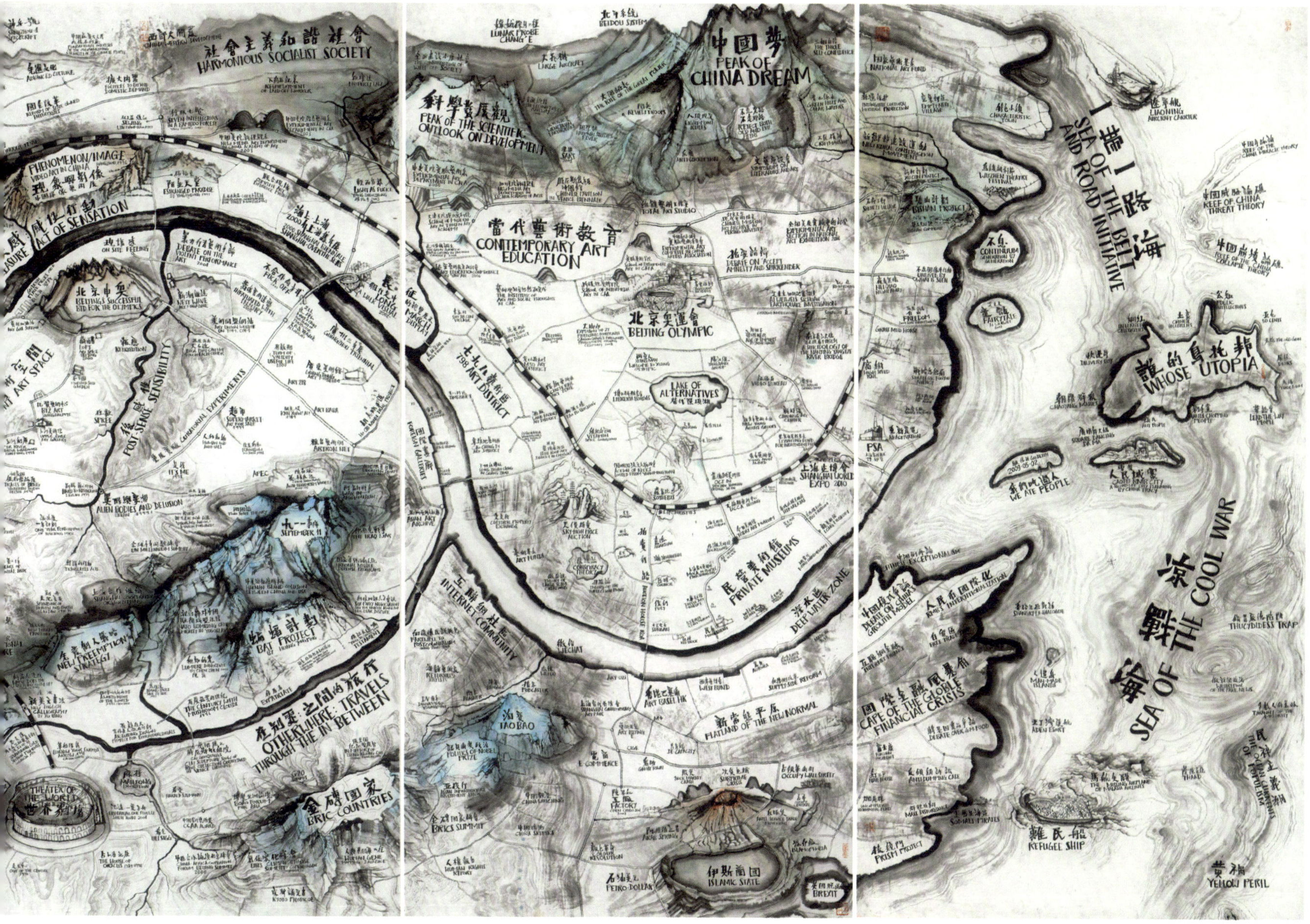

HARMONIOUS SOCIALIST SOCIETY
LUNAR PROBE CHANG'E
BEIDOU SYSTEM
中國夢
PEAK OF CHINA DREAM
PEAK OF THE SCIENTIFIC OUTLOOK ON DEVELOPMENT
PHENOMENON/IMAGE
VIDEO ART IN CHINA
ART OF SENSATION
當代藝術教育
CONTEMPORARY ART EDUCATION
BEIJING'S SUCCESSFUL BID FOR THE OLYMPICS
北京奥運會
BEIJING OLYMPIC
POST-SENSE SENSIBILITY
798 ART DISTRICT
LAKE OF ALTERNATIVES
SHANGHAI WORLD EXPO 2010
SEPTEMBER 11
PRIVATE MUSEUMS
DEEP WATER ZONE
INTERNET COMMUNITY
NEW PREEMPTION STRATEGY
BAT PROJECT
OTHERWHERE: TRAVELS THROUGH THE IN BETWEEN
TAOBAO
PLATLAND OF THE NEW NORMAL
THEATER OF THE WORLD
BRIC COUNTRIES
BRICS SUMMIT
PETRO-DOLLAR
ISLAMIC STATE
BREXIT
LIAONING AIRCRAFT CARRIER
SEA OF THE BELT AND ROAD INITIATIVE
CONTINUUM
FAIRYTALE
WHOSE UTOPIA
WE ARE PEOPLE
SEA OF THE COOL WAR
THUCYDIDES TRAP
CAPE OF THE GLOBAL FINANCIAL CRISIS
REFUGEE SHIP
YELLOW PERIL

CHRISTINA QUARLES .... Christina Quarles is candid about how her gender, sexual and racial identity have affected her day-to-day experience of the world and guided her approach to creating art. Quarles, whose fair skin is in apparent contradiction to her Black ancestry, is frequently identified as white. She expands, in a statement on her website: 'As a Queer, cis-woman, born to a Black father and a white mother, I engage with the world from a position that is multiply situated.' Quarles, who studied both philosophy and studio arts, takes a conceptual approach to image-making. Her drawings and paintings are informed by the ambiguity surrounding public perception and interpretation of her physical appearance, as well as by wider questions around personal identity as manifold and fluid. .... Drawing and painting coexist in Quarles's practice, and she credits her work in paint with enabling her to find a way of expressing the drawn line. Her drawings inhabit the picture plane in engaging and challenging ways, inviting the eye on circuitous and occasionally devious pathways around the image. Her drawings often spread out to the edge of the paper, sometimes dissolving out of frame to hint at the porousness between what is contained within, and without of, the image. This permeability relates to the ways in which the human body is both contained by and exceeds its outlines, its skin. Through a playful use of language, puns and phrases resembling cracked mantras, other works carry the potential for even more open-ended meanings, as in the text panel featured in *Untitled (Jus' Cause)* (2018), which proclaims 'A just cause, jus' because'. .... There is a tender intimacy to Quarles's depictions of bodies, which are often shown at rest, reclining alone or in company. In *Untitled (All There Was To Be Set)* (2018) a figure on hands and knees is positioned on a flying carpet hovering above the ground, while a second person kneels on a patterned tablecloth and reaches back to touch the first. In these vulnerable – perhaps submissive – positions, the human body becomes legible as a collection of surfaces, left blank and made available as a screen for the viewer's imaginative projections. In Quarles's images figures grasp at the promise of tactile contact, sometimes reaching out for their own limbs, as in *Untitled (Lite of My Life, Yew Lite Up My Night)* (2018) in which a reclining nude touches their own, upwardly extended foot. If contemporary society stokes the fantasy of an optimized physique, within which all systems run smoothly to fulfil ideals of glowing health and exultant wealth, Quarles's depictions of figures subject to fragmentation and displacement offer a more sincere take on what it is like to live within one's body and in the company of others.
.... Ellen Mara De Wachter

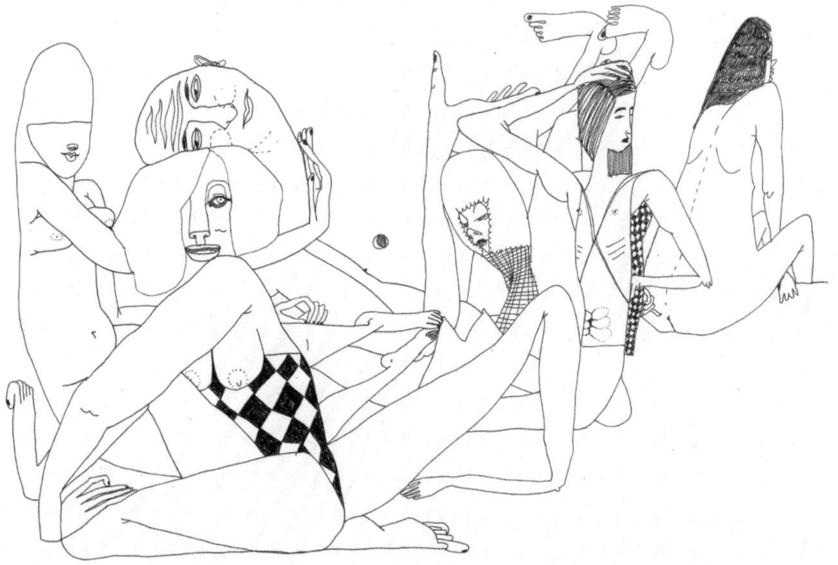

1.

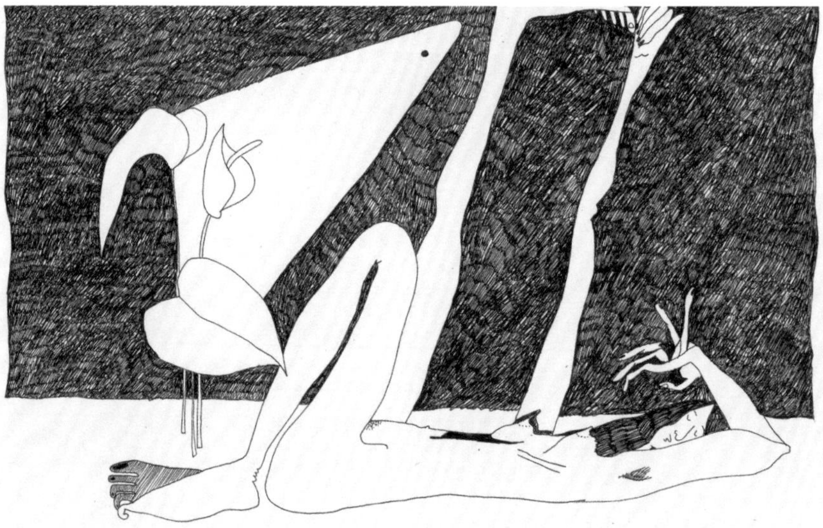

2.

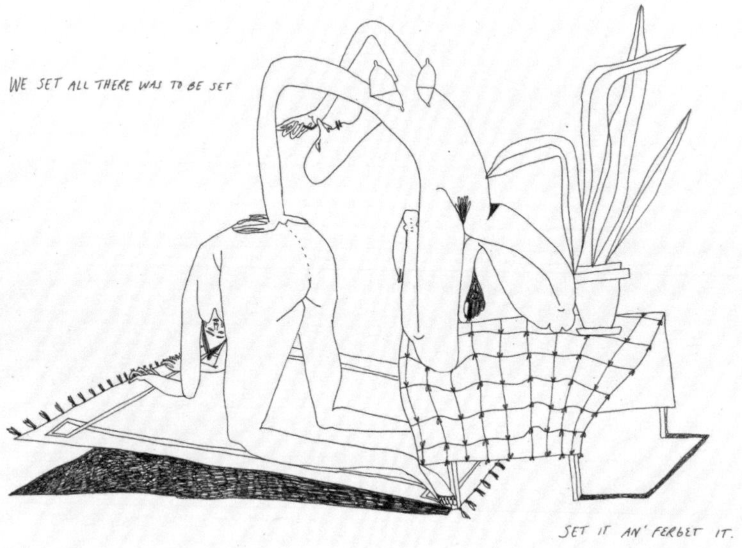

3.

Born 1985, Chicago. Lives and works in Los Angeles.

1. *Untitled (Together, We'll Weather)*, 2018, ink on paper, 33 × 48.3 cm (13 × 19 in)
2. *Untitled (Lite of My Life, Yew Light Up My Night)*, 2018, ink on paper, 33 × 48.3 cm (13 × 19 in)

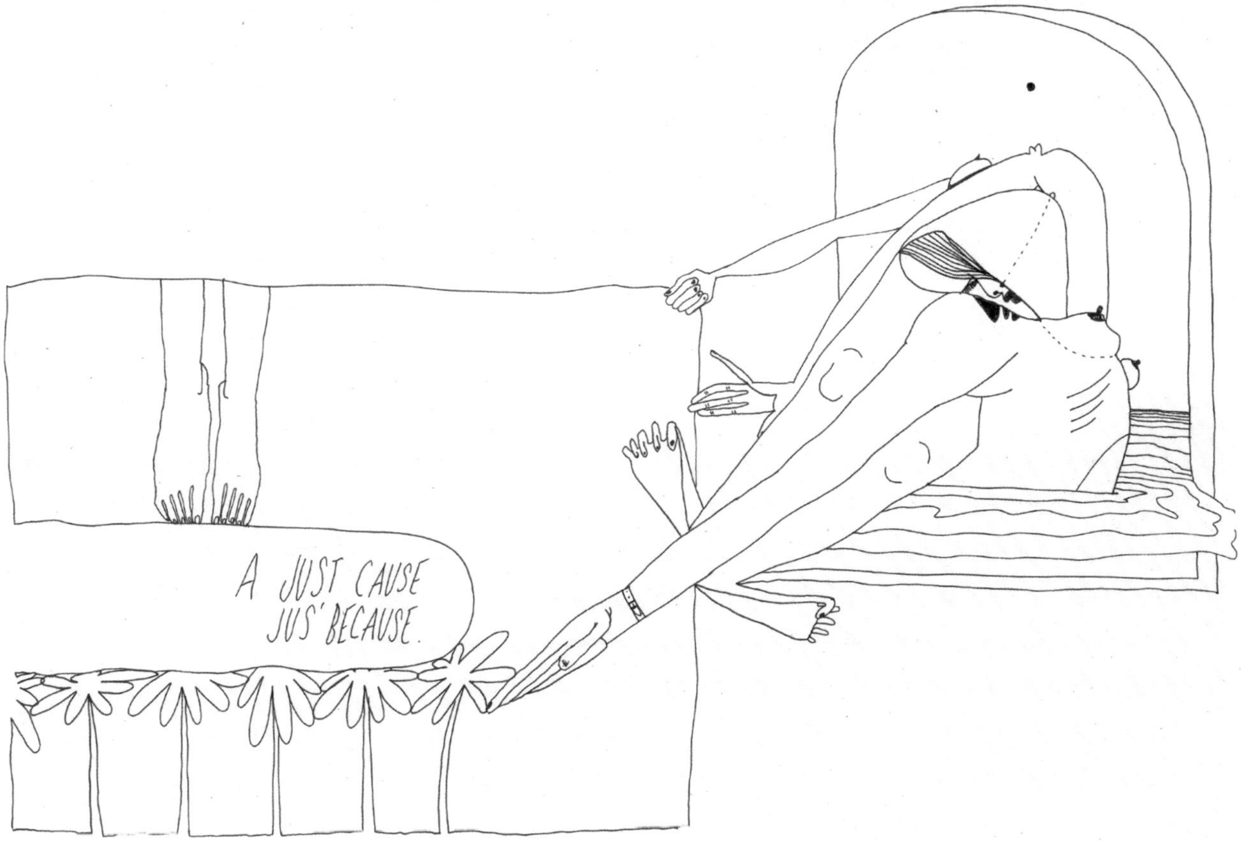

4.

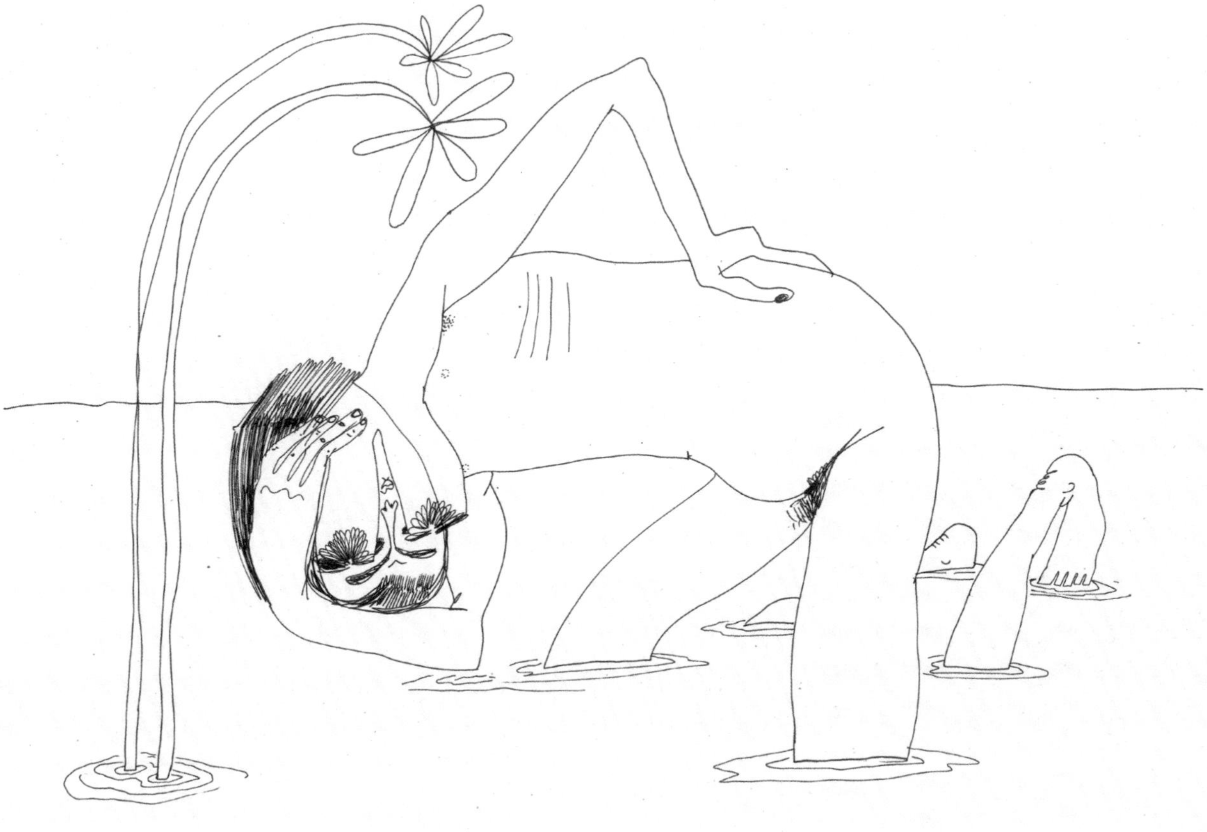

5.

3. *Untitled (All There Was To Be Set)*, 2018, ink on paper, 33 × 48.3 cm (13 × 19 in)
4. *Untitled (Jus' Cause)*, 2018, ink on paper, 33 × 48.3 cm (13 × 19 in)
5. *Untitled (Shallow Ground)*, 2018, ink on paper, 33 × 48.3 cm (13 × 19 in)

HANNAH QUINLAN & ROSIE HASTINGS

.... Marching through a leafy park, leather-clad protestors wearing thigh-high boots, backless dresses and bras argue with a police officer who is mounted high upon a horse. One woman gives another a leg-up, holding her firmly with muscular arms so that she can challenge the law, eye-to-eye. Rendered in black and white with bright highlights and deep shading, *Get Your Self Clean #2* (2018) is velvety with tactile sensuality – fabrics seem squeaky and the horses' coat silky. This graphite pencil on paper drawing is about not only the social space of queer life but also the gendered nature of urban architecture and public space: it questions who is allowed where, and when. Artist duo Hannah Quinlan and Rosie Hastings described the questions that preoccupy them in a 2020 interview with *Queer Direct*: 'Who is able to take risks? Who is allowed agency over their own pleasure? How to be visible without being exploited? How to lay claim to public space?' Initially investigating male sex culture in the UK, demonstrated by their moving image work *UK Gay Bar Directory (UKGBD)* (2016), which responded to the systematic closure of LGBTQ+ social spaces, Quinlan and Hastings consider the political impact of behaviour patterns. They use the idea of the spectrum of male power – as demonstrated in sex clubs – as a metaphor for how power manifests in other spaces, not least the boardroom, and how this might be redistributed. *The Sleepers* (2017) suggests the aftermath of all-out egalitarian hedonism, depicting a group of people who have collapsed, soporific, after what seems like an all-night party. Vibrant blues, yellows and pinks pop across the composition, loose limbs entangled, arched backs echoing one another. .... While their style winks at the stylized, highly masculinized homoerotic art of Tom of Finland (1920–71), the majesty of how Quinlan and Hastings use rhetoric and storytelling in their scenes recalls the Renaissance Masters. Inspired by a trip to the Vatican, such influences are evident in the large-scale drawing *Funny Girls* (2019). Groups of statuesque people gather amid the grand architecture of a sex club, merging risk and pleasure. In the left-hand corner, two people kneel before a woman while others watch. The reclining pose of a man next to a pointed finger recalls Michelangelo's *The Creation of Adam* on the ceiling of the Sistine Chapel (c.1508–12) – God, here, a woman – while the perfect perspective of arched windows and domed doorways suggest Raphael's *The School of Athens* (1509–11), which depicts the formation of knowledge, with Plato and Aristotle conversing. For Quinlan and Hastings, such scenes should be mined for cultural, social and political purposes, proposing new power structures and, ultimately, strategies of inclusivity.

.... Louisa Elderton

1.

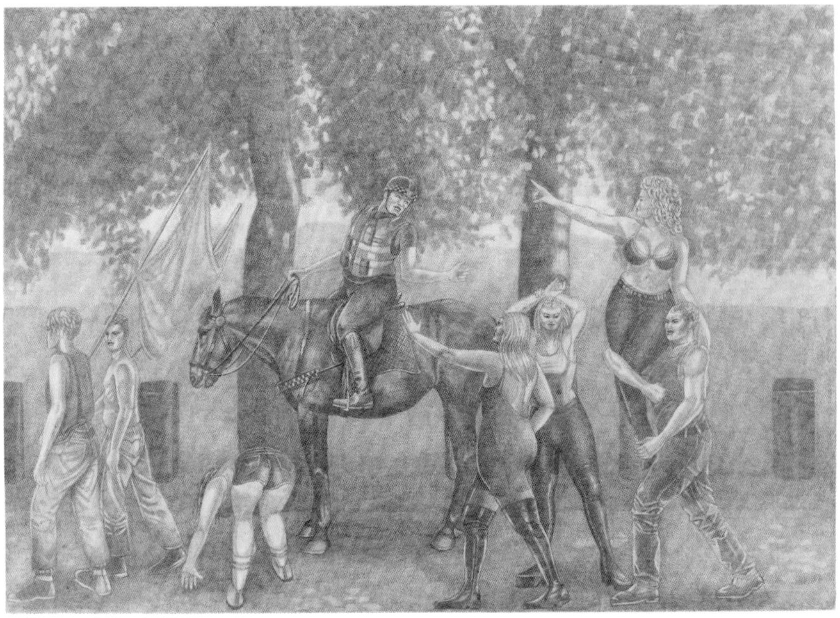

2.

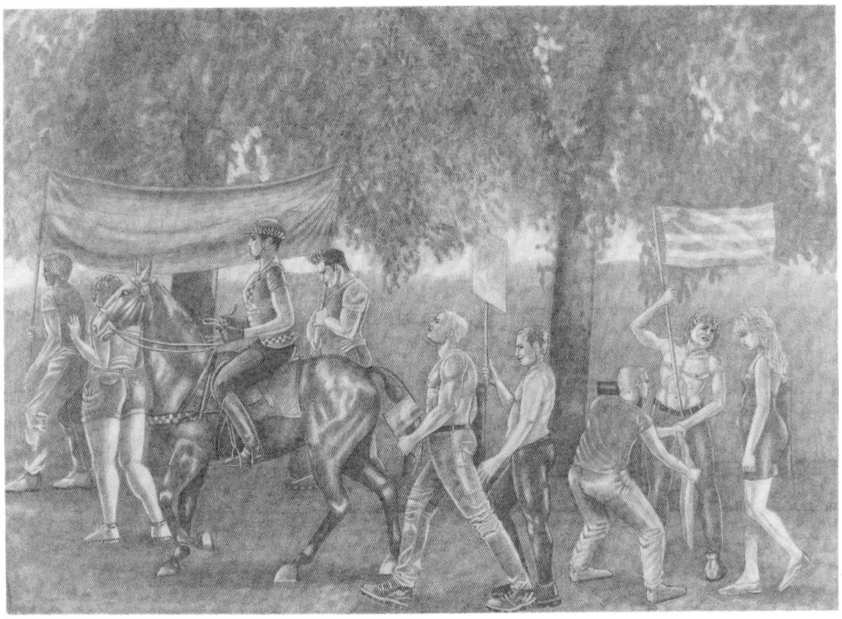

Hannah Quinlan: born 1991, Newcastle upon Tyne, UK. Rosie Hastings: born 1991, London. Both artists live and work in London.

1. *Get Your Self Clean #2*, 2018, graphite pencil on paper, 16.5 × 23.4 cm (6 ½ × 9 ¼ in)
2. *Get Your Self Clean #1*, 2018, graphite pencil on paper, 16.5 × 23.4 cm (6 ½ × 9 ¼ in)
3. *The Dudes*, 2017, Polychromos coloured pencil on paper, 137.2 × 203.2 cm (54 × 80 in)
4. *The Sleepers*, 2019, Polychromos coloured pencil on paper, 81 × 150 cm (31 ⅞ × 59 in)

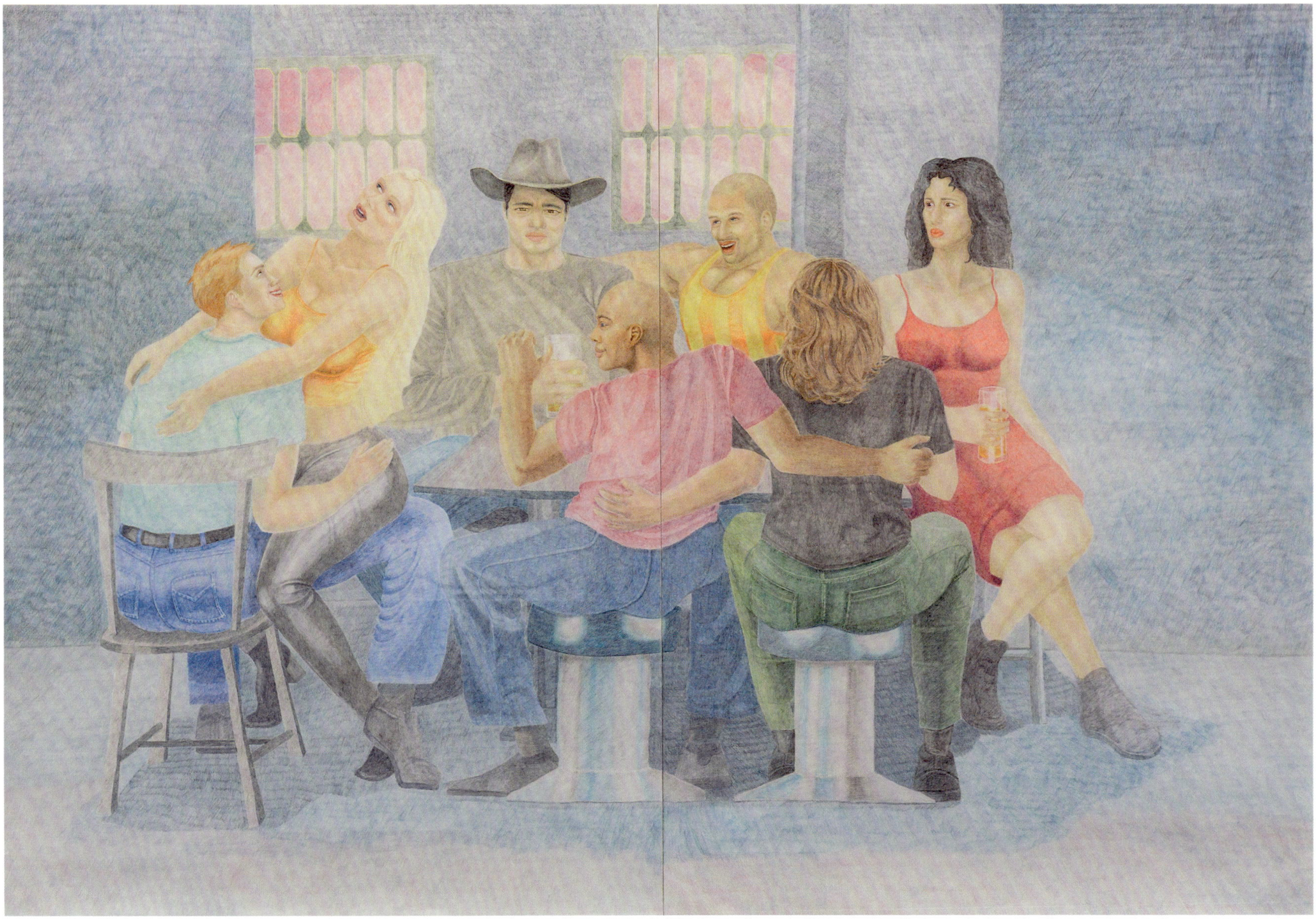

3.

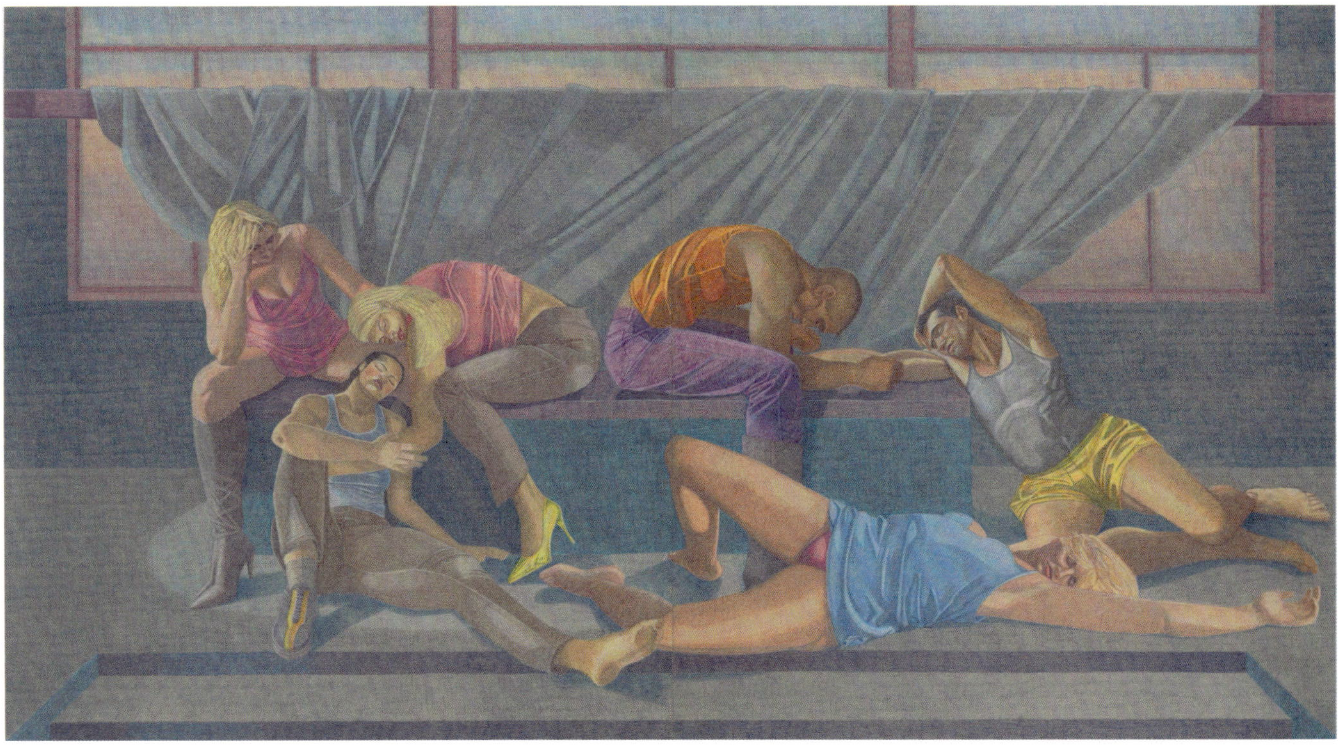

4.

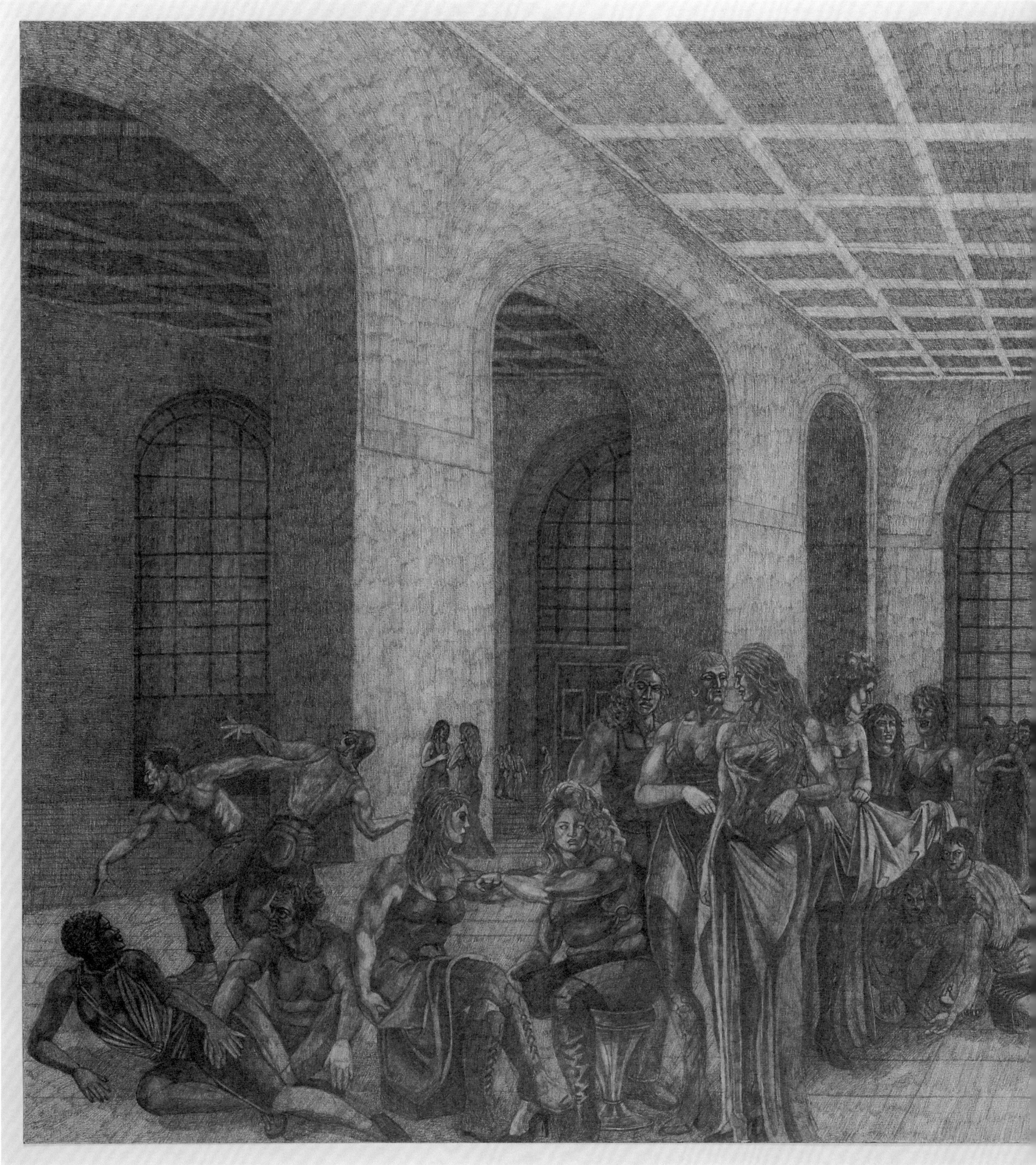

4.

 5. *Funny Girls*, 2019, graphite pencil on paper, 59.5 × 116 cm (23 ⅜ × 45 ⅝ in) ....

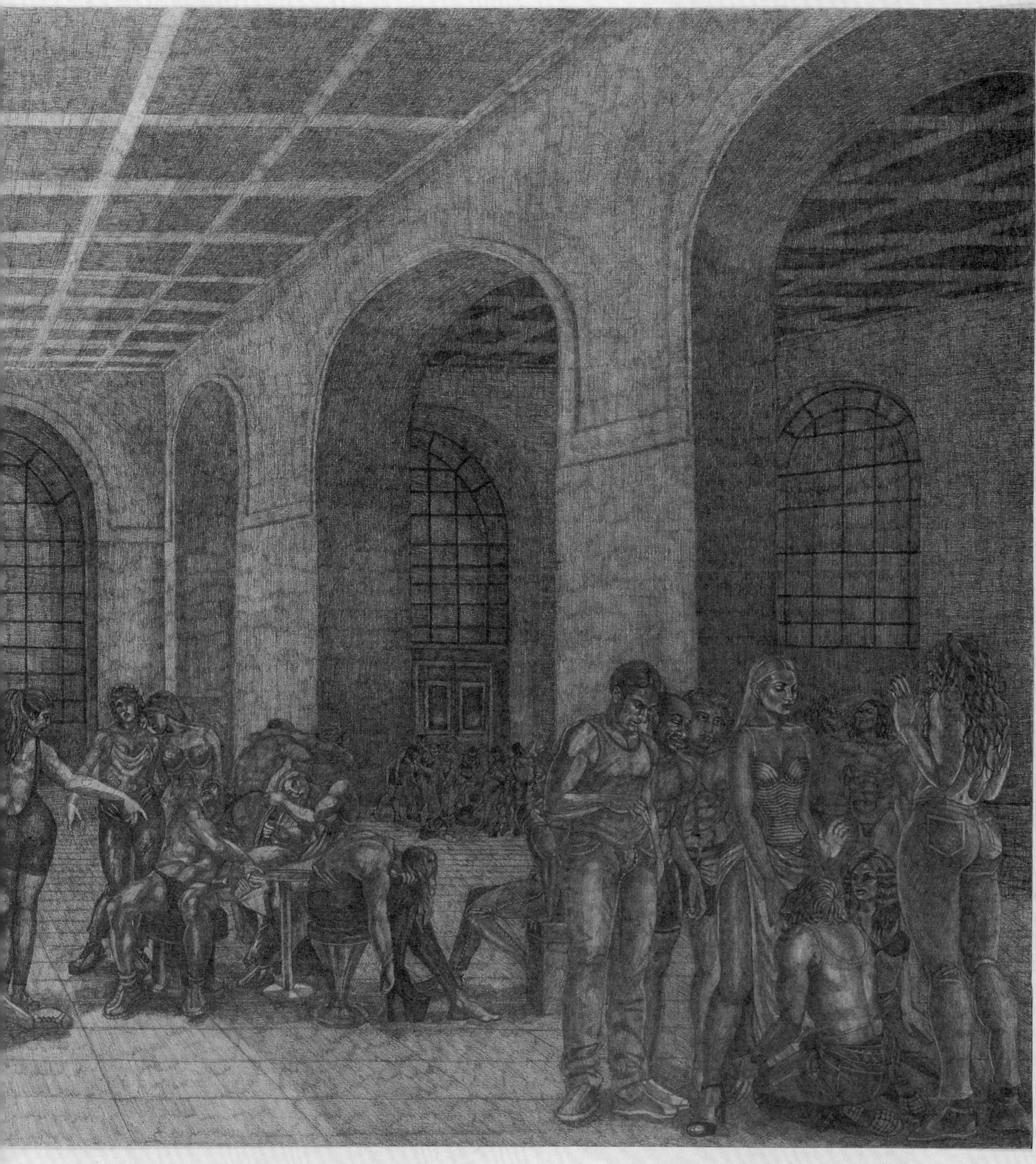

NATHANIEL MARY QUINN .... Nathaniel Mary Quinn has visions from which he makes representations of people he has known. His portraits are unorthodox, showing an emotional essence through masterfully rendered visceral fragments, sourced from magazines and personal photographs to portray Quinn's memories. Often mistaken for collage, each work is a hybrid composite that has a collage aesthetic reflective of complex, interior subjectivity. Drawn through a process that includes a gouache substrate on Coventry vellum paper, with layers of wet and dry media applied using construction paper to mask off completed sections, the artist is blind to the amalgamated figure until the end reveal. This process of 'expressionistic cubism' makes visible the character of an individual in a formal way that is similar to life unfolding – a complex circuitous accumulation of experiences. .... A novelistic impulse exists in Quinn's work, as backstories infuse his memories. *Big Rabbit, Little Rabbit* (2017) portrays the artist as a small child cradled on his father's lap, drawn on multiple sheets of paper to imply the memories are larger than life. The figures pose, seated on a regal ottoman, dominated by the dark furry gorilla arm of the father figure; unaligned jagged edges are jiggered across the sheets of paper, interrupted by scalloped design patterns, while a colourful infant blanket emerges to create high contrast. Big Rabbit's supple mouth is pierced by the depiction of a plastic toy rabbit's nose. Quinn's father lacked a formal education and was unable to read or write, so to make money he would hop from one pool table to another, thus acquiring his sobriquet. Quinn became known as Little Rabbit, a term that emotionally connects him to his father's betting skills to shield against the poverty of the drug-ridden projects of Chicago's South Side. His father taught Quinn how to draw, using thick telephone books, challenging each other to fill a book without erasing a line. Unexpectedly, feminine leather boots emerge from a checked grey on black kilt, symbolizing Quinn's mother's matriarchal support. Mary helped Quinn gain admission to an elite boarding school, but after his first month there she died. Returning home at Thanksgiving, he discovered the apartment where he had grown up was empty, and his father and four brothers (including Charles, as represented in *Charles* (2013)) had abandoned him. He was fifteen years old. He took her name at high school graduation to acknowledge her. .... Depicted with a golden tassel, a clean white collar and three ball bearings that look like bullet holes, *Class of '92* (2015) commemorates Quinn's eighth-grade graduation, a major success for any child who grew up like him. From there he went on to attain an MFA, with all the degrees in between dedicated to the memory of his mother.

.... Kathleen Madden

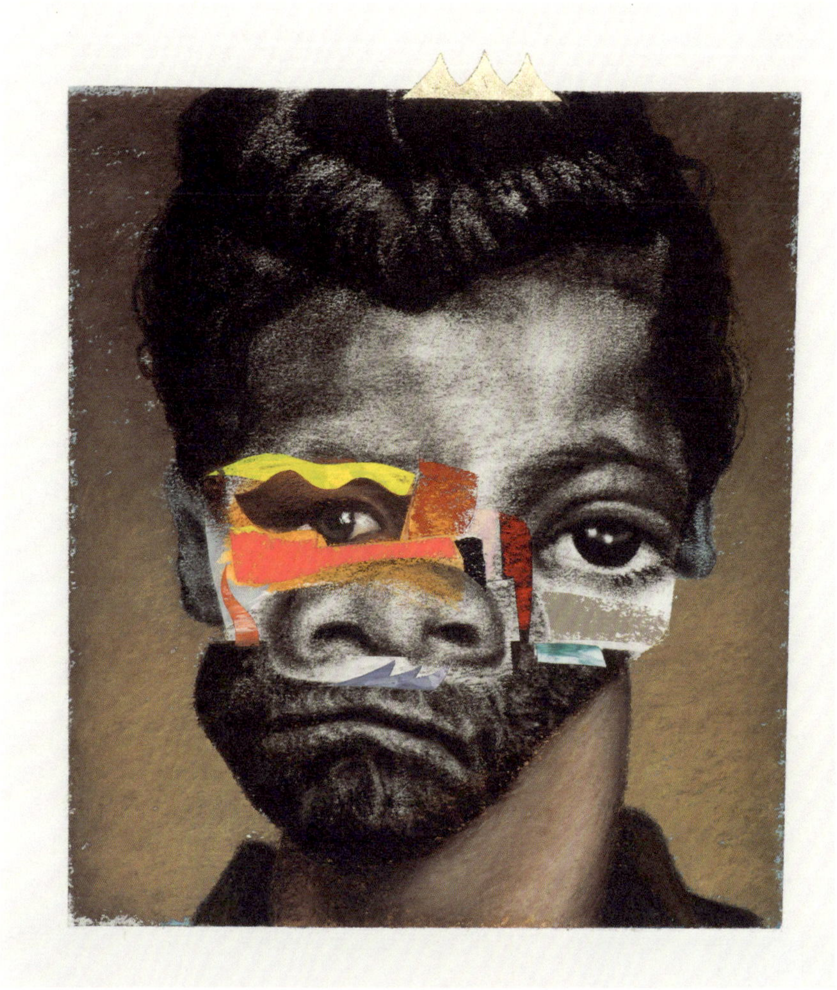

1.

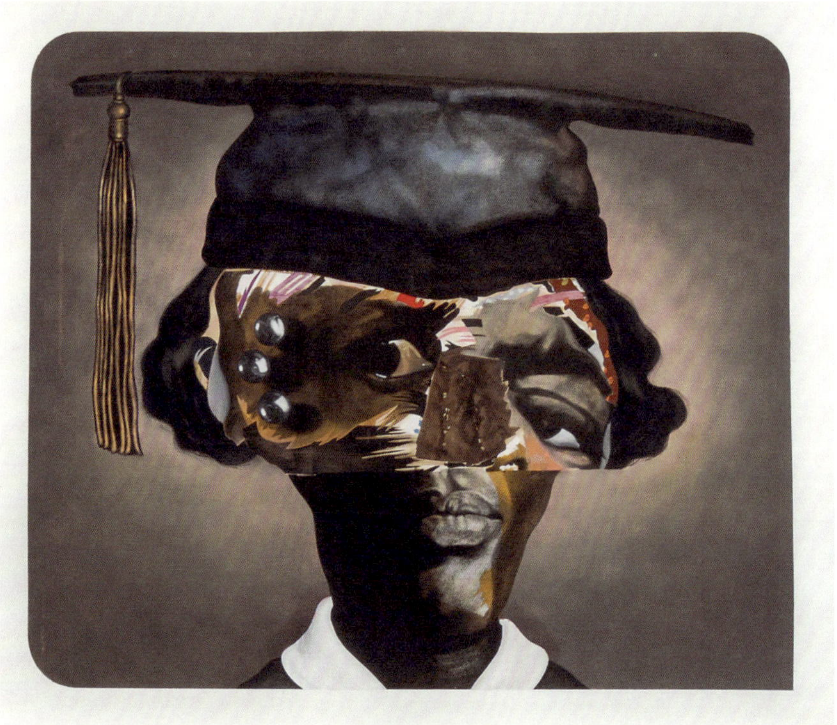

2.

Born 1977, Chicago. Lives and works in Brooklyn, New York.

1. *I Wish A Muthafucka Would*, 2017, black charcoal, gouache, soft pastel, oil pastel and acrylic gold powder on Coventry vellum paper, 30.5 × 30.5 cm (12 × 12 in)
2. *Class of '92*, 2015, black charcoal, soft pastel, oil pastel, paint stick and gouache on Coventry vellum paper, 102.2 × 111.8 cm (40 ¼ × 44 in)
3. *Big Rabbit, Little Rabbit*, 2017, charcoal, gouache, soft pastel, oil pastel, oil paint, paint stick and acrylic silver powder on paper, 182.9 × 142.2 cm (72 × 56 in)

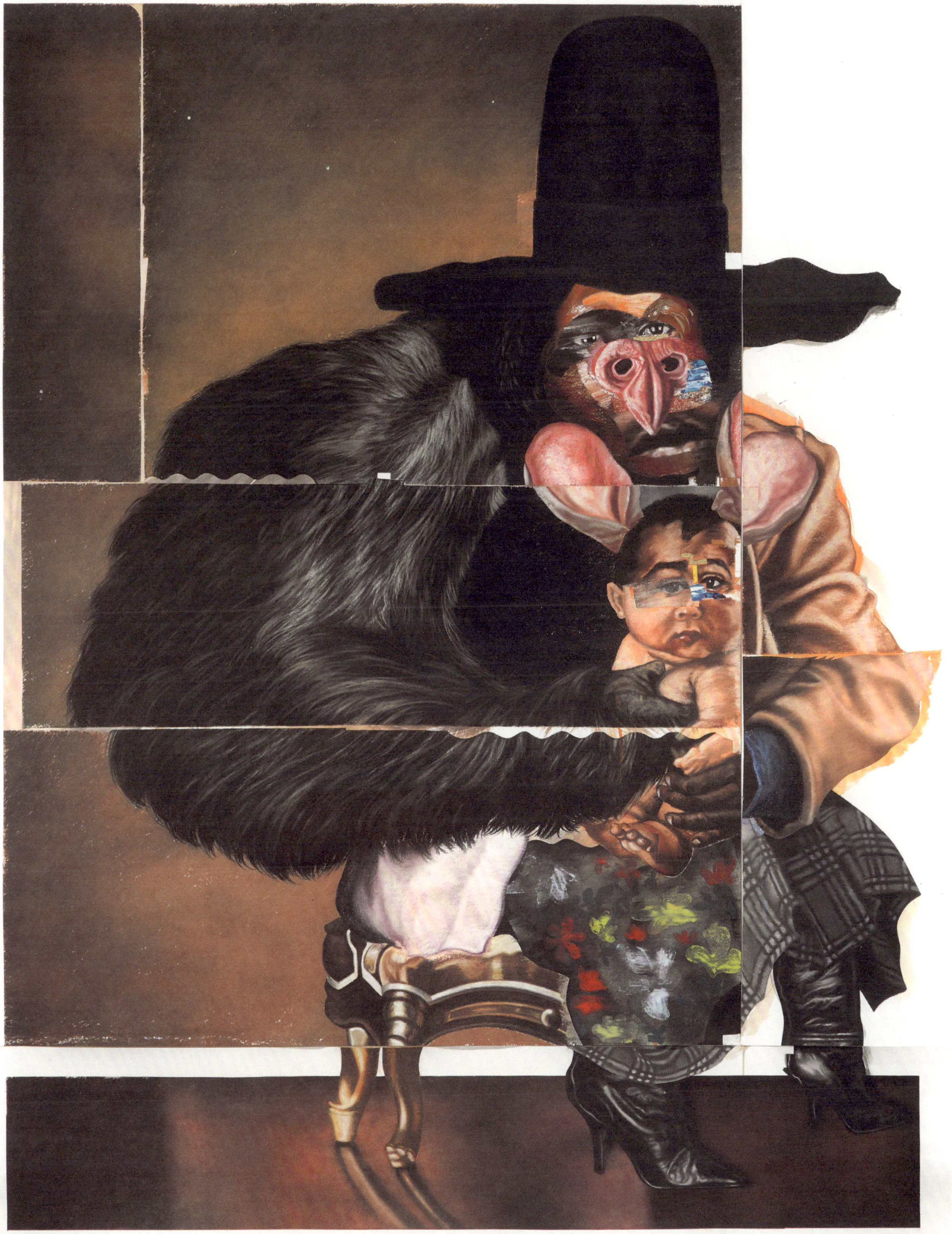

3.

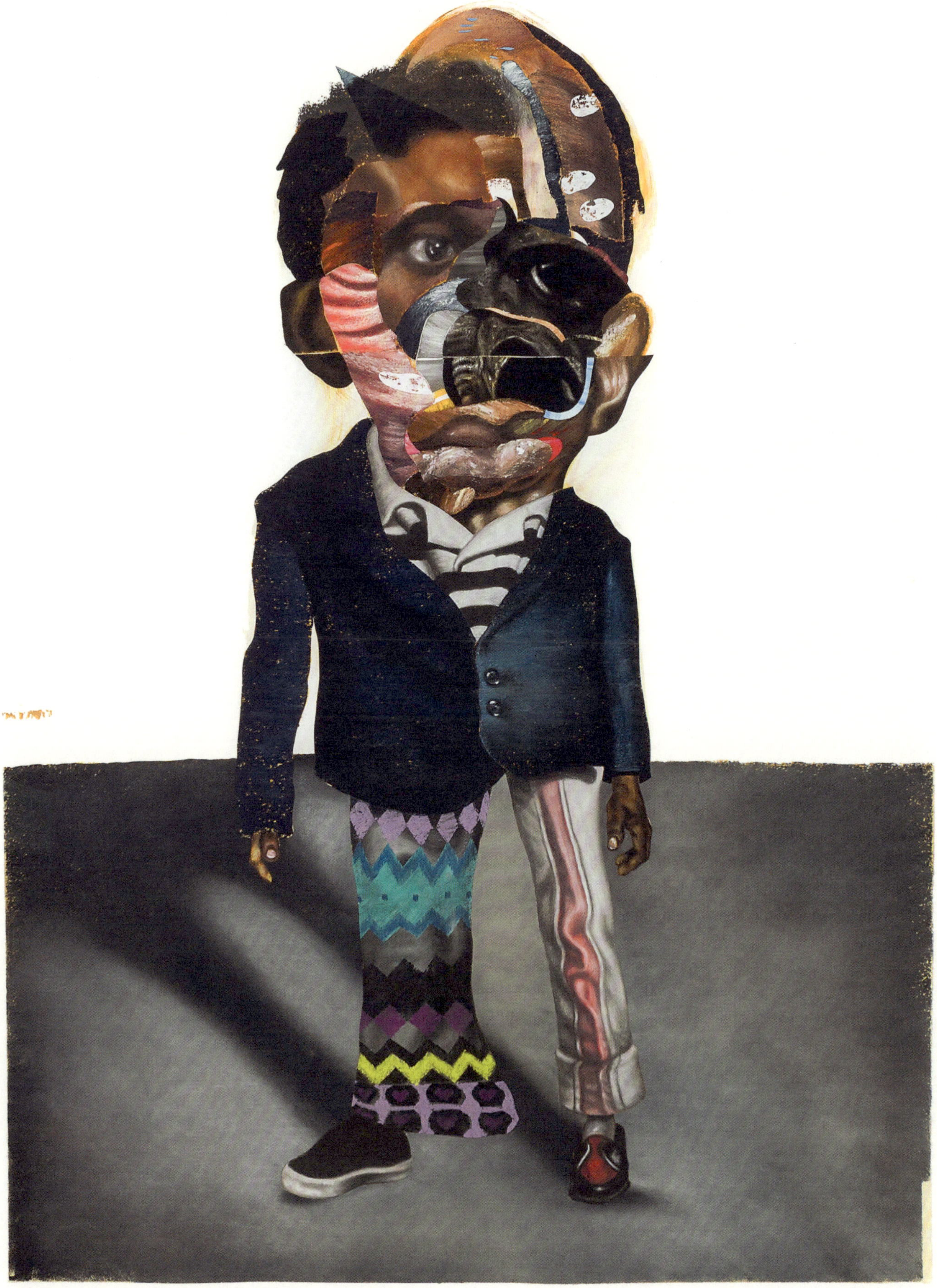

4.

4. *Old Man Slick*, 2018, black charcoal, gouache, soft pastel, oil pastel and acrylic gold leaf on Coventry vellum paper, 127 × 96.5 cm (50 × 38 in)

5. *Charles*, 2013, black charcoal and gouache on Lenox paper, 127 × 96.5 cm (50 × 38 in)

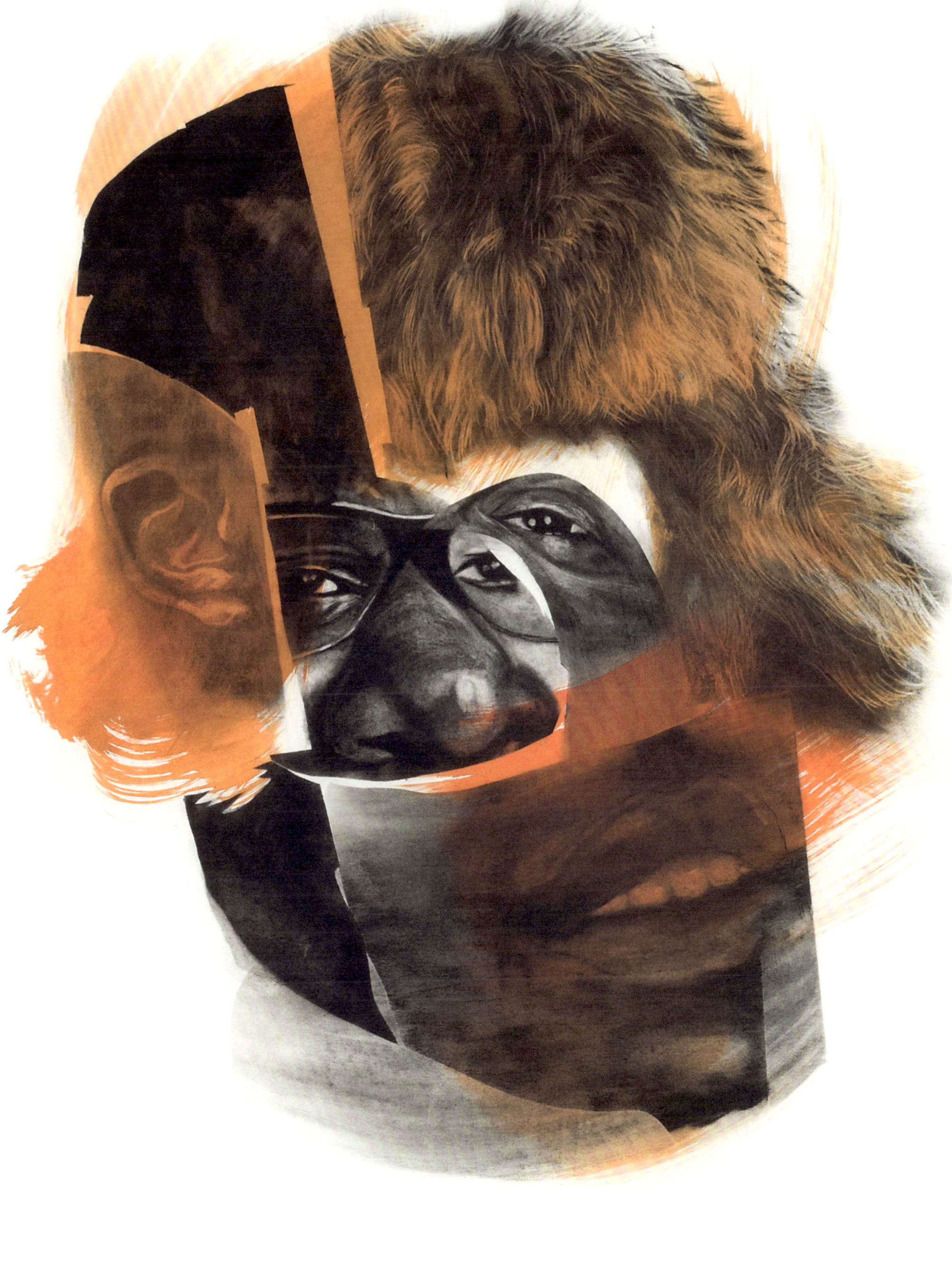

5.

CAMILO RESTREPO .... You can take the artist out of the street, but you can't take the street out of the artist. Camilo Restrepo grew up in Medellín, Colombia in the 1980s, ground zero for the drug wars that devastated much of his country and claimed more than 50,000 lives. After a childhood spent living in the world's most dangerous city, the budding draughtsman turned first to travel and then to art-making. Initially, he took up a photographic camera: early photos featured handmade crack pipes he cheekily titled 'This Is a Pipe', in imitation of Belgian Surrealist painter René Magritte (1898-1967). In time, he swapped those streetwise studies for pen and pencil work, specifically the kind of doodling that has been pegged as 'automatic drawing' since the time of the Surrealists. .... Like with ancient tablets or pieces of parchment, Restrepo's drawings hide multiple meanings beneath their roiling, scuffed surfaces. Correcting while he works, he mixes traditional and unorthodox materials: pieces of newspaper, stickers, ink, pencil, wax, cartoon figures and, by way of final effacement, gobs of his own spit. As with ancient forms of writing, the Colombian's erasures do not fully obliterate the original. Layers of text, line, colour and texture throb beneath the surface; at times, these elements even appear on the drawing's verso. .... Restrepo's subject matter, which he works to the brink of destruction, is the ongoing global battle between fact and fakery. In Colombia, this manifests disastrously at the crossroads of violence and popular culture. In Medellín, for instance, the Netflix series *Narcos* produced a tourist industry that glorifies drug-traffickers Pablo Escobar and Jhon Jairo Velásquez, alias Popeye. Restrepo's job, as he sees it, is to provide a counter-narrative – an alternative set of images and a storyline that are truer for not exalting two of Latin America's biggest mass murderers. .... Consider, for instance, Restrepo's fantastical drawings based on headlines published in four of Colombia's leading newspapers: *El Espectador, El Tiempo, El Colombiano* and *Q'hubo*. These, as well as the works *Los Caprichos (Alias Rambo)* (2014) and *Tight Rope 4 (Mike)* (2015), sport familiar cartoon and movie characters – Homer Simpson, Felix the Cat, Sylvester Stallone's steroidal action hero – together with newspaper clippings that reference actual 'narcos' and the Revolutionary Armed Forces of Colombia (FARC) guerrillas who use those same handles. But it is in his monumental works that Restrepo achieves an eye-popping expansion of his raucous vision. The multi-panel work *Rip Currents 5* (2018), for instance, turns drawing into a cosmogony by filling standard-size sheets of paper that have been glued together into a Hieronymus Bosch-inspired, wall-sized palimpsest rich in colour and line. .... Christian Viveros-Fauné

1. 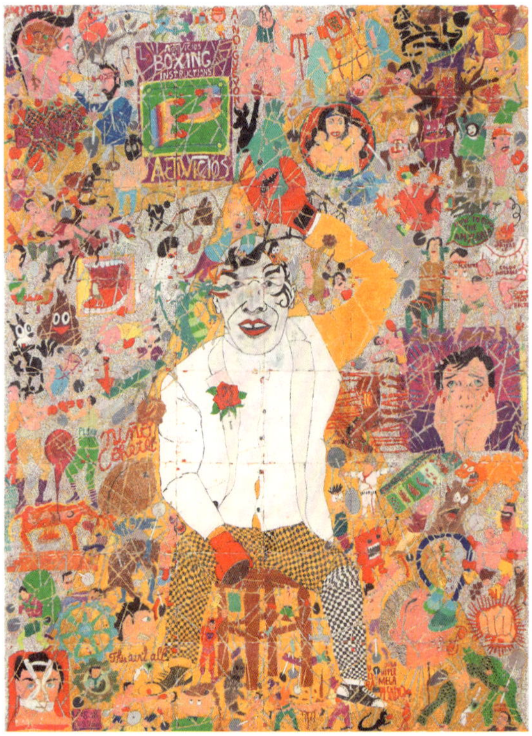

2. 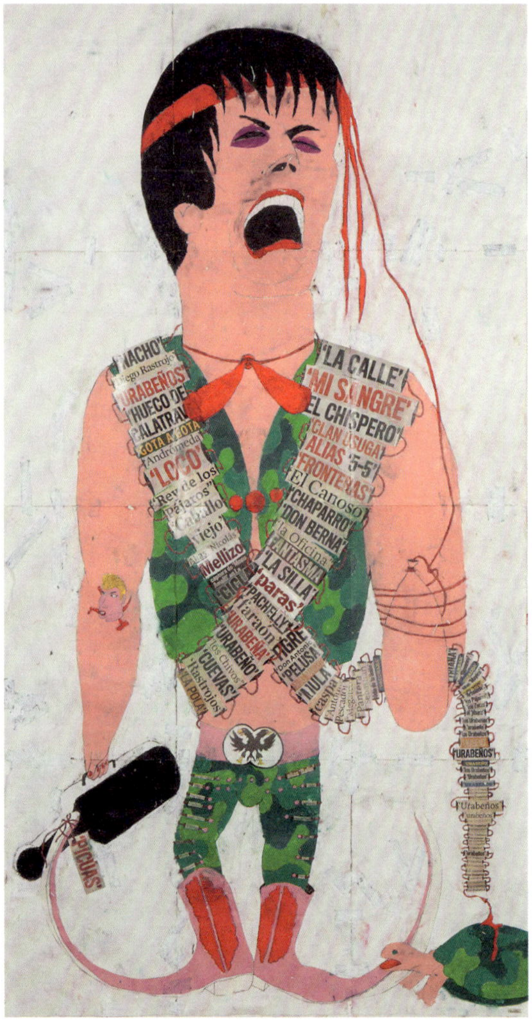

Born 1973, Medellín, Colombia. Lives and works in Medellín.

1. *Tight Rope 4 (Mike)*, 2015, ink, water-soluble wax pastels, tape and saliva on paper, 160 × 122 cm (63 × 48 in)
2. *Los Caprichos (Alias Rambo)*, 2014, ink, water-soluble wax pastels, tape, glue, newspaper clippings and saliva on paper, 119 × 63 cm (46 ⅞ × 24 ⅞ in)
3. *Rip Currents 5*, 2018, ink, water-soluble wax pastels, tape, glue, newspaper clippings and saliva on paper, 237 × 147 cm (93 ⅜ × 58 in)

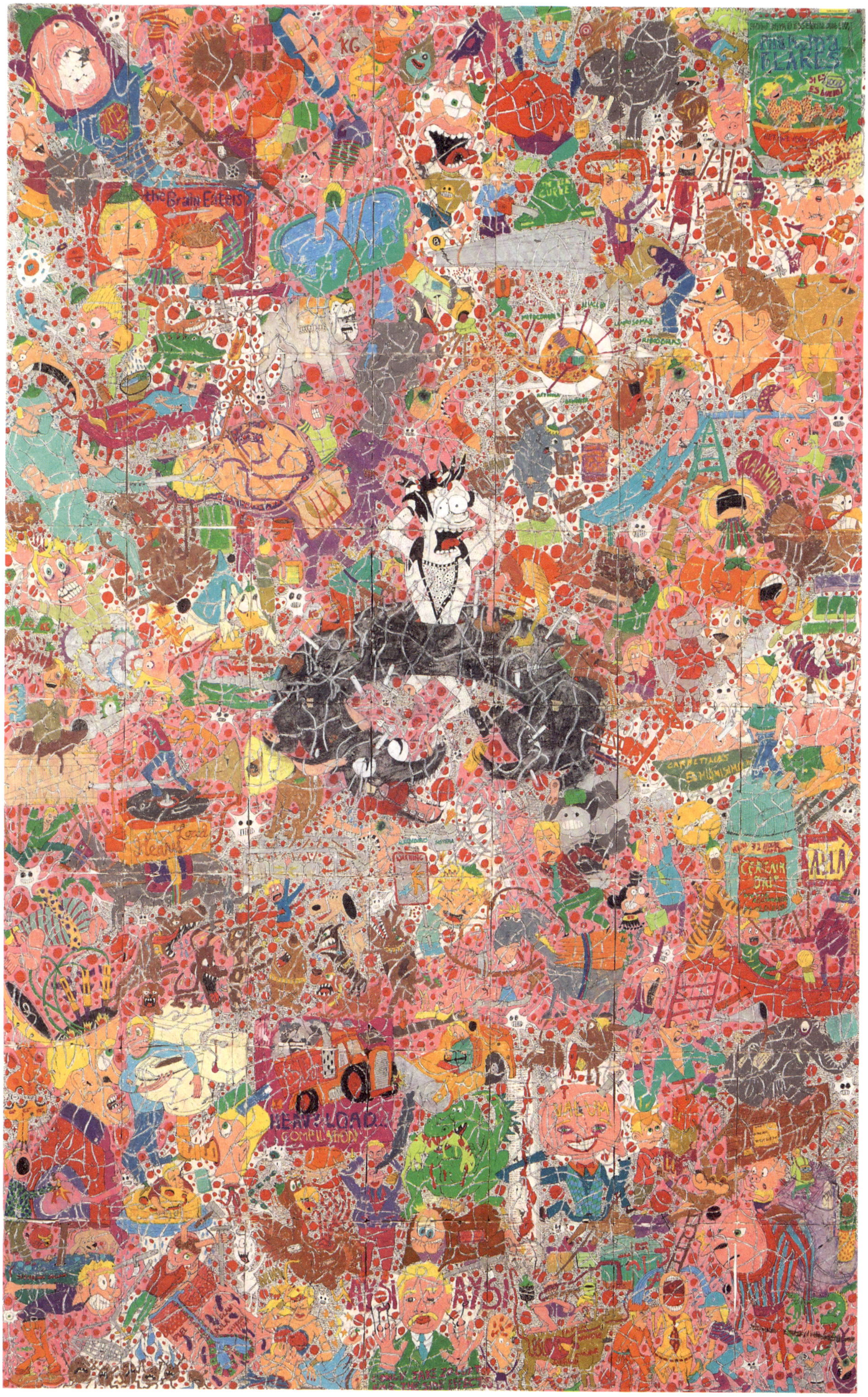

3.

ABEL RODRÍGUEZ .... Looking at the colourful drawings of Abel Rodríguez, the viewer might imagine that the artist spent days, even weeks, carefully studying the rainforest to get the details right. Among the clues to his evident expertise are the varied forms and hues of the drawings' canopies, and the variety of animals roaming the forest floor. .... Yet these are no ordinary jungle landscapes. Despite their remarkable botanical exactitude, the artist painted them entirely from memory. Abel Rodríguez's native name is Mogaje Guihu. He grew up in the Nonuya community near the headwaters of the Cahuinarí river in the Colombian Amazon. He owes his extraordinary understanding of the rainforest and its inhabitants to his uncle, a *sabedor* (man of knowledge), from whom he inherited sufficient wisdom to eventually gain renown as a *nombrador de plantas* (a namer of plants). Rodríguez's detailed grasp of his indigenous community's patch of the Amazon is rare; it is rarer still when exposed to the blind spots of Western science or art. .... His exceptional expertise first drew the attention of Western scientists in the 1980s when he was hired as a guide for Tropenbos International, a Dutch NGO devoted to the study and protection of the tropical rainforest. Following the displacement of his jungle community by the Revolutionary Armed Forces of Colombia (FARC), Tropenbos asked Rodríguez to translate his store of wisdom into an illustrated book. The process birthed an artist with a uniquely holistic outlook on man's relationship to the natural world. .... As word of his talents spread, Rodríguez established a practice that – among other gifts – illustrated not just plant life, but a radically inclusive outlook. Combining an integrated understanding of landscape, ecology, vegetal and animal relations, as well as climate change, his drawings describe an experience of landscape recorded in the communal first person. An outlook that reflects traditional knowledge gained through comprehensive immersion rather than detached observation, his vision both challenges and complements the conventional parameters of scientific know-how. .... Done in Chinese ink, Rodríguez's works on paper challenge traditional art appreciation. At first glance, the majority of his drawings look similar. Upon closer examination, important differences emerge: a tree bursts into leaf in *Terraza Alta II* (2018); a giant anteater shares space with a capybara in *Terraza Alta V* (2018); a thin blue river snakes through the multi-coloured landscape of *Territorio de la Sabana* (2018). A cosmogony is made apparent in these drawings. Among their few Western precedents are the pictures and verses by the visionary Romantic artist and poet William Blake (1757–1827): 'To see a World in a Grain of Sand / And a Heaven in a Wild Flower / Hold Infinity in the palm of your hand / And Eternity in an hour.'
.... Christian Viveros-Fauné

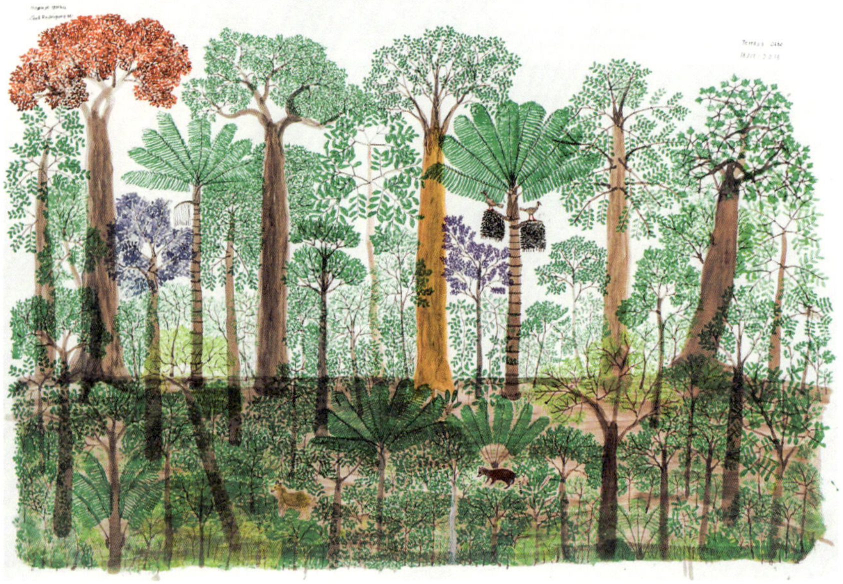
1.

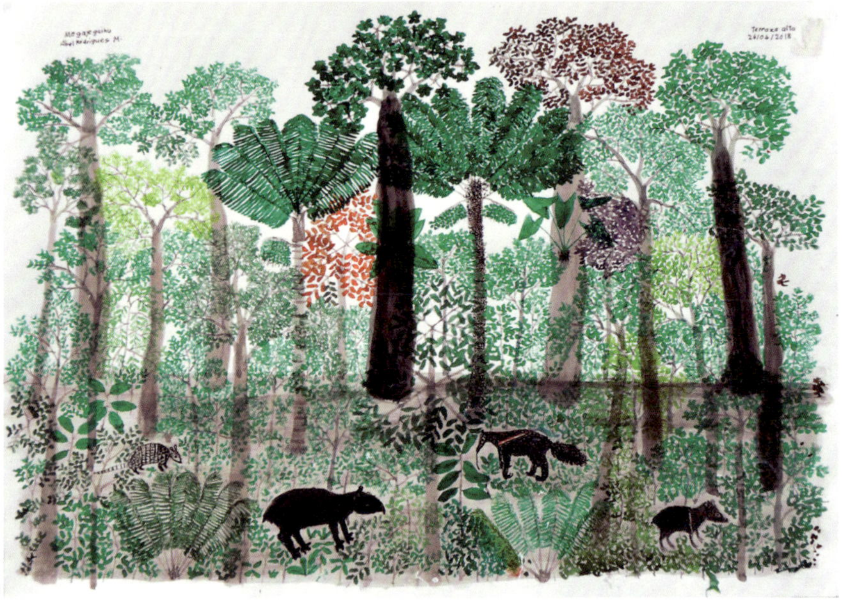
2.

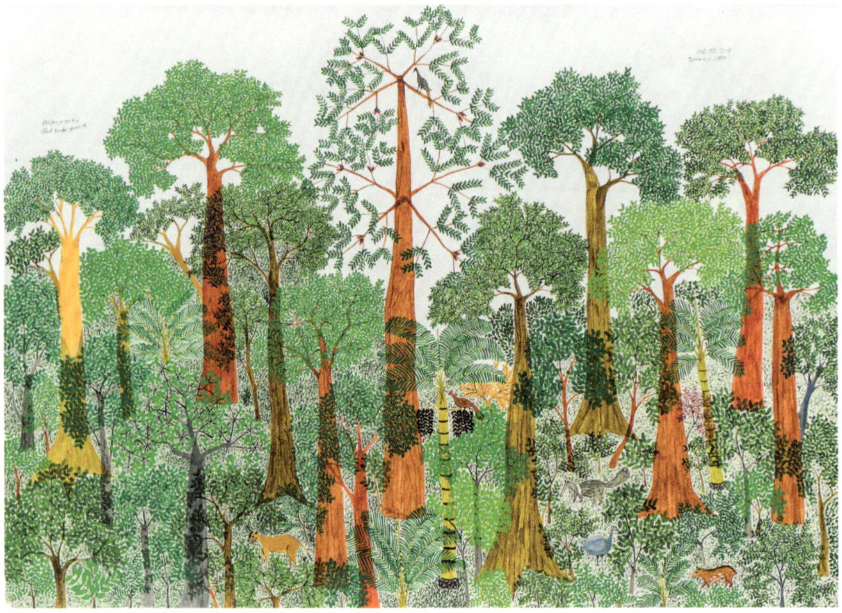
3.

Born c.1944, Cahuinarí region, Colombia. Lives and works in Bogotá.

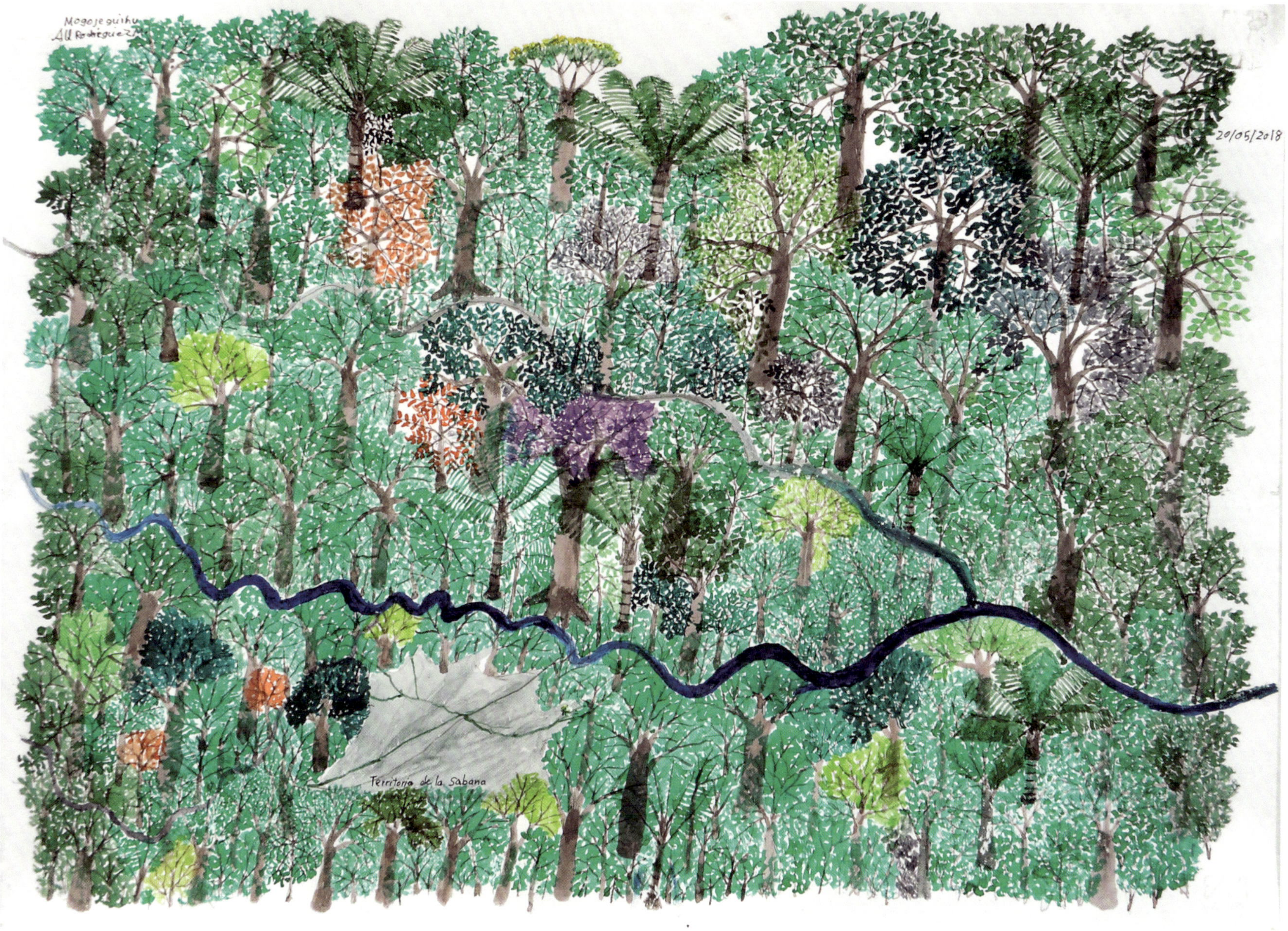

4.

1. *Terraza Alta*, 2019, ink on paper, 50 × 70 cm (19 ⅝ × 27 ½ in)
2. *Terraza Alta V*, 2018, ink on paper, 50 × 70 cm (19 ⅝ × 27 ½ in)
3. *Terraza Alta II*, 2018, ink on paper, 70 × 100 cm (27 ½ × 39 ⅜ in)
4. *Territorio de la Sabana*, 2018, ink on paper, 50 × 70 cm (19 ⅝ × 27 ½ in)

GAMALIEL RODRÍGUEZ……. Gamaliel Rodríguez's ambitiously scaled and patiently rendered drawings of post-industrial landscapes in a state of ecological overthrow are at once factual and speculative. Conflation is central to the artist's method in his ongoing 'Figure' series, started in 2009. The airports, military installations, canals, university buildings, storage warehouses and manufacturing facilities detailed in his more recent drawings are, in the main, fictionalizations of verifiable infrastructures in the United States and the artist's native Puerto Rico. Knowledge of the sites dramatized (rather than merely actualized) in these drawings, while important, is not a prerequisite to engaging the visible bounty recorded. ……. Writing in 1953, Roland Barthes, a thinker invoked by Rodríguez in accounts of his practice, praised the 'aesthetic of silence' characterizing Dutch painter Pieter Saenredam's (1597–1665) 'irremediably unpeopled' paintings of church interiors. He also pointed to the 'detachment and density' typifying Dutch descriptions of objects. One recognizes these attributes in Rodríguez's technically exact drawings, which are frequently based on photographs and sometimes sprawl across multiple panels, as in *Figure 1814* (2017). While precision is constant, it is modulated by the artist's tendency to deform and abstract. There is, for instance, ambiguity to the cumulous vegetation that frequently surrounds his man-made infrastructures, including the canal in *Figure 1821 Lost Port* (2017): they resemble clouds as much as encroaching forests. His earlier 'Issues' series (2011), based on declassified military images, as well as his follow-on 'Dark Thoughts' series (2012–13), aerial views that lapse into haziness, similarly revealed the artist's mediating hand and transformative approach to appropriated imagery. Each series is expressed in a range of different media, from ballpoint pen, graphite, acrylic and gold leaf in the 'Figure' series, to various permanent markers in 'Dark Thoughts'. Rodríguez nonetheless favours ballpoint pen, because of its ability to create the illusion of engraving. ……. Vantage and point of view are integral to Rodríguez's work. *Figure 1839: La travesía / Le voyage* (2019–20), an eighteen metre (fifty-nine foot) long ballpoint pen commission for Massachusetts Museum of Contemporary Art's Hunter Hallway, presents a recessive view of a fictionalized landscape described from an elevated vantage point. Rodríguez's military background strongly informs these aerial views. Prior to studying art, he served as an infantryman in the US Army and acquired proficiencies in map-reading and intelligence. A 2009 exhibition of drawings depicting military weaponry and fuel-generating plants concretized his interest in power, sight, territory and prospect, enduring leitmotifs in his work. While reticent to declare an opinion in his work, his drawings offer a sublimated critique of Puerto Rico's ambiguous status as a US colony (or 'unincorporated territory'). The air-traffic control tower at the centre of *Figure 1828–Aguadilla* (2018) portrays a structure at the Rafael Hernández Airport, on the island nation's north-western tip, which was formerly a United States Air Force base.
……. Sean O'Toole

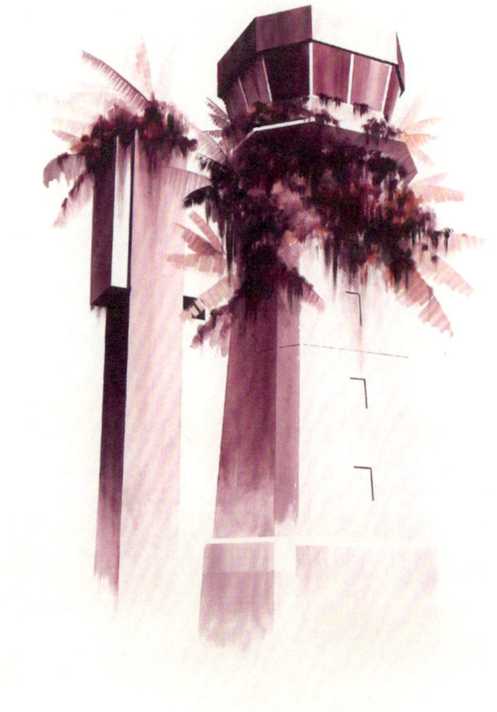
1.

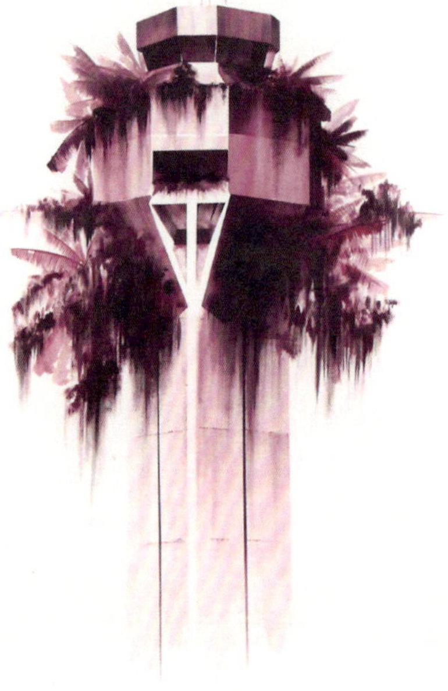
2.

Born 1977, Bayamon, Puerto Rico. Lives and work in Puerto Rico.

1. *Figure 1828 – Aguadilla*, 2018, acrylic and ink on paper, 127 × 97 cm (50 × 38 in)
2. *Figure 1828 SJU*, 2018, acrylic and ink on paper, 127 × 97 cm (50 × 38 in)
3. *Figure 1815*, 2017, graphite on paper, 193 × 254 cm (76 × 100 in)
4. *Figure 1821 Lost Port*, 2017, ballpoint pen, acrylic, coloured pencil and ink on paper, 193 × 381 cm (76 × 150 in)

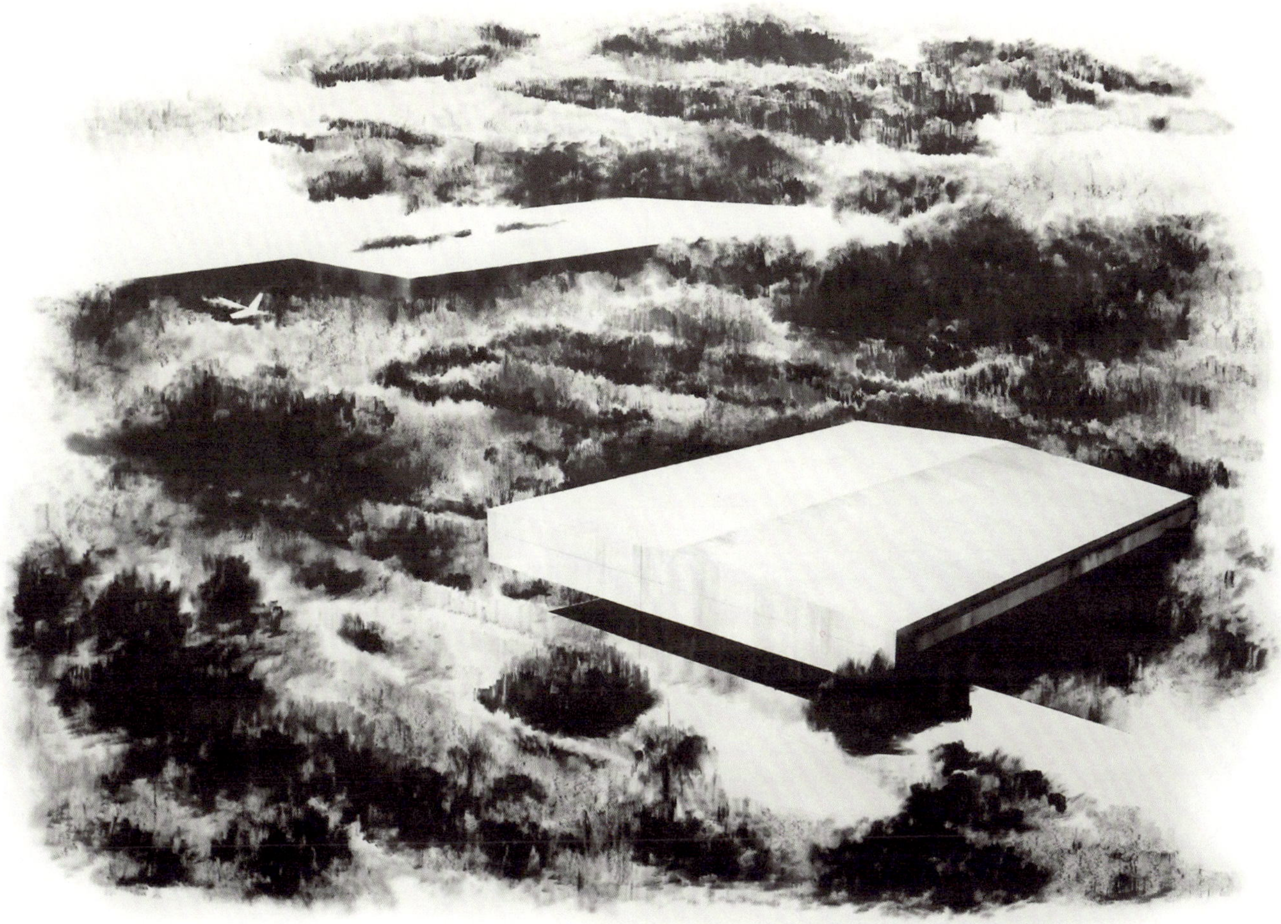

3.

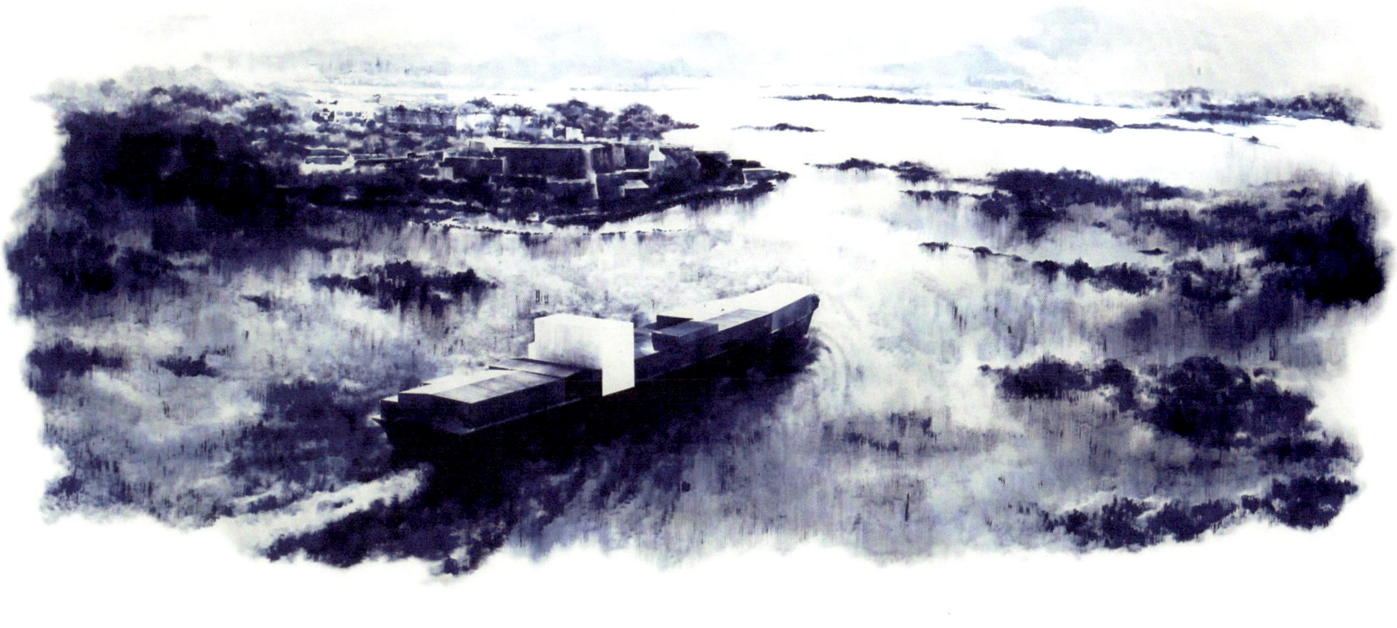

4.

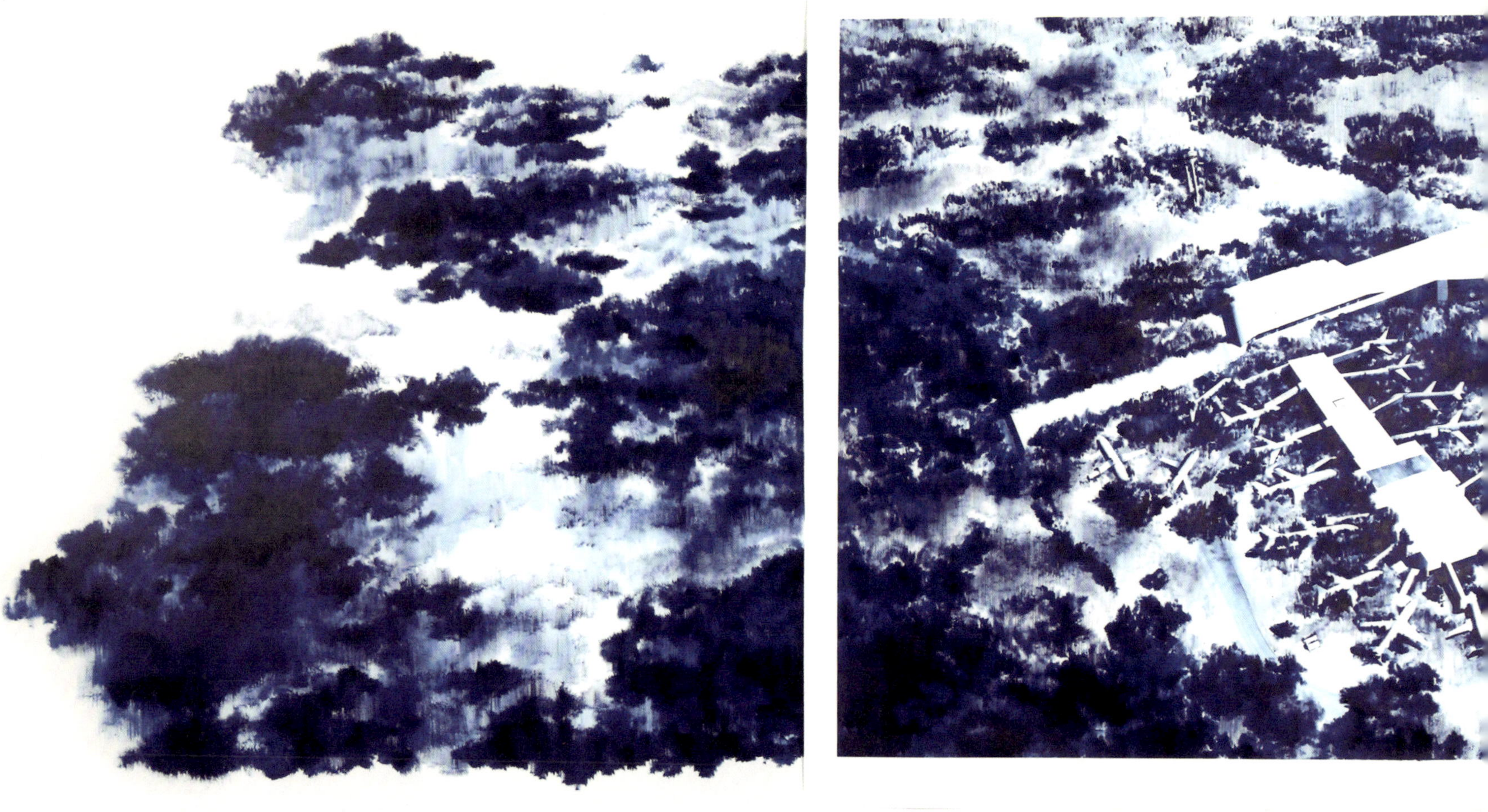

5.

GAMALIEL RODRÍGUEZ

5. *Figure 1814*, 2017, ballpoint pen, acrylic, coloured pencil and ink on paper extended on wall, 193 × 381 cm (76 × 150 in)

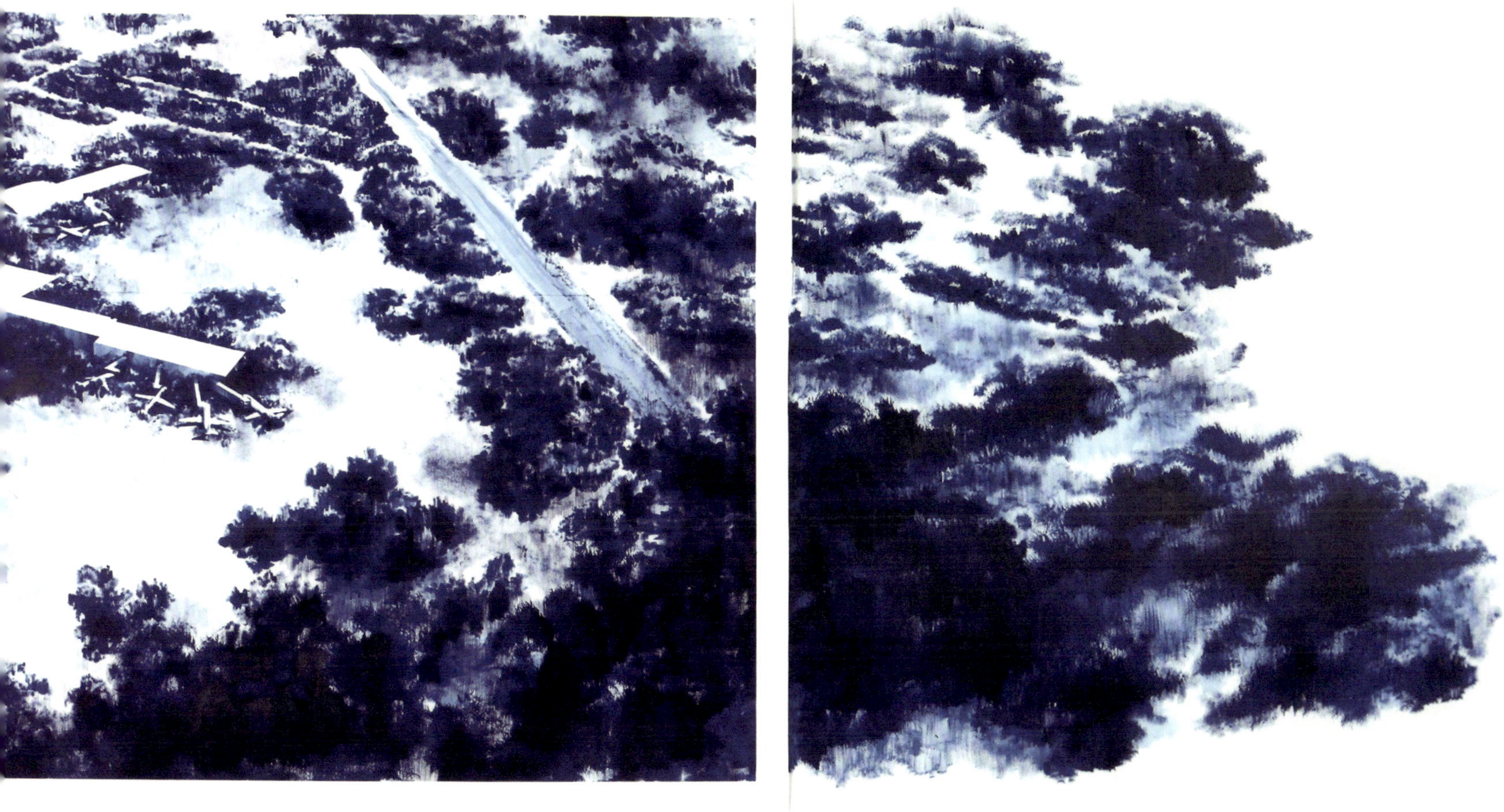

REBECCA SALTER .... In the late 1970s, when Rebecca Salter's art school contemporaries had their sights set on London and New York, she decided instead to head East after graduating to immerse herself in the art and culture of Japan. Enticed by an interest in Japanese prints, she turned her back on ceramics and spent six influential years in the country, studying traditional woodblock printing and mastering a wide range of artistic techniques. Salter's drawings, like the multi-layered, non-figurative paintings and prints for which she is best known, seek to build bridges between Western and Eastern traditions, demonstrating the influence of American abstract painting and mid-century Minimalism as much as Japanese printmaking and calligraphy. .... Employing a variety of techniques, Salter's distinctive abstract drawings are formed from small, repeated marks that emphasize the interplay between presence and absence. Each one reflects the Japanese aesthetic principles that inform all her works. Especially important is the concept of *wabi*, meaning 'simple or 'austere', which encourages an acceptance of transience and imperfection; another is *shibui* (literally 'astringent'), which refers to simplicity and unobtrusive beauty. With muted palettes, some of Salter's drawings recall static displayed on analogue television screens, while others suggest more organic forms such as animal skins, the surface patina of stone or the patterns created by undulating water. From a distance they appear still and ethereal, their neutral tones exuding tranquillity; closer inspection, however, reveals surfaces teeming with activity. .... The ancient technique of pyrography is evident in the large drawing *Untitled AG48* (2014), which is composed of thousands of small burn marks. During its making, Salter found that her heat pen burnt through the thin Japanese kozo paper, scorching the thick backing paper beneath. By reorienting the thin paper, so that the underlying marks could be seen through its translucent surface, she created a gentle rippling effect that recalls murmuration patterns or a crumpled blanket. In *Untitled AM26* (2018), Salter primed one half of the paper with an absorbent gesso so that small ink spots spread and dried at different rates, creating subtle visual shifts across the drawing. Additionally, the work's surface is punctured with tiny holes, which serve to emphasize its materiality and status as an object – another reference to traditional Japanese art where the use of absorbent papers that allow pigment to soak into the page causes image and substrate to fuse into single objects. Working intuitively, Salter painstakingly makes all her marks by hand, an important albeit obsessive approach that infuses her drawings with a fragile, shimmering beauty. It is also precarious, leaving little room for error. Each new work is thus an experimental journey, the success of which can only be evaluated once the final destination is reached.
.... David Trigg

1.

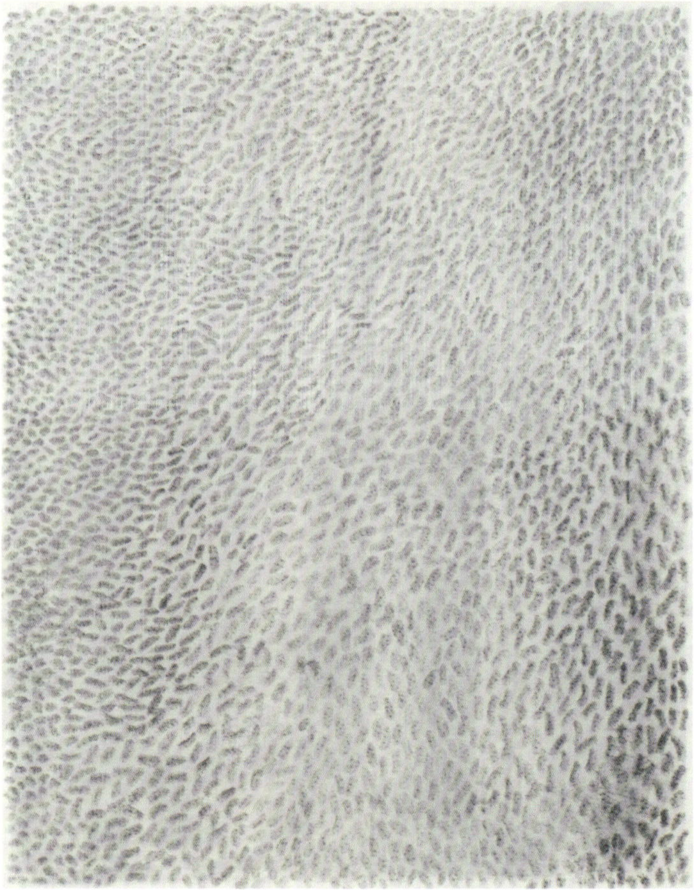
2.

Born 1955, Sussex, UK. Lives and works in London.

1. *Untitled AM26*, 2018, sepia ink on paper, 145 × 115 cm (57 × 45 in)
2. *Untitled AK20*, 2017, graphite and sumi ink on paper, 120 × 96 cm (47 × 38 in)
3. *Untitled AG48*, 2014, pyrography on kozo paper, 94 × 120 cm (37 × 47 in)

3.

MASSINISSA SELMANI .... Before embarking on an artistic career, Massinissa Selmani trained in computer science, a fact that offers a clue to the scientific precision of his delicate drawings. The methodical and painstaking qualities of the process are central to his practice, whether presented as animations, installations or as a series of graphite and coloured pencil drawings. His depictions comprise carefully rendered architectural settings populated by tiny figures and props in elusive locations. These incongruous perspectival arrangements are at once intriguing and absurd. Neat rows of chairs are immaculately arranged on a gradient leading towards a stage that resembles a swimming pool with a car tyre resting on it and two men gesticulating in the distance. Accompanied by a cryptic title, *L'aube insondable #3* (*The unfathomable dawn #3*), (2018), Selmani poetically suggests the ineffable dimension of time. .... The artist grew up in Algiers and moved to France at the age of twenty-five to study art at the École Supérieure des Beaux-Arts in Tours. He has participated in numerous high-profile biennials, as well as presenting his distinctive drawings and paper configurations in a solo exhibition at Palais de Tokyo in Paris in 2018. Importantly, Selmani was included in Okwui Enwezor's 2015 Venice Biennale exhibition, 'All the World's Futures', receiving a coveted special mention award for a suite of drawings and depictions in red notebooks as a tribute to Algerian rural communities and failed utopias. .... Selmani's predilection for drawing can be traced to his teens in Algeria in the 1990s, when he would be intrigued by political cartoons in the newspaper. His source material is derived from cutouts, newspaper clippings, texts and montages transformed into finely rendered drawings with exquisite detail. Influenced by South African artist William Kentridge (b. 1955), he discussed his scenographies in an interview in *Contemporary&* in 2015: 'In my drawings, I like the idea of creating realistic situations that are unlikely to actually occur. The elements making up the drawings are very often copies from press clippings from different countries that I collect on an ongoing basis, dealing with different subjects without any link to my starting point. By associating them, I create scenarios that are frequently absurd.' His drawings are populated with stages, empty happenings, screens, theatres, doorways and ledges. *Soon #9* (2017) is a planar configuration comprising a platform propped up by a mound with an outdoor movie screen above it. Rich with drafting, shading and contouring, Selmani's uncanny and unlikely situations appear both comic and tragic by turns. His drawings meld documentary and fiction in a way that ultimately returns us to the photographs of the Belgian Surrealist poet and theorist Paul Nougé – who also had a scientific background as a biochemist – and his use of humour and surprise, as well as the surrealist character of arbitrariness. .... Natalie King

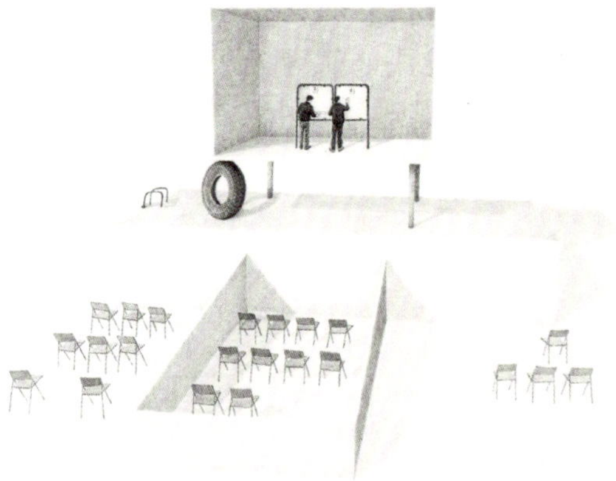

1.

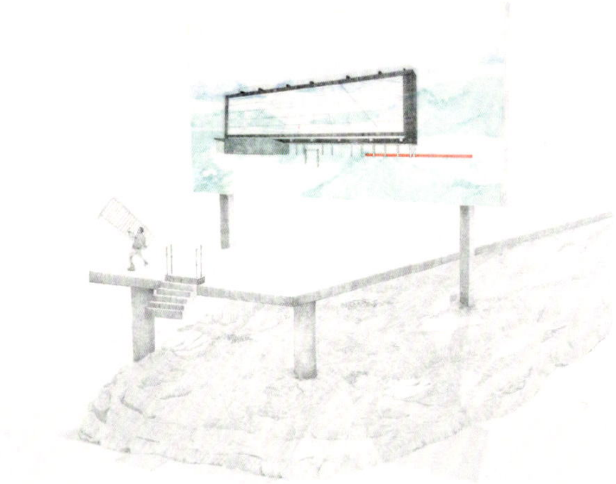

2.

Born 1980, Algiers. Lives and works in Tours, France.

1. *L'aube insondable #3* (*The unfathomable dawn #3*), 2018, graphite and coloured pencil on paper, 124 × 100 cm (48 ¾ × 39 ½ in)
2. *Soon #9*, 2017, graphite and coloured pencil on paper and tracing paper, 129.5 × 97 cm (51 × 38 in)
3. *Détour du lendemain* (*Next day detour*), 2019, graphite and coloured pencil on paper, 78 × 112 cm (30 ¾ × 44 ⅛ in)
4. *Untitled 1 (no plan is foolproof)*, 2019, graphite and coloured pencil on paper, 66 × 91 cm (26 × 35 ⅞ in)

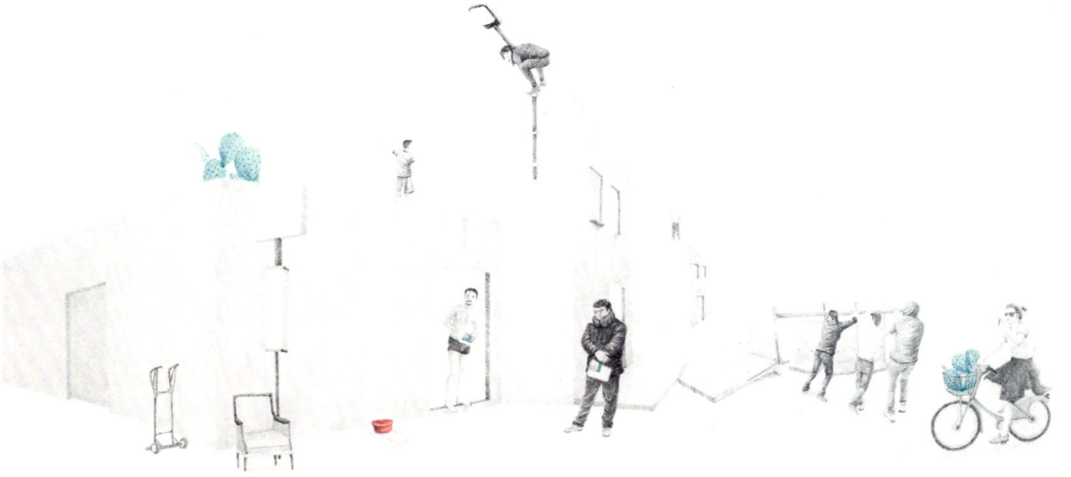

3.

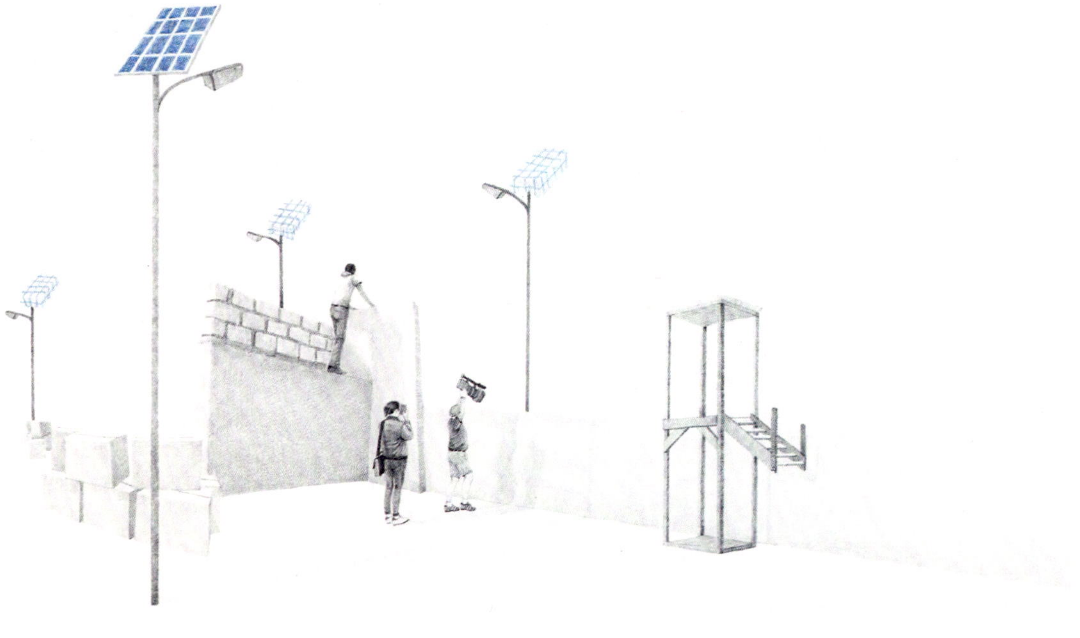

4.

WAEL SHAWKY .... Wael Shawky has always had a flair for the epic. He is best known for his immersive films, installations and performances that synthesize and adapt lengthy texts, often with musical and theatrical components. Central to his practice is an insistence on the multiple, mutable narratives of history, which he emphasizes by interweaving fact, fiction and outright fantasy. As he said at a 2017 Creative Time summit in Toronto, 'History and theatre are caught up in each other... The cabaret is a stage for history, as a performance.' So it is that, in his work, a French epic poem from 778 CE and the curatorial statement of the 2013 Sharjah Biennial were variously turned into *fidjeri*, or Gulf pearl-diving shanties, and Sufi devotional *qawwalis*. Egyptian author Mohamed Mustageb's rural-surreal short stories (intertwined with Shawky's own childhood spent in Mecca and Alexandria), the Crusades narrated from an Arab perspective and the history of oil in the Gulf, meanwhile, all became major film series, which then unfolded across various installations. .... Less ambitious in scope – and more rewardingly intimate as a result – are the quiet ink on paper drawings that he makes alongside these maximalist film projects. Shawky's drawings feature delicate linework and judicious use of negative space. Their subjects, while still hinting at the transmogrified and the grotesque, are whimsical rather than weird. And unlike the saturated, moody colouration of his other works, their palette is gentler too, all pastels and earth tones, although the drawings that accompanied his older *Cabaret Crusades* trilogy (2010–15) did occasionally deploy fiery reds and oranges. Colour is sometimes intimated rather than filled in, as with the beige and blue dotted sky – a sandstorm, perhaps – of *The Gulf Project Camp: Drawing #25* (2019), although elsewhere Shawky does use loose pigment to create a remarkable mouldy-looking effect. .... One hallmark of non-Western science fiction is an emphasis on revisiting and renegotiating the colonial encounter, which might be recast as meeting invading aliens or battling interstellar monsters. In *Gulf Project Camp: Drawing #2* (2019), one of Shawky's more recent Gulf drawings, a sixteenth-century Portuguese galleon anchors offshore near what looks like a bloodstained beach. Centuries later, Westerners would arrive by biplane and, later still, by oil tanker, as in *Gulf Project Camp: Drawing #3* (2019). Strictly speaking, Shawky's drawings are preparatory works, and indeed they have a certain storyboard feel when viewed together, especially given that they are usually hung linearly or in a neat grid. But while they depict moments also seen in associated films – and chimeric creatures that recur as bronze sculptures – they are not so much illustrated stills as storytelling devices and narrative vehicles in and of themselves, albeit ones that do not necessarily follow a linear narrative. .... Rahel Aima

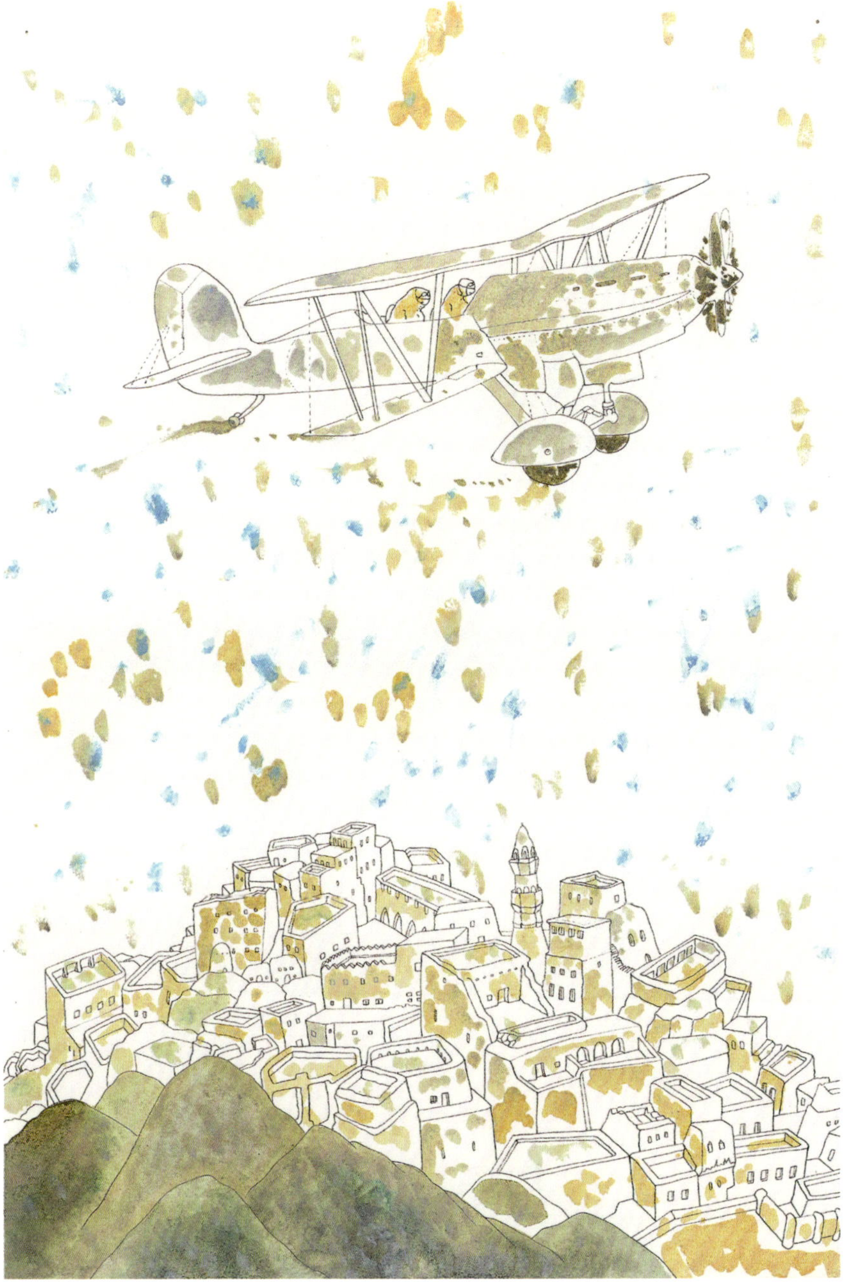
1.

Born 1971, Alexandria, Egypt. Lives and works in Philadelphia.

1. *The Gulf Project Camp: Drawing #25*, 2019, graphite, ink, oil and mixed media on cotton paper, 56.8 × 37.5 cm (22 ⅜ × 14 ¾ in)
2. *The Gulf Project Camp: Drawing #3*, 2019, graphite, ink, oil and mixed media on cotton paper, 50.5 × 70.2 cm (19 ⅞ × 27 ⅝ in)
3. *The Gulf Project Camp: Drawing #2*, 2019, graphite, ink, oil and mixed media on cotton paper, 50.5 × 70.2 cm (19 ⅞ × 27 ⅝ in)
4. *The Gulf Project Camp: Drawing #36*, 2019, fraphite, ink, oil and mixed media on cotton paper, 57.2 × 76.2 cm (22 ½ × 30 in)

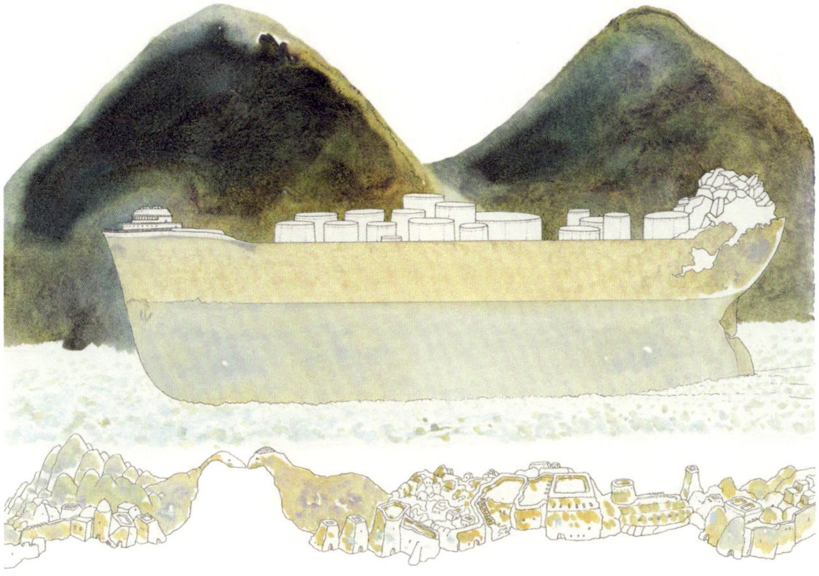

2.

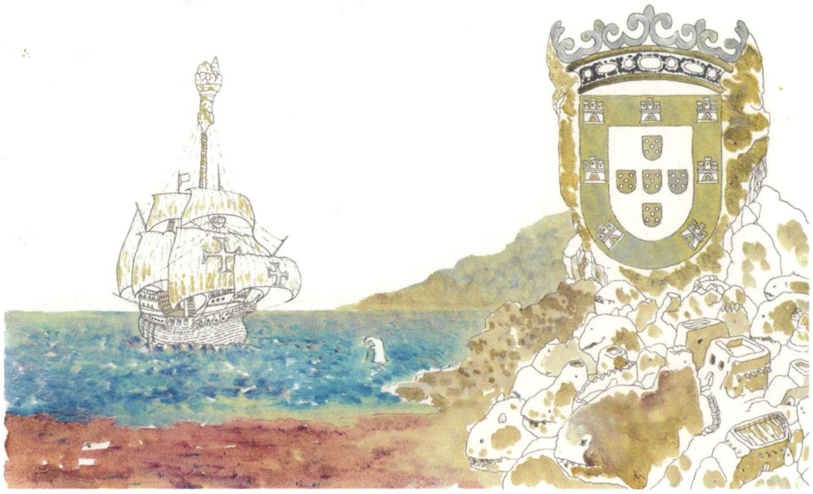

3.

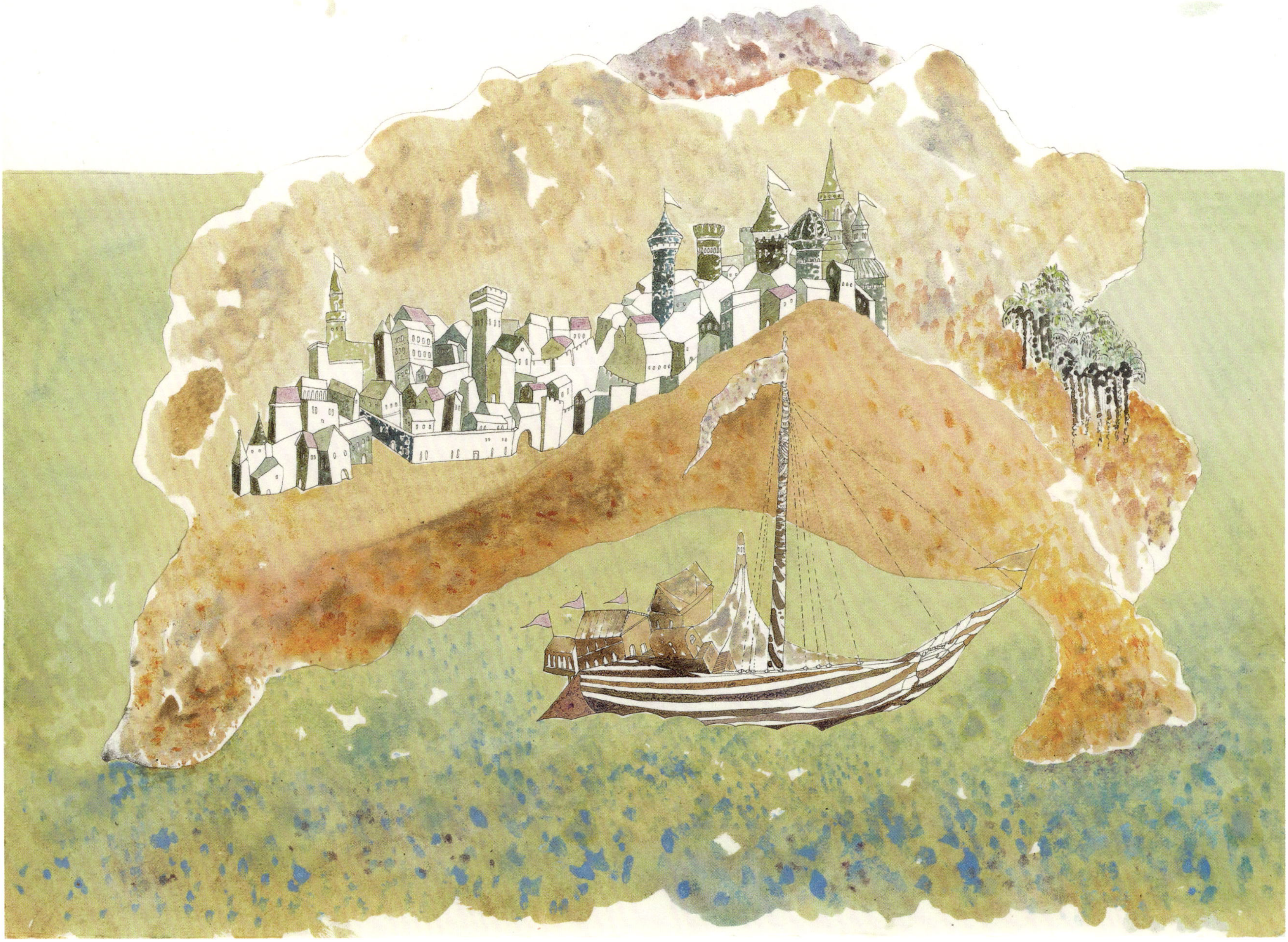

4.

NILIMA SHEIKH .... The tragic love story of a woman named Sohni forms the premise of Nilima Sheikh's *Chenab 5* (2016–17), drawn and painted in casein tempera on a traditional handmade paper from Sanganger, near Jaipur, Rajasthan, India. Sohni swims across the blue waters of a wide river every night and, lit by the silvering stars, she visits her lover Mahiwal, who waits on the opposite bank. She holds on to a baked earthen pot as a float as she swims. Her family find out about the affair and replace the baked pot with an unbaked one, and as Sohni swims that night, the pot slowly dissolves. She can either return and fail her waiting lover or brave the rough waters. She chooses the latter and drowns. *Chenab 5* is one of sixteen panels that form 'Terrain: Carrying Across, Leaving Behind' (2016–17), first shown at Documenta 14 in Kassel, Germany. In the series, Sheikh has drawn and painted similar stories of love, partition, protest and displacement. Her working process is mostly improvisational and she is influenced by Persian, Turkish and Indian miniature painting and manuscript traditions. Text can often be seen interspersed throughout her drawings, for which she draws from the writings of poets such as Agha Shahid Ali, Mahmoud Darwish, Lal Ded and Ocean Vuong.

.... In her five-decade-long career, Sheikh has made paper and scroll-based installations and screens, as well as illustrating children's books and designing sets for the theatre. Her work manifests the direct influence of the Dunhuang Buddhist murals found in Gansu, China, especially in its spatial arrangement, non-linear form and use of multiple entry points into the stories depicted. In the absence of a singular perspective, Sheikh often moves away from establishing a central narrative, allowing for palimpsestic readings. In another panel from 'Terrain: Carrying Across, Leaving Behind', titled *Border* (2016–17), we see a spiral of figures – mostly women – carrying their belongings with them as they walk. One woman carries an entire line-drawn village with her, perhaps in reference to a life she has been forced to leave behind. Sheikh's long-standing collaboration with a family of traditional paper-stencil artists in Mathura, North India, brings repeated architectural, floral and faunal motifs to her work. These are further complemented by her choice of texts, which are mostly quotations and verses from poetry. Sheikh rarely draws in bold lines. Her brush drawings are instead realized in soft, sensitive shapes, usually set against luminous backgrounds; sometimes the works are flecked with gold or spirited by a gentle shimmer. She achieves this special softness through the use of casein and gum tempera and a primarily pastel palette. In her pictures, the natural world floats against a political one, animated by mythical and historical references.

.... Skye Arundhati Thomas

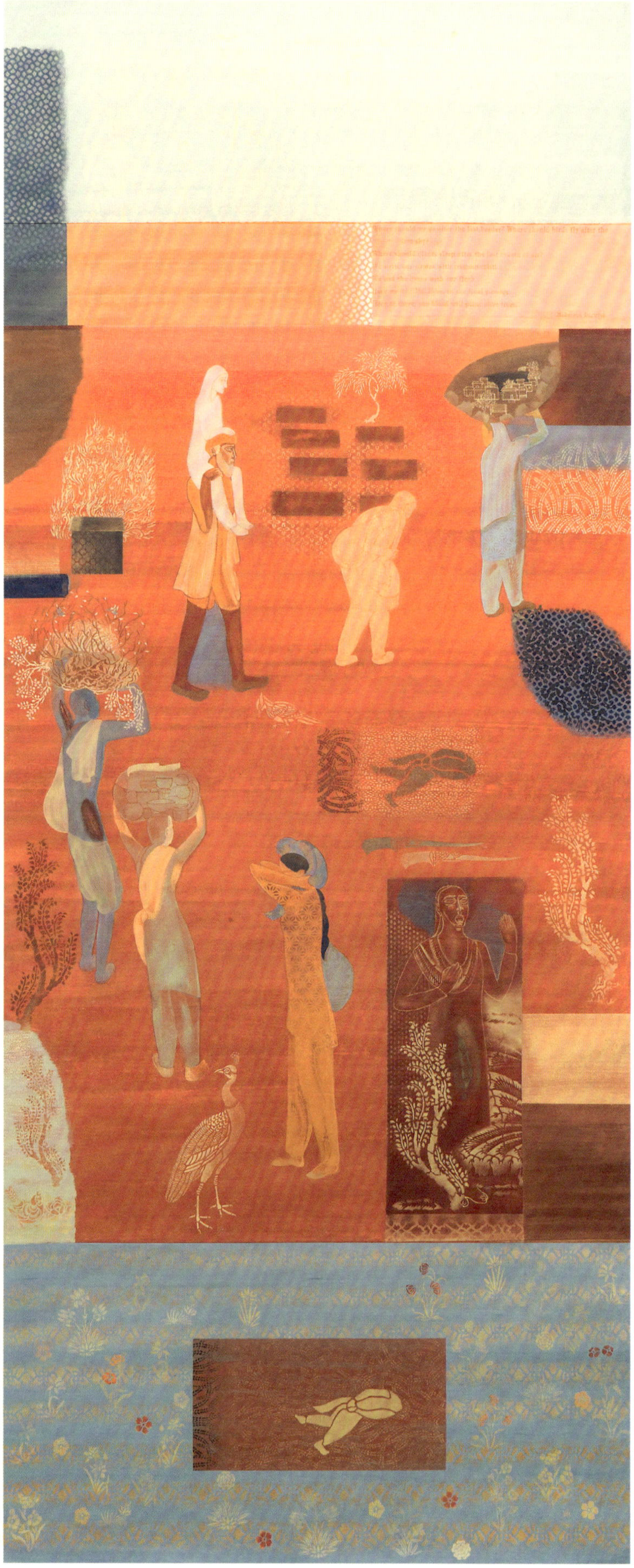

1.

Born 1945, Delhi, India. Lives and works in Vadodara and New Delhi, India.

1. *Border*, 2016–17, casein tempera on Sanganer paper, 213 × 89 cm (83 ⅞ × 35 in)
2. *Chenab 5*, 2016–17, casein tempera on Sanganer paper, 213 × 89 cm (83 ⅞ × 35 in)
3. *Dreaming Home 2*, 2016–17, casein tempera on Sanganer paper, 213 × 89 cm (83 ⅞ × 35 in)

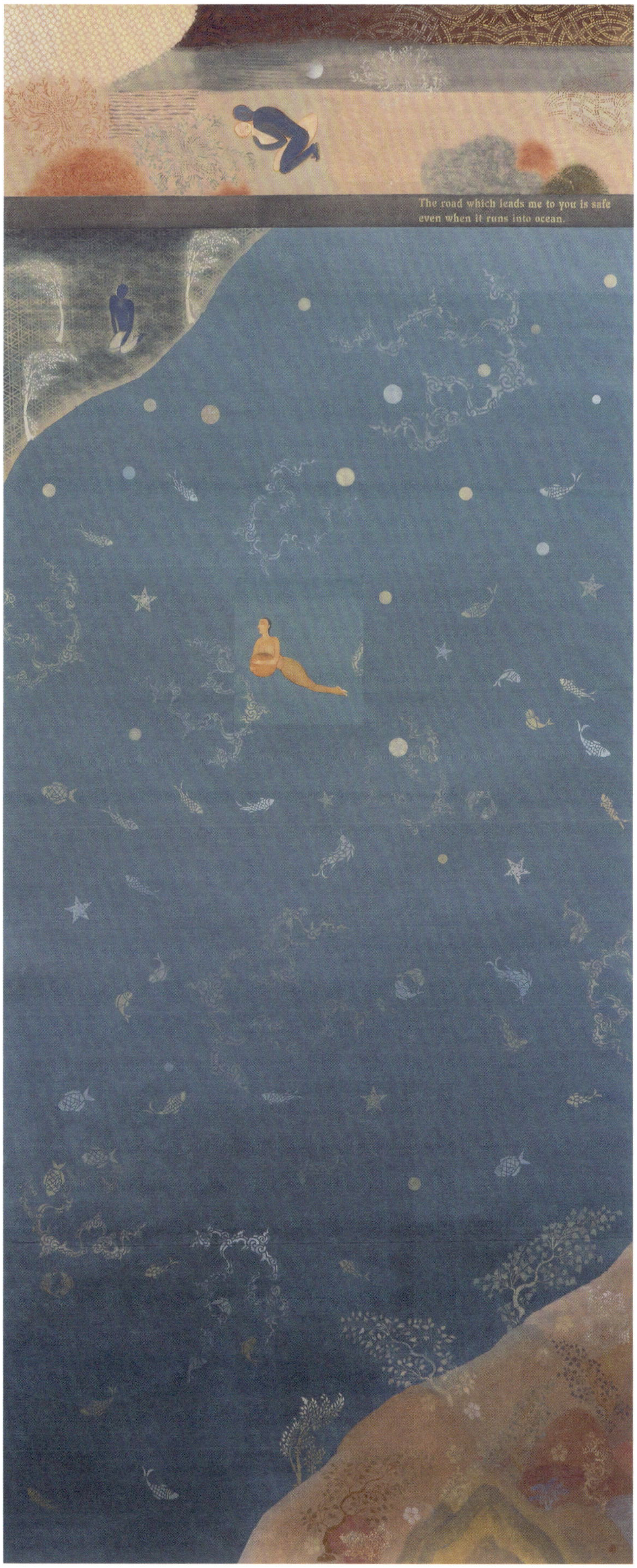
The road which leads me to you is safe
even when it runs into ocean.

2.

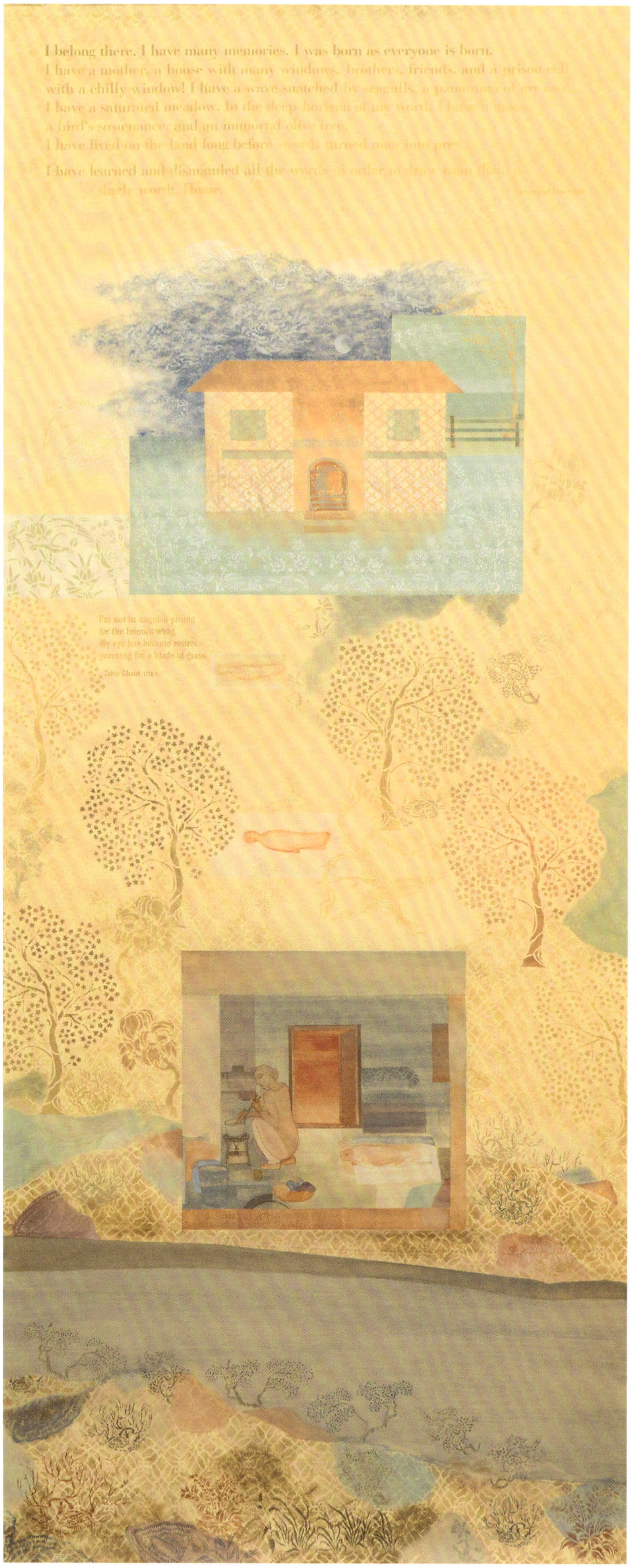
I belong there. I have many memories. I was born as everyone is born.
I have a mother, a house with many windows, brothers, friends, and a prison cell
I'm not in anguish pining
for the huma's wing.
My eye has become restive
yearning for a blade of grass.
Tahir Ghani 17th C.

3.

S A N C I N T Y A   M O H I N I   S I M P S O N .... Sancintya Mohini Simpson's drawings depict displaced women labourers from India set adrift on distant beaches like migratory birds or scattered across fields of crops, drawn from a high, aerial viewpoint. Her small and beautiful watercolour and gouache drawings are painted on wasli paper, a handmade material manufactured specifically for Indian miniaturists. She draws extraordinary but oppressed women who were her forebears, Indian indentured labourers transported from the subcontinent to South Africa, to the coastal province of Natal, from whence their descendants eventually fled to Australia. Splayed across the paper and shrouded in saris and dupattas, her tiny women are gendered marks on the paper's luminous white surface or else they are embedded in bright zones of colour that represent fields, sand and sea, divided into blocks of green, ochre or blue. Her figures – who are exclusively female and all drawn to the same miniature scale – are arranged so that their gestures and contortions suggest stories that are far less happy than the sumptuous colours suggest: cycles of arrival by ship, hard labour and untimely death. At the top right-hand corner of *Natal #4* (2018) a woman hangs, dead, from a tree; meanwhile, other women work in the fields, oblivious to her plight. Assuming Simpson's drawing draws on the traditions of Indian miniature painting, as her materials and subject matter attest, then these are the same woman at different points of her life, flattened together in one space in a clever but traditional sleight of hand. .... In *Kala Pani* (2018) a tiny, clothed woman floats face-down on the deep, dark blue ocean. Towards the top of the sheet of paper, an even smaller-scale ship sets sail towards the horizon. Kala Pani means dark-water, and Kalapani were Indian expatriates, servants and even concubines who boarded ships from India from the sixteenth century onwards. If Simpson's work is a memorial to women who, against the Hindu religious ban on travel across the Dark Water, were transported to South Africa in the nineteenth century, and if her impulse is to celebrate her feminine forebears in harsh South Africa, then this series of drawings is the inversion of her earlier video installations, in which young contemporary *flâneurs* wandering Brisbane – where Simpson is based – are now replaced by women subjected to transportation and suicide. Her miniature paintings continue Simpson's exploration and recovery of feminine experience, now mediated through an erotically loaded traditional vocabulary in which formal beauty was always conflated with female beauty. *Natal #2* (2018), therefore, is a gorgeous miniature painting that oscillates between a politically edged parody of that tradition and its celebration, even as Simpson's clear intention is to reclaim the marginalized edges of history.
.... Charles Green

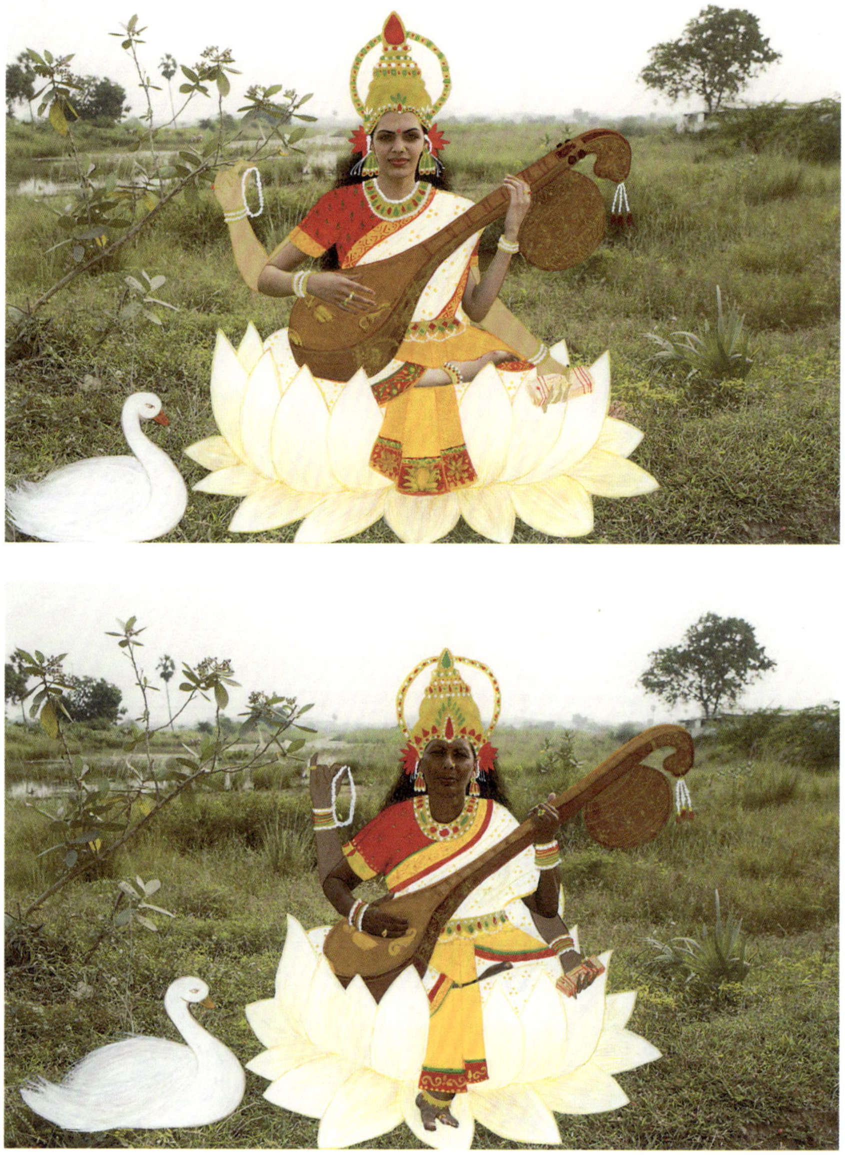

1.

Born 1991, Brisbane, Australia. Lives and works in Brisbane.

1. *Saraswati/Mother* from 'Mother and I' series, 2012–14, archival pigment prints, gouache, watercolour and liquid gold, each 15 × 21 cm (6 × 8 ¼)
2. *Kala Pani*, 2018, watercolour and gouache on handmade wasli paper, 63 × 88 cm (24 ⅞ × 34 ⅝ in)
3. *Natal #1*, 2018, watercolour and gouache on handmade wasli paper, 63 × 88 cm (24 ⅞ × 34 ⅝ in)
4. *Natal #2*, 2018, watercolour and gouache on handmade wasli paper, 63 × 88 cm (24 ⅞ × 34 ⅝ in)
5. *Natal #4*, 2018, watercolour and gouache on handmade wasli paper, 63 × 88 cm (24 ⅞ × 34 ⅝ in)

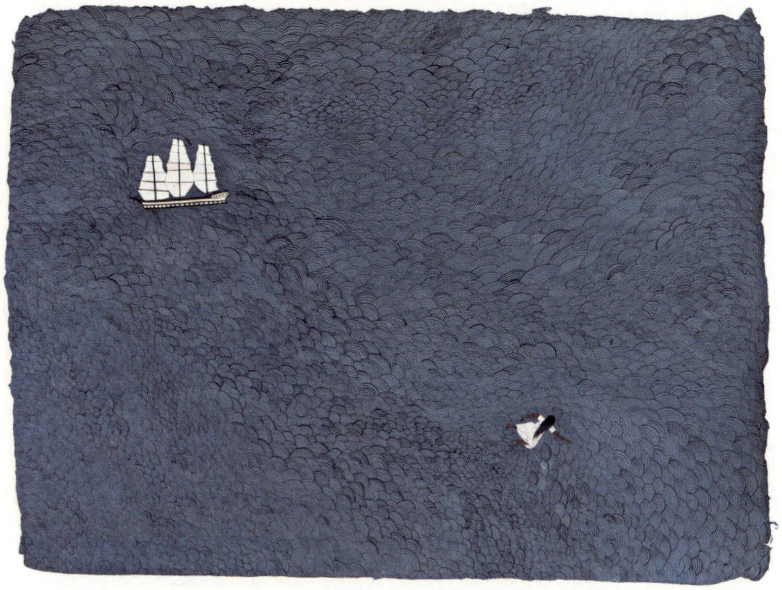

2.

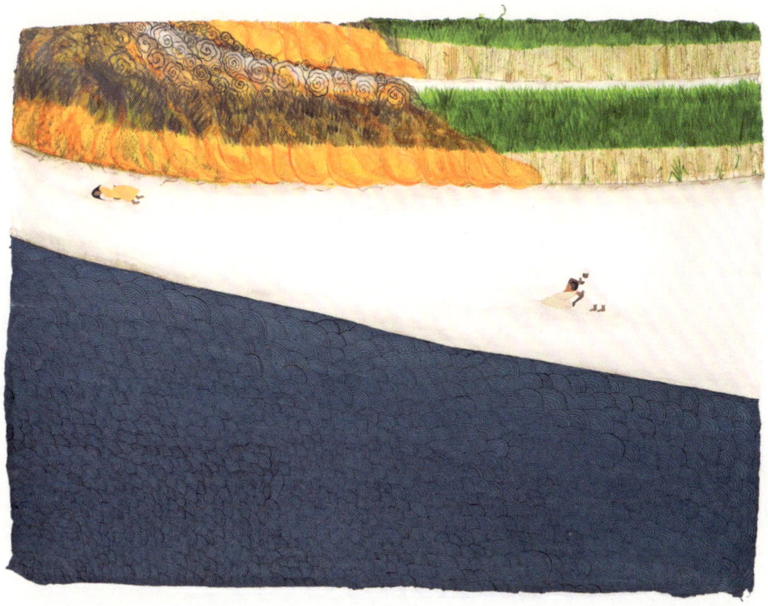

3.

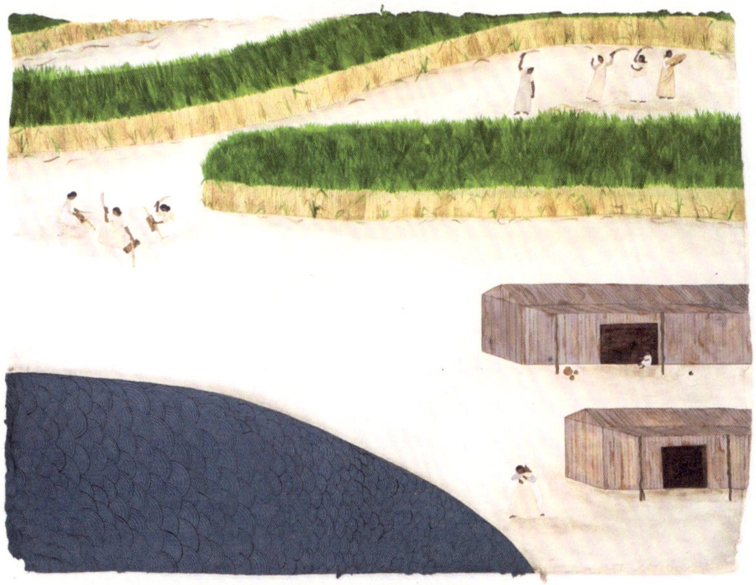

4.

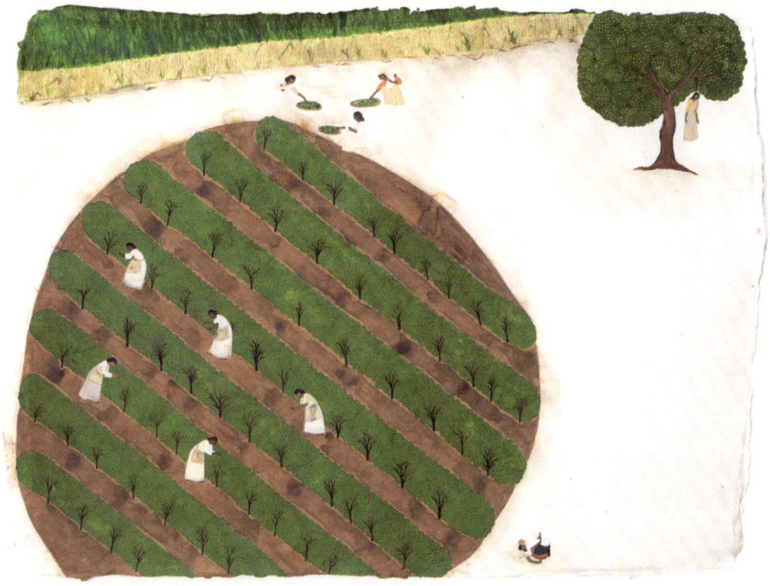

5.

SIN WAI KIN .... Sin Wai Kin (formerly known as Victoria Sin) uses drag to explore the many possibilities of identity, the artificial nature of gender archetypes and the restrictions placed upon the individual by entrenched systems of looking and naming. Born in Toronto in 1991, they began working with drag after moving to London in 2009. In addition to live performance and film Sin produces prints of their face using makeup and facial wipes. Created by applying the wipes to their painted face, these prints can be understood in a number of ways: as an archive of the characters Sin has become, synthetic skins that the artist has shed and as gestures of the myriad possibilities of selfhood. Makeup is a medium through which feminine archetypes have historically been constructed and maintained. In *A Strong Female Figure* (2016) exaggerated features fill a single wipe, a material Sin had elevated from disposable beauty product to fragile canvas. Sin's body has departed, and what remains on the textured surface of the wipe is the labour-intensive mask of the feminine. Lips have been enlarged and painted deep pink, eyebrows raised and arcuated, and the foundation that once covered the skin now fills the entire surface area. .... In a 2019 interview with *Another* magazine, Sin listed Marlene Dietrich, Marilyn Monroe and Jessica Rabbit as influences on their drag, describing them as 'cartoon-ish characters of Western femininity'. A number of the face prints are striking for the manner in which they suggest the idealized and manufactured image of white womanhood. Others combine landscape, portraiture and mythological creatures significant to East Asian cultures. For *Dragon Womxn* (2019) the face is painted in greens and yellows, the application of colours around the chin suggestive of scales. In *Maybe once you were a planet* (2019) the possibilities of the self assume astral dimensions. Eyebrows have become mountains, behind which a giant white sun rises against a blue sky. .... Sin approaches drag as a medium of speculative fiction: a space where identity and gender can be intensified, transformed and multiplied. During *If I had the words to tell you we wouldn't be here now* (2019) – a performance at Toronto Museum of Contemporary Art – Sin narrated a monologue while wearing a gown that clung to oversized prosthetic breasts. 'I am, I am, but also, but really I am...' they said. In the background a drumroll teased a revelation that never comes. In Sin's work, identity is a journey without a terminus. The printed faces are part of a wider reckoning with ideological structures that teach us to limit our understanding of identity, while also demonstrating the innate artificiality of female archetypes.
.... Rosanna Mclaughlin

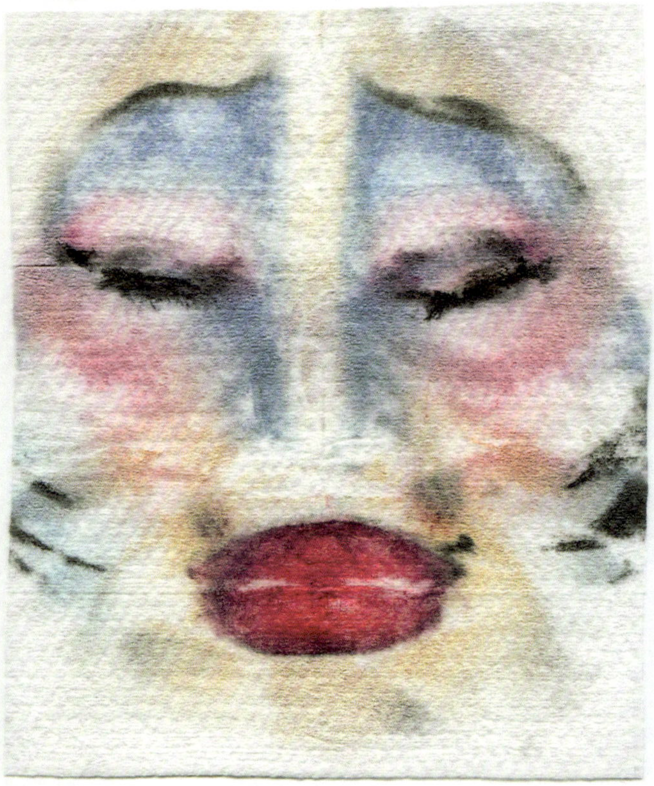

1.

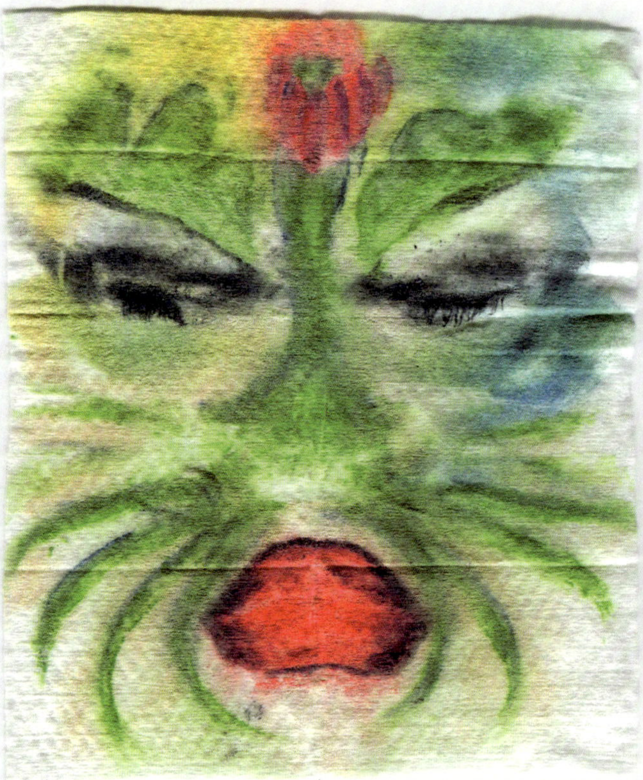

2.

Born 1991, Toronto. Lives and works in London.

1. *You have not been given the words to describe how multiple yourselves are*, 2019, makeup on facial wipe, 20.8 × 17 cm (8 ⅛ × 6 ⅝ in)
2. *A dream of wholeness and parts*, 2019, makeup on facial wipe, 20.8 × 17 cm (8 ⅛ × 6 ⅝ in)
3. *She must be used to it, she is so goddamn beautiful.*, 2017, makeup on facial wipe, 20.8 × 17 cm (8 ⅛ × 6 ⅝ in)

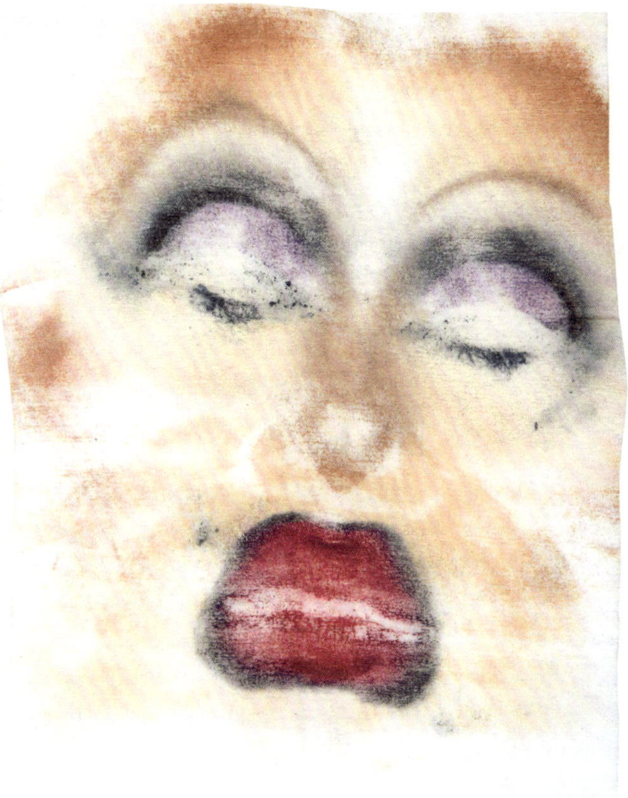

3.

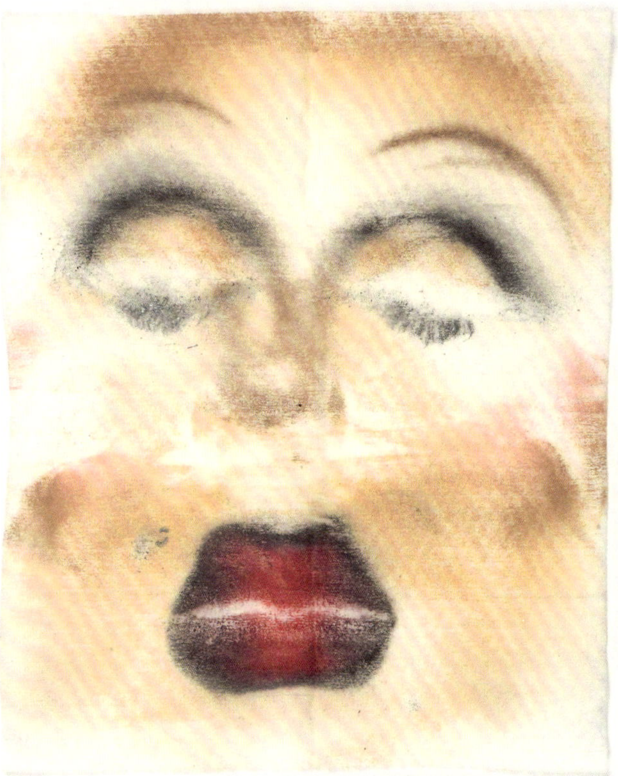

4.

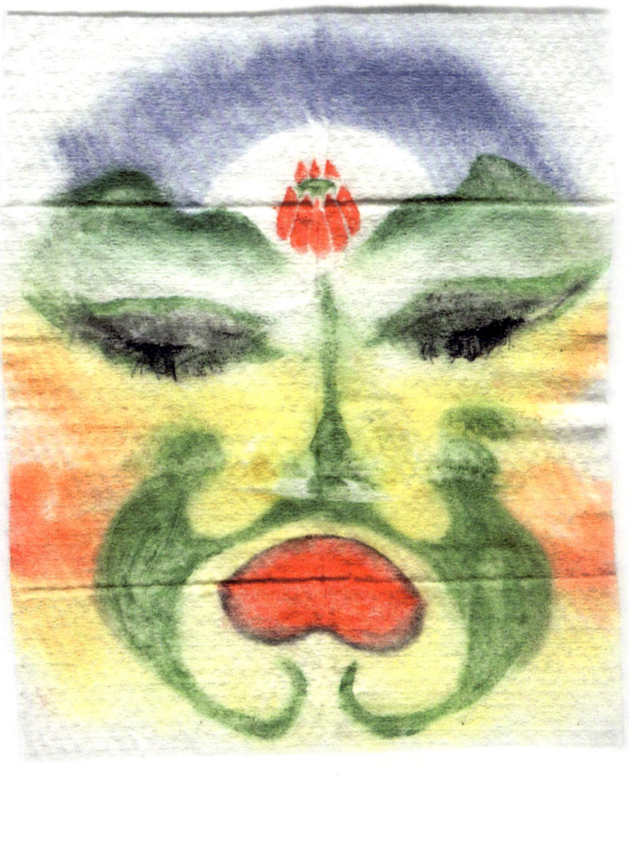

5.

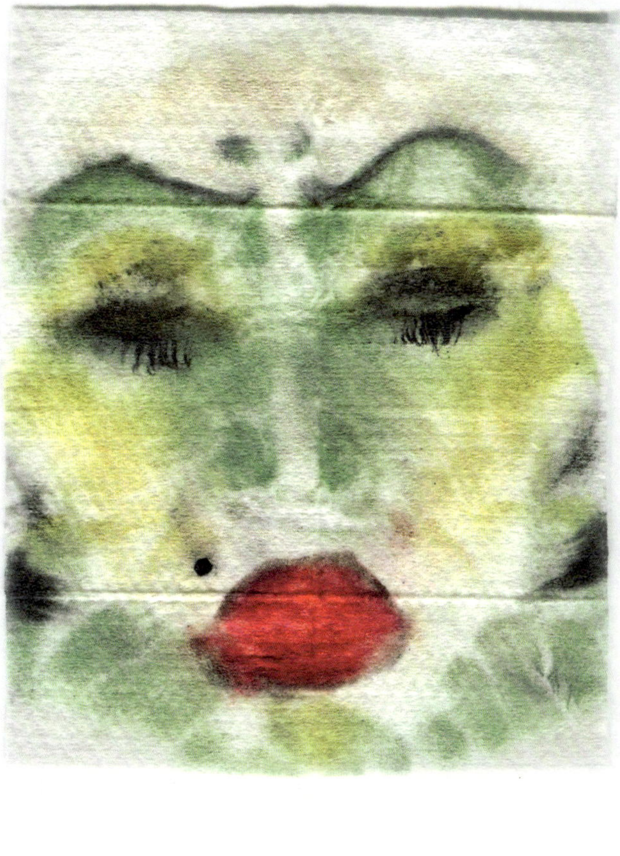

6.

4. *A Strong Female Figure*, 2016, makeup on facial wipe, 20.8 × 17 cm (8 ⅛ × 6 ⅝ in)
5. *Maybe once you were a planet*, 2019, makeup on facial wipe, 20.8 × 17 cm (8 ⅛ × 6 ⅝ in)
6. *Dragon Womxn*, 2019, makeup on facial wipe, 20.8 × 17 cm (8 ⅛ × 6 ⅝ in)

EDUARDO STUPÍA....... 'An explosion in a shingle factory.' The description once used by the critic of *The New York Times* to characterize Marcel Duchamp's (1887–1968) Cubo-Futurist provocation *Nude Descending a Staircase (No. 2)* (1912) fits the art of Eduardo Stupía to a tee. For decades, his complex compositions have played catch-me-if-you-can with viewers' eyes and conventional pictorial sensibilities. If his pictures routinely oscillate between figuration and abstraction, they also consistently establish harmonies from repeated tangles of lines, marks, blots, dots, erasures and stains. Working mainly in black and white, and drawing on a diverse range of media that includes pencil, charcoal, acrylics, graphite, watercolours and ink, the Argentine artist creates pictures that are characterized by fields of expansive mark-making. Unlike the legendary North American variant of all-over application, Stupía's bottom-of-the-world version relies principally on drawing as a methodology. Even when using paint on canvas, he faithfully devotes equal attention to each area of his surfaces. What draws the viewer's gaze are not brushstrokes and drips, but the repeated use of a wavering line that appears, alternately, crabbed and seismic. .... The basic building blocks of Stupía's practice are twofold: drawing and collage. His pictorial signs and drawings at times resemble cursive scribbles in an unknown language; they also recall Chinese scroll paintings, which for centuries have featured a timeless combination of landscape and calligraphy. In Stupía's case, the disparate elements of his compositions are not so much seamlessly resolved as roughly juxtaposed. 'I am not an illustrator,' he has asserted. Instead, he claims, his artworks contain the attributes of controlled chaos: 'Pictorial signs and drawings and the written word are like magnetic fields that attract and repel one another with equal intensity he told the Spanish-language magazine *Arte Al Día*. .... The septuagenarian Stupía has long described his work as made up of 'abstract landscapes'. But stare at one of his drawings for a while and you will think you recognize conventional objects and vistas – even as they fall apart the second they cohere into visual sense. His prosaically titled etching and ink drawing *Landscape* (2017), for instance, appears to hide hundreds of faces, bodies and figures, the way fluffy clouds do the face of Jesus or a welter of randy bunnies – depending on who's looking. A similar work on canvas, *Untitled* (2015), describes an endless number of clusters of frustrated and spiky geometries: at a glance, they look like they might have been drawn with an Etch A Sketch. Another pencil, graphite and charcoal work on canvas, *Landscape* (2012) – Stupía prefers non-allusive titles – describes a moonscape that is both familiar and foreign. The drawing channels the biomorphism of Roberto Matta (1911–2002) and Yves Tanguy (1900–55), but in monochrome, made far more shadowy, labyrinthine and strange.
.... Christian Viveros-Fauné

1.
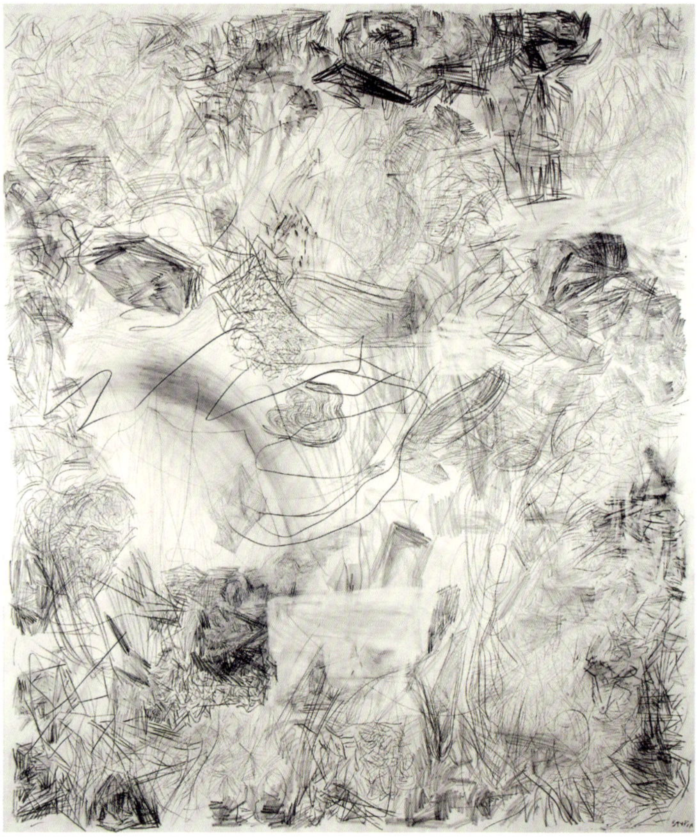

2.
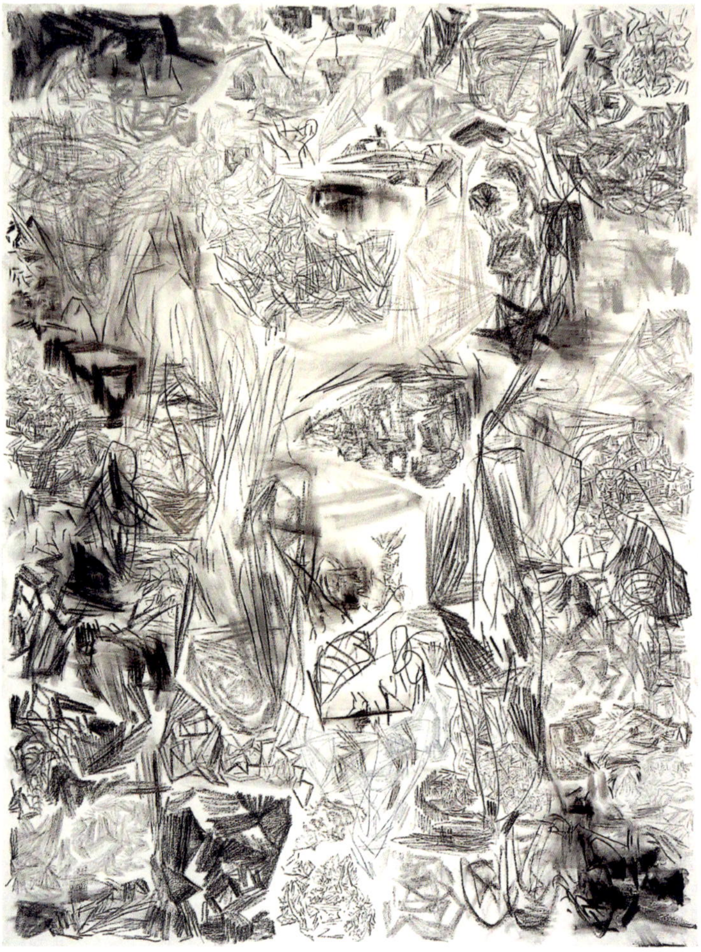

Born 1951, Buenos Aires. Lives and works in Buenos Aires.

1. *Untitled*, 2016, pencil, graphite and charcoal on paper, 140 × 120 cm (55 × 47 in)
2. *Untitled*, 2015, pencil, graphite and charcoal on canvas, 180 × 140 cm (71 × 55 in)
3. *Landscape*, 2012, ink, charcoal, graphite, pencil, pastel and acrylic on canvas, 200 × 300 cm (79 × 118 in)
4. *Landscape*, 2017, etching and ink on paper, 165 × 230 cm (65 × 90 ½ in)

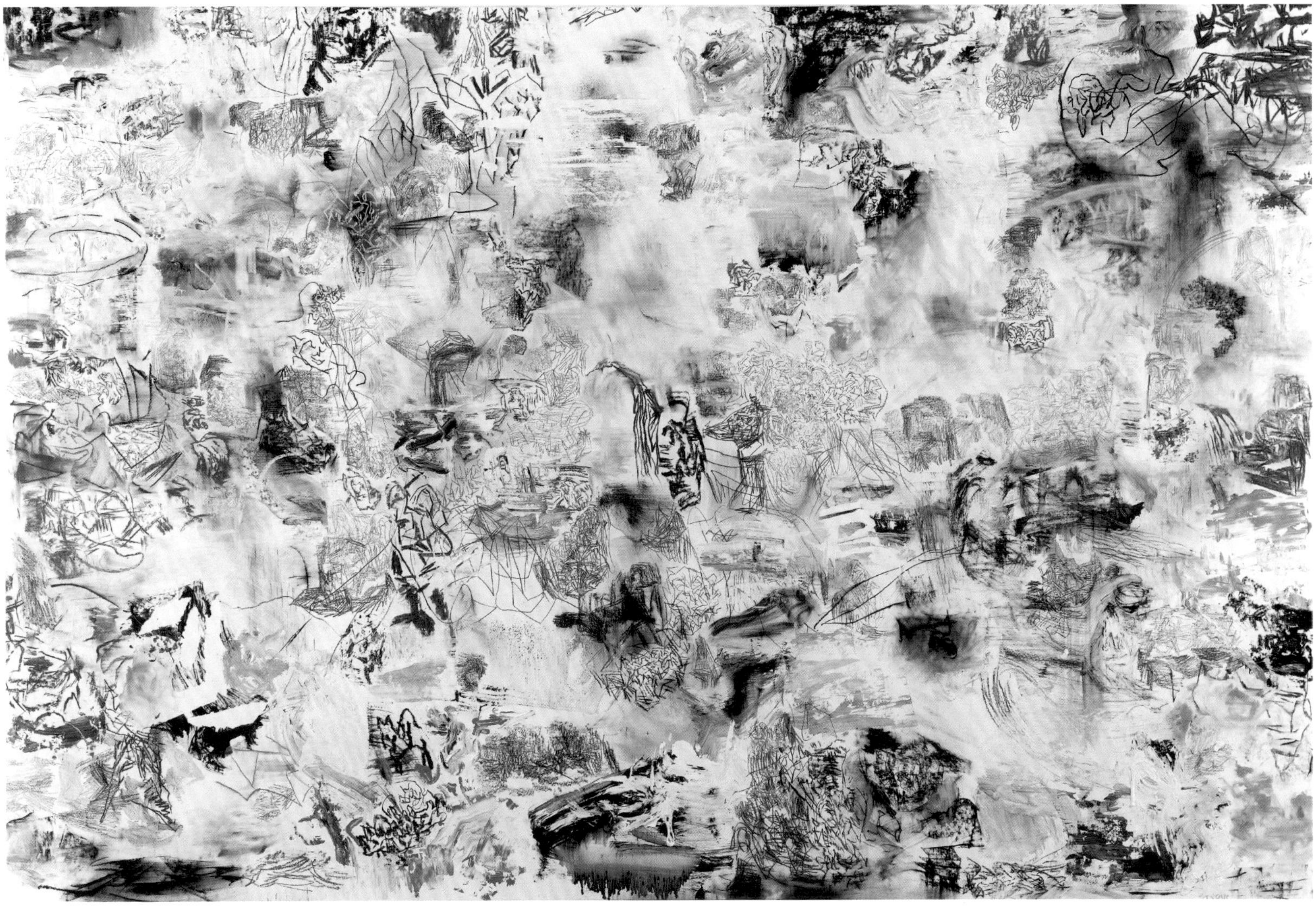

3.

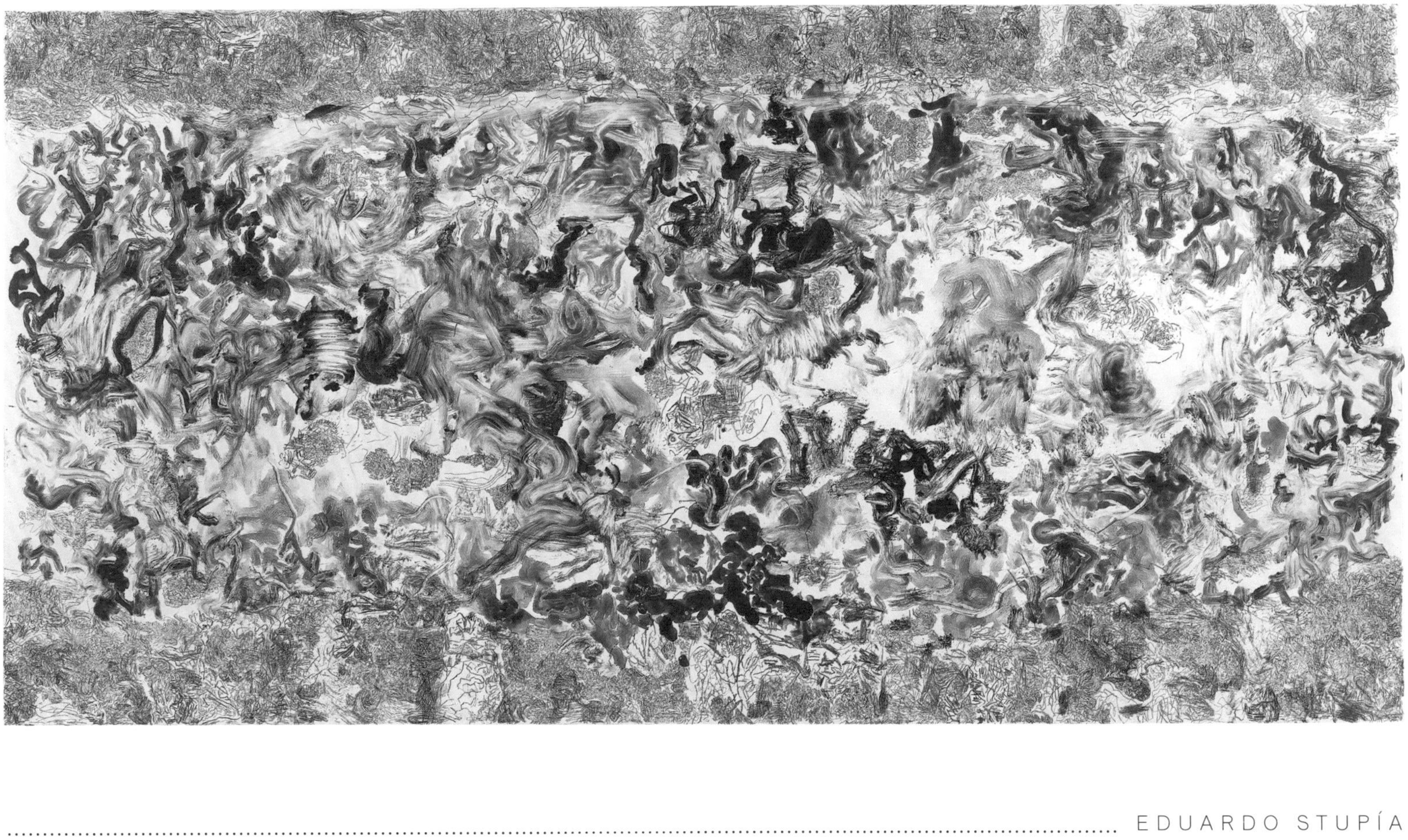

4.

A N G E L A   S U .... Intrigued by early maps and drawings of machines and natural forms from the era of European colonialism, Angela Su makes black and white drawings that have the deceptive appearance and authority of anatomical studies. But they are not scientific or authentic representations of human bodies. Rather it is the discrepancy between her personal and subjective interpretation of what a body looks like and its objective representation that fascinates the artist. Having studied for a degree in biochemistry in Canada, she subverts the assumed embodiment of scientific truth inherent within anatomical diagrams. Her process involves taking apart a drawing of the human body, breaking it down into internal organs, bones and various parts, before then reassembling everything into a new organism, which could be a plant, an insect or even still a person. Su's reinvented drawings maintain the authoritative air of science but in fact work to destabilize the accepted understanding of the human body. In *Rorschach Test No. 1* (2016) she puts three sets of commingled genitalia together, one above the other. One is male, one female and the third a she-male. Their totality is a depiction of some orgy-like sex act. The scientific presentation gives the viewer licence to look at, and into, the body when otherwise such an act would have been considered voyeuristic, pornographic and even a little bit perverse. Su heightens the effect by drawing on drafting film, a mix between plastic and paper used by architects. These films are smooth, translucent and sensual, and she describes the experience as like drawing on skin.

.... Su also engages the body when she embroiders on fabric, using hair instead of thread, finding the lengthy and labour-intensive process both contemplative and enjoyable. Whether working stitch by stitch or stroke by stroke, her practice is preceded by a considerable amount of research. Her reading of the 1997 book *The Body in Parts: Fantasies of Corporeality in Early Modern Europe*, for example, inspired her to take up embroidery and create her series 'Blasons Anatomiques du Corps Féminin' (Anatomical Coats of Arms of the Female Body), a collection of French poems from the Renaissance in which the female body was at once fetishized, revered and scorned, with each one being dedicated to a specific part, from hair to the knee to a teardrop. Su embroidered these texts on fabric, starting with the poem on hair. Gothic in tone, her drawings and embroidery works are fantasies of corporeality underlined by her childhood fascination with monsters, freaks or witches, and her reflections on the interrelations between our state of being and scientific technology. More recently, her embroideries and drawings of bodily fragmentation and schizophrenia make visible the physical and psychological experiences of living in Hong Kong.

.... Carol Yinghua Lu

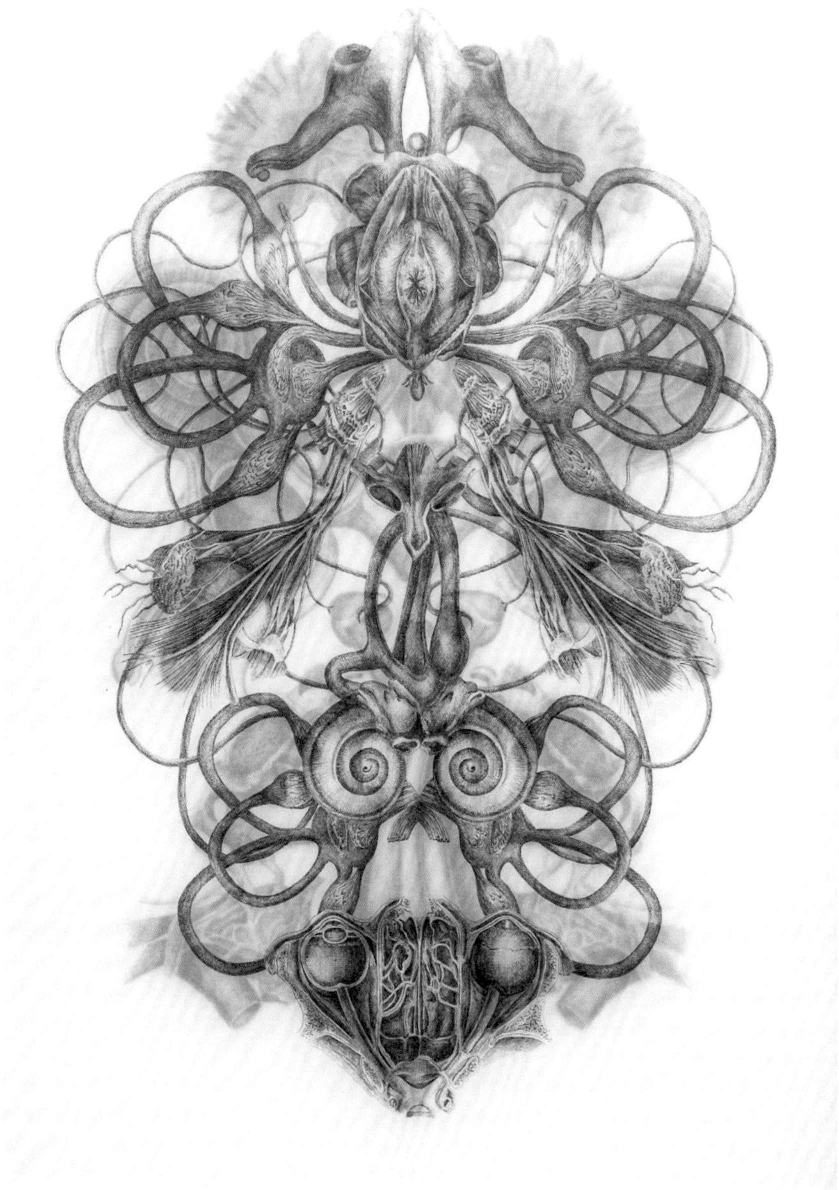

1.

Born 1958, Hong Kong. Lives and works in Hong Kong.

1. *Rorschach Test No. 1*, 2016, ink on drafting film, 155 × 100 cm (61 × 39 ⅜ in)
2. *Juno*, 2019, hair embroidery on fabric, 169.5 × 72.1 cm (66 ¾ × 28 ⅜ in)
3. *Augustina*, 2019, ink on drafting film, 169.5 × 72.1 cm (66 ¾ × 28 ⅜ in)

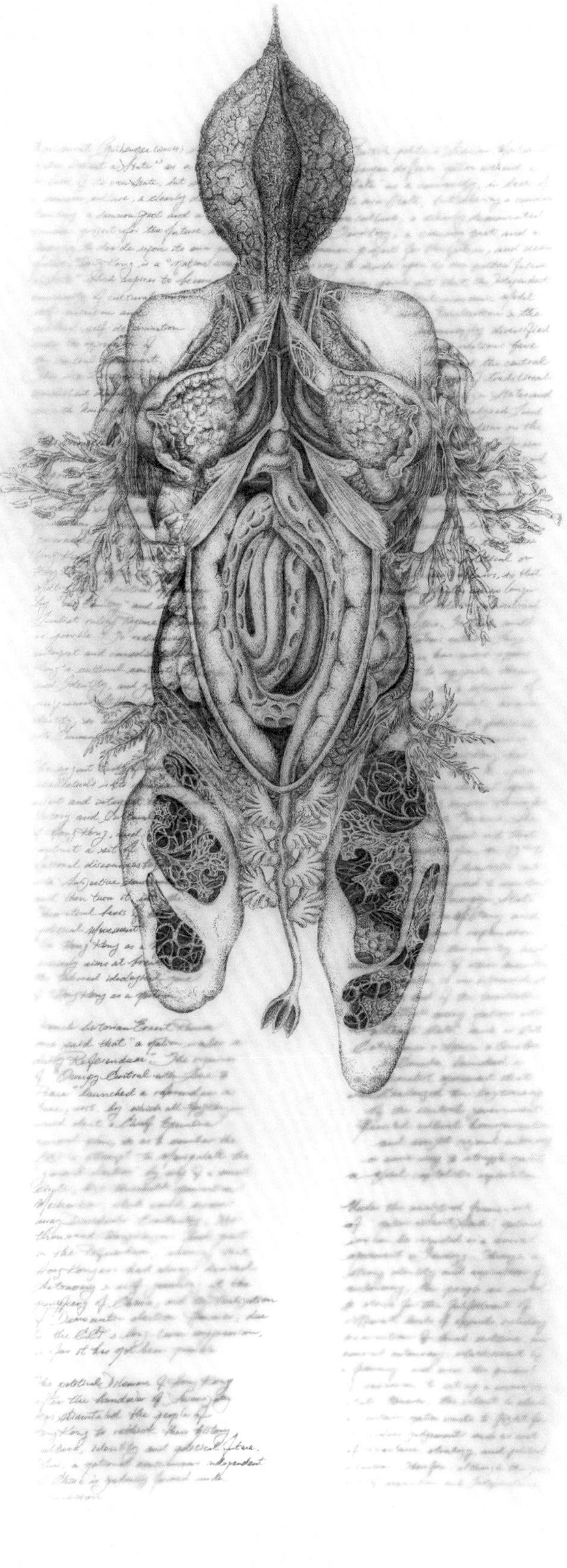

2.

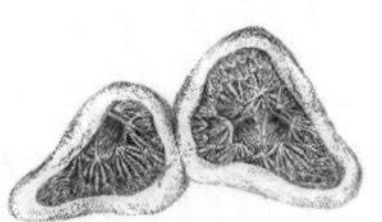

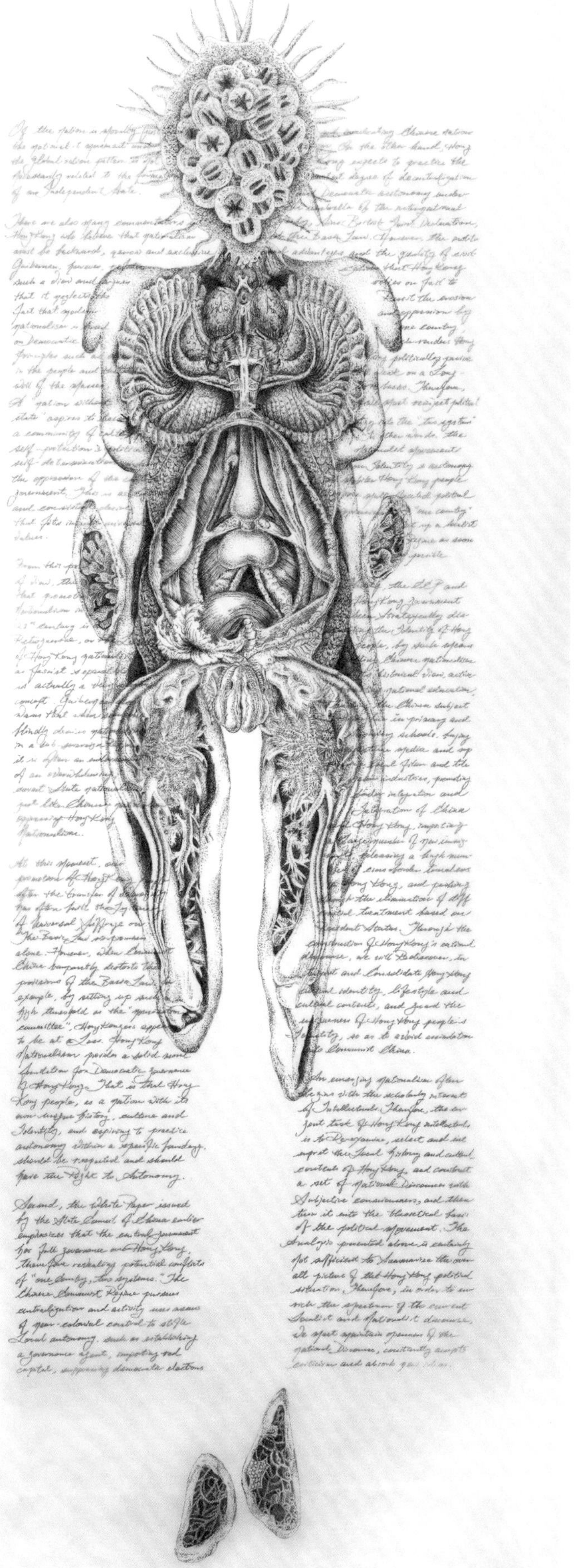

3.

JOSÉ ANTONIO SUÁREZ LONDOÑO.......

'Painting,' Pablo Picasso said, 'is just another way of keeping a diary.' Rarely has that phrase – which has given cover to countless instances of rote journal-keeping – defined an artist's oeuvre more than in the case of José Antonio Suárez Londoño. The Colombian artist's métier is not painting but drawing, yet he has turned what might otherwise be a modest practice into an ever-expanding visual encyclopedia. .... Done in, among other media, pencil, ink, gouache and watercolour on notebooks and bits of scrap paper, the Medellín-born artist's efforts encompass both individual drawings and a multi-volume visual autobiography. For decades, Suárez Londoño has kept up entries in regular instalments – like a picture-peddling version of Norwegian author Karl Ove Knausgaard's six-volume autobiographical novel *My Struggle* (2009–11). Together they constitute a taxonomy of thought that, to employ a phrase French philosopher Michel Foucault once used to describe a short story by Jorge Luis Borges, bears the stamp of our age, our memory and our geography. .... Suárez Londoño owes the inspiration for his signature process to two eureka moments. In the mid-1990s, while residing temporarily in Daytona Beach, Florida, he bought a black marker and a small notebook, which he slowly filled while reading Brian Eno's diaristic *A Year With Swollen Appendices* (1996). Soon after, in 1997, Colombian writer Héctor Abad Faciolince suggested that he and the artist collaborate: Suárez Londoño would produce a drawing a day for a year and Abad Faciolince would respond with writing. The project never materialized, but it helped launch the artist's best-known work: yearly notebooks that he fills with seemingly unconnected drawings of objects, landscapes, portraits, textile patterns, reproductions of Old Master paintings and colour studies. .... Like a modern-day Francisco Goya (1746–1828) labouring over the *Caprichos* (1797–8) and *The Disasters of War* (1810–20), Suárez Londoño charts time passing as a welter of images that he often accompanies with gnomic text. A sort of inventory of the world – among other subjects, he favours pictures of maps, animals, plants, intertwined figures, dancers, machine parts and letters, as well as indices of natural phenomena – his images are usually accompanied by a hand-written time stamp and miniscule notes in French, English or Spanish. As most accountants know, counting brings clarity; Suárez Londoño's drawings accrue like receipts, recording a life's joys and wages. .... Suárez Londoño's work abounds with references to artists, writers, objects, songs, news items and specific artworks. One of the sources he has mined can be seen in his multi-part *The Journal of Eugène Delacroix* (1999). In response to the diary of the great French Romantic painter (1798–1863), the Colombian produced 365 drawings inside a calendar year, working on his already expansive subject from 1 January to 31 December 1999.

.... Christian Viveros-Fauné

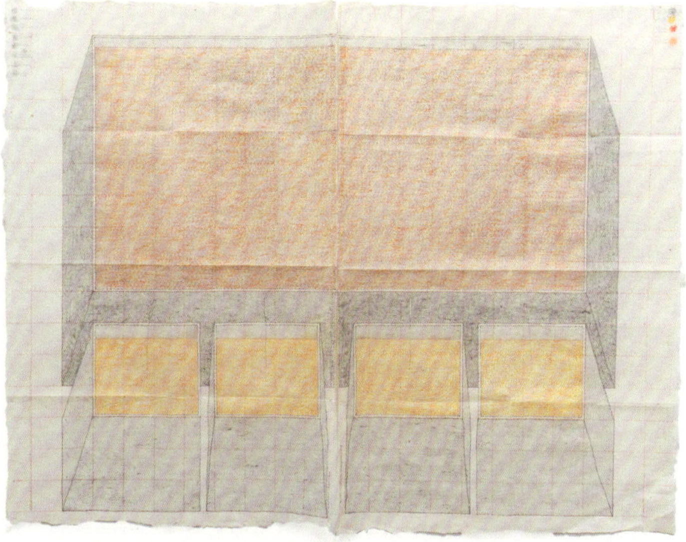

1.

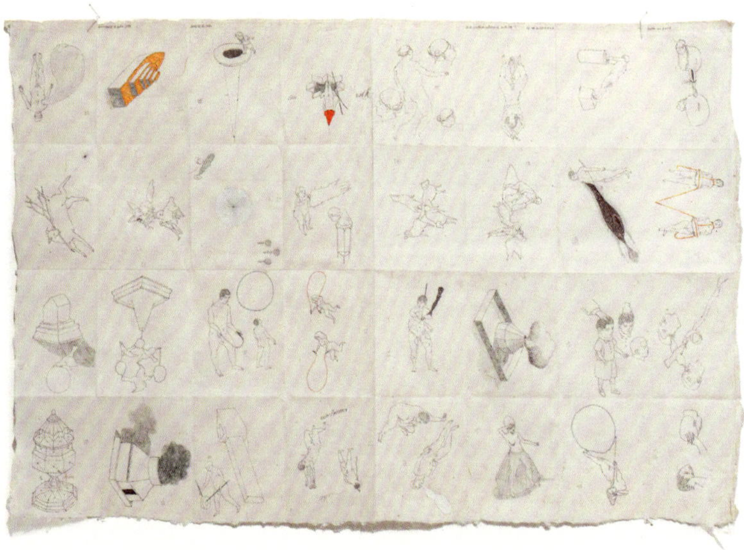

2.

Born 1955, Medellin, Colombia. Lives and works in Medellin.

1. *Dibujo*, 2019, ink, watercolour, gouache and pencil on paper, 77 × 101 cm (30 ¼ × 39 ¾ in)
2. *Dibujo*, 2019, ink, watercolour, gouache and pencil on paper, 50 × 76 cm (19 ⅝ × 30 in)
3. *The Journal of Eugène Delacroix*, 1999 (detail), ink, watercolour, gouache and pencil on paper, wooden frame, one of 12 frames, each 80 × 120 × 6 cm (31 ½ × 47 ¼ × 2 ⅜ in)

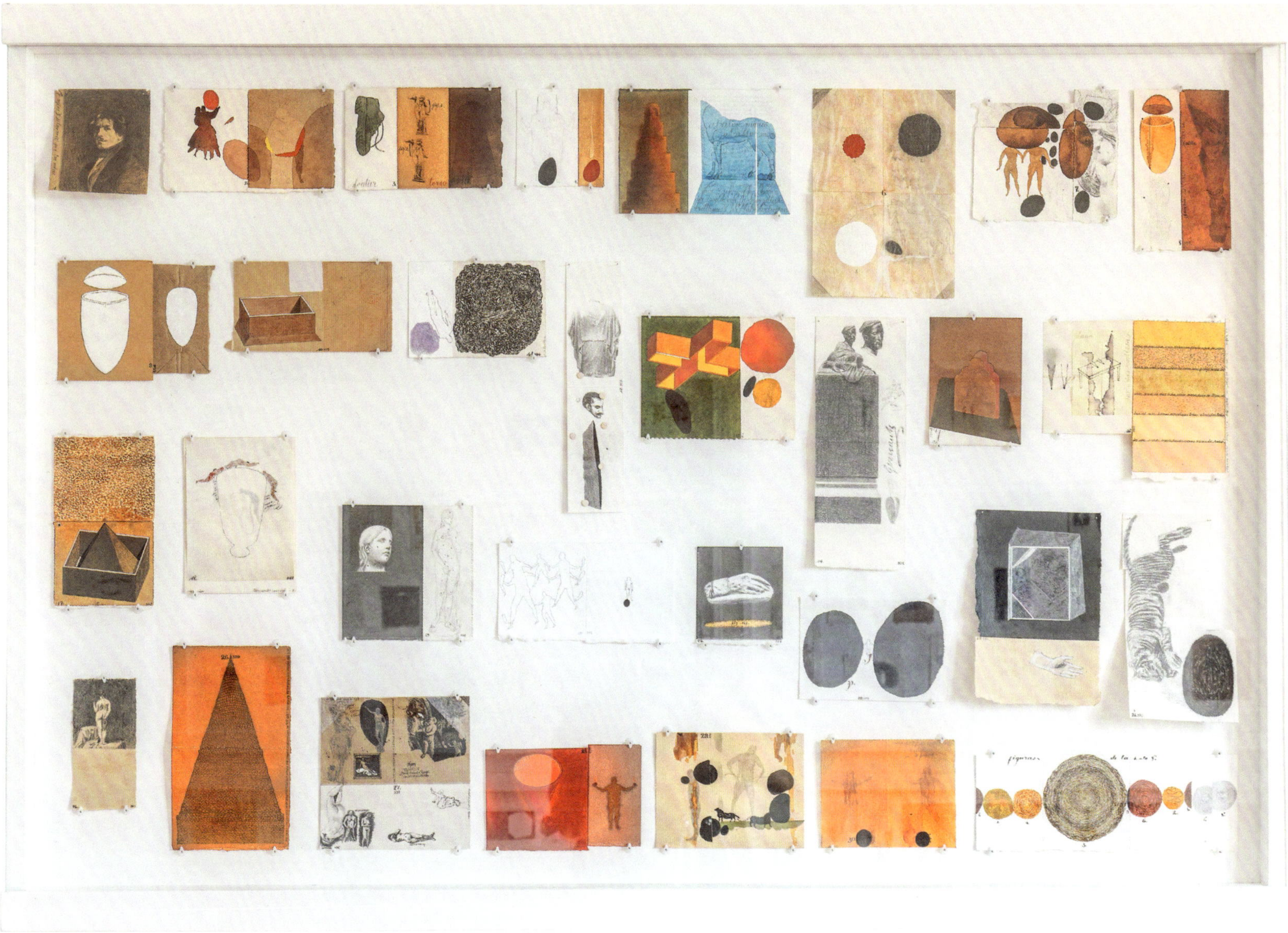

3.

PAMELA PHATSIMO SUNSTRUM.......

Growing up with sci-fi novels and high fantasy movies in the 1980s, Pamela Phatsimo Sunstrum is fascinated with exploring parallels between ancient cosmology and advanced theories in science; both investigate fundamental questions such as who we are, why we are here, how the universe was made and what it is made of. These are not merely abstract questions for the artist. She relates to them by creating an alter-ego – Asme (as me) – as well as the figures of her ancestors, or time-travelling parallel versions of herself who don Victorian dresses or appear as doubles. Juxtaposing elements drawn from her experience of growing up in different parts of Africa, South East Asia and the United States, Sunstrum creates her own universe that reflects this exposure to diverse cultures. A blue lake, a smoking volcano, tropical plantations – these recurring natural scenes emerge subconsciously from her childhood memories. Her surreal drawings of collaged imagery feature what appear to be mainly African figures in scenes that cannot easily be identified as belonging to a particular place or a specific point in time. Often discussed in terms of Afrofuturism, her practice is characterized by multiple layers of imagery placed over one another, with traces of drawing visible under thin layers of paint....... Sunstrum's imagery originates from different cultural and historical genealogies, as well as geographical contexts ranging from volcanic or subterranean to cosmological landscapes. Her elaborate reconstructions of scenes, some real and some imagined, suggest complex narratives, rooted in discourses of postcolonialism, neocolonialism and transcultural identities. Art history offers another source in the construction of her modern-day mythology and she has referenced the trope of the classical hero who sets out on a quest or faces an apparently insurmountable challenge....... In her drawings on paper or wood panels, Sunstrum often models her characters after portrait photographs taken by African photographers in photo studios in West and South Africa. These formal representations of subjects dressed in their finest Western suits or traditional kaftans, posed against painted backgrounds or drapery are, to the artist, emblematic of colonial representations of African people in the history of photography. While borrowing their postures and dress, Sunstrum typically leaves the faces of her figures blank, rendering them anonymous and creating a sense of distance between her representations and her sources, as in the charcoal, ink and gouache drawing *Desirée* (2018). Her characters are usually set against sweeping and light-drenched vistas evocative of European romantic paintings; she deliberately dresses them in outfits of mixed origins, combining references from decorative arts, collections of old costumes, handmade finery and vintage clothing. In drawings such as *The Dove* (2018) and *Buffalo* (2017), the dynamic patterns on the characters' clothing, the carpet and the mountains in the background give a strong sense of rhythm.

.... Carol Yinghua Lu

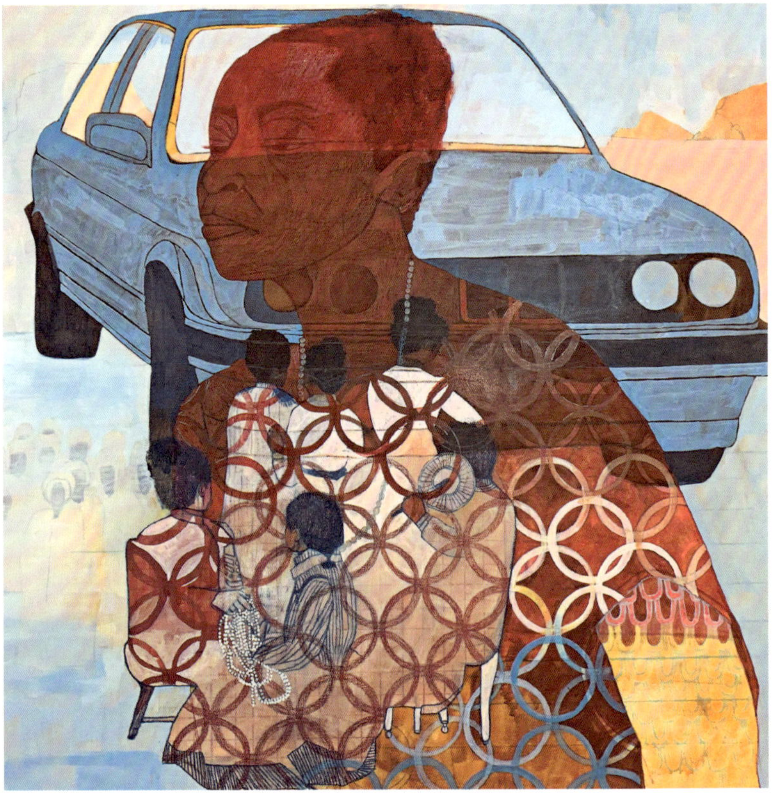

1.

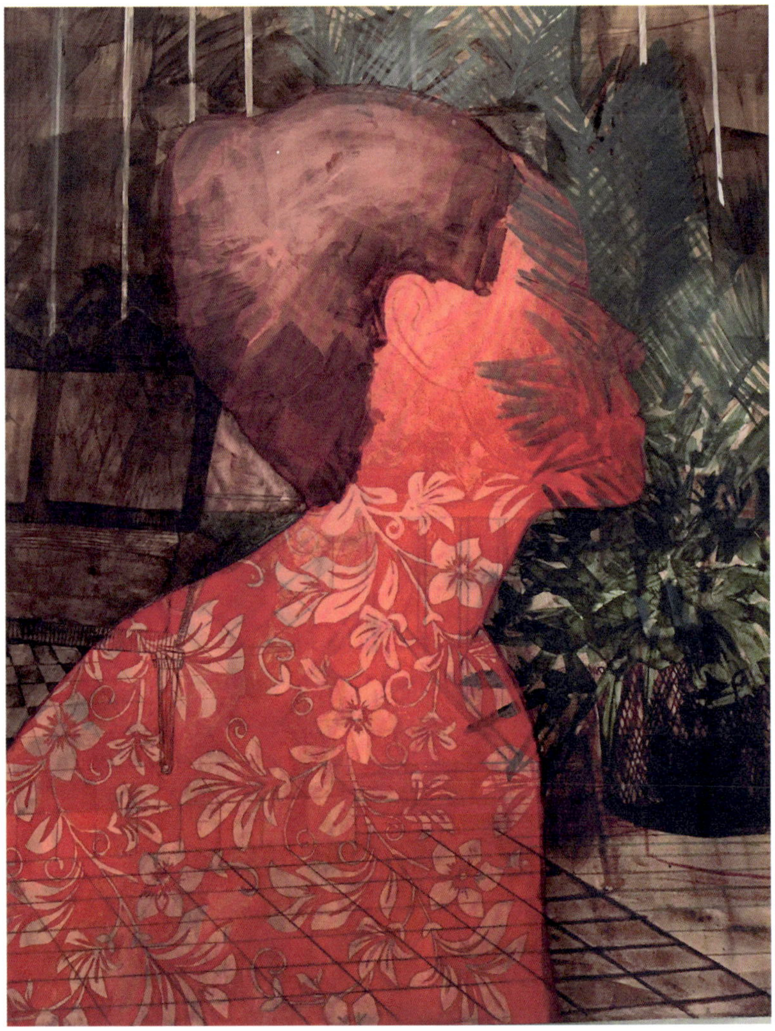

2.

Born 1980, Mochudi, Botswana. Lives and works in Ottawa and Johannesburg.

1. *Gusheshe II*, 2019, pencil and acrylic on wood panel, 76 × 76 cm (30 × 30 in)
2. *Wallflower*, 2018, pencil and acrylic on wood panel, 50 × 40 cm (19 ⅔ × 15 ¾ in)

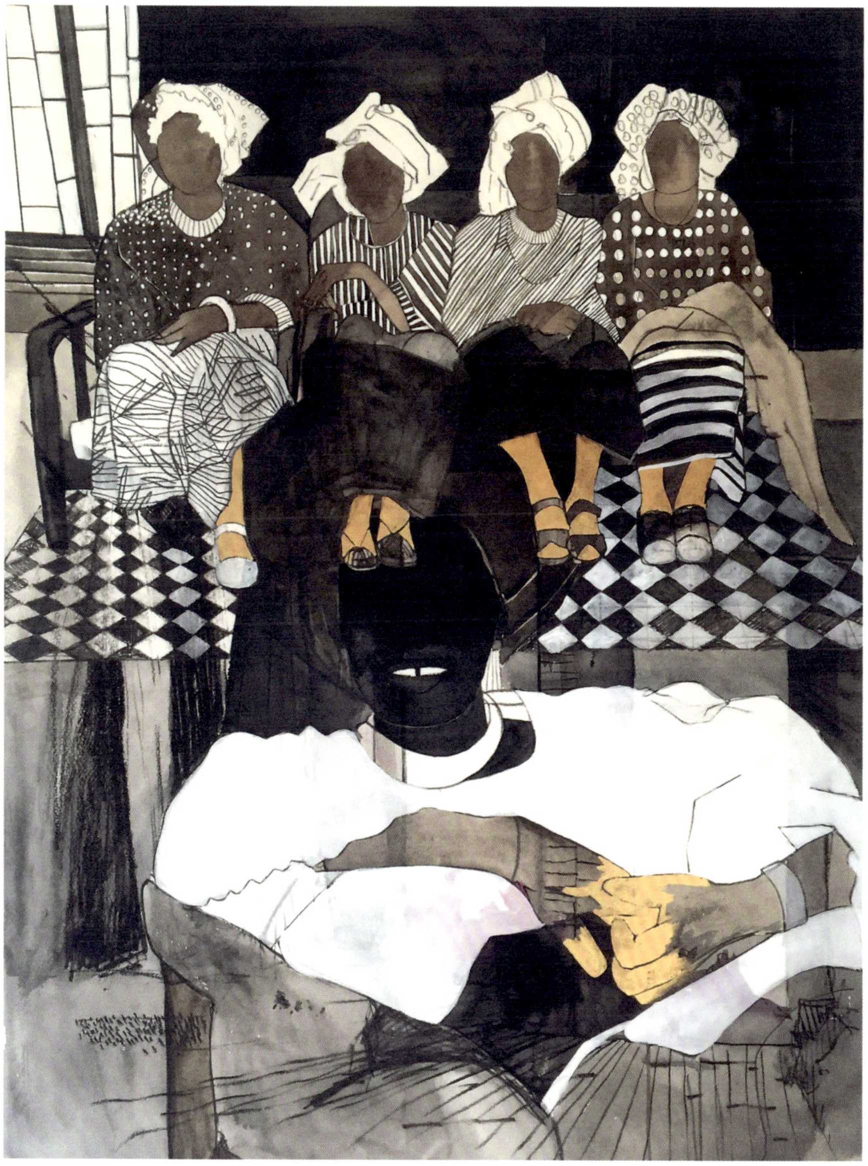

3.

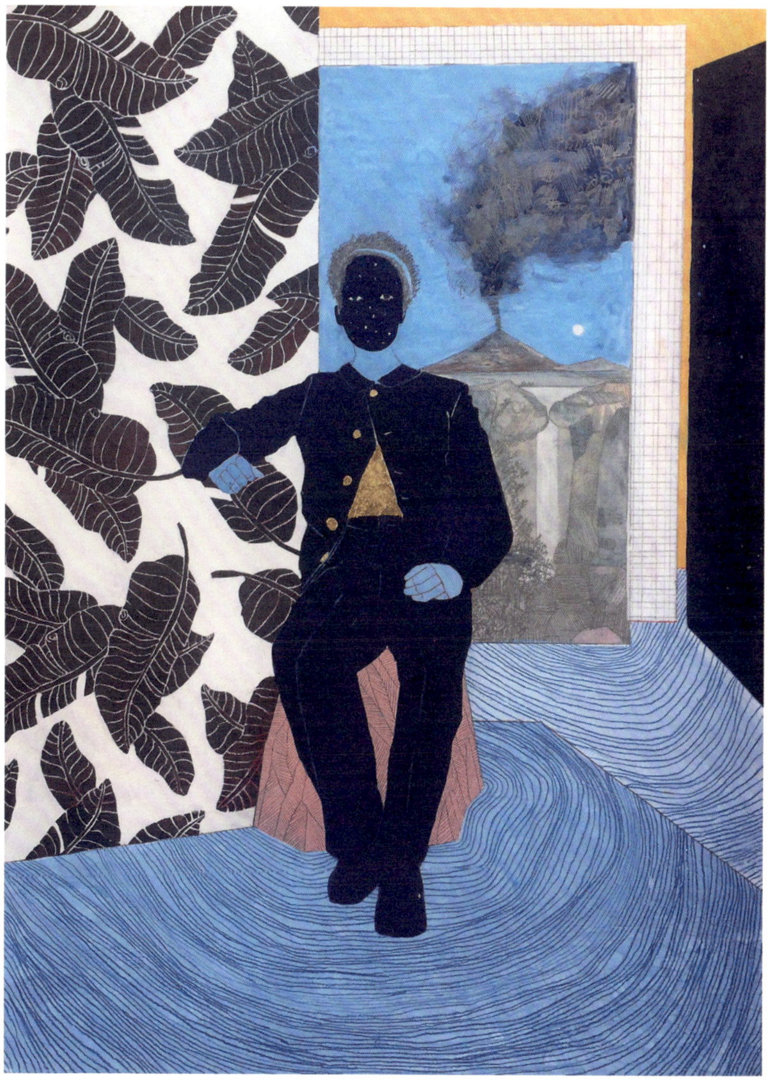

4.

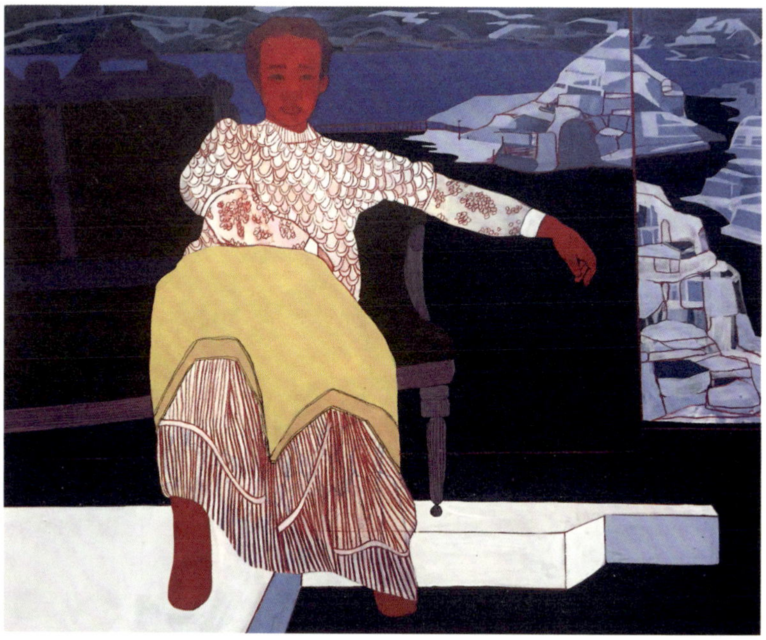

5.

3. *Desirée*, 2018, charcoal, ink and gouache on paper, 76 × 55 cm (30 × 22 in)
4. *Buffalo*, 2017, pencil, gouache and watercolour on wood panel, 40.5 × 30.5 cm (16 × 12 in)
5. *The Dove*, 2018, pencil and acrylic on wood panel, 40 × 50 cm (15 ¾ × 19 ⅔ in)

BHAGYASHREE SUTHAR .... Bhagyashree Suthar often draws with wax. She uses the encaustic technique – a favourite with the ancient Egyptians and Greeks, who would use beeswax or crystallized tree sap to make portraits. The wax Suthar uses is more industrial, sourced from her hometown of Jodhpur, India, and otherwise used in cosmetics or pharmaceuticals. The portraits she makes are not of people, but rather of fantastical landscapes dominated by geometric and architectural structures. She heats the wax – sometimes colouring it with multiple transfers from vividly hued kite paper – and delicately applies this on to her drawings on canvas or wood. Her compositions are full of shapes that are governed by the Fibonacci sequence: their spirals grow exponentially, looping in and out of the canvas or frame. While her drawings have architectural references, the symmetrical patterns of nature also inspire her. When she is not using wax, she turns to a process that is even more intricate, drawing dense topographies of symmetrical lines that have a three-dimensional quality, working primarily in ink on paper. Her shapes fluctuate like optical illusions, curving both inwards and out. .... Suthar grew up in a family of furniture makers, and the complex interaction between structure and design is made visible in her work. In *Untitled* (2019) she has drawn a labyrinth of indigo-pigmented patterns in ink on paper. There are starfish and swirling stairways; decked pathways and sharp-tipped pyramids; and domed ceilings that open to patchwork skies. We are in a city that is tumbling in on itself, as though spinning around a tilted axis. In her work, Suthar bends space, and in viewing her pieces it feels as though we are on unstable ground – about to fall into an altered state of gravity. When Suthar works in wax, once the material has cooled, she uses a combination of tools to draw further into its surface. Her drawings thus sit in layers: both of material and of ornamentation and motif. 'Imagining the city of the future has long been a source of fascination for me,' she said in a 2016 interview with *The Better India*, and her drawings are infused with a utopian, futuristic tinge. She is speculating as to how space and dimension will change in the futures to come, and experimenting with how form could evolve and learn from natural symmetries. There are no accidents in Suthar's work; she leaves no room for them. She is extremely precise with the structures in her drawings and everything is composed to an almost perfect degree of measurement. There is an integral logic to what is going on here: Suthar is building cities, plotting their fine details with her extended and sharp lines. .... Skye Arundhati Thomas

1.
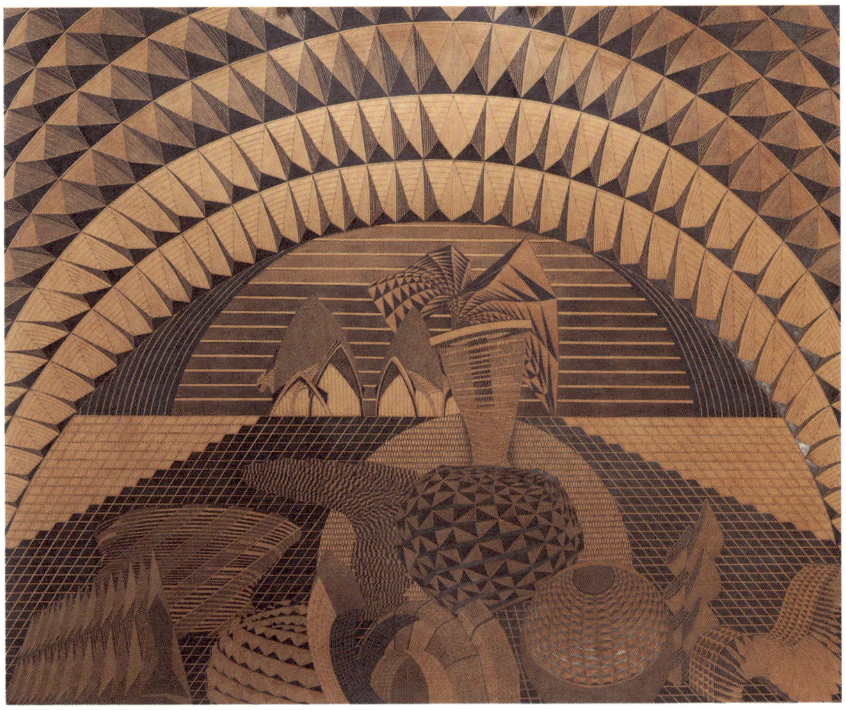

2.
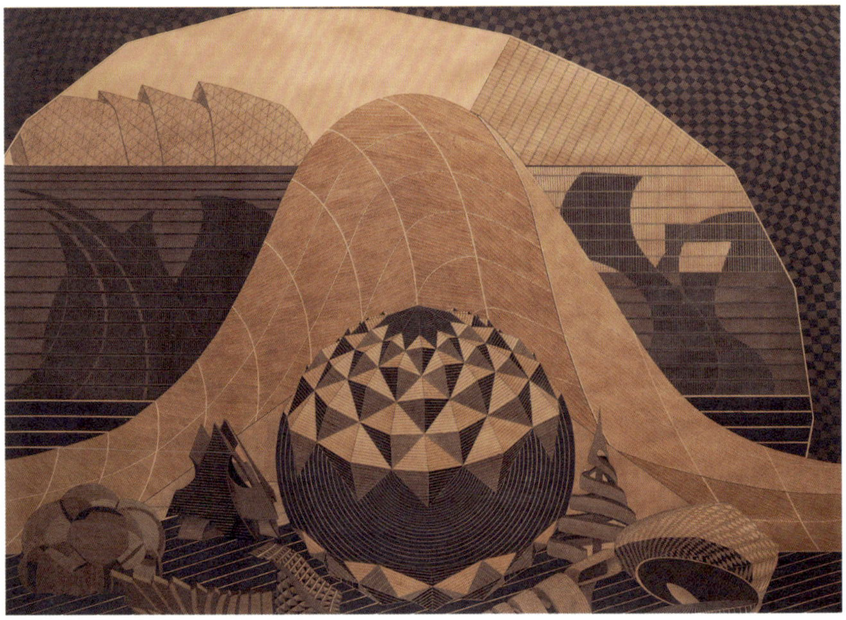

Born 1991, Jodhpur, India. Lives and works in Vadodara, India.

1. *Untitled*, 2017, pen and ink on paper, 121.9 × 152.4 cm (48 × 60 in)
2. *Untitled*, 2017, pen and ink on paper, 121.9 × 152.4 cm (48 × 60 in)
3. *Untitled*, 2019, indigo pigment, pen and ink on paper, 152.4 × 182.8 cm (60 × 72 in)
4. *Untitled*, 2019, pen and ink on paper, 143.2 × 213.3 cm (56 ⅜ × 84 in)

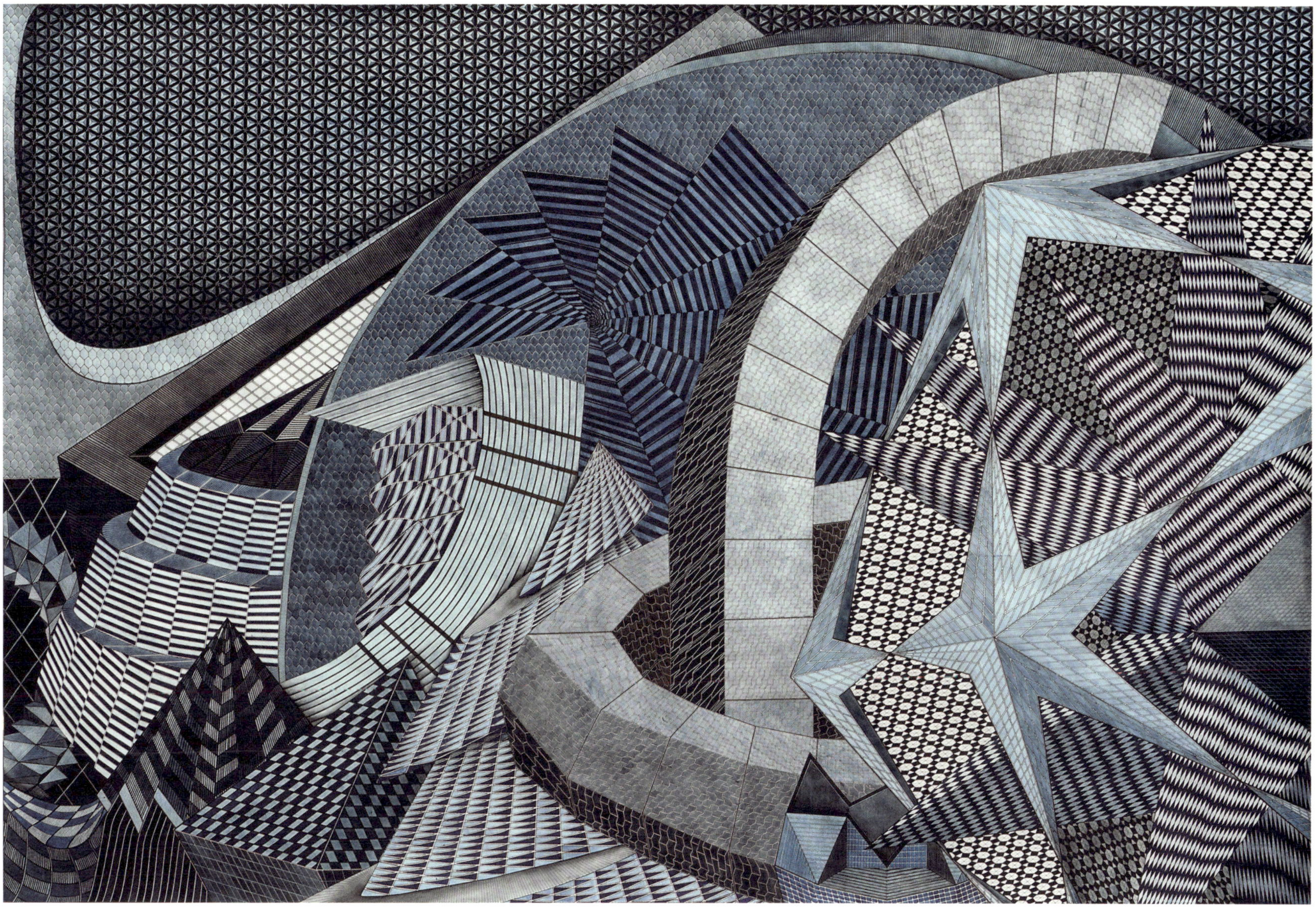

3.

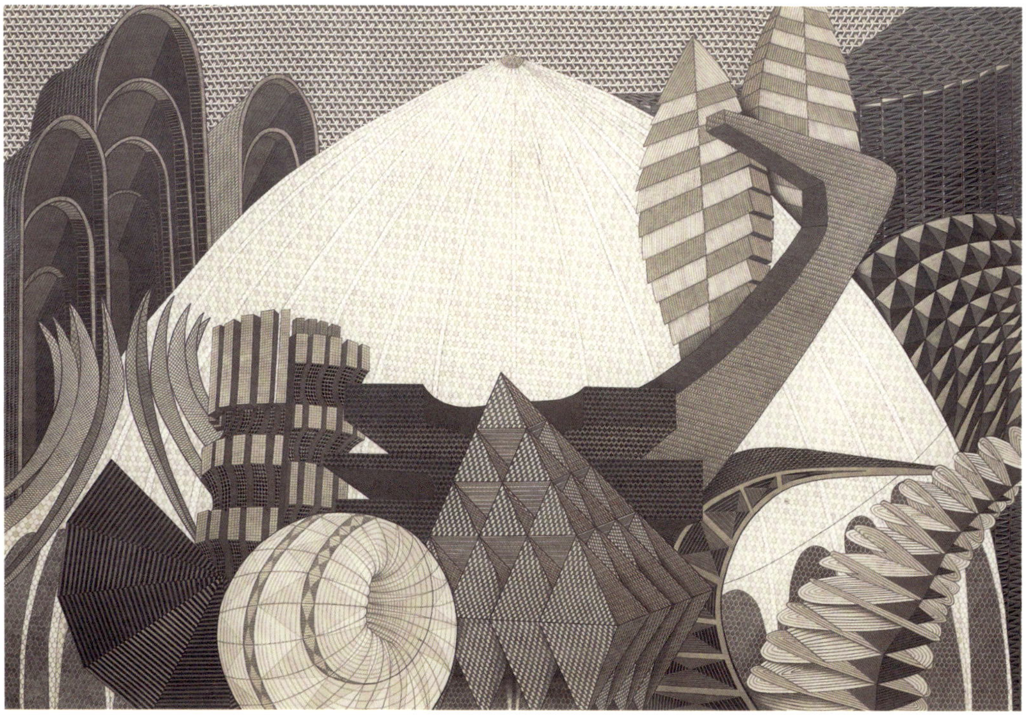

4.

EMMA TALBOT……. Emma Talbot's art developed in the emotionally raw context of bringing up two sons without her partner, following his death in 2006. The intimacy of small works on paper suited her psychological stories of piercing emotional honesty, which detailed the couple's previous life together. Talbot's idiosyncratic pictorial language came out of those reflections on love and loss. Distended heads signal that thought dominates her figures, but their faces are blank – so the features don't carry the burden of meaning and viewers can therefore project themselves into the narrative. Rhythmic patterning, with the waves of long hair often providing the template, build up to swirling intensity. Talbot has also developed a unique calligraphy to integrate her inner monologue into the work – not her everyday handwriting, but a mixture of upper and lower cases and differing sizes that enables the maximum variation of emphases. Sometimes, indeed, her drawings are pure text……. From that relatively confined starting point, Talbot's methods and scope have expanded rapidly so that, in the words of curator Iwona Blazwick, she 'makes radiant drawings and polychromatic sculptures on an epic scale; and combines word and image to express the lyricism and the pain of subjectivity'. Large paintings on silk in multi-panel installations, textiles suggesting protest banners, sculpture and animation confidently tackle such global topics as the future of humanity, the balance of people and nature, and the addictive consequences of the digital. The personal is mapped on to the collective, with Talbot's remembered experiences and speculations on the subconscious linked to a mixture of references from popular and literary culture to explain, as she says, 'what it's like to be me, alive today'……. Small, text-free watercolours are still an important part of her practice, retaining much of her long-established language, but now grouped into suites of linked works with mythical undertones. *Sounders of the Depths* (2019) shares its title with Talbot's major show that year at GEM Museum for Contemporary Art in The Hague, which traced a path across several installations between birth and death as – in her words – 'epic moments that everyone has experienced or will experience, but which we are unable to remember or imagine'. The living were portrayed as sleepwalking between those two defining events. An accompanying text work enjoins us to 'listen / to the body of the world gasping in horror / once gathering in seeds, heavy with fruit, now barren and depleted / an open cry'. No wonder the sun in *Solar Flare* (2019) seems more ominous than generative, even before we get to *The Future Exploded* (2019). Fast forward and the aged woman using old methods in *The Future, Collecting Water* (2019) seems to come from a post-technological vision of what the future might hold.

……. Paul Carey-Kent

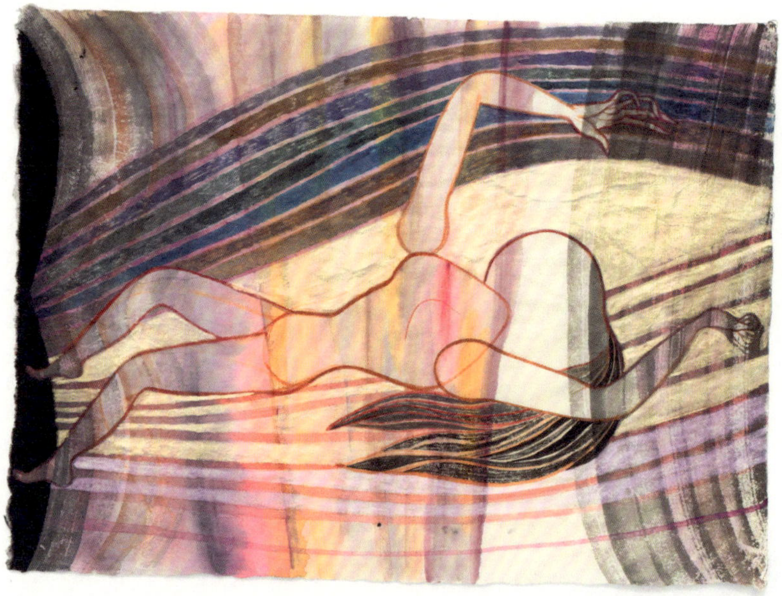

1.

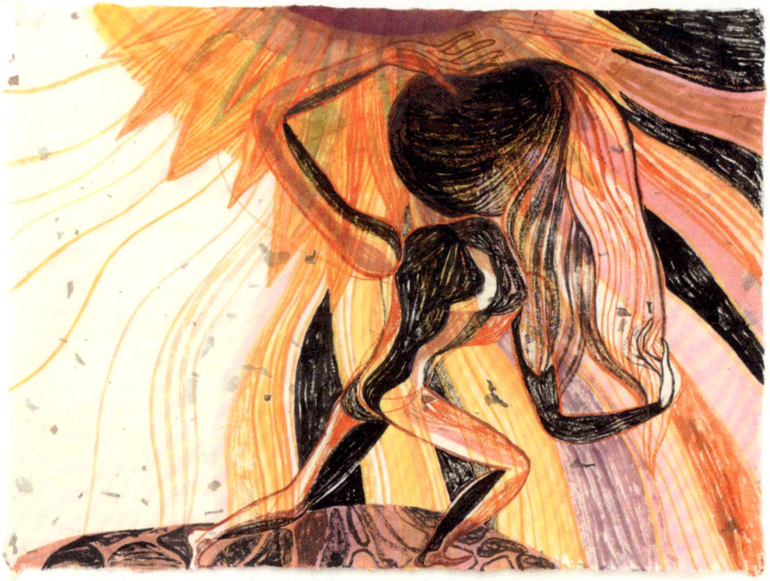

2.

Born 1969, Oldswinford, West Midlands, UK. Lives and works in London.

1. *Sounders of the Depths*, 2019, watercolour and gouache on lokta paper, 29.7 × 42 cm (11 ¾ × 16 ½ in)
2. *Solar Flare*, 2019, watercolour and gouache on lokta paper, 29.7 × 42 cm (11 ¾ × 16 ½ in)
3. *The Future Exploded*, 2019, watercolour and gouache on lokta paper, 29.7 × 42 cm (11 ¾ × 16 ½ in)
4. *The Future, Collecting Water*, 2019, watercolour and gouache on lokta paper, 29.7 × 42 cm (11 ¾ × 16 ½ in)
5. *From the Planet*, 2019, watercolour and gouache on lokta paper, 29.7 × 42 cm (11 ¾ × 16 ½ in)

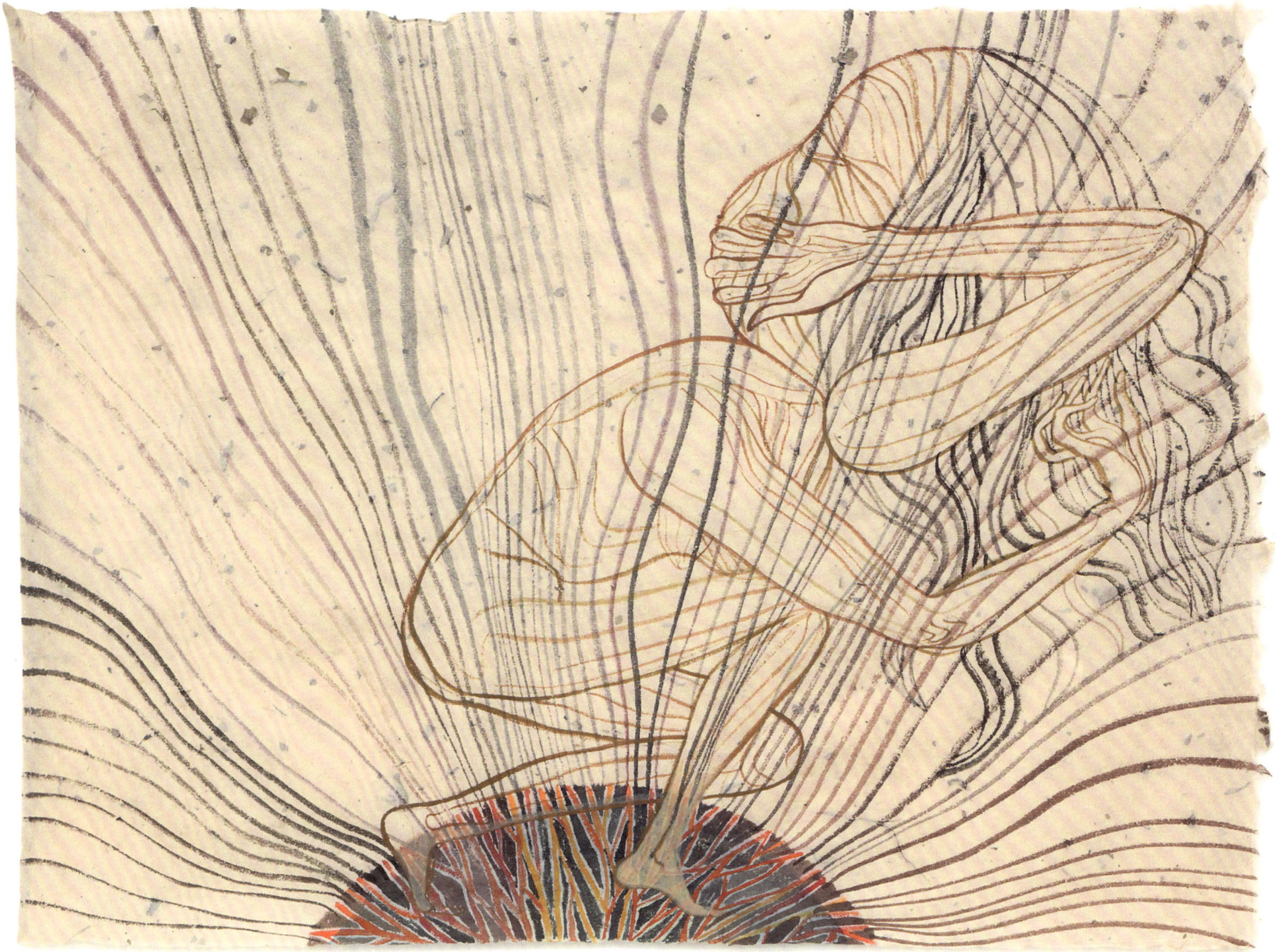

3.

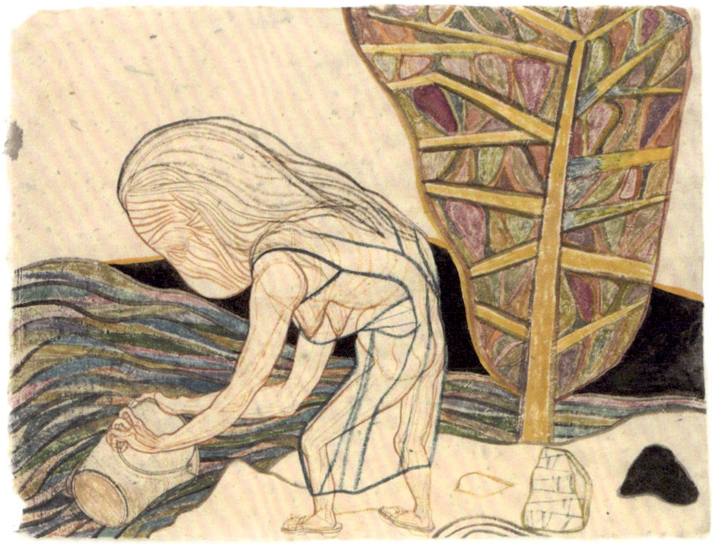

4.

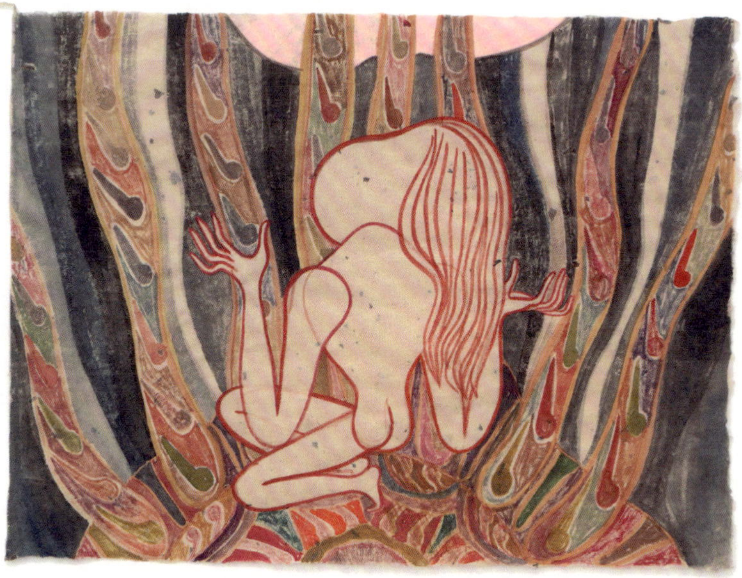

5.

KYLE THURMAN .... When Pennsylvania-born, Brooklyn-based Kyle Thurman was an adolescent, he was advised to consider a career as a soldier or an athlete, which has informed a substantial ongoing series of work. Entitled 'Suggested Occupation', it started at the end of 2015 with the artist making drawings in response to images of male soldiers and athletes he spotted in newspapers. Thurman's almost daily drawing practice offers a regular reminder of the very different lives he could have been leading. .... In *Suggested Occupation 13* (2016–18) Thurman depicts a young man wearing a bullet-proof vest and combat trousers, seated and asleep, his hands clasped on his lap. A fainter figure to one side is awake, reading or looking at something in his hands, just out of sight. They might be on their way back from a military exercise or sortie. The perhaps surprising choice of a bubble-gum pink paper enhances the tenderness of the image depicted – plus nobody looks tough when they're asleep. This is precisely where Thurman's critical thinking becomes evident – by extracting imagery of male figures from the original contexts in which they appear, he takes control of the narrative, sets his own scene for their redepiction and reinterpretation. How the media presents images of men, and how consumers respond to them, plays a significant role in how patriarchal and hetero-sexual paradigms are created, maintained or changed, and Thurman's works, in an understated though thoughtfully conceived and executed way, unpick these male stereotypes and archetypes. *Suggested Occupation 22* (2018), for example, depicts what might be soccer players after scoring a goal – their triumphant cries are almost tribal in their masculinity, yet the hand of one man on the chest of the other, allied to the gentle clasping of the two men's hands, could be interpreted as being decidedly homoerotic. Thurman's drawing reinforces that these two states are not mutually exclusive. .... *Suggested Occupation 4* (2016) shows two men lying on the ground; one has the other in a headlock. A figure stands behind wearing army trousers, his hands in his pockets. It is unclear if the men are engaged in a close-combat training activity or whether they are fighting, either in play or for real. Again, there is a sexual tension underlying the image, increased by the onlooking figure being bare-chested, while his face and expression remain unseen. The uncertainty of the dynamics leaves the drawing open-ended, unresolvable. Often seemingly 'unfinished' in the sense that they appear like sketches, with some sections shaded or coloured with pencils, pastels or markers, Thurman's drawings capture, often at close to life-size, fleeting moments of male interaction that challenge normative ideas of masculinity. .... Matt Price

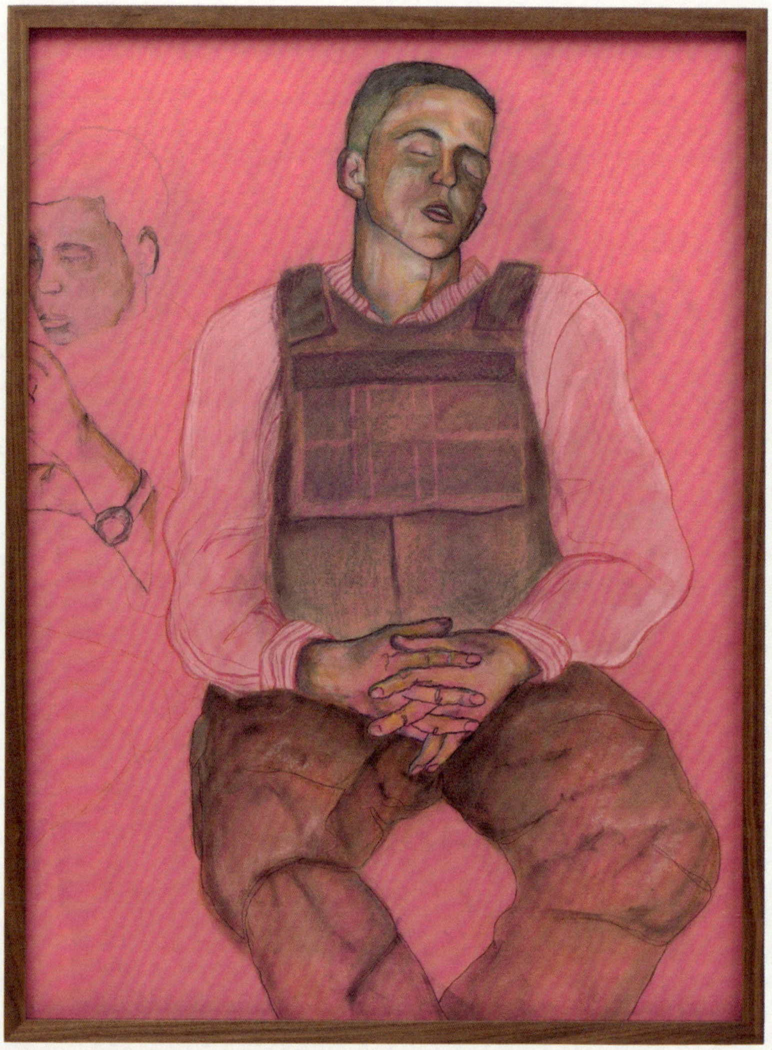

1.

Born 1986, West Chester, PA. Lives and works in Brooklyn, New York.

1. *Suggested Occupation 13*, 2016–18, charcoal, coloured pencil, marker and pastel on seamless paper in artist's frame, 114.3 × 86.7 × 4.5 cm (45 × 34 ⅛ × 1 ¾ in)
2. Installation view, 'Whitney Biennial 2019,' Whitney Museum of American Art, New York

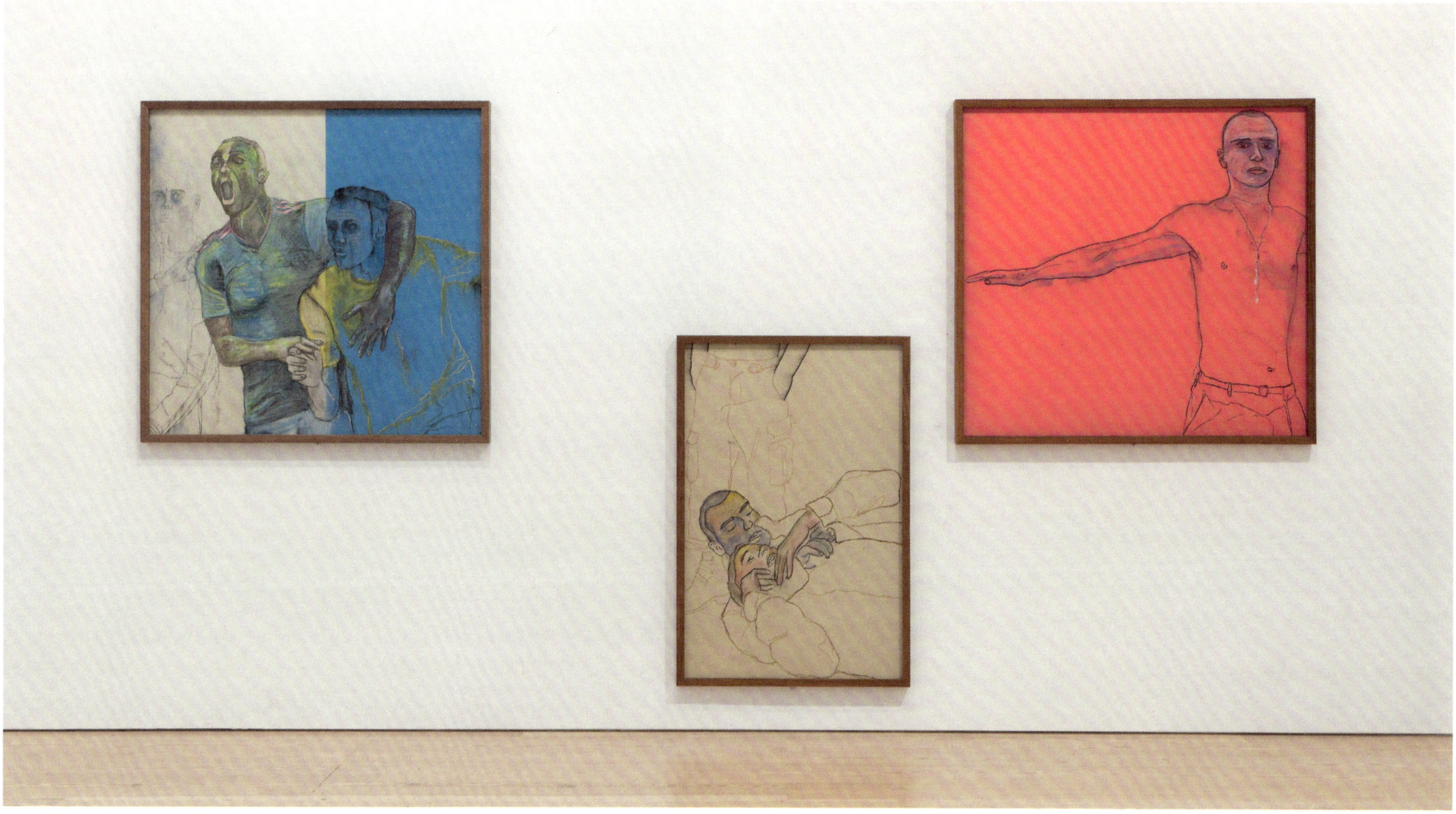

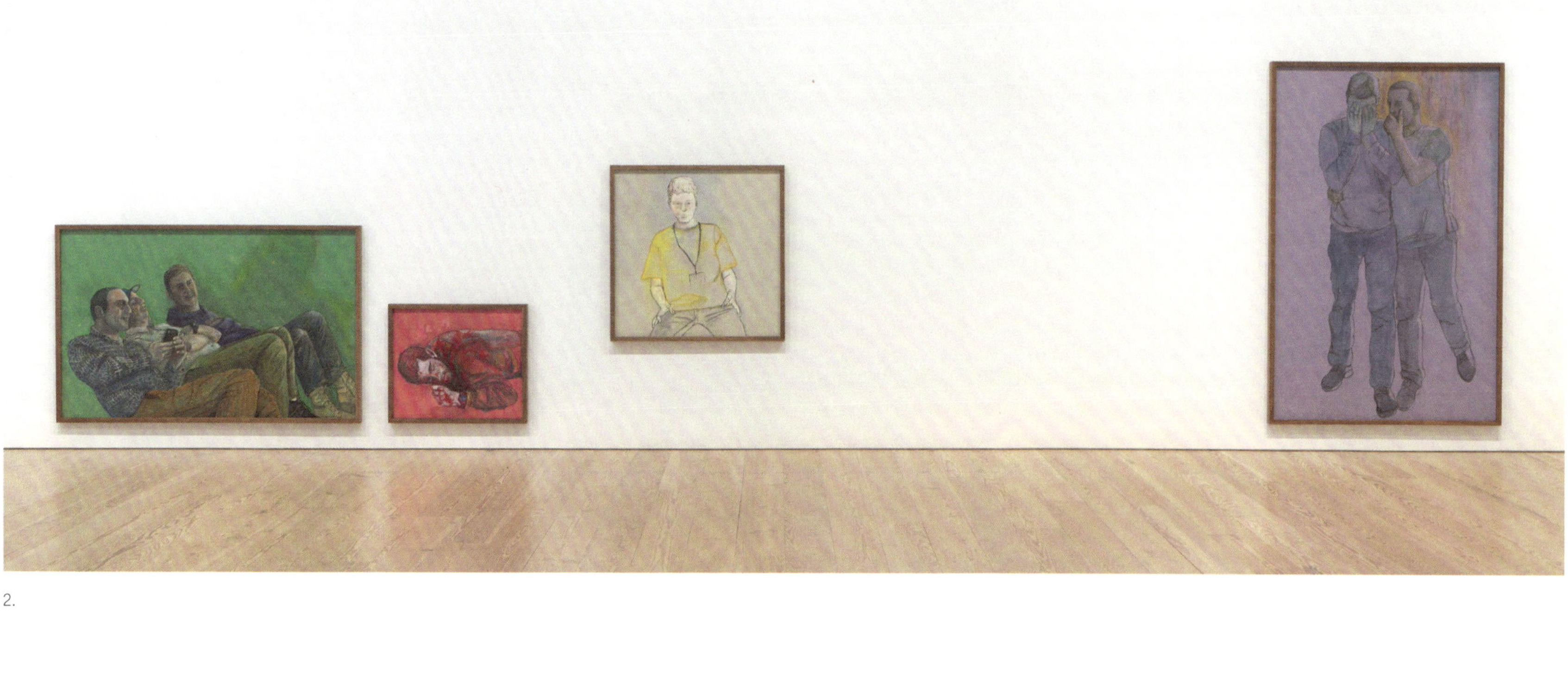

2.

VIKTOR TIMOFEEV....... Working across a variety of media, Viktor Timofeev creates haunting landscapes suffused with existential dread. In *(AB/AB)/B* (2018) multitudes of small, featureless figures cling to a large industrial-looking structure. These figures appear doomed to carry out a Sisyphean task, climbing to the apex only to fall back down and start their ascent again. On closer inspection, the structure reveals itself to be another, larger version of the same figure. The head has been cut open, revealing a maze-like grid in place of a brain. Like many of Timofeev's works, *(AB/AB)/B* is made using coloured pencil, with a palette of greys, reds and blues. A blurring effect gives the impression the entire scene is spinning, enhancing the sense of peril and hopelessness. Some figures crawl through the pathways of the maze; others leap over the edge into the masses below....... In his novel *Invisible Cities* (1972), Italo Calvino wrote that, 'Cities, like dreams, are made of desires and fears, even if the thread of their discourse is secret, their rules are absurd, their perspectives deceitful, and everything conceals something else.' A similar philosophy underpins Timofeev's drawings. His environments are filled with vague terrors, governed by unknown powers, rife with allegorical meanings that remain just beyond reach. *(AB/AB)/B* could be a depiction of the psychological turmoil of an individual or of an entire population toiling under totalitarian rule. Like waking from a distressing dream, the significance of which you are unable to fully place, the use of surreal imagery increases the mood of foreboding....... In an interview with the publication *TZVETNIK*, Timofeev described his works as 'a patchwork of worlds: passing thoughts, fantasies, desires, what-ifs, curiosities, hallucinations, relations, urgencies'. While each of his drawings appears to portray a different scenario, they share certain factors in common. The most prominent of these is the grid, which forms a base layer in many of his compositions. No figures are present in the large wall drawing *Godflower X* (2019), made with hard pastel, but the ground is completely covered in a maze-like grid that stretches to the horizon line. It is not possible to ascertain how tall the walls of this architectural structure are, nor can you see what lies beneath. Out of the dark crevices, twisting forms rise like monstrous weeds towards a blank sky. Their stems and leaves do not look like those of plants, but a hybrid of mangled steel and human sinew. This is a place of death and danger, of which there is no end and from which there is no escape.
.... Rosanna Mclaughlin

Born 1984, Riga, Latvia. Lives and works in New York.

1.
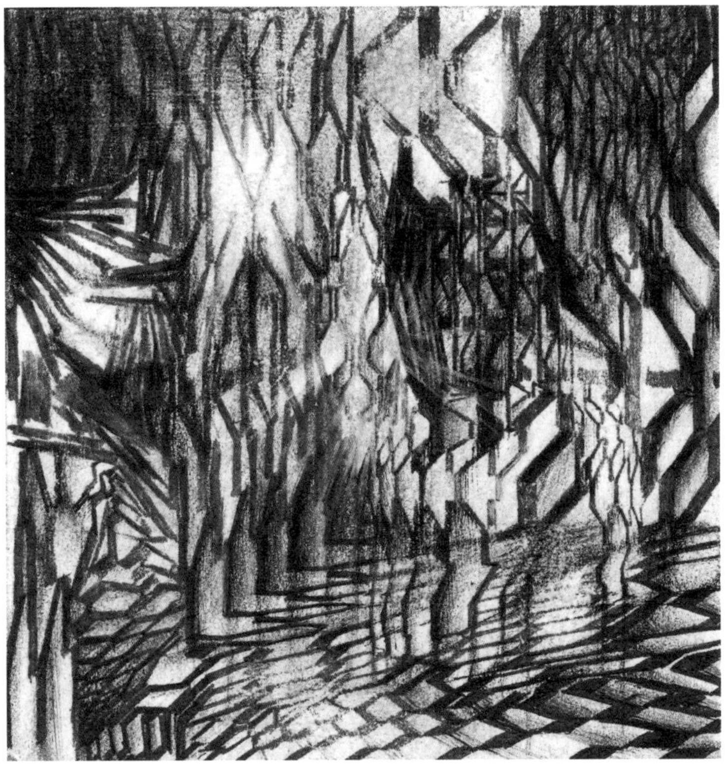

2.
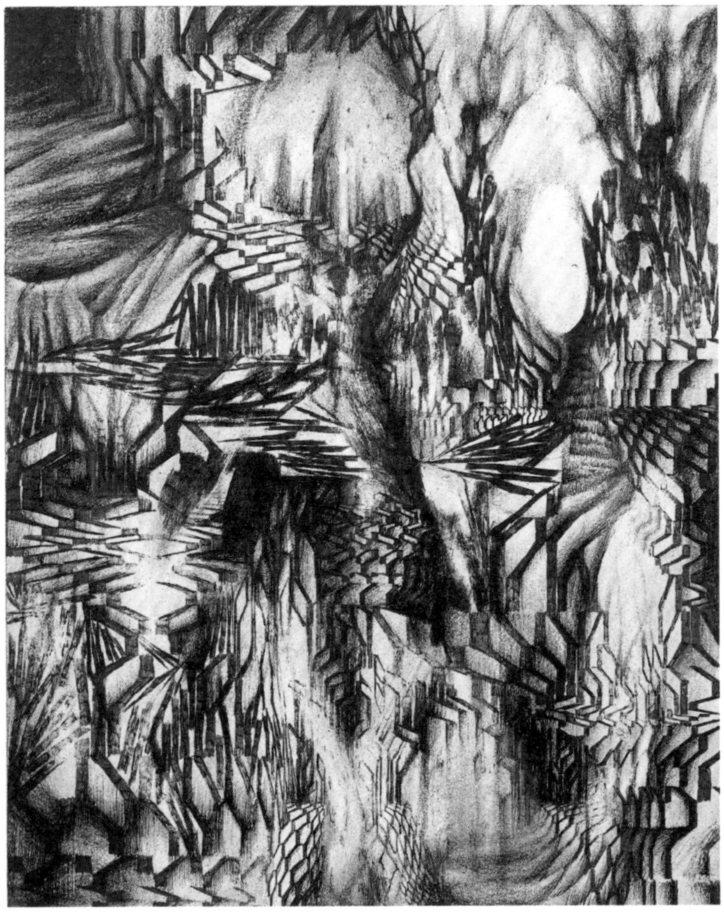

1. *12.17.2009* from 'Dailies (2009 ×19)', 2019, ink and pencil on paper, 15 × 15 cm (5.9 × 5.9 in)
2. *Floating Ossuary*, 2019, ink and pencil on paper, 35 × 28 cm (13 ¾ × 11 in), from 'I had amnesia once or twice', Polansky Gallery, Brno, Czech Republic
3. *(AB/AB)/B*, 2018, coloured pencil on paper, 35 × 25 cm (13 ¾ × 9 ¾ in), from 'God Room', Alyssa Davis Gallery, New York
4. *AB + AB*, 2018, coloured pencil on paper, 35 × 25 cm (13 ¾ × 9 ¾ in), from 'Cosplay at the Family Dinner', The Sunroom, Richmond, Virginia

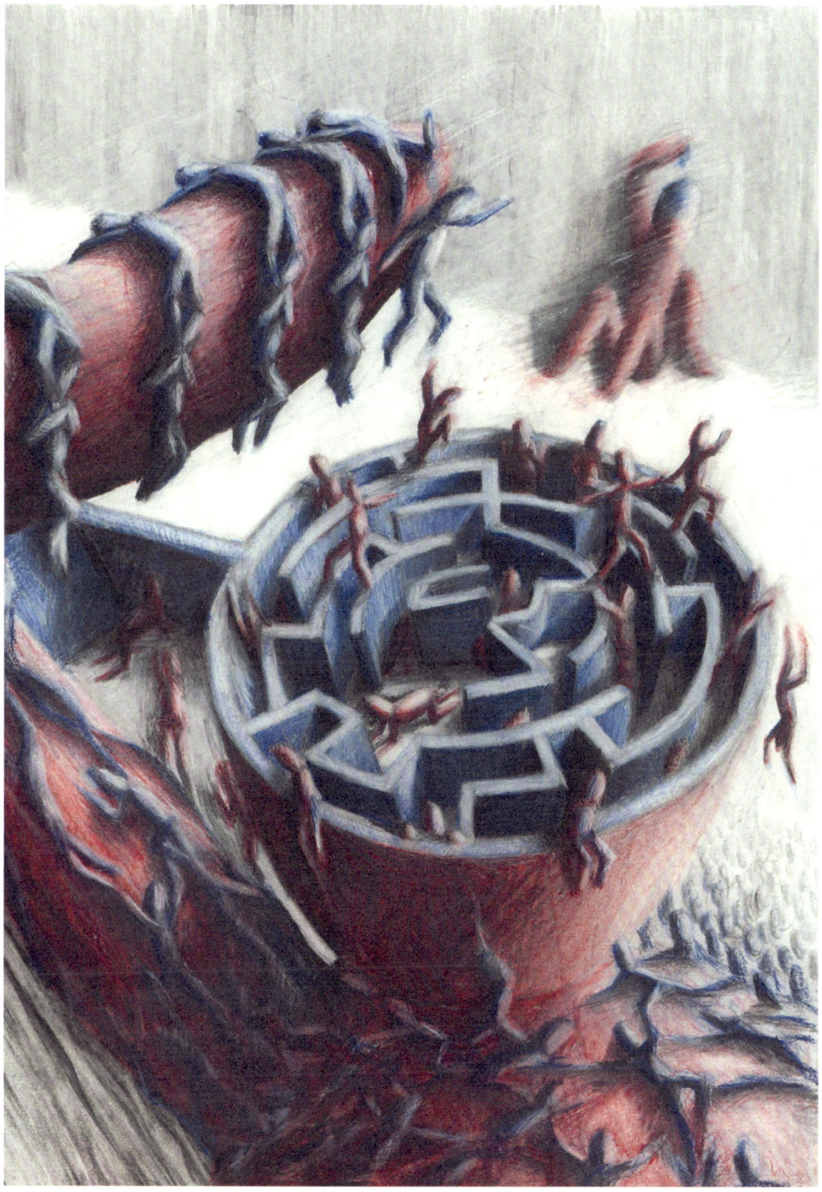

3.

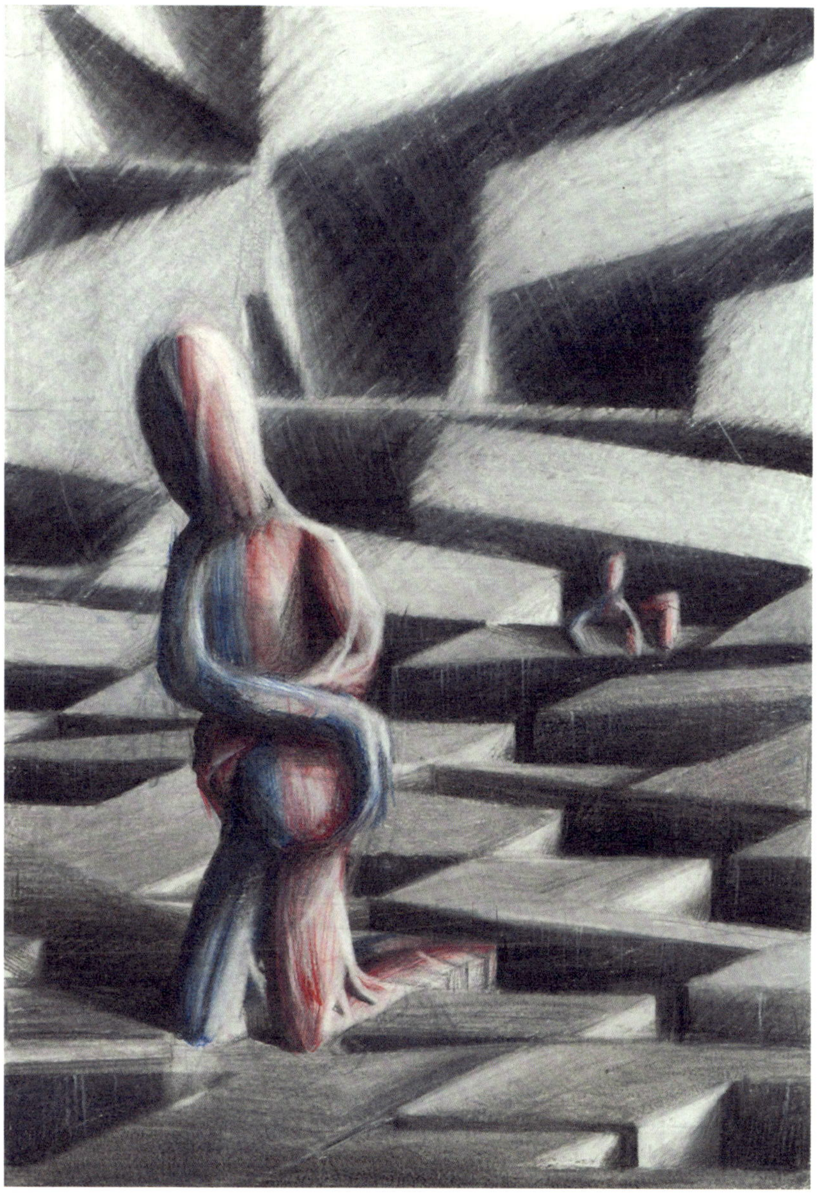

4.

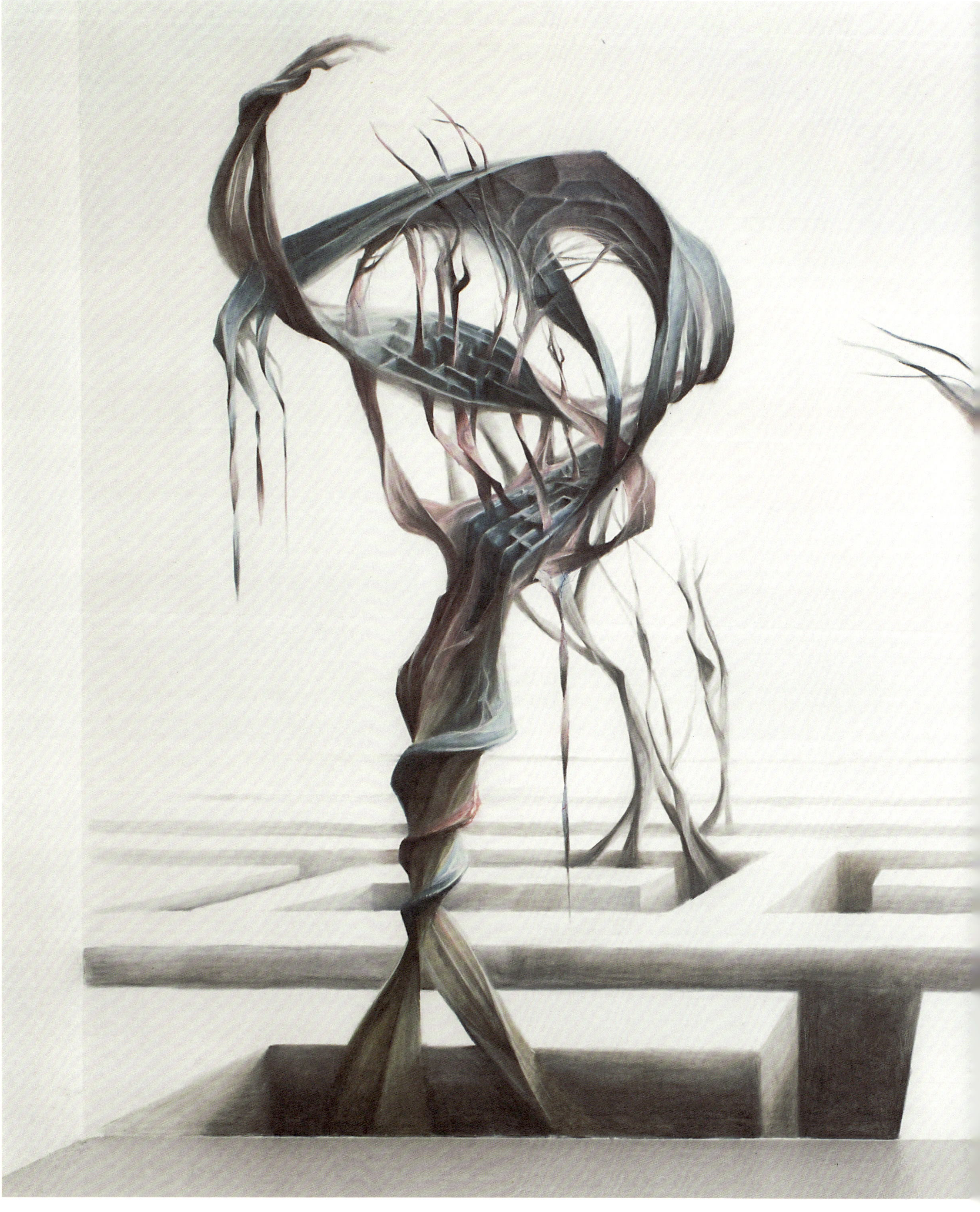

5

VIKTOR TIMOFEEV

5. *Godflower X*, 2019, hard pastel on wall, c.250 × 500 cm (c.196 × 98 in), installation view, 'Modern Nature', Drawing Room, London

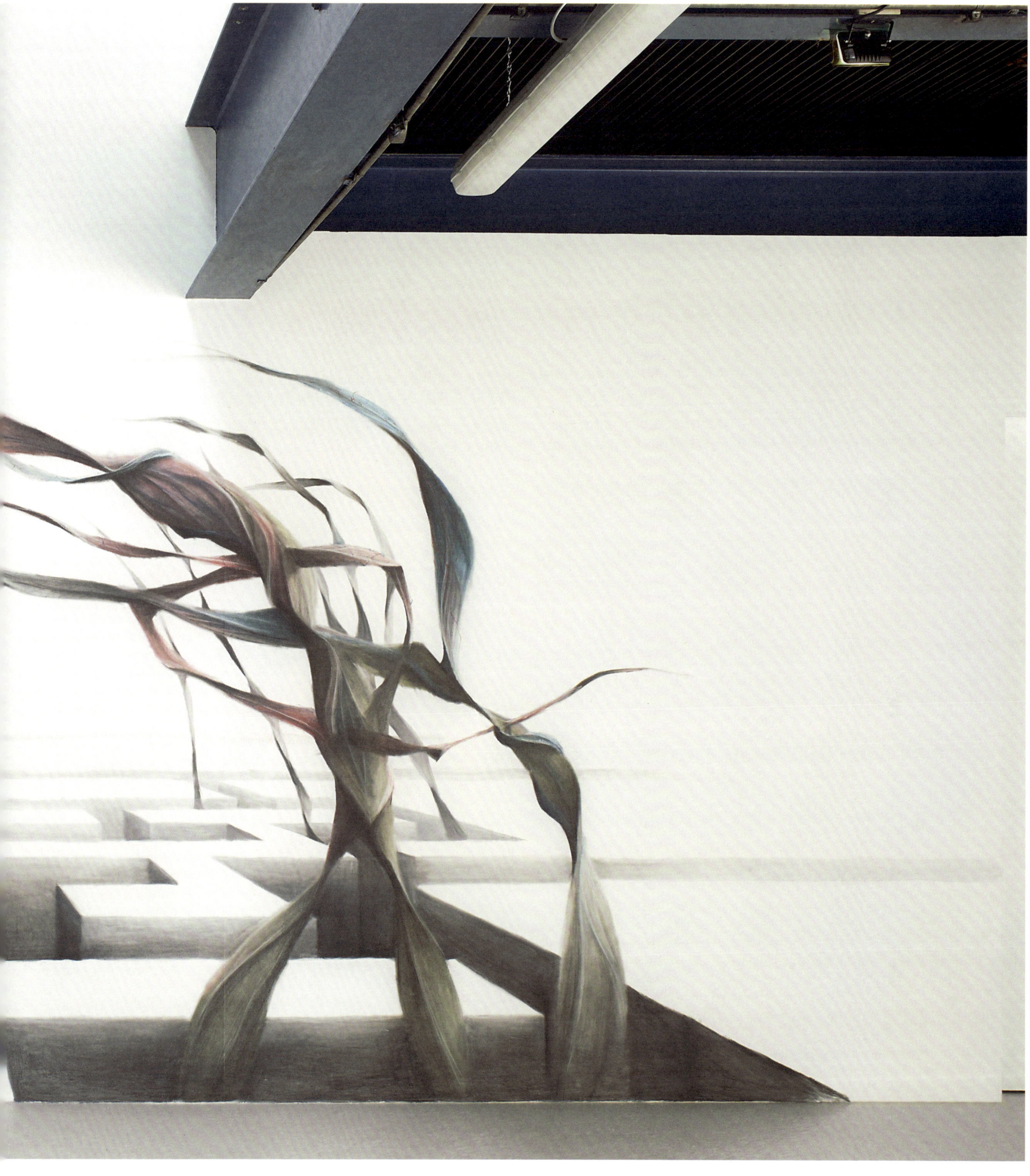

BARTHÉLÉMY TOGUO .... From multimedia installations addressing the global plight of migrants or the Black Lives Matter movement to reams of portraits or abstract watercolour and ink paintings on paper, in Barthélémy Toguo's work there is always the pendulum swing of heated lashing out at or tender embrace of the world in all its terrifying and grand conditions. Similar to the late American artist Nancy Spero (1926–2009), whose printed collages of newspaper type and historical figures called out political injustice and crimes of war around the world, Toguo concerns himself with the ethics of observation, and frequently uses drawing as a direct means of accounting for his own times and recounting the past as well. .... A series of ink, watercolour and photo-collage works on paper is titled 'Bilongué' after a neighbourhood in Douala, the largest city in the artist's native country of Cameroon. He lived and worked there for some months in 2015 while preparing work for Okwui Enwezor's curated exhibition in that year's Venice Biennale, and was impressed by how the residents' way of life was shaped by solidarity, as he noted in a statement accompanying the show of these works at a Cape Town gallery: 'When there is a need, one runs to help the other. It is a flat area so there is a lot of stagnant water. When water floods the house of a neighbour everyone helps them, and so it goes on. I went to capture the images of their faces to tell them that in this difficult city of Douala, they exist as heroes.' Many pieces from this group, including *Bilongué 2* (2020), portray one such person, with a colonial-era photograph affixed to the centre of the paper. Cameroon was a colony or territory of Germany, France and the UK at various points from the mid-nineteenth to the mid-twentieth centuries, and here these echoes of history are built into the faces of present-day dwellers, but with the colour of their features drawn on top, as if refusing their effacement. .... In *Dynastie* (2012), a scroll-like water-colour on paper that runs twenty metres (sixty-six feet) horizontally, the artist's hand is looser in rendering his subjects, but the free-flowing imagery of animals, limbs, fruits and weapons speaks of a beautiful and savage largesse that resonates with the sprawling nature of time. Rendered in a limited palette of black, red and green, the wet-on-wet technique of Toguo's colour application makes every lizard or knife a fuzzy pool of dark and light values, so that each creature and tool comes alive by the same gesture and can, presumably, be duly unmade as well.

.... Paige K. Bradley

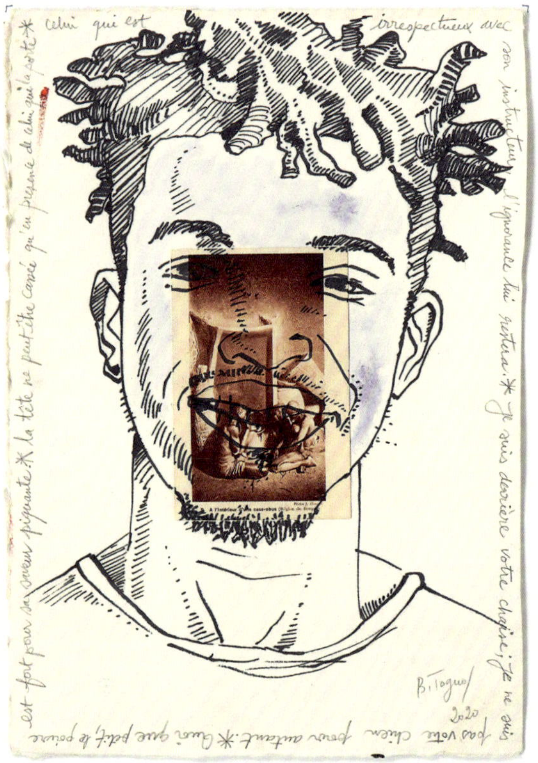

1.

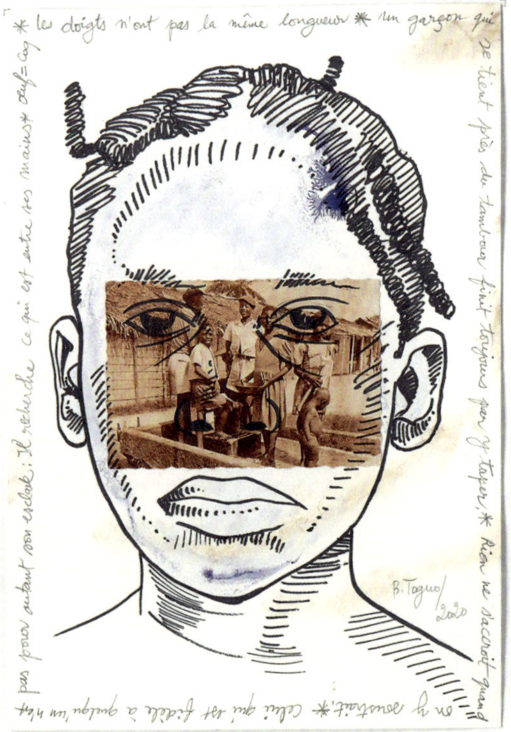

2.

Born 1967, Mbalmayo, Cameroon. Lives and works in Bandjoun, Cameroon, and Paris.

1. *Bilongué 10*, 2020, ink, watercolour and collage on paper, 38.5 × 27 cm (15 ⅛ × 10 ⅝ in)
2. *Bilongué 2*, 2020, ink, watercolour and collage on paper, 38.5 × 27 cm (15 ⅛ × 10 ⅝ in)
3. *L'Homme aux fruits rouges (The man with red fruits)*, 2018, watercolour on paper, 27 × 38 cm (10 ⅝ × 15 in)
4. *Poursuite of the Dragon (Pursuit of the Dragon)*, 2018, watercolour on paper, 28 × 38 cm (11 × 15 in)

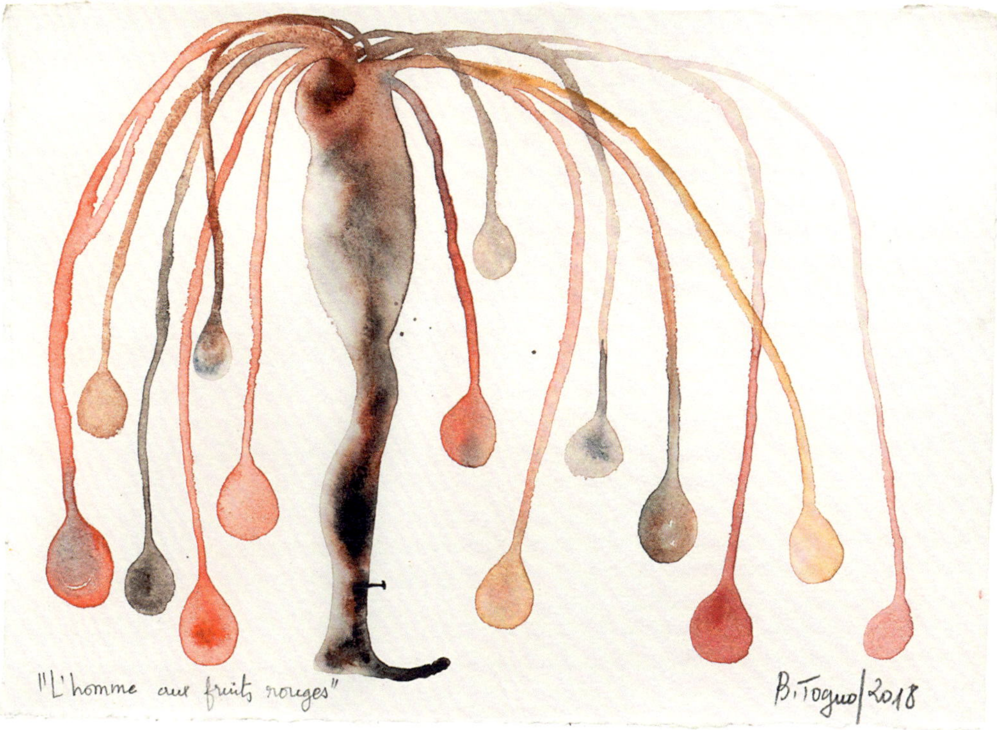
"L'homme aux fruits rouges"
B. Toguo / 2018

3.

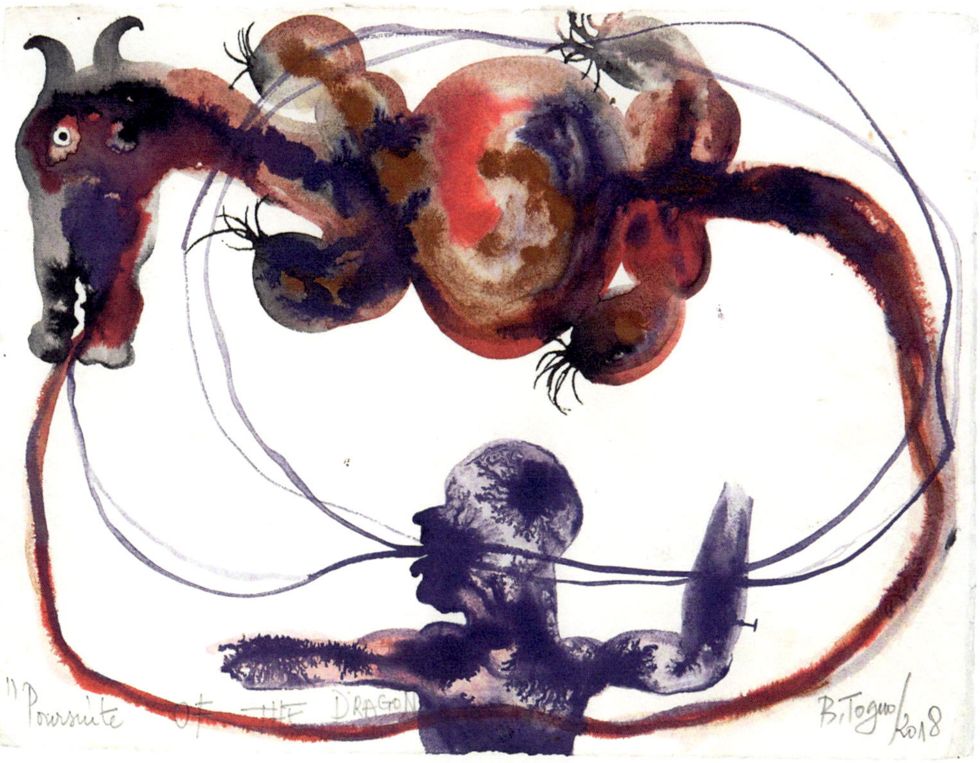
"Poursuite OF THE DRAGON
B. Toguo / 2018

4.

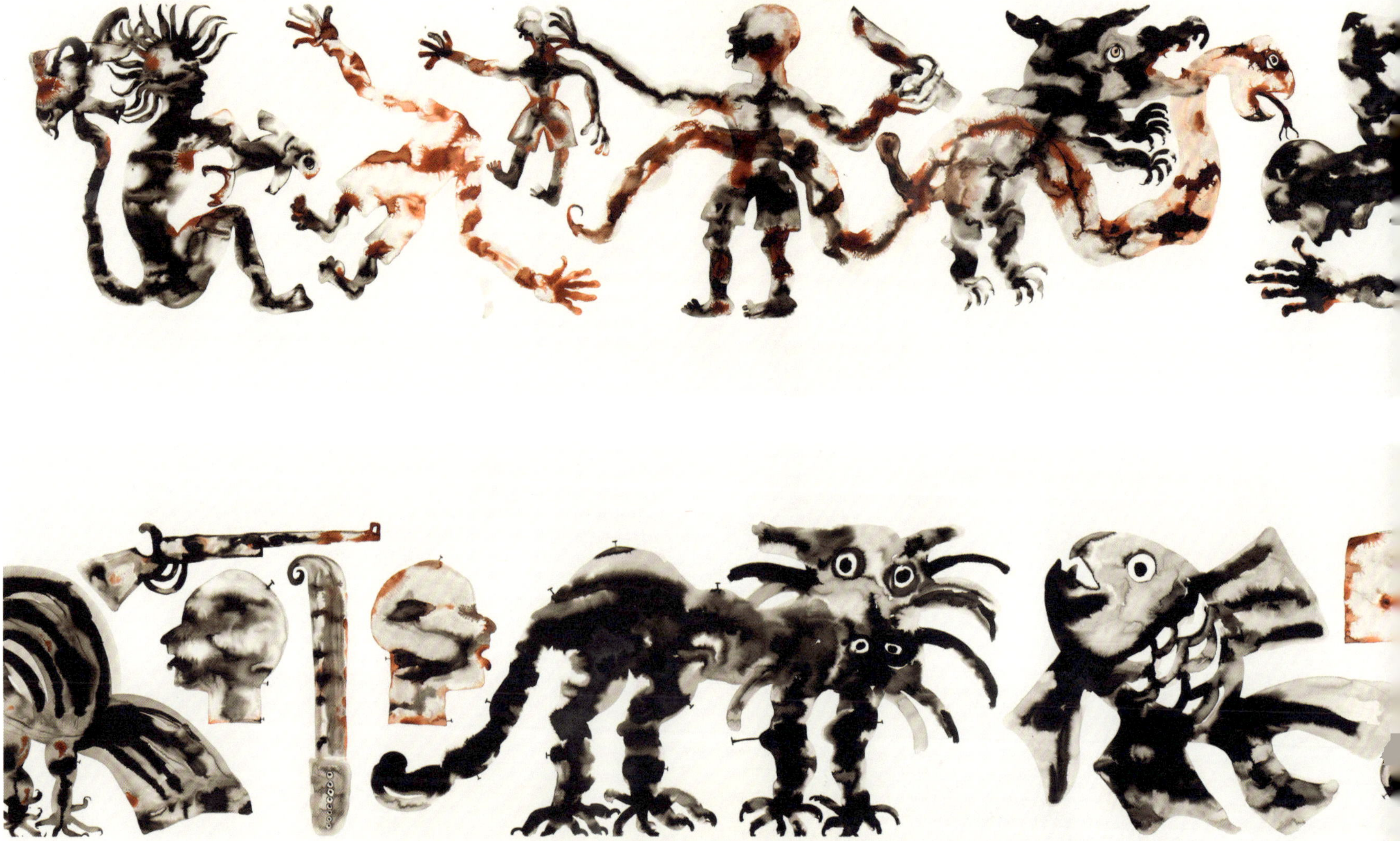

5.

5. *Dynastie*, 2012, watercolour on paper, 1.13 × 20 m (44 ½ × 788 in)

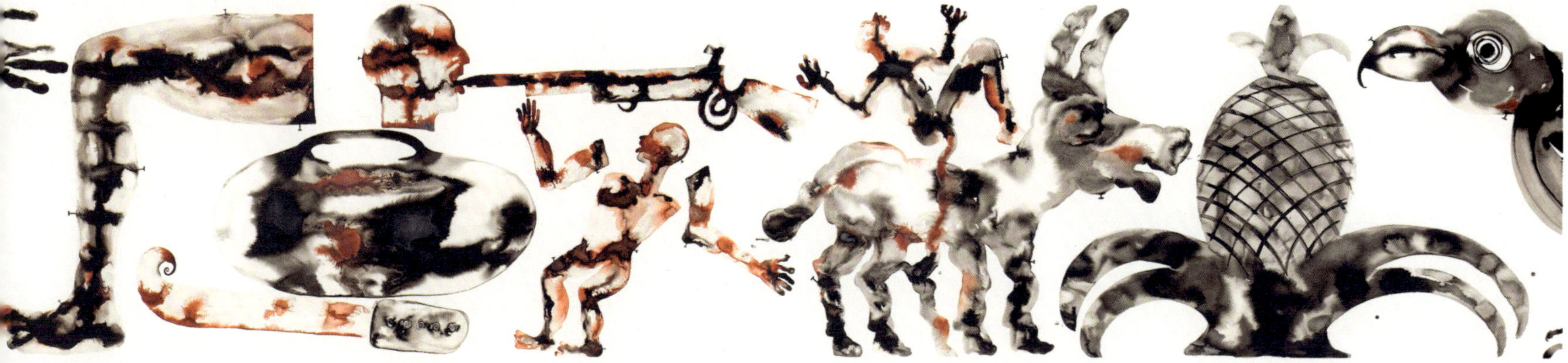

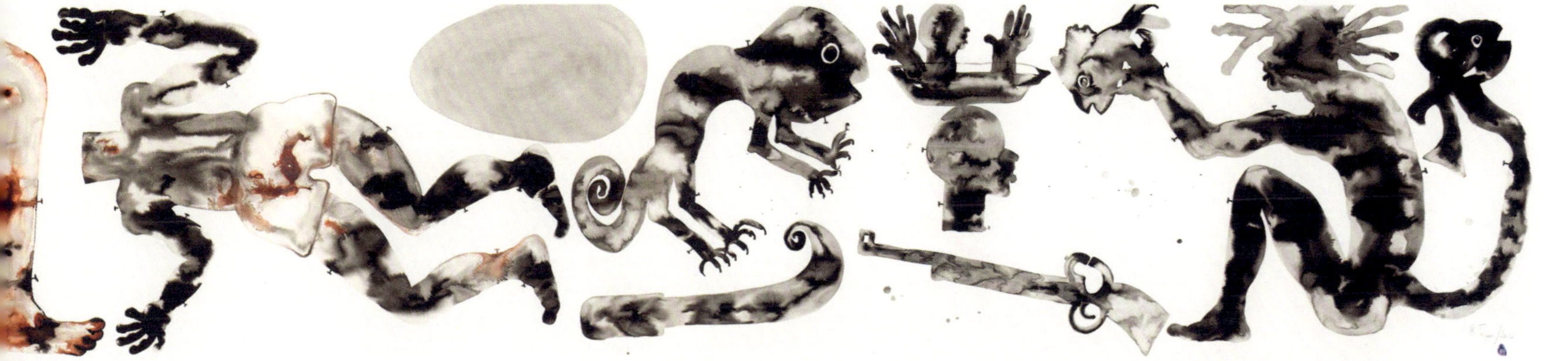

ACHRAF TOULOUB .... Working in video, sculpture and drawing, Achraf Touloub positions his practice at the point where the symbolic logic of tradition meets technologically structured modernity. He maintains that these two belief systems converge more than they clash, and that each one holds equal power in shaping the globalized world. Mostly, the technological is insinuated in his work, rather than explicitly depicted. Given his use of conductive copper ink, we might even understand his drawings as giant circuit boards. But, at first glance, Touloub's large monochromatic drawings have a soothing naturalistic quality to them. Built up through repetitive fractal patterns, they feature a recurring squiggly leaf-like pattern that would not look out of place on a William Morris wallpaper, or a sheet of OSB engineered wood. Their woven, almost textile-like quality reminds the viewer of the links between nineteenth-century jacquard looms and the earliest punch-card computers. .... In Touloub's 2017 Venice Biennale presentation in the central 'Viva Arte Viva' exhibition, fittingly hung in the Pavilion of Traditions, the drawings were inset into or shown alongside mixed-media assemblages of nylon that had been stitched into with similar looping patterns and hung with chains, a recurring motif found in his installation art. There is a seamless extension of line from page to sewn fabric and 3D printed sculpture. The latter are produced by reducing reference images into lines that are then vectorized and 3D printed – a kind of machine-outsourced drawing. The palette is washed out and restful too. Tranquil blues, pinkish reds and greys predominate, and are joined by dulled greens and the rare shy yellow. But the longer you spend looking at them, the more dynamic they get. Like a Buddhist *thangka* painting, they appear multi-temporal, depicting multiple time frames all in the same work. .... Touloub's figures are faceless and mostly semi-abstract but not androgynous, leaning on colour symbolism to uphold gender. So it is that in *Chorus II* (2018), overlapping curvy forms, repeated at different scales, which suggest a mother holding an infant, are rendered in pink. In *Gare du Nord* (2017), bulkier, more planar forms are seen from the back, as if in a crowded station as the French title suggests, and drawn in blue. In *The Birth* (2019), meanwhile, the titular event is condensed to a much more abstract, geometric language: a circular head on a square pillow, with an elongated leaf-like body and another smaller circle for a baby, or at least its emergent head. At the same time, each of these works features inset windows, which gives them a hyper-contemporary feel that suggests nothing so much as videoconferencing, or browsing a webpage with embedded iframes, videos or other media.
.... Rahel Aima

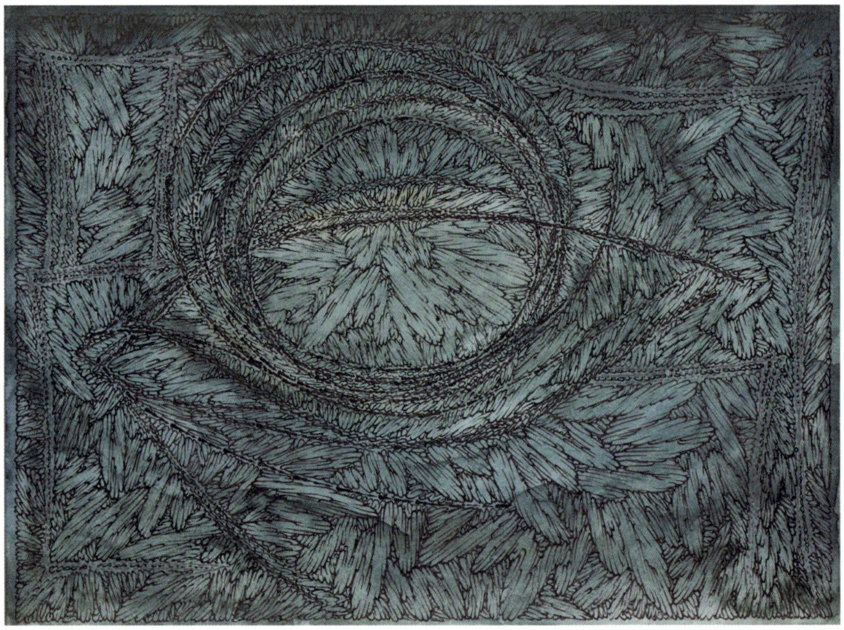
1.

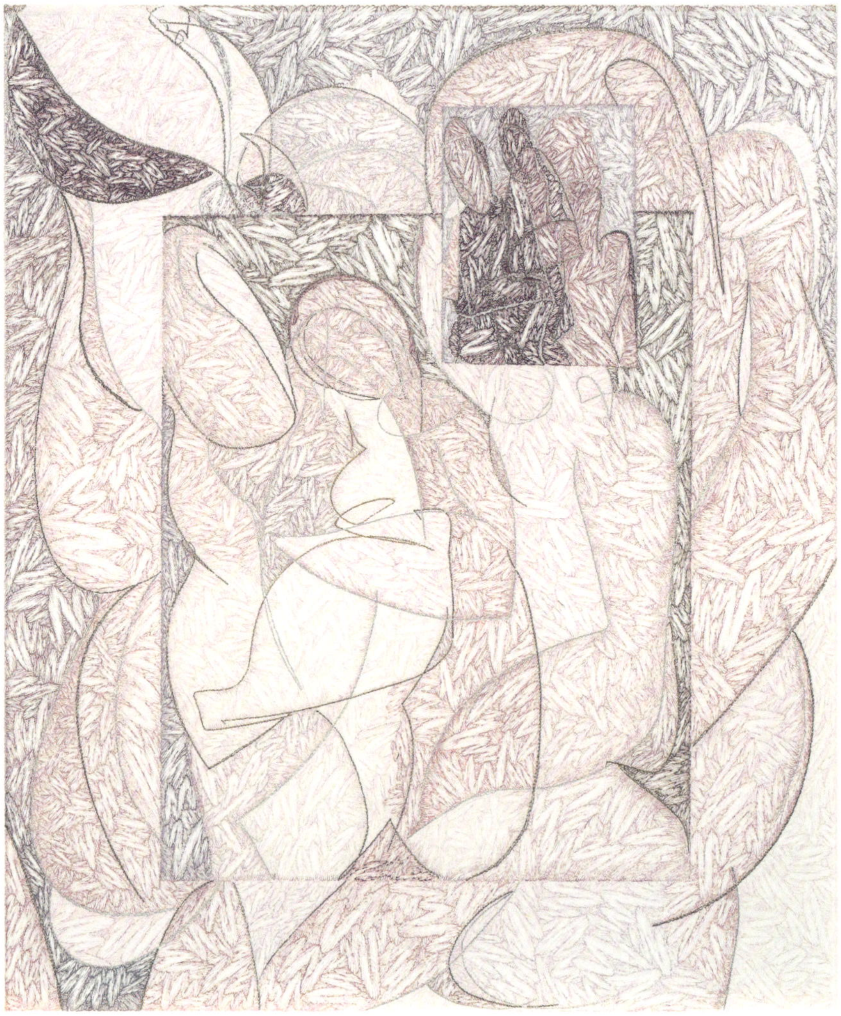
2.

Born 1986, Casablanca, Morocco. Lives and works in Paris.

1. *Discord Landscape*, 2019, watercolour and ink on paper, 29.2 × 40.2 cm (11 ½ × 15 ⅞ in)
2. *Chorus II*, 2018, ink and acrylic on paper, 114 × 97 cm (44 ⅞ × 38 ⅛ in)
3. *Gare du Nord*, 2017, ink and acrylic on paper, 109.5 × 169.3 cm (43 ⅛ × 66 ⅝ in)
4. *The Birth*, 2019, ink on paper, 46.2 × 70.2 cm (18 ⅛ × 27 ⅝ in)

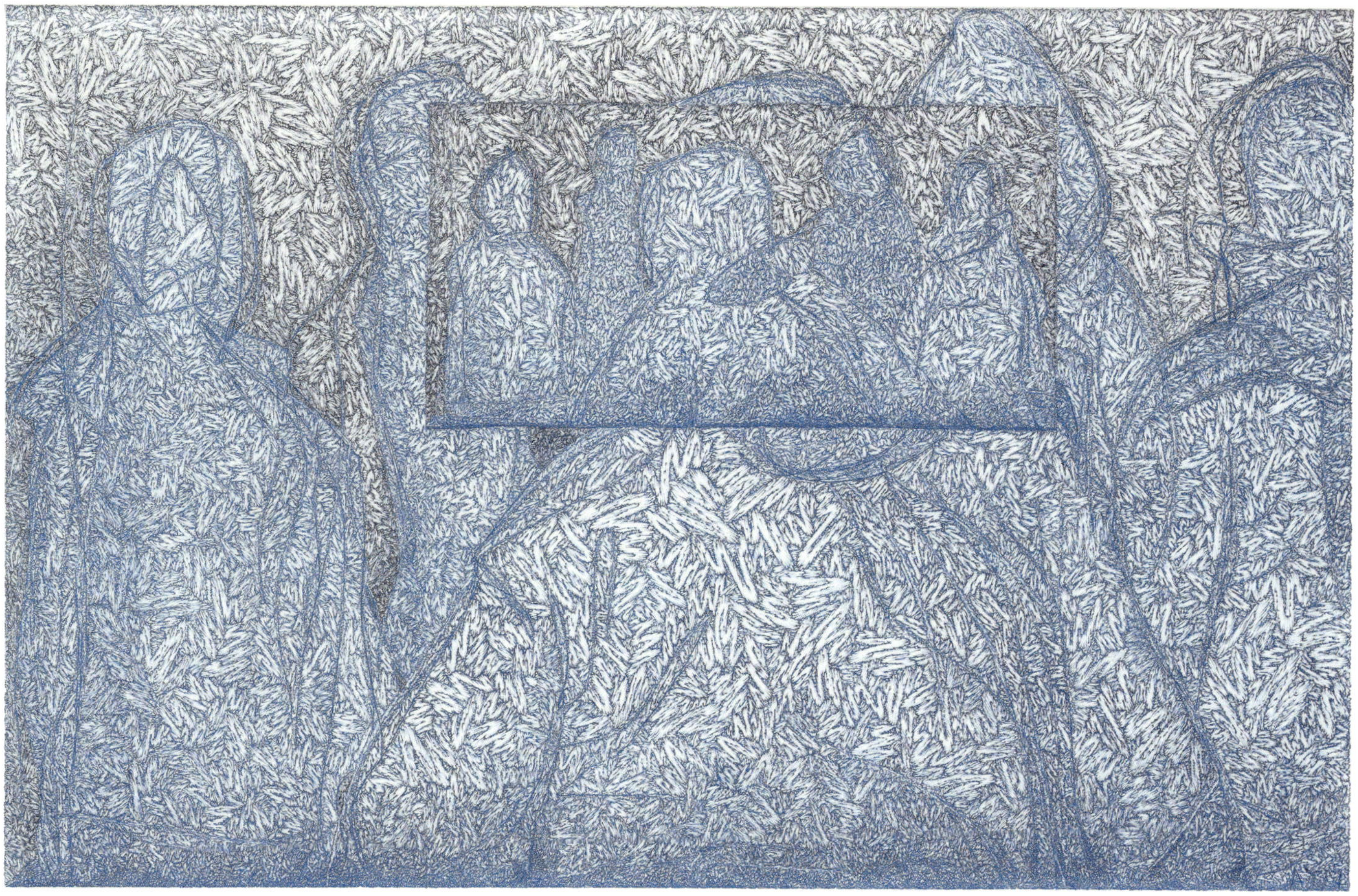

3.

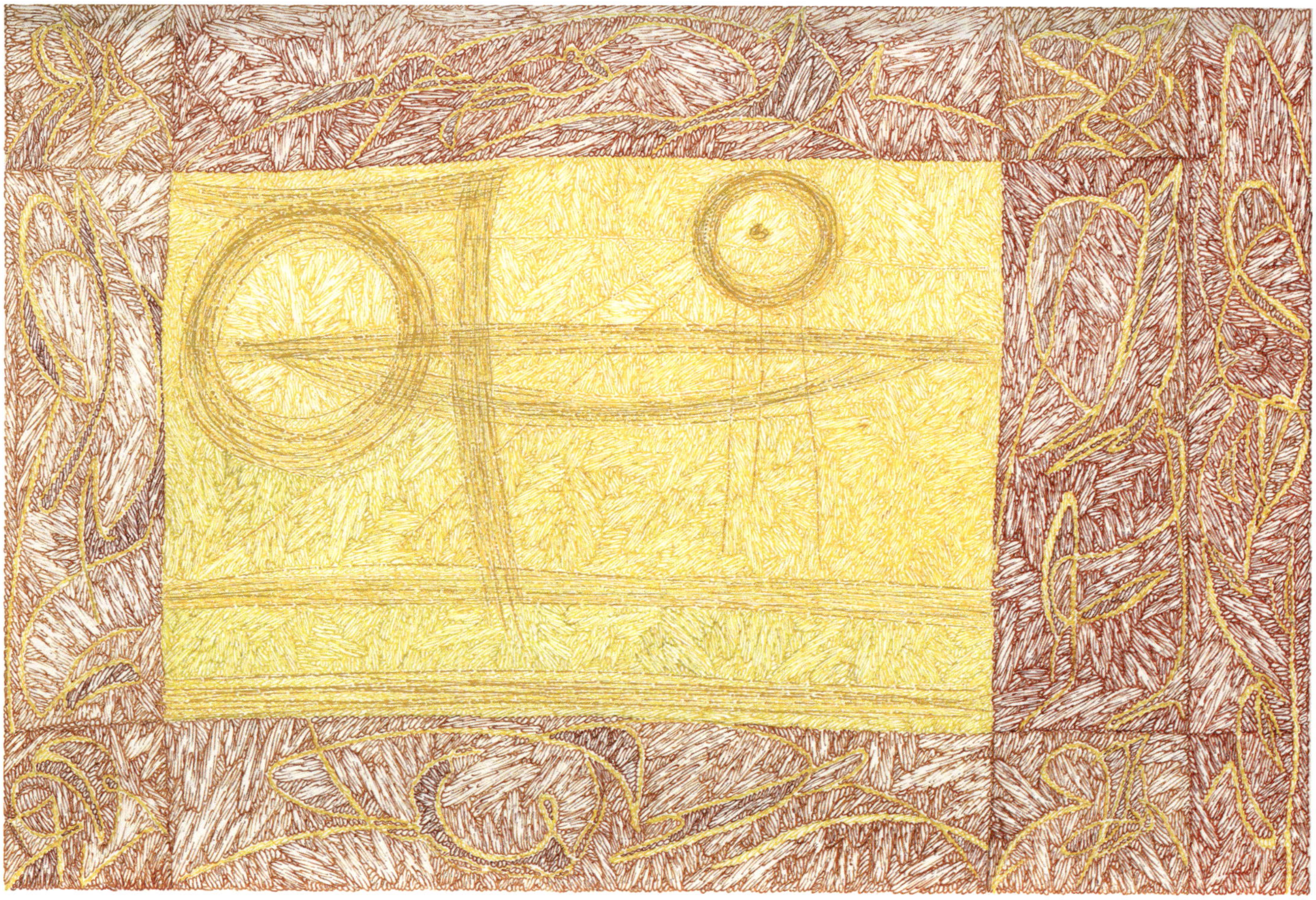

4.

N I C O L A T Y S O N....... Nicola Tyson, who was an adolescent punk in her native London, has exhibited the photographs she took as a teenage follower of the subsequent 'New Romantic' scene before she moved to New York in 1989; she has published a book of letters to dead male artists, satirically countering the way they assumed they could represent women; and she is best known for taking forward the painterly inhabiting of female bodily experience pioneered by the Austrian artist Maria Lassnig's (1919–2014) depictions of *Körpergefühl* (body sensation) and *Körperbewusstsein* (body awareness). Yet Tyson's paintings are based on drawings, only some of which she selects as suited to further development: instinctual drawing is her primary generative practice. In her own words, ahead of a 2016 retrospective of work on paper at New York's Petzel Gallery, 'When I begin to draw, I have no idea what's going to appear. I work swiftly, to stay just ahead of the cage of language, the linear mind and rational decision-making. I just let the forms grow themselves.' Indeed, she sometimes closes her eyes as she draws and tries to look at the image as little as possible until it is done. Error is embraced – Tyson says she rarely needs to erase anything, as apparent 'mistakes' are 'incorporated or used as a springboard for gear changes in mark-making'. That process of seeking an uncensored connection to her hand – rather than her eye or brain – is, explains Tyson, the only way to find a 'truthful' image........ Such a striving towards the automatic can lead away from representation, but Tyson keeps the figurative in play, albeit the abstract qualities of her mark-making are just as prominent. Take *Dancing #3* (2012): abstraction meets bodily sensation as figures break down into separate shapes, including the frozen impression of long hair in movement, while the exaggerated scale of a hand and arm grab attention as the focal points of the couple's charged touching. It's hard to tell whether the subject of *Extraordinary Powers of Hearing* (2015) is human or animal, but there is no doubt about the focus on a dark central disc that suggests not so much an ear as the internal interpretative space through which sound is experienced. Perhaps that simply illustrates how what Tyson's hand draws from her subconscious triggers the tangents of our own. Indeed, *Grazing Sheep and Sky Object* (2015) veers towards more explicitly surreal territory: sheep, defined by negative space and consequently resembling animals cut into a chalk hill, graze beneath what could be the sun but has just enough otherness to read more unexpectedly as a mouth or a UFO.
.... Paul Carey-Kent

1.

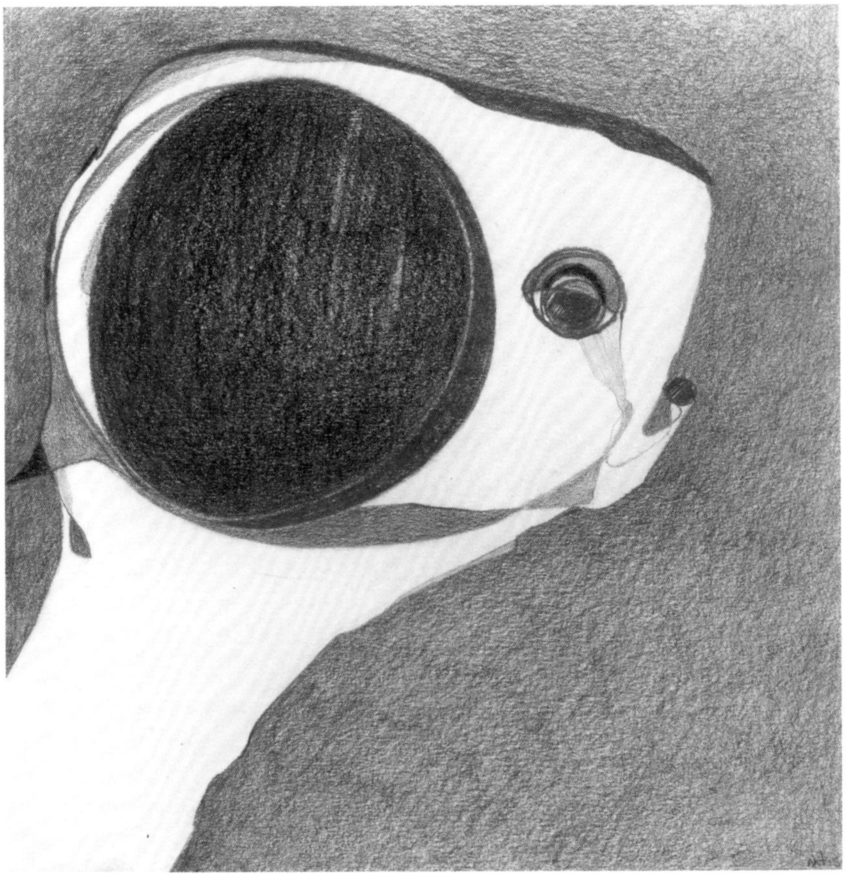

2.

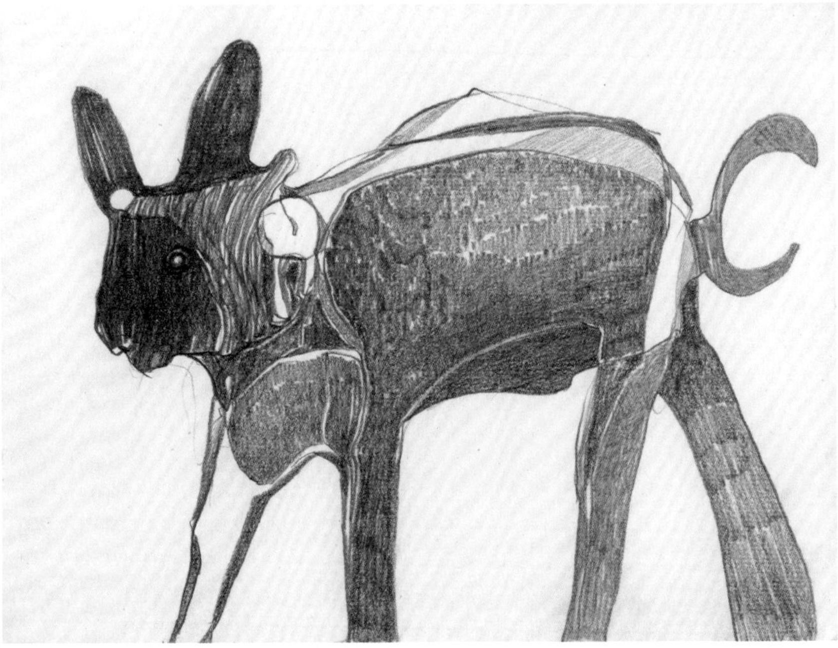

Born 1960, London. Lives and works in New York.

1. *Extraordinary Powers of Hearing*, 2015, graphite on paper, 19.1 × 19.1 cm (7 ½ × 7 ½ in)

2. *Hoarse*, 2019, graphite on paper, 20.6 × 27.9 cm (20 ⅝ × 27 ⅞ in)

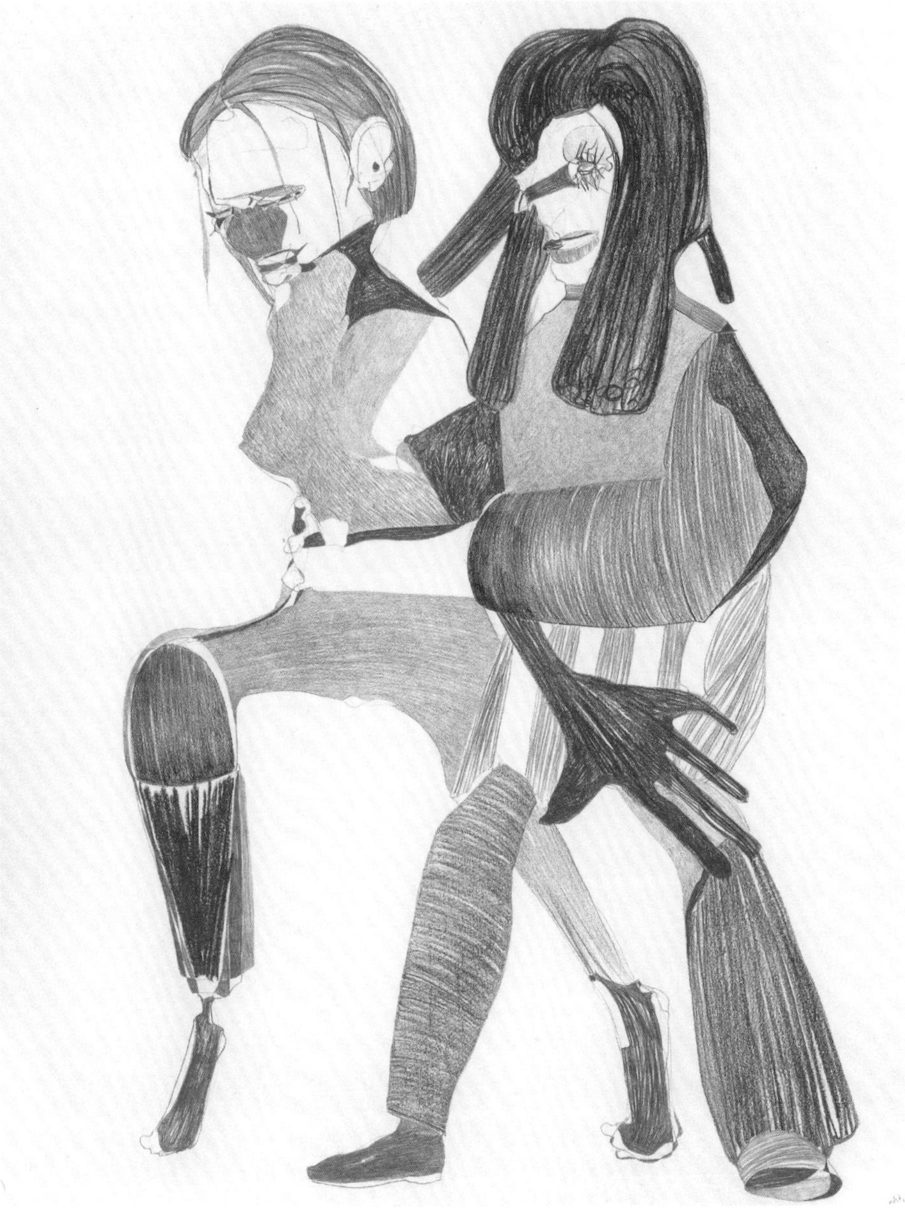

3.

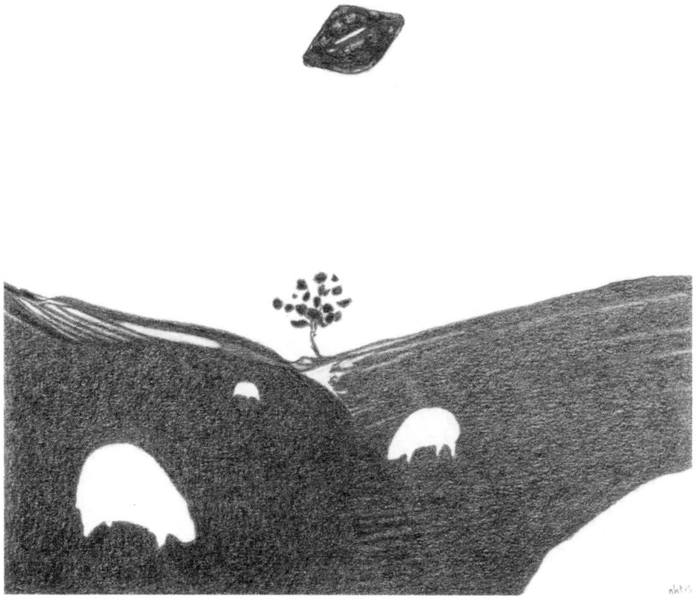

4.

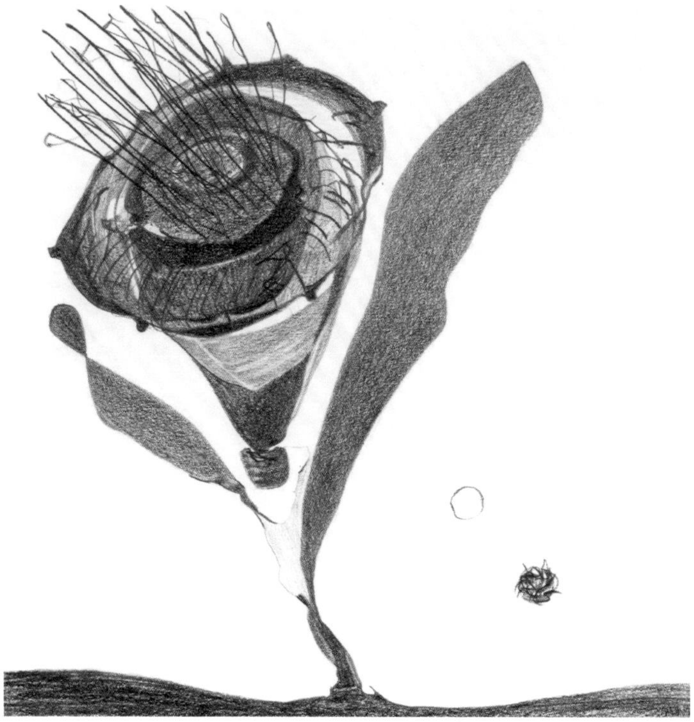

5.

3. *Dancing #3*, 2012, graphite on paper, 127 × 76.2 cm (50 × 30 in)
4. *Grazing Sheep and Sky Object*, 2015, graphite on paper, 19.1 × 19.1 cm (7 ½ × 7 ½ in)
5. *Pollen*, 2015, graphite on paper, 19.1 × 19.1 cm (7 ½ × 7 ½ in)

JOHANNA UNZUETA....... Pain provided the unlikely catalyst for Johanna Unzueta's drawings and murals. The Chilean-born, New York-based artist began producing her distinctive geometric abstracts in 2013 after suffering from carpal tunnel syndrome aggravated by the production of her physically demanding textile sculptures. Expanding her explorations of labour and production, these complex, diagrammatic compositions on paper and gallery architecture profoundly impacted her approach to art-making and now hold a central place in her multi-disciplinary practice. As she said in a 2020 interview in *Artforum*, 'Drawing changed my life: the way I see, the way I speak.'....... Working on large sheets of paper infused with indigo and other natural dyes, Unzueta produces her freestanding pastel and watercolour drawings using a distinctive vocabulary of shapes derived from embroidery hoops and organic forms. Her designs, which typically comprise patterns of overlapping circles, ovals, ellipses and thread-like lines, emerge intuitively, often relative to her own body measurements. Each one is sandwiched between sheets of transparent acrylic and supported by chunky timber bases. Allowing the drawings to be viewed in the round, these framing devices encourage intimate engagement. Sometimes the paper is punctured with small needle holes, further emphasizing the work's materiality. A field of these drawings was displayed in Unzueta's major solo exhibition 'Tools for Life' at Modern Art Oxford in 2020. The installation included *December 2014, January, February, March 2015 NY* (2014–15), which is defined by a coral pink circle surrounded by eight interlocking green discs. Within these are numerous ovals intersecting with smaller circles in muted shades of pink, green and blue. Yet Unzueta's compositions are not purely formal; her concern with the relationships between nature, unseen human labour and globalized commerce are also in view. For instance, some drawings contain elements resembling flower petals or insect wings, while others suggest the warp and weft of woven fabrics. Furthermore, each one appears like a complex Venn diagram – conceivably a metaphor for the intersecting and conflicting processes of globalization that Unzueta addresses in her figurative felt sculptures of industrial machinery and tools....... The sculptural dimension of Unzueta's drawings is underscored by her site-specific murals responding to gallery architecture. These temporary works fill walls and cover facades, such as at Sala de Arte Público Siqueiros in Mexico City, where the two-part drawing *Nictinastia* (2017) was installed between the museum's windows. While their geometric designs are familiar from Unzueta's works on paper, the inclusion of threads and cords reflects her preoccupation with textile-based processes. Drawn with thick oil pastels and charcoal, these temporary installations are impermanent and vulnerable to change. Similarly, the dyes Unzueta uses will fade over time – intimations of a world in flux and the transience of life itself. .... David Trigg

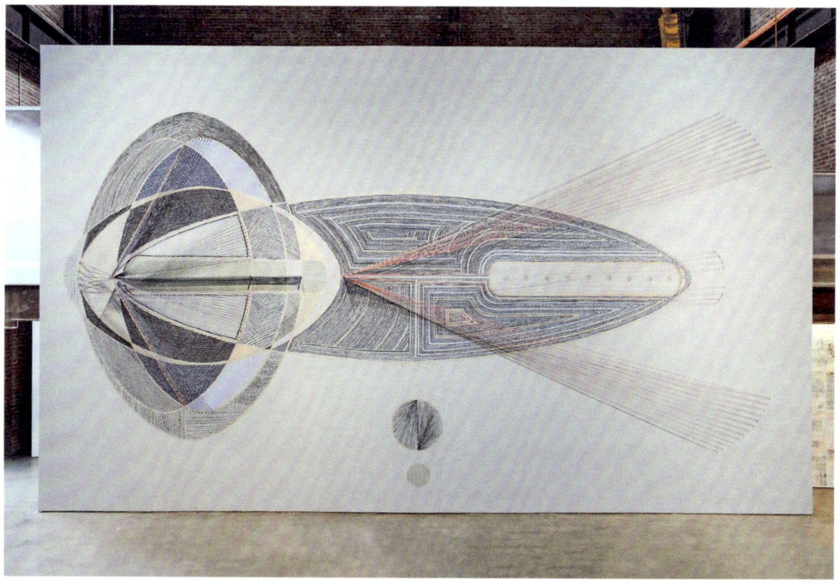

1.

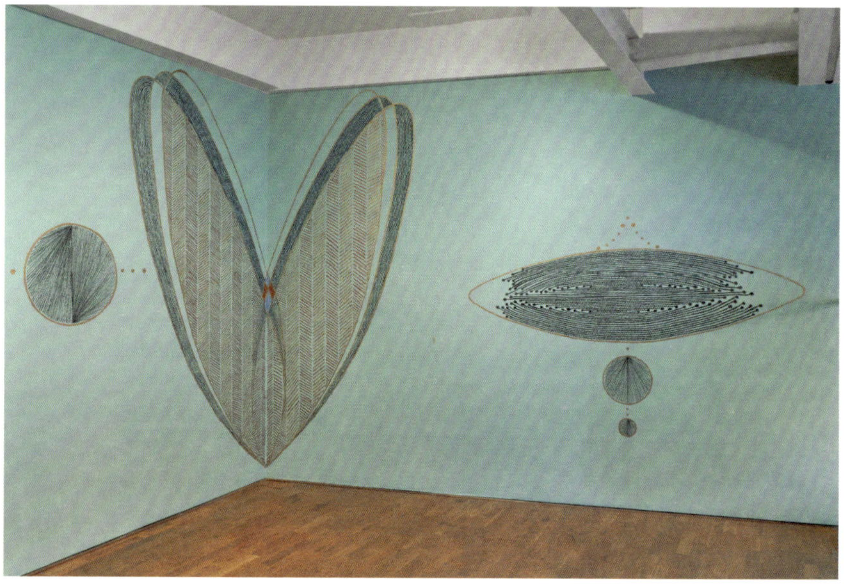

2.

Born 1974, Santiago, Chile. Lives and works in New York.

1. *Grace and Gravity*, 2019, latex paint, oil pastel, charcoal, metal rods and dyed cotton thread, c.600 × 900 × 45 cm (236 ¼ × 354 ⅜ × 17 ¾ in), installation view, 'Searching the Sky for Rain', Sculpture Center, New York
2. *Nocturnal*, 2020, oil pastel and charcoal on wall, installation view, 'Johanna Unzueta: Tools for Life', Modern Art Oxford, UK
3. *Nictinastia*, 2017, oil pastel, metal rods and PVC rope, c.600 × 1,200 cm (236 ¼ × 472 ⅜ in), mural project for Sala de Arte Público Siqueiros, Mexico City
4. Installation view, 'Johanna Unzueta: Tools for Life', Modern Art Oxford, UK, 2020

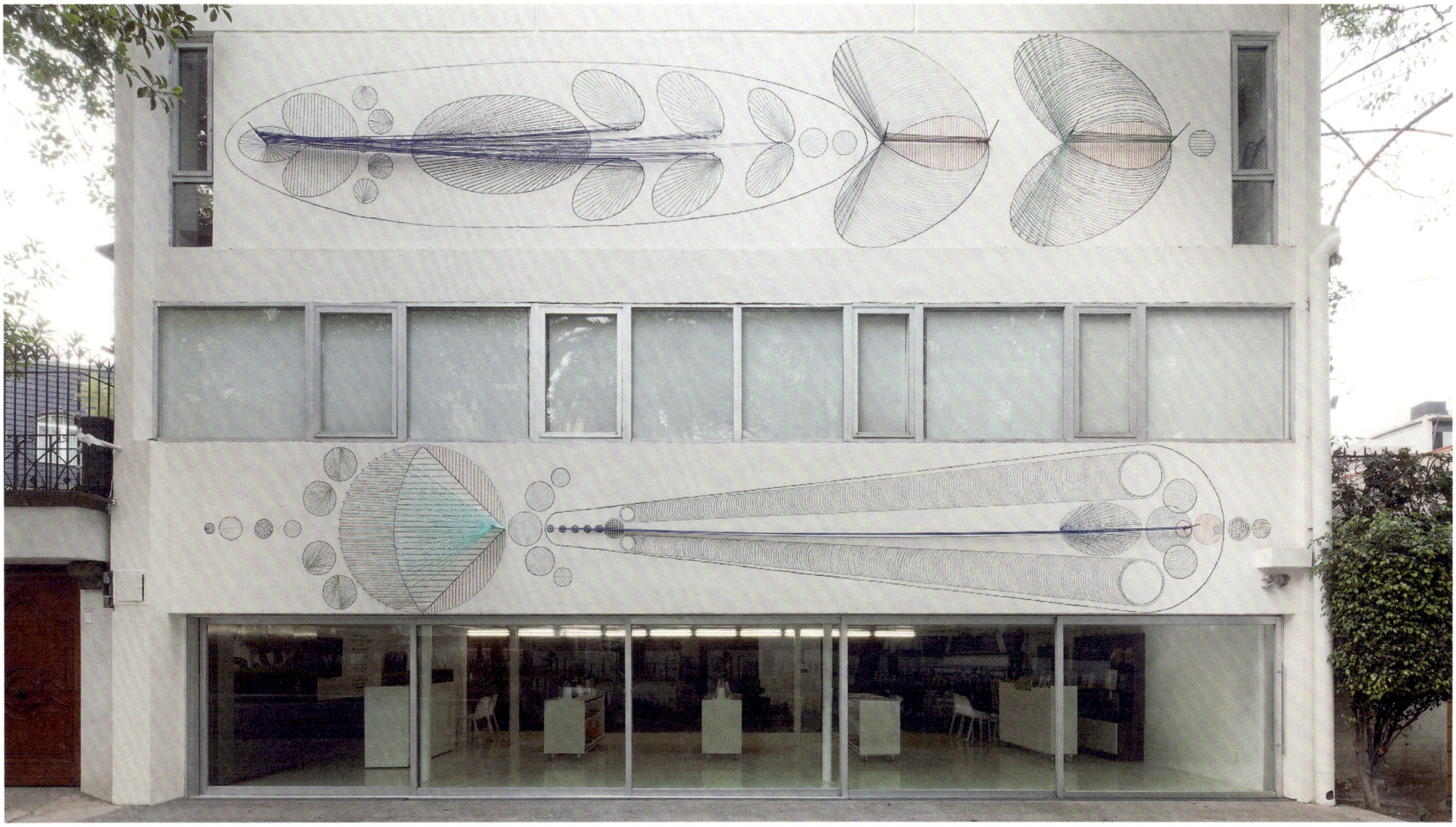

3.

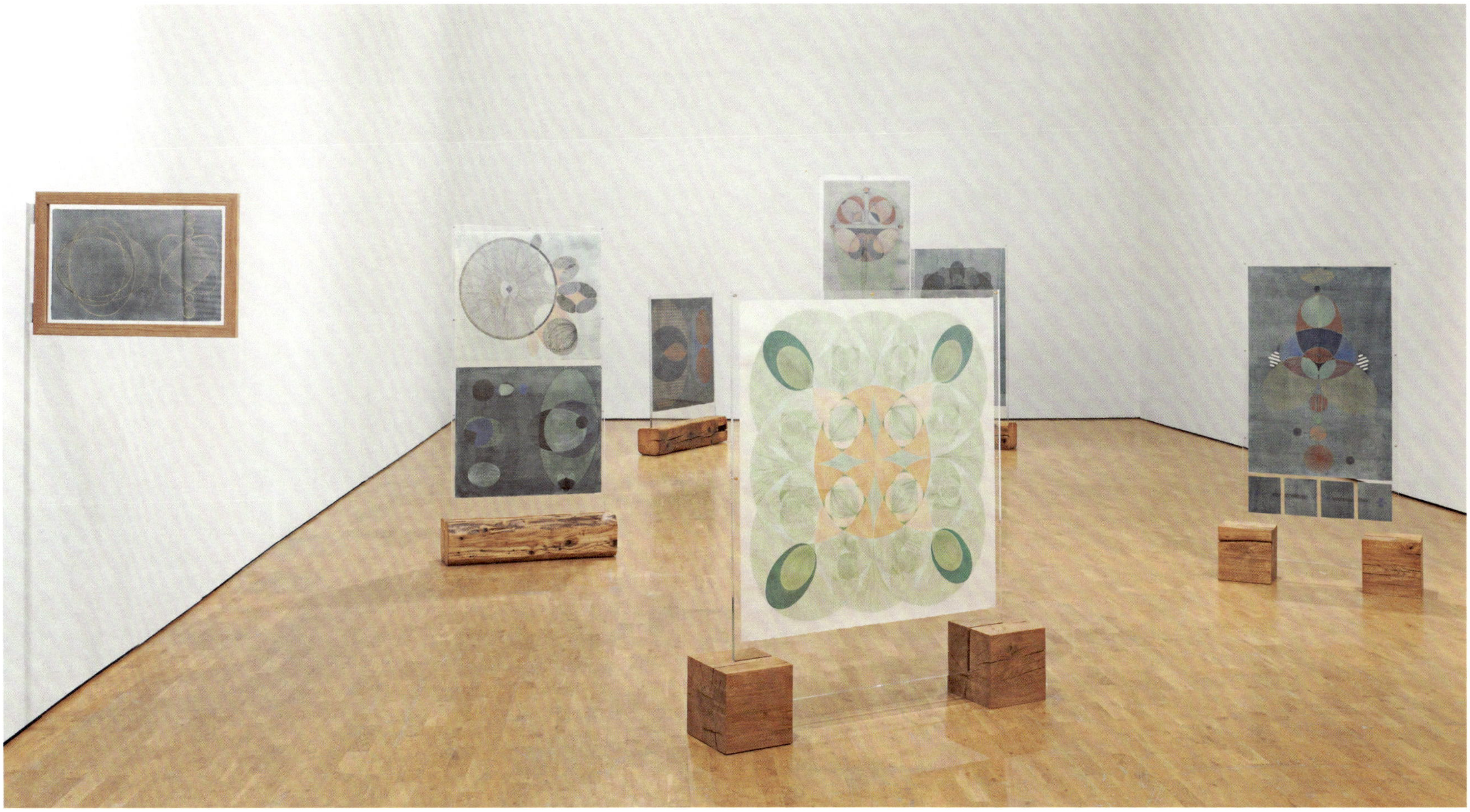

4.

HANNELORE VAN DIJCK....... In mid-2016 Belgian artist and draughtswoman Hannelore Van Dijck presented *Four Flags* as part of a group exhibition called 'Summer Dust' at the Verksmiðjan art centre in Hjalteyri, a town of thirty-five people in northern Iceland. Located in a massive concrete structure that was once the largest herring factory in all of Europe, the art centre featured the work of eleven artists responding to the site and to one another. Van Dijck's contribution was an adaption of her signature charcoal rubbings into a suite of billowing flags on an old building overlooking the water. Like drawing in the wind, her gentle marks become fleeting by responding to the weather and breeze. The flags don't designate place or nationality, rather they signal an ephemerality: a billowing flow of fabric and texture. Working outdoors provided a new setting for Van Dijck's meticulous rubbings and obsessive lines....... Her delicate markings are signposts of place or non-place; large charcoal drawings and rubbings are often rendered in situ over architectural surfaces and interiors, walls and archways. Charcoal in hand, she can draw for days – part of an endurance practice, she marks domestic interiors with shadings and stains. Her drawings evoke permanence and impermanence, further suggested in the title of her 2018 solo exhibition at Gallery Sofie Van der Velde in Antwerp, Belgium, 'The lasting one, that didn't last, that still lasts', about the transience and passing of time. Van Dijck's shadings in charcoal and chalk cover vast surfaces in monochromatic markings that are integrated with the architecture that hosts them. Applied on walls, her smudges have a rhythm in their minutiae and delicate texture, and it comes as no surprise that Van Dijck studied illustration in Ghent, Belgium, ensuring that drawing is her preferred medium, subsequently adapted and modified to different settings....... In an artist's statement for The Drawing Center, New York in 2012, she reflected on the subtlety of her practice and the importance of context and space: 'My drawings are composed of elements sourced from a variety of places close to my personal life. Dreams and reality are mixed. The images are often settings without characters or activity. It is the context that generates the tension. In the composition of a wall drawing, I start with what the original location offers me and try to comprehensively consider the effect of my installation on the essence of the space. Drawing, exhibition and context are one.'....... By working in close contact with her medium, Van Dijck produces fragile, tenuous and transient compositions that are elusive yet have deep psychological impact, her drawings and stained interiors suggesting erosion and fading memories.
.... Natalie King

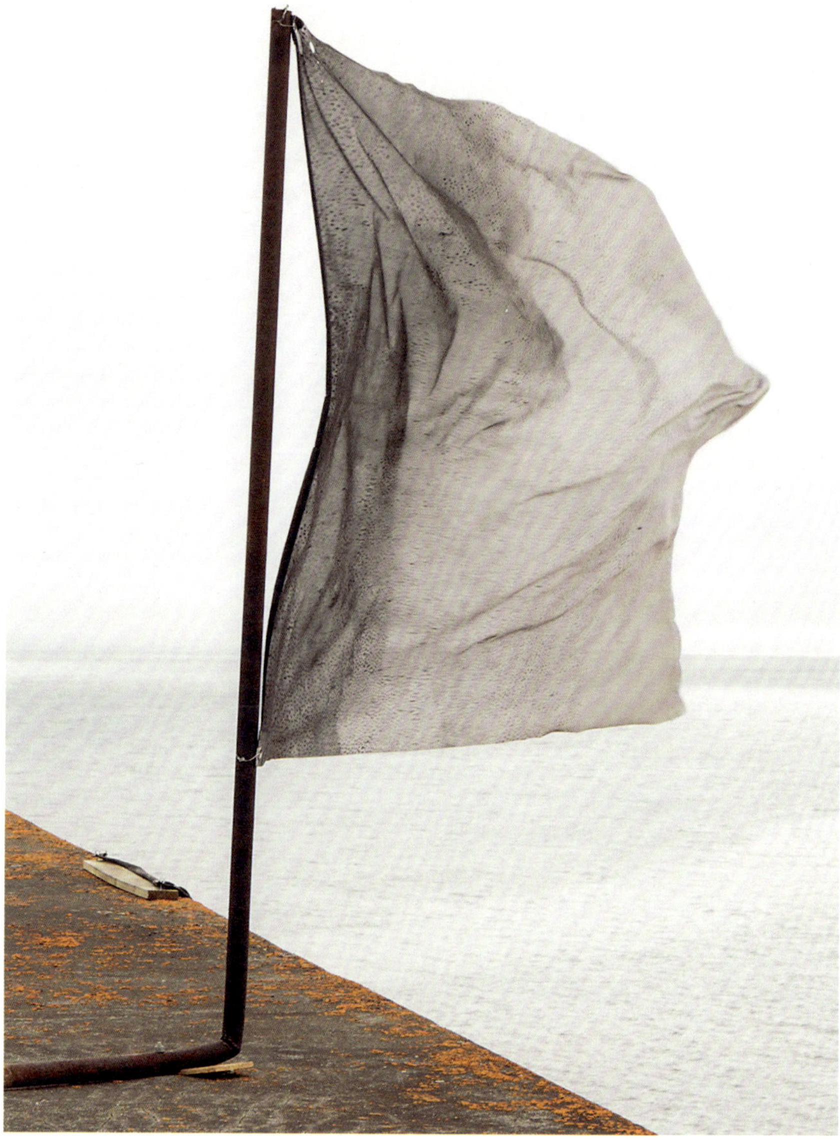
1.

Born 1986, Wuustwezel, Belgium. Lives and works in Geel, Belgium.

1. *Four Flags*, 2012–17, charcoal and fabric paint on textile, dimensions variable, installation view, 'Summer Dust', Verksmiðjan, Hjalteyri, Iceland, 2016
2. *Circulation de l'air*, 2019, charcoal wall drawing, dimensions variable installation view, 'Storytelling', MAC Musée d'art contemporain de Lyon, France
3. *Walls*, 2015, charcoal wall drawing, dimensions variable installation view, 'Collection with loose ends', Kunsthaus NRW Kornelimünster, Aachen, Germany

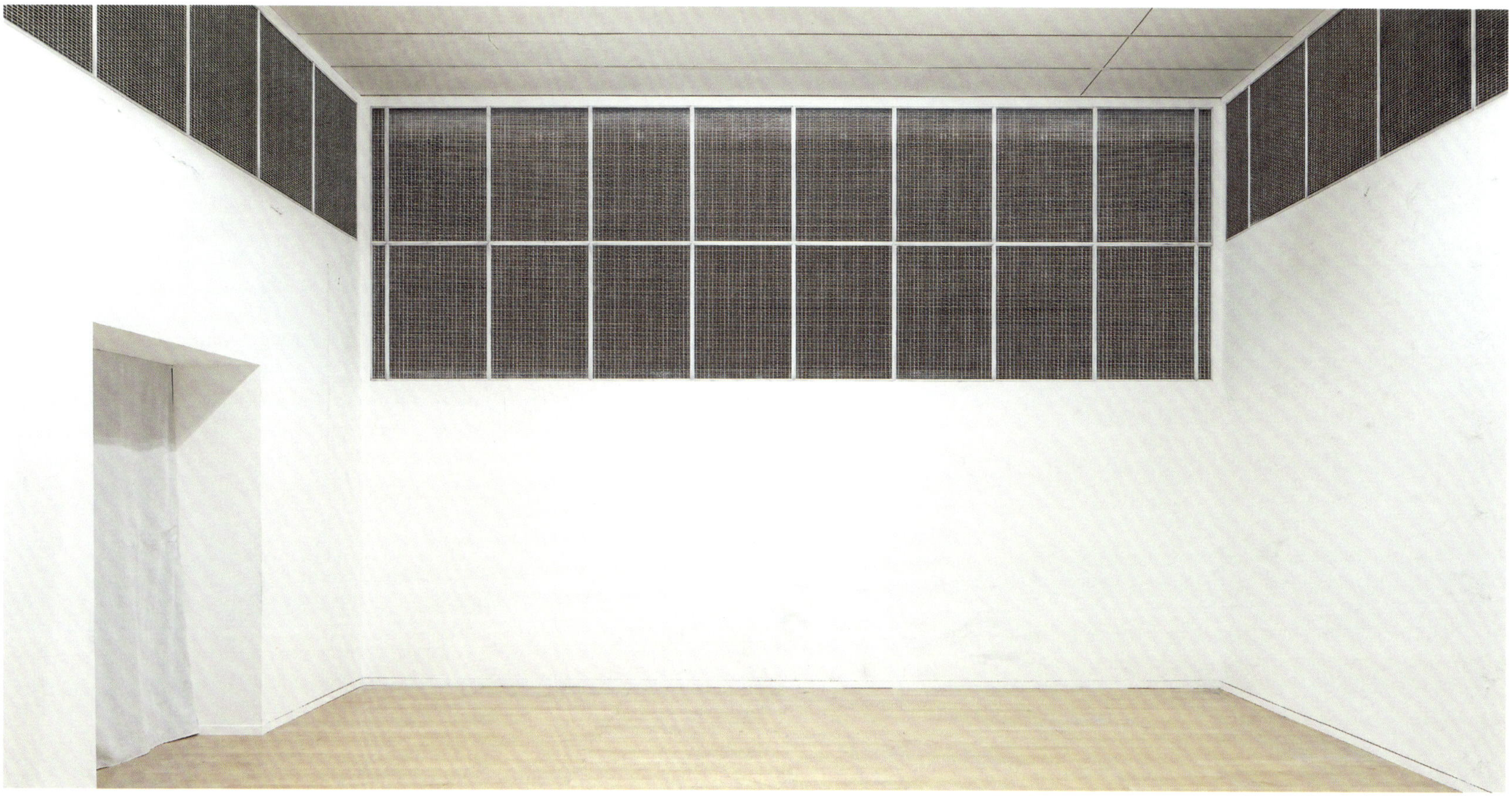

2.

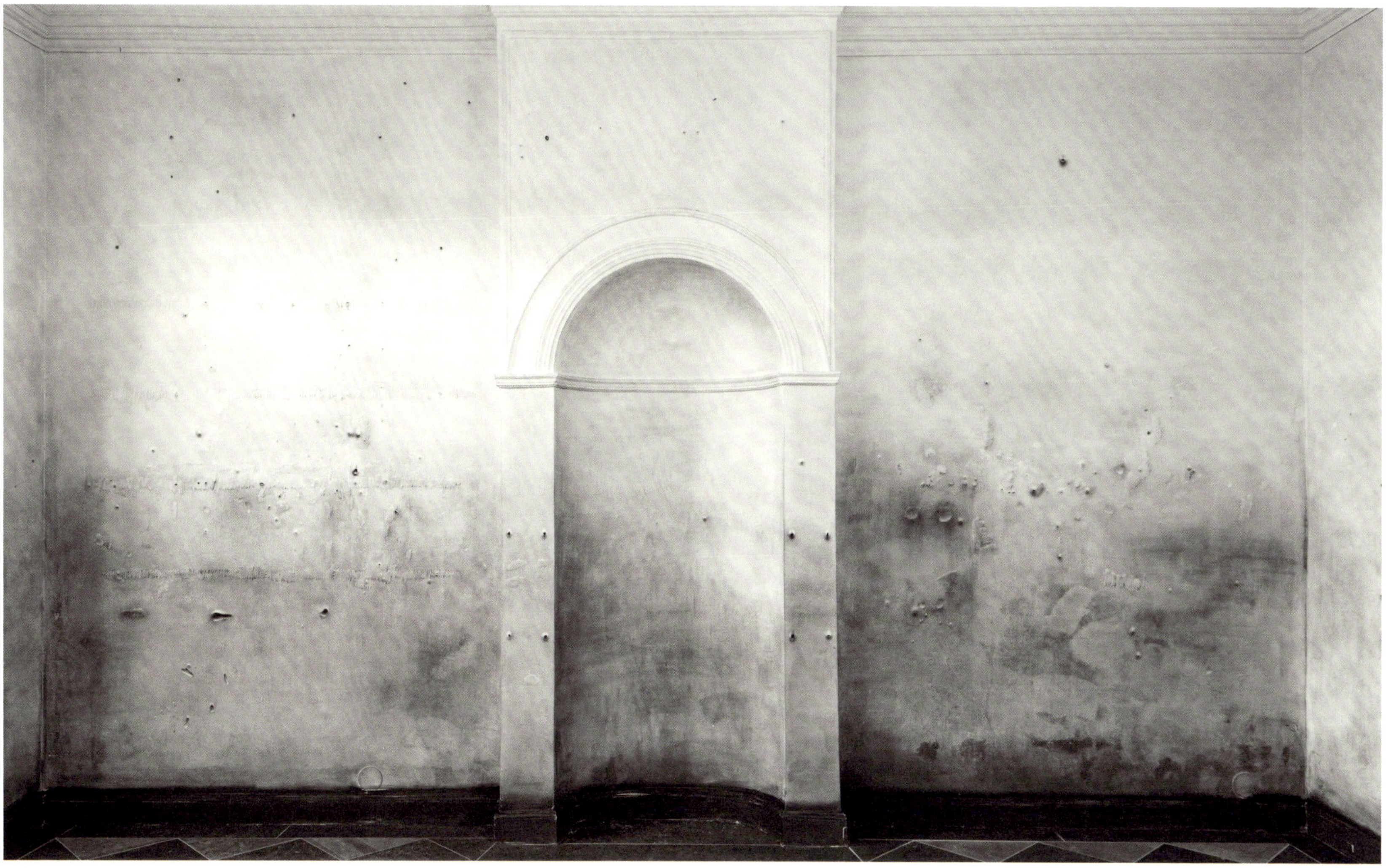

3.

JOSÉ VERA MATOS .... Peruvian artist José Vera Matos's large-scale drawings are shape-shifters: you just can't quite pin them down. His seemingly abstract compositions can comprise dense rectangular columns or more disparate arrangements of circles, triangles, squares and tetrominos (S-, T-, Z- or L-shapes). Take, for example, *¿Con que fin escribió Guaman Poma su crónica? (For What Purpose Did Guaman Poma Write His Chronicle?)*, (2019), in which a series of red spiky graph-like contours intersect. They could be saws whose teeth nearly grate, the visual mapping of sound waves or even blocks falling haphazardly in a game of Tetris. Upon closer inspection, however, these non-figurative forms have another register that also produces meaning: language. .... In *Objeto antiguo, objeto marginal* (*Old Object, Marginal Object*) (2019), Vera Matos uses a stylograph fountain pen – which has a thin hollow tube or needle instead of a nib – on bamboo paper to hand transcribe the chapter 'Marginal Objects: Antiques' from French sociologist and philosopher Jean Baudrillard's *The System of Objects*, published in 1968. One in a series of eight drawings that use turquoise blue and black ink, he reconfigures these handwritten words to make intricate structures of jagged lines. The resulting patterns are so complex as to seem like an invented syntax of signs that we long to decipher. Baudrillard's book considered how different objects are consumed in different ways. He believed that a capitalist society is driven by the need to purchase items, but that this is a socially constructed situation underpinned by fetishizing objects. In other words, we do not have genuine needs related to genuine uses but, rather, a belief that we must buy things to have a sense of meaning in our lives. By this logic, objects say something about their users and have a social significance rooted in a specific moment in time. .... It is such analysis of objects that appeals to Vera Matos. He has an interest in why contemporary societies are so fascinated with ancient objects from pre-Columbian cultures (the visual arts of indigenous peoples of the Caribbean, North, Central and South Americas until the late-fifteenth and early-sixteenth centuries). The artist believes that we seek meaning and symbolic value from these objects as a way of not only understanding them but also accessing past cultures and perhaps, by extension, owning them in the spirit of colonialism. In turn, we sever their sacred history because of a process of appropriation and even domestication of such entities. This will to have total understanding – entire possession – of the world is what Vera Matos uses as a springboard to explore the beauty of the elusive. Like Baudrillard, he sees the excessive search for knowledge as being fruitless, one that inevitably culminates in some kind of delusion rather than transmitting clarity.
.... Louisa Elderton

1.
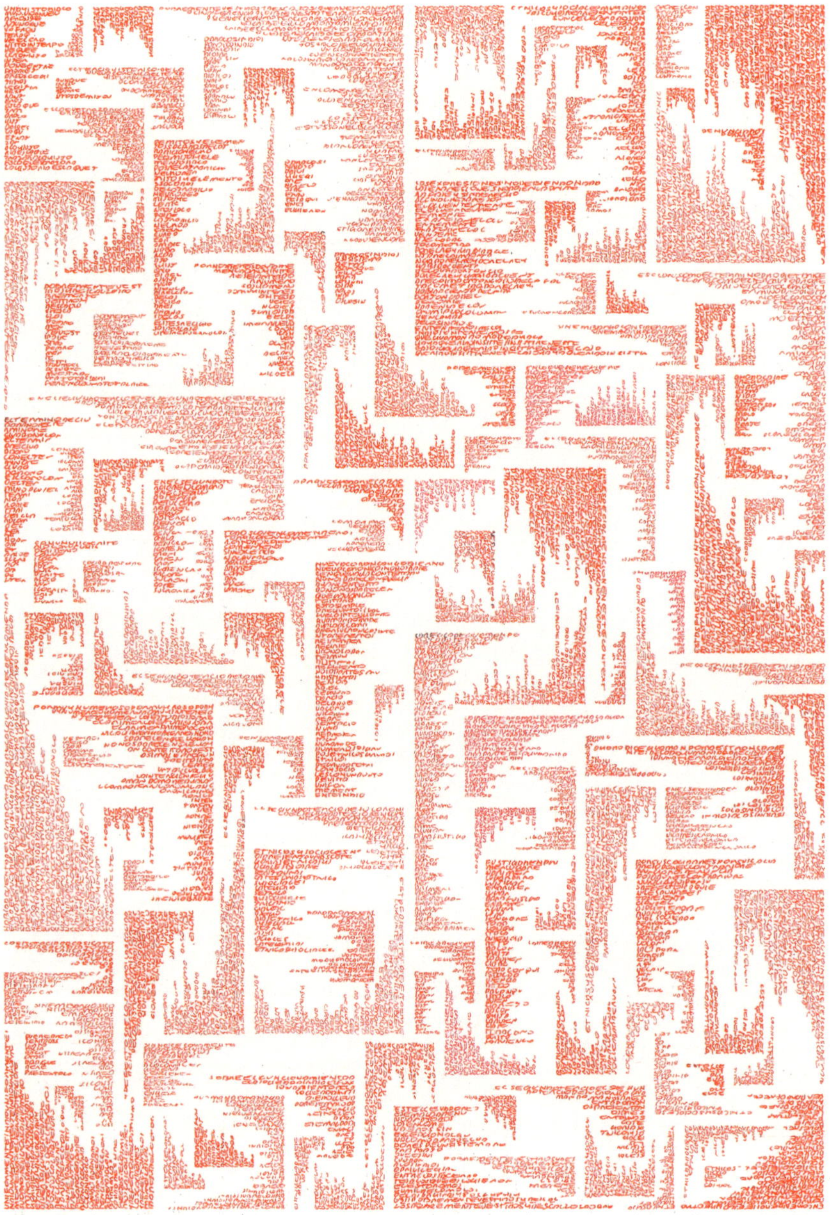

Born 1981, Lima, Peru. Lives and works in Lima.

1. *¿Con que fin escribió Guaman Poma su crónica? (For What Purpose Did Guaman Poma Write His Chronicle?)*, 2019, (detail), hand transcription of text by Jean Philippe Husson, stylograph on bamboo paper, 65 × 50 cm (25 ⅝ × 19 ¾ in)
2. *Siete Ensayos de Interpretación: de la Realidad Peruana* (*Seven Essays of Interpretation of the Peruvian Reality*), 2015, stylograph on cotton paper, 40 × 30 cm (15 ¾ × 11 ¾ in)

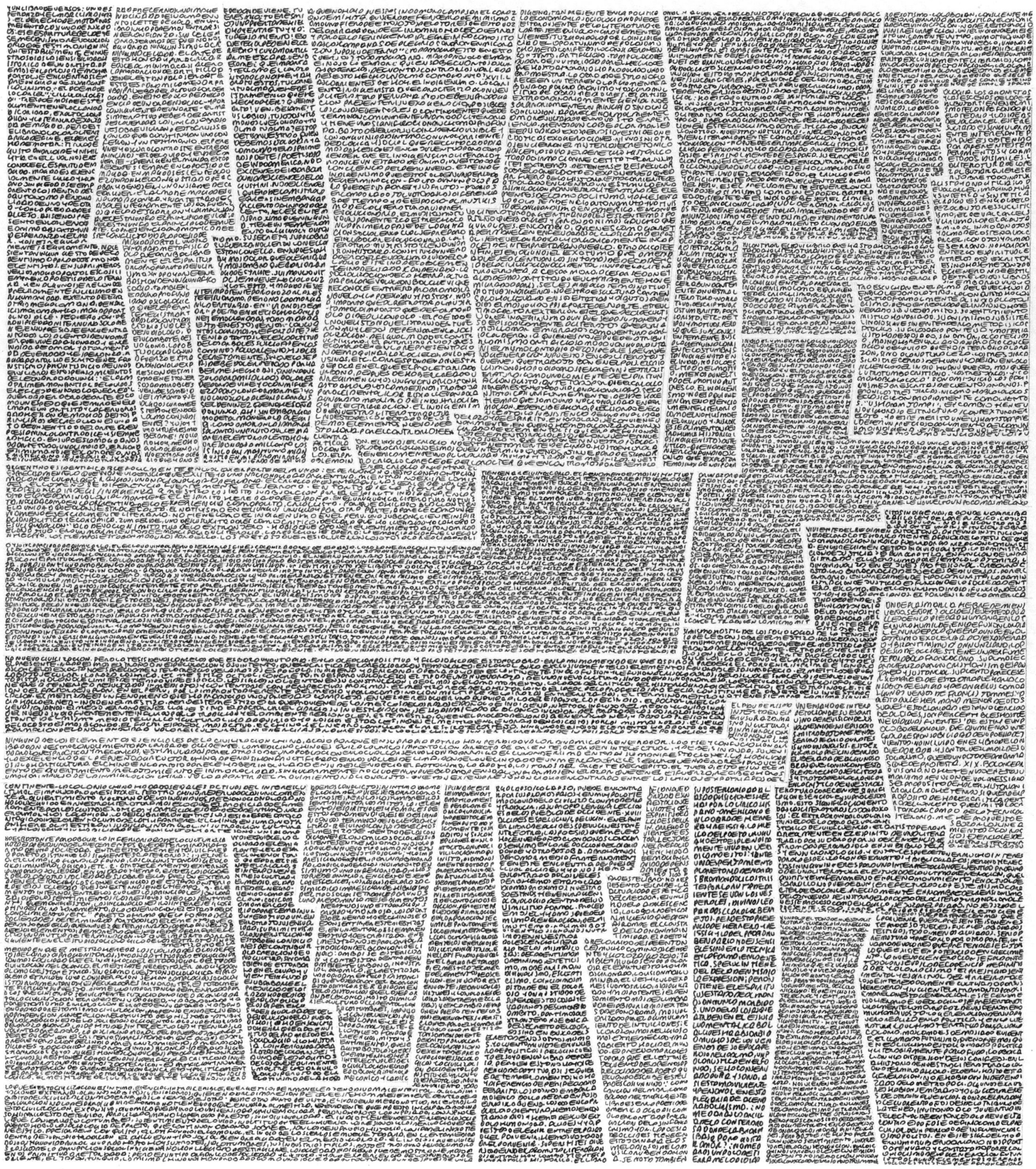

2.

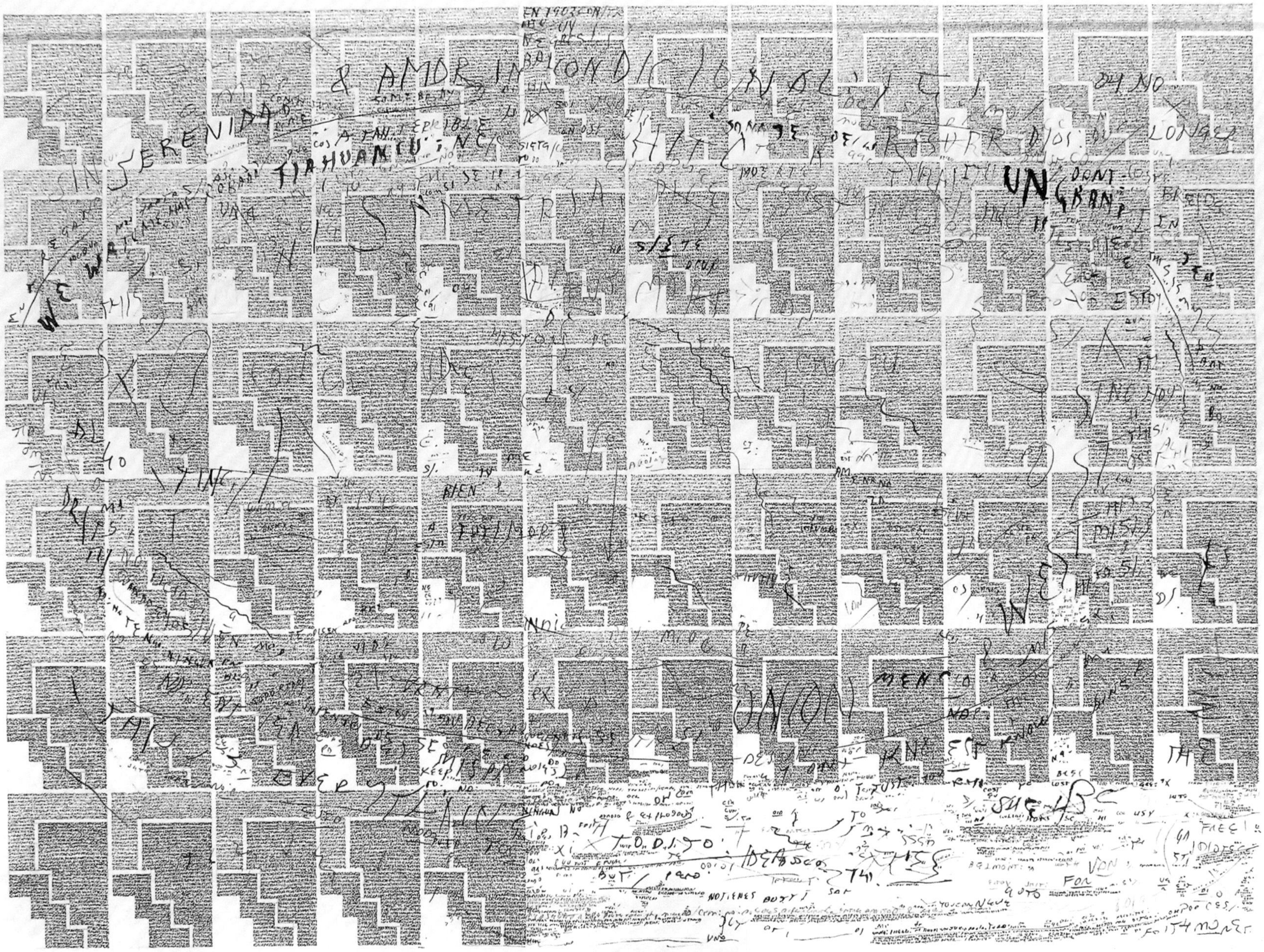

3.

3. *Untitled*, 2016, stylograph, ink and graphite on bamboo paper, 55 × 70 cm (21 ⅝ × 27 ½ in)

4. *Objeto antiguo, objeto marginal* (*Old Object, Marginal Object*), 2019, hand transcription of the chapter 'Marginal Objects: Antiques' in Jean Baudrillard's *The System of Objects*, stylograph on bamboo paper, 59.5 × 42 cm (23 ⅜ × 16 ½ in)

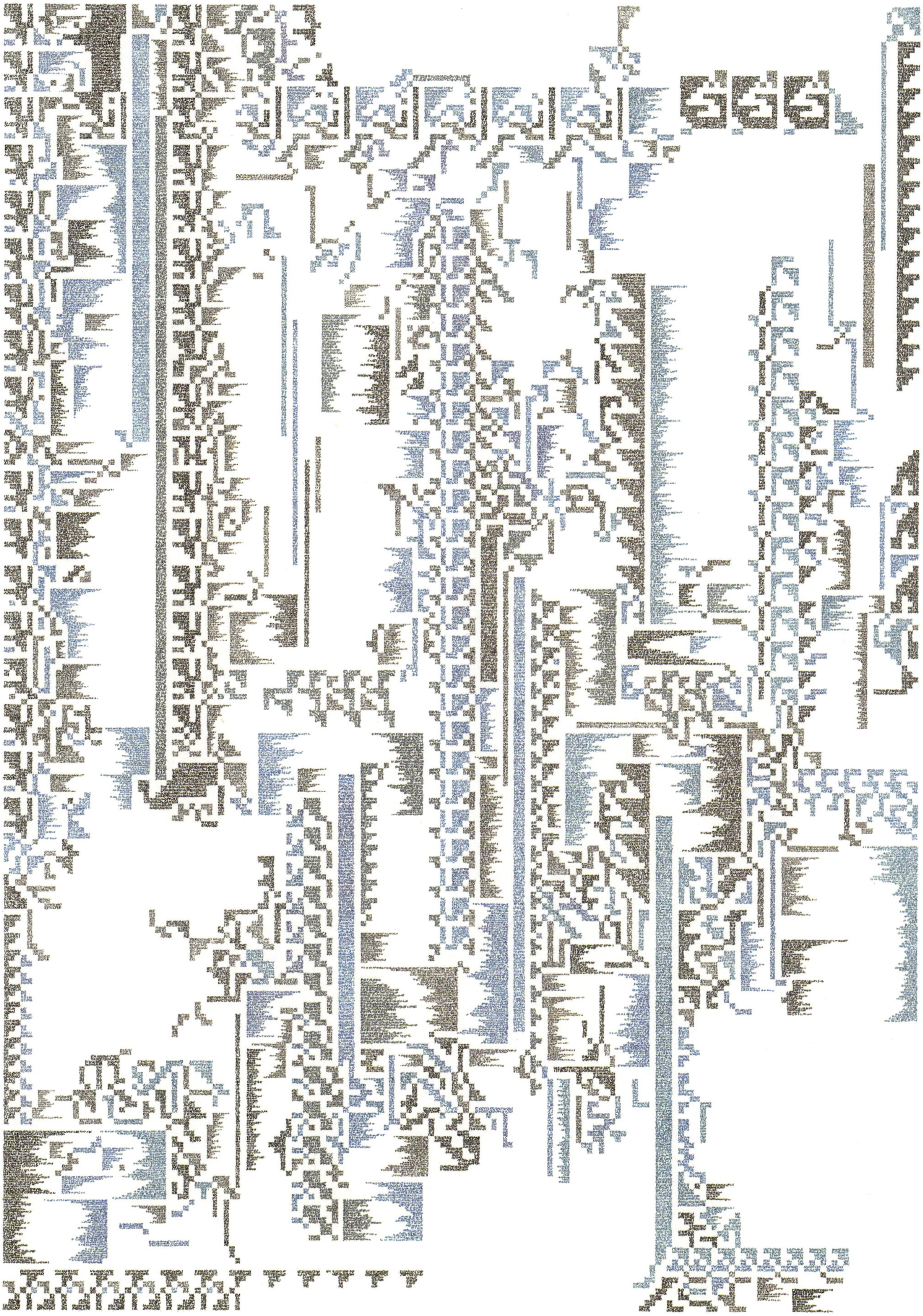

4.

DIANE VICTOR .... Haunting...unsettling...morbid are words that come to mind when looking at Diane Victor's work. She confronts and intimidates the viewer into rethinking and reconsidering socio-political issues surrounding abuse, violence, power, moral corruption, prejudice, bias, inequality, vulnerability and the fragility of life. Victor is recognized as one of South Africa's most acclaimed visual artists, demonstrating exceptional technical expertise in drawing, printmaking, etching and lithography; she also practises *fumage*, a technique that involves 'drawing' with the smoke or ash of a candle, as used by the Austrian Surrealist artist and art-philosopher Wolfgang Paalen (1905–59). Victor draws evanescent patterns on white paper with smoke or carbon residue. Smoke creates dramatic effects that intensify the narratives and sense of irony in these drawings. The medium is fugitive and the resulting works are extremely fragile and easily damaged. This reinforces the issues the artist depicts in her works, of vulnerability and the fragile nature of human life. Her selection of materials and technique is thus fundamental to the process and subject matter. In works such as the triptych *No country for Old Women* (2013) movement and structure are shaped through the use of line, while mass and intensity are created by smoke or ash. .... Sometimes, as is the case here, Victor's smoke images are captured on glass panels that are laminated and fitted into steel frames. The shape of these frames alludes to the stained-glass windows in Gothic architecture and places the work within medieval religious iconography. Another reference is the work of Hieronymus Bosch (*c.*1450–1516), the Early Netherlandish painter whose pictures centre around themes of religion, suffering and torture. *No country for Old Women* honours the female victims of domestic and social abuse and serves as a reminder of the ongoing brutal violence perpetrated against women. One of the victims depicted is a young girl who was gang-raped and disembowelled; another, the artist's aunt, was violently murdered. .... Victor's choice of *fumage* has further significance. There is a duality in the concept of a burning candle: it provides warmth and light but can inflict pain and damage. The subtle touches of smoke in these works result in an interplay of dark and light that mirrors the artist's decision to cast light on darker issues such as the failings of society to protect the vulnerable and the innocent. In *Shadow Boxer* (2015) she dramatically depicts her own figure with boxing gloves, defending herself against an assailant, her own shadow. The boxing gloves resemble the shape of kidneys that one assumes refer to her kidney operation. With her facial expression and boxing gloves rendered in finely drawn detail, the carbon residue elsewhere in the drawing emphasizes the dynamic tension and abrasion in the human interaction. Technique and material unite with subject matter to reinforce the vulnerability and transience of life.
.... Elbé Coetsee

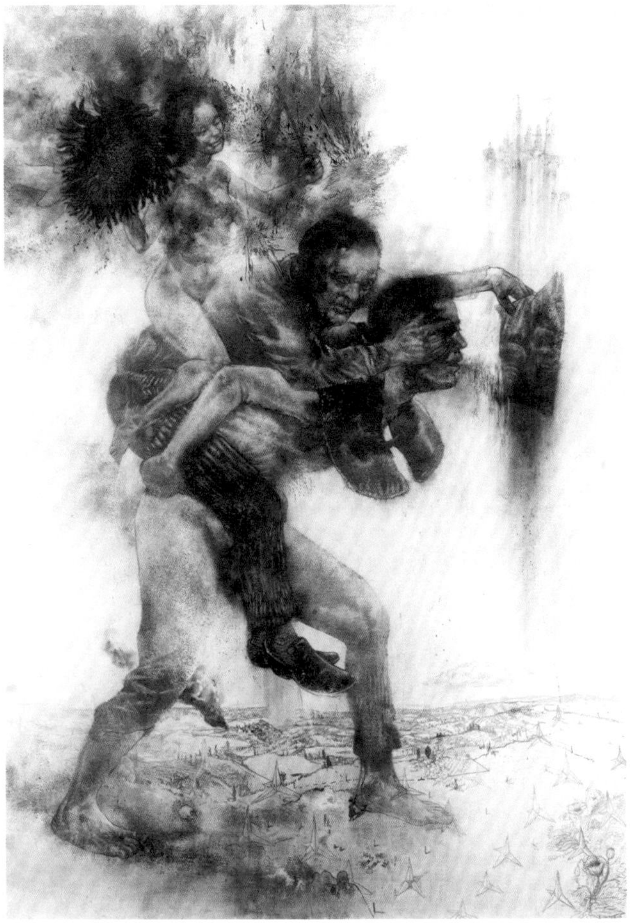

1.

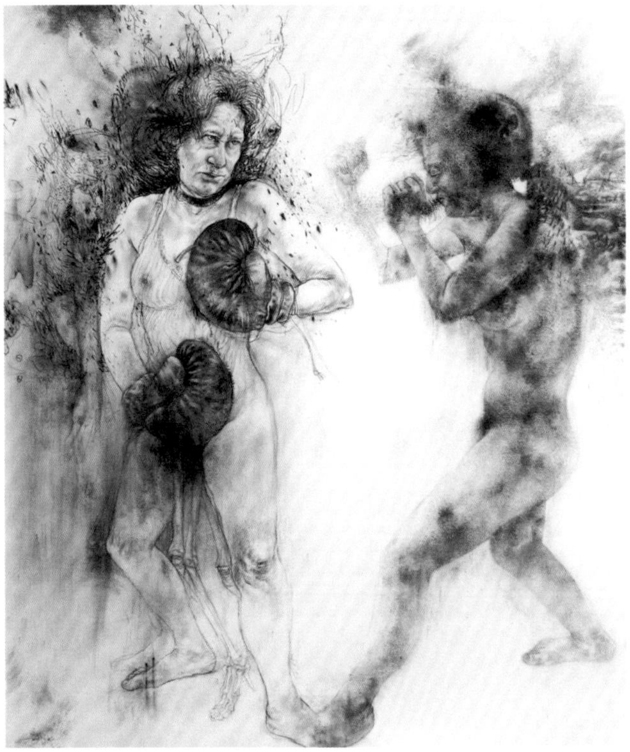

2.

Born 1964, Witbank (now eMalahleni), South Africa. Lives and works in Johannesburg.

1. *The grass is always greener*, 2017, charcoal and ash on paper, 195 × 140 cm (78 × 53 in)
2. *Shadow Boxer*, 2015, charcoal, pastel and ash on paper, 150 × 128 cm (59 × 50 in)
3. *No country for Old Women*, 2013, steel structure, glass and smoke, 3 panels, overall: 500 × 420 cm (196 ⅞ × 165 ⅜ in), installation view, ABSA Klein Karoo National Arts Festival (KKNK), Oudtshoorn, South Africa

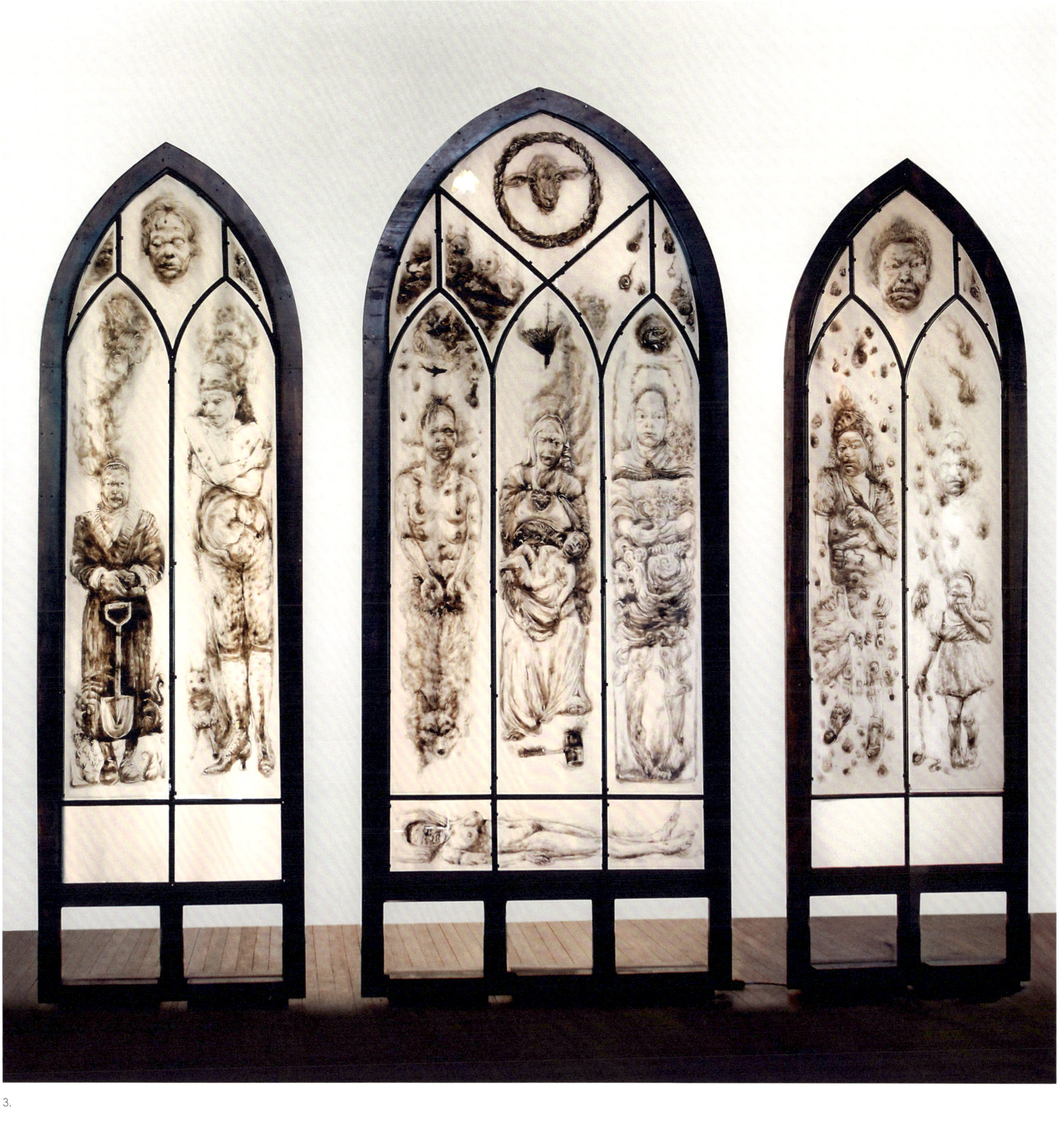

3.

H A J R A W A H E E D.......Hajra Waheed appropriates and
reinterprets archival materials, from historical documents
and declassified government, and oral histories, as a means
to examine colonial and state power and reclaim marginalized
histories. Through works that encompass collage, sound, video,
sculpture and installation, she creates intricate narratives
that address recurring issues surrounding structures of power,
surveillance, privilege and public histories. In doing so, she
exposes hidden, forgotten or omitted aspects of social, political and historical narrations. These wider socio-political and
cultural concerns resonate with her personal experiences of
being raised in Dhahran, Saudi Arabia. The major administrative
centre for the Saudi Arabian Oil Company (ARAMCO), Dhahran
was a geopolitical hotspot guarded by US and Saudi airbases
and with strict controls on access. As a child, Waheed developed an obsession early on with identifying aircraft, tracking
flight routes and keeping a log of her observations in a cryptic
visual language. Such interests and aesthetics have since
found their ways into her artistic projects, frequently collaged
on old graph and notebook papers to give them a patina of
formality........'Drone Studies', for instance, is an expansive
body of works that embodies her near-obsessive exploration
of mapping. It includes 'Architectural Studies 1–17' (2011),
a number of diagrammatic drawings with cut-out details on
aged paper. Each page bears a floor plan that corresponds
to historic sacred sites, mosques from around the world
and aircraft fragments adhered to the paper with Mylar tape.
Referencing the American U-2 spy plane shot down over the
Soviet Union in 1960, these sheets evoke lost pages from an
imaginary notebook kept in the U-2's cockpit. Another series,
'Still Against the Sky 1–3' (2015), takes as its subject mapping
as a means of perceiving and understanding the world from an
individual point of view. Based on found materials from space
research, surveillance documents and unidentified memoirs,
the resulting collage is a stunning pleated map of the galaxy,
with each individual star carefully etched on to transfer paper.
......Resource extraction is another long-term focus of the
artist's research, leading to projects such as 'Plume 1–24'
(2017), a series of found images of clouds of smoke that evoke
memories of the Kuwaiti oil fires in 1991. 'The ARD: Study
for a Portrait 1–28' (2018), which probes the complexities
of corporate-state relations through a study of the Arabian
Research Division, founded in 1946 as a research, translation
and intelligence gathering unit in ARAMCO. Waheed often
uses historical archives as the source for her collages, to
destabilize official histories, opening up spaces for new
imaginaries and interpretations.
.......Carol Yinghua Lu

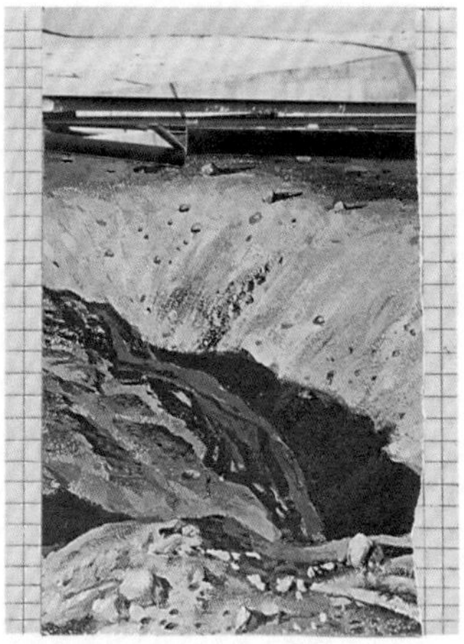

1.

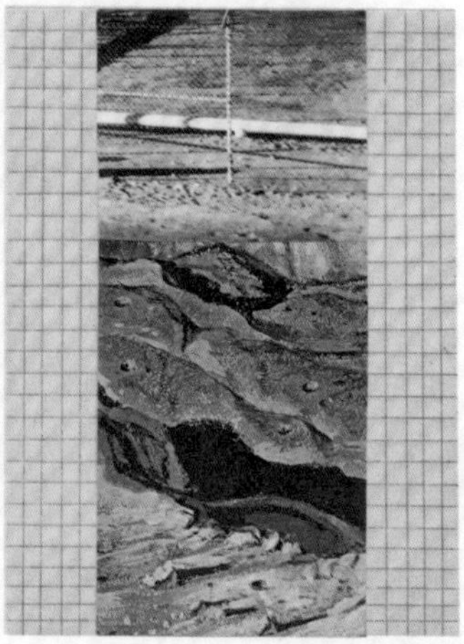

2.

Born 1980, Calgary, Canada. Lives and works in Montreal.

1. *Untitled 1–10* (detail, page 8/10), 2019, etching, photographic collage on paper,
 34.3 × 26.7 cm (13 ½ × 10 ½ in)
2. *Untitled 1–10* (detail, page 7/10), 2019, etching, photographic collage on paper,
 34.3 × 26.7 cm (13 ½ × 10 ½ in)

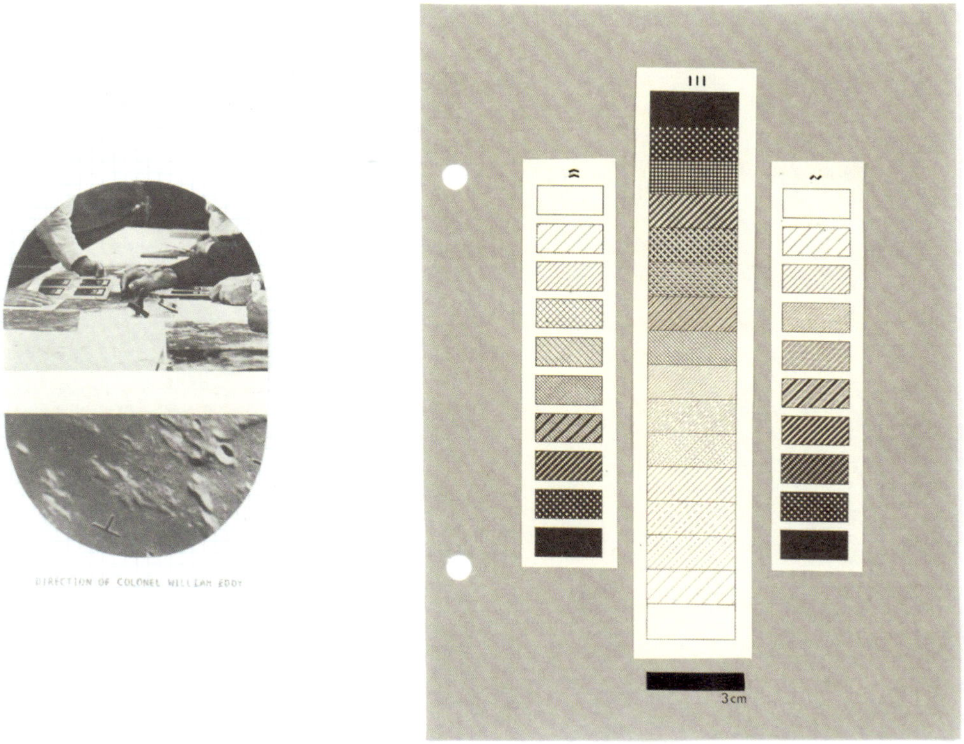

3.

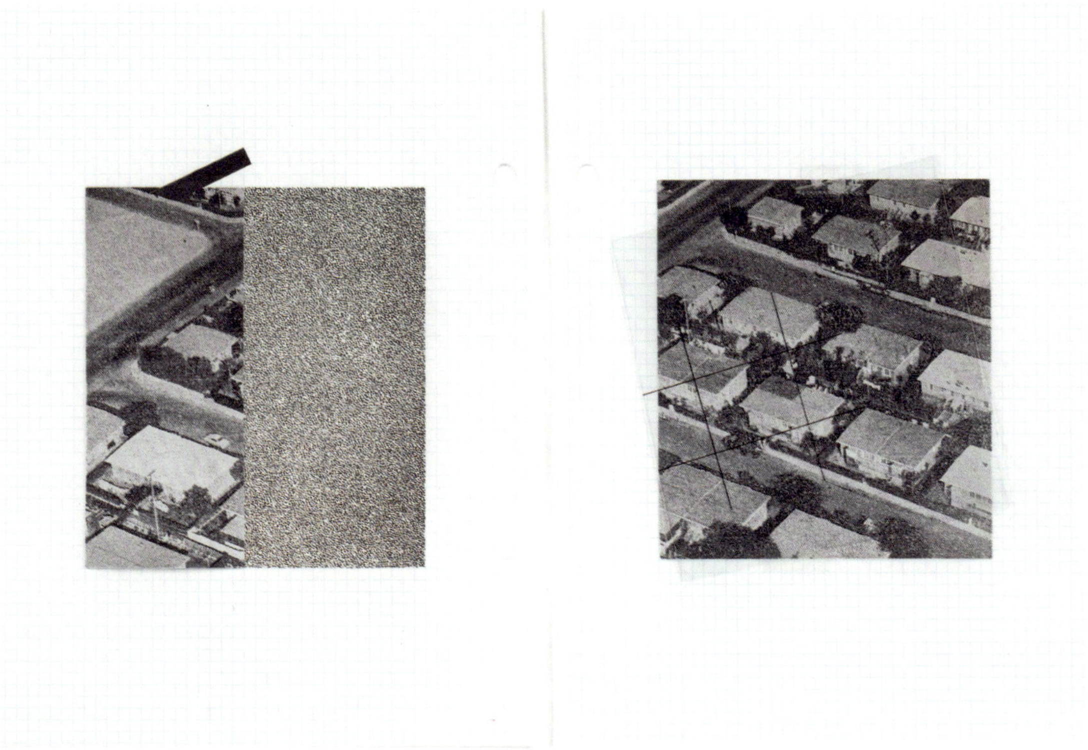

4.

3. *The ARD: Study for a Portrait 1–28* (detail, page 4/28), 2018, Mylar, photographic collage, archival tape, xylene and graphite transfer on paper, 35.6 × 45.7 cm (14 × 18 in)
4. *The ARD: Study for a Portrait 1–28* (detail, page 3/28), 2018, Mylar, photographic collage, archival tape and ink on graph paper, 35.6 × 45.7 cm (14 × 18 in)

BARBARA WALKER'I consider myself a research-based practitioner,' said Barbara Walker ahead of her 2017 residency at London's Drawing Room. 'Eighty per cent of my work is research, which I immerse myself in. It is a grounding for my ideas and the issues I'm tackling.' The thrust of that research is archival investigation to identify those – particularly people of colour – overlooked in the historical narrative. Walker then aims to present them as subjects, delineating an alternative to establishment perspectives that obfuscate the heterogeneity of this history. Take, for example, the way in which she revisits the role of Caribbean servicemen in the British Army in her series 'Shock and Awe' (2015–ongoing). During the World Wars these men were often assigned menial roles and then – despite significant contributions – were not accorded a hero's welcome home and scarcely featured in the public record. Walker celebrates them in enormous drawings rendered directly on the wall, such as *Untitled* (2019), a variation of a drawing from 'Transcended' series (2017), which garnered considerable acclaim at the 57th Venice Biennale, in the Diaspora Pavilion. In *Backdrop* (2018), a work on paper, she centres the Black figures while the other soldiers are blind-embossed to leave just a trace of whiteness. Walker also intervenes to alter the relative visibility of people in contemporary communities. For 'Sub Urban: New Drawings' (2015) she derived large-scale charcoal wall drawings from her own photographs of anony-mous individuals in and around the English town of Farnham. Both that project and 'Show and Tell' (2008–ongoing) address the stereotypes projected onto people through their dress codes. As the artist in residence at The New Art Gallery in Walsall, UK, for three-months in 2011, she drew portraits of members of the public who visited the gallery, but without showing their faces. Depicting heads from behind, or with faces otherwise obscured, and figures from the neck down, the audience were invited to mentally 'complete' their portraits by reading the information provided – clothing, hair and jewellery. Alongside exposing potential prejudices and stereotypes, it triggers such questions as: To what extent is fashion respon-sible for providing the styles through which we may be defined? Or do individuals take the lead in how they choose to look, while consumerist interests follow? Walker's materials and techniques serve to reinforce her themes. Charcoal, especially used on walls, is an easily-smudged and impermanent medium compared with the traditional commemoration of subjects through oil paintings on canvas. Walker underlined in a 2008 interview with *a-n* that 'the removal of detail (through erasing, tearing away, cutting out, blotting, whitewashing) serves to place emphasis upon what I see as a compelling absence of Black representation in our national archives and, by extension, in the collective memory of British society.' This is confounded when she publicly washes away her wall drawings, re-enacting such erasure from history, yet leaving a residue of marks that act as an 'anti-object', suggesting that truth can never be obliterated.
.... Paul Carey-Kent

1.

Born 1964, Birmingham, UK. Lives and works in Birmingham.

1. *Place, Space and Who*, 2019, (detail), charcoal and white chalk wall drawing, c.300 × 180 cm (c.10 × 6 ft), installation view, 'Barbara Walker: Place, Space and Who', Turner Contemporary, Margate, UK
2. The artist working on *Montana*, 2015, charcoal wall drawing, 400 × 420 cm (157 ½ × 165 ⅜ in) for 'Sub Urban: New Drawing', James Hockey Gallery, University for the Creative Arts, Farnham, UK
3. The artist removing charcoal wall drawings, 400 × 460 cm (157 ½ × 181 in), from 'Show and Tell', The New Art Gallery, Walsall, UK

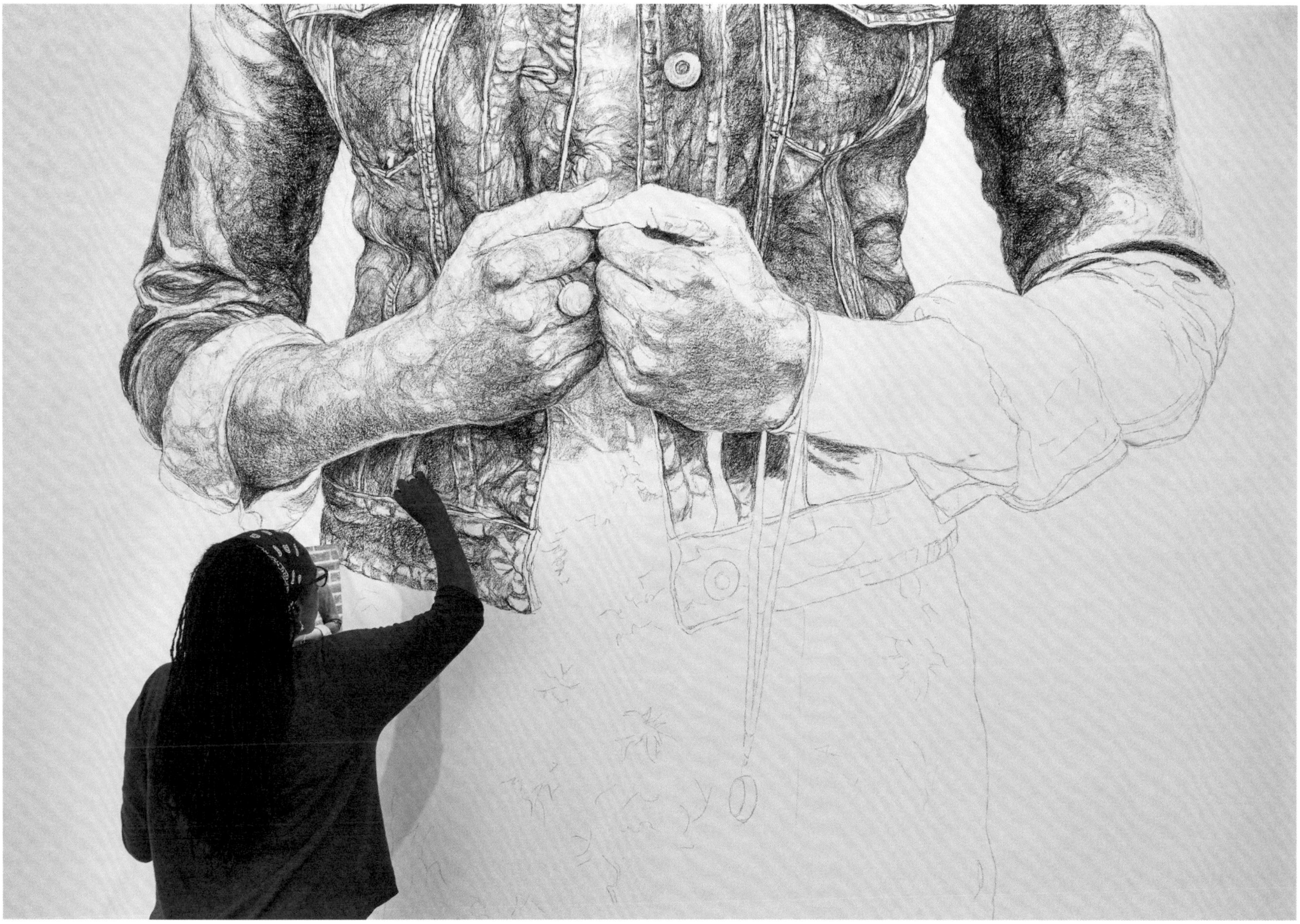

2.

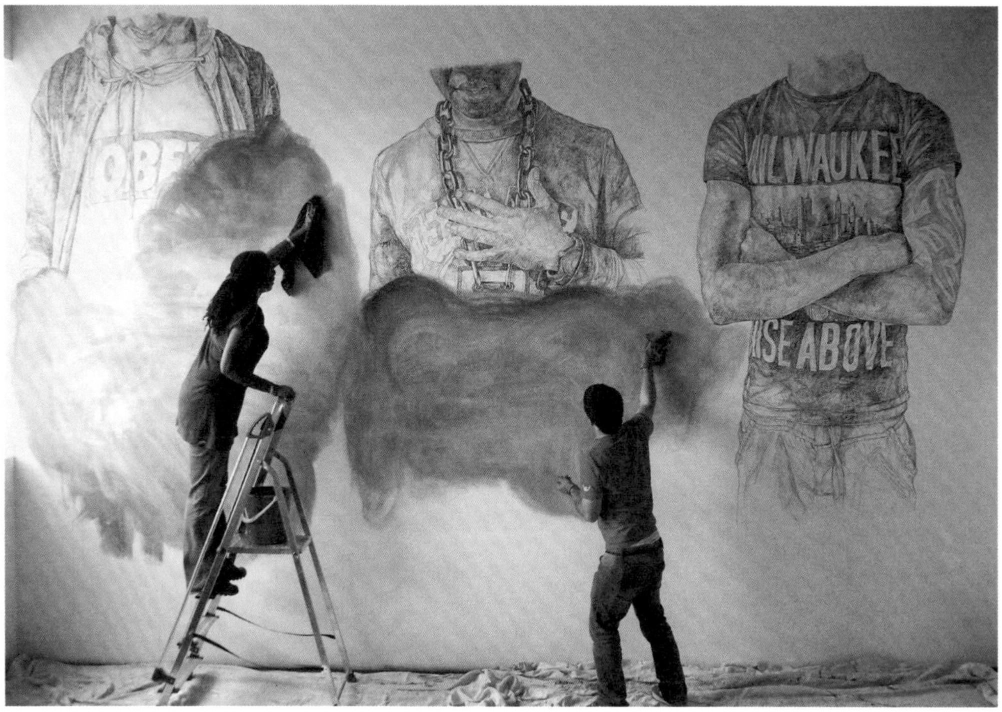

3.

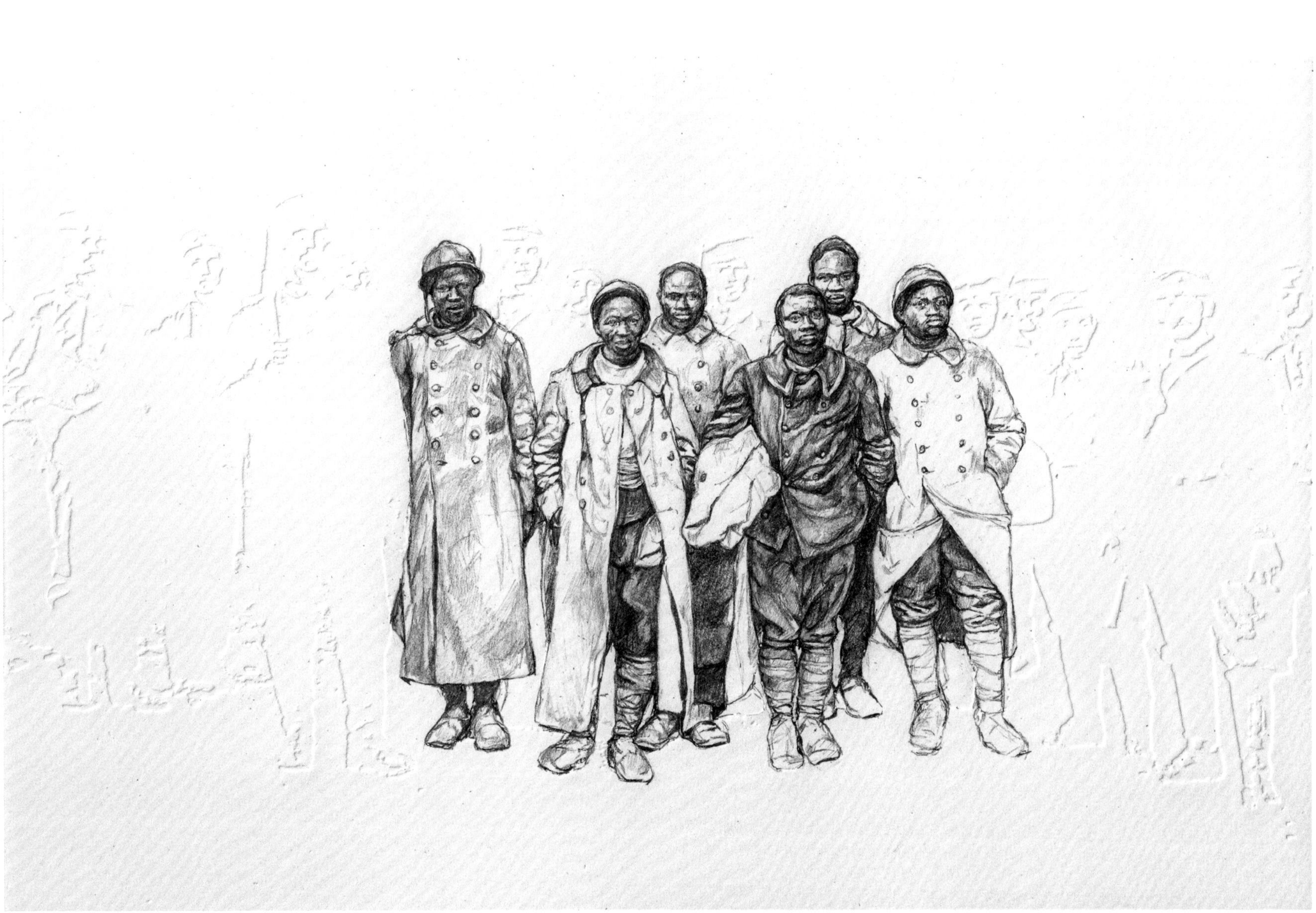

4.

4. *Backdrop*, 2018, graphite on embossed paper, 47 × 61 cm (18 ½ × 24 in)
5. *Untitled*, 2019, conté, black chalk and charcoal wall drawing, 280 × 90 cm (110 ¼ × 35 ½ in), installation view, 'Protest and Remembrance', Cristea Roberts Gallery, London

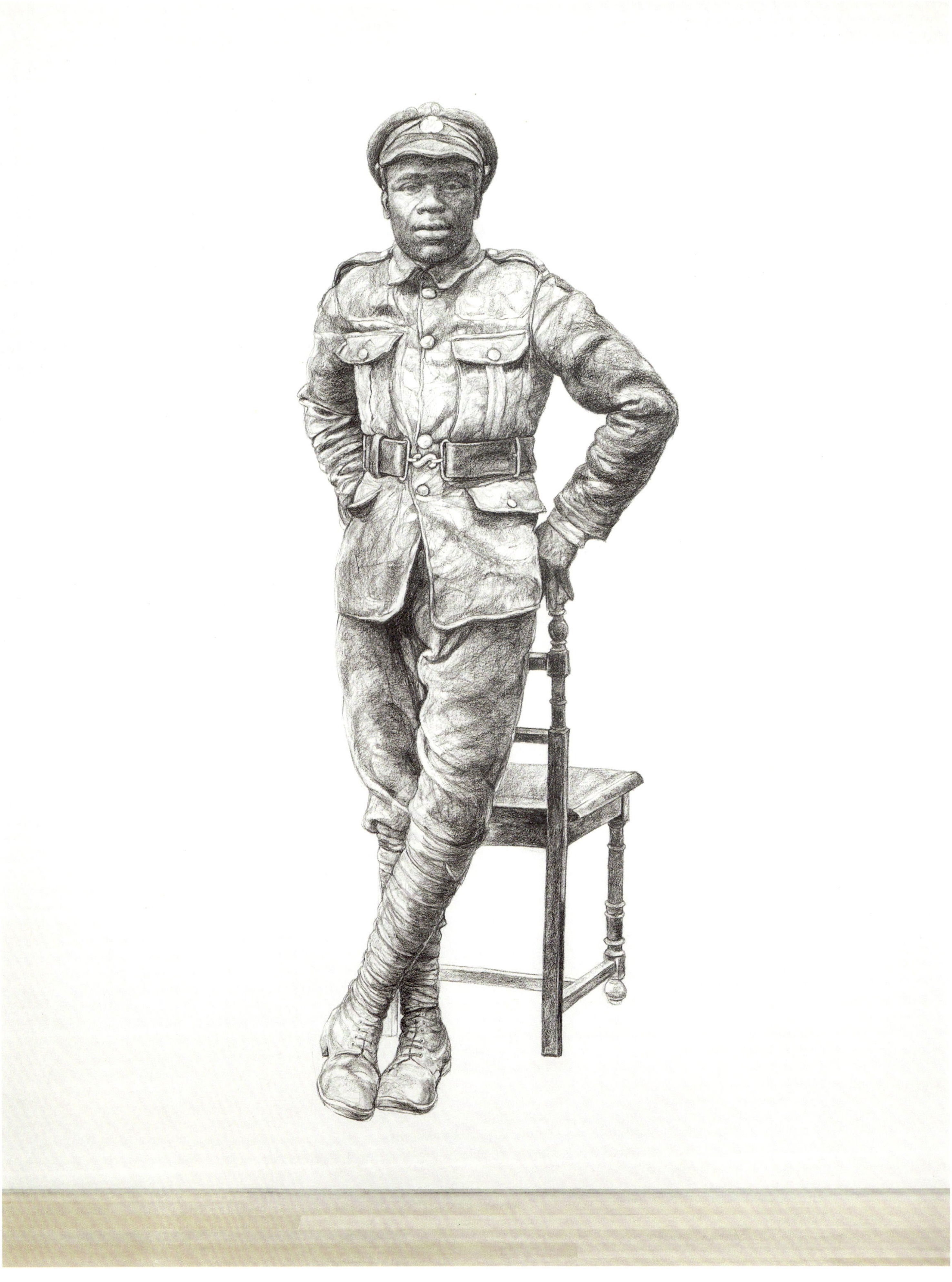

5.

EVELYN TAOCHENG WANG .... Evelyn Taocheng Wang questions what constitutes identity, and the potential for this to morph and change. The cultural construction of selfhood as mediated by autobiography is a core theme, her sharp observations of Eastern and Western cultures finding entangled form upon the page. Rendered using materials such as mineral colours and tea on rice paper, *Eight View of Oud-Charlois, No.4* (2019) depicts the quotidian lives of her suburban neighbours in Rotterdam – where the artist is now based, having grown up in Chengdu, China. Edged with bubble-gum pink fabric, it recalls the illustrated pages of a storybook, words and images relating across a margin. Two parents in giant puffer coats guide their young child towards the MCD supermarket, while a dog waits patiently tied to a tree. Part of a series of eight works, the delicate lines and subtle strokes of colour contrast with the banality of the scenes; Wang elevates the mundane to seemingly magical or fairytale status. .... Studying classical Chinese painting before moving to Frankfurt to attend the Städelschule, followed by a stint at De Ateliers in Amsterdam, the artist mines her own life as primary material for her work. As she said in a 2018 interview with *Mousse*: 'I don't see being personal as dangerous or even taboo for doing art.' *Massage Parlor* (2016), an installation comprising burgundy massage tables, purple curtains and related drawings and paintings, drew directly from the conversations that Taocheng Wang had with clients in an Amsterdam massage parlour where she worked to fund her studies. 'Those conversations were hollow, shallow, trashy, and sexual, but speak about the immigrant's gender issues as a woman.' The artist even titled certain drawings off the back of her experiences here, such as *A Hong Kong-Dutch Client Licking My Arm during the Massage Treatment* (2015). .... This interest in storytelling also underpins Wang's use of literary references, presenting fictionalized characters and differing versions of mythologies, which are retold in new cultural contexts. Two works from 2017, *A Female Grasshopper Shits Behind A Fake Hill* and *Someone Mysterious Hung Herself Up Among Towers* each comprise a large-scale drawing alongside and a small framed text. In the first, small figures and giant insects roam through a landscape; in the second, a person dressed in red gazes out from a building. Depicting scenes from *The Dream of the Red Chamber* by Cao Xueqin, a masterpiece of Chinese literature published in 1791, the semi-autobiographical themes relate to sexuality, its psychological scope mirroring the rise and fall of the author's own family, as well as memorializing the women from his youth. Wang uses such themes of identity and culture to foreground the quests and explorations of women. For her, identity is a moving concept, one changing with time and space, opening, closing and continually transforming along the way.

.... Louisa Elderton

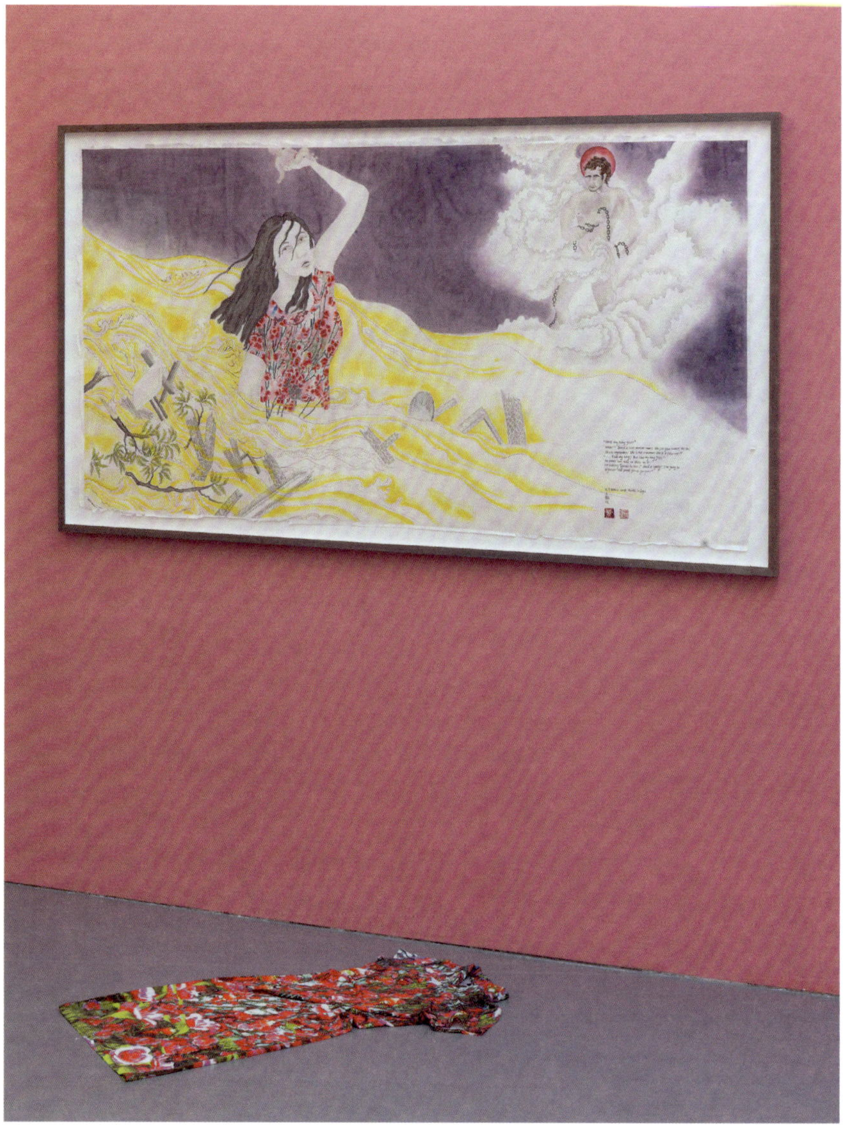

1.

Born 1981, Chengdu, China. Lives and works in Rotterdam, The Netherlands.

1. *Save my baby first*, 2017, watercolour on rice paper, mounted on rice paper, 94 × 176 cm (37 × 69 ¼ in) and agnes b dress, installation view, 'Four Season of Women Tragedy', Galerie Fons Welters, Amsterdam
2. *Eight View of Oud-Charlois, No.4*, 2019, mineral colour, tea, acrylic and fabric sewed on rice paper, 63.7 × 123.5 cm (25 × 48 ½ in)
3. *A Female Grasshopper Shits Behind A Fake Hill*, 2017, ink, mineral colour on rice paper, 180 × 96 cm (70 ⅞ × 37 ¾ in) and pencil on A4 paper, 29.7 × 21 cm (11 ¾ × 8 ¼ in) and *Someone Mysterious Hung Herself Up Among Towers* 2017, ink, mineral color on rice paper, 180 × 96 cm (70 ⅞ × 37 ¾ in) and pencil on A4 paper, 29.7 × 21 cm (11 ¾ × 8 ¼ in), installation view, 'Sensitive Attitude', Friends of S.M.A.K., De Vereniging, Ghent, Belgium, 2019.

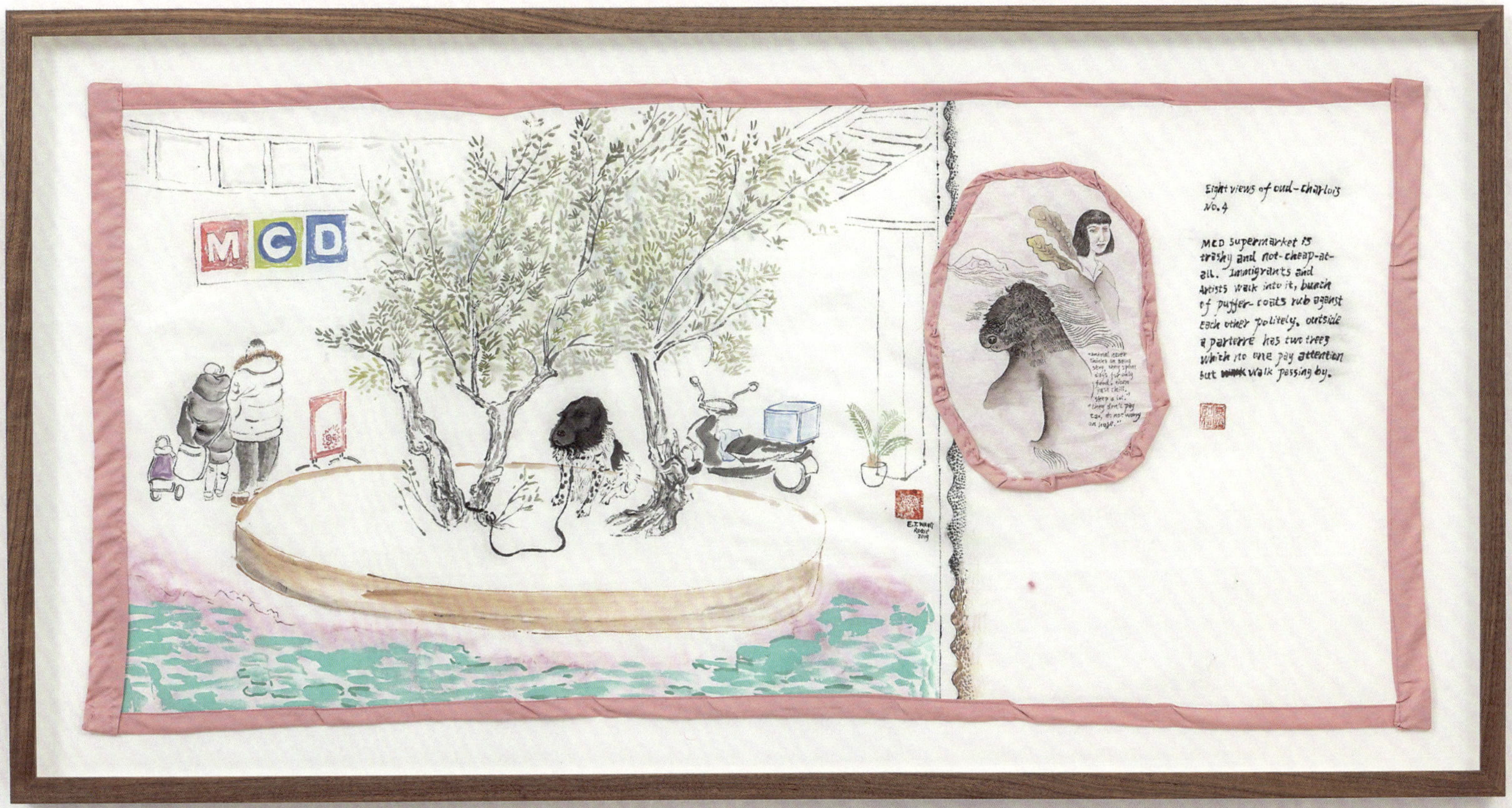
MCD
Eight views of oud-charlois
No. 4
MCD supermarket is trashy and not-cheap-at-all. Immigrants and Artists walk into it, bunch of puffer-coats rub against each other politely. outside a parterre has two trees which no one pay attention but walk passing by.

2.

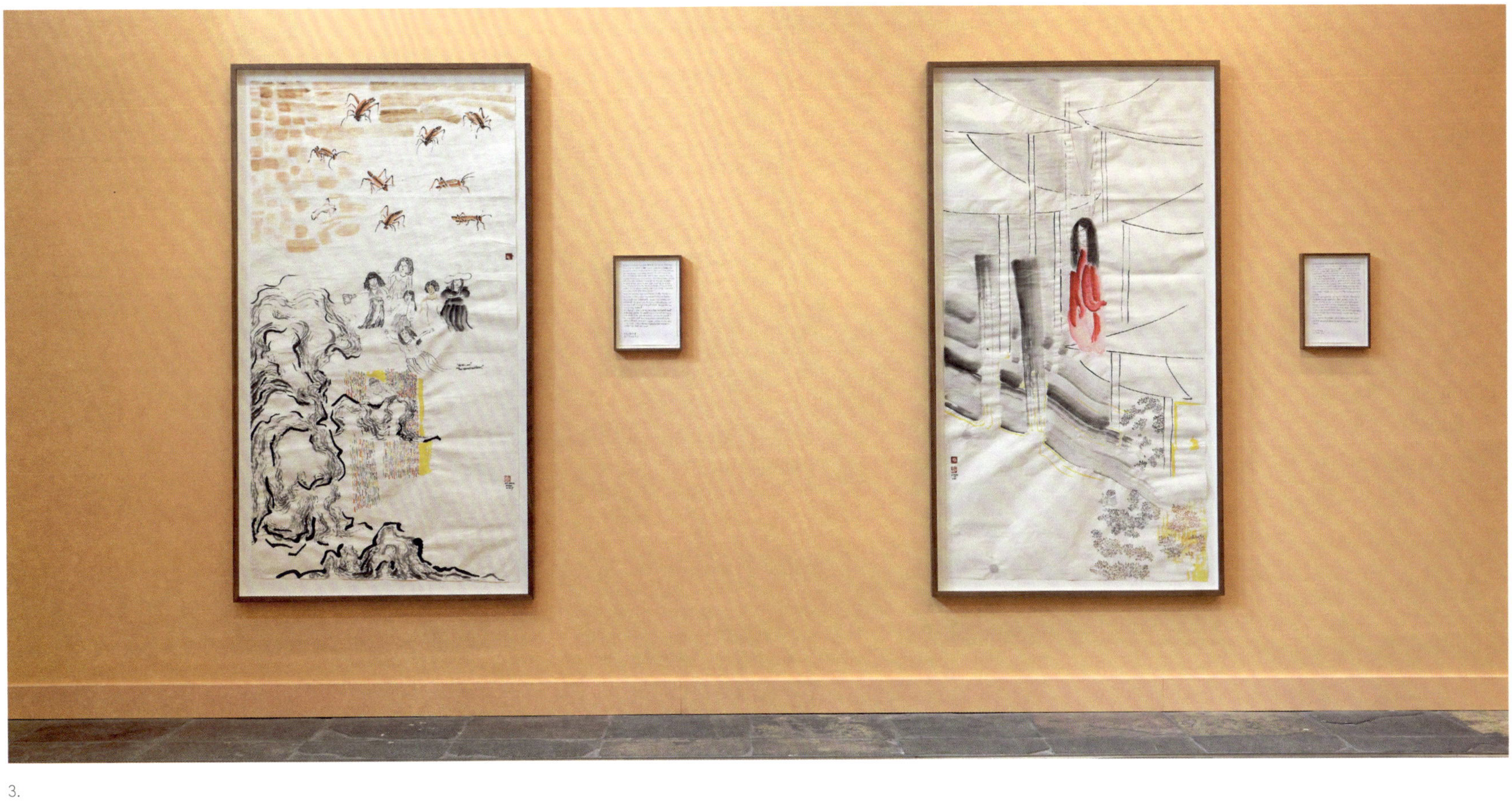

3.

CHARMAINE WATKISS .... Charmaine Watkiss had a serpentine route to becoming an artist: she was a shoe designer for several years, studied film and spent time helping artists to make video, then worked for two decades as a digital designer. Only in 2014 did she decide to train as an artist, graduating from the MA Drawing programme at Wimbledon College of Arts in 2018. Narrative and self-presentation are at the core of her drawing practice, which is founded on what she calls 'memory stories'. They cast Watkiss, life-size, as the conduit for common experiences and histories connected to the African Caribbean diaspora – she is the daughter of Jamaicans who came to post-war Britain in the 1960s, when immigration from former colonies was being encouraged to help with the significant labour shortage. .... History as a driver of self-identity is directly present in Watkiss's first 'memory story' drawing, in which she wears a coat emblazoned with images of City of London insignia, money, docks, tobacco leaves and sugar cane. *Lost/Found* (2015) came out of wondering why a street close to her east London home in Bermondsey was called Jamaica Road. As Watkiss states on her website, her research revealed 'a tale of how the borough of Southwark's participation in the Transatlantic slave trade, and the importation of goods – particularly Tobacco and Sugar along the docks – helped to create the wealth in the commercial district of London which we recognise today.' Typically, the imposingly scaled graphite and ink drawing is enhanced by carefully restricted watercolour that indicates another time and place. .... The time actually taken to make drawings of refined technique on such a striking scale also plays into Watkiss's subject matter – most directly in *We Are Here* (2017), a work in pencil, gouache and ink that depicts her playing cat's cradle. If the game takes her back a matter of decades to childhood, her dress takes us back to deep time, for it is subtly seeded with stars. Such is her declared interest beyond the diaspora in 'ancestral lineage and stories of the cosmos'. In *The Return* (2018) Watkiss – or, rather, one of two selves holding the hull of a historically resonant boat – wears indigo, referencing it as another of the slave trade's major crops. This particular Watkiss seems, with two faces, to look to both the future and the past – or to England and Jamaica – simultaneously. The drawing summarizes the tenor of her way of telling the stories behind difficult issues including slavery, discrimination and inequality – with enough charm to lure a wide audience into paying attention to matters that deserve not to be forgotten. .... Paul Carey-Kent

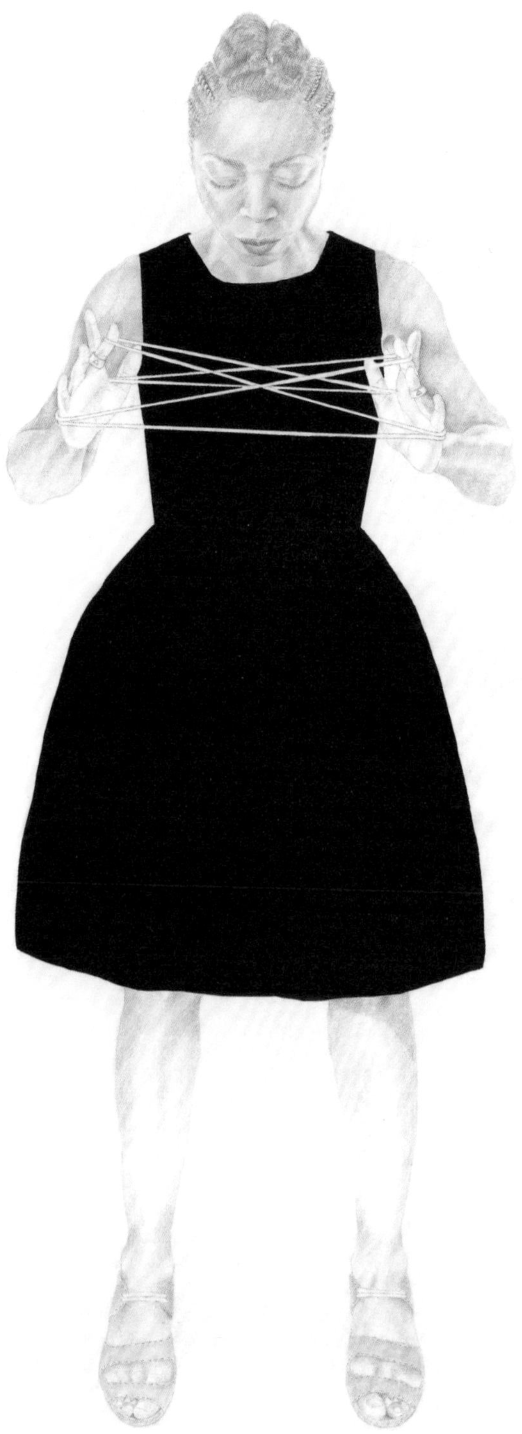

1.

Born 1964, London. Lives and works in London.

1. *We Are Here*, 2017, pencil, gouache and ink on Fabriano paper, 148 × 78 cm (58 ¼ × 30 ¾ in)
2. *The Return*, 2018, pencil, graphite powder, carbon and handmade indigo watercolour on Canson paper, 175 × 130 cm (68 ⅞ × 51 ⅛ in)
3. *Lost/Found*, 2015, pencil, watercolour and ink on Fabriano paper, 148 × 78 cm (58 ¼ × 30 ¾ in)

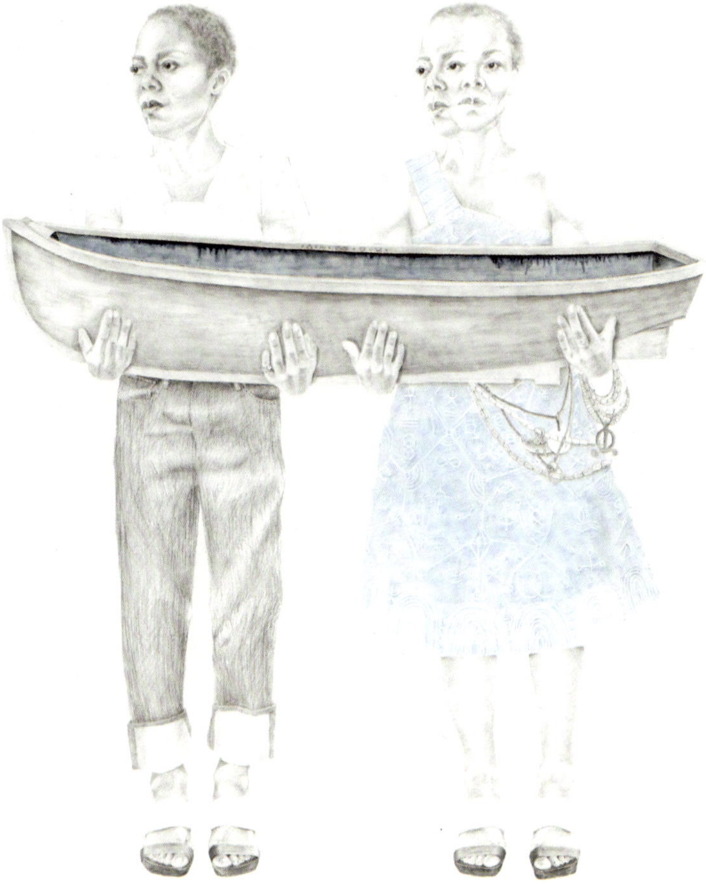

2.

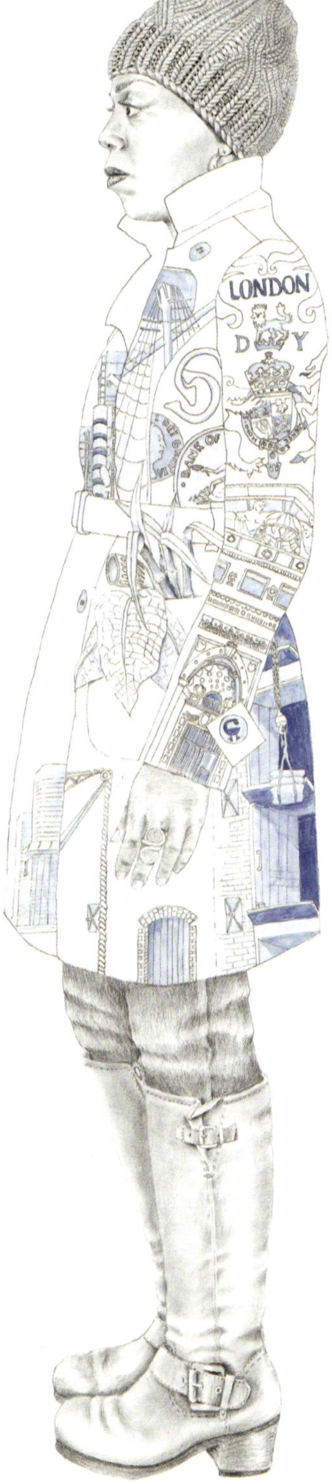

3.

MARTIN WILNER....... There can't be many practising psychoanalysts who are as well established in the contemporary art world as Martin Wilner. A self-taught artist, his fascination with drawing was inspired by the comic books he read growing up in New York in the 1960s and 1970s. While undertaking postgraduate studies, Wilner discovered the work of Art Spiegelman, who, as a graphic novelist and fellow child of Holocaust survivors, was an early influence. Psychiatry and psychoanalysis, as well as being Wilner's profession, are inseparable from his artistic practice. Like a client consultation, Wilner sets parameters of time and space, which are often manifested in the form a body of work takes. 'The Case Histories' series, for example, are analytic works made during one calendar month, with daily communication with an individual reimagined as a rectangular drawing (sometimes in colour) corresponding to that date on a calendar grid. As the month progresses, so does the image, growing into a curious visual study of the person being analyzed. Some feature more eclectic imagery, styles and eras than others. On the reverse, Wilner often writes dense, almost impenetrable notes, in capital letters, in patterns or within doodles, suggesting that this artist-psychiatrist might be as ripe for analysis as whoever is on the couch....... Another ongoing series, 'Journal of Evidence Weekly', begun around the turn of the millennium, regularly takes the form of concertina-style journals (hundreds of them, in fact), involving highly detailed, heavily annotated drawings of people Wilner sees during his daily journey into work, especially on the subway. As well as documenting his fellow commuters, these seemingly unending self-analytical arabesques tell us much about the artist: his fascination with people, his unwavering commitment to his work, his self-discipline, his attention to detail and his desire to navigate the thin lines between realism and caricature, observation and speculation, self and society....... Wilner's spirit and technical virtuosity shine in a work such as *Arkopoly* (2014), from the series 'Game Pieces'. Like a Monopoly board, imagery follows the sides of a square, though here real estate is replaced by the history of the universe – creatures at various points along the evolutionary chain, iconography from civilizations long gone – all spiralling inwards (some in pairs as if destined for Noah's Ark), towards a swirling foetal void within the cosmic black abyss. 'Go' is a Big Bang, while a pair of dice remind us of the role of chance in the development of life as we know it. Motifs are interconnected by umbilical-cord-like feelers emanating from tusks and fingertips, tails and toes. Here, contemplating life and the universe, Wilner seems more liberated, joyful even – drawing connections between mind and matter with both wonderment and insight, and in a language of his own.
.... Matt Price

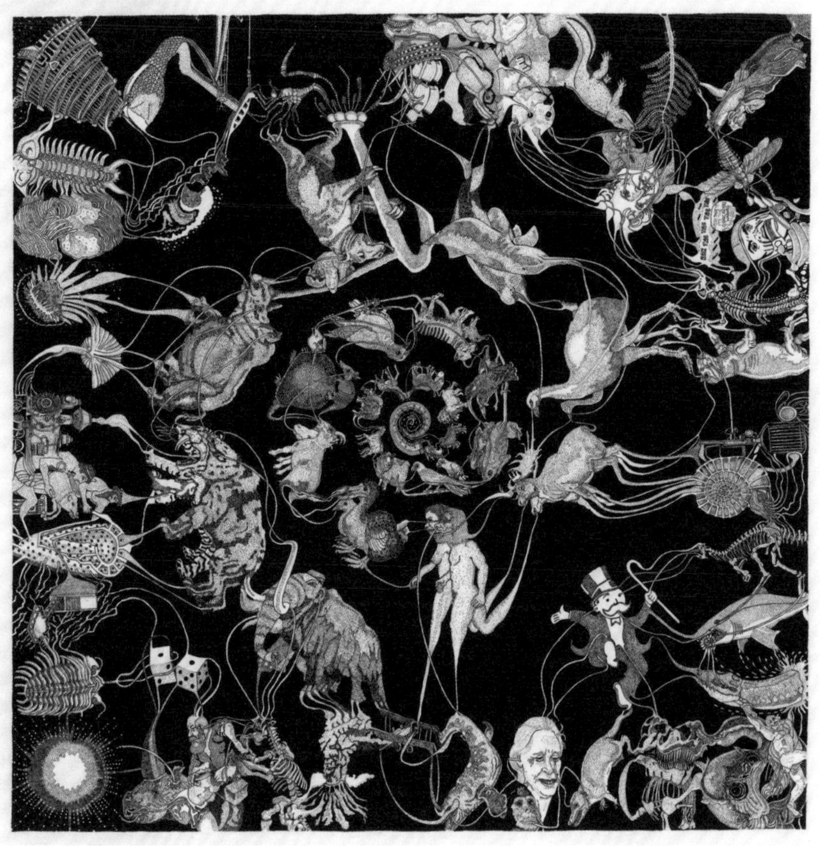

1.

Born 1959, New York. Lives and works in New York.

1. *Arkopoly*, 2014, pen and ink on Bristol board, 61 × 61 cm (24 × 24 in)
2. *The Case Histories | October 2014: Marco Breuer*, 2014, pen and ink on Bristol Board on recto; graphite on Bristol board on verso, 42 × 43.5 cm (16 ½ × 17 ⅛ in)
3. *The Case Histories | April 2015: David Black*, 2015, pen and ink on Bristol board on recto; graphite on Bristol board on verso, 42 × 43.5 cm (16 ½ × 17 ⅛ in)

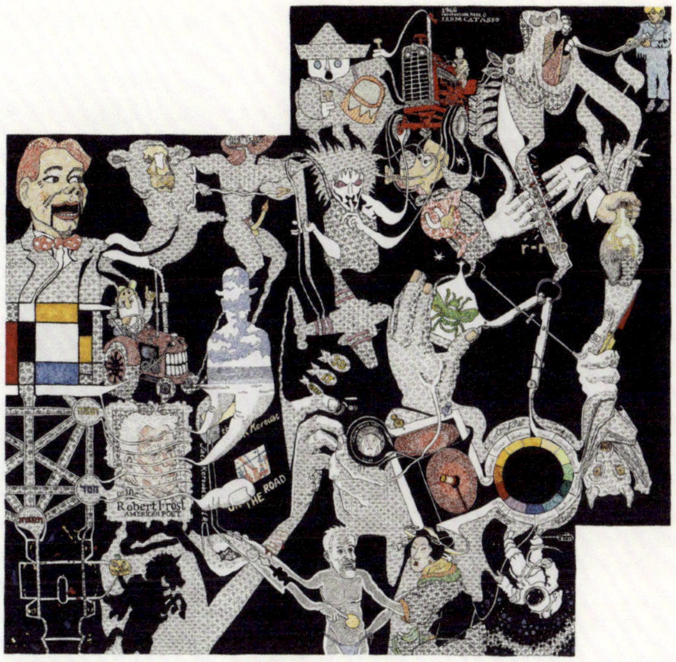

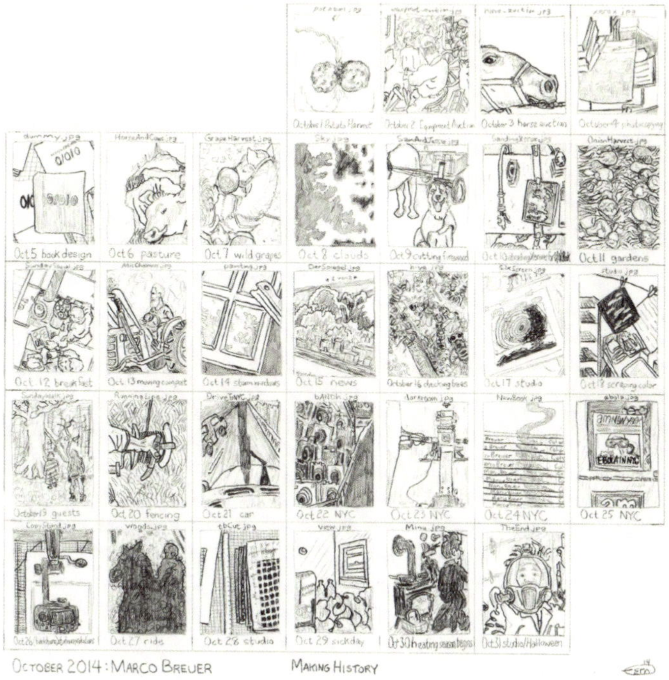
October 2014: Marco Breuer
Making History

2.

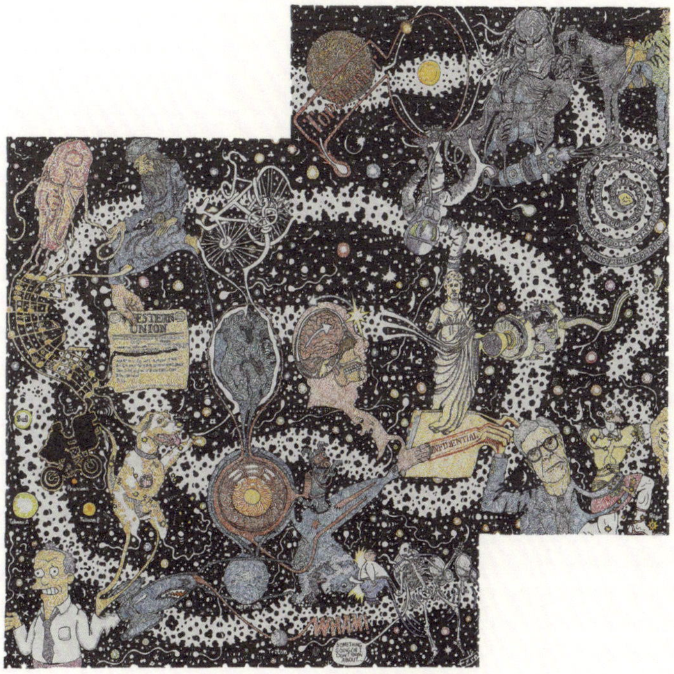

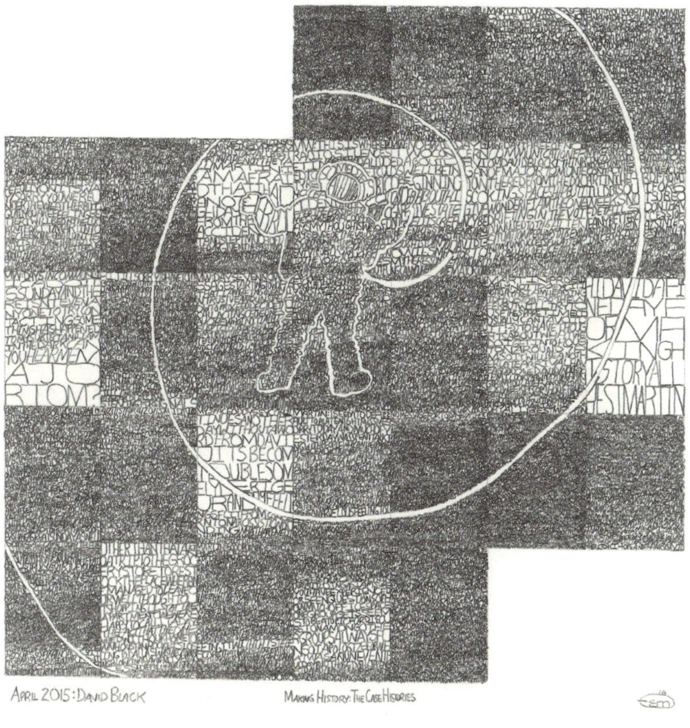
April 2015: David Black
Making History: The Case Histories

3.

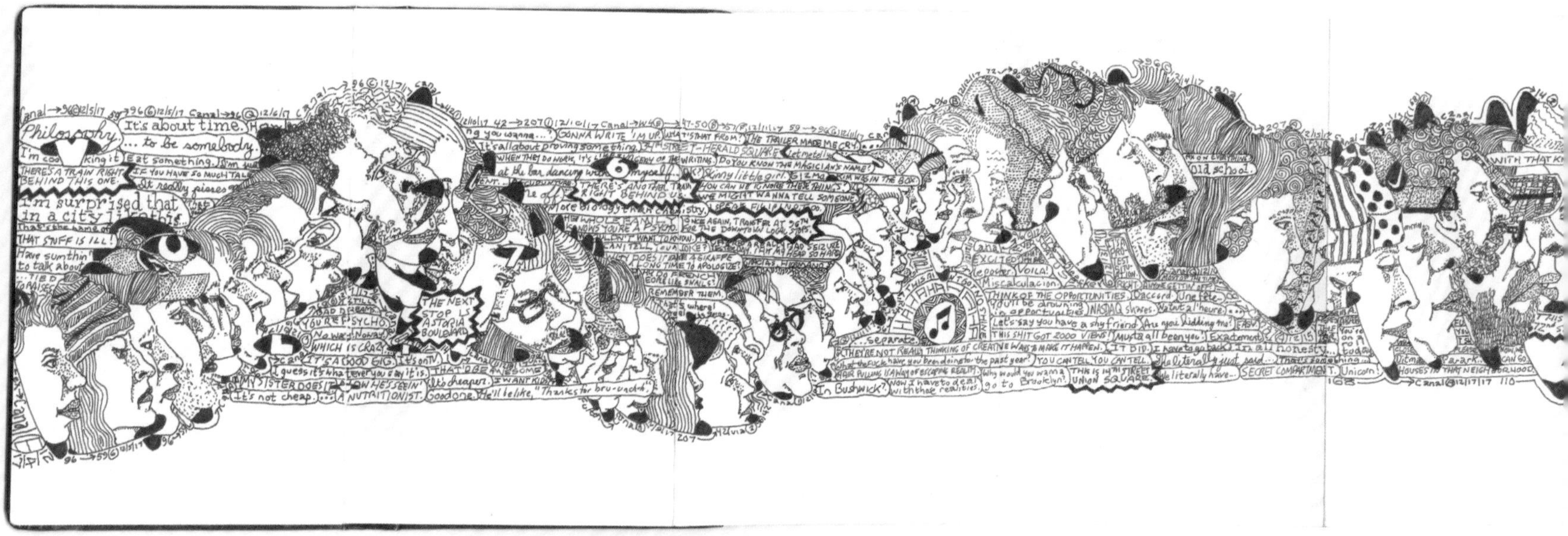

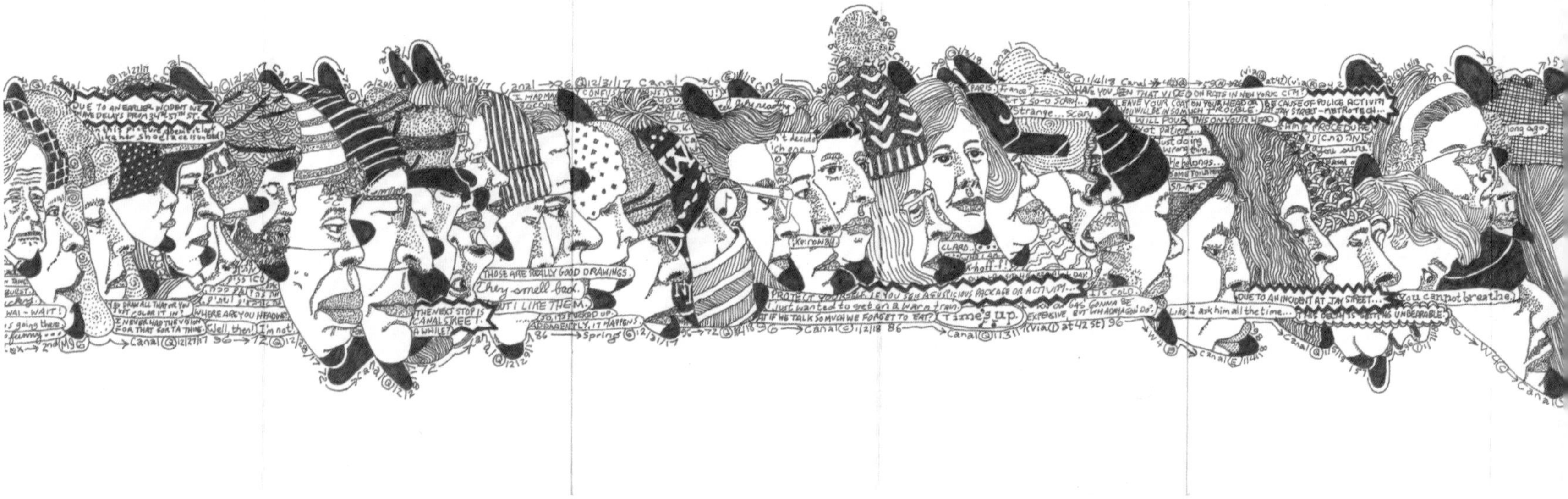

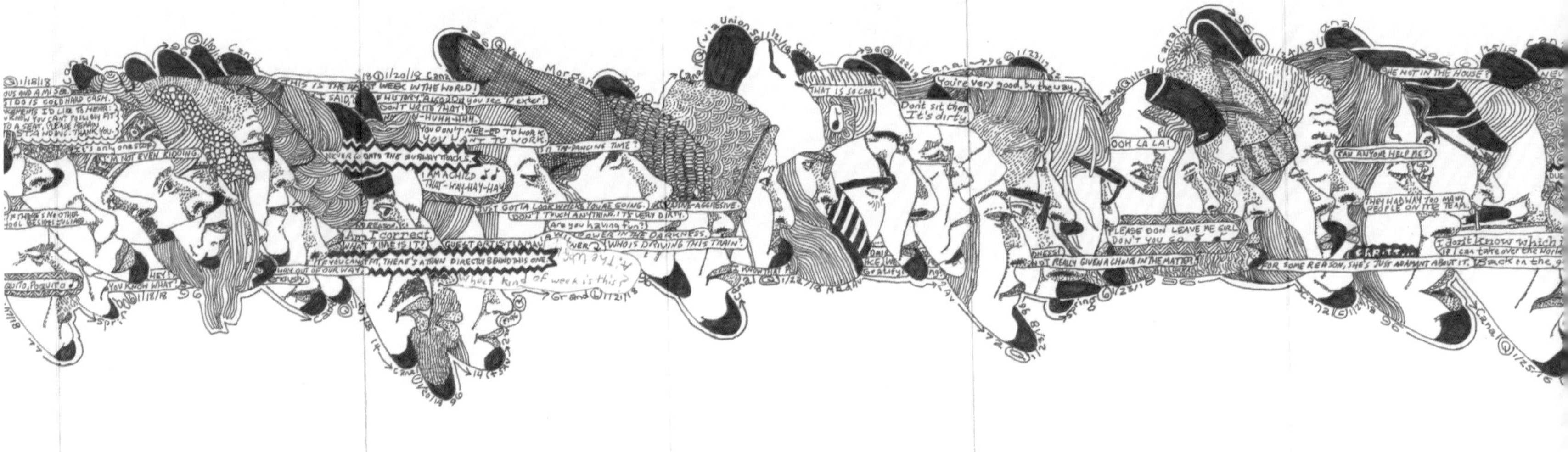

4.

4. *Journal of Evidence Weekly: Vol. 176*, 2017–18, pen and ink on bound accordion book, 14.4 × 215 cm (5 ⅝ × 84 ⅝ in)

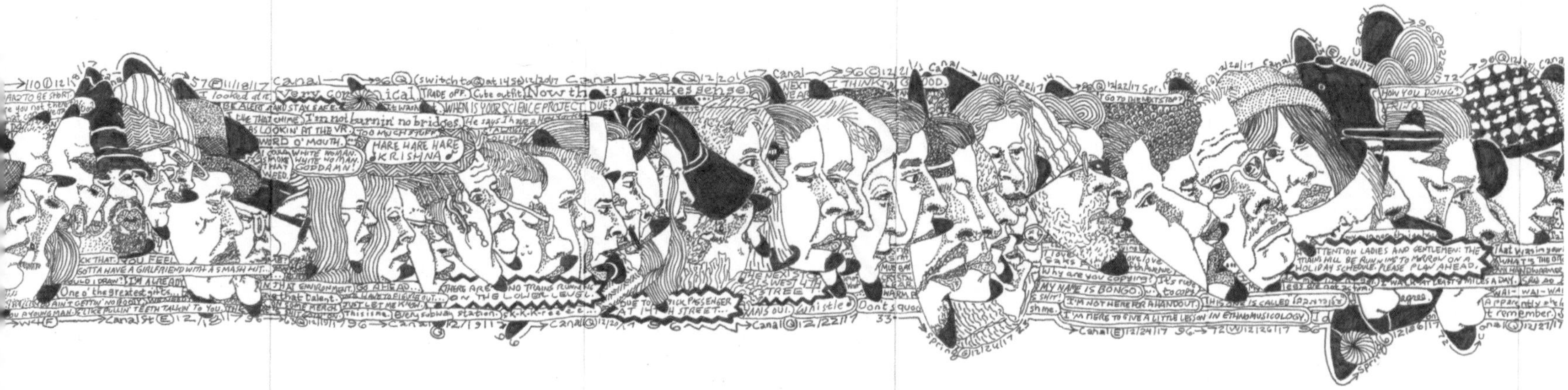
Now this all makes sense.
I'm not burnin' no bridges
HARE HARE HARE KRISHNA
WHEN IS YOUR SCIENCE PROJECT DUE?
MY NAME IS BONGO.
I'M HERE TO GIVE A LITTLE LESSON IN ETHNOMUSICOLOGY.
HOW YOU DOING

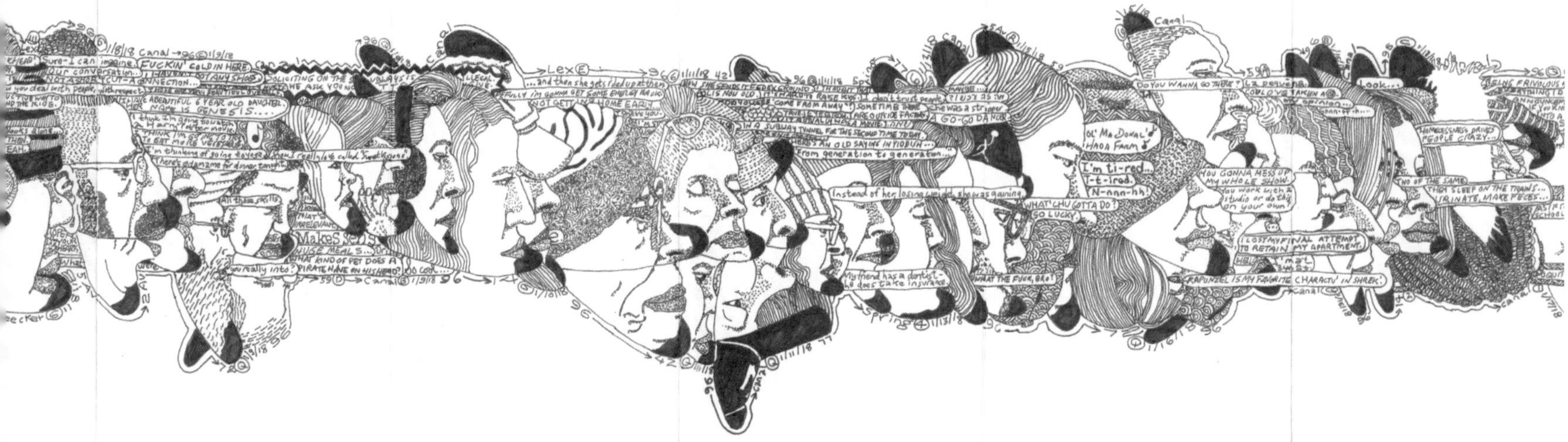
FUCKIN' COLD IN HERE
Ol' MacDonald HADA FARM
I'm ti-red.
from generation to generation...
Look...

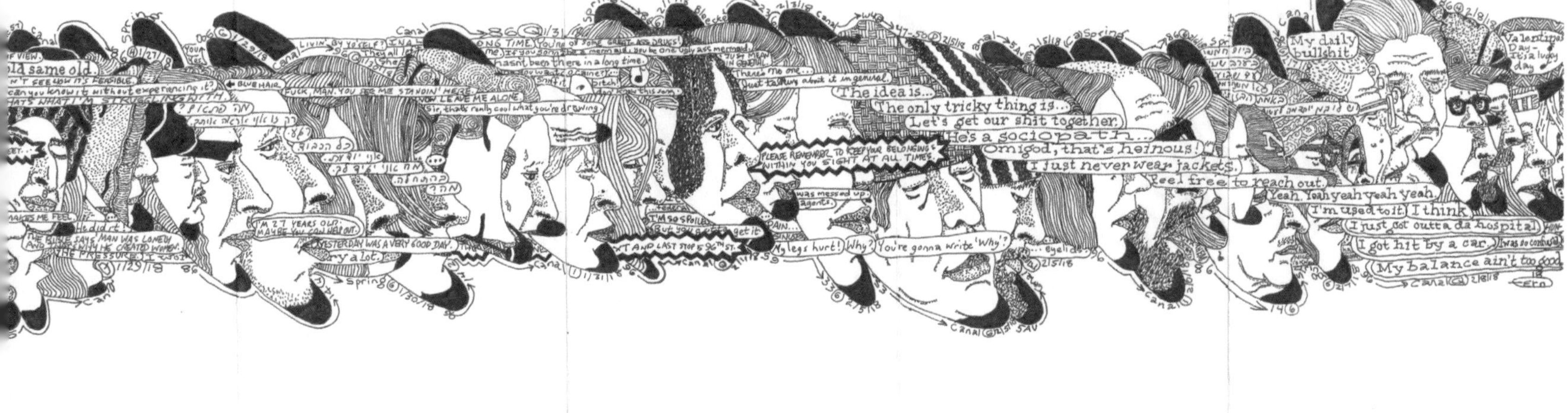
The idea is...
The only tricky thing is...
Let's get our shit together.
He's a sociopath...
Omigod, that's heinous!
I just never wear jackets.
Feel free to reach out.
Yeah yeah yeah yeah yeah
I'm used to it!
I think
I just got outta da hospital
I got hit by a car.
My balance ain't too good
My daily bullshit
You're gonna write 'Why'?
My legs hurt!

JOHN WOOD AND PAUL HARRISON.......

Drawing has been part of John Wood and Paul Harrison's creative collaboration since the duo first met in the early 1990s. At the time they lived in different towns and would post drawings to each other, initiating an aesthetic dialogue that has blossomed into a long-term artistic collaboration. Wood and Harrison's work is often humorously self-reflexive and their interactions, whether harmonious or conflictual, are the subject of several works. Their photograph *We Don't Like Each Other* (2019) shows the artists grim-faced and holding up a placard stencilled with the work's title. In addition to being an end in itself, Wood and Harrison's drawing practice is also an essential part of their process when working in other media, especially performance and video. It facilitates a visual conversation about ideas, during which they might communicate their thoughts by sketching over each other's drawings. The studio workshop is Wood and Harrison's primary forum, whether for the construction of sets for videos, rehearsing performances or drawing, which is a quick and efficient method for setting out the overall structure of a work. When preparing to shoot a video, they pin drawings to the wall to create storyboards, moving them around as a way to edit sequences....... Indebted to the history of Minimal and Conceptual art, Wood and Harrison's work is often executed in black and white or simple colour schemes. For their video performances, they tend to wear basic, unbranded clothing and to match their outfits. For their seminal work *Twenty-Six (Drawing and Falling Things)* (2001), a series of twenty-six short films in which they interact with everyday objects and architectural environments, the artists wore black clothing and performed against white backgrounds to resemble stick figures within the monochrome landscape of pencil drawings....... Wood and Harrison's work is the product of two dry wits influenced by the history of slapstick performance and cinema. It revels in the absurdity of everyday life and routinely deflates the stereotypical overblown ego of the artist, as in their self-referential drawing *No Thought or Effort* (2013), which claims that 'no thought or effort has gone into this at all', a statement that patently contradicts itself. The apparent simplicity of Wood and Harrison's work belies a philosophical finesse and conceptual mischief. Their deadpan humour often pushes at the limits of logic, exposing the treachery of language. At first glance, their drawing *Red / Green / Blue* (2013) seems banal to the point of tautology. Yet the joke is on the mind, as the punchline only lands once cognitive faculty has caught up with the visual sense, to realize that the words and colours are mismatched.

.... Ellen Mara De Wachter

1.
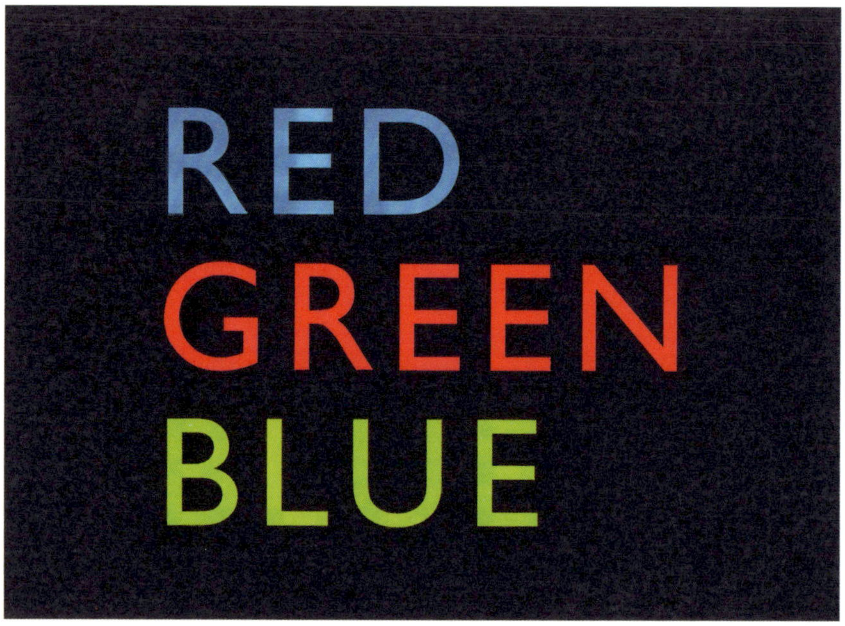

2.
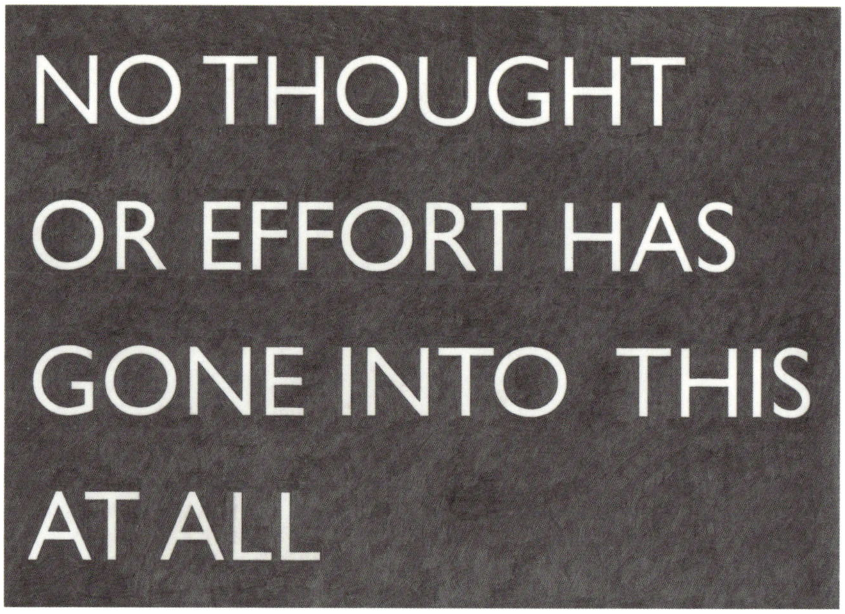

John Wood: Born 1969, Hong Kong. Lives and works in Bristol, UK. Paul Harrison: Born 1966, Wolverhampton, UK. Lives and works in Liverpool and Bristol, UK.

1. *Red / Green / Blue*, 2013, permanent marker on paper, 29.7 × 42 cm (11 ¾ × 16 ½ in)
2. *No Thought or Effort*, 2013, pencil on paper, 29.7 × 42 cm (11 ¾ × 16 ½ in)
3. Installation view of selected drawings, 'John Wood and Paul Harrison: Things That Happen', Carroll/Fletcher Gallery, London, 2012

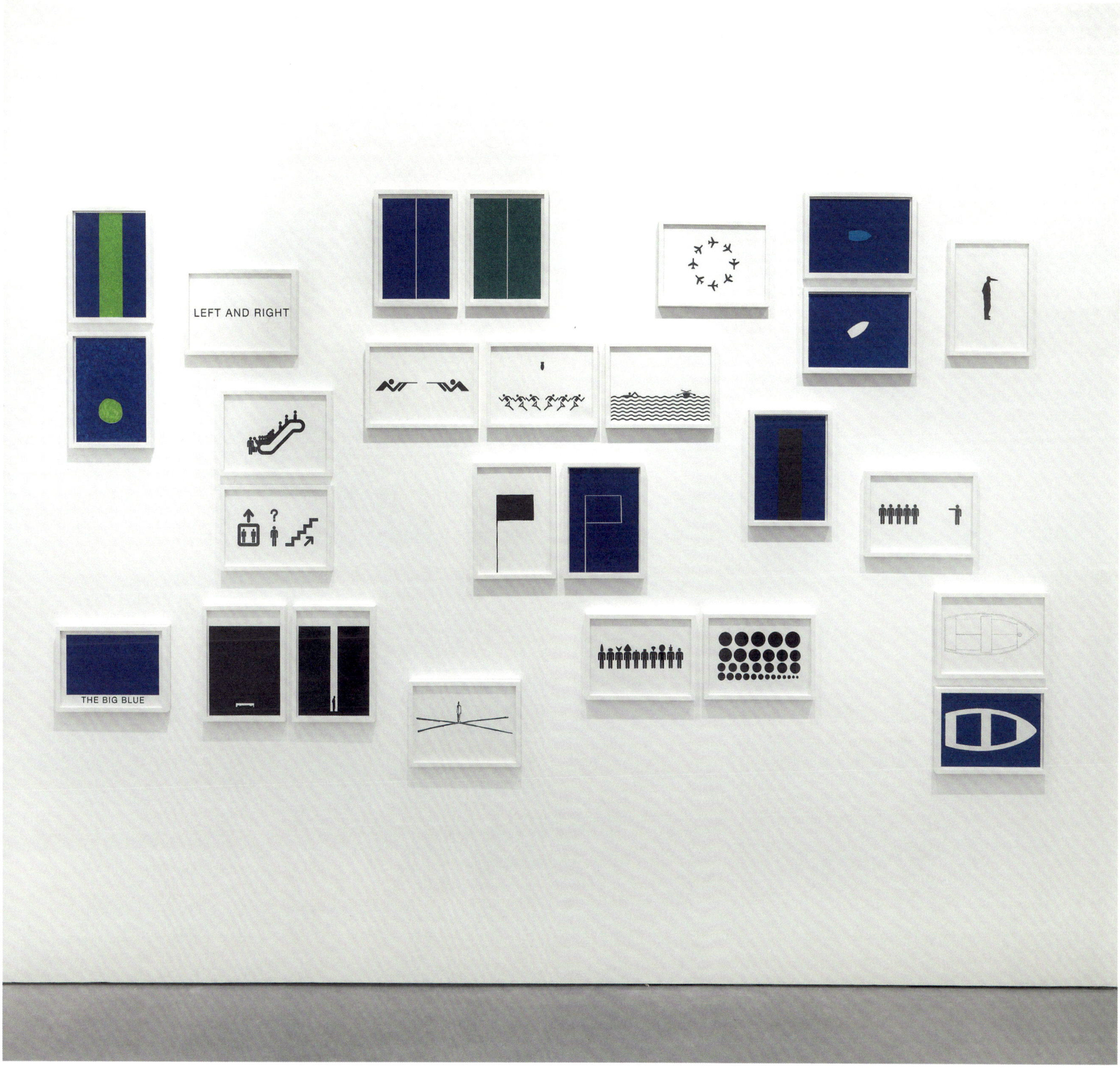

3.

YUICHI YOKOYAMA……. Yuichi Yokoyama, who began his career as an oil painter, switched to Manga as a way to 'draw time'. He began working with the Japanese art of comics and cartooning in 2000, and his first major solo of entirely manga works – at the Kawasaki City Museum, Japan, in 2010 – was titled 'I draw time'. He does not mean this as a metaphor: Yokoyama intentionally stretches time and space through his work. His drawings present stories that speculate towards a future, and they are often fantastical – full of cool characters and elegant machines that freely move around the page with a great sense of speed and personality. This momentum is especially created by Yokoyama's energetically drawn lines and explosively rendered onomatopoeia. He works in ink on paper, sometimes assembling collages, as in *Member of the world map* (2012–13), where small, cutout layers of drawings are joined with masking tape. This work is reckless but still sentimental, composed of many faces and glassy eyes – each seemingly brimming with tears, or great passions. Yokoyama takes the buoyancy and playfulness of cartooning and turns it painterly. He also pays notable attention to space: there is always a precise architecture in which the narratives play out. ……. While Yokoyama's is a kind of 'neo-manga' – whereby his work gives the late-nineteenth century art of comics a twenty-first century contemporaneity – he stays true to the essence of traditional manga. The Japanese word translates to 'whimsical or impromptu pictures' and there is an inherent sense of urgency and immediacy to his practice, as well as a suspension of disbelief. Interestingly enough, Yokoyama does not cite specific manga influences – it is not that he grew up reading manga, or American or European comics – but simply took to the medium as a way of making work that was more complex and layered. The consecutive scenes and narrative building typical to manga allowed Yokoyama to 'put more frequency and detail' into his art, as he explained in a 2011 interview with *Comics Alliance*. There is less emphasis on dialogue in his work; language merely serves to accentuate his use of line. In some places he introduces colour, which is atypical to traditional manga, as in 'Color Engineering' (2010), a series of works on paper and canvas. He paints into the fine lines of his drawing, introducing gradients and tones that almost look like digitally produced special effects. But Yokoyama only works by hand. His drawings idiosyncratically combine the dual aspirations of drawing and speed: in viewing them we are thrown into a continuous, unbroken limbo of time.
……. Skye Arundhati Thomas

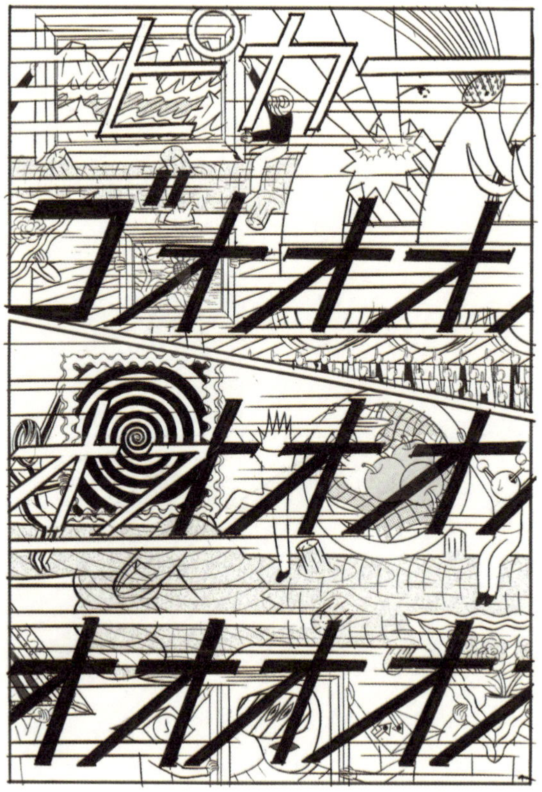

1.

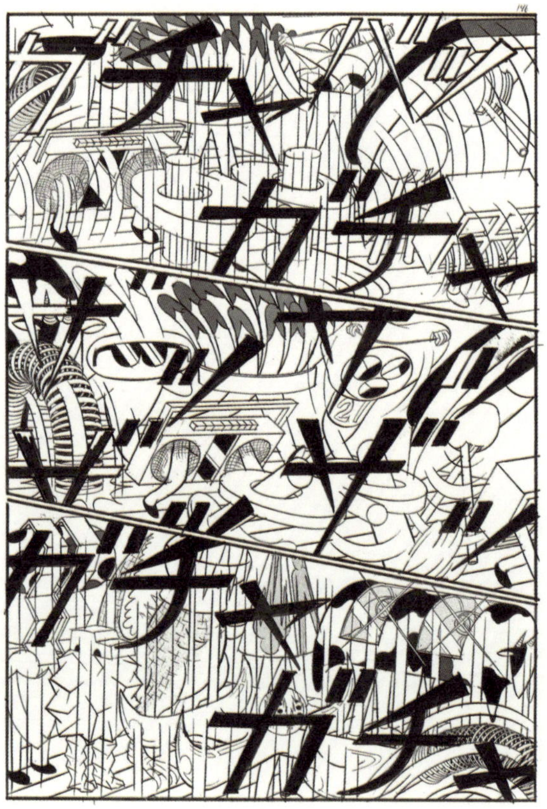

2.

Born 1967, Miyazaki, Japan. Lives and works in Saitama, Japan.

1. *Plaza*, 2018, ink on paper, 32 × 22 in (12 ⅝ × 8 ¾ in)
2. *Plaza*, 2018, ink on paper, 32 × 22 in (12 ⅝ × 8 ¾ in)
3. *Member of the world map*, 2012–13, ink on paper, collaged and masking tape, 20 × 20.3 cm (8 × 8 in)

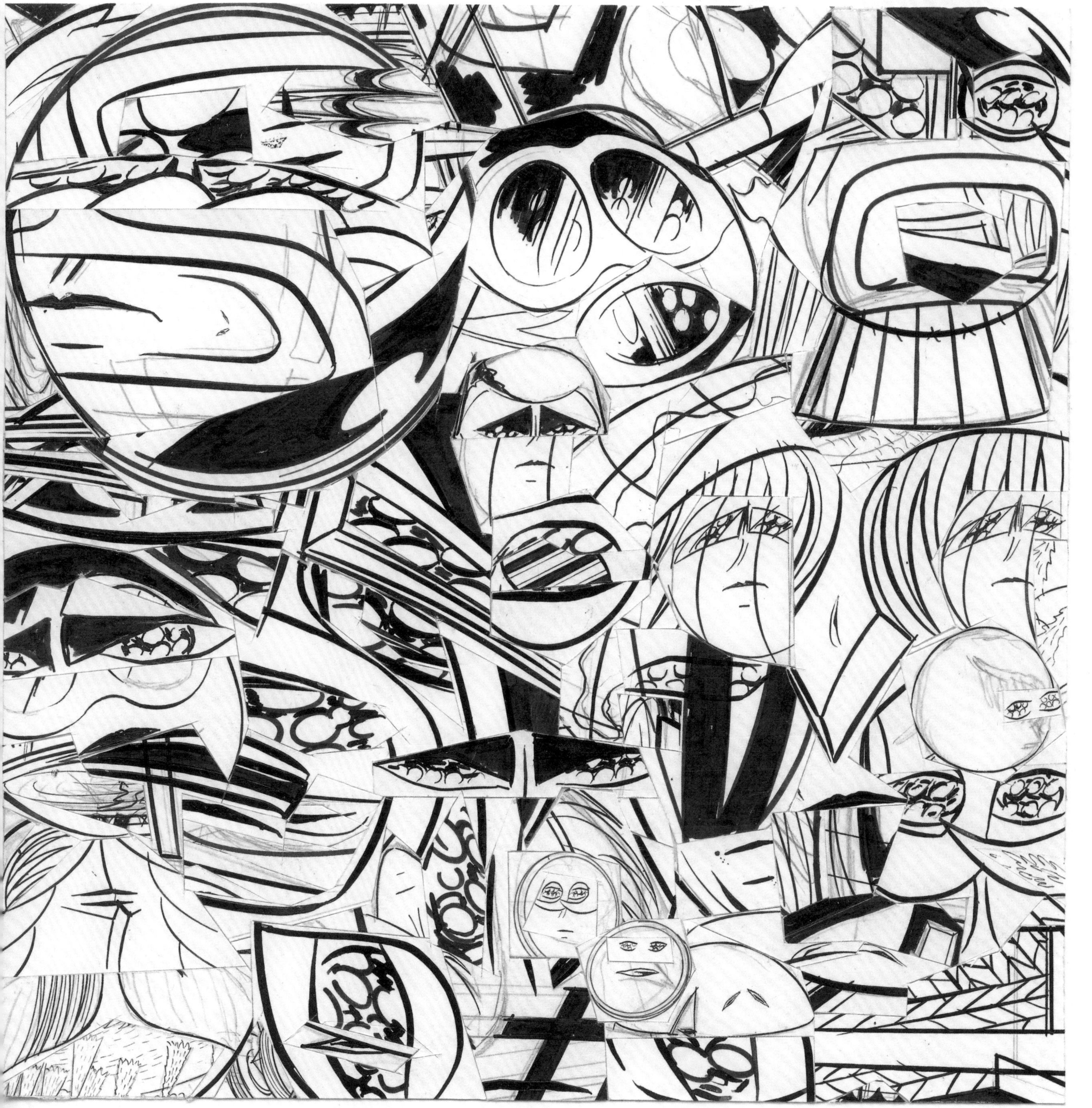

3.

HONZA ZAMOJSKI .... Some might consider Polish artist Honza Zamojski a poet, a prophet or a provocateur. His work is in part a profound meditation on the nature of human thought, communication and our place within the universe, in part a tongue-in-cheek rebuttal of such sober soul-searching and speculation. Wordplay is a significant aspect of his oeuvre, often taking centre stage, as it does in the drawing *Untitled [Goooood]* (2018) whereby a pyramidal configuration of letters turns even lackadaisical viewers into obedient readers as their eyes work down the image. What starts out as prayer-like concrete poetry ('O, GO, GOD') evolves into an aesthetic epiphany or a bawdy climax ('GOOOOD, OOOOOO'). The eyes are struck by how the majority of letters are Os, book-ended by just a handful of Gs and Ds, signalling how meaning and emotion can be generated by just three rounded letters in minimal, geometric formation. .... Zamojski's practice regularly involves sculptures, installations and animations in various mediums, though drawing is never far away – indeed, it often permeates his three-dimensional work. Take, for example, his drawings of hands with single letters wedged between each digit to spell out a four-letter word (ranging from the innocuous to the vulgar). These sometimes leave the paper behind only to reappear as wall drawings or three-dimensional painted steel sculptures. Such translations are effective, the artist's predilection for textual, graphic and geometric visual languages offering strong formal associations and endless critical opportunities. Bold, straight black lines might be used to create giant letters across a gallery wall as if shouting, or to strike through words on a small-scale drawing, as if silencing or cancelling out their meaning. *Untitled [Fear]* (2018), from the series 'World War Free', sees the word 'FEAR' repeated five times, aligned vertically on a small sheet of paper, each iteration partially obfuscated by a black strip at a slightly different angle and position relative to the word; despite such formalist nuances among the stripes, the pacifist sentiment could not be clearer. .... At times, Zamojski's figurative imagery verges on the cartoonish: there's always some kind of curious simplification or reduction of the iconography going on, suggestive of visual languages from earlier periods or civilizations, whether cave painting, classical or medieval traditions. *Untitled [The Crowd]* (2019) comprises five rows of naked human bodies, their heads absent and replaced by oversized faces on their torsos; two figures have only one leg. The drawing is like a strange diagram from an ancient alchemical manuscript, made all the more cryptic by the artist using carbon copy paper in its creation. Lines, patterns and geometric shapes take on symbolic, almost religious or metaphysical significance in Zamojski's work – like civilization itself, perhaps, both deeply meaningful and utterly ludicrous at the same time.
.... Matt Price

1.
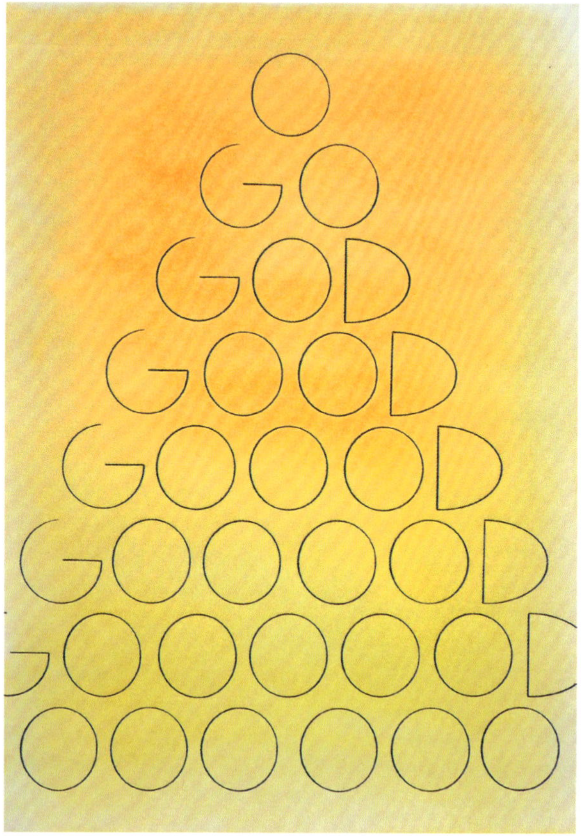

2.
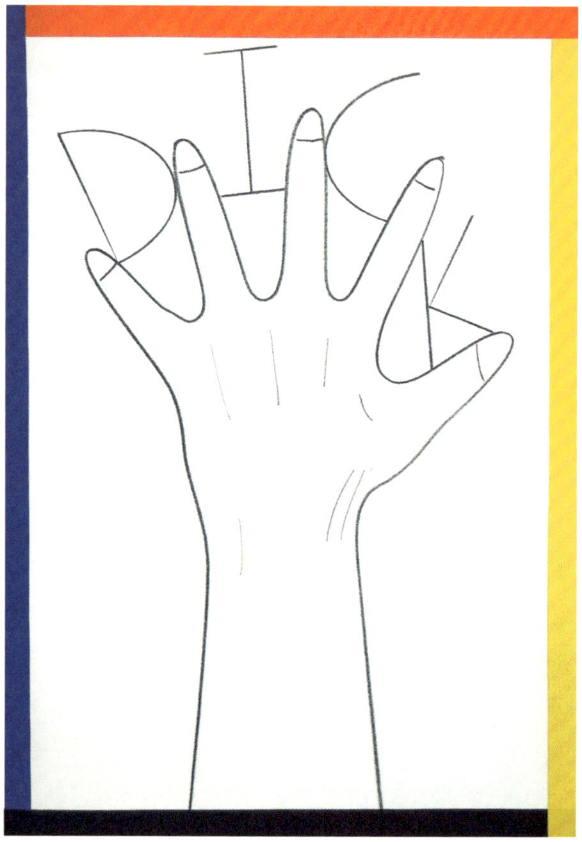

1. *Untitled [Goooood]*, 2018, drawing on paper (made using carbon copy paper) and dry pastel on paper, 48.9 × 34.5 cm (19 ¼ × 13 ⅝ in)
2. *Untitled*, 2015, drawing on paper (made using carbon copy paper) and adhesive colour paper, 34.8 × 24.8 cm (13 ¾ × 9 ¾ in)
3. *Untitled [Fear]* from 'Word War Free' series, 2018, drawing on paper (made using carbon copy paper) and adhesive colour paper, 22.6 × 14 cm (8 ⅞ × 5 ½ in)
4. *Untitled*, 2016, drawing on paper (made using carbon copy paper), 34.8 × 24.8 cm (13 ¾ × 9 ¾ in)

Born 1981, Poznań, Poland. Lives and works in Poznań, Poland.

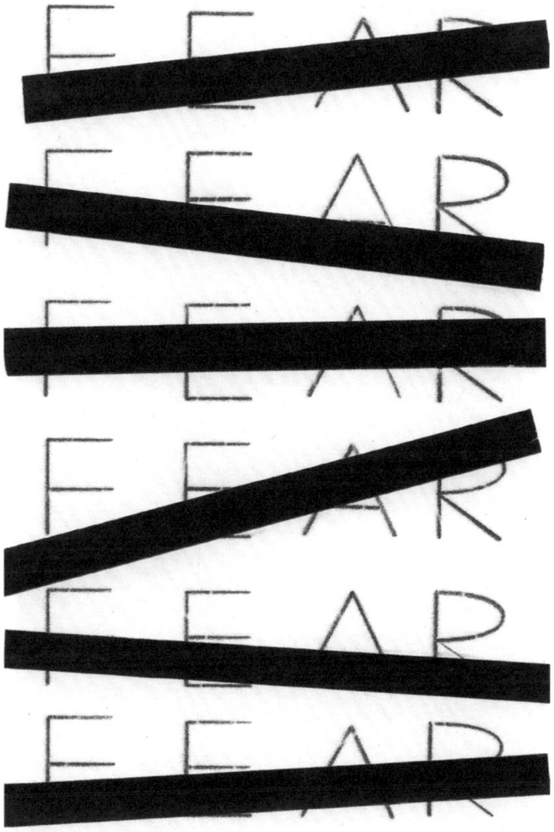

3.

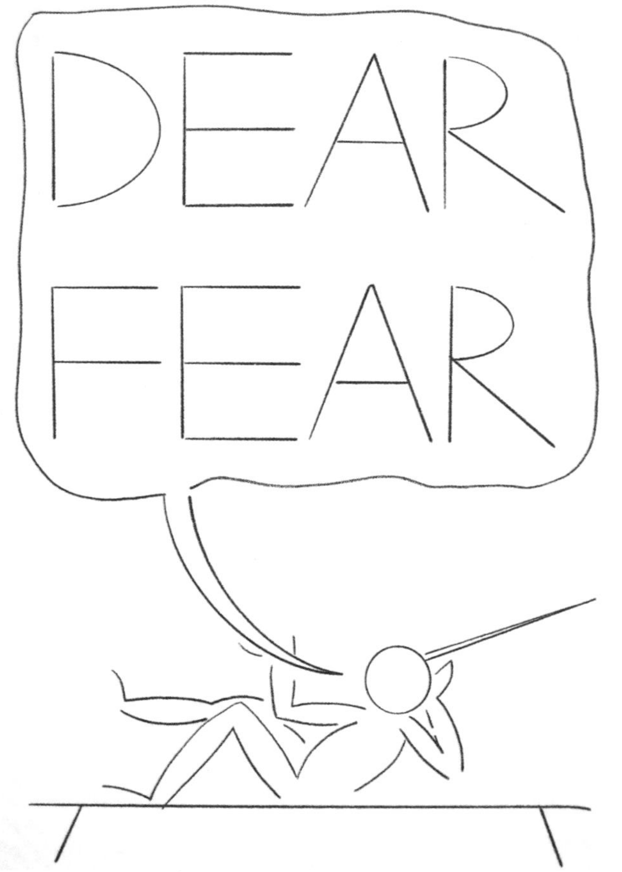

4.

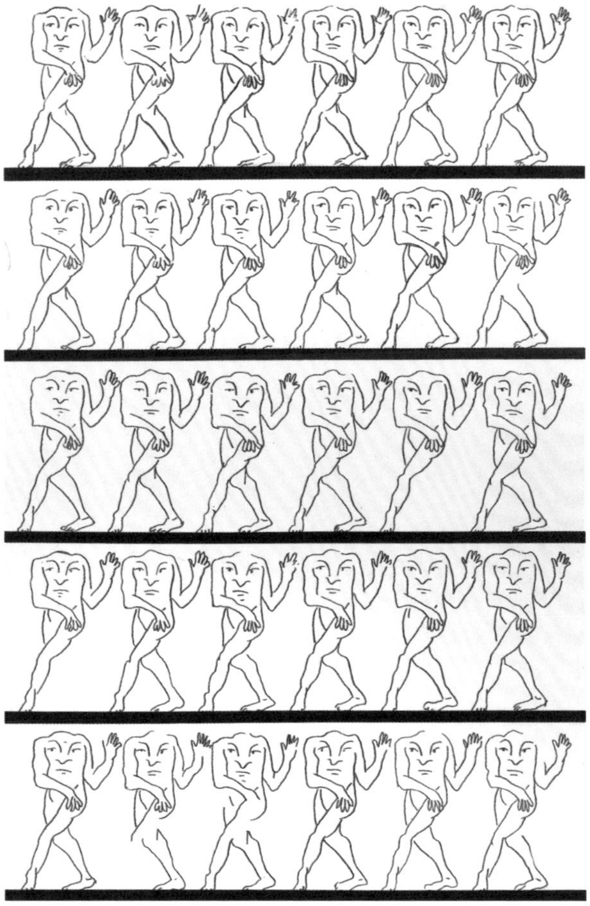

5.

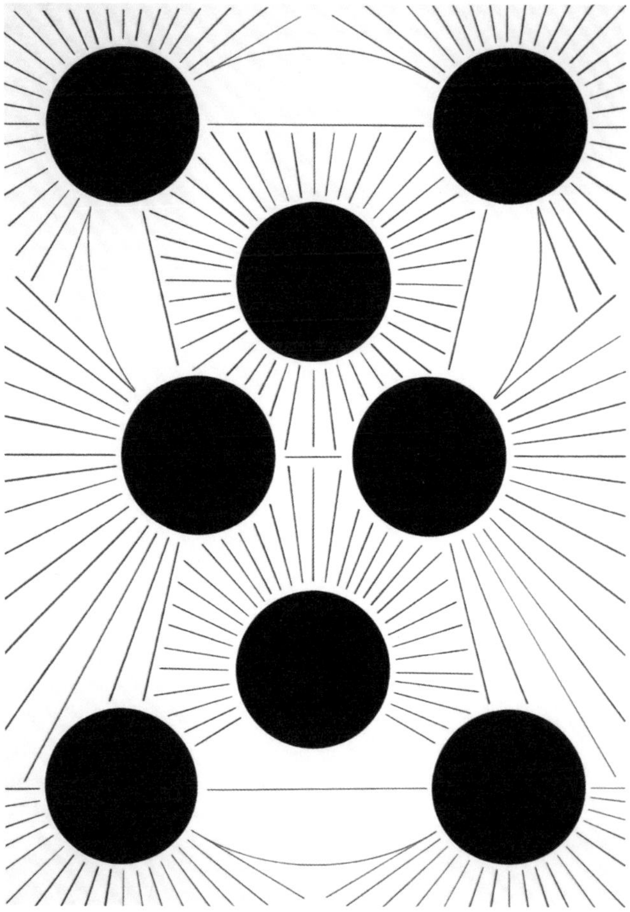

6.

5. *Untitled [The Crowd]*, 2019, drawing on paper (made using carbon copy paper) mounted on MDF, and adhesive colour paper, 60 × 40 cm (23 ⅝ × 15 ¾ in)

6. *Magnetism*, 2018, drawing on paper (made using carbon copy paper) and adhesive colour paper, 69 × 48.9 cm (27 ⅛ × 19 ¼ in)

Z A R I N A .... Zarina was a cartographer who didn't believe in borders. While she repeatedly drew maps, border divisions and floor plans in her work, she actively undid the physical and political boundaries that they represented. She was more interested in the idea of 'home', and how this cannot be tied to place or geography. For instance, in her series of eight 'Letters from Home' (2004), she used extracts from letters written to her by her sister, overlaying and outlining her sister's hand-writing with drawings of houses, floor plans and maps. The evocative, monochromatic metal-cut and woodblock prints gesture towards the letters in a way that seems to suggest that for Zarina, her sister – and the childhood they shared – *was* home. The artist's family was forced to relocate from India to Pakistan because of Partition, and she herself left India in 1958 with her husband, a military officer working in international diplomacy. .... When she was a child, growing up in the northern Indian city of Aligarh, Zarina's father took her to visit Mughal monuments of the sixteenth and seventeenth centuries. The red rocks, arched windows and long corridors enchanted her. 'The precious stones from the ornamental designs have been removed by vandals,' she wrote in a letter to a friend, Lisa Liebmann, in 1984, 'making the wall even more beautiful with its surface cracked and tactile.' A similar style of fractured, ghostly ornamentation appears in Zarina's work, as in *Aleppo* (2013), where she has punched out holes in gold-leaf paper. In reference to the destruction of the eponymous city, the work is a composition of irregular black outlines, a kind of architectural floor plan interspersed with the hole-punch designs that are reminiscent of *mashrabiya* – the hand-carved wooden lattice-work used to cover windows that is typical of Arabic architecture. Zarina's drawings are often accompanied by collage, and because of her minimal, determined choices of material – despite being dominated by simple juxtapositions – her works are precious and exquisite. *Dividing Line* (2001) is a single, darting line across a page. It is a representation of the so-called Radcliffe Line – the geopolitical border that divides the Indian subcontinent, named after the British imperial lawyer Cyril Radcliffe. This dividing line separates India from Pakistan, and is perhaps one of the most brutal and violent borders in the world – considering the history of Partition, to which Zarina alludes. But she does not indulge in representations of either side of the border; instead, she reminds us that the arbitrarily drawn-up border continues to exist and continues silently to exert its power. Zarina made small, precise works, composed of gentle gestures. 'I know the work has density of emotion,' she said in Liebmann's 1988 piece for *Artforum*, 'it will create its own space around it.'
.... Skye Arundhati Thomas

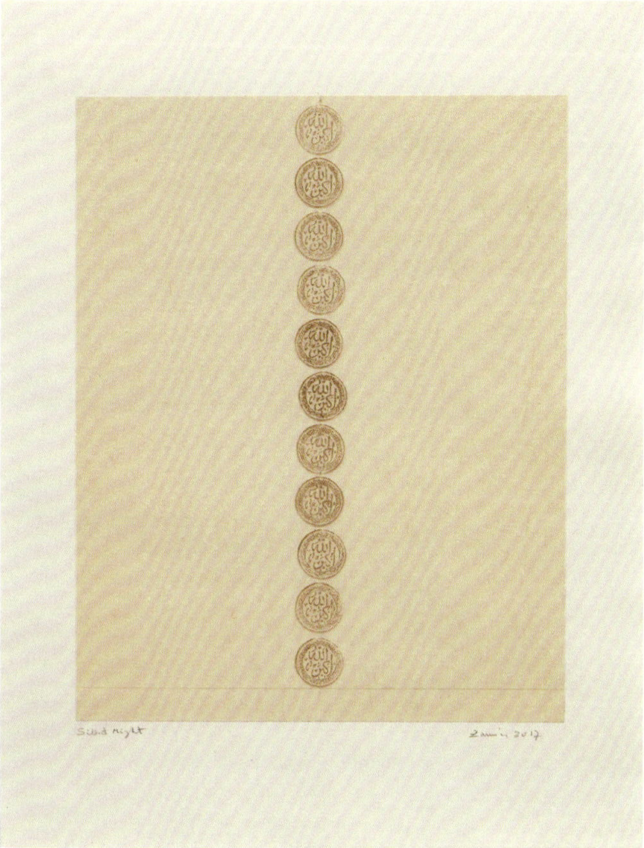

1.

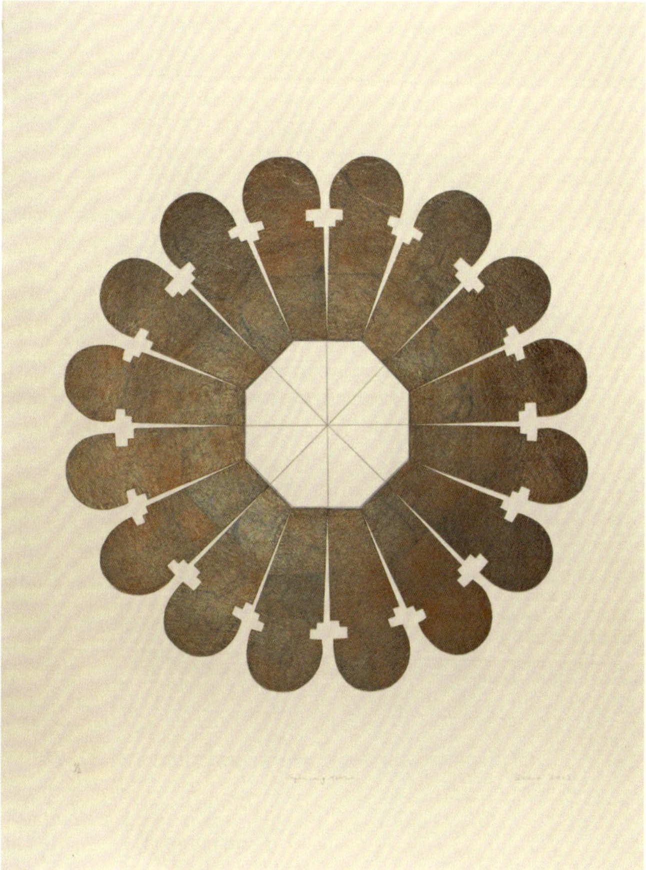

2.

1. *Silent Night*, 2017, collage with rubbings on Indian handmade paper mounted on Somerset antique paper, 40.6 × 32.4 cm (16 × 12 ¾ in)
2. *Spinning House*, 2013, collage with pewter leaf on etching with silver pencil mounted on Somerset textured cream paper, 99.1 × 76.2 cm (39 × 30 in)
3. *Aleppo*, 2013, collage of Indian handmade paper dyed with sumi ink and punched gold-leaf paper on Arches Cover buff paper, 38.1 × 31.8 cm (15 × 12 ½ in)

Born 1937, Aligarh, India. Died 2020, London.

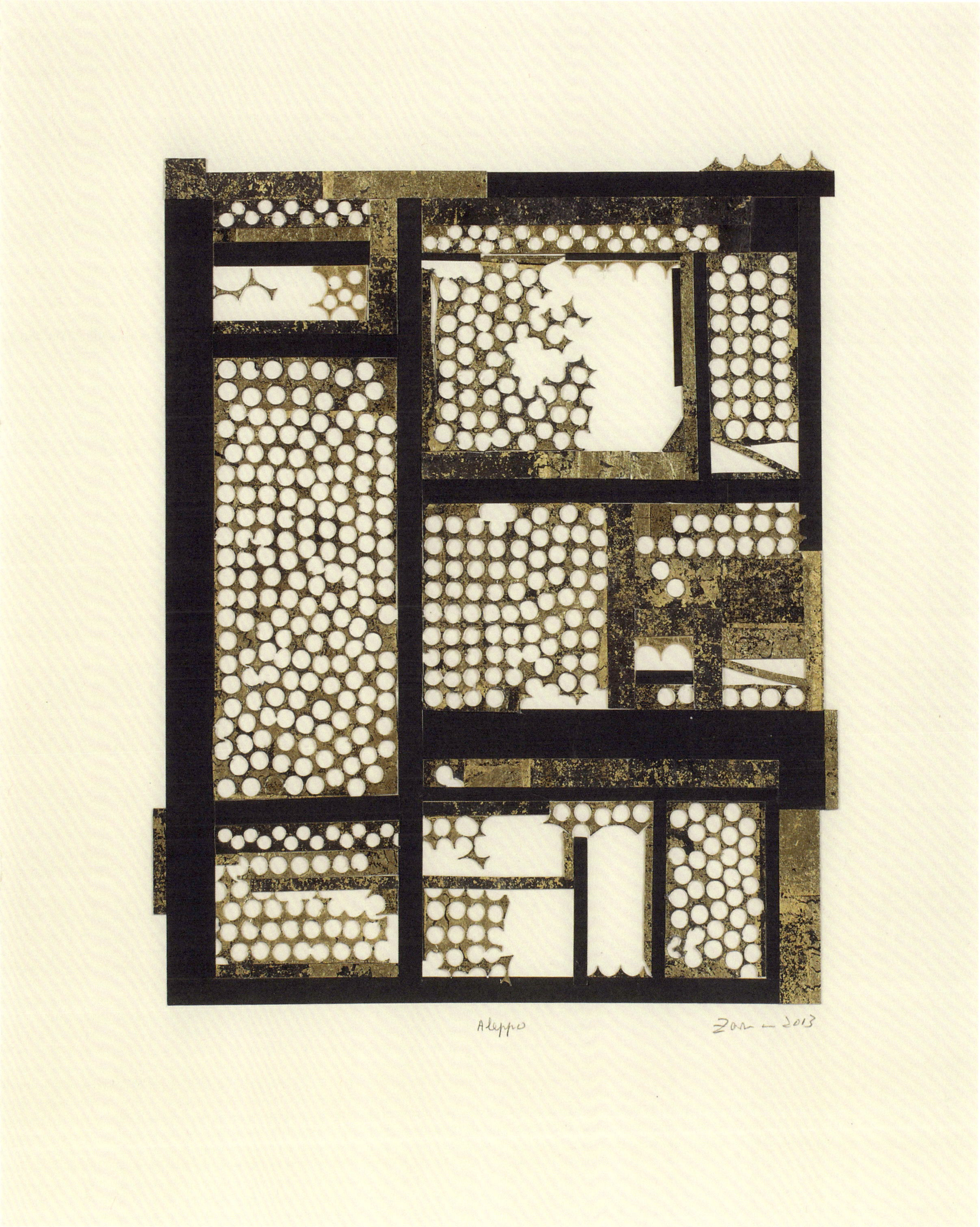

3.

SERGIO ZEVALLOS....... Sergio Zevallos's artworks chart the processes of political indoctrination that lead to aggressive forms of bigotry and xenophobia. Zevallos belonged to the queer art collective Grupo Chaclacayo from Lima, Peru, in the 1980s, making work in response to sexism, racism and homophobia during an era of bloody conflict between the Peruvian state and the Maoist group Shining Path. More recent drawings focus on education, exploring how violent philosophies are systemically imprinted on to the minds of generations of children. .... The pencil and graphite work *A War Machine Series 03* (2019) has the appearance of a school crest for a grim educational establishment. To make it Zevallos traced archival images of children and weaponry. Two schoolboys sit facing each other at separate desks. Assault rifles issuing forth from their groins point towards a drawing of a little girl giving a salute while wearing a dress and pigtails. As if she is a figment of a collective imagination and libido, she is surrounded by lines that emanate from the boys' heads and genitals. Two scrolls placed at the top and bottom of the composition contain the motto 'Propriedad Privada, Dios Patria Ley' (Private Property, God, Fatherland, Law). The work shows how quickly a pen can become a gun, a school uniform military fatigues, a boy a soldier, and a girl a symbol to be guarded and exploited. .... Describing Zevallos's interest in the sexual politics of education for the exhibition Documenta 14, in Kassel, Germany, in 2017, writer and curator Paul B. Preciado noted: 'The school is also the place where the masturbatory hand is made to write. Subsequently, successive institutions teach this same hand to become a masculine hand, to work or to carry a weapon.' Zevallos's drawings often have the appearance of pages torn from school exercise books. For *HK G3 Series* (2018), multiple images – produced on lined, plain and gridded sheets, sometimes overlaid with tracing paper – are attached to a wall. On one sheet, a diagram of an erect penis is superimposed on to an architectural plan, indicating how sexually coded power dynamics taught at school seep into the design of society. While many of the 'lessons' in *HK G3 Series* are bleak, sometimes the figures in the artist's images fight back. A drawing of a schoolgirl tied to a chair indicates how ideas of racial supremacy are drilled into children: 'zum gluck bin ich eine weiße' (luckily I'm a white one) is written in a speech bubble attached to her mouth. In a similar drawing the same girl raises her leg and appears to release a thick stream of urine – a protest, perhaps, against chauvinistic lessons.
.... Rosanna Mclaughlin

1.
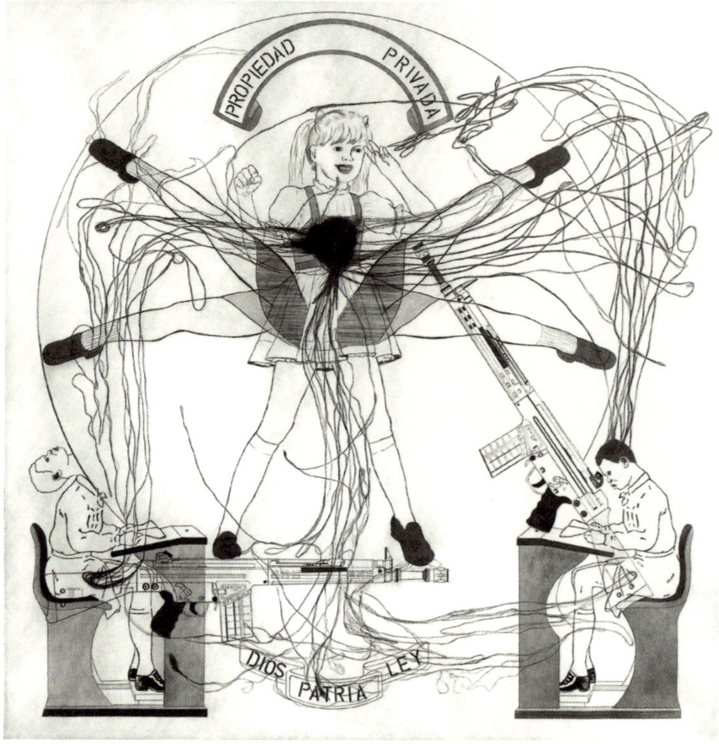

2.
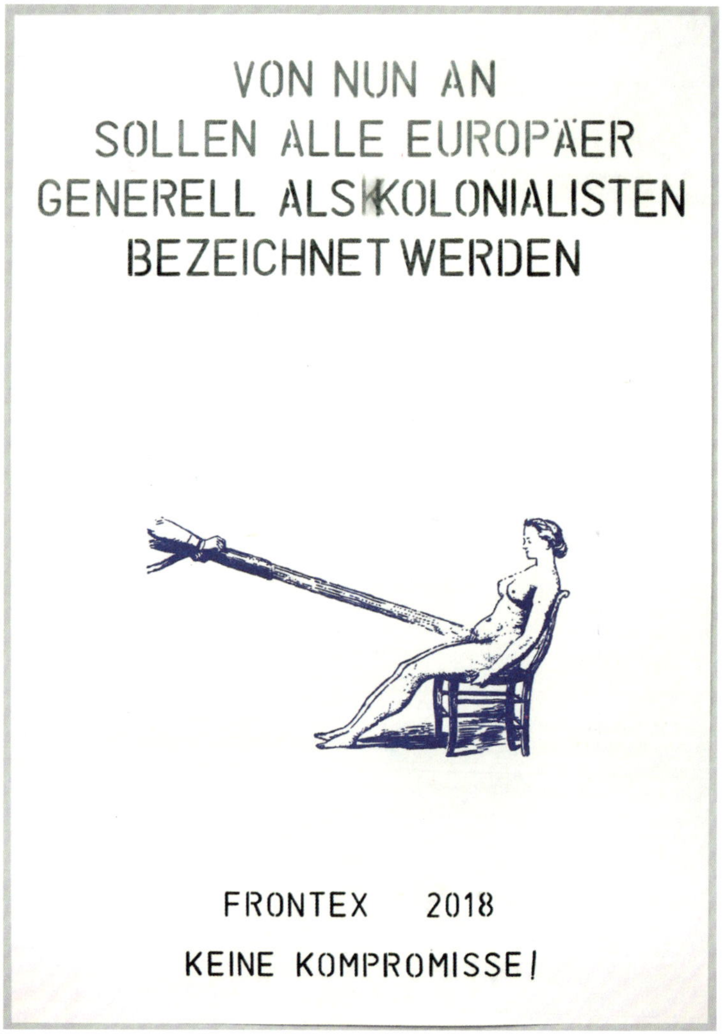

Born 1962, Lima, Peru. Lives and work in Lima and Berlin.

1. *A War Machine Series 03*, 2019, graphite, pencil and tracing technique on paper, 150 × 150 cm (59 × 59 in)
2. *HAITI German Series*, 2018, graphite, pencil and tracing technique on paper, 84 × 59.4 cm (33 × 23 ⅜ in)

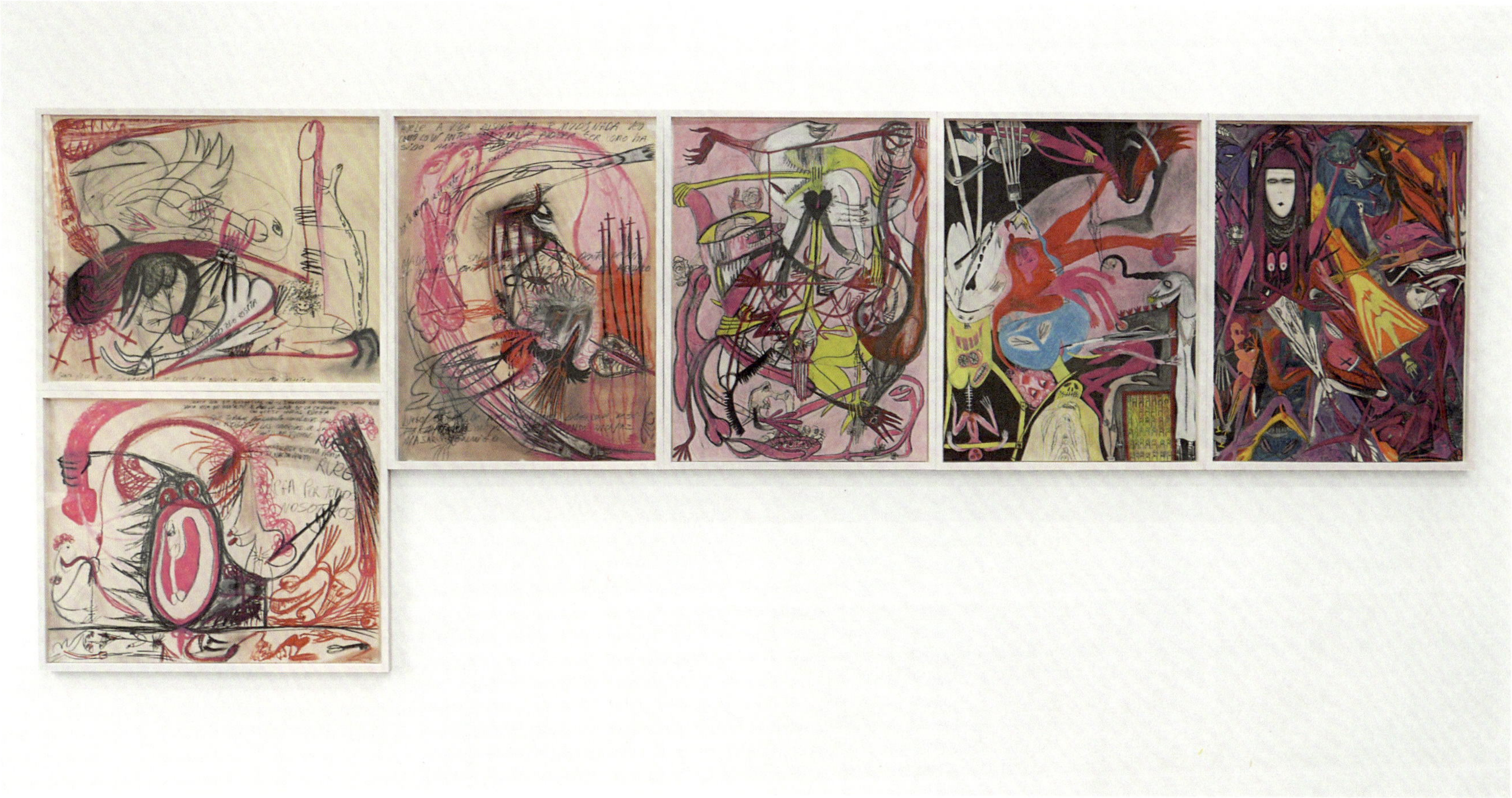

3.

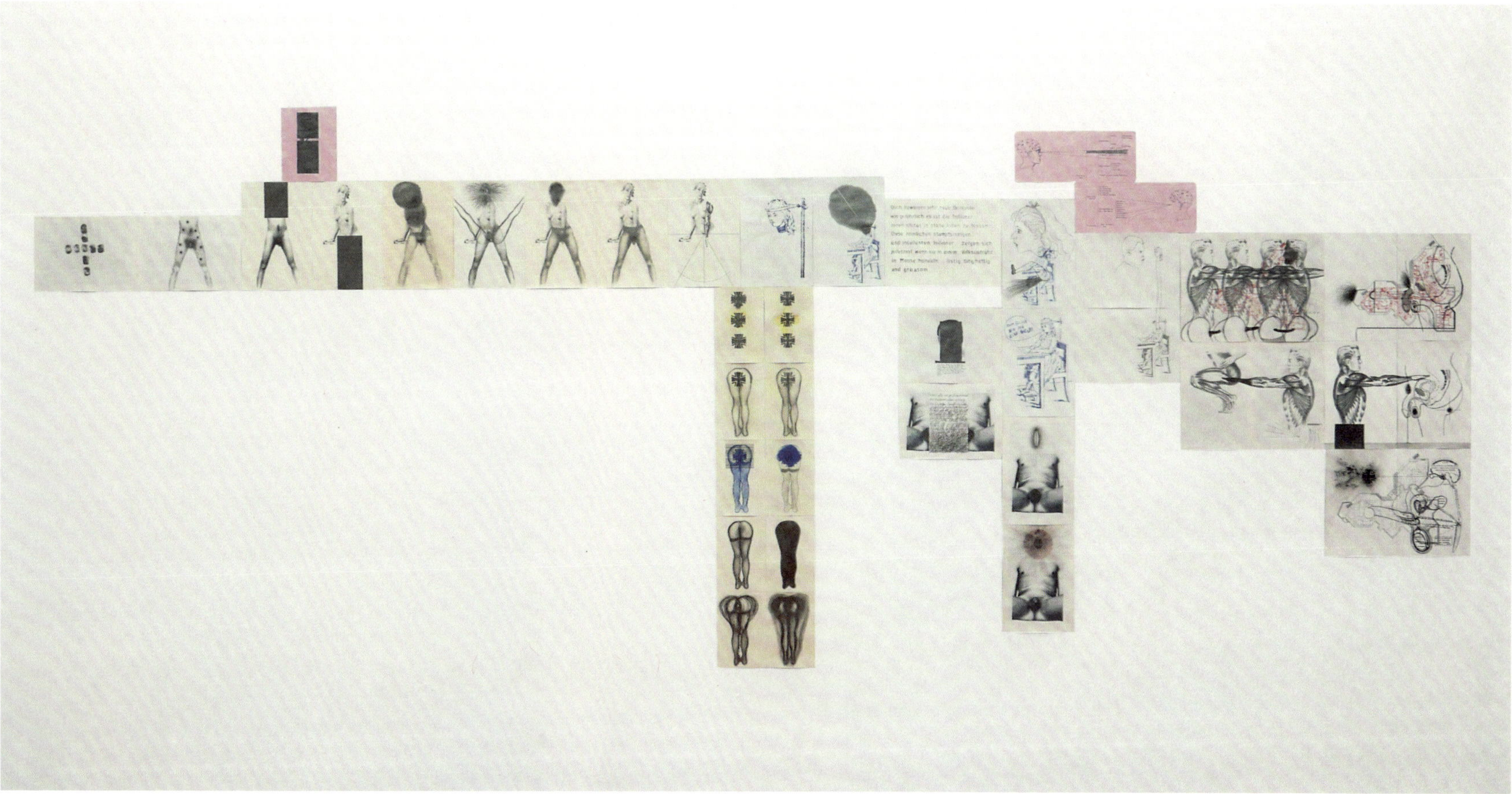

4.

3. *Rosas Series*, 1982, charcoal and colour chalk on paper, each 89 × 69 cm (35 × 27 ⅛ in), installation view, 'Sergio Zevallos | New Journey to the Equinoctial Regions, Awardee of the HAP-Grieshaber-Preis der VG Bild-Kunst', Deutscher Künstlerbund Project Space, Berlin, 2018
4. *HK G3 Series*, 2018, graphite drawing and carbon paper tracing on sheets of printed notebooks, overall: 155 × 410 cm (61 × 161 ⅜ in), installation view as above

INDEX.......

PICTURE CREDITS

All artworks © and courtesy of the artists. p.10, fig.1: Courtesy of Hauser & Wirth. Photo: Martin Parsekian. p.11, fig.3: The Louvre Museum, Paris. p.12, fig.4: MoMA, New York. Gift of The Howard Gilman Foundation. Acc.no: 593.2006. © 2020. Digital image, The Museum of Modern Art, New York/Scala, Florence. © ARS, NY and DACS, London, 2020. p.13, fig.5: © Nancy Grossman. Courtesy of Michael Rosenfeld Gallery LLC, New York. p.14, fig.6: © William Kentridge. Courtesy of Marian Goodman Gallery. p.15, fig.7: MoMA, New York. Acquired through the generosity of Marlene Hess and James D. Zirin, Catie and Donald Marron, Alice and Tom Tisch (in honor of Christophe, Cherix), Marnie Pillsbury and Committee on Drawings and Prints Fund. Acc.no: 319.2017.1-35. © 2020. Digital image, The Museum of Modern Art, New York/Scala, Florence. p.16, fig.9: Whitney Museum of American Art, New York. Purchase, with funds from Charles Tanenbaum. Inv.: 2001.167. © 2020. Digital image Whitney Museum of American Art/Licensed by Scala. p.16, fig.8: Museum of Fine Arts, Houston, Museum purchase funded by the Caroline Wiess Law Accessions Endowment Fund. © Guillermo Kuitca. Courtesy of Sperone Westwater, New York. p.18.2, p.19.4: Photo: Issa Freij. pp.20-21: Courtesy of Milani Gallery. pp.22–4 Courtesy of artSümer. p.22.1: Collection Istanbul Museum of Modern Art. p.22.2: Private Collection. p.23.3 and p.23.4: Collection Evliyagil Museum, Ankara, Turkey. Photo: Abdulhenan Doğan. p.24.5: Photo: Kayhan Kaygusuz. pp.26-7: Courtesy of Sfeir-Semler Gallery Beirut/Hamburg. p.27.3: Collection The Art Institute of Chicago. p.27.5: Collection Mathaf: Arab Museum of Modern Art, Doha. p.27.6: Collection The Art Institute of Chicago. p.28.2: Photo: Sahar Coston-Hardy. pp.32–33: Photo: Andy Keate. pp.34–35: Courtesy of Paula Cooper Gallery, New York. Photo: Steven Probert. p.34.0: Collection of Linda and George Kurz, Cincinnati, OH. pp.36–37.3: Courtesy of OSL contemporary. p.37.4: Courtesy of Kunstnernes Hus and OSL contemporary. Photo: Christina Leithe. pp.38–39: Private collection. p.44, p.45.2, p.46, p.47: Private collection. Photo: Highlevel GmbH. p.45.3: Collection Patsy Bulchandani, Mumbai. Photo: Highlevel GmbH. p.48: Photo: Sylvain Deleu. p.50: Photo: Jan Verboom. pp.52–53: Courtesy Alexander Gray Associates, New York; Galerie Barbara Thumm, Berlin © Teresa Burga/Artists Rights Society (ARS), New York. p.54.1: Collection National Museum Reina Sofía, Madrid. p.55.2: Collection: Federico Klemm Foundation, Argentina. p.55.3: Private collection. p.56.1: Private Collection, Switzerland. Photo: Markus Muehlheim. p.57.2: Courtesy of Galerie Jocelyn Wolff, Parism and Meyer Riegger, Berlin, Karlsruhe. p.57.3: Collection Vincent Honore. p.57.4: Courtesy of Galerie Jocelyn Wolff, Paris. p.57: Photo: François Doury. pp.58–59: © ADAGP, Paris and DACS, London 2020. p.59.3: Courtesy of Selma Feriani gallery. p.59.4: Frac Centre Collection. Courtesy of Frac Centre. Photo: © Blaise Adilon. pp.60-63: Courtesy of Chapter NY, New York. p.60.1: Photo: Paul Saulveson. p.61.2: Photo: Jason Mandella. p.61.3 and p.63.6: Flying Studio. p.61.4: Photo: Jeff Mclane. pp.64–65: Courtesy the artist and Seventeen, London. Photo: Damian Griffiths. pp.66-67: Courtesy of Paul Morris and David Zwirner. p.66.1 and p.66.2: R. Crumb © Robert Crumb, 2019. p.67.3: © Robert Crumb, 2015. p.67.4: © Robert Crumb, 2014. p.67.5: © Robert Crumb, 2016. pp.70–71: Courtesy of Matthew Brown Los Angeles. pp.70-71.2: Photo: Dawn Blackman. p.71.3: Photo: Paul Salveson. p.72.1: Collection of the University of Warwick, UK. p.73.3 and p.73.5: Private collection. p.73.4: Collection The Glucksman, University College Cork, Ireland. pp.72-73: Courtesy Cristea Roberts Gallery and Miriam de Búrca. p.72: Photo: Peter White, FXP Photography. p.73.3: p.73.4 and p.73.5: Photo: Jack Hems. pp.75–77: Courtesy Vigo Gallery and Ibrahim El Salahi. Photo: Justin Piperger. pp.78–79: Courtesy of Galeri Nev Istanbul. p.78.2: Photo: IKSV (Istanbul Foundation for Culture and Arts). pp.80–83: Courtesy of Marlborough, New York and London. p.81.3: Collection The Davis Museum, Wellesley, Massachusetts. pp.86–89: © Tom Friedman. Courtesy the artist and Stephen Friedman Gallery, London. p.90.1: Collection Pennsylvania Academy of Fine Art. p.91.2 and p.91.3: Courtesy of Brooklyn Museum. ppp.94-95: Courtesy of Goodman Gallery, Johannesburg, Cape Town and London. p.96.1: Courtesy of VERBO 2017, Mostra de Performance Art, Vermelho Gallery, Sao Paulo, Brazil. Photo: Edouard Fraipont. p.97: Courtesy of Arróniz Contemporary Art Gallery. p.97.2: Photo: Fabian Cañás. p.97.3: Photo: Ramiro Chaves. p.98.4: Courtesy of Museo Universitario del Chopo. Photo: Fabiola Menchelli. p.100.1, pp.100–103: Courtesy of Pippy Houldsworth Gallery, London. p.101.3: Private collection. p.102.1: Private collection, Sweden. p.102.5: Collection of Amy & John Phelan. pp.108–109: Photo: Julio Osorio, Maria Teresa Hamon and Renato Ghiazza. pp.110-111: Courtesy of Line Ota Fine Arts, Tokyo/Singapore/Shanghai. p.110: Takahashi Ryutaro Collection, Tokyo. pp.112-114. Courtesy of Brennan & Griffin, New York. p.112 Private Collection. p.113.2: Collection MoMA. Fund for the Twenty-First Century, Object number 530.2017. Copyright © 2019 Naotaka Hiro. p.114.3: Photo: Charles Benton. pp.116.1–117: Courtesy of Galeri Nev, Istanbul. pp.120–122: Courtesy of Hollybush Gardens, London. Photo: Andy Keate. p.120.1: British Council Collection. p.120.2: Private collection. p.122.4: Halamish Collection, London. p.124.1 and p.125.3: Courtesy of Hauser & Wirth. pp.124–125: Photo: Martin Parsekian. pp.126-7: Published In Brick Literary Magazine. Toronto. Issue 102, 2018. p.128.1: Photo: Jan Verboom. p.129.3: Photo: Mario Todeschini. pp.130–131: Courtesy of Platform A Gallery, Middlesbrough, UK. p.130.1 and p.131.3: Photo: Anthony Chambers. p.131.2: Photo: Colin Davison. p.132.1: Photo: Stefan Korte. p.132.2: Photo: Rubin Museum and David de Arm. p.133.3: Photo: White Space Beijing. p.133.4: Photo: White Space Beijing and Yang Hao. p.135.2 and p.135.4: Photo: Agostino Osio. p.135.3: Collection British Museum, London. Courtesy of the Trustees of the British Museum. pp.136–137: Private collection. p.140.1 and p.141.3: Photo: Ojārs Pētersons. p.140.2: Photo: Ansis Starks. p.143.2: Ella Fontanals-Cisneros' Collection, USA.pp.146–147: Courtesy of Galerie Peter Kilchmann, Zurich. p.147.3: Photo: Nicole Wilhelms.pp.148–149: Courtesy of Blum & Poe, Los Angeles/New York/Tokyo. p.148.2: Photo: Makenzie Goodman. p.149.3: Photo: Joshua White. p.150.1: Courtesy of Aspen Art Museum. Photo: Tony Prikryl. p.150.2: Courtesy of the Museum of Contemporary Art, Cleveland. Photo: Timothy Safranek Photographics. p.151.3: Courtesy of the Rose Art Museum. Photo: Charles Mayer Photography. pp.152–.153: Courtesy of the artist and Elmarsa Gallery, Tunis/Dubai., Photo: Firas Ben Khelifa. p.152.1 and p.153.3: Private Collection, Tunisia. p.154.1, p.154.2, p.155.4: Courtesy of Fabian Lang, Zurich. Photo: Nick Paton. p.154.2, p.155.3, p.155.4: Private collection. pp.156–157 © Nick Mauss, Courtesy of 303 Gallery, New York. Photo: John Berens. p.159.4: Collection MONA, Australia. p.160.2: Private collection. p.161.3: Courtesy of Bluecoat, Liverpool. pp.162–163: Courtesy of Lehmann + Silva, Porto. p.164–165: Courtesy of GAGPROJECTS. p.168.1: Courtesy of Magenta Plains, New York. p.169: Courtesy of Maria Bernheim Galerie. pp.170–171: Courtesy of Iván Navarro & SKETCH, Bogotá. pp.172–173: Courtesy of Milani Gallery, Brisbane. p.172, p.173.4 and p.173.5: Photo: Christian Capurro. p.174: Courtesy of Mendes Wood DM gallery. p.174.1: EKARD Collection. p.174.2: Collection Jan and Karen Coene. p.175.3: Collection Van Tilborg. p.176.4 and p.177.5: Collection Van Abbemuseum. Courtesy of Lumen Travo gallery. pp.178–.179: Courtesy of SMAC Gallery, Cape Town. pp.180–183: Courtesy Toyin Ojih Odutola and Jack Shainman Gallery, New York. p.184.1 and p.186.4: Courtesy of Galería Luisa Strina, São Paulo. Photo: Edouard Fraipont. p.184.2: Courtesy of Galería Alarcon Criado, Seville. Photo: Bernardo Ortiz. p.185.3: Courtesy of Galería Luisa Strina, São Paulo. Photo: Oscar Monsalve. pp.188-189: Courtesy of Gordon Robichaux, New York, and Herald St, London. Photo: Gregory Carideo. p.188.1: Collection Avo Samuelian and Hector Manuel Gonzalez, New York. p.188.2: Collection Toby Webster, Glasgow. p.191.3: Photo: Henryk Weiffenbach.pp.192–193: Courtesy of Experimenter, Kolkata. pp.194–195: Photo: Max Slaven. pp.196–197: Courtesy of Christine König Galerie. p.198–.199: Courtesy of Richard Saltoun Gallery. p.200 and p.201.2: Courtesy of BALTIC and Galerie Crèvecoeur. Photo: Rob Harris. p.201.3: Courtesy of Workplace, Gateshead, and Galerie Crèvecoeur. p.201.4: Collection Arts Council England. Courtesy of Tramway and Galerie Crèvecoeur. Photo: Keith Hunter pp.202–203: © Deanna Petherbridge. Photo: Stephen White. p.203.4: Tate Collection. © Deanna Petherbridge. Photo: John Bodkin. p.204.1 and p.204.2: Photo: Qiu Anxiong. p.205.3: Photo: Zhang Tianjian. p.207.3: Collection Guggenheim Abu Dhabi. p.208.4: Collection of Solomon R. Guggenheim Museum, New York. Gift of the artist with additional funds contributed by the International Director's Council, 2017. pp.210.–211: Courtesy of Pilar Corrias, London and Regen Projects, Los Angeles. Photo: Damian Griffiths. pp.212-213: Private collection. p.213.3: Photo: Tim Bowditch. p.213.4: Photo: Packshot Studio. pp.214-215: Collection British Museum, London. Photo: Packshot Studio. pp.216–219: Courtesy of Almine Rech. p.216.2: Collection Whitney Museum of American Art, New York.. p.217.3: Collection Brooklyn Museum. pp.220-221: Courtesy of Steve Turner, Los Angeles. p.220.1: John McEnroe Collection. p.221.3: Leonardo DiCaprio Collection. pp.222-223: Courtesy of Instituto de Visión. pp.224–227: Courtesy of Nathalie Karg Gallery, New York. p.226.5: Austin Peavy State University (APSU), Tennessee. p.230.1 and p.231.3: Courtesy of Galerie Anne-Sarah Bénichou. © Adagp Paris. p.230.2 and p.231.4: Courtesy of Selma Feriani Gallery. © Adagp Paris. pp.232-233: © Wael Shawky. Courtesy of Lisson Gallery. pp.234–235: Collection of Kiran Nadar Museum of Art, New Delhi. pp.236-237: Courtesy of Milani Gallery, Brisbane. p.241.3: Photo: Oscar Balducci. p.241.4: Photo: Viviana Gil. pp.242–243: Courtesy of Blindspot Gallery. pp.244–245: Courtesy of GALLERIA CONTINUA, San Gimignano/Beijing/Les Moulins/Habana. Photo: Ela Bialkowska, OKNO Studio. pp.248-249: Courtesy of Akara Art. p.248: Kiran Nadar Museum of Art. p.249.3: Kasturbhai Lalbhai Museum. p.249.4: Architectural Digest Design Show, 2019. p.250.1 and p.251.3: Private collection. pp.250-251: Courtesy of Galerie Onrust, Amsterdam. p.252.1: Collection Sascha Bauer. Photo: Joerg Lohse. p.253: Photo: Joerg Lohse. p.254.1: tzvetnik.online, 2019. p.254.2: Courtesy of Polansky Gallery, Brno. p.254.3: Courtesy of Alyssa Davis Gallery. p.255.4: Courtesy of The Sunroom, Richmond, Virgina. p.256.5: Photo: Andy Keate. pp.258–261: Courtesy Galerie Lelong & Co. and Bandjoun Station. pp.262–263: Courtesy of Galeria Plan B. Photo: Trevor Good. p.263.3 Private collection. pp.264-265: Courtesy of Petzel, New York. p.266.1: Photo: Heidi Bohnenkamp. p.266.2: Courtesy of Proyectos Ultravioleta, Guatemala City. Photo: Ben Westoby. p.267.3 Photo: Ramiro Chaves. p.267.4: Courtesy of Modern Art Oxford. Photo: Ben Westoby. p.268.1: Courtesy of Be-Part Waregem. Photo: Mariana Frandsen. p.269: Courtesy of Galerie Zink & Gallery Sofie Van de Velde. Photo: Carl Brunn. pp.274-275: Private collection. p.274.2: Courtesy of Goodman Gallery. p.278.1 and p.279.2: Courtesy of James Hockey Gallery. Photo: Stephen White. p.279.3: Photo: Vanley Burke. pp.280-281: Courtesy of Cristea Roberts Gallery. p.280.4: Photo: Chris Keenan. p.281.5: Photo: Jack Hems. pp.282-283: Courtesy of Courtesy of Antenna Space, Shanghai; Carlos/Ishikawa, London, and Galerie Fons Welters, Amsterdam. p.282.1: Photo: Gert Jan van Rooij. 283.3: S.M.A.K., De Vereniging, Ghent. Photo: Dirk Pauwels. p.286.1 and p.287.3: Photo: Andre Ribuoli. p.287.2: Courtesy of Hales Gallery. Photo: Cathy Carver. p.288.4: Courtesy of Galerie Jean Brolly. Photo: Andre Ribuoli. p.290.1: Private collection, London. p.290.2: Courtesy of Gallery Von Bartha, Basel. p.291.3: Photo: Kate Peters. p.292: Courtesy of 888 books. p.293.3 © Courtesy of ANOMALY. p.294.1 and p.295.6: Courtesy of Leto Gallery, Warsaw. p.295.3: Courtesy of onestar press, Paris. p.295.5: Courtesy of DREI Gallery, Cologne. pp.296–297: Courtesy of Luhring Augustine, New York.